DUMFRIESSHIRE

DUMFRIESSHIRE

A Frontier Region

Andrew McCulloch

ORIGIN

First published in Great Britain in 2018 by
Origin, an imprint of Birlinn Ltd

West Newington House
10 Newington Road
Edinburgh
EH9 1QS

www.birlinn.co.uk

ISBN: 978 1 912476 28 2

The publishers gratefully acknowledge the support of
the Friends of the Archives
towards the publication of this book

British Library Cataloguing-in-Publication Data
A catalogue record for this book is available on request from the British Library

Typeset by Biblichor Ltd, Edinburgh
Printed and bound in Malta by Gutenberg Press Ltd

Contents

FIFTEEN: *Early Improvement*

SIXTEEN: *Eighteenth-Century Life*

SEVENTEEN: *The Nineteenth Century*

EIGHTEEN: *Modern Times*

Plates

1 Interior of a Neolithic dwelling at Skara Brae, Orkney.
2 The Ruthwell Cross, an example of Northumbrian sculpture.
3 Medieval warfare:
    (a) A 'berefray' or siege tower
    (b) A trebuchet wound down ready to fire.
    (c) Firing the severed heads of captives into a stronghold to demoralise the garrison.
    (d) Sappers undermining the foundations of the castle walls.
4 Images of Robert the Bruce:
    (a) Pilkington Jackson's fancifully flattering representation of Robert Bruce.
    (b) Brian Hill's bland and somewhat characterless representation of Robert Bruce.
    (c) Robert Neave's more candid portrayal of Robert Bruce.
    (d) Robert Bruce's effigy in Rosslyn Chapel, reputedly a copy of Bruce's death mask.
5 Caerlaverock castle.
6 Imaginary siege of Caerlaverock castle.
7 Comlongan castle, Clarencefield.
8 The original part of Hoddom castle, near Lockerbie.
9 Drumlanrig castle, the creation of William 1st duke of Queensberry.
10 Excerpt from the estate map of Hightae illustrating the amalgamation of small runrig holdings into larger enclosed farms.
11 Estate plan of Kirkpatrick Fleming showing the division of the commonty between the adjacent landowners.
12 Thomas Telford.
13 The Rev Dr Henry Duncan.
14 Robert Burns by Alexander Reid.
15 Scottish essayist and historian Thomas Carlyle (1795–1881).
16 (a) Terregles House.
16 (b) The gardens of Terregles House.
17 Georgian mansions:
    (a) Dalswinton, Auldgirth.
    (b) Knockhill, Ecclefechan.

Preface

Like a new-born elephant, this work is the product of a long gestation. But writing it has been a fascinating exercise, and I hope I have managed to convey something of this to the reader. The title is deliberate because in former times Dumfriesshire was indeed a frontier region which straddled the main western route into Scotland – a path regularly trodden by English invaders as they plundered their way northwards leaving a trail of devastation behind them. Frequently their predatory endeavours were focused on reducing Dumfriesshire, and south-west Scotland generally, to a blackened wilderness. It was also the principal battleground in the Wars of Independence which lasted intermittently for close on three centuries. And this combined with the barbarities associated with the ferocious family feuds which were endemic throughout the region accounted above all for its sanguinary past.

The only other history of Dumfriesshire is Sir Herbert Maxwell's *History of Dumfries and Galloway*, but it was published towards the end of the nineteenth century when there was only a limited amount of information available and critical research was in its infancy. Now the aspiring historian is privileged in having access to the mass of books, articles and other information which have since come into the public domain. Most of them are available in the Ewart Library, Dumfries, and they have been of invaluable assistance in writing this book, none more so than the *Transactions of the Dumfries and Galloway Natural History and Antiquarian Society*. These contain an abundance of articles dealing with all aspects of Dumfriesshire's past, many of them contributed by recognised authorities in their particular field.

Writing a county history such as this begs the question of where to draw the line between, on the one hand, narrating a bare sequence of events affecting Dumfriesshire in isolation, rather like producing a collection of beads without a string. And, on the other, how far to digress into contemporary history to explain the background to these events.

In fact the line varies according to the period in question. Broadly speaking, the earlier sections can be confined to Dumfriesshire. After that its history becomes inextricably bound up with that of southern Scotland and elsewhere, as it would remain throughout the Middle Ages until the Treaty of Union of 1707. Then it becomes easier to concentrate exclusively on Dumfriesshire, particularly when dealing with land improvement, early industrialisation, and the development of roads and railways. That said, much that was happening nationally during this time – the aftermath of the

Union, the Jacobite rebellions, the friction within the Church, education, politics and the current Land Reform proposals, to name but a few – affected Dumfriesshire as much as elsewhere. Therefore they merit some digression.

I admit that some of my conclusions may be controversial, or at least not in line with received thinking. I make no apology for this. Rightly or wrongly, they are the product of extensive reading and research, and – I would add – a good deal of thought. I have also attempted to liven up the narrative with the odd story culled from the records. But to avoid clogging the text, I have confined these (like the more interesting nuggets of information) to footnotes. References to primary and secondary sources, on the other hand, have been consigned to endnotes.

I must record my thanks to the staff of the Historical Section of the Ewart Library in Dumfries who have invariably dealt cheerfully and helpfully with my deluge of requests for help and information. Above all I am indebted to Graham Roberts, the Dumfries & Galloway Council Archivist. Not only has he kindly read through the earlier chapters and offered some helpful suggestions, but he has given me valued assistance with the later ones. I am particularly grateful for the encouraging interest he has consistently taken in the book since its original conception. Equally so for his help in securing a grant towards the publication costs from the Friends of the Archives, to whom I must record my grateful thanks. I hope that, thanks to the kind assistance of all concerned, this book will commend itself to the reader.

A J McCulloch

Table 1

Earlier Kings of Scots

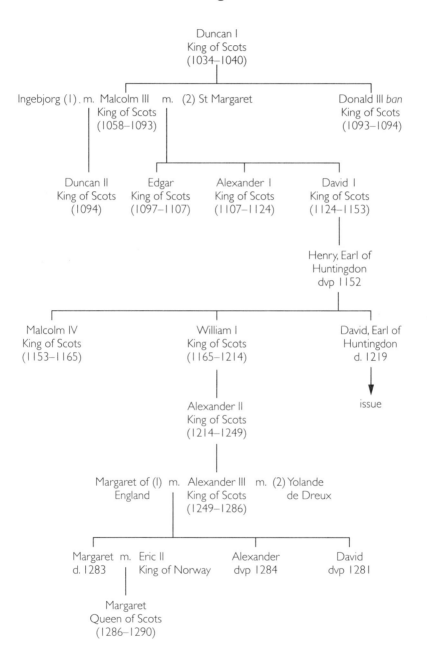

Duncan I
King of Scots
(1034–1040)

Ingebjorg (1) . m. Malcolm III   m.   (2) St Margaret   Donald III *ban*
King of Scots   King of Scots
(1058–1093)   (1093–1094)

Duncan II   Edgar   Alexander I   David I
King of Scots   King of Scots   King of Scots   King of Scots
(1094)   (1097–1107)   (1107–1124)   (1124–1153)

Henry, Earl of
Huntingdon
dvp 1152

Malcolm IV   William I   David, Earl of
King of Scots   King of Scots   Huntingdon
(1153–1165)   (1165–1214)   d. 1219

Alexander II   issue
King of Scots
(1214–1249)

Margaret of (1) m. Alexander III m. (2) Yolande
England   King of Scots   de Dreux
                     (1249–1286)

Margaret m. Eric II   Alexander   David
d. 1283   King of Norway   dvp 1284   dvp 1281

Margaret
Queen of Scots
(1286–1290)

dvp – died in the lifetime of father

Table 2

Bruce lords of Annandale

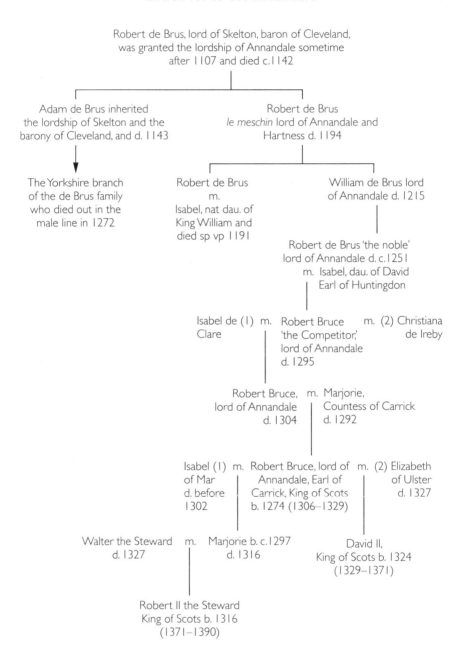

Robert de Brus, lord of Skelton, baron of Cleveland, was granted the lordship of Annandale sometime after 1107 and died c.1142

Adam de Brus inherited the lordship of Skelton and the barony of Cleveland, and d. 1143

Robert de Brus *le meschin* lord of Annandale and Hartness d. 1194

The Yorkshire branch of the de Brus family who died out in the male line in 1272

Robert de Brus m. Isabel, nat dau. of King William and died sp vp 1191

William de Brus lord of Annandale d. 1215

Robert de Brus 'the noble' lord of Annandale d. c.1251 m. Isabel, dau. of David Earl of Huntingdon

Isabel de (1) m. Clare

Robert Bruce 'the Competitor,' lord of Annandale d. 1295

m. (2) Christiana de Ireby

Robert Bruce, m. Marjorie, lord of Annandale d. 1304

Countess of Carrick d. 1292

Isabel (1) m. of Mar d. before 1302

Robert Bruce, lord of Annandale, Earl of Carrick, King of Scots b. 1274 (1306–1329)

m. (2) Elizabeth of Ulster d. 1327

Walter the Steward d. 1327

m. Marjorie b. c.1297 d. 1316

David II, King of Scots b. 1324 (1329–1371)

Robert II the Steward King of Scots b. 1316 (1371–1390)

| sp | – without children |
| vp | – in the lifetime of father |

Rival claims to the throne

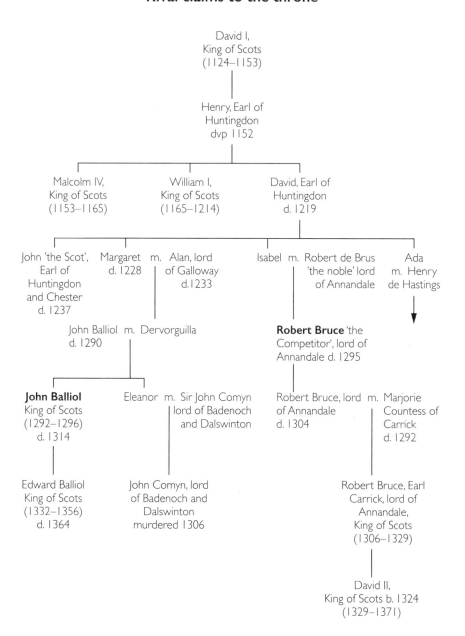

David I,
King of Scots
(1124–1153)

Henry, Earl of
Huntingdon
dvp 1152

Malcolm IV,	William I,	David, Earl of
King of Scots	King of Scots	Huntingdon
(1153–1165)	(1165–1214)	d. 1219

John 'the Scot',
Earl of
Huntingdon
and Chester
d. 1237

Margaret   m.   Alan, lord
d. 1228   of Galloway
                          d.1233

Isabel m. Robert de Brus
                    'the noble' lord
                    of Annandale

Ada
m. Henry
de Hastings

John Balliol m. Dervorguilla
d. 1290

Robert Bruce 'the
Competitor', lord of
Annandale d. 1295

John Balliol
King of Scots
(1292–1296)
d. 1314

Eleanor m. Sir John Comyn
                     lord of Badenoch
                     and Dalswinton

Robert Bruce, lord m. Marjorie
of Annandale   Countess of
d. 1304   Carrick
                                       d. 1292

Edward Balliol
King of Scots
(1332–1356)
d. 1364

John Comyn, lord
of Badenoch and
Dalswinton
murdered 1306

Robert Bruce, Earl
Carrick, lord of
Annandale,
King of Scots
(1306–1329)

David II,
King of Scots b. 1324
(1329–1371)

| dvp – died in the lifetime of father |

Table 4

The Black Douglases

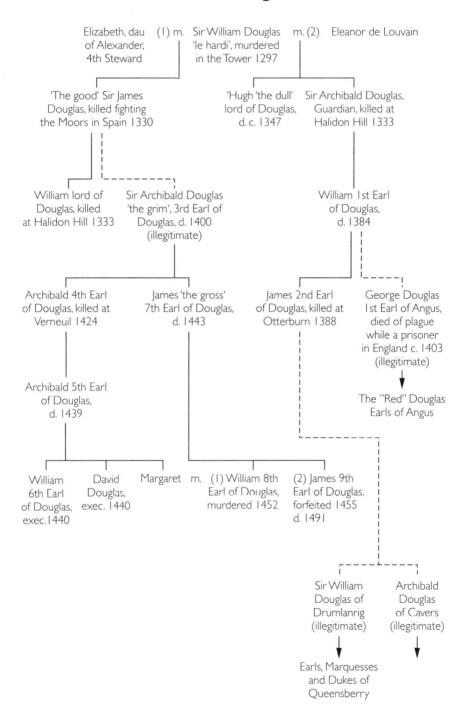

Elizabeth, dau   (1) m.   Sir William Douglas   m. (2)   Eleanor de Louvain
of Alexander,   'le hardi', murdered
4th Steward   in the Tower 1297

'The good' Sir James   'Hugh 'the dull'   Sir Archibald Douglas,
Douglas, killed fighting   lord of Douglas,   Guardian, killed at
the Moors in Spain 1330   d. c. 1347   Halidon Hill 1333

William lord of   Sir Archibald Douglas   William 1st Earl
Douglas, killed   'the grim', 3rd Earl of   of Douglas,
at Halidon Hill 1333 Douglas, d. 1400   d. 1384
                     (illegitimate)

Archibald 4th Earl   James 'the gross'   James 2nd Earl   George Douglas
of Douglas, killed at 7th Earl of Douglas, of Douglas, killed at 1st Earl of Angus,
Verneuil 1424   d. 1443   Otterburn 1388   died of plague
                                                                while a prisoner
                                                                in England c. 1403
                                                                (illegitimate)

Archibald 5th Earl   The "Red" Douglas
of Douglas,   Earls of Angus
d. 1439

William   David   Margaret   m.   (1) William 8th   (2) James 9th
6th Earl   Douglas,   Earl of Douglas,   Earl of Douglas,
of Douglas, exec. 1440   murdered 1452   forfeited 1455
exec. 1440   d. 1491

                                        Sir William   Archibald
                                        Douglas of   Douglas
                                        Drumlanrig   of Cavers
                                        (illegitimate)   (illegitimate)

                                        Earls, Marquesses
                                        and Dukes of
                                        Queensberry

Table 5

Maxwells

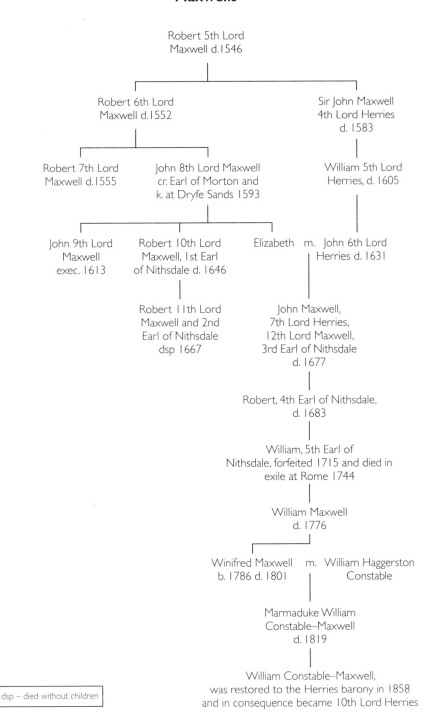

Robert 5th Lord
Maxwell d.1546

Robert 6th Lord
Maxwell d.1552

Sir John Maxwell
4th Lord Herries
d. 1583

Robert 7th Lord
Maxwell d.1555

John 8th Lord Maxwell
cr. Earl of Morton and
k. at Dryfe Sands 1593

William 5th Lord
Herries, d. 1605

John 9th Lord
Maxwell
exec. 1613

Robert 10th Lord
Maxwell, 1st Earl
of Nithsdale d. 1646

Elizabeth   m.   John 6th Lord
Herries d. 1631

Robert 11th Lord
Maxwell and 2nd
Earl of Nithsdale
dsp 1667

John Maxwell,
7th Lord Herries,
12th Lord Maxwell,
3rd Earl of Nithsdale
d. 1677

Robert, 4th Earl of Nithsdale,
d. 1683

William, 5th Earl of
Nithsdale, forfeited 1715 and died in
exile at Rome 1744

William Maxwell
d. 1776

Winifred Maxwell   m.   William Haggerston
b. 1786 d. 1801   Constable

Marmaduke William
Constable–Maxwell
d. 1819

William Constable–Maxwell,
was restored to the Herries barony in 1858
and in consequence became 10th Lord Herries

dsp – died without children

Table 6

Johnstones

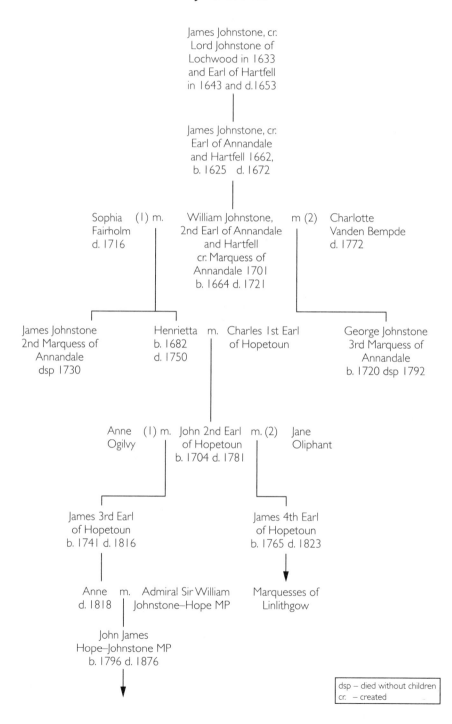

James Johnstone, cr.
Lord Johnstone of
Lochwood in 1633
and Earl of Hartfell
in 1643 and d.1653

James Johnstone, cr.
Earl of Annandale
and Hartfell 1662,
b. 1625   d. 1672

Sophia   (1) m.   William Johnstone,   m (2)   Charlotte
Fairholm   2nd Earl of Annandale   Vanden Bempde
d. 1716   and Hartfell   d. 1772
                         cr. Marquess of
                         Annandale 1701
                         b. 1664 d. 1721

James Johnstone   Henrietta   m.   Charles 1st Earl   George Johnstone
2nd Marquess of   b. 1682   of Hopetoun   3rd Marquess of
Annandale   d. 1750   Annandale
dsp 1730   b. 1720 dsp 1792

Anne   (1) m.   John 2nd Earl   m. (2)   Jane
Ogilvy   of Hopetoun   Oliphant
                    b. 1704 d. 1781

James 3rd Earl   James 4th Earl
of Hopetoun   of Hopetoun
b. 1741 d. 1816   b. 1765 d. 1823

Anne   m.   Admiral Sir William   Marquesses of
d. 1818   Johnstone–Hope MP   Linlithgow

John James
Hope–Johnstone MP
b. 1796 d. 1876

dsp – died without children
cr. – created

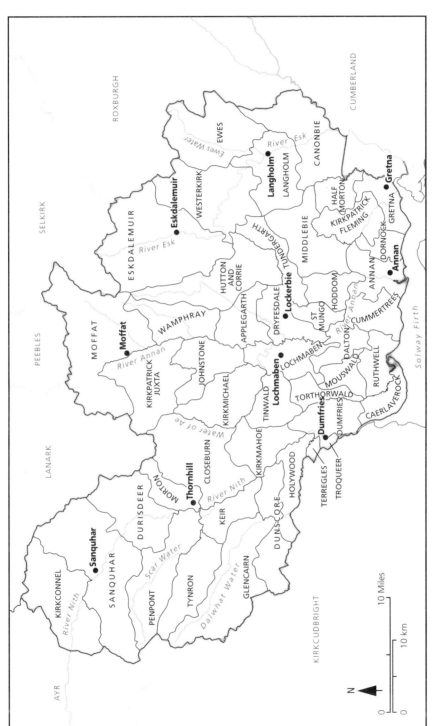

Dumfriesshire – map of the parishes

ONE

The Beginnings

EARLY SETTLERS

In prehistoric times Dumfriesshire lay under an ice sheet which covered much of the northern hemisphere, and which in Britain extended as far south as the Midlands. Although punctuated by warmer spells, known as interglacials, when temperatures rose to almost tropical levels, the Ice Age persisted for over two and a half million years, and at its maximum intensity the ice was more than a kilometre (upwards of 3,000 feet) thick.

Around 15,000 years ago the onset of warmer conditions caused the ice to melt. But it proved a false dawn. Some 13,000 years ago a temporary cessation of the Gulf Stream caused a return to arctic conditions and the re-appearance of glaciers in the high mountains.* This lasted for about 1,500 years until the Gulf Stream re-established itself, when temperatures rose by roughly 10°C within the space of about half a century. As the ice retreated, the land was colonised first by arctic tundra, followed by grass and heather, and later willow and juniper scrub. And as the climate continued to warm, Scots pine and birch were established, providing a habitat for a variety of smaller fauna such as lemmings, voles and arctic foxes. Later, oak, hazel and elm became the dominant species in southern Scotland, and this attracted larger animals such as elk, deer, wild boar, wild horses and aurochs (wild ox),† as well as beavers, lynx and wolves, not to mention a diversity of birdlife.

From about 10,000 years ago the combination of an abundance of food in the form of nuts and berries, the profusion of wildlife, and a warmer climate, encouraged bands of Middle Stone Age – or Mesolithic – hunter gatherers to migrate as far as present-day Scotland.‡ Because the melting ice had caused a rise in the sea level worldwide, those reaching south-west Scotland would have found the present-day coastal regions and the lower reaches of the main river valleys inundated by the sea. For example the Nith estuary would have covered most of lower Nithsdale as far as Auldgirth to form a large, island-studded bay, the largest of the islands being the

---

*   This was the result of a vast inland lake which covered much of northern Canada bursting its ice dam and releasing gigantic quantities of fresh water which exploded tsunami like into the North Atlantic and blocked off the Gulf Stream.
†   They continued to exist in Scotland until about 2000 BC.
‡   Artefacts associated with these people which have been retrieved from the bed of the North Sea reveal that their ancestors migrated along its southern reaches from the Continent, which was then dry land.

ridge of high ground which extends south-eastwards from Georgetown, on the outskirts of Dumfries, towards Caerlaverock. Further east, the low-lying plain round the head of the Solway Firth, including part of south-eastern Dumfriesshire, would have been completely submerged.

While virtually all traces of the Mesolithic people have disappeared, the remains of shell middens at various locations along the raised beaches,* where there would have been a supply of fresh water, suggest that these were their main camp sites. That settlements associated with these people have been identified in the Western Isles, one of the earliest being at Kinloch on the island of Rum, suggests they were skilful and intrepid sailors. Traces of the kind of coracles they used have come to light at various sites in northern Europe, while it is evident from discoveries of the remains of harpoons, fish hooks and fish spears that they derived their living from the sea as well as the land. They would also have used nets, but being perishable none have survived.

Essentially a nomadic people, these early settlers would have migrated inland – up the main river valleys – in search of food and to engage in hunting expeditions according to the season. This is evident from isolated finds of mainly flint implements such as arrow and spear heads. They also used bone, horn or flint scrapers for scouring the flesh from animal skins, which was their main – and probably their only – source of clothing. Yet, notwithstanding that these scrapers would have been in everyday use, only five have come to light in Dumfriesshire, three of them in the parish of Glencairn in Nithsdale.[1]

While there is more abundant evidence of Mesolithic settlement further west – mainly along the eastern shores of Luce Bay, in Wigtownshire, and around Loch Dee and Clatteringshaws, in Kirkcudbrightshire (discovered in the course of forestry operations) – some has come to light in Dumfriesshire. Perhaps the best – and certainly the earliest – example consists of the remains of hearthstones, indicative of an early settlement dating from around 8,000 years ago, which has been identified at Redkirk Point near Gretna.[2] The discovery of ten arrowheads in the vicinity of Gretna itself points to the upper reaches of the Solway as a likely focus of Mesolithic settlement.[3]

There is also evidence of a Mesolithic site at Glencaple,[4] as well as others along the lower reaches of the Nith and the Annan valleys where artefacts associated with them have come to light in the course of ploughing operations. That apart, the scarcity of Mesolithic remains in Dumfriesshire suggests that it was thinly populated and that the people were constantly on the move. This is evident from discoveries of arrowheads at Keir, Penpont, Closeburn and Sanquhar which are indicative of migratory routes up the Nith and Cairn valleys, while other finds at Beattock and Eskdalemuir point to similar routes up the Annan and Esk valleys.[5] There these people would have

---

* Caused by isostatic reaction as the landmass freed from the weight of ice gradually rose so that the sea retreated to the present shoreline.

established temporary camps to serve as a base for hunting expeditions, probably returning to their permanent coastal settlements with the onset of winter.

The Mesolithic era is thought to have lasted for some four millennia – from around 10,000 to about 6,000 years ago, when there is evidence of a gradual change from a hunter gathering to a primitive farming community. For example, traces of fire point to these early farmers clearing patches of native forest by the rudimentary technique of 'slash and burn'. And, apparent from pollen samples preserved in contemporary peat deposits, planting the potash-enriched soil with crops of emmer wheat and barley. These practices are associated with the appearance of New Stone Age, or Neolithic, immigrants who had acquired their skills through contact with the people of continental Europe where farming was already well established. As well as being tillers of the soil, they were also pastoralists who concentrated on rearing cattle and pigs, as well as sheep and goats. Whereas their cattle are thought to have been of the Shorthorn type, and their sheep akin to the Soay breed, their goats were probably not dissimilar to the small, grey animals which roam the Galloway hinterland today and who could well be their descendants.

Modern research based on an analysis of DNA samples suggests that, instead of assimilating with the native Mesolithic people (apart from taking their women), the Neolithic incomers drove them out of the more fertile regions which they proceeded to cultivate, and where they pastured their livestock. Meanwhile the Mesolithic people, consigned to the peripheries, remained as small, widely dispersed groups pursuing their traditional way of life as hunter gatherers. Further evidence suggests that the arrival of the Neolithic people and their productive use of land heralded an expanding population.[6]

As well as being farmers, the Neolithic people are associated with other skills, notably the fashioning of more sophisticated flint and stone implements, and the manufacture of decorated pottery. A quantity of shards came to light at Carzield, near Kirkton, in the course of laying a gas pipeline in the 1990s. This was an important find, for in addition to the pottery shards it included charred grains of primitive emmer wheat and barley, and a cache of burnt hazelnut shells, as well charcoal remains, all indicative of habitation.[7] The surviving Neolithic dwellings represent a considerable improvement on those of the Mesolithic which seem to have been quite rudimentary. While it is difficult to be specific at this distance in time, arcs of stake-holes identified at known Mesolithic settlements are thought to have been sockets for anchoring supports for a wigwam-like timber framework which would have been covered with hides, brushwood, turf or bark.[8] Whereas some were probably little more than windbreaks, the scooped-out hollows identifiable at some of these sites are thought to indicate larger, more permanent dwellings.

Neolithic dwellings were more sophisticated. The best examples, admittedly associated with late Neolithic times, are those on Orkney, notably at Skara Brae which was occupied from about 3100 to 2500 BC. This consists of the remains of ten semi-subterranean, single-roomed houses and a workshop, all revetted against the bank with stone slabs. The houses conform to a standard design which consisted of a hearth at the centre of the room, box beds let in to opposite walls, and a stone dresser presumably for storage. Additionally some were equipped with what was evidently a lavatory complete with an outflow. A more modest example was found at Beckton Farm, near Lockerbie,[9] and doubtless evidence of similar dwellings is waiting to be discovered in Dumfriesshire.

Besides the numerous flint arrowheads that have come to light,[*] the most important artefacts associated with the Neolithic people are their stone axe-hammers. Fashioned from flaked flint, or ground down from hard-grained stone, they were mounted in wooden hafts and used mainly for forest clearance. In fact, such was the demand for good quality, hard-wearing stone that it led to the development of a primitive manufacturing industry and a flourishing trade in these articles. Numerous examples have been found in Dumfriesshire, fourteen having come to light in and around Dumfries itself.[10] Because there is no suitable stone available locally, it would have been imported in a rough state from the nearest 'axe-factory' at Langdale in the Lake District,[†] and fashioned for use by local craftsmen.[11]

Evidently the Neolithic people were quite peripatetic. For example, an analysis of bone fragments found in a cemetery at Stonehenge suggests that some of those buried there came from as far afield as Orkney.[12] Closer to home, confirmation of this comes from the discovery of a bow, nearly two metres long and dating from about 3600 BC, which was found preserved in peat at Rotten Bottom.[‡] This was made of yew wood, and because yew is thought to have been non-native to Scotland at the time it was probably imported from the south.[13]

Evidence of these peoples' beliefs and rituals is apparent from their burial tombs. The fact that some have been found to contain traces of grave goods and shards of pottery speaks to a belief in an afterlife, the pottery being the remains of containers for food to sustain the deceased on his journey to the afterworld. Mostly dating from the early Neolithic, the burial sites consisted of stone-built, compartmentalised (or chambered) tombs covered with earth or turf, and varying in shape from roughly square, to round, to oblong mounds, while some had an entrance passageway. Others were equipped with a forecourt which is thought to have been a focus for ritual activity, while the discovery of traces of henbane at some sites elsewhere suggests the use of hallucinatory, performance-enhancing drugs.

Sets of paired post-holes identified at some sites are thought to have been sockets for timbers used to support a platform for exposing corpses to the elements. Once the flesh had rotted away, doubtless assisted by carrion and other predatory birds and

---

[*]   Recent experiments have shown that it can take only about twenty minutes to fashion (or knap) a sharpened flint arrowhead from a piece of flint.

[†]   Langdale Pike was a source of greenstone, an igneous rock which readily lent itself to 'knapping' into a rough axe-head. Whereas it is reckoned that a skilled craftsman could do this in less than an hour, refining it into a usable implement would have taken much longer.

[‡]   In the Moffat hills between the summit of Hartfell and the head of the Grey Mare's Tail.

rodents (or 'excarnated' to use the technical term), the bones were deposited in the tombs, to be replaced through time by subsequent generations of defleshed corpses. Six examples of the oblong type of burial cairn have been identified in Dumfriesshire: three in Nithsdale, in the parishes of Keir, Glencairn and Kirkmahoe, another in the parish of Kirkpatrick Juxta, while the remaining two were found in alignment with each other at Windyedge near Canonbie.[14]

Other structures associated with the Neolithic people are the so-called timber halls, some of which have come to light in Dumfriesshire. They are thought to have been centres of religious activity, or the houses of a ruling elite, or both. The evidence suggests that they consisted of a large rectangular area, while the remains of post-holes along the perimeter could indicate supports for a roof. From the charred remains which have come to light, archaeologists conclude that these halls were routinely burnt after a century or so of use, perhaps as pyres for their lordly occupants.[15] Traces of one have been identified at Holywood, in lower Nithsdale, and two others at Beckton Farm and Kirkburn, both near Lockerbie.[16] More recently the remains of an earlier timber hall have been discovered in Lockerbie itself.[17]

Meanwhile land was increasingly brought into cultivation. This meant that, whereas early Neolithic society consisted of groups of people living in isolated communities, from about 3000 BC onwards it became more structured and hierarchical, probably marking the emergence of priest chieftains. Consequently society became increasingly stratified and more tightly controlled, which made it possible to conscript and organise the labour needed to undertake major projects. Therefore it was no coincidence that this period witnessed the building of the standing stones and henges (ditched enclosures with a surrounding bank) associated with the Neolithic people. Although their precise purpose is not known, theory has it that they served as social or religious centres for the holding of rituals. Alternatively they could have been ruling centres for the newly emerged priest chieftains, or simply primitive calendars to mark the changing seasons by the position of the sun in relation to the stones. In fact they could have been a combination of all three.

The largest in Dumfriesshire – and indeed in Scotland – is the Twelve Apostles, notwithstanding that it consists of eleven upright stones (there would originally have been twelve), adjacent to the Cluden Water just north of Newbridge. The other two which can be positively dated to the Neolithic are the 'Loupin' Stones' adjacent to the White Esk, immediately south of Eskdalemuir, and the 'Girdle Stones' some six hundred yards downriver below Cote. Since they, like the Twelve Apostles, are situated close to a river, this could be taken to suggest that these stone circles were built along the principal migratory routes. Other stone circles identified at Kirkhill, Whiteholm Rig and Whitecastles, in the parishes of Wamphray, Tundergarth and Hutton and Corrie, are thought to date from Bronze Age times.[18]

An impression of the Neolithic people can be gained from an analysis of some skeletal remains which were found in a tomb at Isbister on Orkney. According to the excavation report, the average height of the men was 170cm (5ft 7in) and that of the women 163cm (5ft 4in). All of them – male and female – were extremely muscular, while more than half the adults showed signs of some degeneration of the spine as a result of heavy labour – presumably from early childhood. Several of the women had skull deformities resulting from carrying heavy loads supported by browbands. What was particularly apparent was their low life expectancy, the high incidence of child mortality and death of women in childbirth. As the report goes on to say, 'Most of those surviving to puberty died before the age of thirty, and only a few individuals could hope to reach fifty.'[19]

THE AGE OF METAL

Fragments of pottery dating from around 2500 BC onwards reveal the existence of a new and more sophisticated type of vessel known as the beaker. This is associated with the arrival of immigrants known (unoriginally) as the Beaker people. They are distinguishable by certain skeletal differences in that they had rounder heads in contrast to the longer-headed Neolithic people, as well as being taller and more robust, and above all they are characterised by their burial practices. Whereas the Neolithic deposited the defleshed bones of the dead in communal graves, the Beaker people inserted theirs hunched up in a foetal position in individual stone cists within a burial cairn. Later it became the practice to cremate their dead and deposit the ashes in an urn which was placed in a burial cairn. More than thirty of these have been identified in Dumfriesshire, most of them in the west, notably at Closeburn and Auchencairn in mid-Nithsdale, and in the parishes of Dunscore, Glencairn and Sanquhar.[20] Alternatively the urns, referred to as cinerary urns, were placed in cemeteries of which a number have come to light – at Kirkburn, Lockerbie; Dowglen Hill, Westerkirk, at Palmerston, Dumfries, and at Carronbridge.[21]

The Beaker people are associated with the introduction of bronze-working of which the earliest evidence appears in southern England around 2700 BC, although it was not until some five hundred years later that there is firm evidence of its spread to Scotland.[22] The emergence of metalworking was of incalculable importance. As Professor Oram put it, 'the discovery of metallurgy is, along with the development of agriculture, one of the great technological revolutions in human history.'[23]

Whereas stone-using technology, although refined over time, remained basically unchanged, metalworking required a diversity of new skills. These ranged from the ability to identify ore-bearing rocks, to extracting the metal, smelting it, manufacturing the moulds for casting it, and refining the finished product. Through time Bronze Age craftsmen acquired the skills needed to create the intricately designed pieces of metalwork, of which some examples can be seen in the Dumfries museum.

Since its constituents of copper and tin are unevenly distributed throughout Britain and Ireland, bronze-working led to a significant expansion of trade. This was accompanied by a redistribution of power to the possessors of the ore, and away from the main Neolithic centres in places like Orkney, and would have been the main reason for their abandonment about this time. Because tin is only found in Cornwall, this led to an expansion of trade – mostly seaborne – between the south-west and other parts of Britain.[24] Copper, on the other hand, is more widely distributed throughout the country.

There was also a demand for gold, particularly in the late Bronze Age when it became the fashion for the emerging warrior chieftains to deck themselves in gold ornamentation as a mark of power and status. An example is a gold lanula (a form of loop) dating from this time which was found at Sanquhar.[25] Since gold was found mainly in Ireland, it would have led to a flourishing trade with south-west Scotland,[26] and doubtless other regions on the margins of the Irish Sea. Although there were small gold deposits in the hills around Wanlockhead, they are unlikely to have been worked at this early date.[27] Trade was by no means limited to the British Isles, for even in early Bronze Age times (from around 2700 to 1500 BC) there is evidence of trade links between the people of Britain and the inhabitants of the Low Countries and adjacent parts of Germany,[28] which later expanded to include much of continental Europe.

The weaponry associated with the early Bronze Age people consisted mainly of short daggers. Perhaps this was due to a lack of the technical skill needed to manufacture more sophisticated types of weaponry. But more likely it was due to a lack of demand, given that this appears to have been a time of relative peace, and – thanks to the prevailing warm climate* – reasonable prosperity. Clearance of the native woodland continued apace – mostly with the aid of stone axes of which a number have been found in Dumfriesshire, particularly Nithsdale.[29] Consequently more land was brought into cultivation, draft oxen being used to haul the primitive ploughs, while the higher ground was abandoned to rough grazing and pasture. At the same time the existing small scattered and irregular fields were converted into larger ones, and the presence of a number of clearance cairns (piles of stones removed from these fields) in Upper Nithsdale suggests that the practice extended to marginal land as well.[30] The discovery of the remains of a contemporary solid wooden wheel at Blair Drummond in Stirlingshire points to the use of ox-drawn carts, while there is evidence of the use of metal spades.[31]

As the peasant farmers colonised the land and brought it into cultivation they established small isolated settlements. Although they are known to have existed elsewhere in late Neolithic times, it was around 1500 BC that there is the first reliably dated evidence of roundhouses in Scotland.[32] They consisted of a series of wooden posts driven into the ground to form a circle. The posts were then interleaved with wattles which were plastered with mud, clay and probably cow dung to give some protection against the elements, while the conical roof would have been covered with straw, bracken or turf.† That the Bronze Age people were also hunters is evident from

---

* The climate had oscillated considerably throughout the preceding millennia, as indeed it always has done, this being primarily a function of Earth's ever-changing position in relation to the sun.

† Recreated examples of roundhouses can be seen at Butser Ancient Farm near Petersfield in Hampshire.

the discovery of what are termed 'burnt mounds'. These are thought to be camp sites where meat was cooked, one example having been identified at Muirhead near Lockerbie.[33]

This period, namely the mid-second millennium BC, is generally regarded as marking the transition from the early to the middle Bronze Age. At the same time, the climate which had remained generally warm since the last mini-'Ice Age' at the turn of the third millennium began to deteriorate as the weather changed from the relatively stable continental pattern to the more variable Atlantic.[34] Winters became colder and summers cooler and wetter, while accumulated sand dunes dating from this period point to the onset of gale-force winds. This resulted in a shorter growing season when much of the marginal land went out of cultivation and was allowed to revert to pasture, while the uplands were abandoned. This would remain the situation until the climate began to improve during the seventh century BC.[35]

Yet the population continued to grow.[36] Because it put additional pressure on already shrinking resources, society became generally more violent as people struggled with one another for survival. This can be inferred from the discovery of more sophisticated weaponry, such as dirks, long-bladed swords, or rapiers, and spear- and mace-heads, as well as socketed axes (designed for the insertion of a haft) dating from this period.[37] The fact that finds of middle Bronze Age metalwork, and particularly weaponry, are more prolific in Dumfries and Galloway than elsewhere in Scotland[38] could suggest that it was more densely populated with a correspondingly increased competition for resources. True or not, the fact remains that warfare was becoming endemic and life for the majority of the people increasingly precarious. Therefore it only needed a major upset to cause a complete breakdown of society.

It occurred with the cataclysmic eruption of Mount Hekla in Iceland in 1159 BC (the precise date can be determined by tree ring analysis). Since nothing remained of it, the force of the explosion must have been enough to blow the whole mountain apart,* while an estimated 5.6 billion cubic metres (equivalent to several cubic miles) of cinders, ash and pumice, or tephra, exploded into the stratosphere. Blown by winds across the British Isles and Northern Europe, it caused a prolonged dimming of the sun. The extent of the catastrophe is evident from core samples taken from the Greenland ice cap, while the rings in oak trees preserved in Irish peat bogs narrowed dramatically for eighteen years after the event.[39] Because this inhibited the growth of crops, and even grass, the resulting famine is thought to have wiped out virtually half the population of Britain.[40]

The consequent chaos, lawlessness, and general anarchy, as people vied with one another for shrinking resources, would have encouraged them to put themselves under the protection of a local dominant individual or 'strong man', albeit at the cost of being reduced to the status of landless labourers.[41] Therefore, instead of consisting

---

* I was told this by a local vulcanologist during a visit to Iceland in 1978. Evidently the present Mount Hekla emerged in the course of another eruption which occurred in the early twelfth century.

mainly of peasant farmers as in the past, society became more hierarchical as these dominant individuals established themselves as warrior chieftains. This in turn led to a demand for more sophisticated personal adornment as a status symbol which was a feature of the late Bronze Age. The violence continued as warrior chieftains competed with each other for control of land and resources, suggested by the long slashing swords dating from this period which have come to light. Far more lethal than the type of weaponry they replaced, they were used in mounted combat as well as on foot, evident from the discovery of fragments of horse harness in contemporary hoards of metalwork.[42]

Reflecting the prevailing turbulence, the late Bronze Age people began surrounding their settlements with defensive earthworks. Although primarily associated with the Iron Age, they had already become a feature of later Bronze Age times[43] and are quite prolific in Dumfriesshire. The change from the late Bronze Age to the Iron Age is generally thought to have occurred around 700 BC. In reality the transition would have been far more gradual – and patchy – than such an arbitrary date would suggest. Doubtless there were a number of reasons for this, one being a reluctance on the part of the aristocracy and their craftsmen to adapt to a new technology, particularly when there were so many vested interests at stake. Nevertheless, the fact that iron is harder than bronze, and capable of producing superior weaponry, and more durable farm implements, must have been a compelling argument for change.

Ironworking spread to Britain partly through the medium of trade with the Continent where it was already well established, and with the arrival of immigrants possessing the necessary skills. Generically referred to as Celts,* they appear to have established an ascendancy over the Bronze Age people, evident among other things from the fact that their language came to predominate. In fact there are two groups of languages associated with these people. Those who settled in Ireland spoke what is termed *q-Celtic*, the forerunner of Irish Gaelic, or Erse, from which the Gaelic of Scotland and the Isle of Man are derived. Others spoke what is described as a *p-Celtic* variant which was the language of the ancient Britons and forerunner of Cornish, Welsh and Cumbric. The last of these became the speech of southern Scotland until displaced by Anglo-Scandinavian in the east and Gaelic in the west around the mid-twelfth century AD.

Since iron ore is more widely dispersed than copper and tin, it led to a falling-off in long-distance trade. Therefore the Iron Age people tended to be more insular and less cosmopolitan than their Bronze Age predecessors. This would remain the case until the development of trade links with the emerging markets of the Mediterranean in about the first century BC, when locally produced wool, animal skins and hunting dogs would have been exchanged for oil, wine and other luxuries which were the perquisite of the Iron Age aristocracy.[44] Because iron was more widely available, and

---

* The Celts did not necessarily have a common ethnic identity. Rather, it was a collective term used to describe a people with a common culture and certain linguistic similarities.

metal no longer the main source of wealth, it was replaced by agricultural produce such as grain and livestock as the principal medium of exchange.

This meant that land was increasingly at a premium. Combined with the population explosion which is known to have occurred during the last centuries BC, this would account for the extensive forest clearance and expansion of cultivated land, which is apparent from an analysis of contemporary pollen samples.[45] In Dumfriesshire farming would have been mainly pastoral, giving point to Professor Piggott's portrayal of Iron Age society as one of 'Celtic cowboys and shepherds, footloose and unpredictable, moving with their animals over rough pasture and moorland'.[46] This is supported by archaeological evidence which shows the north Solway plain as an important centre of pastoral farming in late Iron Age times,[47] while their livestock consisted mainly of cattle (kept for their meat rather than their milk), sheep and pigs. Also horses which were used primarily for warfare, racing and light farm work (the heavy work was done by oxen); in fact the Iron Age people were noted horsemen, as well as being dedicated horse dealers.[48]

Cultivation of the land reclaimed from the native forest was facilitated by the introduction of the heavier iron-tipped plough associated with the Celts, of which an example was found in a peat bog near Lochmaben[49] That corn was cut with iron sickles is evident from the discovery of the remains of one at Applegarthtown.[50] By 250 BC the improvement in the climate which had taken place since the turn of the fourth century encouraged the colonising of hitherto neglected moorland, evident from the rapid expansion of hill settlements in the Southern Uplands which have been carbon dated to around that time.[51] Consisting of groups of dwellings, they are known as 'platform settlements', so-called because they were built on a 'platform' – or foundation – created by hollowing out the hillside and dumping the excavated material on the downside. The fact that a number of these have been identified in upper Eskdale and Ewesdale suggests that the region was probably quite densely populated.[52]

Competition for land would have been mainly responsible for the endemic conflict between family groups which was a feature of Iron Age society. It frequently took the form of mutual cattle raiding (which would persist throughout the Border country and elsewhere until as late as the seventeenth century). That horses were used in combat, and presumably for rounding up cattle, is evident from the discovery of a contemporary hoard of bridle bits, rein rings, harness mountings, and others dating from this period at Middlebie.[53] The prevailing inter-family – and later inter-tribal – warfare was mainly responsible for the building of hillforts which are mainly associated with the Iron Age. They varied in size, although the more prestigious must have been very large edifices. Judging from the remains of the surrounding ramparts and ditches, building them must have represented a huge investment of labour, while the discovery of heavy metal chains suggests the use of slave labour.[54]

Most of the hillforts in Dumfriesshire were situated in Annandale, the most prominent being the one on top of Burnswark near Lockerbie which is thought to have been a local ruling centre. On the other hand, there are proportionately fewer in

Nithsdale, the outstanding one being the hillfort which crowns the top of Tynron Doon near the head of mid-Nithsdale. But the fact that they are more numerous in Eskdale* suggests that it continued to be quite densely populated. Dominating them all is the massive Castle O'er which is situated above the confluence of the Black Esk and the White Esk in upper Eskdale. During later Iron Age times it was expanded to accommodate nine large family roundhouses, and this too could have been a local ruling centre.

Another type of dwelling dating from Iron Age times are crannogs, which are thought to have been high-status settlements. Situated on lochs or marshy ground, they were built on a foundation of tree trunks with an infill of stones and weighted down with boulders to form an artificial island. This served as a platform for building a cluster of roundhouses, the island being connected to the mainland by a causeway. Three have been identified in Dumfriesshire – one near Sanquhar, while the other two are located in the Castle Loch at Lochmaben,[†] and in a small loch near Friars Carse in Nithsdale.[55] (There is another in Loch Urr just over the county boundary in Kirkcudbrightshire.) There were doubtless more, but because crannogs were built on water or marshland it meant that once abandoned they would have quickly disintegrated.

The existence of roundhouses within the confines of the larger hillforts suggests a resident population, while there would have been ample scope to accommodate an influx of people in times of danger,[56] but only temporarily because the length of their stay would have been limited by the availability of food and water. As well as serving as a refuge, and possibly a local ruling centre, the discovery of pieces of metal at the Mote of Mark near Dalbeattie in Kirkcudbrightshire suggests that craftsmen were employed at these centres under the patronage of the local chieftain. Equally importantly, the larger hillforts served as a venue for ritualistic celebrations to mark the principal events in the year, and possibly the sacrifice of animals. Although human sacrifice is a well-attested tradition among the Celts, there is no evidence of it being practised in south-west Scotland.

Sacrifice was merely one means of propitiating the numerous gods in the Celtic pantheon. Since these people, like their Bronze Age predecessors, perceived most of their gods as inhabiting water which they regarded as the principal source of life, sacrifice involved casting votive offerings into pools and marshes. Probably consisting of booty and trophies of war, they included ornamental work and pieces of jewellery, of which a number have been found in lochs and peat bogs. A striking example was the large haul of metalwork retrieved from the Carlingwark loch at Castle Douglas in 1866.

---

* Evident from the 1:50,000 OS map (no 79) which shows a large number of settlements; but the fact that most are blanketed by forestry makes it difficult to identify them.

† The remains of this crannog, which is thought to date from the time of the Roman occupation, is only visible after a spell of dry weather and a consequent lowering of the water level (see Wilson J B, 'The Crannog in the Castle Loch, Lochmaben' *TDGNHAS*, lvii (1982), pp 88 et seq).

An important feature of the later Iron Age was the emergence of tribal group-ings. These are identifiable from the map attributed to the second century AD Greek geographer Ptolemy. This shows the land to the south of the Firth of Clyde being occupied by the Damnonii, while the Votadini controlled eastern Scotland south of the Forth. However, most of southern Scotland was inhabited by the aggressive Selgovae whose territory extended into Dumfriesshire, while to the west were the Novantae. What the map omits to show is that the territory of the Brigantes, a particularly warlike tribe who occupied much of northern England, extended into modern Dumfriesshire. This was significant, because the inhabitants of that enclave were a perpetual source of trouble to their neighbours, as well as to the Romans during their occupation of the region.

ROMAN INTERLUDE

Dumfriesshire was on the northern edge of the Roman empire, but like the rest of southern Scotland it only came under Roman rule intermittently during their near-four centuries' occupation of southern Britain. Nevertheless evidence of their presence is ubiquitous, particularly in the many Roman artefacts which have come to light in the course of ongoing excavations. Perhaps even more so from the remains of their forts, fortlets and marching camps, many of which have been identified through aerial survey and crop discolourations. Similarly their road network which is still partially detectable.

The Roman occupation of Britain began in AD 43 when the Emperor Claudius, anxious to secure a military triumph to strengthen his position at home, dispatched an expeditionary force to subjugate it and incorporate it into the Roman empire. Consisting of four legions, each comprising 5,000 men and a like number of auxiliary troops, it landed on the Solent. From there it proceeded to conquer much of southern England, at which point Claudius arrived in Britain to take command in person. Having gained possession of Colchester and established it as the ruling centre of Roman Britain, he forced the local tribes to make peace against the surrender of hostages. Thereafter he returned to Rome leaving the governor Aulus Plautius with the somewhat vague instruction to 'conquer the rest'.

This proved easier said than done. In the course of the next two decades he and his successors had to contend with two major revolts, one by Boadicea and the other under Caratacus. They were suppressed but only with difficulty, the latter being achieved through the conclusion of a peace treaty with Cartimandua, queen of the Brigantes, which effectively secured the Romans' northern flank. A powerful and warlike tribe, the Brigantes controlled the territory comprising most of northern England from the line of the Humber and Mersey, which extended into south-eastern Dumfriesshire.

In AD 69 they rebelled. It stemmed from a dispute between Cartimandua and her ex-husband Venutius whom she had driven into exile. As soon as news of the revolt reached him, the Emperor Vespasian ordered the governor Petillius Cerialis to suppress it, which he did with the utmost ferocity. In AD 72 he consolidated his success by founding the city of Carlisle where he installed a garrison to serve as a permanent Roman presence in the region.[57] From there he launched a successful invasion of modern Dumfriesshire where he established rudimentary forts at Birrens (known as Blatobulgium) near Ecclefechan, and Dalswinton (the first of four identifiable forts built there), for purposes of controlling Annandale and Nithsdale. No doubt he intended to build other ones, but he was recalled to Rome following the expiry of his term of office.

Building on his achievements, his successor Julius Agricola spent the next few years campaigning against the people of central Scotland and beyond. Having defeated them at the battle of Mons Graupius in AD 83, he consolidated his control over southern Scotland by ordering the construction of a line of forts from the Firth of Clyde to the Tay. Thereafter he spent the rest of his governorship strengthening his position still further by establishing additional forts and fortlets to accommodate the enlarged military presence in the region.

He was also responsible for initiating a road system. Apart from facilitating communications, and hence the administration of the region, it enabled troops to be rushed to trouble spots in the event of outbreaks of native unrest which occurred from time to time, and suppress them before they got out of hand. One road which can be identified with certainty is that which, presumably starting from Carlisle, crossed the Sark near Springfield. Continuing north-westwards past Birrens, probably following a track which had existed since Stone Age times, it linked up with a newly built fort at Ladyward immediately north-west of Lockerbie. From there it would have extended as far as Milton, another newly built fort, near Beattock. At the same time a fortlet was established beside the Iron Age hillfort on Burnswark.

The forts at Ladyward and Milton were doubtless intended to control mid- and upper Annandale. Similarly, another one which was established at Drumlanrig would have guarded the entrance to Upper Nithsdale and the hill country to the west, while the fortlet at Durisdeer, which is thought to date from this period, guarded the entrance to the pass through the Lowther Hills into upper Clydesdale. The fort at Drumlanrig infers the existence of a road of sorts connecting it with Dalswinton, which itself may have been linked by another road to the Agricolan fort at Glenlochar on the Dee. Further east, Agricola was responsible for building a fort at Broomholm on the Esk, immediately south of Langholm.

Rectangular in shape, and generally built to accommodate between five hundred and a thousand men, the forts conformed to a standard design. At the centre was the headquarters building which included an assembly hall. Behind it were the administrative offices, and ranged on either side were the barrack blocks, stables and storehouses. The fort was surrounded by at least one, and usually more, ramparts. Initially they were built of earth and turf excavated from the surrounding ditches, but later they were replaced with stone. The buildings themselves were originally timbered with thatched roofs, though they too were later built of stone. Finally entrance gates were placed at either end.

Around the turn of the second century AD the Romans were engaged in a war against the tribes on the lower Danube. It was not going well. Having suffered two major reverses, they were compelled to draw reinforcements from their armies in other parts of the empire, including Britain. Consequently their occupying force in southern Scotland became so attenuated that in 105 the Emperor Trajan decided to abandon the region and withdraw to the Tyne Solway line. So ended what is known as the Flavian period of occupation.* Nevertheless the principal forts such as Milton and Dalswinton which guarded the main river valleys continued to be occupied, while the Romans maintained a careful surveillance of the region with the aid of native spies and scouts.

Nevertheless, freed from Roman rule, the tribes of southern Scotland became increasingly restive, but in 122 Trajan's successor the Emperor Hadrian came to Britain. Having appraised the situation, he ordered a wall to be built from Wallsend, near the mouth of the Tyne, to Bowness on the southern shore of the Solway Firth. Known as Hadrian's Wall, it was eighty-four miles long and equipped with turrets and milecastles (so-called because they were built at a distance of one Roman mile apart). These were designed to accommodate the contingents of soldiery who were stationed at the Wall to maintain peace and stability among the people on either side. Meanwhile the mutually advantageous trade between them was allowed to continue, although access across the Wall was limited to sixteen heavily guarded checkpoints. This was as much to control the movement of people from one side to the other as to prevent Brigantian troublemakers from stirring up unrest among their fellow tribesmen in Dumfriesshire.

However, the growing militancy of the Brigantians on one side, and the tribespeople on the other, meant that what was originally intended as a demarcation line became a defensive fortification. Therefore the garrison was strengthened by an increased military presence, cavalry as well as infantry, and new forts, such as Vindolanda, Housteads, Chesters and Corstopitum (Corbridge), were built to accommodate them. Those at Birrens and Netherby were also strengthened, while another fort was built at Bewcastle in Roxburghshire, to accommodate the troops needed to control the Brigantian enclave beyond the Wall.[58]

In 144 the governor Lollius Urbicus scored a decisive victory over the tribesmen of southern Scotland. Following this, Hadrian's successor Antoninus Pius re-occupied the region and built a second wall – the Antonine Wall – which extended from the Forth to the Clyde. At the same time he took the Brigantian territory in southern Scotland under direct rule, apparently in punishment for an unprovoked attack on the Novantae.[59] Known as the Antonine period, it witnessed the building of further

---

*   So called after the ruling dynasty of Roman emperors.

forts and fortlets such as those at Raeburnfoot at Eskdalemuir, and Barburgh Mill near Auldgirth. Another was built close to the site of an Iron Age fort on Ward Law immediately above Caerlaverock, while the fort at Netherby is thought to date from this period. Other forts, such as those at Durisdeer, Ladyward, Milton and Broomholm, were enlarged and strengthened, and it was probably at this time that a second fort was established on Burnswark which, like the existing one, is thought to have served as a training camp. In a change of policy, the fort at Dalswinton was abandoned in favour of another one further down the Nith at Carzield which was the lowest fordable point on the river.

It was probably about this time that the road through Annandale to Milton was extended up the Beef Tub before striking north-west to link up with the Roman camp at Little Clyde, and ultimately the important Roman centre at Crawford. Meanwhile a road was most likely built to link Drumlanrig with the fortlet at Durisdeer since there is evidence of its extension north-eastwards through the Lowther hills to Crawford, while there would have been a trackway heading north from Drumlanrig to the fort at Sanquhar. It is thought that a road may have linked Carzield with the main route through Annandale, and – perhaps more certainly – there would have been a road of sorts up Eskdale from Netherby via the fort at Broomholm to Raeburnfoot.[60] There are also traces of a road connecting Raeburnfoot with Newstead in the Border country, while another headed westwards through Dryfesdale presumably to link up with the main Annandale route.[61]

As the name implies, fortlets such as those at Durisdeer, Barburgh Mill and Ward Law were smaller than forts; and surrounded by a single rampart and ditch, they were designed to accommodate some eighty troops. Apart from guard duties, which included patrolling the adjacent stretch of road and signalling information down the line, they were responsible for ensuring that the road was properly maintained, and for escorting convoys of provisions and other goods passing along it. Finally there were signalling stations and marching camps, the latter being essentially temporary structures. That there were a larger number of forts, fortlets and camps in Dumfriesshire than elsewhere in southern Scotland suggests that the Romans regarded it as a particularly troublesome region, perhaps because it was a buffer zone between three warring tribes. On the east were the aggressively hostile Selgovae who controlled much of the Border country including upper Eskdale, while the territory to the west was occupied by their adversaries the Novantae who were generally more amenable to Roman rule. Between them was the Brigantian enclave which comprised lower Eskdale and the adjacent part of Annandale.

During the Antonine period civilian settlements grew up alongside the forts. For the most part they would have been occupied by retired soldiers and serving soldiers' women (it was only later that soldiers were allowed to marry) and children. Also native traders, because these settlements functioned as markets where soldiers could buy, or barter for, locally produced goods. Much however was requisitioned. This applied in particular to corn as well as cattle which were much in demand not only for their meat and milk but also for their hides. These were processed into leather for making saddles, shoes, clothing, bags, shields and tents, all essential to the soldiers' equipment.[62]

As a rule the Romans administered their conquered territories through the agency of tribal chieftains, replacing hostile ones with those willing to collaborate. Nevertheless Roman functionaries maintained a close watch on the native inhabitants and insisted on attending – or being represented at – their meetings. This was only partially successful because covertly hostile tribal leaders and self-appointed troublemakers could always hold clandestine meetings to plan a rebellion, as happened from time to time. Whereas friendly tribes were treated relatively leniently, and hostile ones very much less so, outbreaks of unrest were suppressed with merciless severity.

Generally speaking, Roman rule bought peace and a measure of prosperity. But it came at a price. Because the Romans tried to run their conquered territories at a profit, or at least render them self-financing, heavy taxes were imposed on the subject people. Additionally, they were required to provide forced labour when called on to do so, perhaps for a pittance, or more often nothing at all. Similarly, much of the farmers' produce was either requisitioned or they were forced to sell it to the occupying troops at a discounted price. Probably most resented of all was the regular conscription of able-bodied men for military service in other parts of the empire, from where they were unlikely to return. It was this, combined with the exactions of unscrupulous tax-gatherers, which was mainly responsible for the revolts that periodically broke out in Britain and elsewhere.

In 155 the Brigantes rebelled again. Although they were brutally suppressed, and the population massacred, the Emperor Antoninus Pius seems to have decided that there was nothing to be gained from a continuing occupation of southern Scotland. Therefore he had Hadrian's Wall put back in commission and ordered a phased withdrawal to the Tyne–Solway line. This encouraged the tribesmen of southern Scotland to go on the offensive, and on his accession in 161 the Emperor Marcus Aurelius ordered the governor Calpurnius Agricola to crush them. Having achieved this, and extracted promises of future good behaviour against the taking of hostages, he completed the withdrawal, and abandoned all the forts with the exception of Birrens which was maintained as an outpost.

Their promises proved hollow. During the reign of Marcus Aurelius's son, the Emperor Commodus, the Roman writer Cassius Dio tells us that the tribesmen, namely the Caledonii and Maeatae, 'crossed the Wall [and] did a great deal of damage, and cut down a general and his troops', presumably slaughtering the Roman garrison at Birrens. Commodus responded by ordering the governor Ulpius Marcellus to drive them back. Described as a man of austere incorruptibility and an excessively strict disciplinarian,[63] he inflicted what was described as 'a major defeat on the barbarians'. In time-honoured fashion he followed up his victory with a mass execution of prisoners. Nevertheless the tribesmen remained defiant. In 196, taking advantage of an outbreak of civil war between the supporters of the Emperor Severus and those of his co-Caesar Albinus, they launched a successful attack on the northern frontier and had to be bought off with a large bribe. But it was merely postponing the inevitable.

In the summer of 210 the tribesmen rebelled again. This time it was war to the knife. The Emperor Severus ordered the governor to conduct a punitive campaign against them and, as it was put, 'slaughter everyone in sight'. Nevertheless the situation was serious enough to bring him to Britain, and assisted by reinforcements from other parts of Britain he regained control of southern Scotland. Determined to build on his success, he spent the following winter planning a campaign against the tribesmen beyond the Tay. But it never materialised, for – already terminally ill – Severus died in February 211. His sons Caracalla and Geta competed with each other for the succession, the dispute compounded by their opposing attitudes towards southern Scotland. Whereas Caracalla took the view that continued occupation was more trouble than it was worth, Geta was determined to retain it. Caracalla prevailed by the simple expedient of having Geta murdered. Thereafter, we are told that 'he made treaties with the enemy, evacuated their territory and abandoned their forts'. Finally, having ordered the re-commissioning of Hadrian's Wall, and the refurbishment of Birrens, Netherby and Bewcastle where there was a continuing military presence, he returned to Rome.

The situation beyond the northern frontier appears to have remained quiescent for the rest of the century. However in the early 300s war broke out again when the Picts (a term applied by the Romans to the northern tribes in general) invaded southern Scotland and attacked Hadrian's Wall. In 305 they were driven back by the Emperor Constantius Chlorus. When he died the following year, his son Constantine was proclaimed emperor. Renowned for declaring Christianity as the official religion of the Roman empire, he continued his father's campaign against the Picts, and so did his son the Emperor Constans who eventually made peace with them.

In the 360s the Roman position in Britain began to crumble under the impact of attacks by the Picts from the north (in breach of their treaty with Constans), the Scotti* from Ireland, and the Saxons from across the North Sea – an alliance referred to by Roman commentators as 'the barbarian conspiracy'. In 367 the Emperor Valentinian sent his leading general Theodosius to Britain to bring the situation under control. Having achieved this, he consolidated his success by having Hadrian's Wall put back in commission.

In the course of his campaign Theodosius is credited by contemporary writers with regaining control of an unnamed province which had been overrun by the native Britons. This is thought to have comprised the territory extending from the

---

* Hence the name Scots and Scotland, although another two centuries were to elapse before they began to settle there, when they were responsible for introducing the Gaelic language which, being a regional variant of Erse, is non-native to Scotland.

Wall to as far south as the Ribble – a region which had been devastated by the 'barbarian' invasion. Called Valentia after the emperor, it is believed to have been the forerunner of the British kingdom of Rheged which later expanded to include much of south-west Scotland. In fact it may already have absorbed much of modern Dumfriesshire by the time the Romans abandoned Britain in the early fifth century.

Notwithstanding Theodosius's successes, the northern tribes continued their raids. Although they were repeatedly driven back, Roman rule was becoming increasingly precarious as troops were progressively withdrawn to defend their homeland against invaders from the east. The eventual departure of the Romans from Britain would have gone virtually unnoticed by the inhabitants of southern Scotland. This was mainly because the dearth of Roman artefacts during the latter stages of their occupation of Britain suggests that, there at least, all contact with them had long since ceased. Consequently Iron Age society would have remained much the same as it had existed before the arrival of the Romans.

THE POST-ROMAN ERA

The Roman withdrawal marked the onset of what was traditionally known as the Dark Age, so-called because of the relative scarcity of information about this period, although thanks to modern research we now know far more about it than in the past. Yet Roman influence remained, particularly in some of the larger towns such as Carlisle, which continued to be centres of Roman culture (*romanitas*). Meanwhile the spread of Christianity among a predominantly pagan population is evident from place-names prefixed by *eccles* or its equivalent, such as Ecclefechan, Eaglesfield and Eccles near Penpont, which are taken to imply the existence of an early church.[64]

The people living beyond the Solway Firth – and elsewhere for that matter – would have been mainly peasant farmers and landless labourers engaged in livestock rearing and scratching a subsistence living from the none-too-fertile soil, while paying tribute to a ruling elite. It was a precarious existence, rendered the more so by at least two natural disasters which occurred during that time. One was an outbreak of bubonic plague in about 514 which is believed to have affected the western Britons in particular. Thought to have spread from the infected crews of trading vessels from the Mediterranean seaports, it was reported to have been 'so sudden and sharp that the living were unable to bury the dead'.[65] The other was a succession of particularly lean years between 536 and 545 which were the result of a catastrophic eruption of Mount Krakatoa in Indonesia. Vast quantities of tephra were spewed up into the stratosphere which led to a prolonged dimming of the sun, and the consequent drop in temperature, combined with drought conditions, was responsible for successive crop failures and consequent widespread hunger and starvation.*

---

* The prolonged cold spell is evident from tree ring analysis, while its attribution to the eruption of Mount Krakatoa was the subject of two TV documentaries in July and August 1999, and repeated in May 2000.

Meanwhile a Christian settlement was established at the important trading centre of Whithorn in Wigtownshire. During the fifth century it is thought to have come under the influence of Pelagianism, a heresy which had been anathematised by the Pope. Therefore a certain Nyniau,* allegedly the son of a Romano-British chieftain, is believed to have been sent there by the religious authorities at Carlisle to eradicate it.[66] Much has been written about him and most of it speculative; in fact all that is known with reasonable certainty is that he was an early – or possibly the first – bishop of Whithorn. In his *Historia Ecclesia* written some three centuries later, Bede the Northumbrian monk of Jarrow credits him with converting the southern Picts to Christianity. If so, his apparent disregard of the people living in modern Kirkcudbrightshire and Dumfriesshire, who after all were much closer to home, suggests that most of them were already converts.

If not they must shortly have become so, because this region came under the control of the expanding Christianised kingdom of Rheged (or Yrechwydd). Thought to have been based initially on Brougham, and later Carlisle, virtually all that is known about it comes from Welsh sources where it is referred to as 'the land of the north'. This would account for the theory that it was based on the Roman province of Valentia which was established by the Roman general Theodosius in the late fourth century. There is no certainty as to how far it stretched, although at its maximum extent it is thought to have embraced much of present-day Cumbria, including the Eden valley, modern Dumfriesshire, part if not the whole of Galloway,[†] and southern Ayrshire.

The king who is thought to have been responsible for its expansion into south-west Scotland was Urbgen. Meaning literally 'city born' he is better known as Urien. Member of a family of British kinglets based in Wales, he was the leader of a confederacy of British princes who had banded together to resist the aggressive and warlike Anglian rulers of Bernicia.[‡] Therefore he was most likely responsible for the British victory over the Bernicians at Arderdydd, possibly identifiable with Arthuret a few miles north of Carlisle, in about 573. This may have encouraged the ruling elite in south-west Scotland to put themselves under his protection, which probably explains the absorption of the region into his kingdom.

Urien's principal confederate was Rhydderch Hael, king of Strathclyde and better known as the patron of St Mungo, otherwise St Kentigern. Like Ninian, Kentigern was credited with a number of miracles which were designed to enhance his reputation as a holy man and render him eligible for canonisation. Early writers ascribe him a virgin birth, his mother having allegedly been a British princess from Lothian. When her royal father learnt that she had become pregnant out of wedlock he was so

---

* Latinised to Ninianus, hence Ninian.
† The long-held theory that Dunragit at the head of Luce Bay meant 'fort of Rheged' and marked the western extremity of the kingdom has been discounted.
‡ A recently established Anglian kingdom, it broadly comprised the counties of Northumberland, Durham and north Yorkshire.

enraged that he ordered her to be thrown from a cliff top into the sea. Miraculously she survived. Therefore her unrelenting father is alleged to have had her cast adrift in an open boat in the Firth of Forth, and while tossed to and fro on the waves she gave birth to Kentigern.

The story goes that they were rescued by St Serf who, finding mother and infant washed up on the shores of Fife near his centre of Culross, took them under his wing. And it was there that Kentigern allegedly spent his boyhood. During this time he is supposed to have performed a number of miracles such as restoring St Serf's pet robin – and also his old cook – to life, and (perhaps allegorically) summoning fire from heaven to re-light some lamps which some mischievous youths had put out. When Kentigern eventually left Culross he is credited with crossing the Firth of Forth dryshod. That Macquarrie goes on to say that he 'then caused the tide to rise so that St Serf could not follow him' (shades of Moses' Egyptian pursuers being cut off by the Red Sea) suggests that for some reason Kentigern had incurred his wrath, had escaped from him, and that the enraged saint was trying to recapture him.[67]

Reaching Glasgow, Kentigern put himself under the protection of the Christian king of Strathclyde, who subsequently had him appointed bishop of the diocese.[*] During this time he reputedly performed further miracles such as sowing sand and reaping wheat. But when the king was supplanted by Morgan, a pagan Briton, Kentigern took refuge in Wales. There he remained until summoned back to Glasgow by Rhydderch Hael who had recently overthrown Morgan and seized control of the kingdom. In the course of his return journey Kentigern is believed to have visited Hoddom and founded a primitive monastery there.

Back in Glasgow, Kentigern is credited with performing further miracles – his clothes never got wet in the rain, and he recovered for the queen a ring which she had imprudently given her lover. Further, he is alleged to have caused fresh mulberries to be produced in January for a visiting Church dignitary, while so arranging matters that some milk which had been accidentally spilt into the Clyde was miraculously transformed into a stone of cheese. More realistically, he was responsible for converting the people of Strathclyde to Christianity, a task that would occupy him for the rest of his long life until his death in about 615. Although St Mungo is the only dedication to him in Dumfriesshire, the name of his alleged disciple St Conal is thought to have been preserved in Dercongal, the former name of Holywood abbey.[68]

Meanwhile, following his victory at Arderdydd, Urien continued his campaign against the Bernicians. But sometime between 586 and 593 he was killed along with his son Owain while laying siege to the Bernician stronghold of Bamburgh. After his death Aedán mac Gabráin king of Dal riata assumed the leadership of the confederacy of British princes – surprisingly considering he was a Scottish Gael of Irish

---

*   This is thought to have been co-extensive with the kingdom of Strathclyde which at that time was confined to the region of the lower Clyde. Therefore, when the kingdom expanded southwards in the early tenth century, the diocese was correspondingly enlarged.

extraction. Nevertheless his record as a successful warlord may have persuaded them to put their trust in him. If so it proved misplaced, for in 603 he was defeated by the Bernician king Ethelfrith at the battle of Degsastan* when both sides are said to have suffered huge casualties.

Ethelfrith's victory and the resulting disintegration of the kingdom of Rheged opened the way for the Northumbrian† expansion westward towards Carlisle, and within a few years they had overrun the whole of northern England as far as the Cumbrian coast. In about 613 Ethelfrith defeated a British force at Chester having first slaughtered a group of monks who had come to pray for peace. Meanwhile the Northumbrians' control of present-day Cumbria effectively separated the Britons of Wales from their northern compatriots who in consequence developed their own variant of the Welsh language known as Cumbric.

In 616 Ethelfrith was defeated and killed by Edwin, a member of the royal house of Deira. Edwin was responsible for extending the Northumbrian kingdom as far as the Firth of Forth and bringing Lothian under his rule. It was here, on the shores of the Forth, that he established the stronghold of Edinburgh to which he gave his name. Following this, he turned his attention to the west where he consolidated Northumbrian rule over the whole of northern England as far as the Irish Sea. From there he went on to take possession of the Isle of Man. In 632 Edwin was defeated and killed by Ethelfrith's son Oswald, recently returned from Iona where he had sought refuge following his father's death. Having gained possession of Northumbria, Oswald sent a delegation to the community at Iona requesting them to send a mission under Aidan, a prominent churchman, to convert his subjects to Christianity, which he appears to have achieved in a remarkably short time.

Oswald was probably also responsible for the Northumbrian advance beyond the Solway into Dumfriesshire, evident from Jocelyn's life of Kentigern which states that they reached Hoddom in the early decades of the seventh century.[69] In what may have been an attempt to win over the ruling élite of Dumfriesshire and Galloway, Oswald arranged for his brother and successor Oswy to marry Urien's great-granddaughter Rhienmelth.‡ Evidently the attempt failed because the Northumbrians appear to have encountered considerable resistance. At least so it would seem from the fact that, whereas they are credited with establishing themselves at Hoddom at a relatively early date, it was not until the end of the seventh century that they brought western Galloway fully under control.[70] Possible supporting evidence comes from the contemporary storming of the Mote of Mark, near Dalbeattie, when the ramparts were fired

---

* The site of the battle has never been properly identified. An earlier suggestion that Degsastan is identifiable with Dawston Burn in Upper Liddesdale has been discounted in favour of somewhere in northern England.

† The reference to the Northumbrians stems from the fact that, sometime after Degsastan, Ethelfrith took over the neighbouring Anglian kingdom of Deira (comprising southern Yorkshire) which together with Bernicia comprised the ancient kingdom of Northumbria.

‡ Ominously her name meant 'princess of darkness'.

and the fortress demolished.[71] Similarly the vitrification* of the fort on Trusty's Hill near Gatehouse of Fleet.[72]

Having gained control of south-west Scotland, the Northumbrian – or Anglian – colonisers settled in the more fertile regions, mainly as small-time farmers, having slaughtered the native inhabitants, or driven them out into the poorer uplands to the north, or enslaved them. Since place-name evidence points to the Northumbrians establishing districts known as 'shires' in neighbouring Kirkcudbrightshire,[73] they would presumably have done the same in Dumfriesshire. In which case the 'shires' would have comprised the three main river valleys, the Nith, the Annan and the Esk, and been the forerunners of Nithsdale, Annandale and Eskdale. Yet there is little surviving evidence of the Northumbrian presence in Dumfriesshire. Apart from the discovery of fragments of crosses in an old kirkyard at Hoddom which are taken to be evidence of the existence of a mother church or minster, a more obvious relic is the intricately carved Ruthwell Cross which is incorporated in the local church. In addition, some late Anglian stones have come to light in the parishes of Closeburn and Glencairn,[74] while the remains of a timber hall (perhaps on the site of the Neolithic one) have been identified near the town centre of Lockerbie.[75]

On the other hand, the Northumbrians' presence in the region is well attested by place-name evidence. They include places ending in –ton, derived from the Old English *tūn* meaning a settlement, and its derivatives –toun and –tone as in Johnstone, and 'ham' a village, as in Edyngham, which was the site of an old church on the outskirts of Annan.[76] Other place-names point to the region being well wooded. For example names like Tinwald, Torthorwald and Mouswald are derived from the Old English *weald* meaning 'a woody place'. Similarly the word *grafa*, as in Hardgrove (between Kinmount and Dalton), was the Old English word for a coppice, while *ryding*, as in Spittalridding Hill, Belridden, Riddingwood and Lawridding, near Amisfield, meant 'a clearing'. This suggests that the Northumbrian Angles were clear-felling parts of the native woodland and bringing them into cultivation.

In 685 the Northumbrian advance northward was abruptly checked. Having overrun the territory as far as the Forth and penetrated modern Fife, Oswy's son and successor Egfrith overreached himself. Ignoring the advice of his friends and courtiers alike, he insisted on extending his campaign to the region beyond the Firth of Tay. But the local Picts were ready for him. Luring him and his men as far as the vicinity of present-day Forfar, the Picts turned on them and virtually annihilated them at the battle of Nechtansmere (now Dunnichen) where Egfrith was killed. Following up their success, they drove the Northumbrians back through Fife and across the Firth of Forth.

---

* This involved burning the earth and timber walls and reducing them to a slaggy mass which when cooled fused together.

This marked the northern limit of their expansion on the east. On the other hand, they were more successful in the west where they eventually overran the British (or Brittonic) kingdom of Strathclyde. By 750 they had gained possession of Kyle, which comprised central Ayrshire, and in alliance with their former enemies the Picts they captured the British capital of Al Cluyd on Dumbarton Rock in 756. This gave them virtual control of the whole of southern Scotland, and at the same time it marked the zenith of their power. After that the Northumbrian kingdom began to disintegrate, mainly as a result of disputes over the kingship as successive rulers were deposed, expelled or murdered. Consequently it was left gravely weakened and vulnerable to attack by the Vikings.

THE VIKINGS

From the late eighth century onwards the Norse and Danish Vikings feature prominently in the annals of western Europe, first as hit-and-run raiders and later as traders and settlers. Driven by a combination of land hunger resulting from an expanding population, the prospect of loot, and doubtless a sense of adventure, these intrepid seafarers concentrated their attacks initially on the coastal regions of Britain and northern Europe. Rowing up the principal rivers in their highly manoeuvrable clinker-built longships, they terrorised local populations, burning their settlements, plundering religious houses and carrying off their treasures. Later, having driven out the existing inhabitants they settled in the more fertile regions to become farmers, while others set themselves up as traders. This is apparent from recent excavations at York which show abundant evidence of its being an important centre under Danish Viking rule in the tenth century.

During the latter part of the eighth century Norse Vikings were establishing settlements in the Northern Isles and the Hebrides,[77] evident from the Norse-derived place-names there. Yet it was on the south coast that their first recorded attack on mainland Britain occurred in 787. According to the Anglo-Saxon chronicle three Viking longships put in at Portland on the coast of Dorset. When the reeve of Dorchester, assuming they were merchants, rode up and demanded payment of the tax due by foreign traders they killed him. Although a small, localised incident, it was a foretaste of what was to come, for in June 793 a band of Norse Vikings sacked the monastery at Lindisfarne. Its treasures were seized while the monks were slaughtered, thrown into the sea and left to drown, or carried off as slaves.

Referring to the outrage, his account obviously larded with hyperbole, the Anglo-Saxon chronicler recorded that: 'this year [793] came dreadful forewarnings over the land of the Northumbrians, terrifying the people most woefully. There were immense sheets of lightning rushing through the air [accompanied by] whirlwinds and fiery dragons flying across the firmament. And [soon after] the harrowing inroads of heathen men made lamentable havoc in the Church of God [at Lindisfarne] by rapine and slaughter.' More prosaically, a clearly shocked Alcuin, the famous scholar of York, declared: 'Never before has such an atrocity been seen.'*

Meanwhile the Norse Vikings who had established themselves in the Northern Isles and the Hebrides were extending their raids down the west coast. In 794 they sacked the monastery on Iona. Returning there in 802, they sacked it again – and yet again in 805 when the monks were slaughtered and the abbey burnt. It was finally abandoned the following year when the survivors fled to Kells in Ireland taking with them their illuminated copy of the Gospels known as the Book of Kells.

By the turn of the ninth century the Norse Vikings had extended their plundering raids to Ireland where they carried off men, women and children into slavery. In the early 800s they established a kingdom based on Dublin, and in keeping with the Viking practice of intermarrying with local populations they assimilated with the native Irish. During the latter half of the ninth century their Norse-Irish descendants estab-lished other coastal settlements in the region, including the forerunners of the modern cities of Waterford, Wexford, Cork and Limerick. Meanwhile others were raiding the Isle of Man, and later mainland Britain, focusing their attacks in particu-lar on the coastal regions from the Solway Firth to North Wales.

Throughout this time Norse Vikings were carrying out a series of raids on the coastal regions of northern Europe from the mouth of the Elbe to the Bay of Biscay, and penetrat-ing far up the main rivers they looted and pillaged at will. Their raids began in the reign of the Emperor Charlemagne and continued with unabated ferocity throughout that of his son Louis the Pious. Following the latter's death in 840, civil war broke out between his sons over the carve-up of the Frankish empire. In 845, taking advantage of this, the Vikings attacked the region of Paris. Unable to repel them, Louis' youngest son, Charles the Bald king of the West Franks, bought them off with the grant of settlement lands.

This seems to have kept them quiet for the best part of forty years. But when in 884 the crown passed to Charles's five-year-old grandson Charles the Simple,† the Vikings renewed their attacks. Finally in 911, following the time-honoured policy of recruiting one Viking warband to help fight off the others, Charles endowed a leading chieftain Rolf, or Rollo,‡ with lands in the vicinity of Rouen. This was conditional on him and his followers converting to Christianity, swearing fealty to him,§ and undertaking to

---

*   Bowing to the current fashion of sanitising history, revisionist historians are apt to gloss over such atrocities dismissing them as the biased views of disaffected pagan-hating churchmen expressed in contemporary chronicles. Instead, the Vikings are presented initially as traders and later settlers who assimilated comfortably with their neighbours. This was far from the case – at least to begin with. Professor Dunville was particularly scathing about that school of thought. As he observed in his Whithorn lecture, 'I venture to suggest that if Vikings arrived at the door of this church tonight few of us would leave with our lives, and those who did might wish they had not.'

†   meaning straightforward rather than stupid.

‡   A son of the jarl of Møre, a kinglet in western Norway, the story has it that he was physically so huge that the small Norwegian ponies were unable to carry him and consequently he had to walk. Hence the epithet applied to him of 'the ganger'.

§   The story has it that when Rollo came to do homage to Charles he demonstrated his independence by grabbing the front legs of his throne, and upending it he tipped the luckless king on to the floor.

defend the 'maritime parts'. These lands formed the nucleus of the duchy of Normandy, which was subsequently expanded under Rollo's ducal successors, one of whom – William the Bastard* (later the Conqueror) – would seize the English throne in 1066.

Meanwhile in the early 860s Danish Vikings launched a series of attacks on the coastal regions of Northumbria under their chieftain Ragnar Loðbrok. They ended in disaster when the Northumbrian king Aelle drove them off, took Ragnar Loðbrok prisoner and had him put to death. The story goes that he was thrown into a snake-pit, and as he writhed in the toils of these venomous reptiles this pirate chief is alleged to have gasped with his dying breath that 'the little pigs [i.e. his sons] will grunt when they hear how it fares with the old boar'. True or not, grunt they did. In 865 his sons Ivar *beinlaus* (the boneless) and Halfdan landed on the coast of East Anglia with a large force. Having conquered the region they split their army in two, and while Ivar invaded the kingdom of Wessex, Halfdan headed north. Raising a force King Aelle hurried south to meet him, and in the ensuing battle his army was defeated and he himself killed, thus precipitating the final disintegration of the Northumbrian kingdom.

Halfdan proceeded to establish a Danish kingdom based on York which comprised virtually the whole of present-day Yorkshire. He was almost certainly responsible for a further sacking of Lindisfarne in 875. Tradition has it that the fleeing monks took with them the coffin containing the relics of St Cuthbert and the much-venerated Lindisfarne Gospels. Seven miserable years followed, in the course of which they 'passed through deserted lands ravaged by Viking invaders' and were reduced at one point to subsisting on a cheese and a salted horse's head. Finally they reached the Cumbrian coast where they attempted to sail for Ireland. But blown off course by contrary winds, when the Gospels were washed overboard but miraculously recovered still in their jewelled case, they are supposed to have found sanctuary at Whithorn. Like many other traditions, this was a myth designed to attract pilgrims to that centre, because it is generally believed that the relics of St Cuthbert ended up at Durham.

The disintegration of Northumbria following Halfdan's victory resulted in the emergence of semi-independent ealdormen. The best known was Eadwulf lord of Bamburgh who controlled much of the coastal region from the Tees to the Forth, while the early records of the church of Durham suggest that the region between the Pennines and the Irish Sea comprised a separate lordship,[78] although it was about to come under Danish rule. Following his conquest of Yorkshire, Halfdan extended his kingdom westwards across the Pennines, driving out the existing inhabitants to make way for Danish settlement. Then advancing down the Eden valley, he took Carlisle in 876, sacking it and laying waste to the surrounding countryside so comprehensively that it remained virtually deserted, with Carlisle

---

* So-called because he was an illegitimate son of his father Duke Robert by his mistress Harlette, a tanner's daughter from Rouen.

reduced to little more than a ghost town, as it would remain for some two centuries afterwards.[*]

Crossing the Eden, the Danes invaded modern Dumfriesshire, forcing the Northumbrian – or Anglian – settlers out of the more fertile region into the upland country to the north, taking over their estates or carving out new ones for themselves.[79] These are identifiable from place-names ending in 'beck' (from *bekkr* meaning brook), and 'by' or 'bie' (from *byr* which can mean anything from a township to a small habitation). The fact that almost all these names occur to the east of the river Annan suggests that this was where they settled. Whereas place-names ending in 'bek', 'bie' or 'by' represent earlier settlement, those ending in 'garth' such as Applegarth and Tundergarth are thought to be associated with a later stage.[80]

In most cases the Danish settlers would have given their own names to the estates they appropriated.[81] Later, however, when these estates were taken over by mainly Flemish settlers, they substituted their own names while retaining the suffix 'by' or 'bie', of which there are numerous examples. Initially the Danish settlers would have acknowledged the authority of York, but when in the early decades of the tenth century the region came under the control of the Strathclyde Britons they would have been forced to switch their allegiance to a British lord under pain of expropriation or slaughter.

While the Danish Vikings were overrunning the regions beyond the Pennines, Norse-Irish raiders based on the Isle of Man were attacking the western seaboard of mainland Britain, evicting the local people and taking over their settlements. Initially targeting their raids on the coasts of Galloway, the inner Solway and Cumberland,[†] they later extended them to as far south as the Wirral in Cheshire. In the early 900s they established a colony there having driven out the existing inhabitants – churchmen, nobles and commoners alike. For example Aelfred son of Brithulf, clearly a nobleman, is recorded as fleeing across the Pennines to escape 'the pirates', while Tilred abbot of Heversham, in Westmorland, took refuge in distant Norham where he put himself under the protection of the Northumbrian lord of Bamburgh.[82]

Meanwhile, having driven out the local people, the Norse-Irish raiders were establishing colonies in the more fertile regions round the Solway Firth. Whereas some settled in the Machars of Wigtownshire and along the Borgue coast in Kirkcudbrightshire, others established themselves in Dumfriesshire, evident from place-names ending in 'thwaite' such as Murraythwaite, Thorniethwaite and Twathat. Derived from the Norse *thveit* meaning 'clearing', this suggests that the region was still heavily wooded, and like their Anglian predecessors these settlers had to clear-fell their lands to make way for cultivation. That these places are, broadly speaking,

---

[*]   R C Reid, 'Applegarth before the Thirteenth Century' *TDGNHAS*, xiv (1926–28), 165. According to the chronicler Florence of Worcester, it was destroyed by the Danes and remained uninhabited until the 1090s.

[†]   To avoid confusing modern Cumbria, the name assigned to the former counties of Cumberland and Westmorland, with that of the ancient kingdom of Strathclyde or Cumbria, these counties are henceforth referred to by their former names.

situated to the west of the Annan, while the Danes had established themselves in the lands to the east, could be taken to suggest that the river marked the boundary between these two mutually hostile communities. Notwithstanding their common Scandinavian roots, the antagonism between the Norse-Irish and the Danes is well illustrated by the achievements of Rognvald, a Norse-Irish adventurer from Dublin. Having established a base on the Northumbrian coast, he overran the Danish kingdom of York and proclaimed himself king in 919.

Meanwhile the Strathclyde Britons took advantage of the collapse of Northumbrian rule in the west to extend their kingdom southwards. Having gained control of Dumfriesshire and eastern Kirkcudbrightshire as far as the river Urr, they overran the Solway Plain and advanced up the Eden valley driving out the Danish settlers or reducing them to servitude. But fearing they were about to encroach on the kingdom of Mercia, which was under his control, Athelstan king of Wessex and *bretwalda* (i.e. overlord) of England forestalled them. In July 927 he summoned the king of Strathclyde, the king of Scots, and the Northumbrian lord of Bamburgh to meet him at Eamont Bridge near Penrith. There, doubtless under pressure, they acknowledged his overlordship, while the two kings undertook to suppress 'idolatry'[83] – clearly a reference to their pagan Danish and Norse-Irish subjects. But it was to prove a token gesture, for in 935 the Scottish king Constantine rebelled when he was joined by the king of Strathclyde, and later the Norse-Irish Rognvald's son, Olaf king of York. But, two years later, their revolt was suppressed following their defeat by Athelstan at the battle of Brunanburh.[*]

In 939, taking advantage of Athelstan's death and the new king Edmund's youth, the Strathclyde Britons resumed their advance southwards, gaining control of the whole of north-west England as far as Stainmore Pass on the Yorkshire–Lancashire border. But they misjudged Edmund. A man in much the same mould as his warlike half-brother Athelstan, he was determined to drive them back. Therefore in 943 he invaded Strathclyde and, as we are told, he ravaged the country far and wide, eventually forcing their king to submit.[84] Edmund's terms were harsh. He effectively dismantled Strathclyde by annexing the southern portion which extended broadly from the Solway to Lancashire to his kingdom. But appreciating that taking over the northern half would bring him into conflict with the Irish and the Scots, Edmund handed it over to the Scottish king Malcolm I on condition that he became his 'fellow worker by sea and by land'.

Although northern Strathclyde would remain a separate kingdom for another seventy-five years, its kings were subject to Malcolm I and his successors as kings of Alba, later kings of Scots. Therefore when its last king Owain the Bald died without issue in 1018, northern Strathclyde reverted to Malcolm II, the reigning king of Alba, when the inhabitants of modern Dumfriesshire came under his rule and that of his successors as kings of Scots.

---

[*] Its precise location is unknown although it is thought to have been somewhere in Yorkshire.

TWO

Early Medieval Times

THE ELEVENTH CENTURY

Northern Strathclyde represented a substantial addition to Malcolm II's kingdom, extending as it did from Loch Lomond southwards as far as the Solway Firth. To the east it included much of Teviotdale, while its western boundary was probably the river Urr, beyond which lay the independent lordship of Galloway.[1] It was divided into a number of lordships, those comprising modern Dumfriesshire being Stranid (or Nithsdale) on the west, Estrahanent (or Annandale), and Eskdale and Ewesdale (probably a single lordship), and lower Liddesdale (the Britonnic names for the last three have not survived). The territory between the Nith and the Urr (roughly eastern Kirkcudbrightshire) appears to have been a separate entity which was probably under the control of the lords of Nithsdale.[2]

Following his acquisition of northern Strathclyde, King Malcolm handed over the rulership of northern Strathclyde to his eldest grandson, Duncan, who was appointed prince of Cumbria (the two regions are synonymous). Duncan is believed to have been responsible for introducing a small Gaelic aristocracy into the region but 'without greatly altering [its] Brittonic character', as it has been put.[3] Endorsing this, Barrow asserts that the inhabitants of Annandale 'would have been mainly British or Brittonic [again the two are synonymous], although there were doubtless some Anglian families, survivors from the Northumbrian era, with a thin overlay of Danish and Norse Viking stock'. Meanwhile 'the Cumbric variant of the ancient British tongue would have predominated throughout much of the south-west'.[4]

But this was about to change, because Gaelic was already spreading from Galloway into Nithsdale, although it was not until the end of the eleventh century that the latter became a predominantly Gaelic-speaking lordship.[5] Later, English (or the Anglo-Scandinavian variant which was the forerunner of Scots) penetrated the region from the opposite direction, to the extent that, as Barrow asserts, 'by 1200 at the latest English was fully dominant in Eskdale, Annandale and lower Nithsdale'.[6] Nevertheless, Cumbric is believed to have been spoken in parts of Annandale and Nithsdale until as late as the mid-twelfth century.

The spread of English, or its Anglo-Scandinavian variant, throughout southern Scotland stemmed from Malcolm II's takeover of part of the former kingdom of Northumbria following his defeat of the lord of Bamburgh at the battle of Carham in 1018. Broadly comprising modern Berwickshire, it extended from the Tweed to the

Lammermuirs. This meant that, with his acquisition of northern Strathclyde, Malcolm's original kingdom of Scotia or Alba now included the whole of southern Scotland with the exception of Galloway. Nevertheless the English border continued to fluctuate according to the fortunes of war and diplomacy until 1237 when, in terms of the treaty of York, it was fixed at more or less its present line.

Malcolm II died in 1034 when his grandson Duncan, prince of Cumbria, became king as Duncan I. But because there was no properly established law of succession most kings had to contend with rival claimants to the throne. In Duncan's case the principal claimant was Macbeth. In 1040, having defeated and killed Duncan,* he usurped the throne only to be killed in his turn by Duncan's son Malcolm in 1057. The following year Malcolm defeated Macbeth's stepson Lulach, briefly king of Scots, and became king as Malcolm III. In 1061 he invaded England in a bid to gain southern Strathclyde. Details of the campaign have not survived, but it must have been successful because he appears to have extended the southern boundary of his kingdom to as far as Lancashire. However, ten years later he was forced to withdraw to the Solway.

In 1066 a revolution took place in England when Duke William of Normandy defeated the Anglo-Saxon host at the battle of Hastings. Although he quickly established Norman rule over England south of the Humber, the people of the north under their native lords remained defiant. In 1069 a rebellion broke out in Yorkshire which William, who was notorious for his brutality, crushed with merciless severity reducing the region to a virtual desert and the people to starvation. Taking advantage of this, Malcolm invaded Northumberland in an attempt to annexe it to his kingdom, but he was driven back by Earl Cospatrick, whom William had entrusted with the defence of the north. In 1071 William launched a retaliatory invasion of Scotland, in the course of which he advanced as far as Abernethy in Fife. Realising that further resistance was useless, Malcolm submitted. A truce was agreed, in terms of which he undertook to pay homage to William for his kingdom and surrender southern Strathclyde.

In 1079, notwithstanding the truce, Malcolm launched another invasion of Northumberland. This time it was repelled by William the Conqueror's eldest son, Robert, who subsequently built a new castle at a strongpoint on the Tyne. The forerunner of the modern city of Newcastle, it was intended as a defence against the Scots as well as a base for enforcing Norman rule over the north-east. It was here, and in the north generally, that resistance was strongest, and rendered the more so when the powerful Earl Cospatrick, who had defeated Malcolm in 1070 but had subsequently fallen out with William, joined it along with his son Dolfin.

By 1090 Dolfin had established himself as lord of Carlisle and the adjacent region which – provocatively – he claimed to hold for King Malcolm. William Rufus's response was swift and brutal. In 1092 he reportedly 'went with a great army to Carlisle', drove Dolfin out and, as we are told, he 'garrisoned the castle with his vassals'.

---

* Far from being the old man as portrayed in Shakespeare's *Macbeth* Duncan was about forty at the time.

Further, '[he] sent many people with [their] women and cattle to dwell there and till the land'. In other words he 'planted' an immigrant population in the region, presumably for the purpose of reclaiming the extensive marshland at the head of the Solway Firth. Described as 'churlish folk', meaning that they were carls, effectively peasants, these people are thought to have comprised a mix of Normans, Bretons, French and Germans. And their enforced settlement of the region suggests that it had remained seriously underpopulated ever since its devastation by Halfdan and his host in 876.[7] But not all of them were 'churlish folk', because some are believed to have been 'drengs'[8] – a Northumbrian term meaning that they were freemen and therefore men of status, generally occupying quite a substantial holding in return for certain specified services for their lord.[9]

Some migrated to (or were 'planted' in) Annandale. Here they appear to have taken over the Danish settlements which they re-named after themselves while retaining the existing suffix 'by' or 'bie'. For example Lockerbie took its name from Locard, Sibbaldbie from Sibbald, Warmanbie from Weremund, and Wysebie from Wice. These men were Flemings, whereas the origin of Piers whose name is preserved in Pearseby is less certain. The Gille of Gillesbie, on the other hand, could suggest a native origin. Richard, the originator of Rickerby, was most likely Norman; and, as its name implies, Canonbie was a monastic cell. An exception was Johnstone where the suffix 'tūn' is an Anglian word meaning settlement. That the modern parish of Johnstone comprises poorer land to the north of Annandale could suggest that the John who gave his name to it was a Northumbrian Angle who had been driven out of his original holding by the Danish invaders and had re-settled there.

Having regained control of southern Strathclyde, William Rufus constituted Carlisle and much of Cumberland a lordship similar to those his father the Conqueror had established on the Welsh marches.[10] These lordships had been granted to the Conqueror's leading supporters for the purpose of imposing Norman rule on them as a preliminary to extending it to Wales. Therefore, applying the same principle, Rufus put his trusted adherent Ivo de Taillebois in charge of the lordship of Carlisle for the purpose of imposing Norman rule there as a preliminary to extending it to the lordships of Annandale, Eskdale and Liddesdale.

When Ivo de Taillebois died in the late 1090s, William Rufus appointed Roger fitzGerold lord of Carlisle for the purpose of continuing de Taillebois' work of establishing Norman rule there. And to equip him with the necessary power, Rufus dictated his marriage to de Taillebois' wealthy widow Lucy de Bolingbroke. Since she was a substantial landowner in Lincolnshire, it was perhaps no coincidence that the 'churlish folk' who were 'planted' in the region of Carlisle are believed to come from there. When fitzGerold died in about 1106, Henry I appointed Ranulf de Meschin his successor. Great-nephew of the Conqueror, and son of the vicomte du Bessin who was mainly responsible for Henry's victory at Tinchebrai earlier in the year, Ranulph de Meschin was himself an experienced soldier. Therefore he was given what was tantamount to vice-regal powers, and at Henry's insistence he married Lucy de

Bolingbroke, who seems to have been a virtual perquisite of the lordship. Small wonder that after Ranulf's death in 1130 she paid the crown five hundred marks for the right to remain unmarried for five years![11]

William Rufus was killed in August 1100 – allegedly by a stray arrow while hunting in the New Forest. Although not directly implicated, having been in another part of the forest at the time, Rufus's brother Henry was widely suspected of having a hand in it. He was known to have had a tetchy – and at times a downright hostile – relationship with Rufus, while he had much to gain from his death. Furthermore his subsequent actions appear to have been premeditated. Immediately on hearing of his brother's death, and in order to pre-empt his elder brother Robert, he hurried to Winchester where he seized the royal treasury, and three days later he had himself crowned king.

Like William he was determined to complete the conquest of the north preparatory to extending Norman rule to Scotland. Therefore, at his bidding, Ranulf de Meschin established two baronies on the Scottish border. Partly defensive, they were also intended to serve as a bridgehead for Norman penetration into the adjacent Scottish lordships. One was based on Burgh-by-Sands for the purpose of controlling the Solway fords, which were the main access route into south-west Scotland, while the other comprised the later barony of Kirkandrews which controlled the route into Liddesdale. Whereas the one was entrusted to Robert de Trivers (or Reviers), the other was assigned to Turgot Brandos. A Fleming who had been granted lands in Yorkshire, Turgot Brandos was responsible for building the motte-and-bailey stronghold known as Liddel Strength which overlooks the Liddell Water near its confluence with the Esk. This then was the situation which confronted David, future king of Scots, when he became prince of Cumbria sometime after 1107.

KING DAVID

Malcolm III's death in 1093 in the course of another incursion into Northumberland precipitated a four-year dispute over the succession. Initially his brother Donald *ban** declared himself king, but he was opposed by his nephew Duncan, Malcolm's eldest son by his first wife Ingebjorg. Duncan prevailed, and having defeated Donald and expelled him from the kingdom he proclaimed himself king as Duncan II. His reign lasted a bare six months until his death at the hands of a resurgent Donald *ban* in alliance with his nephew Edmund (Malcolm III's son by his second wife Queen Margaret[†]). Donald *Ban* and Edmund became joint kings, one ruling Scotland beyond the Forth and Clyde, and the other the region to the south.

---

*   Meaning white-haired.
†   Great-niece of the English king, Edward the Confessor, and descendant of the house of Wessex, she was renowned for her piety and her many public works which included founding the priory of Dunfermline (later upgraded to an abbey by her son David I). Subsequently canonised, she is one of the leading cult figures in Scottish history.

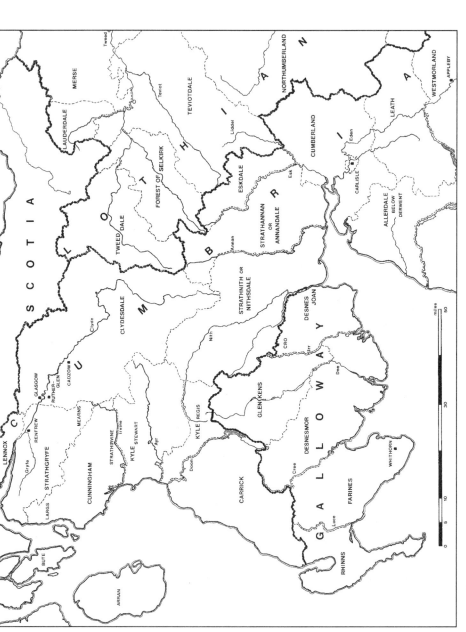

Twelfth-century lordships in Strathclyde and Galloway

R. D. Oram, 'Kingdom, Strathclyde 1092–1153', *TDGNHAS* vol. lxxii (1997), pages 11–40)

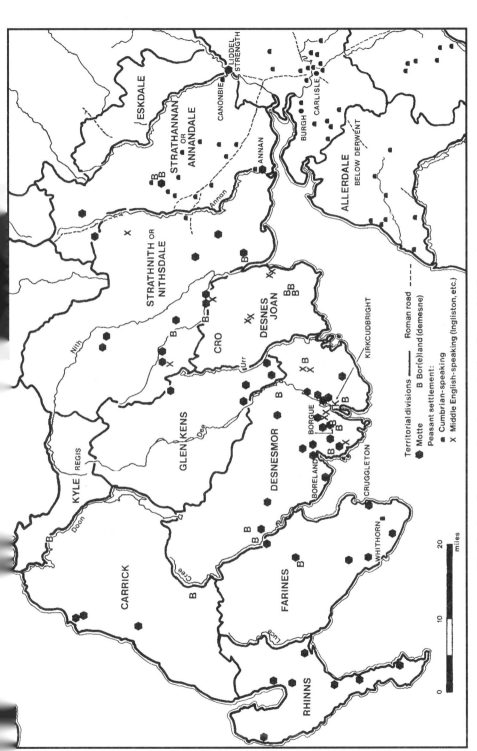

Distribution of mottes and settlements in Dumfries and Galloway in c.1150

(From J G Scott, 'The Partition of a Kingdom: Strathclyde 1092–1153' *TDGNHAS* vol. lxxii (1997), pages 11–40)

In 1097 Edmund's brother Edgar invaded Scotland at the head of an English army. Having defeated Donald *ban* and Edmund, he assumed the kingship of the whole realm as a vassal of William Rufus, having sworn an oath of fealty to him in return or equipping him with an army. Donald *ban* was blinded, though his life was spared (the Church frowned on regicide), while Edmund was banished from the realm to eke out the rest of his life as a humble monk at Montacute abbey in Somerset. Edgar's ten-year reign witnessed the start of Anglo-Norman settlement in Scotland, but it was on a limited scale and mainly confined to the south-east.

Meanwhile, following Malcolm's death, his younger sons Alexander and David, along with their sisters Edith and Mary (his children by Margaret), took refuge at the English court. Whereas Alexander returned to Scotland during the reign of his brother Edgar whom he succeeded in 1107, the others remained in England. In November 1100 Edith (her name was Normanised to Maude) married the recently crowned Henry I. Like his brother William Rufus and his father the Conqueror, Henry has been described as 'masterful, stern and cruel'. But unlike them, he was credited with a reputation for learning – hence the epithet 'Beauclerk' applied to him. He was also much the ablest of the Conqueror's sons, being endowed with that combination of political skill and ruthlessness which was characteristic of the Normans and essential to the consolidation of their conquest of England.

Since his eldest brother Robert inherited the duchy of Normandy, and William the kingdom of England, Henry was allegedly palmed off with five thousand pounds of silver given him by his father the Conqueror on his deathbed. The story goes that Henry took the precaution of having the silver weighed in front of his dying father's eyes to make sure he was not being short-changed. Some three thousand pounds of this was used to purchase the lordship of Cotentin from his ever-impecunious brother Robert.* Consequently it was from that region that a number of the 'new' men with whom Henry surrounded himself at the outset of his reign were drawn. Among them was Robert de Brus, future lord of Annandale.

Henry's marriage to Edith (or Maude) was essentially a political union which was intended to identify him with the former Anglo-Saxon dynasty,† and thus gain the support of the native English. This was partly in anticipation of his brother Robert attempting to wrest the crown from him on the grounds that it had been willed to him by Rufus. Since Robert had been given the duchy of Normandy as his birthright, Henry may have taken the view that he was entitled to the reversion of the English crown. Whether he did so or not, the fact remains that he made sure he got it!

The crown carried with it a claim to the overlordship of Scotland. This stemmed from the oath of fealty which King Edgar had given William Rufus as the price of his (Rufus's) helping him gain the throne. At the same time it ensured that Edgar's

---

* Robert subsequently tried to claw it back in an unlikely alliance with his brother William Rufus, but Henry managed to resist their predatory endeavours.
† From whom she was descended through her mother Queen Margaret.

ten-year reign was a time of peace and relative prosperity. Unlike his brother Alexander who returned to Scotland, the youngest David remained at the English court where he became a protégé of the future Henry I. According to the chronicler William of Malmesbury it was there that he had 'the rust of Scottish barbarousness rubbed off him'. Later, following Henry's accession and subsequent marriage to his sister Edith, David became a man of standing at the English court as 'the queen's brother'.

King Henry anticipated correctly. In 1101 his brother Robert made a determined effort to wrest the crown from him, having enlisted the support of a number of Norman barons from both sides of the Channel. Henry, on the other hand, secured the backing of the Church, and – thanks in part to his marriage – the support of the English people. The combination was enough to give him the advantage and a truce was eventually agreed. But mistrustful of his brother, Henry decided to go on the offensive and seize the dukedom of Normandy. This was achieved in September 1106 following his victory over Robert at the battle of Tinchebrai in which David, now in his twenties, would almost certainly have taken part;[12] and similarly Robert de Brus.

Following his success, Henry ordered the confiscation of all the lands belonging to his brother Robert's supporters, including those of his (and Robert's) close relative William count of Mortain.[*] One of the largest landowners in England, his estates included some fifty manors in Yorkshire, all of which were forfeited. Thirteen of them were given to Robert de Brus, doubtless as a reward for his part in Henry's victorious campaign. Since he had already been given lands there, the addition of these manors meant he was now the leading baron in the district of Cleveland. This was deliberate, because Henry needed to establish a 'strong' man like de Brus in a region where Norman rule was still relatively tenuous, and it was here that he established a ruling centre at Skelton.

In about 1119, in keeping with the fashion among Norman barons, Robert de Brus founded an Augustinian priory at nearby Guisborough, and through the course of time he and his son, the younger Robert, endowed it with a number of churches in Annandale. Meanwhile, as a mark of confidence in him, King Henry extended de Brus' authority to the region beyond the Tees with the grant of the lordship of Hartness, a substantial fief which extended as far as the river Eden.[†]

King Edgar died in 1107 having willed a division of his kingdom between his brothers Alexander and David. Whereas Alexander succeeded to the kingship, his share of the realm being broadly confined to the region beyond the Forth and

---

[*]   His father Count Robert was a half-brother of the Conqueror and one of the leaders of the expeditionary force which defeated the English host at Hastings. He was rewarded with huge tracts of land which included virtually the whole of Cornwall and much of Yorkshire, and as such he was a major beneficiary in the land distribution which followed the Norman conquest. This was the inheritance which he bequeathed to Count William.

[†]   This passed to the Annandale branch of the family. Through course of time they disposed of much of the lordship, reducing it to the area round Hartlepool which was forfeited by Robert Bruce, the future king, in 1306.

Clyde, most of southern Scotland was bequeathed to David. Alexander tried to deny him his inheritance. But concerned to establish his protégé David in southern Scotland as a means of extending his own influence there, King Henry was ready to support his claim by force. Raising an army, he sent it north to David's assistance. A formidable host, it consisted of a number of barons, including Robert de Brus,[13] and their levies, as well as a detachment of Flemings drawn from their enclave on the lower Tyne.[14] The threat was enough to force Alexander to concede David his inheritance, and in consequence he was styled prince of Cumbria.* Yet he still had to impose his authority over the region – a challenging task given the diversity of its inhabitants. Besides a residue of Angles, they included Gaels and Cumbric (or Brittonic) people, as well as the descendants of the Norse-Irish and Danish settlers, all of them mutually inimical or downright hostile.

It was doubtless at Henry's behest that Robert de Brus remained in Scotland to assist David in the task, for which he was well qualified having successfully imposed Norman rule in Yorkshire. Therefore it was probably about this time that David granted him the strategically important lordship of Annandale.[15] Flanked by the semi-independent lordship of Nithsdale to the west and potentially hostile Galloway beyond, it controlled the inner reaches of the Solway Firth, besides straddling the main access route from Carlisle into central Scotland.

In 1113 Henry arranged for David to marry his relative Maude de Senlis,† reputedly the richest woman in England, who possessed some seventy estates and manors scattered throughout the realm. Collectively referred to as the honour of Huntingdon,‡ they were spread over eleven English counties although mainly concentrated in the Midlands and East Anglia. A lady in her early forties, and therefore some years older than David, she was the widow of Simon de Senlis, who had recently died on a crusade leaving her with two sons and two daughters. As a result of his marriage David became a leading English baron as earl of Huntingdon and, in her right, one of the largest landholders in the kingdom.

By the time he succeeded his brother Alexander as king of Scots in 1124 David was already well experienced in managing both his English estates and his Scottish lands, and was therefore well qualified to administer his new realm. Moreover, having been part of the Norman establishment in England for upwards of thirty years, he was intimately acquainted with the feudal system of government and its concept of supreme

---

*   Or more accurately 'prince of the Cumbrian region'.

†   Her father Waltheof was formerly earl of Northumberland, while her mother Judith was a daughter of Lambert count of Lens and the Conqueror's full sister Adela. The story goes that, because Waltheof's loyalty was suspect, the Conqueror gave him his niece Judith in marriage so that she could in effect act as a spy in the bed. So when Waltheof came out in rebellion in 1075 and blabbed to her in his cups about his plans she duly reported them. Therefore when the rebellion was crushed, and Waltheof beheaded, she was allowed to keep his lands, to which others were added as a reward. On her death they passed to their daughter Maude.

‡   Meaning literally 'that which gives a man (in this case a woman) distinction', an honour was the term generically applied to all the lands comprising an endowment, be it an earldom, a barony, or whatever.

power being vested in the king. Therefore he was determined to impose it on Scotland. But first he needed to establish a class of military knights to buttress his authority. Here his English estates proved a fertile source of recruits, most of them landless younger sons whom he encouraged to settle in Scotland with promises of land.

When he became king, David was approaching his mid-forties, and during his near-thirty-year reign he achieved a complete transformation of the realm, its Church, and all aspects of government. So much so, that by the time of his death in 1153 he had put Scotland firmly on the map and established it as a thriving European kingdom. He was profoundly influenced by Henry I, sharing in full his administrative skills and gift of political organisation, and would remain on generally close terms with him until his (Henry's) death in 1135.

David was renowned for his generosity to the Church and its institutions – an extravagance for which his remote descendant James VI of Scotland, deploring the alienation of so many valuable rights, ruefully dubbed him 'ane sair sanct for the croun'. But ever a realist, David perceived that gaining the support of the Church – through bribery where necessary, and securing the appointment of amenable bishops, was crucial to establishing his authority over the realm. With this in mind he undertook a comprehensive overhaul of the organisation and structure of the Church. He already had some experience of this, having been responsible while prince of Cumbria for resuscitating Kentigern's diocese of Glasgow which had become virtually defunct. The incumbent at the time was Bishop Michael, who owed his appointment sometime after 1109 to the combined influence of David and Henry I. But because the episcopal centre of Glasgow was under King Alexander's control, Bishop Michael based himself on the former ecclesiastical centre of Hoddom as a suffragan of Archbishop Thomas of York.

When Bishop Michael died in 1114 David secured, with Henry's assistance, the appointment of his chaplain John as the new bishop. Energetic and methodical like David himself, Bishop John embarked on a reorganisation of the diocese. The need for it is evident from the comments of an anonymous clerk of St Mungo's Church, Glasgow. Writing in about 1120 he observed that:

> In the long period which has elapsed since St Mungo's death different tribes belonging to different races have poured in from all parts and settled [in] this deserted region. Racially distinct and differing in speech and ways of life, they have found it hard to live peaceably together and having practised heathenism rather than holding to the Christian faith.[*]

Bishop John was also concerned to identify which of the churches in his diocese belonged to the Church of Kentigern so that he could claim them on behalf of the Anglo-Norman Church as its successor.[16] Therefore in 1124, at his request, David

---

[*] A C Lawrie, *Early Scottish Charters*, chap I, p 45. The reference to heathenism suggests that there was extensive Danish settlement in Strathclyde.

held an inquest to determine the issue. Consisting of the oldest men with supposedly the longest memories in the region, the jurors' conclusions were summarised in a contemporary charter which lists the churches identified as belonging to the diocese.[17]

Those in Annandale included Hoddom, Abermilk (now St Mungo's), Dryfesdale, Esbie and Trailtrow, the last four having been daughter churches of Hoddom at the time it was a minster or mother church. Also 'Trevergilt' (thought to be Torgill), Edyngham (adjacent to the town of Annan) and the unidentified churches of 'Colehtoun' and 'Brumeschcycd', the latter of which is thought to have been the forerunner of a religious house at Applegarth.[18] On the other hand, the jurors were unable to determine the extent of the lands attaching to these churches since there was no formal parish system. In an attempt to resolve matters, the bishop transferred all the episcopal lands in Annandale to Robert de Brus as overlord,[*] who in return is thought to have undertaken to divide the Annandale lordship into parishes to be attached to each church.[19]

This was of a piece with King David's policy of establishing a parish system throughout the realm, which was one of his major achievements. His criterion was that a parish should be large enough to produce sufficient teinds[†] to support a resident priest, maintain the church and its outbuildings (probably little more than primitive hovels), and where appropriate support an assistant vicar. Consequently many – if not most – parishes were co-extensive with the multiple estates which already existed in the region. Because there were instances where the establishment of a parish meant encroaching on the rights of secular landowners, this gave rise to a number of disputes. One example was that which arose between Robert de Brus' son, the younger Robert, and the bishop of Glasgow, and which was determined by another inquest in 1175.

King David also encouraged the new monastic orders, which had originated in France and spread to England, to establish houses in Scotland. This was achieved by awarding them grants of land and revenue-yielding rights and privileges. His first endowment was a religious house for the Tironensian Order at Selkirk which he founded in 1113 while prince of Cumbria, and which was later transferred to Kelso. Perhaps his most outstanding creation was Melrose abbey which he founded for the Cistercian Order in 1136. Later it acquired substantial lands in Nithsdale and still more in Eskdale. In 1140 David and his son Earl Henry were jointly responsible for founding Newbattle Abbey, which was constituted a daughter house of Melrose, while Earl Henry was the founder of Holm Cultram, another Cistercian house, in Cumberland.

---

*   The grant was confirmed by the then bishop of Glasgow to the younger Robert de Brus sometime between 1141 and 1152 (*CDS* i, 30).

†   Teind was an obligation levied on all occupiers of land to render a tenth part of its annual produce to their local church for the sustenance of the incumbent. This would include such things as corn, hay and other crops, young livestock, poultry and animal products such as butter and cheese.

At much the same time King David was jointly responsible with Bishop John for founding Jedworth (later Jedburgh) abbey for the Augustinian Order. It was probably at David's behest – and certainly with his encouragement – that Turgot de Rossdale* founded a religious cell at Hallgreen, near the confluence of the Esk and the Liddel Water.[†] This was a daughter house of Jedburgh, the settlement which grew up nearby being appropriately named Canonbie. Later, Guy de Rossdale (presumably his son) gave it forty-two acres of land in the vicinity, the charter being granted with the consent of *his* son Radulf.[20]

King David also encouraged the Knights Hospitaller and the Knights Templar to establish foundations in Scotland with the grant of lands. Founded in the 1020s, the Order of the Knights Hospitaller, or the Knights of St John, was dedicated to caring for sick, poor or injured pilgrims to the Holy Land, while the Templars, who were founded in about 1118, were responsible for the protection of all pilgrims. In Dumfriesshire the Knights Hospitallers established a hospital at Trailtrow on the west bank of the Annan near Hoddom, while the Templars were granted a number of small holdings throughout the region,[21] their name being preserved in the village of Templand.

Although primarily motivated by religious considerations, David had sound practical reasons for encouraging the Cistercians to establish themselves in Scotland. An order which made a cult of austerity and frugality, its monks were also practical farmers who cultivated their lands themselves. Therefore they were drawn to the more isolated regions where they were able to concentrate on sheep farming which was their speciality, and where there was scope for reclaiming marginal land and bringing it into cultivation. Sheep farming was extremely profitable, because Scottish wool was greatly prized by the cloth manufacturers of the Low Countries who were prepared to pay a high price for it. Renowned as innovators, the Cistercians were also responsible for pioneering new farming techniques, and being widely copied they helped significantly towards the development of Scotland's economy.

Through course of time these monastic houses became huge property-owning corporations. This was the result of the growing practice among the wealthier land-owners, and later well-to-do merchants, of endowing them with lands, churches, and other assets – usually in return for saying masses for the souls of themselves and their families in perpetuity. While these houses would be responsible for employing a priest, usually one of its canons, to minister to the parishioners, his stipend was generally only a fraction of the value of the attaching teinds, so that remainder accrued to the house's growing wealth. As these institutions acquired ever more

---

* Son of Turgot Brandos whom Ranulph le Meschin had established in what was to become the barony of Kirkandrews.

† The priory is believed to have been demolished by the English following their victory at Solway Moss in 1542 and consequently nothing now remains of it. It is supposed to have been situated just over a mile south-east of Canonbie at the northern end of the flat land adjacent to the confluence of the two rivers.

churches, and other valuable endowments, their growing affluence became so ostentatious, and was so widely resented, that it was an important contributory factor to
the Reformation of the sixteenth century.

FOREIGN SETTLEMENT

King David was responsible for encouraging foreigners to settle in Scotland with grants
of land as a means of buttressing his authority, much as the Norman kings had done in
England. Initially his scope for doing so was limited to the royal demesne lands in southern Scotland, but later, as more land fell into the crown through forfeiture, conquest, or
a failure of heirs, the scope for foreign settlement was correspondingly increased.

The original settlers were generally landless younger sons, mostly from the honour
of Huntingdon, who regarded Scotland as a land of opportunity. As more land
became available David was able to widen the catchment area to include people from
elsewhere, notably Yorkshire and Somerset, and also from the Continent. For example, the forfeitures resulting from the failed rebellions in Moray (broadly the region
between the Highland line and the Great Glen) during the 1120s and 1130s yielded
lands which were mainly granted to Flemings.* As well as being regarded as the finest
fighting soldiers of the time, they were prepared to settle in poorer quality lands
where only rye could be grown – unlike the Anglo-Normans who insisted on grants
of land in wheat-growing areas because the consumption of wheaten bread was seen
as a mark of status.

Foreign settlement opened the way to the establishment of feudalism in Scotland.
But it was a slow process, for only the lands allotted to the incomers could be granted
under feudal tenure. However, through course of time many native lords were
encouraged – forcibly or otherwise – to convert their lands into fiefs and become part
of the feudal nexus. Nevertheless some two centuries were to elapse before Scotland
was completely feudalised, apart from the north-west where the traditional clan-
based system of tenure continued to survive.

Essentially a militaristic society, feudalism had developed in eastern France
during the eighth and ninth centuries. Thus by the time David extended it to
Scotland, it had become a well-developed system of government. It envisaged all
power, patronage and influence flowing from the king as the ultimate owner of the
land, the fount of justice and supreme warlord. He would make extensive land grants
(fiefs) to trusted men of standing (his tenants-in-chief), investing them with a
degree of power appropriate to the size of their holding. But there were attaching
obligations. Initially they consisted of military service of up to forty days a year, but
through time they were expanded to include other forms of service. Most important

---

* They included people like Berowald the founder of the Innes family, and Freskin the ancestor of the
Murrays and the earls of Sutherland. Erkembald the ancestor of the Douglases, on the other hand, was
given lands of much the same quality in south Lanarkshire.

of all, the tenants-in-chief were obliged to do homage to the king, acknowledging him as their feudal superior, and swear a solemn oath of fealty.

They in their turn would make grants of land to their own knightly tenants – or 'infeft' them, to use the technical term – on much the same terms. Thus was established a hierarchy ranging from the most powerful tenants-in-chief down to the smallest landholder. At the lower end of the social scale came the bondmen and serfs who were obliged to provide their lord with food, labour and military service as required. Since these people would have owed similar obligations to their native lord, the imposition of feudalism probably made little difference to them.

The king was expected to live off his own. This meant that, whereas he was entitled to all the revenues accruing to the crown, he had to provide for himself, his household and his court, as well as finance the costs of government, and pay for military service in excess of the forty days' obligation by his tenants-in-chief. His main source of revenue consisted of rents from the royal demesne lands, later augmented by rents and tolls from the burghs. Additionally there were feudal casualties, which was a capital sum payable by heirs on entering into possession of their family estates, as well as other feudal incidents such as the wardship of under-age heirs. They also included the gift of marriage of well-dowered heiresses when the prospective husband was required to pay handsomely for her hand. And finally there were windfalls which could include the reversion of lands to the crown through forfeiture, or a failure of heirs, as well as the profits from justice, mainly in the form of fines and purchases of immunity.

The first Anglo-Norman of consequence to be given lands in Scotland was Robert de Brus, who became King David's principal tenant-in-chief. Just as King Henry granted him lands in Yorkshire to equip him for the task of establishing Norman rule in the region, so David gave him the lordship of Annandale as a base for establishing the royal authority over south-west Scotland. He must almost certainly have issued Robert de Brus with a charter confirming the grant at the outset, but it was not until after he became king that he was able to ratify it by issuing him with a royal charter. This still survives, and although undated it was almost certainly granted early in his reign, possibly at the time of his inauguration. Thereafter the Annandale lordship remained in the hands of his Bruce descendants for upwards of two hundred years. Initially Robert de Brus maintained a court at Annan, but later his son the younger Robert transferred it to Lochmaben.

In about 1130 King David granted the lordship of Liddesdale to Ranulph de Soules, the royal butler and a member of his household. This was a hereditary appointment which would remain in the hands of his descendants for some two centuries. De Soules was most likely a landless younger son; his family originated from Soulles in the lordship of Cotentin and had come to England following the Norman Conquest when they were given lands in Northamptonshire. Later, his nephew and successor Ranulph 'the wicked lord of Soules' established his ruling centre at the de Rossdales' former stronghold of Liddel Strength, and it was there in

1207 that he was murdered by his servants who allegedly boiled him to death in a cauldron.[22] Later his descendant Sir Nicholas de Soules moved the family's ruling centre from Liddel Strength to a site further up the Hermitage Water (a tributary of the Liddel). There he built a massive earth and timber fortification which was the forerunner of Hermitage castle.

At much the same time, Walter fitzAlan was established as a tenant-in-chief in the west.[*] Member of a Breton family established in Shropshire, he was a typical landless younger son who was encouraged to settle in Scotland with the grant of lands.[†] They consisted of two separate fiefs – Strathgryfe in northern Renfrewshire, and northern Kyle in Ayrshire. Both occupied key strategic positions, the one guarding the upper reaches of the Firth of Clyde, and the other the western approaches. David appointed him *dapifer*, or steward of his household. Later, when Walter's grandson was given the title of *senescallus* (i.e. seneschal or steward) of the realm, the office was made hereditary. Adopting it as their surname, his Stewart descendants eventually inherited the crown and would rule Scotland, and later England, for upwards of three centuries.

Situated between Walter fitzAlan's fiefs was the lordship of Cunninghame. This was granted, along with lands in Lauderdale in Berwickshire, and others at Borgue in Kirkcudbrightshire, to Hugh de Morville. Another landless younger son, his family came from Valognes in the lordship of Cotentin, and following his accession to the throne King Henry encouraged them to settle in England with the grant of lands in the honour of Huntingdon. Therefore when David married Maude de Senlis they became his tenants. This was doubtless why Hugh de Morville became one of his tenants-in-chief in Scotland, as well as being given the hereditary appointment of constable of the realm.[‡]

Lying to the east of Annandale was the lordship of Eskdale which included Ewesdale. Sometime in the 1140s King David granted northern Eskdale, comprising the baronies of Dunfedling and Westerker (roughly the modern parishes of Eskdalemuir, Westerkirk and Ewes), to Robert Avenel. Member of a Norman family established in Northamptonshire, and most likely tenants of the honour of Huntingdon, he was almost certainly another younger son who was encouraged to settle in Scotland with the grant of land. At much the same time David granted the barony of Wauchope, another Eskdale fief, to Walter de Lindsay the ancestor of the Scottish Lindsays.

Between them lay the barony of Staplegorton which was granted to Sir Geoffrey (Galfrid) de Conisburgh. He was responsible for building the original castle there,

---

*   According to Barrow, Walter fitzAlan took service with King David in about 1136 (*Anglo-Norman Era*, 13).

†   He was the youngest of three brothers. Whereas the eldest inherited the ancestral lands at Dol in Brittany, the second acquired the family lands in Shropshire and was the ancestor of the fitzAlan earls of Arundel.

‡   The office passed to his descendants the lords of Galloway and was eventually forfeited by their representative John Comyn earl of Buchan who was an opponent of king Robert Bruce.

which was the forerunner of Barntalloch.[23] His family were tenants of earl Warenne in Yorkshire,* and it was because of this that he was among those responsible for escorting the earl's daughter Ada when she came north to marry King David's son Earl Henry in 1139. The family's link with the royal house was maintained by Sir Geoffrey's nephew and heir, Sir William de Conisburgh, who was a member of the court of Earl Henry's son, King William.† That the family remained in possession of these lands until at least the end of the following century is evident from the appearance of Duncan de Conisburgh in the list of landowners in the sheriffdom of Dumfries who paid fealty to Edward I in 1296.‡

By the 1150s feudalism, already well-entrenched in the south, was spreading to other parts of Scotland, notably Fife and the district of Moray where the process was accelerated by the forfeitures resulting from the suppression of a rebellion there. As more land became available for re-grant, so the flow of immigrants increased until it peaked around 1200, after which it began to diminish. These new landowners brought with them a host of retainers, clerks, servants and other dependants,§ and in their wake came merchants, craftsmen and others, mostly native English with a scattering of continentals, including French, Flemings and Bretons. They in turn attracted other settlers, many of them peasant farmers and their families who helped swell the immigrant population, to the extent that by the late thirteenth century it is reckoned that the majority of the inhabitants of southern Scotland were immigrants. This would have helped accelerate the spread of English in the region.[24]

The more exalted settlers constituted a French-speaking aristocracy who (initially at least) appear to have kept their distance from their Scottish counterparts. However, through course of time the distinction became less apparent as a result of intermarriage¶ and the progressive breakdown of the language barrier. David I and his grandsons Malcolm IV and King William were essentially Anglo-Normans. Indeed so closely did they identify themselves with the immigrant aristocracy that, as the English chronicler Walter of Coventry observed, 'the more recent kings of Scots profess themselves to be rather Frenchmen, both in race and manner, and language and culture, and after reducing the Scots to utter servitude they admit only Frenchmen to their friendship and service'. To describe the Scots as reduced to utter servitude is

---

* Where their name is still preserved in the township of Conisbrough near Doncaster.

† Evident from his appearance as a witness to King William's charter confirming a grant of land to Jedburgh abbey (*RRS* ii, no 5).

‡ Having conquered Scotland, King Edward ordered that every churchman, every landholder and his eldest son and heir, and many leading burgesses, swear an oath of fealty to him. This was done in the presence of their local sheriff who recorded their names on a roll to which the signatories attached their seals. These were dubbed Ragman Rolls on account of their resemblance to a prop used in a popular game in contemporary court circles.

§ Ritchie, *The Normans in Scotland*, 313. Quoting from late twelfth century documents, he lists them as falconers, fletchers (arrow makers), foresters, lorimers (makers of bits, stirrup-irons and metal mountings for bridles), porters, sergeants, tailors and taverners.

¶ A case in point were the parents of King Robert Bruce. Whereas his father was primarily an English baron, his mother was a native magnate.

doubtless hyperbole, although these kings probably regarded them as an inferior people. On the other hand, the reigns of Alexander II and Alexander III marked a return to gaeldom.

The grant of a fief carried with it an obligation to build a castle, or in the case of a tenant-in-chief several castles. Primarily defensive fortifications, they were intended to serve as the lord's residence, as well as his ruling centre or *caput*. At the upper end of the scale were the massive motte-and-bailey fortifications of the tenants-in-chief. The motte was designed to accommodate the lord and his family, and to serve as his ruling centre. Consisting of a wooden tower, probably no more than two storeys high (otherwise it risked becoming unstable or collapsing altogether), it was built on a man-made earthen mound and surrounded by a wooden palisade. Connected to it was the bailey, also built on an artificial mound and enclosed within a palisade. It consisted of an exercise yard with outbuildings for the accommodation of servants, soldiery and craftsmen such as smiths, as well as stabling for horses, a brewhouse and a chapel. As an added defence, the whole complex was generally surrounded by a ditch or water-filled moat.

A principal feature of the castle was the main hall where the floor was covered with straw or rushes, furniture being limited to a trestle table and benches. Here the lord and lady, and their family, retainers and visitors, would foregather for the main meal of the day. This was likely to be more copious than varied since it would have consisted mainly of beef or mutton, particularly in stock-rearing areas, or venison and other game killed in the course of the chase. Although spices such as pepper and cumin were being brought back by crusaders from the Middle East, they were probably still a comparative rarity in Dumfriesshire. Nevertheless, excavations of contemporary castle middens show evidence of an improved standard of living.[25]

The sub-tenants' mottes were correspondingly modest, and here living conditions must have been extremely cramped. While the owner and his wife might have their own sleeping quarters, shared with their daughters (in a larger castle they would have separate apartments), the sons, guests and other men were left to dispose of themselves on the floor of the main hall. One can imagine that with so many people living in close, unventilated proximity to one another there must have been a permanent frowst. In fact the whole atmosphere would have been redolent of wet and reeking leather, straw or rushes, and the all-pervasive smoke from the fire, not to mention the rank smell of unwashed human bodies. Small wonder that the Middle Ages have been described as 'a thousand years without a bath'.

The siting of these castles was mainly dependent on a readily available supply of water, and where possible a good all-round view so that a watch could be maintained against a possible attack. The remains of these man-made mounds – creations of native landowners and foreign settlers alike – are readily identifiable throughout southern Scotland. They are particularly numerous in the south-west, some twenty-nine having been identified in Dumfriesshire. A fine example of a former motte-and-bailey castle, notwithstanding that it was partially washed away in a flood, is that of the de Brus lords at Annan. Similarly its successor at Lochmaben which is now incorporated in the local golf course.

A late twelfth century development was the hall house. This was a compact dwelling built of stone with a timber-roofed hall, and below it a subterranean basement which was used for storage and the accommodation of the household servants. Yet it was virtually unprotected. A peel or pele, on the other hand, consisted of a rudimentary building of turf and clay reinforced with timber, which was surrounded by a defensive wall and usually a water-filled ditch. From the fourteenth century onwards it was increasingly the fashion to build castles of stone, which meant it was possible to add more storeys. At the same time they offered a better defence against attack, and unlike their timber-built predecessors they could not be set on fire by besiegers using burning arrows steeped in pitch. Among the earliest in Dumfriesshire were the Maxwell stronghold of Caerlaverock, Auchencass (later Auchen Castle) and Tibbers, which were built by the Kirkpatricks and Sir Richard Siward respectively. However, it was not until the reign of James V that landowners were legally obliged to build castles of stone.

ROBERT DE BRUS

Robert de Brus lord of Annandale belonged to a knightly family from Brix (or Brius) in western Normandy who were almost certainly feudal tenants of the dukes of Normandy. Apart from that nothing is known about his background. His forebears are thought to have been men of standing at the ducal court, and if true it has been suggested that they may originally have been of Viking stock.* Ritchie postulates that Robert was a second generation settler in England, that his father – also Robert de Brus – fought for William the Conqueror at Hastings, and that 'he died towards 1090'.[26] This can probably be discounted, for had that been the case he would have featured in the Domesday Book as the owner of lands with which he would surely have been rewarded.

Another source has it that Robert de Brus came to England as a protégé of the Conqueror's nephew Hugh d'Avranches earl of Chester, and that he was responsible for bringing Robert to the notice of Henry I. This is unlikely because Hugh d'Avranches was an intimate of William Rufus and therefore no friend of Henry, evident from the fact that when Henry succeeded to the throne Hugh was consigned to a monastery where he died the following year. More convincingly, Kapelle asserts that Robert de Brus came to England by invitation of King Henry as one of the 'new' men with whom he surrounded himself in place of the supporters of William Rufus.[27]

---

* This is unlikely because DNA research shows that between them the Norman settlers in England and Scotland had only a tiny amount of Scandinavian genes and that almost without exception they came from modern France and Belgium (see A Moffat, *Britain: A Genetic Journey*, 229–30).

Robert de Brus came to Scotland in about 1107, almost certainly at Henry's behest, to help the future King David establish his claim to southern Scotland, which his brother Alexander was attempting to deny him. Therefore it was to equip him with a power base in the region that David gave him the lordship of Annandale. The relevant charter which was granted after David became king in 1124, and which is preserved among the archives of the duchy of Lancaster, is quite short:

> David, by the grace of God King of Scots, to all his barons, men and friends, French and English, greeting. Know that I have granted to Robert de Brus, Estrahanent, and the whole land from the march of Dunegal of Stranit as far as the march of Randulf Meschin; and I will and grant that he shall hold that land and its castle well and honourably, with all its customary usages such as those which Randulf Meschin has in Carduill [Carlisle] and in his land of Cumberland . . .[28]

The witnesses include Hugh de Morville and Ranulf de Soules, which suggests that they were men of standing at King David's court before they became crown tenants. That Estrahanent was the Brittonic name for Annandale, and Stranit (or Stranid) for Nithsdale, reflects a surviving Cumbric influence in the region, while the reference to 'English' subjects suggests that English-speaking immigrants from Northumbria and elsewhere had already settled in southern Scotland, probably in quite large numbers. Similarly the reference to 'French' is indicative of an existing Anglo-Norman presence there.

Robert de Brus established his ruling centre at Annan, probably because of its proximity to a crossing point over the river, as well as being well placed to guard the Solway fords which served as the main western route into Scotland. Furthermore its proximity to the sea meant that English reinforcements could be rushed there in an emergency.[29] It was here that he built a motte-and-bailey castle. Although part of it was later washed away by the river, the surviving earthworks are massive, and the castle must have represented a huge investment of (doubtless conscripted) labour. Evidently it was intended to serve as a military base as well as a ruling centre, because it is believed to have been garrisoned principally with Flemish soldiery drawn (presumably on Henry I's orders) from their enclave on the lower Tyne. Later, Robert de Brus built two subsidiary castles – one on the Water of Milk, a tributary of the Annan, and the other further up country at Auldton near Moffat.[30]

Annandale was a large fief which comprised roughly half the area of modern Dumfriesshire. Specifically it extended from the Lochar Water on the west to the lands of Liddel and the lordship of Eskdale, then part of the demesne lands of David as prince of Cumbria, on the east. At that time Annandale would have been a poor, backward and thinly populated region consisting mainly of marginal and hill country, and despite the inroads made by previous settlers it was still heavily wooded. These 'damp oakwoods of excessive size and density', as they have been described,[31] would have abounded in game, including elk and other species of deer, lynx, wolves, and possibly brown bears which are known to have existed in Scotland at the time. Also the 'coney', or rabbit, which the Normans were responsible for introducing into England – as a source of food rather than for sport, because these creatures were judged unworthy of their hunting skills and regarded as only fit for snaring.

Since hunting was the barons' favourite pastime, the hunting rights enshrined in the Forest Laws were a jealously guarded privilege, evident from King David's grant to Robert de Brus of exclusive hunting rights over Annandale. Although undated, the charter which was issued at Staplegorton, probably sometime in the 1130s, gave Robert

> and his heir 'in forest' the Valley of the Annant on both sides of the water of Annan, as the bounds are from the Forest of Seleschirche [Selkirk], as far as his land stretches towards Stradnitt [Nithsdale] and towards Clud [the Clyde]. No one to hunt in said forest save himself, under forfeiture of ten pounds, and none to pass through save by the straight way marked out.[32]

It has been suggested that the king issued the charter on the spot after a day's sport had been interrupted by unauthorised persons straying onto the hunting preserve.[33]

Evidence of the barons' dedication to hunting is apparent from the condition attaching to Robert Avenel's grant of lands in upper Eskdale to the monks of Melrose. While reserving to himself and his heirs the exclusive right to hunt 'the hart, boar and roe', he specifically forbade the monks and their servants 'to hunt with hounds or nets, or set traps save only for wolves'. So they too clearly enjoyed the chase. That falconry was another popular sport is evident from Avenel's injunction to the monks not 'to take the nests of falcons and tiercels (goshawks)' and to refrain from damaging the trees 'where they are usually built'. Another example of the nobles' dedication to hunting was Robert de Brus' grandson William de Brus' reservation of the right to hunt 'the stag and hind, hog and roedeer' from his grant of the lands of Kinmount to Robert de Hodelme.[34]

Hunting was exclusively the preserve of the nobility. For most people life was a hand-to-mouth existence depending almost entirely on subsistence farming – principally stock rearing supplemented by rudimentary cultivation. Whereas cattle were run on the marginal land, the hill country to the north was mainly dedicated to sheep, although cattle would be ranched out there during the summer months when there was sufficient grass available. The coastal regions consisted of extensive salt marshes which account for the existence of a number of saltpans. Examples include those at Rainpatrick, Redkirk Point and Cummertrees, which were the subject of grants by the de Brus lords – mainly to religious houses such as Melrose and St Bees priory in Cumberland.

The de Brus lords also established a port (or more likely enlarged an existing one) at Waterfoot adjacent to the mouth of the Annan, some two miles downstream from Annan itself. This would have enabled them to trade with other ports on the Irish Sea littoral, or perhaps further afield. Fisheries were a valuable asset, and similarly the right to fish in rivers and erect stake nets along the shore. For example the first Robert de Brus granted a fishery at Torduff Point, near present-day Eastriggs, to the monks of Holm Cultram.[35] Confirming it, his son Robert specifically reserved to himself and his heirs 'sturgeon and whale' as well as the chance bonus of 'wreck of the sea'.[36] The charter also gave the monks the right to 'build a house on the sand' (sic), while the younger Robert granted Ivo de Kirkpatrick a fishery on the Esk for an annual rent of a pound of pepper.[37]

Because the first Robert de Brus would have regarded himself as primarily a Yorkshire landowner, the management of his English estates being his first priority, he was probably a fairly infrequent visitor to Annandale – particularly during his later years once he had brought it under control and could delegate its management to an overseer.[*] In fact it has been suggested that he regarded Annandale as primarily a sporting estate.[38] Since Blakely asserts that 'there was already an estate structure in place before [Annandale] was granted to him',[39] Robert de Brus probably limited himself to converting the native landowners' estates into feudal holdings, leaving it to his son Robert, and possibly the latter's successors, to encourage outsiders to establish themselves there. The original tenants may be identifiable (but not invariably) from those who took their name from the lands they owned. Whereas Robert de Brus might have established some incomers as tenants, it seems that on the whole this was left to his son the younger Robert.

A probable example of a native tenant family were the Johnstones, although it was not until later in the century that they first appear on record when the younger Robert de Brus confirmed John in possession of lands comprising much of the modern parish of Johnstone.[40] It was here that he built a motte which was the forerunner of Lochwood.[41] Later, between 1220 and 1250, John's son Gilbert (later Sir Gilbert) Johnstone witnessed a number of de Brus charters, suggesting that by that time he and his family had become prominent Annandale tenants.[42]

Other possible native landowners included the Irving, Carruthers, Duncurry and Moffat, and probably the Dunwoody and Pennersax, families. Tradition has it that the Irvings came from Irvine in Ayrshire, and that as prince of Cumbria the future King Duncan 'planted' them, along with other families, in the Border region (in their case Eskdale) to help defend it against the English.[43] The first of the family to appear on record is Robert de Hirewine who was living in the early thirteenth century. However it was not until three centuries later that there is firm evidence of the family's connection with

---

[*]   It was not until the time of his great-great-grandson Robert the Competitor that a steward was first appointed to administer the lordship. Initially the office was rotated among his principal tenants, but later he appointed a professional steward.

Bonshaw[44] which they may have acquired through marriage with an unnamed heiress.[45] The Carruthers, on the other hand, probably called themselves after the place of that name in the parish of Middlebie where they settled. Although the name itself is thought to be Cumbric it does not necessarily follow that the family were as well.[46]

The Duncurry family were established in the lands of Comlongan, Cockpool and Ruthwell along the Solway coast. All that is known about them is that, sometime between 1317 and 1332, Thomas de Duncurry resigned them to Thomas Randolph earl of Moray as lord of Annandale, and that he in turn granted them to his nephew William Murray. Perhaps William acquired them through marriage to a Duncurry co-heiress, in which case Moray was merely confirming him in possession of them. But either way they passed into the hands of him and his descendants the Murray earls of Annandale.* The Moffat family are thought to have been established in Moffatdale (hence their name) by the time de Brus was given the lordship of Annandale. Tradition has it that they were of Norse stock – not impossible given the existence of Norse-Irish settlers in Annandale at the time. Their designation 'de Moffet' in contemporary charters has been taken to indicate that they were people of consequence in the district, two of whom – Richard and Thomas Moffet – feature in the Ragman Roll for the sheriffdom of Dumfries.

The Dunwoodies (or Dinwiddies) took their name from Dunwoodie in the parish of Sibbaldbie where they held lands.[47] The first recorded member of the family was Adam de Dunwidie who witnessed a charter by the younger Robert de Brus' son, William de Brus, sometime between 1194 and 1214.[48] Later in the century William de Brus' grandson, Robert the Competitor, appointed Sir Adam de Dunwidie, presumably a son or grandson of his namesake, steward of Annandale.[49] Similarly the Pennersax family took their name from Pennersaughs, near Ecclefechan, where they held lands. Notwithstanding that Pennersaughs was subsequently acquired by Ivo de Kirkpatrick, the family appears to have remained landholders in the region, assuming that the 'Robert de Perressar' who features in the Ragman Roll is synonymous with Pennersax.

Referring to southern Scotland at this time, Barrow asserts that 'we have the impression of a country far from depopulated, but settled loosely and extensively enough for newcomers to enter by royal favour and practise a more intensive exploitation of resources'.[50] Presumably the same applied to Annandale, namely that it was quite thinly populated during the time of the first Robert de Brus. But it was becoming less so as the population increased, mainly as a result of the prevailing warmer weather and consequently increased productivity. As the population began to outstrip production, so landlords and tenants came under pressure to bring more land into cultivation.[51] While this was readily achievable in time of peace when there was sufficient manpower available, conscription for service in the war that broke out in 1136 rendered it less so.

---

* Not to be confused with the Johnstone earldom of Annandale which was a later creation.

This followed King Henry's death in December 1135. Since his only legitimate son William was drowned when the *White Ship* sank in 1120,[*] his heir was his daughter Matilda, widow of the Emperor Henry V and now wife of Geoffrey count of Anjou (although she continued to style herself Empress Matilda). Already in 1127 Henry tried to ensure her succession by browbeating his leading barons and clergy into swearing an oath accepting her as their future queen. It was repeated some years later, perhaps because of the widespread opposition to the concept of a female ruler; quite apart from which the arrogant Matilda was extremely unpopular. But no sooner was Henry dead than the barons reneged and had his nephew Stephen of Blois, son of the Conqueror's daughter Adela, crowned king instead.

In January 1136, taking advantage of the disputed succession, King David invaded England. Ostensibly in support of the claims of his niece Matilda, his real aim was to gain the lordship of Carlisle and to enforce his deceased wife's ancestral claim to the earldom of Northumberland, now vested in their son Henry. Having captured the principal castles in northern England, David went on to besiege Durham. But confronted by King Stephen's superior army, he was forced to agree a truce. Known as the first Treaty of Durham, it represented something of a victory for David, for in spite of being obliged to give up the captured castles he was allowed to retain the lordship of Carlisle and its castle. At the same time, Stephen promised to confirm his son Henry in the earldom of Huntingdon.

He also undertook to invest Henry in the earldom of Northumberland. But because he delayed doing so, David decided to force his hand. Therefore when the truce expired in January 1138, he invaded Northumberland in an attempt to seize the earldom. The campaign was a disaster. His ill-disciplined troops got completely out of hand and are alleged to have inflicted appalling atrocities on the local population as they plundered their way southwards as far as Yorkshire.[†] Reaching Cowton moor near Northallerton on 22 August, they encountered a hastily mustered English army under Archbishop Thurstan of York.

This consisted mainly of levies contributed by the northern lords, including Robert de Brus. Given his long-standing association with King David, this might seem strange; yet it was understandable because he found himself in an extremely invidious position. If he supported King Stephen he would stand to forfeit Annandale, whereas if he threw in his lot with King David it would cost him his Yorkshire lands. Since the latter were clearly the more important, he was compelled to turn out in support of Stephen. Yet it must have been a difficult decision because it meant

---

[*] Henry had something like twenty-five illegitimate children of whom one daughter was married to Alexander I king of Scots but without issue, while another was allegedly the wife of Fergus lord of Galloway and mother of his younger son Uchtred. But of course none of them were entitled to succeed to the throne.
[†] This is according to the highly partial account of Aelred abbot of Rievaulx. Formerly a member of King David's court, he was a friend and contemporary of his son Earl Henry, but as abbot of Rievaulx he naturally sided with the English and was therefore at pains to portray the Scots as a race of bloodthirsty savages.

breaking his long-standing friendship with David. It has been suggested that, in token of this and in recognition of his past services, David consented to an arrangement whereby Robert resigned Annandale to him for re-grant to his second son Robert. This could be true because it would explain why the younger Robert fought for King David while his father and elder brother were on the opposing side.

Before battle was joined, Archbishop Thurstan allegedly sent Robert de Brus and Bernard de Balliol, another northern lord with similarly divided loyalties, as emissaries to David to plead with him to withdraw. Abbot Aelred, the author of the story, relates how the aged Robert 'grave in manner and scant of speech' addressing David as 'my gentlest lord, my most loving friend' implored him not to fight against his Norman allies. Reminding him of how much he owed to their support, he told him that he had been authorised by King Stephen to offer his son Henry the earldom of Northumberland if he would abandon the campaign and return home. Perhaps David was tempted, but at that moment William, the bastard son of his long-dead half-brother Duncan II, intervened and in a wild tirade he denounced Robert de Brus as a traitor. In a fury de Brus threw a baton down at David's feet signifying the breaking of their feudal bond and a renunciation of his oath of allegiance. Having defied his old friend, we are told that he returned to the English lines 'sad at heart' and battle was joined.

Known as the battle of the Standard from the erection of a pole flying the banners of the northern English saints on a wagon, it proved a very one-sided affair. Charging into the fray with suicidal recklessness, the half-naked Scottish spearmen hurled themselves in vain against the solid wall of English mail-clad knights fighting on foot, supported by the deadly accuracy of their archers. Referring to the Gallovidians who insisted on leading the charge, the English chronicler Roger de Howden described how 'like a hedgehog with its quills you would see a Galwegian bristled all round with arrows and nonetheless brandishing his sword and in blind madness rushing forward, now smiting a foe, now lashing the air with useless strokes'.[52] Seeing these bare-buttocked savages hurling themselves into the fray, Robert de Brus is alleged to have remarked: 'Surely these are not men but brute beasts?' But wild savagery availed them nothing against the well-armed English knights, and eventually the Scots broke and fled, David himself being persuaded to abandon the field.

The story goes that in the course of the battle Robert de Brus took his son, the younger Robert, prisoner and had him delivered to King Stephen. In a gesture of contempt for his youth, the king ordered him to be returned to 'the keeping of his nurse or his mother'.[53] Nevertheless David's campaign was ultimately successful, for in the following year Stephen found himself confronted by the Empress Matilda's forces, and unable to maintain a war on two fronts he was persuaded by his wife Queen Matilda* to make peace. This was formalised by the second Treaty of Durham,

---

* Like the Empress Matilda she was also a niece of King David being a daughter of his sister Mary and Eustace count of Boulogne.

in terms of which Stephen allowed David to retain the lordship of Carlisle and conceded the earldom of Northumberland to his son Henry.

This meant that King David's kingdom effectively stretched as far south as the Tees on the east and the river Derwent on the west.* Consequently he moved his capital to Carlisle. In spite of William Rufus's attempt to re-populate the lordship with the 'multitude of churlish folk' it seems that it was still comparatively empty. Therefore David proceeded to colonise it by encouraging a group of Northumbrian (mainly Anglo-Scandinavian) nobles and their followers to settle there with grants of lands. Later a number of people from that milieu became feudal tenants of the younger Robert de Brus in Annandale, while others were established by his neighbour Uchtred lord of Galloway as tenants of his lands beyond the Nith.

Robert de Brus died, probably in his mid-seventies, in 1142. That he was a witness along with King David to a charter granted by his son Earl Henry shortly before his death suggests that they had become reconciled[54] – at least one would like to think so. Following the usual practice of bequeathing the principal family lands to the eldest son, Robert left his Yorkshire estates, as well as certain rights in the family's fief at Brix, to his eldest son Adam.[55] His descendants remained prominent Yorkshire barons until they died out in the male line towards the end of the following century. The second son Robert inherited Annandale, of which he may already have been given possession. The story has it that, because he complained that it was not possible to grow wheat for making wheaten bread in Annandale, which was a mark of status among the Anglo-Saxons, his father compensated him with the lordship of Hartness. True or not, the fact remains that it passed to him and his successors as lords of Annandale until it was forfeited by his remote descendant King Robert Bruce in 1306.

APPENDIX: WHEN DID ROBERT DE BRUS ACQUIRE ANNANDALE?

The charter granted him by King David in about 1124 reads as follows:

> David, by the grace of God King of Scots, to all his barons, men and friends, French and English, greeting. Know that I have granted to Robert de Brus, Estrahanent, and the whole land from the march of Dunegal of Stranit as far as the march of Randulf Meschin; and I will and grant that he shall hold that land and its castle well and honourably, with all its customary usages such as those which Randulf Meschin has in Carduill [Carlisle] and in his land of Cumberland.

That this is a repetition of an earlier charter, which David would presumably have granted to Robert de Brus at the time he was prince of Cumbria, is evident from the reference to Annandale extending 'as far as the march of Randulf [actually Ranulf]

---

* Later, when Henry II recovered these territories from David's grandson Malcolm IV, the border was pushed back to more or less its present line.

Meschin'. For by 1124 Ranulf was no longer lord of Carlisle. In 1120 he fell heir to the earldom of Chester when his relative Earl Richard d'Avranches went down with the *White Ship*. But fearing that the addition of the earldom to his lordship of Carlisle might render Ranulf de Meschin too powerful a vassal, Henry I refused to confirm him in possession of it unless he resigned the lordship, which he did.

Similarly the reference to the grant being accompanied by 'all its customary usages such as those which Randulf Meschin *has* in Carduill [Carlisle] and in his land of Cumberland' also points to it being a repetition of an earlier charter. Otherwise the verb would have been *had*.

The fact that Robert de Brus was given powers similar to those enjoyed by Ranulf Meschin is significant. This is because the latter was granted the lordship of Carlisle for the specific purpose of establishing Norman rule there, and it was for that reason that he was given powers in excess of those normally attaching to a barony title. That de Brus was given similar powers implies that he had still to establish his authority over Annandale, and this too could argue for a repeat of an earlier charter.

Finally the injunction to de Brus to hold 'its castle well and honourably' implies that it was already built. Since he would not have commissioned the work without first having obtained a title to the lordship, he must have acquired it by an earlier charter. Lawrie asserts that the injunction refers to a castle at Lochmaben. This is most unlikely, because it was not until the 1160s that Robert de Brus' son, Robert the younger, built a castle there to serve as his ruling centre. Therefore the castle referred to in the charter must be the motte-and-bailey at Annan.

Taken together, these add up to a compelling argument for an earlier charter which the future King David may have granted to Robert de Brus as far back as 1107.

ANNANDALE FEUDALISED

The younger Robert de Brus' tenure of the Annandale lordship lasted for some fifty years from the time of his father's death, if not before, until his own death in about 1194. Since his elder brother Adam inherited their father's Yorkshire estates, he was able to devote himself much more closely to the management of his Annandale lordship than his father did – at least in his latter years. The more so because he held no office under the crown, nor is there any record of him taking part in affairs of state. In fact his relations with David's grandsons, Malcolm IV and King William, were much less close than those that had existed between his father and King David, while the fact that he seldom appears as a witness to royal charters suggests that he was an infrequent attender at court.

The story has it that in about 1148 he received a visit from Maelmaedhoig Ua Morgair (O'Moore), archbishop of Armagh and papal legate (better known as St Malachy), while on his way from Ireland to Rome. Learning that a robber was about to be hanged, the archbishop pleaded with Robert for his life; but, notwithstanding his promise that the felon would be spared, Robert consigned him to the gallows. Therefore, when the following day the archbishop encountered the robber's corpse swinging on the gibbet, he allegedly punished Robert by pronouncing a curse on his family and the town of Annan. This was generally held to be responsible, among other things, for the outbreak of plague which occurred there towards the end of the century.

The curse may have influenced Robert's decision not to rebuild his castle at Annan when it was partially washed away by the river in flood. Instead, he moved his ruling centre or *caput* to a more central location at Lochmaben where he built another motte-and-bailey castle. This constituted the nucleus of the town of Lochmaben which grew up in the vicinity. The castle must have been completed by 1166, for it was there that King William issued a charter confirming Robert de Brus in possession of Annandale,* and in 1170 Robert founded a church there. Meanwhile the partially destroyed castle at Annan continued to be used to garrison troops employed in guarding the Solway fords.

King David died, well into his seventies, in May 1153. Since his son Earl Henry had died the previous year, he was succeeded by his eldest grandson Malcolm IV. Taking advantage of his youth and inexperience, a number of native lords came out in rebellion. They were eventually defeated with the assistance of Henry II who had recently succeeded to the English throne. But his help came at a price. Malcolm was forced to resign the lordship of Carlisle, which his grandfather had acquired in terms of the second Treaty of Durham. Similarly his brother William was compelled to give up the earldom of Northumberland, which he had inherited from their father Earl Henry.[†]

The two kings appear to have been on friendly terms, because Henry lured Malcolm with promises of a knighthood into taking part in his campaign in southern France. However, on his return in 1159, Malcolm found himself confronted by another rebellion, the ringleader – or at least the figurehead – being the elderly Fergus lord of Galloway. Turning on him, Malcolm is said to have invaded Galloway three times before finally defeating him, when he forced Fergus to abdicate and retire to Holyrood abbey as a humble monk. To consolidate his success, Malcolm dictated a division of the lordship between Fergus's warring sons Uchtred and Gilbert. Whereas Uchtred was allotted eastern Galloway which would have consisted of the territory between the river Urr and the Cree, Gilbert was given the lands to the west comprising roughly modern Wigtownshire and possibly Carrick.

---

* *CDS* i, 105, *RRS* ii, no 80. Significantly the grant was to Robert de Brus *and his heir*, thus ensuring primogeniture. This was deliberately intended to deny younger sons a share in the lordship lands in order to preserve their integrity as a defence against possible English aggression.

† Because he was compelled to surrender it under duress, William refused to recognise its validity and pursued its recovery with relentless – and unavailing – determination for the rest of his long life.

Malcolm died in 1165 unmarried and still in his twenties, when he was succeeded by his brother William whose reign – one of the longest in Scottish history – lasted for almost fifty years. The third brother, for many years William's heir until the birth of his son the future Alexander II in 1198, was David earl of Huntingdon. As well as being pre-eminent in Scotland, he was also a powerful English baron. That apart, his claim to fame is that it was through him that John Balliol and Robert Bruce the Competitor based their claims to the kingship in 1291.*

Meanwhile the younger Robert de Brus was feuing out lands in Annandale, mainly to incomers whom he established as his tenants. There was pressure on him to do so, because King William's charter of 1166 confirming him in possession of the lordship stipulated that it was to be held for ten knights' service. This meant that Robert was bound to provide ten knights and their levies to perform military service for the king when required.† Therefore it was incumbent on him to dispose of landholdings – or fiefs – to tenants on condition that they provided him with the services of a knight and his retinue when called on to do so. These incomers consisted of a mix of Anglo-Normans and Flemings, while others came from the lordship of Carlisle and a few from Yorkshire.

Prominent among the Anglo-Normans was the Charteris family. The first on record is Robert de Carnoto who witnessed King William's charter of 1166 confirming Robert de Brus in the lordship of Annandale.⁵⁶ Since Carnoto was the latinised form of Chartres, the family probably came from there. Arriving in England during the reign of William the Conqueror, one of them – Ralph de Carnoto – appears in the Domesday Book as a tenant of Robert count of Mortain in Northamptonshire. Following the count's son William's forfeiture, Henry I awarded part of his Northamptonshire lands to Roger de Moubray who in consequence became the de Carnoto family's feudal superior. Later, when King David persuaded Roger de Moubray's son to settle in Scotland with the grant of lands,‡ Robert de Carnoto, presumably Ralph's son, probably accompanied him there.

Sometime in the mid-twelfth century Robert de Carnoto was granted a substantial landholding in Annandale by the younger Robert de Brus and became one of his leading feudal tenants. Specifically, it consisted of the barony of Amisfield, including the lands of Trailflat, on the border with Nithsdale, and those of Drumgree on the Kinnel Water. As a leading tenant he acted as a witness to King William's charter of

---

* His eldest daughter Margaret, wife of Alan lord of Galloway, was the grandmother of John Balliol, while his middle daughter Isabel married Robert de Brus' grandson, Robert the noble, and was the mother of Robert Bruce the Competitor (see genealogical table 3).

† *CDS* i, 105 Additionally the charter conferred on him all the judicial powers normally held by a tenant-in-chief, including those of pit and gallows – namely the right to hang or drown convicted felons. Also to hold a court, although cases involving treasure trove, murder, premeditated assault, rape, arson and robbery were reserved to the crown.

‡ These were situated to the south of the Firth of Forth in present-day West Lothian. Later they were forfeited by his descendant Roger de Moubray following his conviction for plotting to assassinate King Robert Bruce.

1166 to Robert de Brus and another one granted by the king, sometime before 1171, to Kelso abbey.[57] The family seems to have had a close association with that institution, for in about 1180 Robert's brother, Walter de Carnoto, granted it the churches of Trailflat and Drumgree in return for the monks offering up prayers for the souls of himself, his brother Robert and their ancestors in perpetuity,[58] the grant being confirmed by Sir Robert Charteris in 1266.[59]

At about this time, Sir Adam de Carnoto, presumably another member of the family, was acting as a witness to charters issued by Robert Bruce the Competitor.[60] Towards the end of the century Sir Thomas de Carnoto, a clerk in the royal household and probably a relative, was appointed chancellor by the guardians of the realm following the death of Alexander III.[61] Finally, three members of the family – Andrew, Robert and William – feature as landholders in the Ragman Roll for the sheriffdom of Dumfries in 1296.

Other Anglo-Normans who became de Brus tenants included the ancestors of the Herries, Jardine, de Boys (or Bosco), Franciscus and de Mauleverer families. Said to have come from Vendôme on the periphery of the Loire valley, the Herries family probably arrived in England during the reign of William the Conqueror when they are thought to have been given lands in Nottinghamshire. The first on record is William de Heriz, probably a younger son, who established himself in the lordship of Carlisle, and as a Cumbrian landowner he witnessed King David's son Earl Henry's foundation charter of Holm Cultram abbey.[62]

At much the same time the younger Robert de Brus granted him lands in Moffatdale and Evandale. This was followed by the grant of further lands in the vicinity of Gretna, evident from the reference to his holding land adjacent to the Esk as a de Brus tenant. Robert also gave William de Heriz the valuable perquisite of a saltpan at Rainpatrick (now Redkirk Point).[63] Thereafter members of the family were frequent witnesses to de Brus charters until the time of Robert Bruce the Competitor when Robert de Heriz was appointed steward of Annandale,[64] while two members of the family – 'Johan de Araz' (sic for Herries) and William de Heriz – feature in the Ragman Roll. During the following centuries William de Heriz's descendants acquired further lands, mainly through purchase, marriage and royal grant, to the extent that by the early sixteenth century they had become a leading family in the south-west.

The Jardines arrived in England during the reign of William Rufus, or possibly Henry I, when they are thought to have been granted lands in Cambridgeshire. Blakely argues for Huntingdon on the grounds that a William de Gardin held lands there in the early thirteenth century. Plausibly enough, for if that were the case the family could have been tenants of King David which would account for a member of the family, possibly a younger son, coming to Scotland. The first recorded member of the family was Umfredus de Gardine who witnessed a number of charters by Robert de Brus in the 1150s.[65] Therefore Robert would have been responsible for granting him lands in the modern parish of Applegarth where he most likely established a ruling centre on the site of the later Spedlins Tower.

Members of the family continued to witness de Brus charters until the 1230s, the last being Sir Humphrey de Jardine,[66] while the 'Humfrey du Gardin' who features in the Ragman Roll was probably his grandson. It seems likely, though firm evidence is lacking, that the Jardines acquired additional lands in the parish of Applegarth through marriage to an heiress of Hugh son of Ingebald whose surname is not recorded. This would explain how the Jardines came to acquire virtually the whole parish, much of which would remain in their hands until the end of the nineteenth century.

The de Boys (otherwise de Bois or Bosco) family are thought to have come from Lisieux, near Caen in Normandy and settled in Yorkshire, though not as tenants of the de Brus lords of Skelton. The first on record is Richard de Bosco, possibly a younger son, to whom Robert de Brus granted lands at Carruthers (now part of the parish of Middlebie) in what has been described as a 'thinly populated corner of Annandale'.[67] According to Reid, Richard de Bosco was also granted lands on the Kinnel Water,[68] and later the family acquired others in Dryfesdale, possibly through marriage.[69] Styling himself 'del Bois', Richard de Bosco witnessed a number of de Brus charters,[70] as did Humphrey de Bosco, presumably his son. Another member of the family, Sir Thomas de Bosco, acted as a witness for Robert Bruce the Competitor,[71] while the 'Humfrey de Boys, chevalier' who features in the Ragman Roll was probably his son.

Walter de Bosco, another member of the family, gave lands at Carruthers to Durham cathedral priory following a visit to St Cuthbert's shrine with his wife and son.[72] During the thirteenth century others of that name, and probably the same family, rose to prominence in the royal service. Originally a clerk in King William's chancery,[73] William de Bosco became Alexander II's chancellor,[74] and later Ralph de Bosco became one of Alexander III's principal clerks.[75] The family died out in the male line during the mid-fourteenth century when their lands passed through marriage to the Crichtons of Sanquhar.

An obvious Frenchman was William Franceis (or Franciscus), who is recorded as holding two oxgangs of land at Moffat in feu of Robert de Brus in the late twelfth century.[76] Later known as Frenchland, it passed to his son Roger who subsequently resigned it to Robert Bruce the Competitor in exchange for land at Warmanby.[77] However he must have disposed of this soon afterwards because the family does not appear in the Ragman Roll. Information about the Mauleverers is equally sparse; in fact it is not even known where they settled. Yet they appear to have been a family of standing because Hugh de Mauleverer acted as a witness to a number of de Brus charters between 1194 and 1249,[78] while Sir Humphrey de Mauleverer acted in a similar capacity for Robert Bruce the Competitor.[79] He may have been the father of 'Hugh Mauleurer, chevalier' who features in the Ragman Roll for Dumfries.

In 1155, the year after his accession, Henry II expelled all Flemish settlers from England. Many of them, including those from the Flemish enclave on the lower

Tyne, took refuge in Scotland. Some settled in upper Clydesdale where their names are preserved in the local townships. Others settled in Annandale. An obvious case in point was the Fleming, or Flamanc, family to whom Robert de Brus granted lands at Kirtleside in the parish of Kirkpatrick Fleming which was named after them. At some point they acquired a saltpan on the Solway near Gretna – evident from a charter by William de Brus granting a saltpan at Rainpatrick (Redkirk Point) to the monks of Melrose which was stated to be situated between those belonging to Richard de Bois and Richard le Fleming.[80] The latter was probably identifiable with the Richard le Fleming whom William de Brus' son, Robert the noble, appointed chamberlain of Annandale.[81] However the family seems to have died out in the male line, or possibly they abandoned their Annandale lands, because they do not feature in the Ragman Roll.

A possible Flemish settler, evident from his name, was Ingebald. He appears to have been granted a knight's fee which broadly comprised the modern parishes of Applegarth and Dryfesdale. He would most likely have been responsible for building the motte-and-bailey castle on the east bank of the Annan at Applegarthtown to serve as his ruling centre. Apart from the fact that his son Hugh appears as a witness to a later de Brus charter,[82] nothing definite is known about the family. Nevertheless Ingebald's lands in Dryfesdale passed to the de Boys family, and those in Applegarth to the Jardines, probably through marriage.

Another Fleming was Simon Loccard who acquired lands in the vicinity of Lockerbie to which he gave his name (*Loccard-bie*).* Thereby hangs a complicated story. One of the Cumbrian settlers in Annandale was Udard, son of Hildred sheriff of Carlisle. Having inherited his father's manors of Gamelby and Glassanby, in Cumberland, he was given the lands of Hoddom† from which he took the name de Hodelme. When he died in about 1174 his lands in Cumberland and Annandale passed to his son Robert de Hodelme. The same year King William embarked on his ill-fated invasion of England, and as a feudal vassal Robert was obliged to take part. This cost him his Cumbrian lands which were forfeited by decree of Henry II.[83] Therefore he was compensated with Simon Loccard's lands of Lockerbie, Simon being given the lands of Lockarton in upper Clydesdale (named after him) instead.

But Simon refused to move. This became the subject of a protracted lawsuit, and when the verdict went against him he was compelled to do so. Therefore Robert de Hodelme was duly established in possession of these lands, which he subsequently made over to his elder son Adam. When Robert died in about 1120 he bequeathed

---

* Perhaps Simon was merely confirmed in possession of these lands, since his family may have been one of the Flemings 'planted' in Annandale at the turn of the twelfth century shortly before the arrival of the first Robert de Brus.

† A substantial fief, it extended well beyond the present-day parish of Hoddom to include parts of St Mungo, Middlebie and Tundergarth (see A M Findlater, 'Hoddom: A Medieval Estate in Annandale' *TDGNHAS*, lxxxii (2008), p 77).

Hoddom to his younger son, another Udard.[*] Meanwhile in the late 1190s the dispute over the Lockerbie lands re-emerged and became the subject of further litigation. The earlier decision was reversed and Adam de Hodelme was obliged to resign his Lockerbie lands, which in consequence were restored to Simon Loccard. Meanwhile Adam de Hodelme was compensated with the lands of Kinmount. Taking the name de Carlyle, his descendants became pre-eminent in Dumfriesshire, one of them marrying a sister of King Robert Bruce.

Another Cumbrian incomer to Annandale was the first of the Crossebi family who may have taken his name from the village of Crosby near Maryport. He was given lands in the parish of Dornock where he established a ruling centre at Stapleton, and later the family acquired a fishery on the Esk.[84] The first recorded members of the family are Bernard and Ivo de Crossebi who acted as witnesses to an agreement between Robert de Brus and Bishop Engelram of Glasgow in 1189, while Robert, Richard and Adam de Crossebi were regular witnesses to de Brus charters down to the time of Robert the Competitor.[85] In about 1214 William de Brus' son, Robert the noble, allowed Robert de Crossebi to enclose the land at Stapleton as a 'free park' or hunting preserve, a valuable privilege besides being the earliest park on record.[86] In 1272 Adam de Crossebi resigned some lands to Robert the Competitor in exchange for others at Gretna;[87] but the family must have disposed of them soon afterwards because their name does not appear in the Ragman Roll.

Exceptionally the Kirkpatricks, although taking their name from the lands where they settled, were not a native family. In fact they came from Yorkshire and are thought to have been of Danish stock. This would stand to reason since Yorkshire was formerly under Danish rule, while the name Ivo (or Ivone) which is habitually associated with the family is Scandinavian. This was the name of the first recorded member of the family who was given the lands of Kirkpatrick by the younger Robert de Brus, followed by the grant of fishing rights in the Annan and the Sark, along with ground for his men to dry their nets.[88] Around the turn of the century Robert de Brus' son William granted Ivo (now styling himself Ivo de Kirkpatrick) lands in the parish of Kirkpatrick Juxta[†] where he built the Garpol motte to serve as his ruling centre.[‡] Later he acquired lands at Pennersaughs near Ecclefechan.[89] In 1232 Alexander II granted Ivo de Kirkpatrick, another member of the family, the barony of Closeburn.[90]

---

[*]   He had a daughter Christian who married William de Ireby a Cumbrian landowner. Their daughter, another Christian, was married three times. By her first husband Thomas de Lasceles she had a daughter Erminia through whom Hoddom passed to her Carruthers descendants. Her second husband was Sir Adam de Grossemuth who held the barony of Dalton, while her third husband was the widowed Robert Bruce the Competitor.

[†]   Whereas the Kirkpatrick family took their name from the lands where they originally settled, in this case it was the other way about in that they gave their name to the parish.

[‡]   This was later superseded by Auchencass (now Auchencastle) which became the family's principal stronghold.

That the Kirkpatricks were a family of consequence in Annandale is evident from the appearance of Roger and Robert de Kirkpatrick as witnesses to charters by William de Brus.[91] Indeed members of the family continued to witness de Brus charters until the time of Robert the Competitor when Sir Humphrey de Kirkpatrick was appointed steward of Annandale.[92] Two members of the family, Johan and Roger de Kirkpatrick, appear in the Ragman Roll, while the 'Stevene de Kilpatrick' who also features in it was probably a grandson of Ivo, the first of the Kirkpatricks of Closeburn.[93]

The Ross family also came from Yorkshire, but unlike the Kirkpatricks they are thought to have been tenants of the senior, or Skelton, branch of the de Brus family. They were given lands to the west of the Kinnel Water near its confluence with the Ae where their name is preserved in the farm of Ross Mains. That they continued to hold these lands until at least the end of the thirteenth century is evident from the appearance of Aleyn de Rossa in the Ragman Roll. Since there is no record of members of the family witnessing de Brus charters, they were probably of minor importance.

The origins of some families established in Annandale are less certain, such as for example the Grahams and the Corries. While not to be confused with the Grahams of Dalkeith, the heirs of the Avenels, it is possible that the Grahams who were granted lands in Dryfesdale were of the same stock. Nothing further is known about them apart from the fact that they were most likely the forebears of the Grahams of Mosskeswra and Gillesbie both of which are in Dryfesdale.

The Corries took their name from the lands which they acquired in the parish of Hutton and Corrie, although they may not have been a native family. Here they built a castle – the Hutton Mote, near Boreland – as their ruling centre, although it was later replaced by the nearby Tower of Lun. The first of the family on record was Hugh de Corri who witnessed a deed of resignation to William de Brus.[94] Thereafter he continued to witness charters by William de Brus and his son Robert the noble.[95] Later, William de Corri, presumably his son or grandson, did the same for Robert Bruce the Competitor, while a 'Nicol de Corry' features in the Ragman Roll. Latterly there were three separate Corrie families – of Corrie, Newbie and Kelwood – all presumably related.

By the time of his death in about 1194 Robert de Brus must have disposed of all the principal fiefs, although the process of subinfeudation* was still far from complete. This resulted in a fragmentation of a single knight's service. For example when Ivo de Kirkpatrick acquired land at Pennersaughs he was obliged to provide one-eighth of a knight's service, while Sir Thomas d'Aunay, a tenant-in-chief of the Yorkshire branch of the de Brus family, was granted lands around Collin on the same terms. In 1237 he donated part of these lands, including Dargavel, to Melrose Abbey.

---

*   The process by which a principal tenant divided his fief among sub-tenants on much the same terms as he held his own lands.

Another example was Roger de Crispin who was granted land at Lochmaben for one-twentieth of a knight's service in exchange for other (unnamed) lands. The process of subinfeudation continued under Robert de Brus' immediate successors, although it was not fully complete until the time of his great-grandson Robert the Competitor.

THREE

Later Bruce Overlordship

NITHSDALE

The Britonnic lordship of Nithsdale was part of the former kingdom of Strathclyde. Extending from the parish of Kirkconnel south-eastwards to the Solway, its lower reaches comprise some of the most fertile land in Dumfriesshire. Although firm evidence is lacking, the lordship may have included eastern Kirkcudbrightshire as far as the Urr, for beyond it lay the independent lordship of Galloway. This region comprised two ecclesiastical deaneries – the Desnes Cro and the Desnes Ioan – which were part of the diocese of Glasgow. This along with other evidence can be taken to suggest that it came under the rule of the lords of Nithsdale, or at the very least they must have exercised some control over it.[1]

The earliest known lord was Dunegal who was probably an older contemporary of King David. Little is known about him apart from the fact that he is recorded as granting property in Dumfries to Jedburgh abbey, while he appears as a witness to King David's charter granting the lordship of Annandale to Robert de Brus in about 1124. There is no record of him witnessing any other royal charters, but the fact that his sons Radulf and Dovenald appear as witnesses to a royal charter of 1136 suggests that he must have been dead by then.[2]

His eldest son Radulf inherited the southern portion of the lordship, including the original castle at Dumfries, namely the Townhead Mote,* which had been Dunegal's ruling centre and which he used as his own. Additionally he would have inherited Dunegal's rights (whatever they were) over the territory between the Nith and the Urr. Dunegal's second son Dovenald, on the other hand, inherited the northern portion of the lordship, including his father's subsidiary ruling centre of Morton castle near present-day Carronbridge,[3] while his third son Gillepatric acquired part of Glencairn. Later, in 1161, Malcolm IV issued a precept enjoining Radulf and Dovenald (and also Fergus of Galloway's sons Uchtred and Gilbert) to ensure the safety of the monks and their retinue while passing through their lands on their way from Holyrood abbey to its daughter house of Trail, on St Mary's Isle at Kirkcudbright, recently given it by Fergus.[4]

---

* This was situated between Dumfries Academy and Castle Street, adjacent to the Nith. After it was abandoned a new castle was built further downstream within the precincts of the present-day Castledykes Park.

Radulf was a considerable benefactor to the Church, a notable example being his granting the lands of Conheath and Caerlaverock to Holm Cultram abbey, Earl Henry's foundation in Cumberland, which was confirmed by Earl Henry's son King Malcolm.[5] He is also credited with founding the Premonstratensian abbey of Dercongal (later Holywood) adjacent to the Nith and endowing it with extensive lands in lower Nithsdale and the Cairn valley. Additionally he granted 'two bovates [of land]' at Dumfries 'free of all custom and service' to the Hospital of St Peter, York.' The wording of the charter has been taken to suggest that Radulf had become part of the feudal establishment and that he held his lands as a tenant-in-chief of the king,[6] in which case his brother Dovenald is likely to have followed suit.

Radulf was twice married. Although the name of his first wife has not survived, she was the mother of his son Thomas whose putative descendants, the lords of Morton, adopted Randolph (a corruption of Radulf) as their surname.[7] His second wife Bethoc, widow of Uhtred lord of Tynedale, was a daughter of Donald *ban* who was briefly king following the death of his brother Malcolm III. By her Radulf had a son whose name was anglicised to Richard and who is recorded as granting a carucate of land at 'Rughechester' (Rowchester), in present-day Roxburghshire, to Jedburgh abbey.[8]

By her first husband Bethoc had a daughter Hextilda who married Richard Comyn and was ancestress of the two main branches of the Comyn family – the lords of Badenoch and the earls of Buchan. It is possible that, on his marriage to Bethoc, Radulf endowed her with the combined barony of Dalswinton and Duncow, and that she bequeathed them to her daughter Hextila. Equally so that she in turn left them to her son William, the ancestor of the Badenoch Comyns. True or not, the fact remains that the Comyns acquired these baronies at an early date, and in the mid-thirteenth century William's grandson, John Comyn, is believed to have been responsible for building the original castle at Dalswinton.[†]

Dovenald's share of the lordship included the barony of Sanquhar with its castle, as well as those of Eliock, Dunscore and Closeburn.[9] Like his father Dunegal and brother Radulf, he too was a benefactor of the Church and its institutions, principally Kelso abbey. This is evident from King William's charter of about 1193 which referred to an obligation by Dovenald (described as the son of Dunegal) to render it *cain* (effectively tribute) of thirteen cows and a like number of pigs annually. It also records an unspecified gift by his brother Gillepatric.[10]

On Dovenald's death the baronies of Sanquhar, Eliock and Closeburn passed to his son Edgar; and, adopting that as their surname, his descendants remained a prominent family in the district. Like his father, Edgar was a generous benefactor of the Church and its institutions to whom he granted a number of churches. They included

---

* *CDS* ii, 1606. That one of the witnesses had the Cumbric name of Gilledonrut Bretnach points to the continuing existence of a Cumbric aristocracy in Nithsdale.

† John Comyn, who was murdered by Bruce in the church of the Friars Minor at Dumfries in February 1306, was his grandson.

Morton and Closeburn which were assigned to Holyrood and Kelso abbeys respectively,[11] while he donated the churches of Dalgarnock and Dunscore to Dercongal abbey.[12] He also gave it a ploughgate of arable land in the parish of Dalgarnock,* along with fishing rights on the Nith, and a right of common pasture for twenty-four animals (presumably cows and horses) and a hundred sheep, as well as permission to build a mill.[13] This was a valuable perquisite because it gave the monks the exclusive right to grind their tenants' corn, although in practice they would have leased it to a miller, doubtless for a substantial rent.

Whereas Dovenald bequeathed Sanquhar, Eliock and Closeburn to Edgar, the barony of Dunscore was left to his daughter Aufreca. She appears to have given most of it to the monks of Melrose who farmed it as a grange.[14] Since it consists mainly of hill ground suitable for sheep farming, its day-to-day management would have been left to the resident shepherds under the supervision of the monks. But the difficulty was that the monks had to cross the Nith to get there, and because the only available ford was some way upriver it involved a lengthy detour. However in about 1250 John Comyn of Badenoch, as lord of Dalswinton came to their rescue by allowing them to use a ford at Friars Carse, and it was there that the monks established a daughter cell.[15]

Radulf died in about 1165[†] when King William annexed his portion of Nithsdale, and the territory to the west as far as the Urr, presumably on the grounds that they had escheated to the crown. At the same time he took possession of the castle at Dumfries. There is evidence to suggest that this high-handed action provoked an uprising which was suppressed with the aid of enlisted troops who were probably drawn from Annandale. Once the situation was brought under control, William consolidated his authority over Nithsdale, and the south-west generally, by creating a sheriffdom based on Dumfries. Comprising present-day Kirkcudbrightshire, Nithsdale, Annandale and part of Eskdale (the remainder being incorporated in the sheriffdom of Roxburgh), it was administered by a sheriff who established a ruling centre at Dumfries castle. As a mark of its newly acquired status, it was officially designated a royal castle, the first – or at least an early – sheriff being Sir Roger Minto.[16]

An important official, the sheriff was responsible for the administration of royal government at a local level. His numerous duties included the management of the royal lands, the collection of crown revenues, enforcing the king's peace, and officiating at the elaborate ceremonies which symbolised the granting of lands. He was also responsible for local defence. This meant ensuring that all landholders produced their stipulated quota of men for military service when required, and for holding regular wappenschawings, or weapon training exercises. Additionally he was responsible for resolving, with the aid of a jury consisting of the oldest men with supposedly the

---

*   Later merged with Closeburn.
†   Barrow claims that he died in about 1185, but this does not tally with Uchtred's 116/ endowment of the Benedictine nunnery at Lincluden with lands described as formerly belonging to Radulf.

longest memories in the community, disputes over landownership. Last but not least, he held a regular court with right to try civil and criminal cases, subject to the jurisdictional powers of the royal justiciar.

It seems likely that Radulf's nephew Edgar joined in the revolt and that he forfeited the baronies of Sanquhar, Eliock and Closeburn. Although this is speculative, it could explain how it was that King William came to grant the barony of Sanquhar to his illegitimate daughter Isabel* on her marriage to Robert de Ros, lord of Helmsley in Yorkshire.[†] This was clearly intended to establish a royal presence in Upper Nithsdale, which suggests that there was continuing opposition to him in the region. Robert de Ros is credited with founding a hospital for the Knights Templar at Sanquhar. Put under the charge of a warden with a staff of nurses and bedesmen, it would have served as an infirmary for the sick and aged, as well as providing temporary accommodation for pilgrims and travellers. It was doubtless to reinforce the royal presence in Nithsdale that King William granted 'the temple lands of Closeburn and Dalgarnock', along with the barony of Tinwald, to Aufreca, another of his illegitimate daughters, on her marriage to Roger de Mandeville.

When Aufreca died in 1232 her lands reverted to the crown. Therefore Alexander II granted them to Ivone de Kirkpatrick, a member of the Kirkpatrick family who had established themselves in eastern Annandale. His son Ivo allegedly married Euphemia, a daughter of Robert de Brus the noble and a sister of the Competitor, although there is no mention of this in the *Scots Peerage*. Ivone de Kirkpatrick had another son – or more likely a grandson – Stephen who features in the records of Kelso abbey in 1278. Stephen's son Roger de Kirkpatrick was an early companion of Robert Bruce the future king, and the story has it that when a shaken Bruce emerged from the church of the Friars Minor in Dumfries having mortally wounded the Red Comyn, Kirkpatrick is supposed to have exclaimed 'I'll mak' siccar [sure]' as he dashed inside to finish him off. Notwithstanding that his father Stephen appears in the Ragman Roll for the sheriffdom of Dumfries as swearing fealty to Edward I, Roger was a staunch supporter of Robert Bruce.[‡]

King William is believed to have constituted Dumfries a burgh in 1186. But there is no certainty about this because the founding charter has been lost, possibly destroyed during the Wars of Independence. The original town grew up round the Townhead Mote, and here the community lived within the confines of the town wall, access being limited to two – or at most three – main gates which would have been locked at night. Giving the town burghal status was primarily intended to facilitate – and therefore encourage – trade, for which it was well placed given that

---

* She was previously married to Robert de Brus, son and heir of Robert de Brus the younger, who predeceased his father.

† These lands ultimately passed to their descendants the Crichtons.

‡ The barony of Closeburn remained in the hands of his descendants until the late eighteenth century. In the following century a daughter of the family married the count of Teba, a Spanish nobleman, and in 1853 their daughter Eugénie married the Emperor Napoleon III.

the sea level was higher than today and vessels could approach within striking distance of the town.

The annexation of Nithsdale was of a piece with King William's policy of expanding his royal authority throughout the realm, evident from the creation of some twelve new sheriffdoms during his reign. Because the semi-independent lordship of Galloway had been a consistent source of trouble, he took advantage of the quarrel which had broken out between Fergus's sons Uchtred and Gilbert to establish a measure of control over it. Notwithstanding that King Malcolm had dictated a division of the lordship lands between them, Uchtred inherited the lordship itself, much to the fury of Gilbert who held strongly to the view that as the elder son he had a better right to it.* Therefore, applying a policy of divide and rule, William supported Uchtred and brought him into the feudal establishment by granting him the territory between the Nith and the Urr. In return, Uchtred would have paid homage to King William not only for these lands but also, it would seem, for the territory beyond which had been apportioned to him by King Malcolm. Consequently he became a tenant-in-chief of the crown.

While he seems to have been given more or less a free hand in the choice of tenants, King William would have dictated the grant of the important barony of Urr to his chamberlain, Sir Walter de Berkeley, so that he could act as his proxy in the region. Similarly Uchtred was prevailed on to grant the lands of Borgue to Hugh de Morville, another prominent member of the Scottish feudal establishment.† On the other hand, he himself would have been responsible for granting lands at Kirkgunzeon to the monks of Holm Cultram who farmed them as a grange. He also granted land at Lincluden in the parish of Troqueer to the Hospital of St Peter, York, for the endowment of a Benedictine nunnery which was founded in 1167.[17] This was followed by the grant of lands at Drumsleet, now part of Maxwelltown, as well as others in the parish of Kirkpatrick Durham in Kirkcudbrightshire.

Doubtless influenced by his wife Gunnild, daughter of the lord of Allerdale one of the Northumbrians whom King David established in the lordship of Carlisle, Uchtred granted fiefs to men from that milieu as an encouragement to them to settle in Galloway in order to buttress his authority. They included Richard fitzTroite, a close relative of the de Hodelme family, who was given the barony of Lochkindeloch (now New Abbey). Another was Gospatrick fitzOrm, constable of Appleby and a cousin of Uchtred's wife, who was given the neighbouring barony of Colvend – a poorer fief since it overlies a bedrock of granite. Further west, the lands beyond the river Fleet, which constituted the barony of Cardiness, were granted to David fitzTerrus a native

---

* Being the son of Fergus's first marriage, which was not recognised by the Church, he was technically illegitimate and therefore ineligible to succeed to the lordship, a fact which he refused to accept. Uchtred, on the other hand, was a legitimate son of Fergus by one of Henry I's bastard daughters, and therefore a cousin of Henry II who recognised their kinship – at least when it suited him.
† Son of the original Hugh de Morville to whom King David granted the lordships of Cunningham and Lauderdale.

of Gilsland and member of the same milieu. He was the founder of the de Kerdenesse family who subsequently forfeited the barony during the Wars of Independence.

These incomers brought with them numerous servants and retainers, as well as labourers to cultivate the lands seized from the previous occupants. Not surprisingly their presence was fiercely resented by the native Gallovidians. The situation came to a head in 1174 when, taking advantage of King William's imprisonment in England, Gilbert instigated a revolt. Turning on the immigrant population, the Gallovidians slaughtered them out of hand, and only the lucky few, including the principal tenants, managed to escape to their homeland across the Solway. The violence seems to have spread beyond Galloway because the foreign settlers in Annandale are believed to have come under attack as well.[18] If true, it points to a continuing deep-seated hostility on the part of the native population towards the incomers. Uchtred himself was captured and according to the English envoy Roger de Howden he was so mutilated that he took his own life.* Gilbert proceeded to arrogate the lordship, and by playing off the two kings – William and Henry II – with masterly guile he managed to retain it until his death in 1185.

To continue the story because it has a bearing on subsequent events, Uchtred's son Roland (or Lachlan) took advantage of Gilbert's death to claim the lordship. Therefore, ignoring the rights of Gilbert's son Duncan, then a hostage at the English court,† he invaded western Galloway and took possession of Gilbert's lands. But because Henry II was obliged to protect his interests, he threatened retaliation. However a compromise was reached, in terms of which Roland was allowed to keep the lordship, while Duncan retained his father's lands of Carrick in southern Ayrshire. Created earl of Carrick by King William's son, Alexander II, he died at an advanced age in 1250 when he was succeeded by his son Earl Neil (or Nigel). On Neil's death in 1258 the earldom passed to his daughter Marjorie, who married as her second husband Robert Bruce of Annandale and was the mother of Robert Bruce the future king.

LATER TENANTS

In 1174, taking advantage of a revolt by Henry II's unruly sons, King William invaded the northern counties in a bid to recover the earldom of Northumberland. Summonses were issued to his tenants-in-chief to muster their levies to take part in the campaign. They included Robert de Brus. But, knowing that this would cost him his lordship of Hartness, he declined. The campaign was a disaster. No general, King William was dubbed by an Irish chronicler as *garbh* meaning brawny which, as was caustically

---

* On Roger de Howden's say-so, Gilbert 'sent in his butchers commanding them to put out his [Uchtred's] eyes, and to emasculate him and cut out his tongue, [and] shortly after that he ended his life' (Anderson, *Annals*). Since killing a ruler was a mortal sin in the eyes of the Church, the alternative was to so maim him as to render him incapable of ruling, even to the extent of encouraging him to take his own life.
† In security for Gilbert's guaranteeing Roland in peaceable possession of the lands he inherited from his father Uchtred.

observed, 'seems a not unfair assessment of his bravery and his intellectual stature'.[19] As he and his army were about to lay siege to Alnwick castle they were surprised by an English force. In the ensuing skirmish William's horse was killed, and falling on top of him it pinned him to the ground and he was captured. Incarcerated in the Tower of London, he remained there until the following February when he was released on humiliating terms.

On his return to Scotland he punished Robert de Brus for his refusal to obey the summons by confiscating the castles of Annan and Lochmaben. But realising that his actions might provoke de Brus into defecting to King Henry, and deliver him control of Annandale, he relented and restored the castles to him.[20] King William went further. In 1183, to ensure Robert's loyalty, he arranged a marriage between his illegitimate daughter Isabel and Robert's son and heir, Robert the younger.* It had a further advantage. Because Isabel's mother, King William's (unnamed) mistress, was a daughter of the veteran Robert Avenel lord of Eskdale, William could count on him as an ally. Since he could now depend on the support of Robert de Brus as well, it meant that the combination of Annandale and Eskdale would represent a powerful bulwark against possible English aggression.

Shortly before his death in about 1186 Robert Avenel retired to become a monk of Melrose, having endowed it with much of upper Eskdale under reservation of the superiority and the sporting rights to himself and his successors. While some of the place-names mentioned in the relevant charter have either changed or disappeared, it is still possible to identify the lands passing under it. Starting at the confluence of the Black and the White Esk, a few miles south of present-day Eskdalemuir, it extended northwards as far as the march with Ettrickdale, its eastern boundary being the high ground which separates Eskdale from Ewesdale, and on the west it marched with the barony of Dryfesdale.[21] Much of it consisted of woodland, but the rest was 'white' hill country ideally suited to sheep farming which was the Cistercian monks' speciality.

Here they were able to put their expertise to good use by running their improved type of sheep on it, and at the same time they clear-felled much of the native woodland. This served a double purpose. For, as well as increasing the area under pasture, the felled timber was used in the construction of sheep pens (or bouchts) and shelters, to build shielings for the shepherds, and for firewood.[22] Therefore it was doubtless at the monks' insistence that, in terms of the charter, Robert Avenel bound himself and his successors to ensure that whenever they exercised their sporting rights they would refrain from causing damage to the 'hedges, meadows, sheepfolds and other enclosures'. In return, the monks undertook not to destroy hawks' nests in the course of their tree-felling operations. Further, they promised that anyone caught poaching would be taken to the Avenels' ruling centre at Staplegorton and handed over to the bailie for punishment.[23]

---

* He predeceased his father without surviving issue in 1191. His widow Isabel re-married Robert de Ros lord of Helmsley when her father gave them the barony of Sanquhar.

Robert Avenel was succeeded by his eldest son Gervase who added to his inheritance with the acquisition of lands in the parishes of Hutton and Tundergarth. Another son, Laurence, obtained – possibly by inheritance – lands in Dryfesdale which his daughter Agnes later resigned to Robert de Brus the noble. Besides the unnamed mistress of King William, Robert Avenel had another unnamed daughter. She was endowed with lands in Ewesdale, including the manor of Unthank. Therefore when she married a member of the Lovell family who were lords of Hawick these lands passed into their hands.

On Gervase's death the lordship passed to his son Roger. He became involved in a dispute with the monks of Melrose when it came to light that they had been indulging in sharp practice. When Roger's grandfather Robert Avenel stipulated that they were to avoid destroying hawks' nests in the course of their tree-felling operations, he conceded that the sanction would not apply if a bird failed to return to its nest the following spring. It then transpired that the monks or their servants were deliberately chasing the birds away to prevent them from returning to their nests so that they could carry on with their tree-felling operations regardless of the sanction. Because Roger de Avenel was unable to put a stop to the practice, he was forced to appeal to the king to intervene – successfully because the monks or their servants appear to have desisted. When Roger died in 1243 without a male heir, the lordship of Eskdale passed to his daughter and her husband Sir Henry Graham of Dalkeith.[*]

Throughout his tenure of the lordship Robert de Brus maintained close links with his father's foundation of Guisborough priory, endowing it with a number of churches in Annandale. But his right to do so was challenged by Bishop Engelram of Glasgow on the grounds that the inquest set up by David I while prince of Cumbria had determined that the churches in question belonged to his diocese. Robert de Brus took issue. Yes, the inquest had concluded that Hoddom and its four former daughter churches of Dryfesdale, Esbie, Trailtrow and St Mungo belonged to Glasgow, and had not been given to Guisborough. On the other hand, those that were – namely Annan, Lochmaben, Kirkpatrick Fleming, Cummertrees, Rainpatrick (Redkirk) and Gretna – had been founded by himself or his father and therefore he had a perfect right to dispose of them as he wished. The findings were recorded in an agreement of 1189 which was endorsed by King William sometime between 1204 and 1207.[24] This confirmed that Hoddom and its former daughter churches belonged to Glasgow, to which as a gesture of goodwill Robert de Brus added those of Moffat and Kirkpatrick (later Kirkpatrick Juxta[†]), while endorsing Robert's gift of the other churches to Guisborough.[25]

---

[*] As an old man he was a subscriber to the entail of 1284 which guaranteed the right of Alexander III's granddaughter and heiress, Margaret of Norway, to succeed to the kingship.

[†] So named in the fifteenth century to distinguish it from the other churches dedicated to St Patrick in the see of Glasgow – namely, Kirkpatrick Irongray, Kirkpatrick Durham, Kirkpatrick Fleming and Kirkpatrick in Nithsdale. It was styled Juxta since it was the nearest to Glasgow (*Fasti*, 210).

Robert de Brus died, probably in his mid-seventies, in about 1194. Since his eldest son Robert predeceased him, he was succeeded by his second son William. Because his tenure of the lordship lasted a mere twenty years compared with his father's fifty, he issued proportionately fewer charters. One, however, records the grant to Gilbert son of John* of 'a coruscate of land' in Warmanby, upriver from Annan, and 'half a carucate' in Annan itself,[†] along with a toft which had been resigned by Dunegal son of Udard.[‡] This Gilbert, who was the ancestor of the Johnstones, witnessed at least two charters by William de Brus' son, Robert the noble,[26] while his (probable) son, Sir Gilbert de Johnston, witnessed some charters issued by Robert Bruce the Competitor.[27]

One new name appearing during William de Brus' tenure of the lordship was William de Henneville. His family are thought to have come from Haineville, near Cherbourg, and around the turn of the century William de Brus granted him lands on the Sark in return for his resignation of other unspecified lands.[28] Later, another William de Henneville (probably his grandson) witnessed a charter issued by Robert the Competitor,[29] to whom he resigned the lands on the Sark in exchange for others 'in the vill[§] of Moffat'.[30] He may be identifiable with the William de Hellebeck who features in the Ragman Roll. In the following century a Thomas de Henvale, presumably a member of the same family, acquired the lands of Collin and Roucan from Eupham de Torthorwald and her husband Robert Corrie.[31]

Given the importance of Annandale as a bulwark against a possible English aggression, King William ensured William de Brus' continuing loyalty by renewing the ties between their two families which had been severed by the younger Robert's death. Accordingly he arranged for William de Brus' son and heir Robert (future Robert the noble) to marry his niece Isabel, daughter of his brother David earl of Huntingdon. For the de Brus family it was an extremely prestigious match and would greatly enhance their status which had declined since the time of the first Robert de Brus. Yet, in spite of being a member of the royal house, she was a lady of limited prospects because all she stood to inherit was a token share of her father Earl David's landholdings in England and Scotland.

This would change following the death of her brother, the childless John earl of Huntingdon, in 1237. This was because most of his lands fell to be divided between herself, her younger sister Ada de Hastings and the daughters of her deceased elder sister Margaret, wife of Alan lord of Galloway.[¶] Isabella's portion included a number of English manors, and when she died in about 1251 they passed to her sons Robert

---

* *CDS* i, 606. This was the John whom Robert de Brus had earlier confirmed in possession of lands in the parish of Johnstone.
† A 'coruscate' or 'carucate' was the amount of land that could be tilled with the aid of a team of eight oxen in any one year.
‡ Not to be confused with Udard de Hodelme.
§ A vill was the smallest territorial and administrative unit.
¶ Namely Christina and Dervorguilla, the mother of the future king John Balliol.

the Competitor and Bernard, who in consequence regarded themselves primarily as English barons. This effectively distanced Robert the Competitor from his Annandale lordship – at least until later life. In his absence he appointed a steward to administer it for him, the office being initially rotated among his principal tenants.

William de Brus died in 1215 and was succeeded by his son Robert the noble whose tenure of the lordship lasted for thirty years until his death in 1245. Although the majority of witnesses to his charters were representatives of the families who had been established in Annandale by his grandfather Robert de Brus the younger, they included one new name, that of David de Torthorwald. That he first appears as a witness in 1230[32] might suggest that the family were comparative newcomers. They were given the lands of Torthorwald (from which they took their name) on the border with Nithsdale, and it was here that they built a motte-and-bailey castle. Occupying a strategic position overlooking lower Nithsdale with the impenetrable Lochar moss in the foreground and Dumfries beyond, it was later replaced by a stone castle.

David de Torthorwald was also given lands in Dryfesdale, including Overdryfe which he sold to Sir Henry Graham lord of Eskdale sometime in the mid-thirteenth century.[33] About the same time Robert Bruce the Competitor, by a special concession, promised David de Torthorwald that no *eschapium* (a fine imposed on the owner of marauding livestock) would be imposed on him for any of his livestock which happened to stray on to his neighbours' lands. But because fines of one penny for every two sheep, or ten hogs, or ten goats, were excepted from the concession,[34] it seems that the *eschapium* only applied to cattle. During the 1270s David de Torthorwald, presumably his son, witnessed at least two charters issued by Robert Bruce the Competitor in one of which he is described as seneschal, or steward, of Annandale.[35] Two members of the family, Sir James and Sir Thomas de Torthorwald, feature in the Ragman Roll, but their support for the English during the Wars of Independence cost them their Dumfriesshire lands.

Another new name appearing about this time was John de Refhols who inherited, or otherwise acquired, the lands of Raffles near Mouswald (called after the family) sometime before 1245.[36] However he must have resigned them later in the century because the name de Refhols does not appear in the Ragman Roll.

An important incomer to Dumfriesshire during the thirteenth century was Sir John Maxwell, who was granted the lands and barony of Caerlaverock. Since the family became pre-eminent in the region, their origins warrant a brief digression. According to Fraser they were originally Anglo-Saxons and can be traced back to the eleventh century when Maccus (from whom their name is derived) and his father Unwin, thought to have been a man of high standing in Anglo-Saxon England, took refuge in Scotland following the Norman Conquest. Maccus became a prominent feudal baron having been endowed with lands in lower Teviotdale, near Kelso, by King David. Sir John Maxwell was his grandson and he too became a man of some eminence. Appointed sheriff of Teviotdale, he later became Alexander II's chamberlain,[37] and it was probably as a reward that in about 1220 he was given the lands of Caerlaverock.

In the previous century Radulf lord of Nithsdale had granted it, along with the neighbouring lands of Conheath, to Holm Cultram. However it seems that the monks had entered into rather an odd agreement with their sister abbey of Dundrennan in terms of which they undertook that neither of them would acquire lands to the east of the Nith without the consent of the other. Therefore when Dundrennan, who had obviously not been consulted on, still less approved of, the grant of Caerlaverock and Conheath to Holm Cultram, raised a formal objection it was upheld. Consequently Holm Cultram had to surrender them to the crown, which explains how they came to be available for re-grant to Sir John Maxwell.

He was responsible for building the original stronghold which was situated on an artificial island consisting of sand and mud dredged up from a natural inlet of the Solway Firth. Although readily accessible by sea,* the building became so wet and the surrounds so muddy that it became uninhabitable. Worse still, it was regularly flooded by abnormally high tides which had so undermined the foundations that the building had become unstable and had to be abandoned. In the 1270s Sir John's nephew, Sir Herbert Maxwell, built a new castle. Thought to have been one of the earliest stone castles in Scotland, and the forerunner of the present castle, it was situated on slightly higher ground to the north. This became the nucleus of the extensive landholding which the Maxwells eventually built up in Dumfriesshire and the neighbouring counties, to the extent that by the sixteenth century they had become the principal power in the region.

CONTEMPORARY LIFE

The thirteenth century was a time of peace and relative prosperity. The treaty of York, concluded between Alexander II and Henry III in 1237, marked a cessation of warfare between the two countries which would last for nearly sixty years. The respite came to an end in 1296 when, goaded by Edward I's increasingly intrusive demands on them, the Scots were lured into invading England, thus precipitating the first War of Independence. Meanwhile Alexander II and his son Alexander III were preoccupied with extending their rule to the north and west. Therefore, well removed from the scene of conflict, the people of Dumfriesshire – and southern Scotland generally – were able to pursue their farming activities in the confidence that, weather permitting, the grain sown would be harvested without fear of destruction of their crops and that, barring accident or disease, new-born livestock would survive to maturity.

It is not known what the population of Dumfriesshire was at the time; nor is it possible to arrive at a meaningful estimate. All that can be said is that, thanks to the prevailing warmer climate and increased productivity, the evidence from England

---

* The sea level at that time was some five metres higher than today.

and north-west Europe points to a population growth from about the turn of the millennium onwards, peaking at around 1300 when it was the highest it had ever been.[38] As a further pointer, Powicke asserts that the population of Scotland in 1300 was in the region of 400,000. Of this nearly half lived in the dioceses of Glasgow and St Andrews where the people were mainly confined to the lower-lying, more fertile lands and the coastal regions.[39] Doubtless the same applied in Dumfriesshire where the upland regions would have been virtually uninhabited.

Yet the population growth was periodically checked by calamities such as harvest failure and consequent hunger and starvation. For example we are told that the winter of 1205–6 was one of 'great, dreadful and long' frosts which killed 'all sheep, cows and horses' left in the open.[40] Again in 1256 the Lanercost chronicle tells of 'a great corruption of the air and inundation of rain throughout the whole of England and Scotland [when] crops and hay were nearly [all] lost'.[41] That there was a further occurrence of freakish weather in 1260 is evident from Bower's apocalyptic reference to 'dreadful claps of thunder [and] terrifying flashes of lightning [which] burned up men in the fields, and animals far and wide',[42] while the harvest failures of 1283 and 1292 were attributable to persistent bad weather.

Yet in spite of these setbacks the population continued to grow, and Parliament was forced to introduce a number of measures to increase productivity. As early as 1209 a statute was passed taking landholders to task for 'wasting their lands and the country generally' by running 'a multitude of sheep and beasts' on them (i.e. overstocking them), and in consequence 'troubling God's people with scarcity, poverty and utter hardship'.[43] This was followed by another statute of 1214 which compelled landholders to bring marginal land into cultivation either 'with oxen or their feet [i.e. with a spade]'.[44] It also stipulated that ploughing was to begin 'no later than fifteen days before the Feast of the Purification [18 January]'.[45]

That overstocking caused livestock to stray on to other people's lands to the detriment of their crops is evident from Robert Bruce the Competitor's waiving David de Torthorwald's liability to a fine in the event of his cattle straying on to his neighbours' lands.[46] And the fact that land was being brought under the plough in Dumfriesshire is evident from the terms of William de Brus' charter to William de Henneville granting him lands on the Sark. They included 'pasture in the wood', while the grant was stated to be in return for de Henneville's resigning certain (unidentified) lands 'newly cultivated'.[47] The reference to 'pasture in the wood' presumably meant pannage, which was the right to graze pigs on the acorn crop in the autumn.

Despite the inroads made by successive waves of immigrants on the native forest, much of Annandale (and Nithsdale for that matter) consisted of woodland. But from about the mid-thirteenth century onwards it was progressively cut back to allow more land to be brought into pasture. This was to increase production to meet the demands of a growing population.[48] A possible example was the grant by Robert de Brus the noble to Robert de Crossebie of the 'commonty' in the wood at Stapleton, near Annan, with right to enclose it as a free park,[49] although admittedly this was mainly for hunting rather than cultivation. At much the same time, the monks of Melrose were busy clear-felling the native woodland in upper Eskdale to bring it into pasture.

In medieval times, and for some centuries to come, the basic social and economic unit was the ferme-toun. Ferme-touns consisted of strips of cultivable land grouped round small, clustered settlements comprising the tenants' hovels and possibly some rudimentary outbuildings and stockpens. Each tenant had an exclusive right to cultivate a number of strips of land according to a system known as 'runrig'. Apart from opening itself up to frequent neighbourly disputes, it was a precarious form of tenure, for when the tenants' leases expired there was no guarantee of renewal. On the other hand, where a lease was renewed it was normally the practice to re-allocate the strips of ground by a form of lottery. This meant that tenants were unlikely to find themselves cultivating the same ground as before.

Known as the infield, the cultivable land was generally cropped according to a two- to three-year rotation with the emphasis on barley and oats. Much of the barley (or bere) crop was used for brewing, and as beer (of a sort) was habitually drunk by all classes it is thought to have accounted for as much as a third of the entire annual barley crop in Scotland.[50] Although nitrogen-fixing pease and beans were beginning to be grown in the more fertile parts of south-eastern Scotland, the practice is unlikely to have spread to Dumfriesshire. Since it was important for the land to be comprehensively dunged, it was generally the practice to fold the cattle on to the stubble during the autumn and keep them there until the spring. But the drawback was that the ground would become so 'poached' as to be virtually incapable of cultivation. With the arrival of the spring grass the cattle would be driven – and in some cases physically lifted – out to the pasture land beyond the infield. This was the outfield, and here a rudimentary form of crop rotation was practised where part would be cropped while the remainder was allowed to revert to grass and weeds.

Yields were pitifully small. Even in the more fertile south-east of Scotland they seldom exceeded five grains of corn for every seed sown, and in the acid soil of Dumfriesshire they would have been less. Productivity was also badly inhibited by weed infestation, mainly because the conventional ox-drawn plough was unable to turn over the soil to a sufficient depth to kill the weeds. A particularly obnoxious weed was corn marigold or 'gool', which flourished in acid soil. Although colourful when in flower, it choked the crops, while its succulent stem prevented the grain from drying out. At its most destructive it is believed to have reduced yields to as little as a tenth,[51] and because this was tantamount to harvest failure it was vital that the weed be kept under control. Therefore landowners frequently employed 'gool riders' to check their tenants' crops for the presence of the weed, those failing to eradicate it being liable to punishment.*

---

*   Even as late as the eighteenth century Grierson of Lag held special gool courts to punish those of his tenants who failed to eradicate it.

Once the corn had ripened it was cut with a sickle, bound into sheaves which were propped up into stooks and left to dry out. The sheaves would then be taken to the barn and laid out on a threshing floor where they were beaten with flails to separate the grain from the stalks. A time-consuming operation, it was traditionally a valuable source of employment during the winter months. If, on the other hand, the summer was particularly wet, as happened from time to time, the corn never dried out and simply sprouted in the stooks, spelling harvest failure and the spectre of hunger and starvation.

Whereas the stalks were used for cattle fodder, a third of the grain had to go to the landlord as rent, and a tenth (or tithe) to the local vicar as his teind right. Consequently the farmer and his family were compelled to subsist on what was left. Not only that, but he had to pay the miller to grind his corn at the estate mill to which he was 'thirled', meaning that he was forbidden to have it ground elsewhere. This was an iniquitous practice, because it meant the miller had a monopoly of grinding the corn of all the estate tenants. Since he would normally rent the mill from the landlord at considerable cost, he would charge as much as he could in order to maximise the return on his outlay. Small wonder that he was traditionally the most unpopular member of the community.

This is evident from a pronouncement by the king's bailiffs when they sat at Dumfries in about 1259 to hear an appeal against the acquittal of one Richard of the murder of Adam the local miller. There was already bad blood between them, probably resulting from sharp practice on Adam's part. Therefore, encountering him in St Michael's churchyard one Sunday morning, Richard publicly denounced Adam as a *galuvet* meaning a Gallovidian and by inference a thief, and was about to attack him. But rather than commit the sacrilege of being involved in a brawl within the precincts of a church, particularly on the Sabbath, Adam made off leaving a frustrated Richard muttering threats of vengeance which were overheard by a female bystander.

The following Thursday, seeing Adam standing at the doorway of his house, this woman warned him to make himself scarce because Richard was coming his way determined on retribution. But Adam stood his ground declaring, 'I have a knife as sharp as his.' So saying he went into his house and reappeared a few minutes later with the knife with which he threatened to disembowel Richard. As Richard approached, Adam rushed at him intending to do just that. Caught unawares Richard drew his sword and in the ensuing fracas he ran Adam through and mortally wounded him, allegedly remarking 'I have not killed thee; thou didst it thyself.' Arraigned on a murder charge before a jury of thirteen burgesses, Richard asserted (with questionable truth) that he had never harboured any ill-will towards Adam, and that he had been the victim of an unprovoked attack. Accepting his statement at its face value, the jury acquitted him. The king's bailiffs upheld the decision, observing that whereas Richard 'had been faithful in all things' (i.e. a man with an unblemished record) Adam being a miller was by definition a thief.[52]

The marginal and hill land beyond the outfield was mainly dedicated to sheep-rearing and the summering of cattle when there was sufficient grass available. Here they would tear up the clumps of rough grass to allow the emergence of new shoots which provide the best grazing for sheep. Whereas some outby land might be attached to an individual ferme-toun, in other cases it was common to the tenants of several ferme-touns. Or it might be let as a separate entity, as Robert Avenel did when he leased the lands in upper Eskdale to the monks of Melrose (prior to making an outright gift of them). The cattle were most likely ranched out, probably checked from time to time by one of the tenants for accident or disease. A particularly serious disease, which occurred in about 1270 and spread rapidly throughout Scotland, affecting Lothian in particular, was 'lungessouth'. As the name implies, it was a respiratory disease and may have been husk or 'hoose'. Ranching entailed the risk of cattle-stealing which was rife. This is evident from an Act of 1175 which stipulated that anyone exposing cattle for sale had to produce a 'lauchful borch of hamehald'[53] – a form of certificate confirming that they were his lawful property.

Notwithstanding the risks, cattle rearing was practised extensively throughout Dumfriesshire. While some of the surplus heifers and bullocks were slaughtered for home consumption, most were taken to the principal markets in northern England where they were in keen demand. Possible evidence of this comes from the township of Galgate, near Lancaster. The name is thought to be derived from Galwaithgate which was that of a twelfth-century road running past Morecambe Bay, and so-called because it was used by cattle drovers from Galloway. Similarly the monks of Melrose are known to have run cattle on their lands at Dunscore, because the records speak to their acquiring stopover grazing rights on the way. Regrettably, ill-treatment of stock seems to have been common practice, for an Act of Parliament refers to 'the spoilation of certain oxin and putting furth their ene' (gouging out their eyes),[54] so it is hardly surprising that a contemporary chronicler described how 'they flie the companie or sight of men'.[55]

Sheep farming could be extremely profitable. This was mainly due to the Cistercian monks' success in breeding an animal with a superior fleece quality for which there was a keen demand. So much so, that by the late 1100s Scottish monastic houses were sending regular shipments of wool to the clothmakers in the Low Countries, as well as those of Florence and Venice.[56] Consequently much of their wealth was founded on the wool trade, and their methods were widely copied – particularly in southern Scotland where the main pioneers were the Cistercian houses of Melrose, Newbattle, Dryburgh and Dundrennan.

But sheep were vulnerable to predation – by foxes, wolves and birds of prey – and worst of all disease. One of the most virulent was 'pilsought' or 'pluk' (probably sheep scab) which is thought to have resulted from overstocking. A particularly serious outbreak which occurred in the late 1200s was variously attributed to infected sheep brought back from Cyprus by returning Crusaders, or to a batch of infected sheep imported from Spain. Since its rapid spread was attributed to hoar frost, sheep were kept penned up in their enclosures throughout the winter and only allowed out after the sun had melted the ground (about the worst thing farmers could do because it merely encouraged the spread of the disease). Wherever there was an outbreak drastic measures were taken to contain it. For example, in the 1290s King John Balliol directed the sheriffs to place an embargo on the movement of all stock, to hold an inquest into each reported outbreak, and to order the immediate slaughter of all infected animals.[57]

Nor were poultry immune to disease. Referring to an outbreak in the following century, Bower records that 'in 1336 there was such a great fowl pest that people altogether shrank from eating – or even looking at – their cocks and hens, because they were regarded as unclean and riddled with leprosy. Therefore, as he went on to say, 'nearly all that species were destroyed'.[58]

Throughout this time a rigid class system prevailed among the farming community, although it would become less so in consequence of the plague epidemics of the following century. At the lower end of the scale were the cottars who were allotted sufficient land for their subsistence in return for providing a specified amount of labour on their lord's demesne. Above them came various gradations of tenants, from the co-tenants of ferme-touns to the so-called 'eight-oxen men' who farmed a substantial amount of land known as an 'oxgang'.* These tenants are not to be confused with feudal tenants who were generally substantial landowners. The difference was highlighted in an Act of Parliament of the reign of Alexander II which drew a distinction between the tenant of a knight's fee, on the one hand, and 'malaris of carls borne' (i.e. rent-payers of a certain social status) and 'they that are of foul kyn' (i.e. of low birth) on the other.[59]

At the top of the farming ladder, but ranking well below the lord from whom they rented their land, were the husbandmen – substantial farmers who might sub-let part of their holding. In that connection the Lanercost chronicler refers to the difficulty an Annandale landowner, Sir Robert de Robertstone, encountered when trying to extract rents from his apparently prosperous tenants (presumably husbandmen). Evidently the reason was that they had 'waxed lewd through their wealth', and after a drinking bout at the local tavern they would proceed 'to violate each other's wives or seduce their daughters'. Then they would purchase absolution from the local archdeacon to the benefit of his purse – but not that of Sir Robert who was fobbed off with a litany of excuses for non-payment of their rent.

When he found out why, he gave his defaulting tenants an ultimatum: refrain from adultery or I will terminate your leases. This had the desired effect. As the chronicler goes on to say, 'desisting from illicit intercourse, [the tenants] applied themselves to labour and farming, and began to make money'. Disturbed at the lack of fines to swell his coffers, the archdeacon remonstrated with Sir Robert, demanding to know on what authority he presumed to enjoin morality on his tenants. To which Sir Robert replied that what mattered to him was that they should pay their rent, and that their

---

* In central and south-east Scotland an oxgang is reckoned to have been the equivalent of about thirteen acres of arable land, and much the same would have applied in Dumfriesshire.

morals were their own affair. 'But', he went on, 'I perceive that as long as you can fill your purse you are quite indifferent to the state of their souls.'[60] So much for Church morality!

Then there were the bondmen. Although technically freemen, they were required to work full time on their lord's demesne, while below them came the serfs. They were literally the lord's chattels, and the fact that they were 'thirled' – or tied – to his land meant that they were conveyed along with it as a pertinent in the event of a sale or change of ownership. In fact they were slaves in all but name. However, the shortage of labour resulting from the fourteenth-century plague epidemics was responsible for the virtual disappearance of serfdom in Scotland – described as 'that great, peaceful, silent revolution which has never found its way into our histories.'[61]

Thereafter former serfs graduated to become landless labourers, and in many cases small-time tenants or cottars. But it was not an unmixed blessing, because it meant they were denied the protection traditionally extended by the lords to their serfs. This was important in view of the prevailing lawlessness – evident from an Act ordering people not to 'truble other mennis lands'.[62] The lords had far-reaching powers over their tenants and other indwellers, including those of *furca* and *fossa* – pit and gallows. Although such punishments were probably only handed out in extreme cases, a baron's court was more likely to have been concerned with resolving disputes, or imposing minor penalties for comparatively trivial offences.

Life for those at the lower end of the social scale was pretty dismal, as was their diet. Since bread was generally unaffordable, being mainly the perquisite of the upper classes, their staple fare would have consisted of oatmeal in the form of porridge, gruel or brose (uncooked meal and water). Probably quite a healthy one provided it was supplemented with protein which was traditionally obtained by cutting the artery in a cow's neck and sucking the blood. But depressingly monotonous, even if leavened by milk, butter and cheese (the peasant farmers invariably kept a house cow), as well as eggs and possibly poultry. Meat on the other hand was generally only obtainable if salvaged from the carcase of a dead (probably disease-ridden) animal, and was probably more readily available in the autumn when the surplus stock were slaughtered.

For those living near a river there might be the chance of a fish (probably poached), and similarly for those living near the coast, although fishing rights were a jealously guarded privilege. At that time Scottish waters abounded in herring though they would become less plentiful, perhaps in consequence of the onset of colder weather from the fourteenth century onwards. Salmon were particularly popular. Rather than hooked with rod and line, the traditional method of catching them was by erecting stake nets across the river estuaries to trap them as they headed upstream to their spawning grounds. 'Haaf' nets were also used in the fast-flowing channels, while spear fishing was commonly practised in shallower waters, or at low tide when there was doubtless an abundance of flounders as well.

Generally speaking, life for all classes was a constant battle against nature. Yet in the following centuries, when the combination of a deteriorating climate and almost perpetual warfare, particularly in southern Scotland, reduced the people to utter destitution, there was a tendency – at least on the part of the chroniclers – to look back on the thirteenth century as a sort of Golden Age. Although life in general may have been better than in the following century, it was only relative and a Golden Age it was not.

ROBERT BRUCE THE COMPETITOR

Robert de Brus the noble died in 1245. He was succeeded by his elder son Robert, later known as the Competitor,* who according to the *Scots Peerage* was born in 1210.† The Lanercost chronicler describes him in fulsome terms as 'a man of handsome appearance, a gifted speaker, remarkable for his influence [and] most devoted to God and the clergy'. In the same vein, the chronicler goes on to say that it was 'his custom to entertain more liberally than all the other courtiers', that he was 'most hospitable to all his guests', and 'pilgrims were never allowed to remain outside his gates, [while] his door was always open to the w-ayfarer'.[63]

In 1234 an event occurred which would have profound implications for the future, because it resulted in the Balliol/Comyn faction establishing an ascendancy over the south-west, which in consequence became the principal battleground during the Wars of Independence. This was the death of Alan, the last of the semi-independent lords of Galloway. Since he left three daughters as co-heiresses, Alexander II used this as a pretext for dismantling the lordship and bringing that notoriously troublesome region properly under control. Therefore, with questionable legality, he decreed the dissolution of the lordship and the division of its demesne lands between the three daughters.‡ But, jealous of their independence, the Gallovidians resisted, and rallying under Alan's illegitimate son Thomas they defied the king.

Alexander responded by invading the province. But his troops suffered a near disaster when they became bogged down in a marshy flow at the head of Loch Ken and were attacked by a Gallovidian force which had been shadowing them as they made their way across the Glenkens.[64] However it was averted at the last moment by the timely arrival of the rearguard under Ferquard Macintaggart earl of Ross who succeeded in driving the Gallovidians off into the hills. Thomas and his leading supporters fled to Ireland, while the task of consolidating the victory and stamping out all further resistance was assigned to Walter Comyn earl of Menteith. He

---

* Since he only became a competitor for the kingship towards the end of his long life, he would not have been referred to as such before then. However, to distinguish him from the other Roberts de Brus I have so described him throughout.

† Possibly later (see A A M Duncan, 'The Bruces of Annandale' *TDGNHAS*, lxix (1994), 89).

‡ The eldest, Elena, Alan's daughter by his first wife, was married to Roger de Quenci, earl of Winchester. The other two – Christina and Dervorguilla – were the issue of his second wife Margaret, daughter of David earl of Huntingdon. Whereas Christina was married to William de Forz earl of Aumale, Dervorguilla's husband was John Balliol, a man of lesser rank who possessed extensive estates in northern England, and it was their son John who would become king.

proceeded to carry out what was euphemistically termed the 'pacification of Galloway' by instituting a campaign of terror accompanied by the utmost brutality. But before he could complete the task, Thomas returned with an army of Irish mercenaries and drove Menteith and his men out of Galloway.

King Alexander dispatched another army there, this time under Patrick earl of Dunbar.[*] He defeated the Gallovidian rebels, but mainly through guile having persuaded Gilleruth (or Gilrod), a local chieftain and Thomas's right-hand man, to defect. Therefore when he encountered Thomas's attenuated force he scored an easy victory. Whereas the prisoners were summarily hanged, the leaders were taken to Glasgow where they were tied to opposing horses and torn limb from limb. Thomas himself was imprisoned in Edinburgh castle where he was thought to have been put to death.[†] Having gained control of Galloway, Alexander proceeded to divide the lordship lands between the three co-heiresses. The result was that by the end of the century modern Wigtownshire had come under the control of the Comyns,[‡] while Kirkcudbrightshire was dominated by the Balliols,[§] both implacable opponents of the Bruces.

Robert Bruce appears to have been a regular attendant at the court of Alexander II, who was his near relative.[¶] In fact, when the succession to the kingship was being adjudicated in 1291/2, he would claim as part of his pleadings that, back in 1238, Alexander II had formally appointed him his successor. Although he was unable to produce supporting evidence, this was plausible given that his maternal uncle, John earl of Huntingdon and Chester, who was next in line to the throne, had died without issue the previous year. And because Alexander's wife Joan (sister of Henry III) had died childless earlier that year, Robert was his nearest male heir.[**]

Earl John was a son of King William's brother, David earl of Huntingdon. A prominent magnate in England where he owned extensive estates, he was also pre-eminent in Scotland, and in addition to being a substantial landowner he was heir-presumptive to the throne. His English estates included the honour of Huntingdon which he had inherited from his father Earl David, as well as those belonging to his mother's

---

[*]   Although well past middle age, Earl Patrick was in fact Alexander II's nephew, his mother being one of King William's illegitimate daughters. His father, also Earl Patrick, married as his second wife Christina, the widow of William de Brus, and this would lead to a dispute between the younger Earl Patrick and Robert the noble over her dower lands in Hartness (*CDS* i, 700).

[†]   Not so, because he was transferred to the custody of his half-sister Dervorguilla and her husband John Balliol when he was warded in the Balliol stronghold of Barnard castle. There he remained for over sixty years until 1296 when at the age of almost ninety he was released on the orders of Edward I.

[‡]   Alan's eldest daughter Elena, who was apportioned virtually all the lordship lands there, left most of them to her middle daughter Elizabeth who was married to Alexander Comyn earl of Buchan.

[§]   Alan's youngest daughter Dervorguilla, later wife of John Balliol, was allotted part of the lordship lands in present-day Kirkcudbrightshire while most of the rest went to her full sister Christina. Following Christina's death without issue, Dervorguilla inherited her share and thus became the dominant power in eastern Galloway.

[¶]   King Alexander was a first cousin of Bruce's mother.

[**] In fact Alexander married again the following year and had a son, the future Alexander III. Thus the issue became dormant until revived by Robert Bruce following Alexander III's death in 1286.

family the earls of Chester, from whom he also inherited the title.[*] Following his death, part of his lands was set aside for the liferent of his widow Helen,[†] while the remainder was divided between his three sisters and their issue.[‡]

It included the earldom of Chester. But because it was an important bulwark against the Welsh, the English king Henry III could not allow it to be divided up between Earl John's co-heiresses. Therefore he annexed it to the crown[§] having compensated them with sundry manors elsewhere. Consequently Robert Bruce's mother, Isabella, was given those of Writtle, in Essex, and Hatfield Regis, as well as a share in the manor of Kempston in Bedfordshire, and part of the Tottenham estate. In addition, she inherited part of the honour of Huntingdon as well as a share of Earl John's Scottish estates. On her death in about 1252 these were divided between her sons Robert the Competitor and Bernard. Robert's share included the manors of Writtle and Hatfield Regis, and on Bernard's death without issue Robert inherited his share as well.

In 1240 Robert Bruce married the thirteen-year-old Isabel, daughter of Gilbert de Clare earl of Gloucester and his wife Isabel, one of the many daughters of William le Marshal earl of Pembroke. Described as 'a tocherless lass with a lang pedigree', her dowry consisted of a mere fifteen pound land in the town of Ripe, in Sussex, which had been given her by her maternal uncle William le Marshal. Nevertheless her highly placed connections, which impinged on the English royal family,[¶] greatly enhanced Robert Bruce's standing. They had two sons – Robert future lord of Annandale, and earl of Carrick in right of his wife, and Richard, who died unmarried.

In July 1249 the fifty-year-old Alexander II suddenly died on the island of Kerrera while about to launch an expedition to reclaim the Western Isles from the king of Norway. Because his son Alexander III was barely eight, this led to a power struggle for control of the regency in which Robert Bruce played a prominent part as a possible heir to the throne. In the first instance Alan Durward, who was married to Alexander II's illegitimate daughter Marjorie, arrogated power – and in effect the regency – to the exclusion of his rival Walter Comyn earl of Menteith. And to ensure continuing peace with England, Durward arranged for the young king to marry Henry III's daughter Margaret.

No sooner had the marriage taken place than Menteith, supported by his younger half-brother Alexander Comyn earl of Buchan, and his nephew John Comyn of

---

[*]   His mother Matilda was the daughter and heiress of Hugh de Kyvelioc (Cweiliog) earl of Chester, a descendant of Ranulf de Meschin one-time lord of Carlisle.

[†]   Daughter of Llewellyn prince of North Wales by an illegitimate daughter of King John, she was suspected of poisoning her husband Earl John.

[‡]   His sisters were the now-deceased Margaret, second wife of Alan lord of Galloway, Isabella wife of Robert de Brus the noble, and Ada who was married to an English baron, Henry de Hastings (see genealogical table 3).

[§]   It still remains one of the titles of the Prince of Wales.

[¶]   Ironically it was through her that King Robert Bruce was related to some of the principal English commanders during the War of Independence.

Badenoch, seized power. Meanwhile concern for his daughter's welfare gave Henry a pretext for intervening in Scottish affairs. Therefore he sent emissaries to Scotland to make secret contact with Durward and his supporters, including Robert Bruce, for the purpose of organising a coup. This took place in August 1255 when Menteith and his principal supporters were decoyed to Stirling castle. In their absence Durward and his supporters took possession of Edinburgh castle, and with it the person of the king. Acting in his name, they set up an English-supporting ruling Council of which Robert Bruce was a member.

In 1258 Alexander III, now seventeen, arrogated full ruling powers and replaced the Durward-led Council with a Council of Twelve. This was evenly balanced between representatives of the Durward and the Comyn factions. Since he was excluded from it, Bruce abandoned Scotland having delegated the administration of his Annandale lordship to a steward. Thereafter he concentrated on his role as an English baron and the management of his estates in the south. As a feudal tenant of King Henry, Bruce fought for him in his baronial war and took part in the battle of Lewes in 1264, when he was captured. Ransomed for a large sum (arranged by his son Robert who had remained in Scotland), he was released in time to fight alongside the lord Edward (future Edward I) at the battle of Evesham the following year, when the rebel barons were defeated and their leader Simon de Montfort killed.

Meanwhile in pursuit of his father's ambition to gain control of the Western Isles, Alexander III sent an embassy to King Haakon of Norway in an attempt to negotiate their cession. It appears to have backfired, because all it did was encourage the Norwegian king to lead an expedition to Scotland to assert his overlordship of the Isles. Basing himself on the Isle of Man, he launched an attack on the Clyde coast which was guarded by Alexander the Steward as the local sheriff. Learning of the approach of King Haakon's galleys, the Steward raised a force which beat off a Norwegian landing party in a skirmish at Largs. Meanwhile a storm blew up which wreaked such havoc among the rest of the fleet as it lay at anchor off the Cumbraes that King Haakon abandoned the expedition and sailed for home. But he never got there because he died at Kirkwall in Orkney at the end of the year.

The following year King Alexander assembled a fleet in the Solway in readiness to launch an attack on the Isle of Man. The threat was enough to force the Manx king Magnus to capitulate and come cap in hand to pay homage to Alexander at Dumfries (a town that Alexander is said to have 'viewed with admiration'). Thereafter he appointed a bailie to administer the island. However his regime was so harsh and oppressive that in 1275 it provoked a rebellion. The leader was Magnus's illegitimate son Godfrey, who drove the bailie out of the island and established himself as ruler. Alexander responded by assembling another fleet in the Solway. This time it sailed. The invasion was successful; Godfrey and his supporters were overwhelmed in a bloody slaughter and Alexander regained possession of the island.

Meanwhile, in Robert Bruce's absence in the south, the stewardship of Annandale was rotated among his principal tenants – Sir Adam de Dunwiddie, Sir Robert de

Heriz, Sir Humphrey de Kirkpatrick and Sir David de Torthorwald.[65] Later he appointed Adam de Crokedyk, his man of affairs and one of his executors, as a professional steward.[66] The witnesses to the charters issued on Robert's behalf include a number of new names, suggesting that they were recent incomers to Annandale. Some were obviously of French extraction, such as Sir William de Mortaigne, Sir William de St Michael, and possibly Sir Ingram de Muscens. Another witness of obvious French origin was Sir William de Boyville whose family was represented by Eustace de Boyville in the Ragman Roll,* although as English support-ers they forfeited their lands during the Wars of Independence. Similarly Rauf (Ralph) de Camera, constable of Annandale, whose family was represented by Symond and William de la Chambre in the Ragman Roll, although they too appear to have lost their lands.

The names of other witnesses sound more anglicised – Sir David de Parco, John de Remundeby, Richard Crispin (owner of lands at Lochmaben) and Sir John Seton. The first three must have disposed of their Annandale lands soon afterwards because their names do not feature in the Ragman Roll, unlike the Setons who were represented by Johan and Richard de Seton. Other contemporary landowners included John de Normanville who owned the lands of Cronyanton and Minnygap in the parish of Johnstone. He features in the Ragman Roll, but his support for the English during the Wars of Independence cost him his lands which King Robert Bruce gave his sister Margaret and her husband William Carlyle.[67] Another was Richard de Bancori who in about 1270 resigned 'the whole land of Locharwood with certain common pasture in the fee of Comlongan' to Robert the Competitor.[68] Whether he owned other lands in Annandale is not known, but if so he must have disposed of them soon afterwards because the name de Bancori does not appear in the Ragman Roll.

In 1270 Robert Bruce embarked on a crusade to the Holy Land in company with Henry III's younger son Edmund earl of Lancaster, while his sons Robert and Richard travelled in a separate company under the lord Edward. These companies were part of the English contribution to a European expeditionary force raised by the French king Louis IX for the purpose of recovering the holy places from the Egyptian mamlu-kes. Having failed to achieve their objective (King Louis died in the course of the campaign), the leaders were forced to make a face-saving truce, leaving the survivors to make their own way home. They included Robert Bruce. In the course of his return journey he visited St Malachy's shrine at the abbey of Clairvaux where he is said to have bought off the century-old curse which the saint had pronounced on his family by arranging for three lamps to burn there in perpetuity. On his return he endowed the abbey with land at 'Esticroft' (thought to have been near Kinmount) to meet the cost of maintaining the lamps.[69] Consequently, as the Lanercost chronicler observed,

---

* Probable members of an Ayrshire family who later changed their name to Boyle and whose current representative is the earl of Glasgow.

'through his good deeds of piety' he alone of all his ancestors was 'buried at a good old age.'*

During his absence his wife Isabel de Clare had died, and soon after his return he married the twice-widowed Christina de Ireby. Daughter of William de Ireby, a Cumbrian landowner, and his wife Christina de Hodelme, she had inherited lands in Cumberland from both her parents, as well as others from her previous husbands. Consequently she was a lady of considerable means. But because the de Hodelmes were Annandale tenants, Robert Bruce's son, Robert, perhaps conscious of his mother's exalted rank, regarded the marriage as something of a *mésalliance* and tried unsuccessfully to deny Christina her legal rights following his father's death.

He himself made a more prestigious marriage, and thereby hangs a tale. One of his fellow crusaders was Adam de Kilconquhar, earl of Carrick in right of his wife Countess Marjorie, who was killed at the siege of Acre. Therefore on his return to Scotland Robert went to visit Countess Marjorie at her castle of Turnberry to break the news of her husband's death. She sounds to have been less than heartbroken, for according to Bower she first encountered the younger Robert Bruce while out hunting and took an immediate fancy to this 'distinguished and very handsome young knight'. Having exchanged 'greetings and kisses', the countess brought him back to her castle where she prevailed on him to stay 'for the space of fifteen days or more' during which time they were secretly married.[70]

A romantic story, but as ever the facts are more prosaic. Since she was not far off being a grandmother,† the countess can hardly have been in her first flush of youth and was in fact some years older than the twenty-eight-year-old Robert. She may indeed have been captivated by him, and even if he reciprocated her feelings (not necessarily the case) he would doubtless have consulted his father before taking such a hasty plunge into matrimony. Besides, the countess's marriage was in the gift of the king, so his consent would have been obligatory, and because she was such a valuable prize Alexander was probably under pressure to earmark her for a member of the Comyn family. Therefore it was extremely unlikely that he would allow her to marry the younger Robert Bruce, and if they were to do so without his consent they stood to incur draconian penalties and possible imprisonment.

Yet the opportunity to gain the Carrick earldom and deny it to the Comyns was too good to miss. For the combination of Carrick and their Annandale lordship would enable the Bruces effectively to ring-fence Balliol/Comyn dominated Galloway and Nithsdale,‡ besides giving them a valuable foothold in Ireland.§

---

*   *Chron Lanercost*, 114. Not strictly true because Robert's great-grandfather, Robert de Brus the younger, who had been responsible for the curse, also survived to 'a good old age', and so did the original Robert de Brus.
†   Her daughter by Adam de Kilconquhar later married Thomas Randolph of Morton, sheriff of Dumfries, and their son Thomas, future earl of Moray and lord of Annandale, was born about 1278.
‡   The fact that the Comyn lords of Badenoch owned the baronies of Dalswinton and Duncow meant they had a commanding influence there.
§   The Irish lands included modern Larne and a large tract of land extending northwards to Glenarm which King John had granted to Marjorie's grandfather Earl Duncan.

Conversely, if the Comyns were to acquire the earldom it would deliver the whole of the south-west into their hands. Faced with such a potential calamity, the elder Bruce probably told his son in effect to marry the countess and chance the consequences. If so, Bower's assertion that the marriage was clandestine was probably true. It did not remain so for long. As soon as he heard of it, a predictably furious Alexander confiscated Marjorie's earldom and all her lands. Later he relented and restored them on payment of a heavy fine, at the same time allowing the younger Bruce to assume the title of earl of Carrick.[71] The marriage was prolific as they proceeded to have a family of five sons and five daughters, the eldest being Robert Bruce the future king, who was born on 11 July 1274.

Having forgiven the younger Bruce, King Alexander employed him as a go-between with his brother-in-law Edward I with whom he was on the friendliest terms.[*] In 1278, as a signal honour, Alexander appointed him his proxy to pay homage to Edward for his English lands (kings did not kneel before other kings). As an English landowner Robert entered the service of King Edward who in 1282 appointed him keeper of Carlisle castle.[72] When the Welsh rebelled in March that year, he was among those to whom Edward issued summonses to perform feudal service in the ensuing war[73] – a hard-fought campaign which ended with the Welsh capitulation in June 1283. Three years later an event occurred that would ultimately lead to a dramatic change in the Bruce fortunes.

---

[*] Evident from the letters passing between them and their families. Apparently Edward was particularly close to Alexander's wife Margaret who was his immediate younger sister, and who died in 1275.

FOUR

The First War of Independence

A DISPUTED KINGSHIP

On 18 March 1286 King Alexander III held a meeting of his Council at Edinburgh castle. This was followed by a banquet which continued until evening by which time a gale was blowing. Nevertheless, ignoring the pleas of his courtiers to remain there for the night, Alexander insisted on making the journey back to his manor at Kinghorn in Fife where his young French bride of five months was waiting for him. Landing safely at Inverkeithing, he and his companions set off along the coastal path towards Kinghorn. But becoming separated from them in the darkness, Alexander lost his way when his horse stumbled and threw the forty-four-year-old king against a rock breaking his neck.

Since his two sons and a daughter by his first wife Margaret, Edward I's sister, had predeceased him, his heir was his sickly three-year-old granddaughter Margaret, the daughter of his deceased daughter Margaret and her husband King Erik of Norway. As a courtesy, emissaries were sent to King Edward to inform him of the news at which, as he later admitted, he was 'greatly distressed'.[1] Meanwhile he replied with polite expressions of regret; but apart from that he evinced little interest in Scottish affairs because he was about to leave for his dukedom of Gascony where he would remain for the next three years.

In late April a Parliament consisting of all the senior clergy, earls and barons was held at Scone to decide on the future government of the realm. They included Robert Bruce, probably now in his seventies, but as vigorous and active as ever. Objecting to the concept of a female ruler, and therefore refusing to recognise the young Margaret as queen, he staked out his own claim to the kingship in uncompromising terms. This was immediately challenged by John Balliol who claimed a superior right, and it resulted in a lengthy wrangle, described as a 'bitter pleading', between them.[2]

But ignoring their claims, the Parliament appointed six guardians to administer the realm on the young queen's behalf. The final choice reflected a careful balance between the Bruce and Balliol factions, the latter including John Balliol's influential Comyn relatives, who represented the Scottish establishment. Nevertheless Robert Bruce considered that his interests were not properly represented, taking particular exception to the choice of his former political opponent Alexander Comyn earl of Buchan* as senior guardian.

---

* He, it will be remembered, was associated with his elder half-brother Walter Comyn earl of Menteith in the seizure of power following King Alexander's marriage. Later a member of the Council of Twelve (from which Bruce was excluded), he became Alexander's principal adviser throughout the rest of his reign.

Therefore in September that year he held a conclave of his friends and supporters at his daughter-in-law Countess Marjorie's castle of Turnberry. It culminated in the drawing up of what was known as the Turnberry Band. In terms of this, the signatories undertook to support Bruce's claim to the kingship, and in a slightly naïve bid for King Edward's support they specifically reserved their allegiance to him. Bruce also took the opportunity to prepare the ground for an invasion of Galloway which was intended to destroy – or at least undermine – the Balliol/Comyn power base in the south-west.

It began in November and lasted throughout the winter. While Bruce's son, Robert earl of Carrick, invaded northern Wigtownshire with his feudal levies, he himself advanced on Dumfries. Having captured the royal castle, he and his men crossed the Nith into Galloway. Advancing south-west, they took the stronghold of Buittle on the lower Urr, which belonged to John Balliol's elderly mother Dervorguilla, now living on her estates in Bedfordshire, and razed it to the ground. From there they headed for Kirkcudbright where they took possession of the royal castle.

Meanwhile the earl of Carrick advanced on Wigtown where he and his men captured the royal castle. This was important because it was the administrative head-quarters of Alexander Comyn earl of Buchan, who was the local sheriff as well as senior guardian. Continuing down the western shore of Wigtown Bay, Carrick and his men attacked Buchan's castle of Cruggleton, and moving on to Whithorn they burnt the cathedral church and so devastated the episcopal lands that the bishop was reduced to a state of near-starvation. Continuing their campaign of destruction, they ravaged the surrounding countryside to such an extent that parts of it remained uncultivated for some years afterwards.

There is no record of the guardians sending an army into Galloway, nor of any local opposition; still less is there evidence of a battle taking place. Yet it is hard to believe that the Bruces' campaign went unchallenged. By the following spring they had withdrawn from Galloway. Why is not known. It may be that Robert Bruce decided that he had gone far enough and that to continue the campaign would risk alienating uncommitted Scottish magnates, or even forfeiting the support of his adherents. Although successful in the short term, the campaign would prove coun-ter-productive because the Gallovidians remained implacably hostile to the Bruces throughout the Wars of Independence.

In February 1289, in a bid to achieve a permanent peace with England, the guard-ians sent a deputation to Gascony to meet King Edward and discuss with him the possibility of a marriage between their five-year-old queen, Margaret of Norway, and his son the four-year-old Edward of Caernarvon. Perceiving that such a union could deliver him effective control of Scotland, Edward responded positively and under-took to obtain the approval of Margaret's father King Erik of Norway. Not difficult because Erik was beholden to Edward for a recent loan; and besides such a marriage would greatly enhance his standing among his fellow European rulers.

Following his return to England later that year, Edward arranged for negotiations for the marriage to take place between representatives from England, Scotland and

Norway. The talks culminated in the treaty of Salisbury, concluded in November 1289, which provided that Margaret of Norway should come to Scotland or England free of any matrimonial engagement before 1 November the following year. This was followed by a marriage treaty – the Treaty of Birgham – which was concluded between the English and Scots in July 1290. To allay Scottish fears regarding their future autonomy, Edward issued letters patent guaranteeing that, in the event of their queen marrying his son, Scotland would continue to be ruled as a separate kingdom independently of England.

So far so good; but there were ominous straws in the wind. While negotiations for the marriage treaty were still under way, Edward jumped the gun by petitioning Pope Nicholas IV for his consent – necessary because the young couple were within the forbidden degrees of relationship. In the event it was readily forthcoming. In June 1290, in anticipation of the royal marriage and before the treaty of Birgham was concluded, Edward appointed the forceful and assertive Bishop Antony Bek of Durham as the young couple's lieutenant in Scotland. Finally, claiming that it was in response to an 'appeal' by its people, he unilaterally annexed the Isle of Man and appointed Walter Huntercombe as custodian. But the fact that Huntercombe's appointment pre-dated the 'appeal' rather negated Edward's justification for doing so.

Following the conclusion of the treaty of Birgham, Edward issued a letter to the guardians and all Scottish magnates. Advising them that the purpose of Bishop Bek's appointment was 'to guard the peace and tranquillity of the realm', it enjoined them to put themselves 'at his [Bek's] bidding in all matters needful for the government and peaceful state of the kingdom [of Scotland]'. Sinister words, particularly as Bishop Bek demanded that as soon as Margaret of Norway arrived in Scotland the guardians were to hand over the principal castles to him as her lieutenant. This was tantamount to being asked to surrender control of the realm, which was more than the Scots were prepared to do. But at that point events took a tragic turn.

Margaret never reached Scotland because she died in Orkney in late September on her way there. Meanwhile the Scottish magnates had assembled at Scone in readiness for her enthronement. When news of her death reached them it caused consternation, the more so because there was no certainty as to who was entitled to succeed to the throne. Worse still, there was every prospect of civil war breaking out over the rival claims of Bruce and Balliol. The magnates' worst fears appeared to be confirmed when, on hearing news of Margaret's death, Robert Bruce rushed to Perth with a large body of men. Since his allies, the earls of Atholl and Mar, were reportedly mustering their forces as well, it looked ominously likely that he was planning to seize the throne by force.

In desperation Bishop Fraser of St Andrews, the senior Scottish prelate, wrote an impassioned plea to King Edward beseeching him to intervene to prevent a civil war. It seems that Edward was willing, fearing that if a civil war were to break out in Scotland it could spread to England. But at that point his wife Queen Eleanor fell ill, and when she died at the end of November he was too grief-stricken to pursue the matter further.

The following January, when it had become clear that neither Bruce nor Balliol would give way and civil war seemed inevitable, the guardians in desperation appealed to Edward to determine the succession. On the face of it this was an eminently sensible request, for Edward was well respected internationally and had been invited to arbitrate the succession to the kingships of Cyprus, Sicily and Castile.[3] Therefore he could be relied on to reach a fair and just solution. Moreover he appeared to be on generally good terms with the Scottish nobility with whom he had been acquainted since his visits to the court of King Alexander and Queen Margaret back in the 1260s, while a number of them held lands of him in England.

Now an elderly widower in his fifties, King Edward had reigned for nearly twenty years, having been at the forefront of English affairs long before then; the ablest and best-advised king of the Angevin dynasty, he was at the height of his formidable powers. Autocratic, dictatorial and august, and a man of commanding physical presence (he was well over six foot tall[*]), he wielded immense personal authority, as well as possessing an unrelenting vigour and tireless energy that would persist into old age. A true cosmopolitan, he was acquainted with most of the rulers in Europe, to many of whom he was related. Consequently he had an essentially Frankish contempt for the Scottish people (as opposed to the nobility) whom he regarded, as he did the Irish and the Welsh, as an inferior race. Nevertheless self-interest dictated that he accommodate them by determining the succession. This was not going to be easy since there were no less than thirteen claimants, including Balliol and Bruce, although most of them were descended illegitimately from the royal house.

The question of Edward's arbitrating the succession was discussed by the English Parliament of January 1291 when it was decided that a court should be set up to decide the issue. As a preliminary Edward invited all the claimants, including Bruce and Balliol, to present their petitions. They were to be quite short, merely setting out their descent from the royal house and specifying the substance of their claim, whether it was for the throne itself or a share of the royal demesne lands, and their grounds for doing so.

Having learnt from experience that a decision was pointless without the means of enforcing it, Edward insisted on judging the issue in the role of acknowledged overlord of Scotland. The idea was not new because most Scottish kings had at one time or another paid fealty to their English counterparts. Indeed it was probably at Edward's instigation that, when the younger Robert Bruce paid homage to him on King Alexander's behalf for his English lands in 1278, the bishop of Norwich attempted to bounce him into extending it to include his Scottish realm. However the bishop was forestalled by a timely interjection from Alexander, who was

---

[*] When his coffin was opened in 1774 his body, even shrunken by age, was found to measure six foot two inches (1.88m) which was extremely tall for the time (Prestwich, *Edward I*, 567)

present – namely, that he held his kingdom 'of nobody but God himself'.[4] Since then the issue had remained dormant.

Faced with the demand that they acknowledge Edward's overlordship the Scottish leaders prevaricated, arguing that because no-one save a king could acknowledge him as overlord they were unable to do so. Accepting this, albeit reluctantly, Edward tried an alternative approach. Therefore he demanded that each claimant should perform homage to him so that the oath of fealty given by the successful candidate would automatically crystallise over the realm once he became king. As a further insurance, Edward re-affirmed Bishop Bek's order that the principal castles be delivered up to his appointees, who would hold them for the duration of the hearing, later known as the Great Cause, on the understanding that they would then be handed over to the successful claimant. Accordingly Sir William de Boyville, an Annandale landowner, was appointed keeper of Dumfries castle. When he died soon afterwards, he was followed in quick succession by two other Dumfriesshire landowners, Sir Walter Curry (or Corrie) and Sir Richard Siward of Tibbers. Siward held it until late 1292 when, at Edward's direction, he handed it over to John Balliol as the newly appointed king.

On Edward's recommendation a joint Scottish and English Parliament, which was convened at Norham on 3 June 1291, decided that the court should consist of a hundred and four auditors under his presidency. Of these he would appoint twenty-four, and Bruce forty, while John Balliol and his brother-in-law Sir John Comyn of Badenoch* would choose the remaining forty between them. It was agreed that the hearing should take place in a disused friary at Berwick (on Scottish soil), and that it should begin on 3 August.

When the day came, the auditors, the claimants and their legal advisers were assembled at Berwick in readiness for the hearing. Presiding in person, King Edward opened the proceedings with a short speech and invited the claimants to present their petitions. These were read out to the court in turn, the intention being that it would decide which of them had the best claim so that Edward could pronounce judgement accordingly. Meanwhile he handed over the presidency to his chancellor, Robert Burnell bishop of Bath and Wells.

Although it soon became apparent that Bruce and Balliol had the strongest claims, the hearing proved far more protracted than expected. For one thing Bruce's petition was longer than all the others put together. His main contention was that, as a grandson of David earl of Huntingdon in contrast to Balliol who was a great-grandson, he belonged to a senior generation and was therefore one degree nearer the royal house. Arguing for primogeniture, Balliol contended that he had the better claim because he was descended from Earl David's eldest daughter, whereas Bruce's mother was the second daughter. Perhaps appreciating the strength of Balliol's claim, Bruce deployed every shot in his locker, some demonstrably improbable. Nevertheless his assertion

---

* Now head of the Comyn faction following the recent death of Alexander Comyn earl of Buchan.

that Alexander II nominated him as his successor back in 1238 might have been true except he was unable to substantiate it – not that it would have made any difference to the outcome.

An important point to be decided was which law should be applied in determining the issue. Was it to be feudal law (which favoured Balliol's claim of primogeniture), or natural or 'imperial' law (which would support Bruce's claim of proximity), or canon law? Because the Scottish auditors were unable to give a definitive answer, Edward ordered opinions to be obtained from certain internationally renowned jurists. Accordingly a deputation of lawyers was sent to France armed with a statement of the facts to consult them. Meanwhile the proceedings were adjourned until October.

Another reason for the delay was an extraordinary assertion put forward by the count of Holland, one of the claimants, which if substantiated would override the claims of both Balliol and Bruce. This was that, for various reasons, David earl of Huntingdon had renounced his rights of succession to the crown both for himself and his descendants. Consequently King William had decreed that, in the event of a failure of his legitimate issue (as had happened), the succession should open up to the descendants of his eldest sister Ada, of whom the count was the senior representative. Claiming that the documents supporting his contention had been lost, he asked for a further adjournment to give him time to find them. Since Edward was at pains to ensure that the proceedings were conducted with the utmost fairness and impartiality, he conceded the count's request. But instead of using the time to institute a search for the 'missing' documents, the count prevailed on a pliable clerk to produce forgeries which he somehow managed to persuade two senior prelates to authenticate by adhibiting their seals to them. In the end he withdrew his claim – perhaps through failure of nerve; or more likely, as Bower suggests, he was bribed by John Balliol.

Finally in November 1292 the court dismissed Bruce's claim. The following day, to insure against it lapsing on his death he formally resigned it to his son, the recently widowed earl of Carrick (his wife Countess Marjorie had died earlier that year). This put Carrick in a quandary, for if he rendered homage to John Balliol for his earldom, which he would be obliged to do, it would imply acceptance of his kingship to the prejudice of his own claim. Therefore, to avoid this, Carrick resigned the earldom to his eighteen-year-old son Robert, the future king (henceforth referred to as the earl of Carrick).

Finally on 17 November Edward's deputy, Roger Brabazon, Chief Justice of the King's Bench, pronounced judgement in favour of Balliol. Three days later he paid homage to Edward at Norham acknowledging him as his feudal superior, and on 26 December he repeated it, this time as enthroned king of Scots when he acknowledged Edward's overlordship of the realm. Replying, Edward is said to have warned him to rule it well and administer justice in such a way that no-one should have cause for complaint lest he 'as lord superior of Scotland should be obliged to apply a guiding hand'.[5] A thinly veiled threat that unless John did as he was told he would intervene – by force if necessary.

A man of more mettle than the 'toom tabard' – or empty cloak – as he is portrayed by the chroniclers,* John made a determined effort to rule effectively. But he found himself increasingly thwarted as Edward's 'guiding hand' – or rather his bullying interference – became ever more apparent. The crunch came when Edward insisted on his right to hear appeals against judgements passed in Scottish courts, including those reached by King John himself. Since this was in direct contravention of the treaty of Birgham, in terms of which Edward undertook that all legal suits affecting Scottish matters should be heard in Scotland, a group of leading Scottish magnates presented a petition to him in name of King John reminding him of his promise.

Edward's response, issued through Roger Brabazon, was uncompromising. Using his knowledge of the law to twist it to his advantage, he asserted that the treaty was a marriage treaty and therefore its validity depended on the royal marriage taking place. And because it never did the treaty had lapsed, and with it his contingent obligations. Furthermore he contended that as lord superior he had every right to hear Scottish appeals and would summon King John himself to answer for his judgements if necessary. This proved no idle threat because John was ordered to appear before the Michaelmas Parliament of 1293. When King Edward requested him to defend a judgement reached in his court, King John attempted to prevaricate, whereupon that awe-inspiring monarch subjected him to one of his terrifying harangues (a similar one would cause the dean of St Paul's to suffer heart failure). Browbeaten into submission, John renewed his homage on abject terms and promised to appear before the next Parliament to defend his judgement. But events supervened.

Meanwhile the Bruces were doing everything possible to undermine King John's authority, particularly in southern Scotland where their power was strongest. They also had supporters in the north, notably the powerful earl of Mar. Therefore, in order to cement an alliance between the two families, Bruce arranged for his granddaughter Christina (a daughter of the younger Robert Bruce) to marry Earl Donald's son Gartney (later his grandson Robert earl of Carrick married the earl's daughter Isabella). Because King Erik of Norway was overlord of the Western Isles, and therefore in a position to make trouble for King John, Bruce entered into an alliance with him. This was sealed with the marriage of his granddaughter Isabella (the younger Robert Bruce's eldest daughter) and King Erik who had remained a widower since the death of his wife Margaret (Alexander III's daughter) in 1283.

Both the younger Bruce and his son the earl of Carrick escorted Isabella to Norway for her wedding under a safe conduct issued by King Edward. Following his return, Carrick was sent by his grandfather to visit his estates in the south. While there he was instructed to attend the royal court at Westminster in order to pay his respects to

---

* This is a classic example of history being written by the victors. Since it was part of Bruce propaganda to traduce John Balliol, making out that choosing him as king was not only wrong but a disastrous aberration which was responsible for all the miseries inflicted on the Scots during the Wars of Independence, the chroniclers obediently followed this line – understandably, because their preferment and pension prospects depended on it.

King Edward, with whom he may already have been acquainted. Ironically in view of later events, Edward appears to have taken a liking to the young earl, perhaps recognising him as a man in his own image, because he arranged for loans to be advanced to him from his exchequer. Not only did Carrick avail himself of the offer, but Edward twice extended the repayment date.[6]

The indomitable old Bruce, now well into his seventies, had a final clash with King John over the appointment of a successor to Bishop Henry of Whithorn when he secured it for his chaplain Thomas Dalton in preference to John's candidate. Nevertheless it proved a pyrrhic victory because Bishop Dalton became a staunch supporter of the English, and a consistent opponent of King Robert Bruce, during the second War of Independence. Latterly the old Competitor seems to have spent most of his time on his English estates, and was still up to enjoying a day's hunting. At least so it would appear from a reference in June 1294 to his being absolved of a fine of a hundred merks for the unlawful killing of a deer in the King's forest in Essex.[7] He died at the end of March 1295 when the lordship of Annandale passed along with his other estates to his son Robert, henceforth referred to as Bruce of Annandale.

CONQUEST AND OCCUPATION

In May 1294 the French king Philip IV sent a force under his brother the count of Valois to occupy King Edward's dukedom of Gascony – an act of aggression that resulted in the outbreak of war between England and France. On 29 June exercising his right as lord superior of Scotland, Edward issued summonses to King John, ten Scottish earls, as well as other magnates, including the three Bruces – father, son and grandson – to muster at Portsmouth by 1 September with their levies in readiness to sail for Gascony to drive out the French. Taking the view that their levies were to be used for the defence of the realm and not to engage in a foreign war which was no concern of theirs, the Scottish magnates prevaricated. However they were saved by the outbreak of a rebellion in Wales which caused Edward to postpone the expedition.

The following year the summonses were re-issued. But the magnates persisted in their refusal to comply, using every possible excuse real or imagined. Nevertheless there were exceptions. Among them were Bruce of Annandale and the earl of Carrick (old Bruce having recently died). In a gesture of defiance of King John, and concerned for their English estates which stood to be forfeited if they refused, the Bruces not only responded to the summons but made a formal submission to Edward. Meanwhile, fearing that King John would be pressured into doing the same, the Parliament of July 1295 stripped him of his ruling powers and vested them in a Council of Twelve. Since the Bruces were regarded as traitors (and would be for some years to come), Carrick's earldom was forfeited, and similarly his father's lordship of Annandale which was given to John Comyn earl of Buchan.[*]

---

[*]   He had succeeded to the earldom following his father Earl Alexander's death in 1289.

Finally, in what was tantamount to a declaration of war with England, the Scottish Parliament sent a high-ranking delegation to France to negotiate an alliance with King Philip. This was concluded in October and cemented with the betrothal of King John's son, Edward Balliol, and King Philip's infant niece Jeanne, daughter of the count of Valois.* King Edward responded by preparing for an invasion. Meanwhile in June 1295 Bruce of Annandale, now firmly in the English camp, was summoned to the English Parliament as Baron Bruce.[8] In October he was reappointed keeper of Carlisle castle,[9] while Carrick appears to have sailed with Edward's expeditionary force to Gascony.[†]

In early March 1296 the Scots mustered an army at Caddonlea, near Selkirk, in readiness to resist the invasion. Meanwhile, having got as far as Newcastle, Edward decided to remain there and leave it to the Scots to make the first move. This was crucial, for if they could be induced to show themselves as the aggressors it would give him an important propaganda advantage. This they obligingly did. On 26 March a Scottish force under the joint command of John Comyn, son of Sir John Comyn of Badenoch, and the earl of Buchan crossed the Solway fords and plundered their way as far as Carlisle where they laid siege to the castle. But Bruce of Annandale, as keeper, counterattacked with such vigour that he drove them back across the border, Buchan himself taking refuge at Sweetheart abbey.

This gave Edward the pretext he needed. On 28 March his army crossed the Tweed at Coldstream and headed for Berwick, the largest Scottish town and a principal emporium of northern trade. He offered the townspeople terms promising them leniency if they surrendered. Their unedifying response was to bare their buttocks at the English, yelling obscenities at them and Edward in particular – most imprudently considering that the town's defences consisted of nothing more than a ditch and a palisade. Consequently the English swept over them at the first assault, and taking possession of the town they killed a number of inhabitants.

Here the Scottish chroniclers, whose politically slanted accounts were written long after the event, indulge in an orgy of hyperbole. Claiming that the capture of the town was followed by a wholesale massacre of the inhabitants lasting for three days, they paint a lurid picture of how the victims 'fell like autumn leaves', and 'the streams of blood pouring from the bodies of the slain' were such that 'mills could be turned by the flow'.[10] Other corpses were allegedly thrown down wells or hurled into the sea. Possibly the latter but certainly not down wells because Edward was planning to rebuild the town and would not want the water supply fouled by decomposing Scotsmen.

As ever the facts are more prosaic. The massacre – if such there was – probably lasted only a few hours until Edward, fearing papal censure, called a halt to further bloodshed. After he had taken possession of the town he ordered the inhabitants to bury the dead, for which they were paid 'a penny a piece [i.e. per corpse] at the King's expense'.[11] The

---

*   The betrothal came to nothing. Jeanne subsequently married William count of Hainault and was the mother of Queen Philippa, wife of Edward III.

†   This can be inferred from King Edward's recognition of his 'good service' (*CDS* ii, 852). See McCulloch, *Scottish Saga*, 89 fn q.

keeper, Sir William Douglas,* was allowed to go free having undertaken to fight for Edward – a promise he would have no hesitation in breaking as soon as he felt able to do so with impunity. Following the capture of Berwick, Edward sent a force under Sir Robert Clifford to conquer the south-west and take hostages from among the local leaders.† Meanwhile the main army was sent up the east coast under the earl of Surrey, while Edward remained at Berwick to supervise the initial stages of the rebuilding work.‡

Surrey may have counted on an unopposed advance to Edinburgh because Dunbar castle, the only stronghold on the way, belonged to the English-supporting Patrick earl of Dunbar. However, Earl Patrick had gone to join King Edward at Berwick having committed the care of the castle to a keeper. In his absence it was attacked by a Scottish force under the earls of Atholl, Ross and Menteith: Earl Patrick's wife Countess Marjorie (a Comyn, being a sister of the earl of Buchan, and therefore a covert Scottish supporter) prevailed on the keeper to hand over the castle keys to her, whereupon she opened the gates to let the attackers in and had the garrison clapped in irons.

When Surrey reached the castle and found it in Scottish hands he proceeded to lay siege to it. But before doing so he offered the three earls – Atholl, Ross and Menteith – surrender terms. Claiming that they had no authority to accept them, they begged permission to send an emissary to King John who was encamped with his army near Haddington to obtain the necessary consent. Surrey agreed and declared a temporary truce. However, when the emissary arrived at the Scottish camp, and doubtless acting on the instructions of the three earls, he urged King John and his Council to take advantage of the truce by making a surprise attack on Surrey's force and lift the siege. Notwithstanding that it was a flagrant violation of the accepted rules of warfare, King John and his Council agreed.

Setting out from Haddington, the Scottish army took a slightly circuitous route to Dunbar keeping to the foothills of the Lammermuirs. Unwisely, for as they swarmed over the intervening high ground they were spotted by the English. Leaving a detachment under his newly knighted grandson Sir Henry Percy§ to

---

* Father of Sir James Douglas, one of King Robert Bruce's principal lieutenants, he was the ancestor of the earls of Douglas. A man with a chequered career, he had already crossed swords with Edward as a result of having raped and abducted (a seemingly not unwilling) Eleanor de Ferrers, a well-connected widow of whom Edward had the gift of marriage. Having put away his wife (a sister of the Steward and mother of Sir James Douglas), he married Eleanor and was pardoned on payment of a fine of £100. Their younger son Archibald, who was appointed guardian of the realm for David II, was the ancestor of the earls of Angus and the Douglases of Drumlanrig, later dukes of Queensberry.

† Specifically, leading men from the Forest of Selkirk, the Moor of Cavers, Liddesdale, Eskdale, Moffatdale, Annandale, Nithsdale and Galloway (Stevenson, *Docs* ii, 36)

‡ It was completed in a remarkably short time, because Edward was able to hold a Parliament there at the end of August.

§ The son of Surrey's deceased daughter (his other daughter was the wife of King John) Percy had been brought up in his grandfather's household. Because Surrey's long-dead wife Alicia was one of Henry III's Lusignan half-siblings, he was a quasi-uncle of King Edward. To continue the links, Alicia's full brother William de Lusignan was the father of Aymer de Valence, later earl of Pembroke, who would become the principal English commander in Scotland, and also of Joanna the wife of John Comyn the younger. Such were the complexities of the inter-baronial relationships which impinged on both the English and Scottish royal houses.

continue the siege, Surrey went off with the rest of the army to intercept them. Battle was joined near present-day Spott when the Scots were forced down into the steep-sided dell of the Spott burn. Trapped in what became a killing ground, the Scottish army was virtually annihilated by a constant hail of arrows fired on them from pointblank range. Two days later, on 29 April, King Edward reached Dunbar when the Scottish garrison surrendered, and the captured knights and magnates were dispatched to various prisons in England. Because the footsoldiers were merely an embarrassment, Edward ordered them to be freed on parole and issued with safe conducts to return home.[12]

After that it was a walkover. Since there was virtually no further resistance, and Scotland was effectively a conquered country, Edward was determined to put the final seal on it by removing all symbols of its nationhood in order to destroy for ever its identity as a separate realm. Therefore, on reaching Edinburgh, he ordered that the Scottish regalia and other relics, including the much-venerated Black Rood of St Margaret, be taken to London and deposited in the Tower. Arriving at Stirling, Edward and his troops found the castle abandoned with only the gate-keeper left to hand over the keys. From there they advanced to Perth where he ordered the Stone of Destiny, that symbol of almost religious significance on which the Scottish kings were traditionally enthroned, to be removed from the abbey church at nearby Scone to Westminster Abbey where it would remain for almost seven hundred years.

Meanwhile King John and the Comyn leaders who had been retreating north-wards in the face of the advancing English, were reduced to wandering aimlessly among the Angus glens with the sole aim of keeping their distance from them. Finally, at the urging of the Comyns, John gave himself up. But Edward's terms were uncom-promising and required nothing less than his deposition. In an age when symbolism was all-important he ordered that it should be accomplished by means of three sepa-rate rituals which were designed to cause John the maximum humiliation. In the last of them he was conducted into Edward's presence arrayed in royal splendour. First the crown was taken from his head, then the sceptre and sword from his hands and the ring from his finger. Finally the royal arms on his tabard or surcoat where forcibly ripped off (hence the chroniclers' sneering reference to him as 'toom [empty] tabard').[13] Then, taken to London along with the Comyn leaders, he was consigned to the Tower.*

Following King John's deposition Bruce of Annandale is said to have reminded Edward of a promise he allegedly made to him – namely, that in the event of John's deposition he would be given the reversion of the kingship. But Edward, who had no

---

* Soon afterwards he was transferred to the relative comfort of a manor in Hertfordshire where he was allowed to hunt in the King's forest (*Documents Illustrative of the History of Scotland 1286–1306*, ed. Stevenson, ii, 425). Although returned to the Tower during Wallace's rebellion, he nevertheless maintained a sizeable household. Finally he was allowed to retire to his family estates in Picardy where he died in 1314.

intention of repeating his attempt to rule Scotland through a puppet king, dismissed his request with the withering retort: *'ne avonis ren autres chosis a fer que a vous reaumys gagner* – have we nothing else to do but win kingdoms for you?'[14] Nevertheless Bruce was at least restored to the lordship of Annandale while Carrick was reinstated in his earldom.

Meanwhile Clifford was encountering resistance in the south-west, particularly in eastern Galloway where support for King John was strongest, and probably in neighbouring Nithsdale as well. Nevertheless he appears to have overcome it without difficulty, and judging from the names of those who submitted to him the ringleaders were members of the Clan Afren, a kindred based in northern Kirkcudbrightshire. In a document dated 27 July 1296 they admitted that their 'fole emprise' (misguided enterprise) was in support of King John, and confessing their faults on behalf of their kindred they 'swore on the saints' that henceforth they would support Edward in his campaign against the Scots.[15]

Having disposed of King John and the Comyn leaders, King Edward resumed what was in effect a triumphal progress. From Montrose he advanced to Aberdeen where he took possession of the royal castle, and then along the Moray coast where his troops captured the castles of Forres and Elgin. Turning south he crossed the mountains to Strathdon, and so to Arbroath, Dundee and finally Perth, leaving detachments of soldiery behind to garrison the principal castles. By 22 August he was back at Berwick having, as the chronicler put it, 'conquered the realm of Scotland and searched it [i.e. taken possession of it] in xxi weeks'.[16]

Since his attempt to rule Scotland through a puppet king had proved a failure, Edward decided to take it under his direct rule. Accordingly he held a Parliament at Berwick to determine the shape of the new administration. After prolonged debate (the Parliament sat until well into September) it was decided to put the veteran earl of Surrey in overall charge with the title of *custos* or warden of 'the *land* of Scotland' (so described to emphasise its diminished status). Under him there would be a treasurer (Hugh Cressingham), a chancellor (Walter Amersham), three justiciars and two escheators, the last being responsible for collecting the revenues and taxes. Supporting them was an army of occupation. Consisting of rough and brutal soldiery who habitually abused their authority by inflicting mindless cruelties on the Scottish people, their conduct was largely responsible for the rebellion which broke out the following year. Probably the most important military appointment was the wardenship of the south-west. This was given to Sir Henry Percy, while Sir Robert Clifford was appointed his deputy, their joint headquarters being based at Carlisle castle, still under the keepership of Bruce of Annandale.

To consolidate his conquest, Edward ordained that every landholder in Scotland should swear fealty, either to him in person at Berwick or to their local sheriff. Besides all secular landowners and their eldest sons, they included the heads of all religious houses and other clerical landowners, as well as the leading burgesses of the principal burghs. The ruling applied to all Englishmen owning land in Scotland who were required to swear a similar oath, and a roll listing those taking it was drawn up for each sheriffdom.

Notwithstanding that the sheriffdom of Dumfries included modern Kirkcudbrightshire, it is possible to gain a reasonably clear picture of contemporary landownership in Dumfriesshire, while the representatives of most of the families established as Bruce tenants in Annandale are easily recognisable. Altogether the roll for the sheriffdom of Dumfries contained nineteen churchmen and ninety-six secular landowners and their sons. The latter included 'Robert de Brus le veil' and 'Robert de Brus le jovene, earl of Carrick'. Not that Carrick owned any land in Dumfriesshire at the time, but his appearance was in conformity with Edward's requirement that the eldest son and heir of each landholder should swear an oath of fealty as well.

In late September, having completed his arrangements for governing the country, Edward departed south. While handing over the newly cut seal of the land of Scotland to the earl of Surrey, he allegedly remarked to him: *bon besoigne fait quy de merde se delivrer.*ˣ Meaning roughly 'it's a good job to be rid of shit', this was an earthy reflection of his contempt for the Scots and his evident relief at returning to the civilised south. He left behind a country seething with resentment. He had ridden roughshod over everything the Scots held sacred, had abolished their kingship and deprived them of their status as an independent realm. And to cap it all, he had removed all the venerated symbols associated with their identity as a separate nation. Furthermore he had set up what was essentially a military dictatorship administered by an unimaginative clerical bureaucracy supported by an ill-disciplined rabble of brutal and licentious soldiery.

REBELLION

It soon became apparent that the administration was not working properly. For one thing Surrey conceived such a dislike for Scotland and the Scots that he spent most of the time on his estates in Yorkshire. This meant that responsibility for Scotland's government fell on the treasurer Hugh Cressingham. Compensating for the stigma of illegitimacy, this smooth, obese official made himself so objectionable to his subordinates that he was hated as much by them as by the Scots. More to the point, it was proving extremely difficult to collect the revenues and taxes needed to meet the costs of administration. Therefore, instead of being a self-financing operation as originally intended, it was proving a constant drain on the English exchequer. Therefore Cressingham was forced to slim down the administration – a risky move in view of the mounting unrest and a growing likelihood of rebellion.

The first stirrings of revolt occurred in the spring of 1297 when a minor disturbance broke out in the West Highlands. It was followed by further outbreaks in the

---

ˣ   Grey, *Scalacronica*, 17. Kings would normally address their subjects in the first person plural, or as in this case using the impersonal pronoun.

north-east which were co-ordinated into a rebellion by Andrew Moray. A Scottish aristocrat, he had been captured at Dunbar and was consigned to prison at Chester from where he managed to escape back to Scotland. As the rebellion gathered pace, King Edward was forced into the risky policy of releasing a number of Scottish magnates, including the Comyn leaders (Sir John of Badenoch and the earl of Buchan), and allowing them to return home on condition that they would use their influence to suppress it. As a pledge of their co-operation they were required to surrender close members of their families as hostages. Although enough to deter these magnates from siding openly with the rebels, they could hardly be expected to make any serious attempt to discourage them. Nor did they.

In late May another revolt broke out in the south-west when the rebels (or perhaps more accurately the freedom fighters) captured a number of castles and slaughtered the English garrisons out of hand. On 4 June Edward ordered Percy and Clifford to 'arrest, imprison and justify [i.e. hang] all disturbers of the peace', while Cressingham was requested to give them 'aid and counsel'.[17] At the same time the sheriffs of Cumberland, Westmorland and Lancaster were instructed to raise levies and send them to Percy and Clifford's assistance.[18] With their help, and that of a number of local landowners, the rebellion was crushed and the castles recaptured, when Edward issued letters of thanks to the landowners for their support.[19]

Meanwhile another revolt broke out in the west under Bishop Robert Wishart of Glasgow and James the Steward which spread rapidly throughout northern Ayrshire, Renfrewshire and the lower Clyde. Unilaterally proclaiming themselves as guardians (which in a sense they were having been among those appointed in April 1286), they were joined by the earl of Lennox. The rebellion gathered strength and looked set to become a serious challenge to the English, particularly when the bishop and the Steward managed to enlist the support of the earl of Carrick. A man of fickle loyalties, his overarching ambition was to gain the Scottish crown which had been denied to his grandfather. Therefore, when the bishop and the Steward held out to him the prospect of securing the kingship of a free, independent Scotland for his father – or possibly himself – at the head of a successful rebellion, the bait was taken. Consequently he abandoned his allegiance to King Edward and joined them in what became known as the 'aristocratic' rebellion.

Carrick's accession to the rebel cause delivered the tenants of his earldom and their levies, but not his father's Annandale tenants. Summoning them to Lochmaben, he explained his defection to the Scots telling them that, 'No man holds his own flesh and blood in hatred, and I am no exception. [Therefore] I must join my own people [i.e. the Scots] and the nation in which I was born.' A somewhat belated rediscovery of his Scottish roots. In the end the Annandale tenants declined to support him, claiming that because 'their lord [the elder Bruce] remained with King Edward' they were bound to follow suit.[20]

In May two further rebellions broke out – one in Fife under Macduff who persuaded the tenants of his under-age nephew the earl of Fife to rebel, and the other in Lanarkshire under William Wallace. Younger son of a knightly family who were tenants of the Steward in northern Ayrshire, and who feature in the Ragman Roll as swearing fealty to King Edward, he allegedly killed the sheriff of Lanark in the course of a private vendetta. Now an outlaw, beyond the pale of forgiveness, and propelled into rebellion, he set about gathering recruits as fast as he could before the English had a chance to rally their forces.

It has been suggested that his recruiting campaign took him as far south as Nithsdale where he captured the English-held castle of Sanquhar causing the garrison to flee. Pursuing them downriver, Wallace is supposed to have overtaken them somewhere near Dalswinton and routed them.[21] This is unlikely because the English were still in possession of Sanquhar castle at the end of July.[22] Nevertheless Wallace's rebellion spread rapidly as people flocked to his banner, and it gained further momentum when Macduff and his supporters joined forces with him. Soon afterwards they were joined by Sir William Douglas who had reneged on his undertaking to Edward. But not for long, for he soon abandoned Wallace to join the aristocratic rebellion where as an aristocrat himself he doubtless felt more at home.

Initially the English regarded Wallace's revolt as a sideshow compared with the aristocratic rebellion, which they perceived as the main threat. Accordingly a number of Galloway landowners were requested to raise 2,000 footsoldiers between them, while Sir Richard Siward was ordered to raise a further 700 from Nithsdale. They were to be sent along with enlisted troops recruited from northern England to join Percy and Clifford at Carlisle.[23] As soon as they arrived, the army set out. While Percy advanced with one force through Galloway, Clifford invaded Annandale with the other and sacked the town of Annan in retaliation for Carrick's defection to the rebels.[24] Crossing into Nithsdale, he and his men devastated the countryside as they headed north. In late June the two forces met up at Ayr, and continuing their advance northwards they encountered the aristocratic rebels at Irvine.

Seeing the size of Percy's army, and realising that defeat was inevitable, the rebel (or nationalist) leaders sent emissaries to him asking for surrender terms. He was amenable. But the leaders deliberately spun out the negotiations in order to tie down his army and give Wallace a chance to muster further support. On 12 July, notwithstanding that they were in negotiation with Percy, Bishop Wishart, the Steward and other leaders issued a proclamation which was intended to frighten the people into supporting Wallace. Namely, that they 'had been told for a certainty that [the English] would have seized all the middling people of Scotland and sent them beyond seas to their great damage and destruction'. In other words they were to be conscripted for service in the campaign which Edward had recently opened up against King Philip in Flanders. Finally the leaders called on 'the whole community of the realm of Scotland' to rise up in rebellion against the English.[25] Hardly calculated to encourage Percy to show leniency!

Nevertheless he seems to have done so, for when the surrender terms were finally agreed the leaders were spared imprisonment against the giving up of hostages for their future good behaviour. Later that year a remarkably forgiving Edward received Carrick back into his peace. But no such accommodation was extended to Bishop Wishart and Sir William Douglas who were taken to Berwick loaded with chains. The latter proved a recalcitrant prisoner, evident from Cressingham's report to the king that 'he is still very savage and very abusive',[26] adding in another letter that he had ordered him to be put in irons.[27] In October he was transferred to the Tower where he died in January 1299[28] – of vexation according to one source,[29] though the Scots suspected (probably rightly) that he was murdered.

Throughout the summer Wallace had been gathering recruits and rallying the people of southern Scotland to his cause. That he and Moray were able to make the progress they did owed much to Surrey's continuing absence in Yorkshire and the fact that Cressingham, who had been left in charge of the administration, lacked the necessary authority. And besides, he appears to have been extraordinarily complacent. Reassured by the triumphant Percy and Clifford that the rebellion in the west had been crushed, and reports from Bishop Cheyne of Aberdeen and Gartney of Mar that they were 'putting down the insurrection in Moray', he remained culpably inactive.[30]

On 22 August, unaware of the seriousness of the situation, King Edward sailed for Flanders in a bid to enlist the support of the north European rulers in his campaign against King Philip. Percy was among his entourage having asked to be relieved of the wardenship of the south-west, when he was succeeded by Clifford. It was only after Edward had arrived in the Low Countries that Cressingham, appreciating the gravity of the situation, reported to him. Edward immediately ordered Surrey north. Hastily mustering an army he reached Berwick where he was joined by Clifford and his army from the south-west, as well as contingents from Cumberland and Lancashire. In early September the combined army set out from Berwick to crush the rebellion.

Meanwhile Wallace, who had been gathering recruits in Fife, was laying siege to the important seaport of Dundee. But when news reached him that Surrey was on the march he abandoned it. Assuming that Surrey was making for Stirling – logically because it was the main access to northern Scotland, Wallace headed there, being joined on the way by Moray and his supporters. Reaching the river Forth on 9 September, they took up a position on the Abbey Craig.* Below it the river describes a series of loops as it meanders down to the head of the Firth, one of them extending to immediately below Stirling castle where there was a bridge. Correctly anticipating that this was where Surrey's troops would cross, Moray and Wallace sent their troops forward to seal off the neck of the loop with the aim of bottling them up.

On 11 September the English army began crossing the bridge, but finding themselves bogged down in the soft ground the cavalry fell an easy prey to the Scottish pikemen. Those considered ransomworthy were taken prisoner while the rest were slaughtered. They included Cressingham who was dragged from his horse and

---

*   Now surmounted by the Wallace monument.

stabbed to death. Meanwhile, seeing the battle going according to plan, Moray and Wallace abandoned their command post on the Abbey Craig to join it. Finally realising that defeat was inevitable, Surrey ordered the bridge to be broken to prevent the Scots from crossing it and attacking the castle. Then, entrusting its keepership to two reliable knights, he rode straight for Berwick followed by the remnants of his army as they trudged their weary way along the road past Falkirk and Linlithgow and back across the border.

After the battle Cressingham's bloated corpse was retrieved from the piles of dead and his skin was flayed off so that strips could be distributed throughout Scotland as a token of the victory, one allegedly being used to make a sword-belt for Wallace. Although he has been credited with the victory, it could equally well have been attributable to Moray, or more likely they were jointly responsible. Either way, they were greatly helped by Surrey's poor generalship in allowing his army to fall into their trap. The victory gave a tremendous fillip to the Scots' morale because it showed that their relatively small army was capable of defeating a numerically superior English army equipped with cavalry in a pitched battle. It also delivered northern Scotland into the hands of the Scots, which it would remain for the next five years. Although the English continued to maintain a substantial presence in southern Scotland, their occupation zone fluctuated according to the fortunes of war.

Following Moray's death in November (as a result of wounds received in the battle) Wallace became a virtual dictator. Later he had himself knighted (provoking the acid comment by the English that 'from a robber he became a knight, just as a swan emerges from a raven') and appointed guardian, ostensibly on behalf of King John to whom he professed allegiance. Since his authority rested on a single victory he needed to build on it by achieving further military successes, the more so because of the covert opposition of the Comyns and their supporters. They greatly resented the supersession of their family's near seventy-year ascendancy, particularly when usurped by someone like Wallace whom they regarded as a parvenu and a man of inferior status. But tainted by their association with John Balliol's failed kingship, they were forced to make a show of co-operation with Wallace, hoping that in the fullness of time they would regain their ascendancy. In any case their hands were tied because concern for their hostages inhibited them from being more proactive.

Despite the efforts of wishful-thinking historians to conjure up an association between Bruce and Wallace, the fact is that there was none whatsoever. In any case Bruce (or Carrick) would have shared the Comyns' view of Wallace, as did most of the Scottish magnates, and like them he would have resented Wallace's ascendancy. Since he saw no future for himself in a Wallace-dominated Scotland, he decided to mend his fences with King Edward and come into his peace[31] (although he would soon defect again). Other magnates who resented Wallace's authority and attempted to resist were given short shrift. As Bower put it, 'if [a particular magnate] did not gladly obey his orders, [Wallace] got hold of him, put pressure on him, and held him in custody until he submitted entirely to his good pleasure'.[32]

Wallace's immediate aim was to recapture the English-held castles, but to achieve it he needed a large standing army. His recruitment methods were brutally effective. Those who attempted to evade the draft were summarily hanged, while taxes were levied – and rigorously extorted – to support and maintain the army, and purchase arms and equipment. Resuming the siege of Dundee, he captured the castle before going on to take the fortress of Dumbarton which controlled the western approaches. More importantly, he captured Stirling castle as a preliminary to advancing on Edinburgh. Here he took possession of the town, though not the castle where the English garrison succeeded in holding out. Therefore, abandoning the siege he and his army headed south, and having failed to take Roxburgh castle they went on to capture Jedburgh.

Crossing the border, they took possession of Berwick town when the English inhabitants were slaughtered almost to a man. Because the castle held out, Wallace left a detachment to continue the siege while he and the rest of the army went on to invade the northern counties. Having failed to capture Alnwick, Newcastle and Durham castles, his troops ran amok committing mindless atrocities on the local population. Moving on to Cumberland, they attempted to take Carlisle castle with similar lack of success. In revenge, they extended their bloodthirsty campaign as far as Cockermouth until a spell of unusually cold weather forced them to abandon it and return home.

In early December, Clifford counterattacked by invading Annandale with a large contingent of footsoldiers. A scratch force of local peasantry was raised to repel them. However their resistance seems to have amounted to little more than yelling obscenities at the English and insulting them with the conventional taunts of 'tailed dogs' which was calculated to goad them into a fury, as indeed it did. Retribution came when the peasantry found themselves trapped in a bog and Clifford's troops made short work of them. Having burnt ten local settlements in reprisal,[33] he withdrew to Carlisle leaving a token force behind to guard the border.

Meanwhile Edward had agreed a truce with King Philip. But forced to remain in Flanders to settle his financial obligations to his allies, he postponed his return until the following March. No sooner was he back in England than he issued summonses for the mustering of an army to crush the rebellion once and for all. By 25 June a force of some 2,000 cavalry and 26,000 footsoldiers had assembled at Roxburgh, and in early July it marched. Withdrawing in the face of their advance, Wallace allowed the English to burn and lay waste to the surrounding countryside as they headed up Lauderdale and over the Lammermuirs towards Edinburgh. Arriving at Leith, they found that only five of the expected seventeen supply ships had arrived, the rest having been delayed by contrary winds. Unwilling to wait, Edward continued his advance, but his troops began to go hungry as they headed westwards through Lothian.

Finally on 22 July they encountered the Scottish army drawn up for battle on a hillside immediately to the south of Falkirk. When battle was joined the Scottish pikemen stood their ground against repeated assaults by the English cavalry, although the archers were cut down almost to a man. The principal magnates who were drawn up behind them with their mounted levies should have come to their rescue, but instead they abandoned the field. Attributing Wallace's defeat to their treachery, Bower claims that it was the result of a plot against him inspired by Comyn jealousy[34] – probably true enough since they were never reconciled to his leadership. Therefore as soon as they saw the battle going against him they would have had no hesitation in leaving him in the lurch. Finally the massed ranks of Scottish pikemen were broken, many being driven down the hill into a morass where they were virtually annihilated. Wallace himself abandoned the field, but reluctantly and only at the urging of those who persuaded him that he would be more useful alive than dead.

The English suffered heavy casualties as well, and this combined with a steady trickle of desertions was enough to persuade Edward to abandon his plan to recover northern Scotland. Therefore, having recaptured Stirling castle he headed south to Ayr with the aim of capturing its castle and taking delivery of the supplies ordered from Ireland. Arriving there at the end of August, he found the castle burnt on the orders of Carrick, now thought to be lurking somewhere beyond the Tay. Clearly Wallace's defeat had given him renewed hope of gaining the kingship. Therefore burning the castle and abandoning his allegiance to Edward would have been designed to restore his credibility with the Scots.

Worse still, the expected supply ships had failed to arrive. Once again Edward was not prepared to wait. Therefore he and his army proceeded south to Cumnock, and on into Nithsdale where they set up camp near present-day Thornhill. While there, Edward took the opportunity to inspect the 'new stone house' (or pele) which Sir Richard Siward* was having built for himself at nearby Tibbers.† Evidently he was so impressed with it that, when in the following year he ordered the building of a new pele at Lochmaben, he commissioned Siward to draw up the plans for it.[35] Arriving at Lochmaben, he ordered the town to be burnt in reprisal for Carrick's defection; and, notwithstanding that it belonged to the loyalist Bruce of Annandale, he had the castle razed to the ground.[36] But appreciating its importance as a centre for controlling the south-west, Edward ordered the building of a wooden pele (stone

---

*   Married to a daughter of Sir John Comyn of Badenoch, Siward had been appointed by Edward as keeper of Dumfries, Kirkcudbright and Wigtown castles. Later he switched his allegiance to the Scots and fought for them at Dunbar when he was taken prisoner along with his son. The following year he was released against the surrender of another son as a hostage, but on condition that he took part in Edward's campaign in Flanders. Here his 'good service' earned an improvement in the conditions of his sons' confinement. Now firmly in the English camp he fought for Edward at Falkirk, and the following year he was appointed warden of Nithsdale.

†   All that is left of Tibbers is a large artificial mound, or mote, about a kilometre downriver from Drumlanrig Castle.

was too costly) on a peninsula at the southern end of the Castle Loch to serve as the local headquarters.

In mid-September Edward reached Carlisle where he distributed forfeited Scottish lands to his supporters. For example 'the castle of Amesfield and the lands of Drumgrey', forfeited by Andrew de Chartres in punishment for fighting for the Scots at Falkirk, were given to Guy de Beauchamp earl of Warwick.[37] Edward also reorganised the command structure in southern Scotland, appointing Sir Robert Clifford captain and lieutenant of the west marches (which extended from Liddesdale to Galloway) with power to receive the men of Nithsdale into his peace.[38] Although many took up the offer they were quick to renege once the Scots looked like recovering the region. His subordinate commanders were Sir Simon Lindsay, appointed captain of Eskdale, and Sir Robert Cantilupe who was given the wardenship of Annandale and keepership of Lochmaben.[39]

Given the importance of Dumfries castle as the western outpost of the English-occupation zone, Edward ensured that it was fully up to strength. Therefore the garrison of twelve men-at-arms and twenty-four footsoldiers was supplemented by twenty-four crossbowmen drawn from Berwick and Lochmaben. Their provisions included ten tuns of wine, a large quantity of malted barley (for brewing beer), as well as oats, pease and beans, copious supplies of fish including ten thousand herrings, and fifty ox carcases.[40] Engineers, carpenters, smiths and masons were dispatched there to refurbish the castle and put the defences in order. Meanwhile springalds and other engines, as well as crossbows, and supplies of iron and steel for the manufacture of ballshot, and counterweights for the siege engines, were delivered there.[41] At the same time the bishop of Carlisle was commissioned to supply as many 'quarreaux' as possible.* Having ensured that all the English-held castles were fully garrisoned, and done what he could to strengthen his position in Scotland, the indefatigable Edward returned to York where he spent the winter planning his next campaign.

SCOTTISH DEFIANCE

Following his defeat at Falkirk, Wallace withdrew beyond the river Forth where he embarked on a recruiting drive. Such was his popularity and personal magnetism that by late August he had raised a large enough force to come within an ace of recapturing Stirling castle.[42] But it was not enough to save his position. At a meeting of the Scottish magnates held later in the year he was deprived of the guardianship and replaced by Carrick and the younger John Comyn as joint guardians in the hopes – forlorn as it turned out – that they would unite their factions behind the Scottish resistance.[43] Wallace seems to have accepted his exclusion from power with good

---

* McDowall, *Dumfries*, 68, these were bolts fired from crossbows. Derived from the French word *carré*, they were so-called on account of their four-sided head.

grace, because he continued to play an active part in the Scottish resistance until August 1299 when he left for the Continent. There he spent the next four years championing the Scottish cause, both at the French court and at the papal curia, while the issue of a safe conduct by King Haakon of Norway suggests that he may have gone there as well, presumably to promote Scottish trade.

At the same meeting it was decided to launch a major offensive against the English. Focusing on the south-west where the English position was weakest, the Scots invaded Annandale and Nithsdale in such force that the garrison at Carlisle castle feared that they too were about to come under attack. So much so that Sir William Mulcaster, the sheriff of Cumberland, dared not leave his post to present his accounts to the treasury officials at York.[44] Appreciating the danger, Edward placed the northern counties on a war footing. In the event it proved unnecessary, for in December the Scots abandoned their attacks on the south-west and turned their attention to recapturing Stirling castle.

Faced with political difficulties at home, combined with an acute shortage of money, Edward abandoned his plans for a campaign in 1299 and decided instead to strengthen the English position in Scotland. Because the Scots were in possession of Caerlaverock and had re-taken Dumfries, it was clear that Lochmaben was their next target. Therefore, as a precaution a contingent of twenty-seven crossbowmen was deployed to protect the workmen engaged in building Edward's new pele there. Similarly the money and supplies shipped to Waterfoot at the mouth of the Annan had to be escorted under armed guard to Lochmaben. Supplies were essential because the dearth of food locally meant that the garrison was permanently on the verge of starvation.[45] As Clifford observed in a letter to Richard Abingdon, the king's victualler at Carlisle, 'because of the great dearness of [i.e. scarcity in] the country, no *vivres* [food] can be got here'.[46]

To strengthen the English position in south-west Scotland, Edward made further changes among his commanders. In June 1299 he appointed Sir John de St John warden of Annandale in place of Clifford, who retained the captaincy of the western garrisons, although he was replaced soon afterwards by Sir Ralph Fitzwilliam.[47] At much the same time Sir Richard Siward was appointed warden of Nithsdale,[48] while Sir Robert Felton replaced Sir Richard de Cantilupe as keeper of Lochmaben.[49] This would prove no sinecure because the expected attack by the Scots soon materialised.

The return of Bishop Lamberton,[*] Sir John de Soules and others from their mission to France in July 1299 heralded a major offensive which came close to driving the English out of Scotland altogether. After recovering lower Clydesdale, Sir John de Soules, now in overall command, split the army. While the main body continued its advance up the Clyde, first to Bothwell, then Biggar and finally into Tweeddale, the rest of the army under Carrick headed south to lay siege to

---

[*]　Bishop Fraser's successor as bishop of St Andrews and senior prelate in the Scottish Church.

Lochmaben.[50] It began on 1 August just as the garrison troops were threatening to desert because of non-payment of their wages.[51] But in spite of every effort Carrick and his men failed to take it.

On 10 August Carrick attended a Council meeting at Peebles which had been convened to discuss future strategy. Here he and Comyn came to blows. According to an English spy who was present, high words passed until Comyn losing his temper seized Carrick by the throat, while the earl of Buchan accused Bishop Lamberton of plotting treason. At that point the Steward and others intervened to break up the fight and order was restored. Because Carrick and Comyn's altercation put paid to any chance of their future co-operation, Bishop Lamberton was appointed senior guardian to keep the peace. And to invest him with the necessary authority he was given the captaincy of all the castles in Scottish hands.[52]

After the meeting broke up, Carrick returned to the south-west to resume his attacks on Lochmaben. But Sir Robert Felton and his men continued to resist all attempts to take it. The following month Carrick scored a minor success when his men beat off a raiding party from Caerlaverock, in the course of which their leader Robert Cunningham was killed. Reporting this to Edward, Felton told him that 'many were wounded on both sides, though fewer of our men than the others', adding that he had ordered Cunningham's head to be cut off and nailed to the 'great tower' (i.e. the now completed pele) at Lochmaben.[53]

In early November the attacks ceased. But only temporarily, because a Scottish Parliament held in the Torwood near Stirling decided to launch another offensive against the south-west. This time the attacks were pursued with such vigour that by the end of the month a combination of casualties and a steady leakage of deserters had reduced the English garrison to a total of some forty footsoldiers and a mere handful of men-at-arms.[54] In desperation Felton was compelled to recruit local sympathisers. But their wages were a further drain on the limited amount of coin reaching him, which was barely enough to meet his existing commitments. Besides the soldiers' pay, they included the wages for those employed in guarding the supplies after they had been offloaded at Waterfoot and 'lay on the beach', coopers for repairing damaged flour and wine casks, and those responsible for escorting the supplies to Lochmaben.

Yet in spite of all these difficulties Felton continued to hold out. This was partly due to the assistance of a number of Annandale tenants and their retainers who, following the lead of the elder Bruce, continued to support the English. Most of them are identifiable from the list of those receiving compensation from Richard Abingdon, the receiver at Carlisle, for the value of horses killed.* They included Sir John and Sir Roger de Kirkpatrick, Sir Humphrey de Bosco, Sir James and Sir Thomas de Torthorwald, Sir Humphrey de Jardine, Sir William Heriz and Sir Hugh Mauleverer.[55] Later, with certain notable exceptions such as the de Mauleverer family, they switched their allegiance to the younger Robert Bruce.

---

* Horses were far more valued than footsoldiers who were regarded as readily expendable.

Relief finally came in January 1300 when Edward, having renewed Sir John de St John's appointment as captain and lieutenant of Annandale, ordered him and his deputy Sir Robert Clifford to establish their headquarters at Lochmaben.[56] Consequently their retinue of fifty men-at-arms represented a vital addition to the attenuated garrison. The following month St John recaptured Dumfries, thus removing the threat from that source, while King Edward's capture of Caerlaverock castle during his campaign in the south-west the following summer ensured the safety of Lochmaben for the immediate future.

His campaign, which began in late June 1300, was mainly intended as a show of strength to overawe the people of Galloway and coerce them into his allegiance. It was planned with characteristic thoroughness. A fleet of fifty-seven ships raised from the Cinque Ports and the main Irish seaports was to assemble at Skinburness, the nearest port to Carlisle. From there they would hug the Solway coast to keep Edward's army supplied as it advanced through Galloway.

His immediate objective was to take Caerlaverock. Apart from Lochmaben it was the most important fortress in the south-west, and because it served as a base for attacking other castles in the region, notably Dumfries and Lochmaben, its capture was vital. Nevertheless it was a daunting prospect because it was virtually impregnable, being protected partly by the sea and partly by the almost impenetrable Lochar moss.* Therefore the largest ship – the *St George* of Dartmouth – was earmarked for the transportation of three siege engines, or trebuchets, across the Solway to the harbour immediately below Caerlaverock. From there they would be manoeuvred into position to bombard the castle.

Arriving there on 9 July, Edward's troops set up camp in front of the castle to await the arrival of the siege engines. The principal feature of these contraptions was the main beam which was balanced on a fulcrum. At one end was a bucket which contained lead counterweights, and at the other a sling in which the missiles – usually rocks and stones, but sometimes rotting corpses, human and animal, and even well-stocked beehives – were packed. This end was wound down with the aid of a capstan, and when released the missiles were hurled with such force as to batter down the walls of a castle. Not surprisingly the sight of these huge engines being manoeuvred into position so terrified the garrison that they offered to surrender. But Edward would have none of it and ordered the siege to continue.

According to one account, the English proceeded to hurl such a murderous volley of 'stones, rocks and *quarreaux* [arrows]' at the castle that 'within one short hour there were many people wounded, maimed [and] killed'.[57] Then the siege engines were brought into action – to devastating effect as the missiles hurled from them breached the walls and knocked the roof in. Realising the hopelessness of their

---

* Evidently the Lochar moss was only accessible during a dry spell. Therefore King Edward's commanders would have had to compel local people to guide the army across it, presumably bridging the Lochar Water. See *NSA* (Caerlaverock), 349.

situation, the constable Walter Benechafe ordered one of the garrison to hang out a white pennant in token of surrender. But as he did so he was struck by an arrow which penetrated his mailed glove and transfixed his head.[58] When the garrison finally surrendered, Benechafe and eleven others were consigned to prison at Newcastle,[59] while the rest were reportedly hanged from the nearest trees.[60]

Leaving Clifford in charge of the castle, Edward and his army advanced up the Nith to Dumfries. Crossing the river into Galloway (presumably by the bridge recently built on the orders of King John's mother Dervorguilla), they headed for Kirkcudbright. While there, Edward was approached by the younger John Comyn[*] and the earl of Buchan asking for a truce. Since their terms – the restoration of King John, recognition of the right of his son Edward to succeed him, and the return to the Scottish magnates of their forfeited English estates – were quite unacceptable, Edward contemptuously dismissed their pleas and resumed his march westwards.

Reaching the lower Cree, he encountered a Scottish force consisting of three brigades formed up on the far side. As soon as the tide went out, his army crossed the river. The Scots were routed, many being killed while the survivors escaped to the fastnesses of the Wigtownshire moors, running it was said 'like hares before grey-hounds'. Some were captured, including William de Chartres, a brother of the laird of Amisfield, who was consigned to prison at Carlisle. Continuing his advance, Edward reached Wigtown on 16 August when he decided to abandon what was clearly an inconclusive campaign.[61]

Arriving at Sweetheart abbey on 25 August, in the course of his return journey, he was met by Archbishop Winchelsey of Canterbury with ominous news. Notwithstanding that this tough-minded and sometimes irascible prelate had crossed swords with Edward in the past, his mission must have caused him some apprehension. At the Pope's request (and under threat of suspension from office if he failed to deliver it in person) he brought with him a bull censuring Edward for his treatment of the Scots and demanding that his claim to overlordship be adjudicated by the papal court. When the archbishop handed it to the king, accompanied by a homily enjoining him to observe its terms, it provoked an explosion of royal wrath.

Nevertheless, pressure from the envoys of King Philip, with whom he was temporarily at peace, was enough to persuade Edward to receive a Scottish delegation who had come to Dumfries to ask for a truce. Already supplied with a copy of the bull, they were well aware of the strength of their position. But when they boldly challenged the king to ignore their request at his peril, it provoked another explosion of royal wrath when he threatened 'with an oath [to] lay the whole of Scotland to waste from sea to sea and force its people into submission'.[62] Nevertheless, bowing to reality, he grudgingly agreed to grant them a truce to last from 1 November until the

---

*   His father Sir John of Badenoch was still alive (he died in May 1302), but because he disappears from the records after 1298 it would seem that he was incapacitated, possibly as a result of a stroke.

following Whitsunday (21 May).[63] Once back at Carlisle, he renewed Sir John de St John's appointment as warden of Annandale and captain of Dumfries and Lochmaben castles, while Sir Richard Siward replaced Sir Roger Clifford as his deputy, both beeing equipped with a contingent of forty men-at-arms.[64]

As soon as the truce expired Edward embarked on another invasion. This was to be conducted on two fronts. One army under his son Edward, now prince of Wales, would set out from Carlisle and advance through Dumfriesshire and Galloway, and from there up the Ayrshire coast. The other, commanded by himself, would advance from Berwick up Tweeddale and into Clydesdale, the plan being that they should join forces on the lower Clyde. From there the combined army would go on to recover Stirling castle as a preliminary to regaining control of northern Scotland.

Reaching Dumfries, the prince sent a detachment up the Nith to capture the Comyn stronghold of Dalswinton while he and the rest of his army advanced westwards through Galloway. Meanwhile the Scottish army under the command of Sir John de Soules, recently appointed guardian,* was deployed on the high, bleak country straddling eastern Ayrshire and Lanarkshire with the aim of preventing the two armies from joining up. The plan was that part of the Scottish army, which was concentrated round Stonehouse, would harass Edward's host as it advanced down the Clyde valley, while the rest under the command of the earl of Buchan would block the prince's advance up the Ayrshire coast. This he succeeded in doing; and, doubtless assisted by the earl of Carrick, he forced the prince and his army back to Loch Ryan.

This enabled de Soules to leave his command post and head south to gather recruits from Annandale and Nithsdale where the people were quick to renounce their feigned allegiance to Edward. This left Lochmaben increasingly isolated, and Felton's hard-pressed successor Sir Robert Tilliol was compelled to warn the king that 'all the country is rising because we have no troops to ride upon them'.[65] Responding to his plea for reinforcements, Edward ordered the prince of Wales to send a cavalry force to Lochmaben. But he was beaten to it by de Soules. As Tilliol reported to the king, he (de Soules) and Sir Ingelram de Umfraville had appeared before the walls at the head of a force of 'twelve score men-at-arms and seven thousand footmen or more' (doubtless a gross exaggeration), and that 'they had burnt our town and assailed our pele'.[66] The attack failed, and the Scottish host withdrew to Annan where they reportedly 'burnt and pillaged the country round about'.[67] Next day they were back. But after several hours' fighting, in the course of which many Scots were killed, they were again repelled. Reporting his success to the king, Tilliol told him that de Soules and his men had gone on to attack Dalswinton before heading for Galloway.

---

* Shortly after the Council meeting at Peebles in August 1299, when Bishop Lamberton was appointed senior Guardian, Carrick resigned. In May 1300 he was replaced by Sir Ingelram de Umfraville; but in early 1301, for reasons unknown, all three guardians resigned and Sir John de Soules was appointed sole guardian.

By September Edward had advanced to within striking distance of Stirling. But because it was too late in the season to lay siege to the castle, he decided to defer it until the following spring and spend the winter at Linlithgow. Meanwhile he sent envoys to France to negotiate a permanent peace with King Philip. But, mindful of his obligation to them, Philip insisted that the Scots be party to the talks.[68] Since he needed a respite to strengthen the English presence in Scotland, Edward reluctantly agreed. The negotiations culminated in the truce of Asnières, and because it was to last until St Andrew's Day (30 November) 1302 the siege of Stirling castle had to be postponed until the following year.

Since the truce of Asnières and the prospect of a permanent peace opened up the possibility a Balliol restoration, the earl of Carrick decided to abandon the Scots and return to Edward's allegiance. No Scottish patriot – at least not at this stage, and motivated entirely by self-interest, he was not interested in the cause of Scottish independence except under a Bruce kingship. Since a Balliol restoration would inevitably result in the proscription of himself and his family, his defection to Edward is readily understandable. Yet Carrick must have feared that, given his record of inconstancy, he had burnt his boats beyond redemption.

Not so, because the astonishingly forgiving king, perhaps influenced by a personal liking for the twenty-seven-year-old earl, was prepared to receive him into his peace. More to the point, Carrick's defection delivered the men of Carrick to the English which greatly strengthened their position in the south-west. Since Carrick's second marriage – to Elizabeth, daughter of Richard de Burgh earl of Ulster, Edward's key supporter in Ireland – took place about this time (his first wife Isabella of Mar having died in childbirth in 1297), it may have been dictated by Edward in order to ensure Carrick's loyalty. Certainly Edward must have had some confidence in his loyalty, for not only was he prepared to receive Carrick into his peace but he appointed him a member of the Council responsible for administering English-occupied Scotland. This meant that Carrick was now pitted against the very people he had recently aspired to lead.

COLLAPSE OF THE RESISTANCE

On 11 July 1302 King Philip's supposedly invincible cavalry suffered a crushing defeat at the hands of the Flemish urban levies at the battle of Courtrai, an event that would alter the whole course of the war. Fearing that it might encourage Edward to renew his hostile alliance with the Flemings, Philip decided to conclude a final peace treaty with him. Informed of this, the Scots sent a high-ranking delegation to Paris to plead that any treaty should be conditional on Edward granting them a permanent peace, and to insist that they be party to the negotiations. Such was the importance they attached to it that Sir John de Soules was released from the guardianship to lead it.*

---

* He was later succeeded as guardian by the newly knighted Sir John Comyn, now lord of Badenoch following his father's recent death.

Determined on nothing less than the conquest of Scotland (he was already planning an invasion for the following year), Edward refused to countenance Scottish participation; still less was he prepared to grant them a permanent peace. Consequently Philip was forced to back down, fobbing off the Scots with hollow promises that their interests would be protected under a separate treaty. Taking him at his word, the Scots remained defiant. Therefore Edward ordered the border castles to be repaired and provisioned, and the garrisons, which had become dangerously undermanned mainly through desertions, brought up to strength. The need for this was evident from Sir Richard Siward's complaint to Ralph Manton, the cofferer, who was responsible for supplying them with money and provisions – namely, that he 'had not above ten men-at-arms at either of these places [i.e. Dumfries and Lochmaben]'.[69] Accordingly both castles were strengthened, and it was probably at this time that Dumfries castle was enlarged,* its garrison being supplemented by twenty-seven archers.[70]

The attack, the most aggressive yet, and almost certainly masterminded by Wallace, newly returned from the Continent, took place in January 1303. But instead of being directed against the south-west as expected, it was aimed at the English garrisons in the south-east. Meanwhile Edward was finalising his plans for an invasion. For the first time levies were to be raised from Scotland. In April the earl of Carrick was asked to contribute 1,000 footsoldiers and as many men-at-arms as possible from Galloway and Carrick, while Sir Richard Siward was ordered to provide levies from Nithsdale.[71] They were to be sent to Roxburgh where the army was due to muster on 12 May.[72]

Eight days later, Edward's envoys concluded a treaty of perpetual peace with the French at Amiens. But relying on King Philip's promises, the Scots continued militant. On 14 June, while at Clackmannan, Edward received alarming news that they had broken into Annandale and Liddesdale with 'a great force of horse and foot' and were doing 'much damage'.[73] The situation continued to deteriorate. On 23 June reports reached the exchequer officials at York that another force had invaded England and was plundering the country round Carlisle, while a third under Wallace was harrying the district between Dumfries and Caerlaverock and reported to be about to 'destroy Annandale'.[74]

Meanwhile Sir John de Moigne, the acting warden of Galloway and Nithsdale, was bombarding the officials at York with requests for money, accompanied by dire warnings that the garrisons of Dumfries and Lochmaben needed urgent relief 'before it is too late'. Unless he received enough to pay them their arrears of wages 'by the bearer of this letter', he went on, there will be 'neither enough knights, nor esquires, nor crossbowmen to mount guard [there]'. The English position in the south-east was equally desperate, because the token force which Edward had left behind under Sir Aymer de Valence was not strong enough to cope with the situation. Therefore he was compelled to detach part of his army and send it south under Carrick and Sir

---

*   The foundations of the enlarged castle still survive in Castledykes Park.

John de Botetourt, recently appointed warden of Galloway and Nithsdale, to his assistance.[75] This was enough to check the Scots' offensive and drive them back beyond the Forth and Clyde.

The Scots were now thoroughly demoralised. It was clear that King Philip's promises that their interests would be protected under a separate treaty were so much empty rhetoric and that they were now on their own. Since there was no further possibility of a Balliol restoration, they may justly have wondered what they were fighting for. This sense of futility combined with a growing war-weariness caused many to consider an accommodation with Edward on acceptable terms as preferable to continuing what was clearly a hopeless struggle. Worse still the Pope, now won over to Edward's side, enjoined them to submit under threat of interdict.

After considerable debate the Scottish leaders decided to put out peace feelers. In December 1303 they informed Edward through intermediaries that they were willing to treat. Responding, he ordered de Valence and Percy to meet Sir John Comyn and agree surrender terms (de Valence being an obvious choice since he was Comyn's brother-in-law). Edward was equally anxious to bring the war to an end. He clearly loathed it, regarding his entanglement with the Scots as demeaning for a man of his international standing, and only driven to continue it at the expense of so much time, effort and money by a fanatical determination to subdue them. Therefore he was prepared to be conciliatory, and his terms were lenient. When de Valence and Percy reported that they were acceptable to the Scottish leaders, Edward authorised them to receive their surrender.

While moderation was the order of the day, there were certain magnates like Bishop Wishart and others whom Edward singled out for punishment. This took the form of exile or imprisonment for varying terms depending on the perceived gravity of their offence. As leader in his capacity as guardian, and head of the Comyn faction, Sir John Comyn was a case in point. He was sentenced to a term of exile, perhaps reduced on account of his abject surrender to Edward and putting all his lands at his disposal.[76]

But Edward's success was not yet complete. While the magnates were prepared to submit, they were unable to control the partisans who were determined to fight on. That they were active in Galloway is evident from Edward's order in late 1304 to post troops there 'to protect the people on this side of the Cree' (i.e. modern Kirkcudbrightshire) who had come into his peace.[77] At the same time Wallace was conducting a guerrilla campaign in the Borders in collaboration with Sir Simon Fraser. A small force was dispatched there under Carrick to hunt them down. He was successful to the extent that Fraser was persuaded to give himself up. Wallace would also have been given the chance to submit, but he refused. Had he done so, then like Fraser he would have been sentenced to a term of exile or imprisonment, but not the traitor's death he eventually suffered. As it was, he continued to conduct an increasingly beleaguered campaign until he was finally captured some eighteen months later, by which time resistance had all but ceased.

Having gained control of Scotland, Edward needed to set up an administration to govern it. Because this was bound to be the subject of prolonged discussion and consequent delay, an interim administration was put in place to run it on an *ad hoc* basis. But instead of entrusting it exclusively to English officials as in 1296, Edward encouraged a number of collaborating Scotsmen to participate. While this has been seen as belated enlightenment on his part, it was more likely dictated by shortage of money since the inclusion of Scotsmen would help reduce the administration costs.

Those responsible for controlling the region beyond the Forth included Sir Richard Siward who was appointed sheriff of Fife and keeper of the bishopric of St Andrews.[78] The appointment of sheriffs in southern Scotland, on the other hand, was entrusted to Carrick (now lord of Annandale following his father's death in April 1304) and Sir John de Botetourt. Whereas the latter remained warden of Galloway and Nithsdale, Carrick, already sheriff of Ayr, appointed himself (with Edward's approval) sheriff of Lanark.[79] At a lower level Sir Matthew Redmayne was appointed keeper of Dumfries castle. To enable him to defend it against partisans from Galloway, he was equipped with a garrison of five men-at-arms, ten crossbowmen and ten archers.

He sounds to have been a controversial character. While profiting from public office was standard practice, the complaints made by certain local landowners suggest that he overstepped the mark. As Scots supporters, their lands had been forfeited; but following their submission to Edward these had been restored to them. Because a ceremony involving the symbolic delivery of earth and stones by the local sheriff was a prerequisite for taking physical possession, Redmayne was charging an exorbitant fee for officiating at them, which he was not entitled to do. Furthermore he and his officials were accused of seeking 'to grieve and distress the poor people' by appropriating their corn, carts and beasts, allegedly for the king's use but in reality for their own. Finally he was charged with acquiring 'by various dubious means the lands of John Haytone and Matthew de Terregles'.[80]

Meanwhile Edward was preparing for his long-deferred siege of Stirling castle, the last remaining fortress in Scottish hands. As a preliminary, he ordered all available siege engines to be brought there – at considerable inconvenience because they were dispersed throughout the realm. Most were transported by sea, but they still had to be hauled from the landing point at the head of the Firth of Forth to within range of the castle. Lead was also needed to manufacture counterweights for the siege engines, and similarly a large supply of 'round stones' for missiles. Whereas stones were readily available, much of the lead was stripped from the roofs of Dunblane cathedral, the convent at Perth, the cathedral and priory buildings at St Andrews, and Dunfermline abbey. Nevertheless Edward was at pains to ensure that in each case the section of the roof covering the altar was left intact,[81] while compensation was eventually paid to these houses for the value of the lead taken.[82]

Some engines were hauled overland, including the two dispatched by the earl of Carrick from Ayr, for which Edward sent him a grateful acknowledgement coupled with a request to let him have 'the frame of the great engine'. Because Carrick was unable to find a large enough wagon to transport it, Edward offered to send help if needed.[83] The same day he wrote to de Botetourt ordering him to go to Carrick's assistance and to collect as much lead as possible while he was about it.[84] The preparations included the manufacture of 'Greek fire', an explosive mix consisting of pitch, sulphur and other ingredients such as saltpetre, which was specially prepared by a Burgundian chemical expert.[85] This was packed into earthenware pots to create what were effectively firebombs. These would then be set alight and hurled from the siege engines into the castle.

The siege lasted for upwards of two months – from early May to mid-July 1304. Eventually the walls were breached and the firebombs reduced the castle to a blackened shell, forcing the garrison to take refuge in caves hollowed out from the underlying rock. Finally they offered to surrender. But Edward would have none of it. He wanted to try out the largest of his siege engines, the *Loup de Guerre* (Warwolf), which had just become operational. Therefore he ordered the siege to continue, and it was only after the engine was found to be working satisfactorily that he accepted their surrender. In punishment for their obstinacy in holding out and putting him to so much trouble and expense, Edward ordered the garrison to be hanged and disembowelled,[86] and it was only after impassioned pleas from his commanders and courtiers alike that he relented and consigned them to prison instead.

In February 1305 he convened a Parliament at Westminster to determine the shape of the new administration. At his request, it was attended by Carrick, Bishop Wishart and Sir John de Moubray as the Scottish representatives. On their recommendation it was agreed to defer a final decision until the next Parliament which would be attended by ten Scottish magnates as commissioners. Following their return to Scotland, the bishop, Carrick and de Moubray convened a Parliament at Scone to choose the commissioners. On 13 July Edward issued letters requesting them to meet twenty English representatives to draw up a set of proposals for approval by the English Parliament which was due to meet in August. The Scottish commissioners consisted of a cross-section of the baronage, including Patrick earl of Dunbar (now styling himself earl of March). Since he failed to turn up, Sir John Menteith was appointed in his place.

On 3 August Menteith's men apprehended Wallace at Glasgow, probably as he was about to take ship for the Continent. Although vilified down the centuries as Wallace's betrayer, Menteith was merely carrying out his duties as a member of the new administration. Moreover he was probably regarded as performing a valuable public service. Perceiving Wallace as a threat to their new-found accord with Edward, the magnates would doubtless have welcomed his capture, while the great majority of war-weary Scots were probably only too glad to be rid of someone who had remained a disruptive force and a disturber of the longed-for peace.

Taken to London he was subjected to a show trial. The indictment was read out specifying the charges laid against him. Denying the charge of treason on the grounds that he had never given his personal oath to Edward, he refused to answer the others. The outcome was inevitable. He was condemned to a traitor's death. It took place on 23 August. Tied to a sledge, he was dragged from Westminster through jeering crowds – and probably watched with indifference by the Scottish magnates assembled in London for the forthcoming Parliament – to the public gallows at Smithfield. There he was hanged, cut down while still alive, emasculated, disembowelled and finally beheaded, his head being stuck on a pole on London Bridge.

The Wallace of history has become so larded with myth and legend that it is hard to distinguish the real man from the folk-hero he has been hyped up to be. This is primarily thanks to sycophantic hagiographers – notably Blind Harry – who, sanctifying him with the halo of martyrdom, have portrayed him as the man who inspired the Scots to throw off the yoke of English domination, and remain defiant to the end. Building on this, Scottish historians have portrayed him as the architect of Scottish independence and the symbol of its nationhood which, thanks to politically inspired propaganda, he continues to be regarded to this day.

Inevitably the facts are more prosaic. Yes, he was a man of undoubted talents and great personal magnetism; brutal as well, but he had to be. His achievements speak for themselves – namely his co-ordinating a (temporarily) successful rebellion, defeating the English in a pitched battle (in co-operation with Moray), ruling the country as a virtual dictator, putting it on a war footing, and forcing a generally hostile nobility to acknowledge his authority. Nor can one deny his work in advocating the cause of Scottish independence at the continental courts, while the increasingly unpopular campaign which he pursued after his return to Scotland was a reflection of his commitment to it. Yet when all is said and done, his achievements were transitory. He failed to secure a Balliol restoration to which he claimed to be committed, and in the end the Scots submitted, albeit reluctantly but simply to put an end to an unendurable and – in the eyes of many – an increasingly pointless struggle.

In late August the Westminster Parliament approved the proposals submitted by the English and Scottish commissioners for the future governance of Scotland. They were enshrined in a series of ordinances issued by Edward for 'the settlement of the *land* of Scotland' (again emphasising its diminished status).[87] Yet he paid the Scots an implied compliment by appointing a member of his family, namely his forty-year-old nephew John of Brittany, as lieutenant in overall charge of the new administration. Under him were the principal officers of state – the chancellor, the chamberlain, and others, while he would be assisted by an advisory council consisting of twenty-two Scottish magnates including the earl of Carrick. Since John of Brittany had to wind up his affairs as seneschal of Gascony before taking up his new appointment, Bishop Lamberton was put in temporary charge of the administration with the title of chief guardian.

Whereas some sheriffs continued to hold office under the new administration, others were dismissed. Sir Matthew Redmayne, the sheriff of Dumfries, was stripped of his office and replaced by Sir Richard Siward who, probably at his own request, was transferred from Fife. Another was Carrick who was relieved of the sheriffships of Ayr and Lanark. This could suggest that, in spite of giving him a say in determining the shape of the new administration, and appointing him a member of the lieutenant's advisory council, Edward had doubts about him[88] – not without reason, as would become apparent. The new administration included the Dumfriesshire landowner Sir Roger Kirkpatrick, head of the Auchencass family, who was appointed joint justiciar of Galloway along with an Englishman, Sir Walter de Burghdon (Edward had ruled that the important office of justiciar could not be held exclusively by Scotsmen).*

Once the new administration was put in place, Edward required every member – the principal officers of state, the justiciars, sheriffs and other officials, including members of the advisory council – to swear a solemn oath. Its terms were comprehensive. They included a promise to give 'good and lawful advice' for the maintenance of the king's peace, to reveal any known hindrances to the 'good government of Scotland', and to advise on how to overcome them. As a member of the advisory council, Carrick would have subscribed to it.

On the whole the new regime involving the participation of Scottish magnates was fair and reasonable, and even enlightened. But because it relied on their full-hearted co-operation in the face of mounting resentment of English domination, it was inherently unstable. Although it could be expected to last for Edward's lifetime, he was now an old man, and once he was gone there was every likelihood of it breaking down under the youthful and inexperienced prince of Wales. Nevertheless Edward must have been heartily thankful to be rid of the troublesome Scots, and the costly and time-consuming digression from his rulership of England, Wales, Ireland and Gascony. Now he could look forward to returning to the international stage where he felt he properly belonged, and embarking on another crusade to the Holy Land to which he had long committed himself.

---

*   *CDS* ii, 1011 Rather than support his feudal lord Robert Bruce, Kirkpatrick remained in allegiance to the English until at least 1313, and it was probably only after Bannockburn that he came into Bruce's peace for the sake of retaining his lands.

FIVE

The Second War of Independence

A FAILED REBELLION

King Edward's confidence in the Scots' acceptance of the new regime proved woefully misplaced. Notwithstanding the inclusion of Scottish magnates in the new administration, there was widespread resentment of English domination, the loss of their independence, and the studiedly diminished status of their realm. Above all the presence of English troops was a constant and visible reminder that theirs was a conquered country. It was a situation that would never last, for sooner or later the Scots were bound to rise in revolt. But who was to lead it? Carrick – or Robert Bruce as he should now be called – had no doubt. He was the man. Therefore, while ostensibly co-operating with Edward, he was secretly gauging the amount of support he could count on from the magnates known to be hostile to the new regime – or aggrieved at being excluded from it – if he were to come out in rebellion.

His principal ally was Bishop Lamberton. While their immediate objective was to regain Scottish independence, their ultimate goals were different. Whereas Bruce was determined to gain the throne, the bishop's main concern was for the independence of the Scottish Church. Because he saw it as under threat so long as the English were in control of Scotland, he took the view that it could only be assured by a successful revolt, and that Bruce was the man to lead it. Therefore he promised Bruce that if he were to come out in rebellion then he, Lamberton, would use his influence as senior bishop to deliver the Church.

Therefore on 1 June 1304, at the very time he was assisting Edward in the siege of Stirling castle, Bruce entered into a pact with the bishop at nearby Cambuskenneth. In terms of this they undertook to consult with each other before attempting any 'arduous business' (a euphemism for revolt).[1] They continued to conspire together, notwithstanding that the one accepted membership of John of Brittany's advisory council, and the other the position of chief guardian. But there was little they could do for the time being, because a revolt was unthinkable so long as Edward was alive. Nevertheless they probably reckoned they had not long to wait, because he was now approaching seventy, in declining health and subject to recurrent bouts of illness.

On the face of it, Lamberton's choice of Bruce as the potential leader of a revolt was surprising. How could someone who was regarded by the Scottish establishment as a traitor, had recently been fighting against them, and who was holding a senior position in an essentially English administration, convincingly pose as a patriot? Still more far-fetched was the idea of someone who was essentially an English aristocrat putting himself forward as a nationalist leader and rallying the people to his cause. Another, apparently insuperable, obstacle was Sir John Comyn. True he was in exile, but he was bound to return sooner or later, in which case his qualifications as a nationalist leader were far superior to Bruce's. Unlike him, Comyn had been unswervingly loyal to the Scottish cause, was head of a family long recognised as the doyen of the Scottish establishment, and commanded wide popular support. Above all, as a nephew of King John he had a better right to the throne.*

The issue came to a head sooner than expected, because Edward in a display of clemency remitted Comyn's already reduced term of exile. Therefore when he returned to Scotland in the summer of 1305, this put Bruce on the spot, for it was essential that he come to an accommodation with him – not easy given their mutual antagonism. Because their negotiations were conducted in private, the only information comes from the highly tendentious accounts of the chroniclers who were not above sacrificing truth in the interests of conforming with the prevailing political climate. Therefore, showing him in a favourable light, Bower claims that Bruce was so moved by 'the shameful subjugation of the country' and 'the cruel and endless harassment of its people' that for their sake he was prepared to allow Comyn the leadership of the revolt and give him his full support. In return, Comyn would assign him all his lands.

Alternatively, Bruce is supposed to have offered Comyn all his lands if he, Comyn, would support him in his bid for the kingship,[2] which Comyn allegedly promised to do. Casting him in the role of a betrayer, Bower alleges that no sooner was their agreement formalised than Comyn showed it to Edward as proof of Bruce's treason. Since this would earn Bruce a traitor's death, and his elimination as a rival, Comyn counted on gaining 'control of all of Scotland', presumably as a puppet king like his uncle, King John.[3] This highly partial and probably fictitious account of what passed between them has earned Comyn the reputation of one of the most traduced characters in Scottish history.

Bower goes on to assert that King Edward planned to have Bruce arrested while attending his court. But tipped off by Edward's son-in-law Ralph de Monthermer, who was a friend of his, Bruce made good his escape and headed back to Scotland having allegedly had the shoes on his horse reversed to mislead his pursuers. As he and his companions approached the border they reportedly encountered a messenger heading in the opposite direction. Apprehending him, they searched him and found he was carrying incriminating letters from Comyn to Edward recommending that he have Bruce consigned to a traitor's death. The messenger was duly beheaded and, as Bower put it, 'God [was] greatly praised for guiding [his] journey in their direction',[4] and no doubt thanked for the chance to kill him.

---

* His mother Alianore Balliol was King John's sister and therefore his right to the throne derived from her grandmother Margaret, eldest daughter of David earl of Huntingdon.

There could be a grain of truth in the story – at least as far as de Monthermer's tip-off is concerned, for, when he was captured fighting for the English at Bannockburn, Bruce ordered his release without ransom. What is certain is that on 10 February 1306 Bruce met Comyn in the Church of the Friars Minor in Dumfries.* According to Sir Thomas Grey, an English knight who wrote his *Scalacronica* while a prisoner in Edinburgh castle in the 1340s, this was at Bruce's behest, although it seems that he never intended that the meeting should take place. Evidently he sent his brothers Thomas and Alexander Bruce to Dalswinton to persuade Comyn to meet him there to settle their differences, the plan being that they should murder him on the way. However the story has it that Comyn gave them such a friendly and hospitable welcome that they could not bring themselves to kill him in cold blood.[5]

If murder was what Bruce had in mind, it must have come as an unpleasant surprise when his brothers returned to Dumfries accompanied by a very-much-alive Comyn. Nevertheless he appears to have invited Comyn to confer with him in private within the sanctuary of the church. Since both Bower and Grey give broadly similar accounts of what transpired, one can only assume that the information came from an eavesdropping friar. In any case the gist of their discussion – or altercation – would have been predictable. Bruce accused Comyn of betraying him by revealing their pact to the king. Comyn is supposed to have replied: 'I shall never be false to my English seigneur [since] I am bound to him by oath and homage', adding that because their pact was treasonable he was duty bound to report it. 'No', exclaimed Bruce, 'I had different hopes of you and your friends. You have betrayed me to the king, you cannot escape my will.' The argument became increasingly acrimonious until Bruce in a fit of rage struck Comyn with his dagger and mortally wounded him.

Tradition has it that when Bruce came staggering out of the church appalled at what he had done, two of his companions – James Lindsay and Roger Kirkpatrick† – caught hold of him and asked him what had happened, to which he allegedly replied: 'I doubt I have slain the Red Comyn'. 'Doubt you not', exclaimed Kirkpatrick, 'I'll mak siccar [make sure]', and dashing into the church he and Lindsay chased away the friars who were tending the wounded Comyn and finished him off with their swords.[6] More likely, Bruce's companions who were waiting outside, hearing the sound of a fracas, dashed inside and hacked him to death there and then.

While no doubt embroidered in the re-telling, Bruce's murder of Comyn within the sanctuary of the Church of the Friars Minor is well attested. Probably unpremeditated, and perpetrated in a fit of rage to which he was prone, it was an appalling – and potentially catastrophic – blunder which bounced him into a rebellion for which he was completely unprepared. That the murder was committed within the sanctuary of a church, and in front of the high altar, was about the worst sacrilege imaginable. Not

---

* Founded by Comyn's grandmother Dervorguilla Balliol it was situated to the north-west of the present-day Vennel.
† Not to be confused with the Sir Roger Kirkpatrick the joint justiciar of Galloway.

only did it earn Bruce widespread condemnation but, more seriously, papal excommunication. Apart from a brief suspension, it remained in force until the last year of his life and would seriously hamper his efforts to establish his kingly authority.

Since Comyn was the most respected and influential magnate in Scotland, leader of its establishment, and head of his family, his murder earned Bruce the lasting enmity of the entire Comyn faction which included much of the nobility. Although they and their allies made a show of reconciliation with Bruce following the triumph of Bannockburn, these potential fifth columnists continued to dog him throughout much of his reign. Worse still, Bruce found himself pitted against King Edward whose formidable remaining energies were concentrated on a single-minded determination to have him hunted down, brought to justice and consigned to a traitor's death. A more unpromising start to his rebellion can hardly be imagined, and few would have given a thought for his chances of success.

Leaving Comyn's still warm corpse to be tended by the friars who had ventured back into the church, Bruce and his companions headed for Dumfries castle and demanded its surrender. The custodian Sir Richard Giraud was prepared to do so, but the more stout-hearted king's justices who were holding a court in the great hall refused and barricaded the doors. However, threats to burn down the building while they were inside was enough to flush them out, when they gave themselves up and were allowed to return to England.[7]

Having burnt his boats Bruce had to move fast in order to strengthen his position as best he could before the English could mobilise their forces. Therefore his immediate aim was to capture the castles in the south-west and put them out of commission. Accordingly he and his supporters took Caerlaverock, followed by Lochmaben, Dalswinton, Tibbers and finally Ayr. Because he lacked the men to garrison them, all he could do was foul the wells to render the castles uninhabitable, demolish their fortifications (not difficult since they consisted of wood, earth and stones), carry off what provisions they could, and destroy the rest. The one exception was Bruce's own fortress of Loch Doon which was situated on an island in the loch. Rather than slight it, he entrusted the keepership to his brother-in-law and close friend Christopher Seton.

Moving on to Glasgow, he was joined by Bishop Wishart. Since Comyn's murder was perpetrated in his diocese, the bishop should properly have excommunicated Bruce on the spot. Instead, contumaciously defying the Church, this doughty old prelate not only granted him absolution but exhorted his flock to turn out and fight for him as if taking part in a crusade.[8] Thereafter he and Bruce embarked on a recruiting drive throughout the west.[9] Meanwhile Sir Simon Fraser, who had been serving with the English since his return from exile, defected to him and embarked on another recruiting drive in southern Scotland.

Bruce's initial success owed much to the delayed arrival of John of Brittany, and even more to the slowness of the guardians, abetted by Lamberton, in reacting to the situation, for it took nearly a fortnight for news of Comyn's murder and Bruce's revolt to reach King Edward. One can imagine his shock, anger and disbelief on hearing that Bruce, to whom he had been so accommodating, had trusted (up to a point), and may even have liked, had so flagrantly betrayed him. Worse still, that he had compounded the treason with the ultimate sacrilege of murdering Comyn within the sanctuary of a church – a particularly heinous crime in the eyes of someone of Edward's strongly held religious beliefs.

Nevertheless he was quick to respond. Bruce's English lands were declared forfeit, and similarly his Carrick earldom and the lordship of Annandale including Lochmaben castle. Whereas the earldom was given to Sir Henry Percy, Annandale was granted to Edward's son-in-law and daughter, the earl and countess of Hereford.[10] But apart from Comyn's murder and Bruce's revolt, Edward had no clear idea of what was happening in Scotland. This was because his commanders on the spot were equally unclear as to the turn of events and were unable to keep him informed. Therefore all he could do was issue them with a general instruction to strengthen the English position there. At the same time he caused Bishop Halton of Carlisle to pronounce sentence of excommunication on Bruce, while successfully petitioning the Pope to issue a bull confirming it.[11]

In late March, in an act of monumental bravado, Bruce had himself crowned king. The ceremony took place on the Moot Hill at Scone, where Scottish kings were traditionally enthroned, on Lady Day (25 March) 1306. The date was significant because it marked the start of a new year and was therefore deliberately chosen to imply a new beginning in the annals of Scottish history. Since the Scottish regalia and other symbols of kingship had been removed to London and only makeshift substitutes were available, it must have been a pretty shoddy affair. The robes and vestments supplied by Bishop Wishart would have had a very second-hand look, while the banner displaying the arms of Alexander III, which had been stowed away in the episcopal wardrobe for the past twenty years, was probably riddled with moth holes. Furthermore only a handful of earls and bishops attended.

Nevertheless the ceremony was so staged as to endow Bruce's arrogation of the kingship with a veneer of legitimacy, and to disguise the fact that he was a usurper. Moreover a usurper faced with the seemingly impossible task of driving the English out of the realm, recovering its independence, and establishing an unchallenged right to the kingship. Nevertheless, staging an inauguration such as this was a shrewd move politically since it was designed to project himself as a rallying point for disaffected Scots. Two days later, on Palm Sunday, Bishop Lamberton celebrated pontifical High Mass in the nearby Augustinian abbey. But hardly had the final blessing been pronounced than Bruce hurried off to take advantage of John of Brittany's continuing absence, and the English inaction, to subdue the region beyond the Tay.

By this time Edward, now fully abreast of the situation, was preparing for another invasion to restore the English position in Scotland. Meanwhile he ordered de Valence and Percy to hunt down Bruce and his supporters and bring them to justice. And so ferociously determined was he to leave nothing to chance that he instructed them to 'byrn and slay and raise [the] dragon'.[12] Harking back to the Welsh wars, raising the dragon standard symbolised that no quarter was to be given, all conventions of warfare disregarded, and captured knights were to be summarily executed without the option of ransom. This was deliberately intended to deter high ranking Scotsmen from joining Bruce.

Setting out from Carlisle and advancing up Nithsdale towards Ayr, Percy re-took the castles slighted by Bruce, and captured his stronghold of Loch Doon. Betrayed by the garrison, the keeper Christopher Seton was taken prisoner and consigned to a traitor's death in Dumfries.* At the same time de Valence set out from Berwick. Advancing rapidly through Lothian, where he was joined by a number of Comyn-supporting knights and their retinues, he crossed over to Fife. Continuing his pursuit of the two bishops, Lamberton and Wishart, he finally caught up with them at Scotlandwell and took them prisoner.

During this time Bruce was busy subduing the region beyond the Firth of Tay, and having mustered a 1,500-strong army he was laying siege to the castle at Aberdeen. But hearing that de Valence had crossed the Forth and was heading in his direction he broke off the siege and advanced to meet him. Battle was joined at Methven near Perth on 19 June when de Valence's army made a surprise attack on Bruce's men. In the ensuing fray the latter were put to flight, many being taken prisoner. Those willing to come into Edward's allegiance were spared, while the more intransigent were executed with varying degrees of cruelty. Among the former was Bruce's nephew Thomas Randolph. Initially reluctant to abandon his uncle, he was spared execution at de Valence's intercession, although Edward ordered him to be detained in prison.[13] Clearly his fate hung in the balance, but in the end he was released against his under-taking to fight for the English.

Meanwhile Edward was preparing for an invasion on two fronts. While he himself would lead an army up eastern Scotland, another would advance up the western route under the prince of Wales. But at that point he fell ill again. Therefore it was arranged that the prince should conduct a single invasion up the western route. Setting out from Carlisle on 8 July he advanced up Annandale, and on the 11th he received the unconditional surrender of the Lochmaben garrison who had been holding out against the new owners, the earl and countess of Hereford. Anticipating a possible local rebellion, the prince set about improving the castle's defences,[14] and on his father's orders he ensured that Dumfries, Caerlaverock and Tibbers castles were fully garrisoned.[15]

Meanwhile, having escaped from Methven, Bruce returned through the moun-tains of Atholl to Aberdeen accompanied by the tattered remnants of his army. But

---

* Many years later his widow, Christina Bruce, founded a chapel on the spot where he was put to death, while Bruce himself earmarked an annuity of five pounds from the rents of Caerlaverock for masses to be said for his soul (*RRS* v, 266). The chapel was demolished in 1715 to provide material for strengthening the defences of Dumfries against a possible Jacobite attack.

it was no safe haven. Any illusions he may have had were rudely shattered when news reached him of the approach of de Valence's army. Since his force, now reduced to some 500 men, was no match against de Valence's well-equipped cavalry and footsoldiers, flight was the only answer. Because the prince's army, now at Perth, cut him off from the south, while the hostile earl of Ross controlled the territory to the north, his only course was to head south-west for Argyllshire. There he could count on the support of the Campbells and MacDonalds. Nevertheless it was fraught with danger because it meant passing through hostile MacDougall territory. This soon became apparent. On 11 August, while making their way through Strathfillan, Bruce and his men were attacked by a force of Highlanders under Alexander MacDougall's son, John of Lorne, at Dail Righ.[*] Outnumbering Bruce's men by some two to one, the Highlanders charged them down cutting them to pieces and putting the survivors to flight.

With a force reduced to a mere 200 men Bruce was in dire straits. Since most of Argyllshire was denied him, his only course was to head south to the friendly territory of Lennox, which was under the control of his supporter Earl Malcolm, and from there to MacDonald-controlled Kintyre. But rather than expose the ladies in his company to further danger, he sent them back across the mountains to Kildrummy castle in Strathdon escorted by his brother Neil and others. The ladies included Bruce's wife Elizabeth, his nine-year-old daughter Marjorie, his sister Mary, and the countess of Buchan, who had officiated at his inauguration.[†] Since the castle was fully provisioned and well-nigh impregnable, Bruce must have assumed they would be safe there until he was in a position to rescue them.

Soon after the royal party's arrival at Kildrummy word came of the approach of the prince's army. Concerned for their safety, Neil Bruce sent the ladies north accompanied by the earl of Atholl, probably intending to take ship for Orkney. As Orkney was part of Norway, where Bruce's sister was queen, it was doubtless assumed that they would find a safe haven there. Reaching Tain they sought temporary sanctuary in the church of St Duthac. On hearing this, the earl of Ross ordered his retainers to capture them. Forcing their way into the church and violating its sanctuary, they seized the refugees. On Edward's orders the men were hanged,[‡] while Bruce's wife and daughter were consigned to separate nunneries in Yorkshire. Mary Bruce and the countess of Buchan, on the other hand, were confined to latticed cages, the one suspended inside the walls of Berwick castle and the other at Roxburgh.

---

[*]   Situated between the modern townships of Crianlarich and Tyndrum where a small memorial stone marks the site of the battle.

[†]   As representative of the earls of Fife who traditionally had the right to place the crown on the king's head, she volunteered to perform the office for Bruce of whom she was reputedly a mistress.

[‡]   They included the earl of Atholl. When he begged for mercy on account of his royal blood (he was an illegitimate descendant of the English King John), Edward with grim humour ordered him to be hanged from higher gallows than the others as a mark of his superior status.

Reaching Kildrummy, the prince brought up his siege engines and proceeded to bombard the castle. After a week of constant and fruitless pounding, the English stooped to treachery. Promised a pardon, the garrison blacksmith was prevailed on to set fire to the castle by torching the grain supply which was stored in the great hall. As the fire took hold the defenders were forced out on to the battlements leaving them with no alternative but to surrender. While most were summarily executed, Neil Bruce and his fellow magnates were taken to Carlisle. There they were hanged, disembowelled and beheaded, Neil being the first of Bruce's brothers to die in his cause.

Meanwhile Bruce managed to win through to the stronghold of Dunaverty on the Mull of Kintyre. But fearing treachery, he remained there for only a few days before taking ship for the island of Rathlin off the coast of Ireland. Since he dared not set foot in Ireland for fear of being captured by Edward's supporters, notably his father-in-law the earl of Ulster, he moved on to the Inner Hebrides where he remained for the next few months. His position could hardly have been worse. Driven out of the country he aspired to rule, and an outlaw with a price on his head, he was under constant threat of capture and the certainty of a traitor's death.

BRUCE AT BAY

Bruce spent the winter of 1306–7 as a refugee among the friendly MacRuarie clansmen in the Inner Hebrides, and assisted by their leaders he embarked on a recruiting drive throughout the Western Isles. His aim was to raise a large enough force to achieve a landing on the mainland and establish a bridgehead from which to renew his campaign. This took time, and therefore it was not until the following year that he felt in a strong enough position to justify the attempt.

During the previous summer Edward, increasingly prone to bouts of illness, had slowly made his way northwards. Reaching Carlisle in late September, he decided to spend the winter at Lanercost priory where he remained until the following March, directing operations as best he could from his sickbed. Unable to take the field in person, he issued a stream of increasingly peremptory orders to his commanders to round up all known Bruce supporters, demanding that they keep him fully informed of their progress. To his intense frustration, evident from the tone of his letters, they failed to do so because they themselves had no clear idea of what was happening, still less where Bruce had gone to ground.

Meanwhile Edward instituted a pogrom against all Bruce supporters. While prepared to be lenient to those who had been coerced into abandoning their allegiance to him and wished to return to his peace, he ordered that the more obdurate be subject to what would now be called 'citizens' arrest'. This meant that, whenever recognised by a member of the public, they were to be apprehended or reported to the authorities when they were liable to be thrown into prison or summarily hanged. The pogrom lasted throughout the winter until March when, under pressure from the papal legate, Edward ordered de Valence to proclaim a general amnesty.[16] At the same time his principal supporters were rewarded with grants of forfeited lands. In Dumfriesshire, notwithstanding that he was fighting for the English, Thomas Randolph's barony of Morton was given to Sir William Latimer, the captain-general of the northern counties.

By January Bruce had mustered a large enough force to attempt a landing on the coast of his native Carrick. Anticipating this, Edward ordered Sir John Menteith to have his fleet of galleys, supplemented by others from Ireland, patrol the outer reaches of the Firth of Clyde between Kintyre, where Bruce was thought to be lurking, and the mainland. Edward was right; Bruce was indeed in northern Kintyre. But hoping to avoid an encounter with Sir John Menteith's galleys, he decided to make the short crossing to Arran intending to use it as a base from which to attempt a landing on the Carrick coast. Therefore he sent part of his force ahead – allegedly under Robert Boyd and James Douglas[*] – to take possession of the island.

At the same time he sent a contingent south under his brothers Thomas and Alexander Bruce to make a diversionary raid on the Wigtownshire coast. Sailing into Loch Ryan they made an unopposed landing. But when they encountered a hastily mustered force under Dungal Macdouall, the leading local magnate, they were routed and most of them taken prisoner. They included the Bruce brothers, both of whom were badly wounded in the fray. Taken to Carlisle, they were tied to a horse's tail and dragged through the city streets to the gallows where they were hanged and beheaded, their heads being impaled on the city gates.[17]

The main expedition fared better. Having allegedly taken possession of Brodick castle by a ruse, and captured a number of vessels bringing supplies of arms and equipment to the garrison, Boyd and his fellow leaders sent word to Bruce that he could safely follow with the rest of his force. So far so good, but many hazards lay ahead. Although Arran is only some fifteen miles from the Carrick coast, the presence of Menteith's galleys rendered the crossing extremely perilous, while attempting a landing was doubly so because Percy had established his local headquarters at nearby Turnberry castle.

Worse still, Bruce's plan miscarried. A local man named Cuthbert is reputed to have been sent ahead to gauge the amount of support for him locally and find out whether the people would rally to him in the event of his making a successful landing. The arrangement was that, if he thought there was enough support to justify the attempt, Cuthbert would light a beacon at a pre-arranged time on Turnberry Head. The bonfire was duly lit and Bruce's flotilla set sail. But on landing he was met by a frantic Cuthbert who told him that the people were so terrified of the English that

---

[*] Son of Sir William Douglas, former keeper of Berwick, the part Barbour assigns him in this exploit is fictitious, for at that time James Douglas was in Edward's allegiance hoping – in vain as it proved – to recover the family lands in Douglasdale which had been forfeited by his father. It was not until after Bruce's success at Loudoun Hill that Douglas decided to throw in his lot with him.

no-one would dare turn out for him, that somebody else had lit the fire and he had been unable to put it out for fear of discovery.*

There was no going back. Instead, with characteristic boldness Bruce ordered his men to make a night attack on the troops encamped in the vicinity of Turnberry castle whom they slaughtered almost to a man. Hearing the victims' screams, and assuming they were being attacked by a much larger force, the garrison cowered within the safety of the castle walls. But on sallying forth at daybreak they found the place strewn with corpses, Bruce and his men having escaped with a large haul of booty to the fastnesses of southern Carrick. It was to be the start of a long and perilous journey, and the story of how from this modest beginning, itself no mean feat, Bruce managed to gain possession of the realm, and obtain universal recognition of his king-ship, must surely rank as one of the most remarkable achievements of all time.

Meanwhile the outlook could hardly have been more unpromising. Indeed the best Bruce could hope for was simply to stay alive until the old king's death. Still at Lanercost, Edward ordered de Valence to establish a cordon in order to corral Bruce in Carrick, while Percy was instructed to deploy his army throughout the region to flush him out. To prevent him from escaping by sea, he ordered as many vessels as possible to be raised from the Cumbrian ports and sent fully manned to join Menteith's fleet in the Firth of Clyde.[18] At the same time levies were raised from Cumberland and Westmorland to supplement Clifford's force in Nithsdale to help him complete the cordon on the east.[19]

In early March Edward left Lanercost, and progressing by slow stages he finally reached Carlisle. There he held a Parliament which was attended by 'a very great number of people and clergy',[20] including the papal legate. One can well imagine their shock at the sight of this bent and emaciated wreck of a once magnificent king as, supported by attendants, he slowly shuffled his way to the throne. At his bidding the papal legate pronounced Comyn's murderers 'excommunicate, anathematised and sacrilegious [and] expelled them from the Holy Church until they should make full atonement'. Turning to the situation in Scotland, and advised that there was strong support for Bruce in the north-east, the Parliament endorsed Edward's instruction to the chamberlain, John de Sandale, to ensure that all the castles in the region were fully garrisoned and put in a proper state of repair.[21]

Because it took time to assemble the cordon, Bruce grasped the opportunity to slip south into Galloway where he spent much of February plundering the region and black-mailing the people as a means of raising money to pay his troops. He extended his campaign into Nithsdale, but when he encountered Clifford's force supplemented by the Cumbrian levies he was forced to withdraw. Taking the offensive, Clifford left Sir John de Botetourt (recently Bruce's comrade-in-arms) to guard Nithsdale[22] while he himself advanced through Galloway, forcing Bruce and his men into de Valence's cordon.

---

* Barbour, *Bruce* (Douglas), 131–3. So the story goes, but it must be stressed that while Barbour's hagiography may bear some approximation to the truth it cannot be taken as gospel.

Hemmed in on all sides, they were confined to the upland country of southern Carrick where they concealed themselves as best they could among the birch and pine forest from the troops deployed to hunt them down. Finally, in their desperation to run him to earth, the troops resorted to using bloodhounds and – on Barbour's say-so – treachery.

In mid-April Bruce and his men were lurking in Glentrool, a long narrow valley which penetrates from the upper Cree valley into the Galloway hinterland. Learning of this, de Valence sent a force to capture him; but, according to Barbour, Bruce and his men beat it off with heavy losses.* This may be an exaggeration, although a skirmish did take place there in May 1307. As a result the English were driven back towards the Cree, thus enabling Bruce and his men to break out into Ayrshire. Ten days later he scored a more significant victory. Through a combination of skilful use of ground and the laying of booby traps, known as 'calthrops',† he defeated a 3,000-strong English army (outnumbering his by some five to one) under de Valence at Loudoun Hill. Success breeds success, and recruits flocked to join him, including James Douglas, who would become one of his principal lieutenants. Similarly there was growing support for him in the north-east where many were ready to turn out for him once he was able to reach them.

Meanwhile, frustrated beyond endurance by his commanders' inability to capture Bruce, Edward was planning another invasion. Summonses were issued to the northern magnates to muster with their levies at Carlisle by late June. On 3 July, determined to lead the army in person, the dying king had himself raised from his sickbed; and, hoisted on to a horse, he set out on what would be his last journey. As ever, he was accompanied by a large retinue which included his grandson the earl of Gloucester,‡ one of the richest and most powerful magnates in the realm. No longer able to ride unaided, the king had to be supported by an esquire on either side, and even then he could only manage a short distance at a time. Therefore his army barely covered two miles a day as it wended its way towards the Solway fords. On the third day he was forced to rest. However on 6 July, indomitable to the last, the king struggled on as far as Burgh-by-Sands on the lower reaches of the Eden. But the effort was too much. The next day he died, probably of a heart attack, within sight of the Scottish hills where Bruce lurked unconquered and still a free man.

Since he had become something of a legend in his own lifetime, it was inevitable that his reputation should be further enhanced after his death, and the chronicler Froissart gives it colourful embellishment. On his say-so, Edward refused to allow even his death to deny him victory over the Scots. Therefore he ordered that his corpse be boiled in a cauldron until the flesh had fallen from the bones. These were to be carried at the head of the army, and only when the Scots were finally subdued were they to be given a ceremonial burial.

---

* His success is commemorated by the Bruce Stone which is situated on a rocky eminence overlooking the Buchan burn near its outflow at the eastern end of Loch Trool.
† These were pits some two feet deep, each containing a sharpened stake embedded in the ground. Concealed under a covering of grass, they were designed to maim both men and horses.
‡ Son of his daughter Joan of Acre, who had died earlier in the year.

News of his death was hushed up until the arrival of the prince of Wales for fear that if it leaked out it would encourage more Scots to defect to Bruce. Even the chancery colluded in the deception by continuing to issue writs in his name.[23] In spite of the old king's efforts to enhance his prestige as the future king, the pleasure-loving twenty-three-year-old prince, now Edward II, was a grave disappointment to him. Physically a big, strong man, nearly as tall as his father, he was an intrepid horseman and described as having 'some share of chivalrous qualities'.[24] But that was all. Lacking his father's authority, his compelling personality and his terrifying presence, he was incapable of commanding the same respect. To make matters worse, he was a very poor judge of character and unable to recognise good advice when given. Nowhere were these failings more apparent than in his choice of favourites to whom he virtually surrendered his ruling powers with ultimately fatal consequences. Nor did he share his father's overwhelming determination to subdue the Scots, although that would come later.

Meanwhile his efforts to pursue his father's campaign seem to have been decidedly half-hearted. For the rest of July the army remained on standby, because it was not until the end of the month that Edward finally set out from Carlisle. Reaching Dumfries on 3 August, he remained there taking oaths of fealty from the Scottish magnates before heading north. Setting out on the 12th he made a brief stopover at Sanquhar, and on the 19th he reached Cumnock where he based himself on the earl of March's castle. He remained there for a week while scouts were deployed to track down Bruce and his men. When they reported that Bruce was believed to be lurking in the south-west, Edward ordered a withdrawal. By 30 August he was at Tinwald where he confirmed de Valence's appointment as guardian and ordered him to hold the line of Clydesdale to prevent Bruce from breaking out to the north. But no sooner had he done so than he sent de Valence to France to negotiate his marriage to King Philip's daughter Isabella, having relieved him of his command and the guardianship. This coincided with the long delayed arrival of John of Brittany, now earl of Richmond following his father's recent death.[25]

The scouts had reported correctly. Bruce was indeed in the south-west conducting another plundering campaign in Galloway. Edward immediately ordered the earl of Richmond and the other commanders to assemble their forces in the south-west preparatory to running him to ground. This played straight into Bruce's hands. His campaign in Galloway was essentially a feint which was designed to cause the English to do just that – namely to draw their forces away from Ayrshire and Lanarkshire. This enabled him to give them the slip, and because the line of Clydesdale had been left unguarded he was at last able to break out to the north.

THE TIDE TURNS

Bruce could at last plan a coherent strategy. Therefore, while James Douglas was sent to harry the Border country and incite the people to rebel, Bruce's immediate objective was to capture the Comyn stronghold of Inverlochy at the western end of the Great Glen. This was to be a combined operation. While he would assault the castle by land, a naval force under his ally Angus Og MacDonald would attack it from the sea. Meanwhile, to prevent the Comyn-supporting John of Lorne from coming to the rescue,* Bruce forced him to agree a truce by threatening to attack his family stronghold of Dunstaffnage. Justifying this in a long and highly tendentious letter to King Edward, John of Lorne claimed that he had been confronted by a greatly superior force under Bruce. Yet it was Bruce who had asked for the truce 'which', as he went on to say, 'I granted [him] until you send me help'.[26] (He must have been pretty stupid to imagine the king swallowing such a yarn!) Having neutralised him Bruce was free to invest Inverlochy, and within a month the garrison had surrendered and the castle was demolished.

Advancing up the Great Glen and capturing the other main stronghold of Urquhart, which he put out of commission, Bruce and his army reached Inverness where they were joined by the bishop of Moray and his tenants. Having forced the castle garrison to surrender by cutting off their water supply, the combined army moved on to Nairn. Here they set fire to the castle and flushed out the garrison forcing them to surrender. These successes were enough to persuade the earl of Ross to ask for a truce, which Bruce granted him on condition that he gave up his two younger sons as hostages. This meant he could embark on his campaign to crush the earl of Buchan's power-base in the north-east without fear of attack from the rear.

Meanwhile the beleaguered English supporters in the north sent frantic pleas to the earl of Richmond for help. But they never reached him, because the messengers were routinely intercepted and killed. Consequently neither he nor his commanders were aware of the extent of Bruce's success. Nor was King Edward particularly concerned about the situation in Scotland since he was preoccupied with mounting baronial opposition at home. When in April 1308 a report finally got through to Richmond it was too late, for by that time Bruce was in virtual control of the north-east having triumphed over the earl of Buchan.

As one of the most powerful magnates in the realm Buchan posed a major threat to Bruce, and because there was no question of coming to an accommodation with him, this was to be a fight to the finish. It proved a hard-fought campaign, the more so because Bruce fell seriously ill, probably through a combination of rough living and stress. Meanwhile, joined by David earl of Atholl† and Sir John de Moubray, Buchan went on the offensive. He tried to persuade the earl of Ross to join him; but, knowing that Bruce would have no compunction in putting his sons to death if he did, he declined. On the other hand the last-minute arrival of a force under his nephew Sir David de Brechin was enough to give him the edge over Bruce.

Or so he may have thought. However, when battle was joined at Oldmeldrum Buchan suffered an overwhelming defeat and was forced to flee south. Building on his success, and to consolidate his authority over the north-east, Bruce embarked

---

*   Predictably because he was half a Comyn, his mother being a sister of the elder John Comyn.
†   Whereas his father Earl John was a Bruce supporter and had been hanged following his capture at Tain, Earl David defected to the English following his capture at Methven.

on a campaign of terror which involved the systematic destruction of every vestige of Comyn power and influence in the region. The task was assigned to his ruthlessly aggressive brother Edward Bruce. Setting about it with a will, he and his men captured and demolished every stronghold, killing the occupants out of hand regardless of age or sex. The slaughter extended far and wide as people were killed indiscriminately and without mercy, their homesteads destroyed, grain stores burnt, and their livestock driven off. Known as the 'herschip [harrying] of Buchan', the scale of the devastation was such that it is said to have remained seared in people's memories for more than fifty years afterwards.[27]

Having destroyed the Comyn power in the north-east, Bruce should logically have turned on the MacDougalls. But because his truce with John of Lorne was still in force, he sent part of his army under his brother Edward, assisted by Robert Boyd and Alexander Lindsay,[28] to subdue Galloway. Grasping the opportunity to avenge his brothers' deaths, Edward Bruce set about the task with characteristic energy and brutality. Descending on western Galloway, he and his men terrorised the people, inflicting savage cruelties on them, and devastated the region as comprehensively as his father had done in 1286–7. According to the Lanercost chronicle they blackmailed the landowners into paying them protection, then no sooner had they done so than they were put to death.[29]

Crossing the Cree, Edward Bruce and his men encountered a local force under Sir Dungal Macdouall* at Kirroughtree, where a skirmish took place. Putting Macdouall and his men to flight, they continued their campaign of destruction as far as 'the fords of Dee'. Here they encountered a much larger combined English and Gallovidian force under the warden Sir Ingelram de Umfraville. In the ensuing battle the English-Gallovidian force was routed and a number of local chiefs killed.[30] Heading southwards towards the Solway coast, leaving a trail of devastation behind them, Edward Bruce and his men took possession of the MacCan stronghold on Hestan island adjacent to the Urr estuary.[31] Logically, his next step would have been to lay siege to the Balliol stronghold of Buittle, now in English hands. But at that point he was summoned north by his brother to take part in his campaign against the MacDougalls, the truce with John of Lorne having expired. At the same time James Douglas was ordered to break off his harrying of the Border country to take part in the campaign.

It began in late July 1308. Correctly anticipating that John of Lorne and his clansmen would attempt to ambush his army while it made its way through the Pass of Brander, Bruce sent a force under James Douglas up the slopes of Cruachan to attack them from the rear. Catching them by surprise, Douglas and his men forced the clansmen down into the pass where the main army drove them back to the river Awe where many were drowned while the rest took flight. Pursuing them down the shores of Loch Etive, Bruce and his army laid siege to the MacDougal stronghold of

---

*   He had been knighted as a reward for his defeat and capture of Thomas and Alexander Bruce, and others, the previous year.

Dunstaffnage. When it fell, John of Lorne's aged father Alexander of Argyll was taken prisoner, John himself having made off in a galley down Loch Awe from where he escaped to England. To reinforce his success, Bruce embarked on a two-month campaign of terror similar to 'the herschip of Buchan' in order to stamp out all remaining opposition in the region and bring it fully under control.

Meanwhile James Douglas returned south to continue his harrying of the Border country. His route took him down the Lyne Water, a tributary of the Tweed, where he encountered a contingent of hostile Scots under Bruce's nephew, Thomas Randolph, and others. In the ensuing skirmish Randolph was captured and dispatched in chains to Bruce. Brought before his uncle, he defiantly rebuked him for stooping to guerrilla tactics, claiming that it was unbecoming of an aristocrat – an aspersion on his successes which so infuriated Bruce that he ordered Randolph to be kept in detention until he had purged his contempt and was prepared to make a formal submission.[32] An inauspicious start to their outstandingly successful partnership when Randolph became his uncle's principal lieutenant and right-hand man.

By October Bruce had gained possession of the earldom of Menteith, and the same month the earl of Ross submitted. He was followed by other Scottish magnates, including Sir John Menteith, and in March 1309 even the cautious old Steward felt he could safely declare for him. Consequently Bruce was now in control of virtually the whole of Scotland beyond the Forth and Clyde. Since he needed to set up an interim government to administer it, he summoned a Parliament. At his dictation it confirmed his right to the kingship and declared John Balliol a usurper. But being an unrepresentative body, with the Balliol/Comyn faction still commanding widespread support throughout the realm, its decree carried little weight.

Meanwhile the English, who were present in strength in southern Scotland, particularly the south-east, continued to pose a threat to Bruce. However, relief came when King Edward, pressed by his father-in-law King Philip, and distracted by his conflict with a fractious nobility, offered him a temporary truce. Grasping the opportunity to reinforce his authority over his newly won territories and stamp out all further resistance, undistracted by war, Bruce agreed. Not that he had the slightest intention of honouring the truce; nor did Edward who used the respite to strengthen the English position in Scotland. In July his intention became clear when he issued summonses for an invasion to take place on 1 November when the truce was due to expire. Meanwhile, to guard against a possible Scottish invasion of the west marches, Edward ordered the northern barons to summon their levies in readiness to defend them.[33]

In the event, baronial opposition forced Edward to postpone his invasion until the following September, and even then some of their leaders refused to take part. When it finally took place it proved inconclusive. Advancing by way of the Tweed and the Clyde, he and his army reached Renfrew where he expected to be joined by reinforcements from Ireland. But because they failed to arrive he had no alternative but to withdraw. Constantly harassed by Bruce supporters, Edward and his army fell back on Berwick where he remained for the winter determined to renew the campaign the following year. Meanwhile he instituted some changes among his commanders: for example, Sir John de Segrave, the former guardian of English-occupied Scotland, was appointed warden of Dumfries and Annandale. His subordinate commanders included Sir Ingelram de Umfraville, who was given the keepership of Caerlaverock, and Sir Dungal Macdouall the custodianship of Dumfries castle, while John Comyn (son of the murdered Comyn) was put in charge of his family's stronghold of Dalswinton.

Edward's plans to launch another invasion in 1311 were thwarted by Parliament's refusal to finance it. This left him with no alternative but to return south. Seizing the opportunity, Bruce went on the offensive. In August his troops descended on Annandale, and driving the English out of the region they poured across the border into Cumberland terrorising the people into buying truces to finance his war effort. The following month it was the turn of the people of Tynedale, and two months later Bruce and his men were attacking the English garrisons in south-east Scotland.

By the following year Bruce was in a strong enough position to attempt the capture of the remaining English-held castles before driving the English out of Scotland altogether. Starting with those in the north, Dundee fell in April, and by November Bruce was laying siege to Perth. This was finally taken by the sort of ruse at which he had become adept. After a six-week siege in the course of which the garrison beat off all attempts to take the castle, Bruce and his men made a show of abandoning it. Lulled into complacency, the garrison relaxed their guard. Then one moonless night in January 1313 Bruce and his men returned, and wading the moat they scaled the walls with the aid of rope ladders hooked on to the battlements. Catching the garrison by surprise they slaughtered them to a man, and by morning they were in possession of the castle.

Meanwhile Edward Bruce was given the task of capturing those in the south-west. His immediate objective was Dumfries. In May 1312, anticipating a possible siege, King Edward ordered the bailiffs of Wark and Sowerby to contribute to the cost of improving its defences, and in early June, in response to a complaint by Sir Dungal Macdouall that his stores were running low, they were replenished.[34] This enabled the garrison to hold out for a further nine months, for it was not until February 1313 that the castle finally fell, and only then because Bruce came to his brother's assistance. Following its capture he ordered it to be demolished,[35] and by the end of March he had gained possession of Buittle, Dalswinton and Tibbers.[36] Meanwhile Lochmaben remained in English hands until at least October when there is a record of wages being paid to the garrison by King Edward's receiver at Carlisle.* This left Caerlaverock, which held out until the following year when Sir Eustace Maxwell switched his allegiance to Bruce.[37]

---

*   *CDS* iii, 336 The garrison included a number of Annandale tenants – Sir Roger Kirkpatrick, Sir William Heriz, Sir Thomas de Torthorwald, Alan de Dunwidie, Walter de Bosco and Henry de Carlyle.

In February 1313, following the capture of Dumfries, Bruce ordered his brother Edward to lay siege to Stirling castle. Since it controlled much of central Scotland, as well as holding the key to the north, its capture was vital. On 23 June, with the garrison facing starvation, the keeper Sir Philip de Moubray presented Edward Bruce with an ingenious proposal. Namely, that if he were to abandon the siege and permit the castle to be re-supplied then he, de Moubray, would confine the garrison to it and allow free access to all comers across Stirling bridge. Further, that unless an English army relieved the castle within a year and a day he would surrender it – a crafty plan to which the unsuspecting Edward Bruce, impatient at being tied down to a lengthy siege, agreed.

When he reported it to his brother naïvely thinking he had scored a bloodless success, Barbour quotes the latter as saying that it was 'unwisely done'. A classic understatement, because Bruce must have been absolutely livid with Edward for allowing himself to be taken in by such a ruse. His strategy for recovering Scotland piecemeal by recapturing the English-held castles without being drawn into a pitched battle was proving extremely successful. Now his brother's ill-judged action would force Edward to bring a large army to Scotland to relieve the castle. In which case, he would be compelled to give battle with the virtual certainty of a crushing defeat and the extinction of all hope of regaining Scottish independence under his kingship.*

In August 1313 a contingent of Scotsmen captured Linlithgow castle, a key strong-point on the road between Edinburgh and Stirling. Barbour gives a colourful, if probably apocryphal, account of how this was achieved. On his say-so, the Scots enlisted the help of a local farmer who was contracted to supply hay for the garrison horses. It was arranged that the attack should take place when the garrison were out on patrol. Therefore, at the appointed time eight armed men concealed themselves in a cartload of hay. Then, just as the sentries were opening the gates to allow it into the castle, they leapt out and killed them. Before the alarm could be raised the rest of the force, who had concealed themselves nearby, dashed out of their hiding-place, stormed the castle and took possession of it.[38]

In February 1314 Douglas captured the key Border stronghold of Roxburgh. Here again Barbour comes up with an unlikely story of how on a pitch dark night Douglas and his men covered themselves with black cloaks, and pretending to be cattle they affected to graze their way up to the castle. With the aid of long spears they hoisted rope ladders equipped with hooks up to the battlements. Having secured them, they scaled the walls and gained access to the castle. Catching the garrison by surprise as they were indulging in a pre-Lenten feast, Douglas and his men slaughtered them almost to a man.[39]

The following month Thomas Randolph, now earl of Moray, laid siege to the virtu-ally impregnable Edinburgh castle. Here Barbour's account sounds more plausible.

---

* Yet in spite of this Bruce created Edward earl of Carrick, having already given him the lordship of Galloway. He is first described as lord of Galloway in a charter dated 12 April 1312 (*RRS* v, no 20), and was created earl of Carrick sometime between that date and 21 October 1313 (*RRS* v, no 35).

Now fully converted to Bruce's unconventional methods of warfare, Moray chose a suitably dark night to make the attempt. Having ordered his troops to station themselves at the main gate at the top of the present-day Royal Mile, he and a band of some thirty men climbed the castle rock with the aid of specially constructed long ladders. Just as they gained the parapet the alarm was raised and the garrison rushed to repel them. After a short but bloody fight, Moray and his storming party overcame them. Then dashing to the main gate they unlocked it, whereupon the troops came swarming in and took possession of the castle.⁴⁰

Bruce's fears regarding his brother's pact with Sir Philip de Moubray proved abundantly justified, because it was responsible for Edward's invasion of 1314. Since Parliament refused to vote him the necessary funds, he was forced to rely on his Italian bankers and other sources to finance it. It was a desperate gamble, and leaving nothing to chance Edward mustered the largest army ever to have invaded Scotland. Consisting of some 18,000 footsoldiers including 5,000 Welshmen and 2,500 armoured knights, it was said that if the baggage train was lined up end to end it would stretch for twenty miles.⁴¹ In addition there was a mass of ancillary personnel – farriers, grooms and blacksmiths to attend to the horses, as well as minstrels, heralds, valets, laundresses, prostitutes and priests.

On 17 June 1314 the army set out from Wark on the English side of the Tweed. To ensure an ample supply of food, it was accompanied by 'herds of cattle, flocks of sheep, and pigs beyond number'. Edward and his entourage, which included Sir Aymer de Valence, now earl of Pembroke,* took up a position immediately behind the vanguard. Advancing up Lauderdale 'covering the entire surface of the land like locusts' as it was described,⁴² the army headed for Edinburgh before turning west. Reaching Falkirk on 22 June, it set up camp for the night. Warned of its approach, Bruce divided his army into four brigades. While he retained one under his command, the others were assigned to his brother Edward, the earl of Moray and Walter the Steward.† Since the last was described as a 'beardless youth' (he was about sixteen), actual command was entrusted to James Douglas. The brigades were then deployed throughout the New Park‡ to prevent the English from reaching Stirling castle.

BANNOCKBURN

The battle took place over two days – 23 and 24 June 1314. During the first day the English endured a long march in sweltering heat from the previous night's camp at Falkirk as they headed for Stirling castle. As the vanguard emerged from the Torwood,§ they could see the Scottish troops milling around in front of the New Park

---

* He had inherited the earldom on the death of his mother Countess Joanna in September 1307.
† Bruce's future son-in-law.
‡ An area of woodland to the south of Stirling castle, it was part of a former hunting preserve of Alexander III.
§ Reckoned to be somewhere near the present-day motorway intersection.

in the distance. Between them was a stretch of open ground along which ran a track, part of an old Roman road. Correctly anticipating that this would be the English line of march, Bruce ordered the ground on either side to be honeycombed with 'calthrops' similar to those used at Loudoun Hill. This was designed to funnel the English into a narrow corridor admitting no more than three or four mounted knights abreast.

Unaware of this, the English cavalry under the earls of Hereford and Gloucester attempted to charge the Scottish positions, but they found themselves caught up in the booby traps. Some kept to the track. Among them was Hereford's nephew Sir Henry de Bohun. The story goes that, catching sight of Bruce ahead of him mounted on a small palfrey, and recognising him from the gold coronet on his helmet, this young knight thought to win immortal glory for himself – and a handsome reward – by charging him down and killing him. But just as he was closing on Bruce, the latter edged aside and raised his axe. As de Bohun went thundering past unable to stop his horse, Bruce brought the axe crashing down on him with such force as to slice through his helmet and cleave his skull, killing him instantly, though at the cost of breaking his axe handle, much to his annoyance. Following behind, the rest of the cavalry attempted to charge the Scots, but constricted by the booby traps they were repulsed.

Meanwhile another cavalry force under Clifford and Sir Henry de Beaumont tried to outflank the Scots on the right and make for the castle. But spotting them in the nick of time, the earl of Moray's brigade fell on them. After a gruelling fight the English were scattered. While some withdrew the way they had come, and some went on to seek sanctuary at Stirling castle, most headed downhill on to the Carse where, on Edward's orders, the rest of the army had set up camp. Although dictated by the availability of water to slake the thirst of men and horses, his decision proved a serious error because the soft ground was unsuitable for cavalry. To compound it, Edward ordered his army to take up a position between two converging streams flanked by soft mudbanks – the Bannock burn and its tributary the Pelstream burn.* This was another major blunder, because it risked the army being hemmed in by the Scots, which is exactly what happened and it would cost him the battle.

Meanwhile Bruce had been swithering as to whether to risk a pitched battle or, having scored a minor success, to retire with honour to the wilds of Lennox. However, that evening Sir Alexander Seton, a Scottish knight who had been pressed into service with the English following his capture at Methven, escaped to the Scottish camp. He assured Bruce that English morale was low and told him that if he were to give battle he would score an easy victory. While Bruce may have dismissed this as wishful thinking, he seems to have placed more reliance on the reports from scouts about the vulnerability of the English position, and this probably clinched his decision to fight.

At first light the Scots formed up in battle order. Having received the customary blessing, they advanced rapidly downhill in echelon with the aim of catching the

---

* Marked on old maps, the Pelstream Burn has since disappeared although parts of its former course are still detectable.

English by surprise and avoiding the withering fire of their archers. Reaching the carse, they formed a line many ranks deep at the narrowest point between the two streams,* their plan being to bottle up the English. While the front ranks knelt with their lethally sharp twelve-foot pikes fixed in the ground, and pointed at such an angle as to spear the underbellies of the oncoming horses and topple their riders, the rest presented a forest of firmly anchored pikes. In a hard-fought and extremely bloody battle which raged all day the English cavalry repeatedly hurled themselves against the Scots in a desperate effort to break their line, only to find themselves impaled on the wall of pikes.

As the heaps of dead and wounded men and horses piled up, they prevented the English footsoldiers, whom Edward had unwisely placed at the rear of the cavalry, from reaching the Scots. The archers, whom he had equally ill-advisedly consigned to the rear, were similarly hamstrung. Unable to get a clear field of fire, they were prevented from loosing off their arrows for fear of hitting the cavalry in front. At one point a contingent managed to cross the Pelstream burn from where they could fire on the Scots' flank to lethal effect. But they were quickly charged down and scattered by a force of light horsemen under Sir Robert Keith.

Once the cavalry had exhausted themselves, the Scots went on the offensive, gradually forcing the English back towards the confluence of the two rivers when they finally broke. Many were drowned as they tried to escape, and eventually the streams became so clogged with corpses that, as Barbour put it, they 'formed a causeway which those behind crossed without so much as wetting their feet'.[43] Once it was clear that the battle was lost, King Edward was prevailed on to leave the field. Showing himself at his best, he had been in the thick of the fight, had already had a horse killed under him, and when some Scottish knights grabbed the reins of his remount and tried to unhorse him, big strong man that he was, he beat them off with his mace. However, aware of the disastrous consequences if he was captured, the earl of Pembroke forcibly led the protesting king away.†

Edward's brother-in-law, the earl of Hereford, accompanied by some fifty knights and their attenuated retinues, managed to escape to the illusory safety of Bothwell castle,‡ where the custodian Walter fitzGilbert gave them sanctuary. But learning of the Scottish victory, and anxious to ingratiate himself with Bruce, he promptly interned them before handing them over to Edward Bruce. Such was the value of

---

*   Thought to be somewhere between 900 and 1,000 yards wide.
†   This account of the second day's battle and where it took place, which is broadly in accord with General Christison's interpretation, is based on W Scott's conclusion in his *Bannockburn Revealed*, combined with my own investigation of the ground, not easy since most of it has been developed. Basing his conclusions on the evidence of the chroniclers who would have been relying on second- or third-hand accounts, Professor Barrow argues for a site further up the hill which makes no tactical sense. All the same, I was encouraged to see from a TV programme presented by Neil Oliver that my account accords with his conclusion, and similarly that of Alistair Moffat in his recently published *Bannockburn: The Battle for a Nation*.
‡   This had been given him by Edward I following its capture in 1301 and was still in his possession.

their ransoms that a grateful Bruce rewarded fitzGilbert with substantial grants of land, including the forfeited Comyn lands in Clydesdale. This was the principal power base of his Hamilton descendants, who would later become the leading power in the realm.

Although the war continued off and on for another fourteen years, with the balance of power remaining firmly with the English, Bannockburn was a turning point. It meant that Bruce could go on the offensive, so that the main theatre of the war shifted from southern Scotland to the northern counties of England. Here the earl of Moray and James Douglas conducted a series of raids, blackmailing the people into buying truces by threatening to burn their settlements and crops, and carry off their livestock. While the main object was to raise money to pay his troops and purchase supplies and equipment for his war effort, it also served to demonstrate Edward's inability (through financial constraints) to defend them, thus helping to undermine his authority.

In November 1314 Bruce held a Parliament at Cambuskenneth. At his insistence it decreed that all Scottish landowners who had inherited their lands (as opposed to those who had been given them by Edward I) would be allowed to keep them provided they swore allegiance exclusively to him.[44] Since it would prevent those possessing lands in England from paying fealty to King Edward, these stood to be forfeited. This meant they were faced with a stark choice: either swear allegiance to Bruce and keep their Scottish lands but lose their English estates; or refuse, in which case it would cost them their Scottish lands. Since they could not have it both ways, a choice there had to be.

To encourage them into his allegiance, the option was extended to Bruce's former opponents. Statesmanlike perhaps but questionably wise, because a number of former Comyn supporters who made a show of swearing allegiance to him for the sake of keeping their Scottish lands remained covertly hostile. Nevertheless the option was denied to all members of the Balliol and Comyn families. Consequently their forfeited lands reverted to the crown, the former Comyn baronies of Dalswinton and Duncow being a case in point.* Whereas Dalswinton was granted to the Steward's cousin Sir Walter Stewart of Garlies,[45] Duncow, which included Carnsalloch and Dusquhen (Dalscone), went to Bruce's long-standing supporter Sir Robert Boyd.[46]

Another member of the Steward's family to be established in Nithsdale was his sister Egidia (or Giles) Stewart and her husband Alexander Meyners (Menzies) who were given the barony of Durisdeer.[47] This formerly belonged to the senior branch of the Lindsay family and had passed to Ingelram de Guines, a Frenchman, on his marriage to Christine daughter and sole heiress of William de Lindsay lord of Lamberton, the head of the family. De Guines had been an English supporter, but on

---

* The murdered Comyn's son, also Sir John Comyn, was killed fighting for the English at Bannockburn leaving two young sons who were then living on the family estates in Northumberland, but they died before reaching adulthood.

inheriting the lordship of Coucy in 1311 he abandoned Scotland for France. Consequently his (or rather his wife's) lands were forfeited and redistributed among Bruce's supporters.[48]

The Lindsays were among the most powerful kindreds in southern Scotland. When William de Lindsay lord of Lamberton was killed in Edward I's Welsh War in 1283, the headship of the family passed to Sir David Lindsay, his nearest male relative whose lordship of Crawford lay immediately to the north of Annandale. Because he had been captured by the English while fighting for Bruce, he was rewarded with lands near Moffat.[49] Sometime after 1320 William Lindsay,* probably his younger brother, was given the barony of Kirkmichael which had been forfeited by Sir Roger de Moubray for his part in the de Soules conspiracy.[50] At much the same time, Sir David and William Lindsay's near relative, John Lindsay, was restored to his family's lands of Wauchopedale which had been forfeited by his father Sir Simon Lindsay.[51]

Much of Eskdale changed hands. To the south was the barony of Kirkandrews on the lower Esk which was forfeited by the English Sir John Wake of Liddel and given to Sir John de Soules 'for homage and service'.[52] But following de Soules' death at the battle of Faughard in 1318 it reverted to the crown. It was later appropriated by Sir James Douglas's half-brother, Sir Archibald Douglas the future guardian.[53] The superiority of northern Eskdale was retained by Sir John Graham of Dalkeith, a descendant of the Avenels, who had the foresight to come into Bruce's allegiance just days before Bannockburn, while the barony of Westerker belonged partly to Sir William de Soules and partly to his uncle Sir John the former guardian.[54] Both their shares subsequently reverted to the crown – Sir William's on his forfeiture in 1320, and Sir John's following his death in France shortly afterwards. Whereas Sir William's share went to Sir James Douglas,† Sir John's was given to the monks of Melrose,[55]

The grant to Douglas was part of the extensive landholding which Bruce was building up for him in southern Scotland for the purpose of establishing him as a major power in the region. This included the lands of Polmoody in Moffatdale, for which Douglas and his successors were obliged to render the king 'twelve broad arrows' annually.[56] He was also given the barony of Staplegorton which had been resigned by John de Lindsay.[57] Until recently it had belonged to the de Conisburgh family, Duncan de Conisburgh having featured in the Ragman Roll for Dumfries, but had probably reverted to the crown through forfeiture and been given to Lindsay.

A number – probably most – of the Annandale tenants had supported the English, some being members of the English garrison at Lochmaben when it was captured by Edward Bruce in 1313. Since few of them had English lands to lose, and perhaps out

---

* A canon of Glasgow cathedral at the time, he subsequently became Bruce's chamberlain.
† *RMS* I, app i, 38, ii, 227, 346 the 'good' Sir James, as the chroniclers sycophantically referred to him, was knighted on the eve of Bannockburn.

of loyalty to the family, but more likely self-interest, they would have readily switched their allegiance to Bruce. But not all. One exception was the de Torthorwalds. The head of the family was Thomas de Torthorwald who, along with his brother James, swore fealty to Edward I in 1296. Both continued to support the English, James being killed fighting for them at Bannockburn. Because Thomas refused to swear allegiance to Bruce, he forfeited the barony of Torthorwald, which was given to Sir John de Soules.[58] Following the latter's death at Faughard it reverted to the crown, and in 1321 Bruce gave it to Sir Humphrey de Kirkpatrick (whose wife was coincidentally a sister of Thomas and James de Torthorwald).[59]

Bruce's immediate family were also beneficiaries. For example he gave his sister Margaret and her husband William Carlyle the lands of Cronyanton and Minnygap in the parish of Kirkmichael, which had been forfeited by the English-supporting John de Normanville.[60] Later he gave their son, the younger William, the lands of Collin and Roucan which were part of the forfeited barony of Torthorwald.[61] At much the same time Bruce gave Sir William de Soules' forfeited lordship of Liddesdale to his much-favoured illegitimate son, also Robert Bruce, who was a frequent attendant at his court.[*] Other forfeitures included the Mauleverers and the Pennersax family whose lands went to Stephen de Kirkpatrick.[62]

Like other aristocratic families the de Chartres, being landowners in Scotland and England, had divided loyalties. Whereas their Scottish lands consisted of Amisfield and Drumgree, those in England comprised lands in Wiltshire. Nevertheless Andrew de Chartres fought for the Scots at Falkirk. But the penalty was heavy, because Edward I ordered the forfeiture of both his Scottish and English lands.[63] This would explain why his brother William de Chartres was among those opposing Edward I during his campaign in Galloway of 1301. In 1304 Andrew de Chartres came into Edward's peace and was restored to his lands in Wiltshire (but not Amisfield and Drumgree since they had been given to the earl of Warwick). Thereafter he became one of Edward's supporters,[64] which would explain his presence as a member of the garrison of Dumfries castle when Robert Bruce captured it in the wake of Comyn's murder.[65] He died sometime before Bannockburn where his son Robert fought for the Scots. Consequently the Cambuskenneth Parliament restored him to Amisfield and Drumgree, now recovered from the earl of Warwick;[66] but because it cost him his English lands the family became exclusively Scottish.

Other families who rose to prominence, and who first appear as Dumfriesshire landholders at this time, included the Crichtons and the Carruthers. The first of the Crichtons to be established as a landholder in Dumfriesshire was William, a younger son of Alexander Crichton, lord of Crichton in Lothian He acquired half the barony of Sanquhar through his wife Isabella, a daughter and co-heiress of Robert de Ros

---

[*]   *RMS* I, app ii, 283. When the younger Robert Bruce was killed at Dupplin without issue, the barony was appropriated by Sir Archibald Douglas as guardian. After his death at Halidon Hill it was filched from his son William (future earl of Douglas) by Sir William Douglas the 'Knight of Liddesdale', and following his murder David II restored it to the younger William.

lord of Wark,* and purchased the other half from her sister Margaret and her husband Richard Edgar. Consequently he acquired virtually the whole of the combined parishes of Sanquhar and Kirkconnel, most of which would eventually pass to his descendants the earls of Dumfries.

The Carruthers family are thought to have been established in Dumfriesshire before the arrival of the first Robert de Brus. But it was not until 1296 that the family first appear on record when Simon de Carruthers, parson of Middlebie, features in the Ragman Roll. Later, Thomas son of John Carruthers was given the lands of Mouswald, to which he added the neighbouring property of Appletreethwaite on his marriage to Joan, daughter and co-heiress of Robert de Aplintoun (or Applyngdene).[67] Another family who are thought to pre-date the first Robert de Brus were the Moffats, Thomas Moffat having acquired lands in the barony of Westerker forfeited by Sir William de Soules,[68] while Ade (Adam) Moffat who was granted the neighbouring lands of Knock would have been a close relative, possibly his brother.[69]

In December 1314 an exchange of prisoners took place at Dumfries when Bruce's wife Elizabeth of Ulster and daughter Marjorie were released after eight years' confinement to separate nunneries in Yorkshire. Not long afterwards Elizabeth produced a daughter, followed by another, because Bruce's son and heir – the future David II – was not born until 1324 when Bruce himself was almost fifty.[†] Meanwhile in 1315 Marjorie, his eighteen-year-old daughter by his first wife Isabella of Mar, married Walter the Steward.[‡]

The same year Bruce sent an expeditionary force to Ireland under his brother Edward to open up a second front in the war with the English. This was intended to prevent King Edward from recruiting Irish levies to supplement his army and cause him to divert troops to Ireland instead. At the same time Edward Bruce was ordered to so devastate the country as to deny it as a source of provisions for English troops. But ruthless and aggressive though he may have been, Edward Bruce was no strategist; nor did he possess the diplomatic skills needed to bind the fractious Irish princes into an alliance. Consequently his three-year campaign, which was blackened by appalling atrocities on both sides, ended in disaster with his defeat and death at the battle of Faughard, near Dundalk, in October 1318.

Meanwhile in July 1315 the Scots laid siege to Carlisle which was under the keepership of a Cumbrian knight, Sir Andrew Harclay. Because it rained incessantly the siege engines became so bogged down that it was impossible to drag them within range of the castle. Therefore Bruce had his men construct a prefabricated drawbridge to enable them to get close enough to the castle walls to sap their foundations. When it too sank in the mud, they tried filling the moat with bags of hay and sacks

---

* A descendant of Robert de Ros of Helmsley who married King William's illegitimate daughter Isabella and was given the barony of Sanquhar as her dowry.
† Another son, John, was born in October 1327 but died young. Since Bruce's wife Elizabeth died the same month it was presumably in childbirth.
‡ He had succeeded his father James the Steward in 1309.

of corn with equal lack of success. Finally a party of men tried to scale the walls with the aid of ladders. But arming themselves with long poles, the English pushed the ladders over, the attackers still clinging to them. When Bruce had exhausted every possible means of taking the castle, news reached him of the approach of the earl of Pembroke with a relieving force. Therefore he abandoned the siege and withdrew to Annandale hotly pursued by the garrison who took a number of knights prisoner.[70]

The following year Bruce and Douglas attempted an assault on Berwick. But it was frustrated by the vigilance of a sentry who raised the alarm and caused them to beat a hasty retreat. The setback was partly mitigated by Sir John de Soules' defeat of an English force under Harclay in a skirmish in Eskdale. In the course of it, Harclay was taken prisoner but was later ransomed. In November a truce was agreed; but in February 1317 Douglas broke it by sending a force to plunder Tynedale. At Easter, William Dacre, a prominent northern baron, carried out a retaliatory raid on Annandale. Such was the resulting devastation that, as he triumphantly reported to the chancellor John de Sandale, '[the country] is utterly wasted and burned, and from Lochmaben to Carlisle there is neither man nor beast left'.[71]

In 1316 the newly elected Pope John XXII issued a bull imposing a truce on the English and Scots as a preliminary to securing a lasting peace. Two cardinals were sent to England to enforce it, one of them – Cardinal Fieschi – being ordered to proclaim it from the pulpit of St Paul's. They sent envoys to Scotland to deliver a copy of the bull, along with a letter from the Pope, to Bruce. Since he was benefiting considerably from Edward's political difficulties at home, he was not interested in a truce. In any case he was well aware of the Pope's bias against him as an excommunicate, that he held the Scots responsible for the war, and that he was entirely unsympathetic to – and probably couldn't even understand – the Scots' aspirations to independence. Therefore Bruce simply ignored the bull.

Yet courtesy demanded that he receive the envoys. According to their report he did so with 'smiling affability'. Having listened to what they had to say, he blandly assured them that no-one was more anxious than he to conclude a lasting peace. Indulging in some mild leg-pulling, he feigned puzzlement as to the identity of 'Robert Bruce, Governor of Scotland' to whom the papal letter was addressed (the Pope refused to acknowledge his kingship) and declined to open it in case it was meant for someone else. When the envoys begged him to dispense with such sophistries and proclaim a truce, he replied that he could not do so without the consent of his Council, and because the members were dispersed throughout the realm it was impossible to convene an early meeting. Finally realising they were getting nowhere, the envoys returned south with the letter unopened and the bull unread.[72]

In defiance of the papal injunction, Bruce sent Moray and Douglas on a plundering raid into Yorkshire. Responding, Archbishop Melton of York reaffirmed the sentence of excommunication on Bruce, while the Pope retaliated by excommunicating Moray and Douglas as well. Since Bruce, Moray and Douglas remained impervious to papal censure, the cardinals placed Scotland under an interdict. Because this prohibited the celebration of mass, baptisms and marriages, and the burial of the dead, with the fearful implication of all unabsolved sinners going to Hell, it was calculated to stir up opposition to Bruce within Scotland, which it eventually did.

In December 1318, following the death of his brother Edward his designated heir, Bruce held a Parliament at Scone to settle the succession. This was a matter of vital importance since his only daughter Marjorie had died in March 1316. She was killed as the result of a riding accident during the last stages of pregnancy, although miraculously the child cut from her womb after her death survived.[*] Therefore it was decided that if Bruce were to die without a legitimate son this child should succeed him. Further, that if he was a minor at the time of Bruce's death the earl of Moray, whom failing Sir James Douglas, was to be appointed guardian. The same Parliament ratified Bruce's grant to the earl of Moray of the lordship of Annandale which had reverted to the crown following Edward Bruce's death. Since he had already inherited the lordship of Nithsdale, he was now overlord of the whole of modern Dumfriesshire with the exception of Eskdale.

The Parliament went on to pass a number of measures which were designed to suppress unrest. Fomenters of discontent were to be arrested, while scaremongering or disseminating rumours harmful to Bruce was made a punishable offence. Anyone daring to utter sedition risked being reported to the authorities and committed to prison, or if the situation warranted put to death. A more savage traitor's death awaited those who had come into Bruce's peace, sworn allegiance to him and defected, or were convicted of plotting against him. The effect of these draconian laws was to establish what was tantamount to a Bruce dictatorship.

CONTINUING CONFLICT

By 1320 there was widespread discontent with Bruce's regime, focusing in particular on the interdict and its effects. Fearing that it might erupt into open rebellion, Bruce and his advisers decided to change tack. Therefore, instead of persisting with their increasingly counterproductive defiance of the Pope, they decided to present a petition to him explaining the Scots' case in the hopes of persuading him to a more conciliatory attitude. Accordingly, in March 1320 Bruce convened an assembly of the leading magnates – lay and clerical – at Newbattle abbey, where it was agreed that the petition should take the form of a letter which would be so framed as to convince the Pope of the justice of their cause.

Dated 6 April 1320, and known as the Declaration of Arbroath because the letter was issued there, it went in the names of forty-four leading magnates. Because they were ordered to have their seals delivered to Arbroath for adhibiting to the letter

---

[*] Named Robert after his grandfather, he succeeded as Steward on his father Walter's death in 1326. In 1371, at the advanced age of fifty-five he succeeded his uncle David II, and as King Robert II he reigned for nineteen years until his death in 1390.

(actually a document), they would not have been aware of its finer details, although its general thrust had been agreed at Newbattle.[73] Mixing historical fact with fiction and special pleading, it is nevertheless popularly regarded as the embodiment of Scottish nationhood, while its ringing phrases provide splendid copy for populist historians. The most oft-quoted is the final peroration: 'as long as but a hundred of us remain alive, never will we on any condition be brought under English rule', which epitomised the Scots' new-found sense of nationhood forged in the heat of repeated English invasions. More discerningly, and contrary to the populist view, the Declaration has been described as acquiring 'a status and prestige which historically it was never intended to enjoy'.[74]

The Pope's reply, received in late August, was strictly non-committal, merely saying that he would ask 'the king of England [to] incline his mind to peace', while enjoining the Scots to do the same. Although, as a concession, Bruce's excommunication was temporarily suspended (it was later re-imposed), Moray's and Douglas's remained in place – and similarly the interdict.

In the early summer of 1320, while the Scottish envoys were on their way to Avignon to deliver the letter to the Pope, evidence emerged of a plot to assassinate Bruce. Known as the de Soules conspiracy, it was so-called after Sir William de Soules, lord of Liddesdale and a member of the extended Comyn family,[*] who was popularly credited with masterminding the plot. Wrongly, because it was almost certainly instigated by King John's son, Edward Balliol. Although living in France, he was a frequent attender at the court of Edward II whom he knew well having been a member of his household. Therefore it is more than likely that Edward connived at it. This stands to reason, for if the plot were successful he would doubtless have counted on replacing Bruce with Edward Balliol as a puppet king, just as his father attempted to do with King John.

The ringleaders consisted of a group of some twenty magnates who were covert Balliol adherents and appear to have enjoyed considerable support.[†] When the plot came to light they were arrested, interrogated and brought to trial before a specially convened Parliament at which Bruce presided in person. Political considerations, as well as the need to make an example of them as a deterrent to others, dictated harsh punishment – hence its name the 'Black' Parliament. Most of the ringleaders were sentenced to death and forfeiture. Among them was Sir Roger Moubray. Because he died in prison while awaiting trial, the law required that his corpse be brought before the Parliament so that decree of forfeiture could be pronounced on it.[75]

Even those not directly implicated were consigned to the gallows. For example Sir David de Brechin's failure to report the plot when he knew about it was enough to secure a conviction. He was condemned to be tied to a horse's tail (the ultimate

---

*   His mother was a sister of John Comyn earl of Buchan.
†   Or so it would seem if Barbour's assertion that when de Soules was arrested he was accompanied by a retinue of three hundred and sixty esquires is correct (Barbour, *Bruce* (Douglas), 430).

indignity) and dragged through the streets of Perth to the market place where he was publicly hanged and his head cut off. On the other hand, some like Sir Eustace Maxwell of Caerlaverock were acquitted for lack of evidence. Nevertheless the extent of the opposition to him must have come as a severe shock to Bruce, probably rendering him morbidly suspicious of a further attempt on his life and all the more ready to crack down on the slightest sign of opposition.

It may have been about this time that, as a reward for their loyalty and support, or possibly in compensation for the hardship they had suffered during the Wars of Independence, Bruce reputedly conferred the status of 'kindlie tenants' on the indwellers of the 'four towns of Lochmaben' – Heck, Hightae, Greenhill and Smallholm. Denoting kin rather than benevolence, it meant that their tenancies were henceforth to be held of the crown and as such were transmissible to their heirs in perpetuity. Additionally they were granted exclusive fishing rights over a four-mile stretch of the river Annan.* An alternative theory has it that the original tenants were granted these pendicles of land in return for providing food for the Lochmaben garrison.[76]

In March 1322, in a show of energy and determination worthy of his father the old king, Edward II defeated his baronial opponents under the leadership of the earl of Lancaster at the battle of Boroughbridge. Therefore, freed from their attempts to curb his ruling powers, he began preparing for another invasion. It proved a fiasco. Pre-empting it, Bruce ordered the evacuation of all livestock from Lothian and Berwickshire as a preliminary to laying waste to the countryside ahead of the English army as it advanced up the east coast. Since the English had counted on living off the land until they reached the supply ships they expected to be waiting for them in the Forth, and found the land completely devastated, they began to go hungry.

Worse still, on reaching Musselburgh they found that the ships had failed to arrive (some had been attacked by Flemish privateers and the rest scattered in a storm), they faced starvation. To add to their plight, disease (probably dysentery) broke out in their ranks and claimed so many victims that Edward was forced to order a withdrawal. Having wantonly sacked Holyrood abbey, his depleted army returned by way of Soutra and Lauderdale, plundering the abbeys of Melrose and Dryburgh as they headed southwards, and by the end of September they were back at Durham.

Two months later the Scots counterattacked, when Bruce led an army across the border. Plundering its way southwards as far as Yorkshire, it encountered an English force drawn up on the edge of the North Yorkshire Moors near Byland. In a daring

---

* Although this form of tenure was abolished in the late fifteenth century, an exception was made in the case of the 'kindlie' tenants of the four towns of Lochmaben, perhaps out of respect for the memory of Robert Bruce, while their rights were confirmed by James VI and Charles II. In the 1660s viscount Stormont, the owner of Lochmaben, tried to evict them. However, the tenants took him to court when it was ruled that they were entitled to remain in possession, the decision being upheld by the House of Lords. Originally quite numerous, there were still about 125 tenancies in the early 1700s. Thereafter the numbers dwindled, most being bought out by the laird of Rammerscales, so that by 1837 they were reduced to 56. This form of tenure was finally abolished by the Abolition of Feudal Tenure (Scotland) Act of 2000.

attack a Scottish contingent under Douglas scaled the escarpment and caught the English by surprise. After a fierce engagement they were put to flight with many prisoners taken, including the earl of Richmond. Walter the Steward and his men pursued the English fugitives as far as Rievaulx abbey in a desperate attempt to capture King Edward, who had based himself there. But they were too late. Warned in the nick of time, he escaped to York; but in his hurry to get away he was forced to leave 'all his silver plate and much treasure' behind.[77]

The prisoners included a number of French knights who had probably come in search of adventure. Anxious to gain favour with the new king Charles IV, whom he saw as a potential ally, Bruce treated them with every consideration and allowed them to return to France. Meanwhile he invited them to remain as his guests for as long as they wanted. More to the point, he waived their ransoms. Because Sir James Douglas was entitled to them having been responsible for their capture, Bruce undertook to grant him additional lands in compensation, and as a pledge of his promise he allegedly gave Douglas an emerald ring. Therefore, when in 1325 he granted Douglas sundry lands, including the barony of Staplegorton, the relevant deed was known as the 'emerald' charter.[78]

In late 1322 Bruce received a peace offer from an unlikely source – namely Sir Andrew Harclay, keeper of Carlisle castle and warden of the English west marches. Concerned for the sufferings of the ordinary people, as the Lanercost chronicler charitably puts it, but more likely for the integrity of his Cumbrian estates, Harclay sent envoys to Bruce offering to discuss terms. A doubtless sceptical Bruce sent him an encouraging reply inviting him to a parley at Lochmaben. In January 1323, travelling there in disguise, Harclay met Bruce and his advisers, including the earl of Moray. Although he may have been a competent enough soldier, Harclay was completely out of his depth when it came to the subtleties of diplomacy, particularly when pitted against such crafty negotiators as Bruce and Moray. As a result he allowed himself to be duped into concluding an agreement which effectively prevented him from defending the west marches and allowed Bruce to invade them with impunity. Worse still it was treason. Therefore when he naïvely reported the substance of the agreement to King Edward, doubtless expecting to be rewarded for his success, the king ordered his arrest. A special court was convened to try him. Presided over by Sir Geoffrey Scrope, Chief Justice of the King's Bench, he was convicted of treason and condemned to a traitor's death.

That is not to say that Edward was averse to the idea of a truce following his defeat at Byland, provided it was on acceptable terms. Already in January, shortly after Harclay's ill-fated mission, he had sent a French nobleman to Bruce's court to sound him out. Since Bruce was amenable, it was agreed that he and Edward should appoint delegations to discuss peace terms. Their talks culminated in the truce of Bishopthorpe, which was concluded on 30 May 1323 and provided for a thirteen-year suspension of hostilities. When war broke out between Edward and Charles IV in August the following year, Bruce took the opportunity to press for a final peace treaty. Again he and Edward appointed commissioners to discuss terms, but the negotiations stalled over Edward's refusal to concede Bruce's demand for recognition of his kingship and Scottish independence. The resulting stalemate lasted for some three years until overtaken by an unexpected turn of events.

In 1325 Edward's ill-used queen Isabella, who was virtually under house arrest, persuaded him to send her to France to mediate with her brother King Charles. Once there she refused to come back. Later she moved to Hainault in the Low Countries where, assisted by Count William, she and her paramour Roger Mortimer lord of Wigmore (later earl of March) raised an expeditionary force to invade England. In September 1326 it landed near Felixstowe. By the following month London was in their hands, and by the end of the year Edward's regime had collapsed. In January 1327 he was forced to abdicate in favour of his fourteen-year-old son Edward III.

Nevertheless hostilities were resumed. In July 1327, claiming that the English had breached the truce of Bishopthorpe, Bruce ordered an invasion of the northern counties when the Scots penetrated as far as Weardale in County Durham. The English dispatched an army from York to confront them. Hopes were high because it was equipped with cannons, a novel type of weapon which had recently been imported from the Low Countries. The Scots proved elusive, and meanwhile it poured with rain which so saturated the gunpowder as to render the cannons useless. Finally the English troops caught up with the Scots at Stanhope, in upper Weardale. In the course of the ensuing stand-off, the Scots made a night attack on the English camp when they came within an ace of capturing the young king. After an inconclusive campaign they gave the English the slip and returned home.

The following month Bruce invaded Northumberland in an attempt to force the English to conclude a peace treaty. It was well timed because Queen Isabella and Mortimer's regime was beginning to crumble, and the widely held suspicion that Mortimer was responsible for Edward II's murder* contributed to its unpopularity. Since the war was distracting them from their efforts to shore up their regime, and Bruce's successes risked undermining their authority, Isabella and Mortimer were under pressure to conclude a treaty. Bruce was equally anxious to do so, provided it was on his terms – namely recognition of his kingship and Scottish independence. This was accepted, albeit reluctantly. After further haggling, agreement was reached on all the major points, including a provision that Bruce's son and heir David, now approaching four, should marry Edward III's six-year-old sister Joan. Finally a treaty – the treaty of Edinburgh (or Northampton as the English referred to it) – was

---

* Tradition has it that he suffered the agony of having a red-hot iron inserted into a catheter rammed up his rectum to burn out his bowels. Recently more weight has been given to the Fieschi letter. So-called after the writer Manuele Fieschi, bishop of Vercelli and a papal legate, it was addressed to Edward III informing him that his father had escaped from prison having overpowered the guards, and that he had become a hermit in northern Italy where he is believed to have died in the 1340s. In fact the ex-king is supposed to have mer his son Edward III at Coblenz in September 1338 when the latter went there to negotiate an alliance with the Holy Roman Emperor against King Philip VI of France.

concluded at Holyrood on 17 March 1328, and on 8 May Mortimer prevailed on a reluctant Edward III to give it his royal assent.

Although greeted with jubilation by the Scots, the treaty was extremely unpopular with the English who regarded it as a betrayal of all they had been fighting for. No-one more so than Edward III. To register his disapproval he and his newly wed queen Philippa of Hainault* refused to attend the wedding of his sister Joan and the young David. Moreover he was determined to abrogate the treaty on the grounds that, because his consent had been obtained under duress and while he was under age, it was invalid. But he had to bide his time because there was no question of challenging it while Bruce was alive and instalments of the indemnity awarded him under the Treaty were still outstanding.

However, he could afford to wait because Bruce was unlikely to live much longer. Although only in his mid-fifties, years of hardship and stress had taken their toll, rendering him prematurely old and increasingly dogged by ill-health. In particular he appears to have suffered from a skin disease, probably erysipelas, although the English chroniclers gleefully claimed it was leprosy, by implication attributing it to divine retribution for Comyn's murder and his other transgressions. In February 1329, probably as a token of thanksgiving for the recent lifting of his excommunication, he went on a pilgrimage to St Ninian's shrine at Whithorn. Setting out from his manor at Cardross in Dunbartonshire, where he spent his latter years, he would have gone by sea as far as Loch Ryan, and from there overland to Whithorn. Returning to Cardross in early May, he appears to have suffered a heart attack (or so Barbour seems to infer) and died there on 7 June 1329 within a month of his fifty-fifth birthday.

Although Bruce was deservedly hailed as pre-eminent in the annals of Scottish history, traditional historians have consistently portrayed him as a one-dimensional heroic figure, the embodiment of Scottish nationalism and endowed with all the qualities of courage, leadership and endurance to which he owed his success. While true enough as far as it goes, this ignores some inconvenient facts which detract from the popular image. Notwithstanding that he had been reared by a Gaelic-speaking family in Carrick, having been fostered out at birth, and had inherited a Scottish earldom, the fact was that he and his family regarded themselves as primarily English aristocrats. Since he would have spent much of his adolescence and early manhood among the English aristocracy, he would inevitably have shared their ideals and aspirations, as well as their prejudices.

Yet, doubtless indoctrinated by his formidable old grandfather, he never allowed himself to be deflected from his overriding ambition to become king of a free, independent Scotland. Indeed, it became such a fixation that he was prepared to go to any lengths to achieve it. He repeatedly betrayed Edward I's trust, each time – astonishingly – forgiven until his murder of Comyn propelled him into revolt. This forced on him a complete transformation from an English aristocrat into a rebel leader, to

---

*   Daughter of Count William and Jeanne of Valois who as a child was betrothed to Edward Balliol.

abandon the conventional type of warfare in which he had been trained, to become a guerrilla fighter and adopt the unorthodox methods which only a man of his talents, inventiveness and versatility could achieve. Finally it meant completely identifying himself with the Scots, with whom he probably felt scant affinity – at least to begin with. That Bruce accomplished all this with such success is a tribute to his remarkable ingenuity, qualities of leadership, and latterly statesmanship.

Historians have laid particular stress on Bruce's humanity. Only partially true, for although prepared to show magnanimity (not always reciprocated) where the situation warranted, he could be remorseless – and downright brutal – when occasion demanded. Indeed he could never have achieved what he did without a willingness to authorise and condone the kind of barbarities inflicted on the people of Buchan, Argyllshire and Galloway, and latterly those of northern England.

Above all, like many a successful commander, Bruce was extremely lucky. Not only that, but he was quick to take advantage of whatever strokes of good fortune came his way, and plenty did. Nowhere was it more apparent than in finding himself pitted against an inferior adversary like Edward II whose initial lack of interest in the Scottish war, and the consequent dilatoriness of his commanders on the spot, enabled him to break out of the south-west and gain control of the north. Later, baronial opposition to Edward (largely of his own making) prevented him from crushing Bruce, which with his superior might he could easily have done. When Edward did eventually confront him at Bannockburn, it was his strategic incompetence that handed victory to Bruce against all the odds. Finally the instability of Queen Isabella and Mortimer's regime forced them to conclude a treaty recognising Bruce's kingship and Scottish independence, which marked the culmination of all his achievements. There is much truth in the aphorism that fortune favours the bold, and Bruce was no exception.

SIX

Bruce Supremacy Regained

RIVAL KINGS

Robert Bruce was succeeded by his five-year-old son David II, and in terms of the statute of 1318 the earl of Moray was appointed guardian and effectively regent. It was probably about this time that, as lord of Annandale, he granted the lands of Comlongan to his nephew William Murray, ancestor of the Murrays of Cockpool and later earls of Annandale.* Moray proved a strong, capable ruler, and so long as he remained at the helm, and Queen Isabella and Mortimer were in control of English affairs, peace was assured. But it was not to last. In October 1330 Edward III instigated a *coup*. Mortimer and Isabella were arrested: Mortimer was hanged while Isabella was placed under house arrest,† and Edward assumed full ruling powers.

Meanwhile the 'disinherited', a group of influential magnates who had been deprived of their Scottish lands by the Cambuskenneth Parliament, saw Bruce's death as an opportunity to recover them. Their leader was Sir Henry de Beaumont who claimed the earldom of Buchan and a half share of its attaching lands in right of his wife who was a niece – and the elder of the two co-heiresses – of Earl John. Others included lord Talbot, son-in-law of the murdered Comyn, and Henry Percy notwithstanding that he had been restored to his father's share of the barony of Urr in Kirkcudbrightshire.‡ Also Thomas Wake of Liddel who was determined to recover the family barony of Kirkandrews in lower Eskdale.

Assuming the leadership, de Beaumont set about raising an expeditionary force to invade Scotland with the aim of securing the throne for Edward Balliol as king, and thus substantiate the claims of himself and his fellow 'disinherited'. Now approaching fifty, Edward Balliol had been nursing an ambition to seize the throne ever since his father the ex-King John's death in 1314. Because this was out of the question so long as Bruce was alive he was forced to bide his time. Now that the opportunity had arisen, he was readily persuaded to take over the leadership of the expedition, and,

---

* Comlongan formerly belonged to the Duncurry family, and it is possible that William Murray acquired it through marriage to an heiress. If so, his uncle the earl of Moray was merely confirming him in possession of it.

† Later released, she became an influential member of the English royal family until her death in 1358 (see Ian Mortimer, *The Perfect King*, 330)

‡ *RRS* v, no. 353. His father Sir Henry Percy, whom Edward I had appointed warden of the south-west, had died – possibly murdered – about the time of Bannockburn.

with the tacit encouragement of King Edward, he and the 'disinherited' magnates succeeded in raising a force of some two to three thousand men. This was to be a seaborne invasion, the plan being that they would land on the coast of Fife and head for Scone where Edward Balliol would have himself crowned king.

However, Moray pre-empted him by having the young David crowned first – on 24 November 1331. But the following July Moray died, allegedly poisoned by his chaplain or a monk in English pay. Since an invasion was thought to be imminent, it was imperative that a new guardian be appointed without delay. Accordingly a Parliament was held at Perth to choose a successor – not easy because there was no obvious candidate. After what was described as a 'gret and lange dyssentyown [argument]'[1] they chose Donald earl of Mar. Although a nephew of Robert Bruce,[*] he was an unlikely choice since he had been a close adherent of Edward II and had only recently returned to Scotland following the latter's deposition.

As it happened he never had a chance to prove himself. Four days later, on 6 August, Edward Balliol's force landed at Kinghorn on the coast of Fife and headed for Scone. Reaching the river Earn, near Dupplin, they found a greatly superior Scottish army encamped on the far side. But anticipating an easy victory the Scots relaxed their guard – with disastrous consequences, because Edward Balliol's men discovered a ford further upstream, and crossing the river they formed up ready to attack. As dawn broke on 11 August they fell on the Scots, catching them by surprise and slaughtered them 'like cattle in the meat-markets' as it was put.[2] The dead included the earl of Mar whose guardianship had lasted just over a week; also Thomas Randolph who had succeeded his father as earl of Moray a bare three weeks before.

From there Edward Balliol went on to capture Perth, and the following month he had himself crowned king at Scone.[†] This meant there were now two kings in Scotland, and the resulting civil war would last for almost a quarter of a century. Following his inauguration Edward Balliol moved fast to secure his family's power base in the south-west where Sir Eustace Maxwell of Caerlaverock[‡] was busy rallying local landowners and their levies to his cause. Having gained control of the region, Edward Balliol went on to lay siege to Roxburgh castle. About this time he gained a substantial fillip, for having received the full amount of the indemnity awarded him under the treaty of Edinburgh, King Edward abrogated it, which meant he could now openly support him.

But it came at a price. This was apparent from letters patent which Balliol issued at Roxburgh acknowledging Edward as lord superior of Scotland and binding himself

---

* Son of Bruce's sister Christina and Earl Gartney, he was also a nephew of Bruce's first wife Isabella of Mar.

† To avoid confusion with Edward III he will continue to be referred to Edward Balliol, and his rival as David II – or King David – although each was recognised as king by their supporters.

‡ He, it will be remembered, had been acquitted of complicity in the de Soules conspiracy for lack of evidence. Given his standing in the region and the importance of Caerlaverock as a virtually impregnable fortress (its defences had been greatly strengthened since its capture by Edward I in 1300), Maxwell was effectively Edward Balliol's anchor man in the south-west.

to pay homage and fealty to him. Still more controversially, he undertook to cede Edward lands in southern Scotland of an annual value of two thousand pounds which were to remain part of England 'in all time coming'. Specifically they included the whole of south-east Scotland, as well as the sheriffdoms of Peebles, Roxburgh and Dumfries. Not surprisingly this was widely resented and would cost Balliol much valuable support.

Meanwhile the Scottish magnates chose Sir Andrew Moray* as guardian in place of the earl of Mar. Following his appointment, he and Sir Archibald Douglas† made a devastating raid on Galloway where the people had risen in support of their 'special lord' Edward Balliol. Then, joining forces with Robert the Steward‡ and John Randolph, the new earl of Moray, they invaded Dumfriesshire causing a number of Balliol-supporting landowners to flee to England for safety.§

When news of their successes reached him, Edward Balliol, who was still besieging Roxburgh, hurried off with part of his army to oppose them. Reaching Annan, they set up camp on the burghmuir outside the town. During the night Sir Andrew Moray and his men made a surprise attack on them when Balliol had a narrow escape. Caught in bed, he barely had time to don a single boot before leaping onto an unbridled horse and riding straight for Carlisle accompanied by the few who managed to get away.¶ From there he sent envoys to Edward III with pleas for help, while an English chronicler asserts that the lady de Guines (formerly Christian de Lindsay) outfitted him with new clothes to replace those he was forced to leave behind in his hurry to escape.[3]

Sir Andrew Moray followed up his success with an abortive attempt to lift the siege of Roxburgh when he himself was captured. Sir Archibald Douglas was appointed guardian in his place, and on the strength of this he appropriated the lordship of Liddesdale which had reverted to the crown following the death of the younger Robert Bruce at Dupplin.[4] In February 1333 Edward Balliol returned to Scotland with levies contributed by a number of magnates, doubtless in expectation of a share in the spoils of victory. His immediate objective was to lay siege to Berwick – a daunting challenge since the Bruce-supporting Scots had spent the last few months strengthening its defences. In May, when the siege looked like continuing indefinitely, King

---

*   Posthumous son of Andrew Moray, the joint victor of Stirling Bridge, he was married to Bruce's sister Christina. Consequently he was the stepfather of his predecessor the earl of Mar, as well as being King David's uncle by marriage.

†   Half-brother of Sir James Douglas who had been killed fighting the Moors in Spain in March 1330.

‡   Bruce's grandson and future Robert II.

§   Evident from Edward III's grant of special protection to Sir Roger de Kirkpatrick, Humphrey de Kirkpatrick, Adam Corry, and others, described as 'Scots from Scotland who lately came with their retinues and purpose to remain [in England for] some time' (*CDS* iii, 1067, 1068). This Humphrey de Kirkpatrick, who was Sir Roger's son, was probably not the same person as the Sir Humphrey to whom Robert Bruce granted the Torthorwald barony if only because their wives had different names (*CDS* iii, 1067: Maxwell-Irving, *The Border Towers of Scotland*, 253).

¶   One who failed to do so was Balliol's younger brother Henry, who was killed in the affray leaving Balliol himself as the last of the line.

Edward sent reinforcements to Edward Balliol's assistance. Sir Archibald Douglas attempted to draw them away from Berwick by launching a diversionary raid across the border. In the course of it he laid waste to the lands of Gilsland which belonged to Ranulf lord Dacre, sheriff of Cumberland and keeper of Carlisle castle.

In a tit-for-tat retaliation Dacre's relative, the Cumbrian baron Sir Anthony de Lucy, invaded Scotland and ravaged Annandale. Responding, William Douglas* drove Lucy and his men back as far as Dornock where he forced them to give battle. In the ensuing fray a number of Annandale landowners were killed, including Sir Humphrey Jardine and Sir Humphrey de Boys, while Douglas himself was taken prisoner. Exercising his kingly powers, Edward Balliol ordered de Boys' lands in Dryfesdale to be handed over to lord Dacre, along with those forfeited by the Bruce-supporting Roger de Kirkpatrick, in compensation for the devastation of his lands of Gilsland.[5]

Having failed to draw the English relieving force away from Berwick, Sir Archibald Douglas broke off his campaign in northern England and headed there with the intention of lifting the siege. Crossing the Tweed, he and his army encountered an English force drawn up on Halidon Hill, which dominates the approaches to the town. When battle was joined on 19 July, Douglas's men were overwhelmingly defeated, he himself being killed along with many other Scottish magnates. Next day the Scottish garrison capitulated leaving Edward Balliol in virtual control of the realm and effective king of Scots.

In October he held a Parliament at Perth to ratify his cession of the lands in southern Scotland to King Edward and the reinstatement of the 'disinherited'. To ensure compliance, King Edward ordered Sir Henry de Beaumont, Henry Percy and Ralph Neville and others to attend the Parliament as a reminder to the members of who was in charge.[6] Notwithstanding this, and in spite of packing the Parliament with loyal bishops and magnates, Balliol had some difficulty in persuading it to ratify his actions. Even then it only did so by a narrow majority – so narrow that King Edward ordered the summoning of another Parliament to endorse its decision. This time it was held in Edinburgh, and because the town was in English hands they were in a stronger position to put pressure on its members. Consequently the decision was confirmed without demur,[7] and in June 1334 Edward Balliol issued a charter formally vesting King Edward in the promised lands in southern Scotland.[8]

It cost Balliol the support of a number of influential magnates, notably Sir Eustace Maxwell who switched his allegiance to the Bruce faction. Consequently his barony of Caerlaverock was forfeited and granted to lord Dacre who retained it until he was driven out by the Bruce loyalists some years later. The English takeover of southern Scotland was accompanied by a wholesale dispossession of the Bruce-supporting landowners whose estates were given to Balliol adherents. In Nithsdale, John Stewart

---

* Future lord of Liddesdale and son of Sir James Douglas of Lothian, he was a member of the junior branch of the Douglases who became lords of Dalkeith.

forfeited the barony of Dalswinton which was given to David earl of Atholl, Balliol's lieutenant in Scotland. Another victim was Sir Alexander Meyners who was deprived of the barony of Durisdeer (it was later restored to him along with the barony of Enoch), while Sir Archibald Douglas's lordship of Liddesdale was granted to Sir Ralph Neville. At the same time Balliol appointed an Englishman, Peter Tilliol, sheriff of Dumfries and keeper of the castle.[9]

In July 1333 Balliol granted the lordship of Annandale, including Moffatdale and custody of Lochmaben castle, to Henry Percy.[10] This was challenged by Edward de Bohun. Claiming that he had been promised them by King Edward, he appealed to him to overrule Balliol's grant to Percy. Accordingly Edward ordered Percy to hand them over to Sir Henry de Beaumont and Ralph Neville who were to hold them until the next Parliament pending a decision. Evidently Percy demurred, for on 2 November Edward issued a letter in peremptory terms commanding him 'on his highest peril' to comply with his instructions and censuring him for not having done so.[11] The upshot was that the Parliament decided in favour of de Bohun. Nevertheless Percy was compensated with the castle, town and forest of Jedburgh, as well as the lands in Annandale which had been forfeited by Sir Walter Corry and his son John.[12] In the event de Bohun's tenure was short-lived, because he died the following year when the lordship of Annandale was given, along with the keepership of Lochmaben, to his brother William, the commander of the English forces in Scotland.

The Corry family appear to have had divided loyalties. Whereas Sir Walter and his son John were Bruce loyalists at the temporary cost of their lands, their near relative Adam Corrie was a Balliol supporter, having fled to England when Sir Andrew Moray and others invaded Dumfriesshire. Now returned to Scotland, he was appointed William de Bohun's steward of Annandale. A close relative of King Edward with whom he was in high favour, de Bohun became one of his leading commanders in the Hundred Years' War, and later appointed constable of England he was rewarded with the earldom of Northampton. Since his commitments in England and on the Continent kept him fully occupied to the exclusion of Annandale, Adam Corrie's stewardship would have been no sinecure.

Since Balliol was in virtual control of the realm, David II and his queen were forced to take refuge in Dumbarton castle under the protection of its keeper Sir Malcolm Fleming, his former foster-father. Meanwhile John Randolph earl of Moray was sent to France to ask for help, which the French king Philip VI was obliged to give in terms of the treaty of Corbeil.* In early 1334 he returned to Scotland having secured promises of French rein-forcements coupled with an invitation to the royal couple to take refuge in France. Arriving there in May, they are said to have been introduced to the French king by Sir Humphrey Kirkpatrick of Torthorwald, who was apparently an habitué of his court.†

---

*   This was concluded between Robert Bruce and King Philip's predecessor, Charles IV, in 1326.
†   Later, King David fought for King Philip during his campaign of 1339–40 against Edward III in northern Europe (A H Burne, *The Hundred Years' War*, 22).

Emboldened by the promise of French reinforcements, the Bruce loyalists went on the offensive. Later that summer the earl of Moray, the Steward and William Douglas overran Balliol's south-western heartland when they attacked – but failed to take – Caerlaverock, now in the possession of lord Dacre. Heading eastwards, they invaded the territories recently ceded to Edward, forcing the newly arrived English officials to take refuge at Berwick where they were joined by Edward Balliol. At that point the Bruce loyalists gained an important, if temporary, advantage when the earl of Atholl switched his support to them, although self-interest dictated his return to King Edward's allegiance shortly afterwards. Still more important was Edward's seemingly perverse decision to release Sir Andrew Moray on ransom* – an error of judgement he must have bitterly regretted.

Meanwhile King Edward was planning another invasion to shore up the English position in Scotland. Since this was to be a winter campaign, and therefore understandably unpopular, he was unable to raise a large enough army to crush the Bruce loyalists. Therefore he spent the next few months at Roxburgh vainly trying to enlist recruits. During that time repeated English raids on his lands caused the earl of March, Edward Balliol's key supporter in the south-east, to defect to the Bruce faction. Finally, his inability to crush the Bruce-supporting Scots combined with a French diplomatic offensive was enough to persuade King Edward to grant them a truce to last from Easter until midsummer 1335.

This gave the king an opportunity to prepare for an invasion which was to take place immediately after the expiry of the truce. Accordingly, in July 1335 he set out from Carlisle with an army of 13,000 men, while another force under Balliol started from Berwick. Advancing up Nithsdale, Edward and his army set up camp at Dalswinton when he appointed the earl of Atholl, newly returned to his allegiance, custodian of the castle, although his tenure proved short-lived. Meanwhile Balliol received a substantial fillip when the earl of Moray was ambushed and captured in the Borders. This was a serious loss to the Scots because it deprived them of his leadership for the next few years, while it was probably scant consolation that William Douglas only narrowly escaped capture himself.

In August King Edward and Balliol's armies met up at Perth where they established a joint headquarters. Here they granted an amnesty, known as the Pacification of Perth. Those Bruce supporters who accepted it were promised safety of life and limb and allowed to retain their lands, and in a bid to win over the Scottish clergy it guaranteed the independence of the Church. Nevertheless many Bruce supporters remained defiant. But not all. When the Steward's lands in the west were threatened with attack by a force of 1,500 Irishmen in a fleet of fifty ships, he quickly submitted, as did many others – to the extent that it enabled King Edward and Balliol to regain control of Scotland. Consequently they withdrew to Berwick where they disbanded their armies.

---

* It was paid out of funds earmarked for the embellishment of Robert Bruce's tomb in Dunfermline Abbey.

But they had reckoned without Sir Andrew Moray. On 30 November, with the assistance of the earl of March and William Douglas, he defeated a force under the earl of Atholl at Culblean in Aberdeenshire, Atholl himself ending a somewhat murky career transfixed to an oak tree by a Scottish spear. Moray's success earned him the leadership of the Scottish resistance, and the following spring he was reappointed guardian. Meanwhile, to secure his newly acquired territories in southern Scotland, King Edward ordered the refurbishment of the principal castles in the region.

They included Caerlaverock where Sir Eustace Maxwell, now returned to Balliol's allegiance, was charged with carrying out the necessary repairs. But the king's faith in him proved misplaced. Maxwell was a professional turncoat who consistently trimmed his sails to the prevailing wind. Whereas Balliol's success encouraged him to return to his allegiance, Moray's victory persuaded him to revert to the Scots. But prudently he delayed doing so until Edward had provided him with the money and materials needed to carry out the repairs.[13] Given Maxwell's prominence in the south-west, his defection was a severe blow to Balliol. But worse was to come. Following the outbreak of the Hundred Years' War in May 1337, King Edward withdrew his troops from Scotland. Thereafter the war with France would occupy him to the virtual exclusion of all further support for Balliol who was left in the lurch.

Meanwhile Edward granted the Bruce-supporting Scots a truce which was to last until Martinmas 1339. By the time it expired, the pendulum of fortune was swinging back to Balliol again. The forty-year-old Sir Andrew Moray died in the spring of 1338. Apart from being a serious blow to the Bruce supporters, it meant they had to find another guardian. Although William Douglas was best qualified in terms of age and military experience he lacked the necessary landed power. Therefore the appointment went to the Steward. This meant that, instead of having an experienced military commander at the helm, the Scots found themselves saddled with a youth in his early twenties. And because he lacked his predecessor's belligerence the offensive slackened.

However the return of the earl of Moray in 1340, released in exchange for two captured English earls, gave the Bruce supporters new heart. Determined to drive the English out of Scotland altogether, Moray opened his campaign with a descent on Annandale (of which he was the rightful lord) in a bid to recover it from the English. This he succeeded in doing, although he failed to take Lochmaben, which remained in English hands. Nevertheless the recovery of Annandale, combined with Alexander Ramsay of Dalhousie's capture of Edinburgh castle, meant that the English were effectively confined to the south-east. Following this, Moray, William Douglas and Ramsay made a series of concerted attacks on them, with the result that by the following year most of Scotland, including the marches, was back in Bruce hands.

FLUCTUATING FORTUNES

By the summer of 1341 it was considered safe – indeed essential – for King David and his queen to return to Scotland. Landing at Inverbervie on the coast of Kincardineshire, well out of reach of the English occupying troops, the seventeen-year-old David was confronted with the daunting task of establishing his royal authority and driving Edward Balliol and his supporters out of Scotland. His principal supporter in southern Scotland was William Douglas who had been rewarded with substantial grants of land in Roxburghshire.

This merely whetted his appetite for more. In 1337, having driven the English out of neighbouring Liddesdale Douglas appropriated it for himself, claiming that he held it in wardship for his under-age godson William Douglas who was the rightful owner.* Notwithstanding this, his support for King David earned him further lands. In January 1342 he was given the former Graham lordship of Dalkeith,† followed by the barony of Kirkmichael which had been forfeited by John de Moubray, son of Sir Roger de Moubray (tersely described in the charter as 'slaine traitors'[14]). In February David issued a charter confirming him in possession of Liddesdale.[15] Later, he created him a knight (hence his designation 'the Knight of Liddesdale') and granted him lands in Ewesdale and Eskdale forfeited by William Lovell.[16]

In an attempt to re-establish the rule of law, David introduced the practice of holding justices ayre – effectively circuit courts – for the purpose of dispensing and enforcing justice. To lend weight to their authority, he presided over as many as possible in person. This meant travelling extensively throughout the realm, in the course of which he visited Dumfriesshire on at least three occasions. In December 1343 he stayed at Middlebie when he appointed the Steward's cousin, Sir Alexander Stewart of Darnley, bailie of Annandale.[17] He was back there in September 1344, this time as guest of William Carruthers of Mouswald whom he rewarded with lands at Middlebie 'forfeited by the late Thomas Lyndby'.[18] William Carruthers was probably the elder brother of John Carruthers‡ who, as steward of Annandale, would have been in attendance on David during his visit. So too would John Stewart his recently appointed chamberlain, now restored to Dalswinton.[19] On his next visit in 1362, David granted John Carruthers' son Thomas half the lands of Raffles, near Mouswald.[20]

Notwithstanding that the English had effectively left him in the lurch, Edward Balliol continued to pose a threat, particularly in the south-west where he commanded widespread support. Therefore David sought to bring the principal local magnates on

---

*   Son of Sir Archibald Douglas, and future earl of Douglas, he was living in France at the time.
†   *RMS* I, app ii, 813. According to the *Scots Peerage* (vol vi, p 197) he acquired it through marriage to a sister of Sir John Graham of Dalkeith, the last of that branch of the Graham family, and the king was merely confirming him in possession of it. Following his murder it passed to his nephew Sir James Douglas of Dalkeith and his descendants the earls of Morton who, some centuries later, sold it to the duke of Buccleuch.
‡   *RRS* vi, no. 282. He is believed to have been the ancestor of the family of Carruthers of Holmains.

side – notably Sir Eustace Maxwell of Caerlaverock and Sir Duncan Macdouall, both men of fickle loyalties who were prepared to support whichever side self-interest dictated. Maxwell seems to have been won over without difficulty, but in Macdouall's case David adopted a carrot-and-stick approach. Come over to my side and you will be rewarded with lands; but if you don't you will stand to lose everything. It worked, and Macdouall was persuaded to defect. Although his support was of dubious value, it was better to have him on side than in the Balliol camp. But, given Macdouall's record of inconstancy, David could not risk handing over control of the region to him. Instead he put Sir Malcolm Fleming, his former protector and a reliable 'strong' man, in charge. In November 1341, to equip him with the necessary power and authority, David granted him all the crown lands beyond the Cree and created him earl of Wigtown.[*]

Meanwhile Sir William Douglas the Knight of Liddesdale's predatory ambitions extended to members of his own kindred, because he set his sights on acquiring the lands formerly belonging to the 'good' Sir James Douglas which were now held by his half-brother, Hugh lord of Douglas, as head of the Black Douglases.[†] A cleric, and seemingly atypical of his race (evident from his epithet 'the dull'), he was not the man to stand up to Sir William's overbearing might. Therefore he was persuaded to hand over the superiority of Westerkirk, Staplegorton, and other lands in the marches, to him.[21] In May 1342 the Knight went further. In an attempt to appropriate the rest of Hugh's patrimony, he prevailed on him to execute a deed entailing it.[‡] Although the first-named heir was Hugh's nephew, the younger William Douglas (son of Sir Archibald) who was still in France, the Knight made sure that he himself came in second place ahead of the 'good' Sir James's illegitimate son Archibald.[§]

But he overreached himself. Since there was a limit to how far he could accommodate the Knight's predatory ambitions without risk to his own position in the marches, David attempted to establish Sir Alexander Ramsay of Dalhousie as a rival power in the region. The previous March, when Ramsay recovered the key stronghold of Roxburgh from the English, David appointed him to the prestigious offices of keeper of the castle and sheriff of Teviotdale. Taking the view that he was entitled to them himself, and correctly perceiving their grant to Ramsay as a threat to his own position, Sir William decided to eliminate him. Therefore, he had Ramsay kidnapped and spirited away to Hermitage castle where he was starved to death. This resulted in a vendetta between the Knight's men and Ramsay's adherents, among whom was the

---

[*]   *RRS* vi, 39: *RMS* I, app i, 119. They had been forfeited by the descendants of Alexander Comyn, earl of Buchan.

[†]   Elder brother of Sir Archibald Douglas, he had succeeded to the Douglas lands on the death of William Douglas, son of the 'good' Sir James, at Halidon Hill in 1333.

[‡]   *RRS* vi, no 51. Referred to as the Douglas Entail, this became a matter of some importance when determining the succession to the Douglas lands following the death of James second earl of Douglas without legitimate issue at Otterburn in 1388.

[§]   *RRS* vi, no. 51, pp 93–4. Known as Archibald the Grim, and a mighty warrior in the image of his father, he subsequently became the third earl of Douglas.

Dumfriesshire landowner John Herries.* Since the Knight's men gained the upper hand, David was forced to concede his appointment to Ramsay's offices.

As warden of the middle marches the Knight was present, along with John Randolph earl of Moray and others, at the Anglo-Scottish peace talks which took place at Lochmaben in August 1343. As a result, the Scots became party to the three-year truce recently concluded between England and France when it was agreed that no war should take place in Gascony, Scotland or elsewhere.[22] Notwithstanding this, the Bruce-supporting Scots subsequently laid siege to Lochmaben, now in the keepership of Sir Walter de Selby. William de Bohun, recently created earl of Northampton, responded by dispatching an army to its relief. But on arriving there they found that another army raised by Sir Anthony de Lucy and the bishop of Carlisle had driven off the besiegers, relieved the garrison and revictualled the castle. Therefore, as the St Albans chronicler put it, 'they went back, having done nothing'.[23]

Meanwhile Edward Balliol was still campaigning against the Bruce supporters in southern Scotland. But time was not on his side; he was now in his sixties, and being the last of his line, unmarried and childless, he had no heir to succeed him. Nevertheless King Edward still regarded him as his Scottish surrogate, having appointed him captain of the army of occupation in July 1342 and renewed it in August 1344. Yet support for him was dwindling, and the Maxwells had finally turned against him. Although Sir Eustace Maxwell, that habitual trimmer, had returned to Balliol's allegiance, he died in March 1342. His brother and successor Sir John Maxwell, on the other hand, was a staunch Bruce supporter.

In June 1345, in breach of his truce with Philip VI, King Edward invaded France, and in August the following year he scored a decisive victory at Crecy. From there he went on to lay siege to Calais when the hard-pressed Philip, invoking the Franco-Scottish alliance, called on David to make a diversionary attack on England. Responding, David mustered an army at Canonbie on the lower Esk. His immediate objective was to capture the nearby castle of Liddel Strength which was under the custodianship of Sir Walter de Selby, until recently keeper of Lochmaben. Since the castle occupied a commanding position overlooking the Liddel Water, this was a daunting undertaking. Nevertheless, by filling the moat with earth and brushwood, David's troops managed to gain the outer wall, and tearing it down with iron tools they stormed the castle and forced Selby to surrender. Any hopes he may have had that capitulation would earn him favourable terms were quickly dispelled. David was determined to punish him for his savage treatment of the people of Annandale during his keepership of Lochmaben. Therefore he ordered that Selby be forced to watch his two sons being strangled before he himself was beheaded.[24]

Crossing the border, David's host burnt the settlements in the vicinity of Carlisle, while threats to attack the town itself were enough to persuade the burghers to buy him off with a sum of 300 merks. Continuing their campaign of destruction as they

---

* A loyal supporter of King David, he was later appointed keeper of Stirling castle.

headed east, his troops quartered themselves on Lanercost priory before sacking it. Having blackmailed William lord Dacre into paying him a large sum of money to spare his lands of Gilsland, David and his army headed for Hexham. Here his troops ransacked the town, and looted and burnt the priory before going on to Corbridge, and finally Durham.

Meanwhile summonses were issued to the northern barons to rally to the defence of their homeland. On 17 October 1346 battle was joined at Neville's Cross, near Durham. Initially there was a stand-off as each side, determined to remain on the defensive, waited for the other to make the first move. Finally the English archers let loose hail upon hail of arrows, and unable to withstand their withering fire the Scots were forced to go on the offensive. It proved a disaster. The vanguard under the earl of Moray and the Knight of Liddesdale was pulverised, the Knight being captured and Moray killed,* while the survivors were forced back on to the second line under King David. As the battle continued to rage, they were forced back on to the rearguard under the Steward and the earl of March. Seeing that all was lost, they turned tail and galloped for home. Not so the king, who stood his ground in spite of being struck in the face by two arrows. Eventually he was forced to abandon the field. Overtaken by Sir John Coupland, a Northumbrian knight, he refused to surrender and in the ensuing hand-to-hand struggle he was overpowered, but not before he had knocked out two of Coupland's teeth. Taken prisoner he was dispatched to captivity in England where he would remain for eleven years.

Some two or three thousand Scots are believed to have been killed, including a number of magnates and many knights and landowners. Among them were Sir Humphrey de Kirkpatrick 'and his brother', Humphrey de Boys of Dryfesdale, and Sir Thomas de Torthorwald. Having switched his allegiance to King David and been restored to the lands of Collin and part of Roucan, Sir Thomas was a member of his bodyguard and was killed trying to defend him.† The prisoners included Sir William Jardine, John and Patrick Herries, and Sir John Stewart of Dalswinton.[25] Also Sir John Maxwell of Caerlaverock, who was dispatched to the Tower where he died shortly afterwards,[26] and most important of all the Knight of Liddesdale.

On his return to Scotland the Steward was appointed 'king's lieutenant', effectively guardian. Since it was expected that the English would follow up their success by invading Scotland to shore up Edward Balliol's position, the Steward's immediate priority was to put the country on a war footing. Or should have been, but the measures he took were patently inadequate. In fact the invasion did not take place until the following May when a 3,500-strong English army under Edward Balliol and two northern lords, John de Neville and Henry Percy, set out from Berwick. Joined by a contingent from Galloway, the combined force invaded Lothian and the regions to

---

* Since Moray had no issue, the earldom passed to the earl of March as husband of his sister 'Black Agnes' the celebrated defender of Dunbar castle against the English in 1338.
† His lands of Collin and Roucan passed to his daughter Eupham and her husband Robert Corry who sold them to Thomas de Henvale (*RMS* I, app ii, 1485, 1597)

the west before turning south. Advancing through Ayrshire and Nithsdale, and slighting the Bruce-held castles, including Dalswinton, on the way, they reached Caerlaverock.[27] As a result they won back most of the territory which had been recovered from the English by the earl of Moray.

In Annandale most landowners took the line of least resistance and submitted. But some were committed Bruce adherents, albeit at the cost of their lands, the forfeitures being recorded in the accounts of Sir Eustace Maxwell, the Balliol-appointed sheriff of Dumfries.[*] Among them were the Carruthers and Kirkpatrick families, and John Herries, who was among the prisoners taken at Neville's Cross, but who later rose to prominence as one of King David's most trusted supporters. Others included William Crichton who forfeited his barony of Sanquhar, Sir William Jardine who lost his lands, and the earl of March who was deprived of the barony of Glencairn. Similarly the baronies of Durisdeer, Ellisland, Tinwald and Torthorwald were appropriated to the English crown,[28] Ellisland being awarded, along with the lands of Terregles, Troqueer and others, to the Cumbrian baron Sir Henry de Multon.[29]

The Johnstones were probably Bruce loyalists – at least for a time, because their lands were reportedly confiscated and given to the English-supporting Carlyles. However, they appear to have defected to the Balliol camp after Neville's Cross, for in 1347 Gilbert Johnstone served on the English-appointed jury which was set up to determine the succession to the Carlyle family lands. This followed the death of Sir William Carlyle, when the jury found in favour of William, the son of Sir William's deceased brother John Carlyle.[30] Since Robert de Crosby was another juror, this suggests that his family were also Balliol supporters. Again the Corrie family seem to have had divided loyalties. On the one side was the Bruce-supporting Sir Walter Corry whose forfeited lands were given to Henry Percy. But Percy's lease of them to Sir Walter's brother John in 1350 suggests that he was a Balliol supporter. Nevertheless he must have gone over to the Bruce party soon afterwards, for in 1357 Robert the Steward as king's lieutenant confirmed the sale of his lands of Wamphray to the Bruce-supporting Sir Roger Kirkpatrick.[31]

Following Edward Balliol's recapture of southern Scotland, King Edward insisted that he establish a court at Caerlaverock, now in English hands following Sir John Maxwell's death in captivity. Further, that he should display all the trappings of monarchy. Therefore, acting as the king he aspired to be, Balliol appointed keepers to the principal castles in the region. A case in point was Adomar (Aymer) earl of Atholl,[†] who was given the keepership of Dumfries castle. Not content with that, Earl Adomar arrogated the keepership of Dalswinton in place of its owner Sir John Stewart, who was a prisoner in England. In that capacity he ordered that the damage caused by Edward Balliol's men in the course of their recent advance through Nithsdale be repaired and the castle put back in commission. In the event Edward

---

[*]   Probable son of Sir John Maxwell, he had sworn allegiance to Edward III.
[†]   Son of Earl David who was killed at Culblean.

Balliol's Indian summer proved short-lived, for in a change of policy King Edward evicted him from Caerlaverock having restored it to the English-supporting Sir Herbert Maxwell.[32] Consequently Balliol was forced to withdraw to his recently built manor on Hestan island, adjacent to the Urr estuary.

THE BLACK DEATH

In 1348 an outbreak of a particularly virulent form of bubonic plague resulted in a temporary cessation of hostilities. It was caused by a bacteria-carrying flea hosted by rats who flourished in the insanitary living conditions of the time. After a short incubation period the victim would develop a high fever accompanied by giddiness, vomiting and severe pain, as well as a swelling of the lymphatic glands in the armpits, neck and groin. Known as buboes, these would grow to the size of an egg, or even an apple, before they burst expelling quantities of pus and blood. This caused the victims such excruciating pain that it frequently drove them mad until their agonies were cut short by a merciful death. Another symptom was heavy bleeding under the skin which left them with a curiously black appearance – hence the term Black Death.

The period from the initial manifestation until death could last for up to a week. It frequently happened, particularly in towns, that the victim was thrown out of the house and left to die in the street for fear of contaminating other members of the household. The corpse was then bundled onto one of the carts which daily patrolled the streets gathering up the dead. They were then taken out to the burghmuir, or some other place well removed from the town, for burial in a mass grave.

There were other forms of plague such as the less common pneumonic plague where the bacillus accumulated in the lungs and killed the victim within two days. Or the equally lethal septicaemic plague which caused certain and sudden death. Either way, the speed of the onset of the plague, the agonising pain, and the grotesque appearance of the victims, rendered it all the more terrifying.

Thought to have originated in central Asia, the disease had penetrated India, China and the Middle East from where it spread to Europe – probably brought by merchants unwittingly carrying it in their galleys. It first appeared in England in August 1348 and continued to rage for the next three years. As the Scottish chronicler John of Fordun, writing in about 1385, put it: 'By God's will, this evil led to a strange and unwonted kind of death, inasmuch as the flesh of the sick was somewhat puffed and swollen, and they dragged out their earthly life for barely two days.'[33] Since it took upwards of a year for the pestilence to spread to Scotland, the Scots smugly assumed that they had been spared the divine wrath visited on their sinful neighbours. Not for nothing did the chronicler Henry Knighton brand it 'the foul deth that Ynglesh men dyene upon'. But the Scots' turn would come soon enough.

On Knighton's say-so, a Scottish army was mustered in the forest of Selkirk ready to take advantage of the Englishmen's plight by invading the northern counties. But at that point the plague suddenly appeared in their ranks when he asserts – probably with some hyperbole – that 'within a short period some five thousand died'.[34] Praying to 'God and Sen Mungo, Sen Ninian, and Seynt Andrew' to protect them, the survivors fled, some dying by the wayside. The rest dispersed to their homes carrying the disease with them and spread it among their families and neighbours. The Scots' terror is readily understandable. As Fordun put it, 'to such a pitch did the plague wreak its evil spite that nearly a third of mankind died of the disease' – a fearsome toll, but probably true enough since his assertion is supported by other chroniclers.

He goes on to say that it attacked 'especially the meaner sort and common people – seldom the magnates',[35] presumably because their living conditions were marginally less squalid. That is not to say that the disease didn't strike the upper ranks of society – even royalty, an example being Edward III's daughter Joan, who died of the plague while on her way to marry a son of the king of Castile. Nor was King David taking any chances, because we are told that he took refuge in the north accompanied by 'many of the more wealthy and more noble men of the kingdom'. This was because of fear of the pestilence 'which was spreading in the southern parts of the kingdom'; therefore he was understandably anxious to escape the 'horrible sights and sounds of the multitude of ill and dead'.[36]

The clergy were among the worst affected. This stands to reason given that their calling put them at particular risk since it involved visiting the sick, administering the last rites to the dying, and giving aid and comfort to the victims and their relatives. According to an English monk, many a priest who caught the disease through hearing the confession of an unsuspecting victim died before the penitent himself. To fill the vacancies left by the clerical victims, the Church appointed unskilled replacements, some of them so illiterate that, even if they could read it at all, expounding the scripture was quite beyond them. The alternative was pluralism where a priest held more than one living, but this led to a decline in pastoral care. Either way it set a trend that would contribute to the emergence of the reformist movement of the sixteenth century.

According to contemporary evidence the people of southern Scotland were particularly badly affected, one source claiming that 'the plague carried off so vast a multitude of both sexes that nobody could be found [to] bear the corpses to the grave'. Consequently 'men and women carried their own children on their shoulders to the church and threw them into the common pit'.[37] Taking up the tale, Bower asserted that 'everyone trembled at it with such fearful dread that children would not dare visit their parents', notwithstanding that they were 'suffering in the last extremity'. 'Instead', he goes on, 'they shunned the contagion as [if] from a serpent'. As a churchman he could not resist adding a homily: 'These plagues occur from time to time because of the sins of mankind.'[38]

This came to be known as 'the first pestilence' to distinguish it from the second outbreak of 1362, and the third and fourth in 1379 and 1417. The 1362 visitation was described as 'a death-sickness among men [which] raged [throughout] the whole kingdom of Scotland like the former one in all respects, both in the nature of the disease and the number of those who died'.[39] These visitations were interspersed by a number of minor outbreaks, and although they would continue throughout the following centuries the practice of numbering them was abandoned.

Fordun refers to another of 1439 where he specifically mentions Dumfries. 'In that samen year', he wrote, 'the pestilence came in[to] Scotland and began at Dumfries', probably imported in a rat-infested trading vessel from which some of the rodents escaped ashore while it was lying at anchor in the Nith. As he went on to say, it was called 'the Pestilence bot [without] Mercy, for they that took it nane ever recoverit, but they died within xxiv hours'. Plague had already been raging throughout England and France, and the outbreak at Dumfries evidently marked the beginning of its onslaught in Scotland.[40] The fact that Archibald fifth earl of Douglas is thought to have been a victim suggests that the upper classes were no less vulnerable than others.

A further outbreak in 1455 caused Parliament to decree that, in the event of the upper ranks of burghal society, namely the officials, burgesses and merchants, falling victim to the plague, they were to be 'quarantined within their houses'. The Act further provided that, unlike the dwellings of the underclasses, theirs were not to be burnt to prevent the spread of the disease. The infected poor, on the other hand, were to be 'put furth of the toun'. This meant banishment to the isolation camps on the burghmuir where they were consigned to the mercies of the 'foul clenzers'. Popularly regarded as the dregs of humanity, their job was to force the victims to dig their own graves and make sure that no-one escaped.[41] Invoking divine assistance, the Act further decreed that prelates were 'to mak generale processionis throu out their dyoceis twyss in the wok [week] for the staunching of the pestilence'.[42]

The plague visitations were all the more terrifying because no-one knew what caused them, apart from a general belief, echoed by Bower, that it was divine retribution for man's sinfulness. Others put it down to the poisonous state of the atmosphere. This was attributed to various causes, ranging from an ominous conjunction of the planets to malodorous vapours or miasma welling up from the bowels of the earth which polluted the atmosphere and penetrated the human body through the pores. Alternatively it was ascribed to some local source of putrefaction such as stagnant water, foul smelling marshes, or even rotting carrion. These beliefs persisted until as late as the nineteenth century when medical science identified the rat-borne flea *xenopsylla cheopsis* infected by the bacillus *yersinia pestis* as the culprit. Other factors were blamed as well. For example the rapidity of the spread of the first pestilence was attributed to a combination of overpopulation and the debilitating effects of a succession of bad harvests.

The resulting mortality had a profound effect on contemporary society. The sharp decline in the population was reflected in a corresponding reduction of the workforce and a serious downturn in trade. In the towns there was a virtual cessation of commerce with financial transactions left uncompleted through the death of one or both parties. Building work and other projects came to a standstill for lack of craftsmen to complete them; nor was it possible to replace the hovels of the poor which were deliberately burnt in an attempt to prevent the spread of the disease. The effect on the countryside was equally devastating with settlements and whole villages abandoned as the survivors fled, many carrying the disease with them. Since the millers, blacksmiths and other artisans joined the stampede, there was a virtual cessation of cultivation, while the shortage of men to tend the livestock meant they were frequently left to run wild.

The consequent dearth of tenants meant that the survivors acquired a scarcity value, which gave them added muscle when it came to negotiating leasehold terms with their landlord. The more so given the landlords' concern to maintain their rental income, and at the same time ensure that their lands remained in cultivation. This was to prevent them from falling into 'utter and irredeemable decay', as it was put. As to maintaining their rental income they were probably crying for the moon, while ensuring that their lands continued to be farmed could only be achieved by offering tenants a better deal in the form of improved conditions of tenure. This could mean extending the leasehold period or giving them handsome inducements to take up abandoned land. The shortage of tenants encouraged many landowners to split their holdings in order to render them more marketable, and because it enabled cottars and others to take on leases it resulted in a widening of the tenant class.

These changes were replicated further down the social scale, because the dearth of manpower opened the way for former serfs to become landless labourers or even small-time cottars. Nevertheless it was at the cost of the protection traditionally extended to them by their landowner. At the same time the shortage of men to work the land forced up the price of labour, while it added to the pressure for statutory labour to be commuted to a monetary wage. The resulting competition for labour gave people a wider choice of employment, and this in turn led to greater social mobility as they abandoned the estates, to which they and their families were bound, in search of higher pay and better working conditions elsewhere.

The reduced population and the shrinking demand for food led to a collapse in cereal prices. This encouraged farmers to turn to stock rearing, notwithstanding the fall in the price of cattle (including oxen), sheep, pigs and horses (although poultry seem to have retained their value). Nevertheless sheep farming remained profitable because the expanding clothmaking industry in England meant there was a seemingly endless demand for Scottish wool. In general, therefore, the effects of the plague can be summed up in the words of one historian, that it 'introduced a complete revolution in the occupation of the land', and that 'few shocks can have been more violent than that caused by the Black Death in fourteenth-century Europe'.[43] Yet the long-term effects were more muted, for once the plague had run its course, population numbers rapidly increased, tribute to an abnormally high birth rate which, although checked by the second outbreak of 1362, continued to grow.[44]

There is no record of the changes resulting from the Black Death being reflected in Dumfriesshire, although they must have to some extent. But there would have been less scope for it because Dumfriesshire was a relatively impoverished county with only a limited amount of arable land where the changes would have been most obvious. Since the hill country to the north was mainly given over to sheep farming, it would have been largely unaffected, except that there may have been fewer shepherds to tend the sheep, with a corresponding increase in ranching. Much of the rest of the county consisted of woodland. Knighton attests to this in his (doubtless exaggerated) assertion that when John of Gaunt invaded Annandale later in the century his men had to cut down so many trees to open up a line of march that 'the strokes of eighty thousand hatchets might have been heard'. In a flourish of poetic licence he went on to claim that when the trunks were burnt the fires gave off such a heat that they 'made the heavens red'.[45]

In spite of warfare, political unrest, and the periodic plague visitations, Dumfries itself appears to have prospered. At least so it would seem judging from the terms of the charter granted it by Robert III in 1395. A comprehensive document, it transferred the burgh to the 'provost, bailies, burgesses and community' while endowing them with a wide range of rights and privileges. These included an entitlement to the rents of the lands and property within its bounds, the revenues from its customs and tolls, and the proceeds of fines levied by the burgh court. Additionally they were granted fishing rights in the Nith (subject to those of the Friars Minor). In return, the burgh was obliged to pay the crown a *reddendo* of £20 annually, half at Whitsunday and half at Martinmas.

Dumfries was primarily a trading centre, and the market place, which was adjacent to the Townhead mote and the church, was where the merchants conducted their business. Together with other middlemen and townsfolk, they comprised a new and growing middle class who eventually gained control of the affairs of the burgh, and in particular its trade. Because Dumfries probably lost out to the more accessible ports of Wigtown and the Isle of Whithorn, and even Kirkcudbright, in the competition for foreign trade, its maritime trade would have been confined to the ports along the inner Solway and the Cumbrian coast. Much of the locally produced wool would have been transported overland to Teviotdale, and from there downriver to the main entrepot of Berwick for shipment to the principal cloth markets in the Low Countries and elsewhere. Surplus cattle, on the other hand, were driven across the border (despite the risk from robber bands) to the principal markets of northern England where they were much in demand.

Nevertheless life for virtually all classes, in town and country alike, was a constant battle against nature, the climate and disease. Infant mortality was consistently high, health was generally poor, and life expectancy so limited that those who survived to the age of forty were considered old. In general, therefore, the best that could be hoped for was 'safety of the person, safety in possessions, a tolerable winter and a kindly summer'.[46]

THE END OF THE BALLIOLS

In 1347 William Douglas, now lord of Douglas following the death of his uncle Hugh 'the dull', returned from France. A formidable warrior like his father Sir Archibald the former guardian, and his uncle Sir James, he was determined to recover his family lands in Douglasdale from the English, and the lordship of Liddesdale from the Knight. Assisted by his maternal uncle, the powerful Sir David Lindsay of Crawford, he seems to have achieved the former without difficulty. This not only secured him a landed base but it encouraged other magnates – particularly those hostile to the Knight – to rally to him. With their help he gained control of the forest of Selkirk, and routing the men of Teviotdale he forced them into his allegiance, thus establishing himself as a leading power in the marches.

News of his successes must have been particularly galling to the incarcerated Knight. The more so because, in spite of being allowed to return to Scotland from time to time on parole, he was unable to rally enough support to prevent the younger William from undermining his position at home. Therefore in July 1352, desperate to secure his liberty, he entered into a treasonable pact with King Edward. Under the terms of this, Edward undertook to release him and restore him to the lordship of Liddesdale, his lands in Moffatdale and those in Eskdale. In return, the Knight promised to perform military service for King Edward against all comers except the Scots. Further, that in the event of an English army invading Scotland he would contribute a force and allow it free passage through his lands which included Liddesdale.[47]

As soon as he was released, the Knight set about reducing the younger William's influence in the marches. He still commanded widespread support in the region, and this became apparent once his campaign was under way, when he was joined by many lesser barons who resented the younger William's influence. Fearing that the Knight intended not only to drive him out of the marches but to appropriate his lands in Douglasdale as well, the younger William resorted to desperate measures. In August 1353 he arranged for some henchmen to ambush the Knight while out hunting in the Selkirk forest when, as Bower tells us, he was 'cruelly and wretchedly killed'.

King David almost certainly sanctioned the murder – probably when the younger William visited him in London earlier in the year.[48] For not only did it go unpunished, but doubtless relieved to be rid of this overmighty subject who posed such a threat to his authority, David rewarded William by confirming him in possession of his family lands. They included those formerly belonging to his uncle the 'good' Sir James, to which he had fallen heir under the Douglas entail, as well as those he had inherited from his father Sir Archibald which included the lordship of Liddesdale. In addition the charter confirmed him in the barony of Drumlanrig which he purchased from his indigent brother-in-law the earl of Mar.[49]

However, the king's confirmation of his possession of Liddesdale was challenged by the Knight's daughter Mary and his nephew James Douglas. Whereas Mary claimed it as part of her legal rights in his estate, James Douglas argued that he was entitled to it as the sole beneficiary under his will.* But their claims were dismissed on the grounds that the Knight had forfeited Liddesdale when he entered into his treasonable pact with King Edward. Therefore it was held that the king's charter to the younger William should stand. Nevertheless its force, and that of other royal charters granting lands in southern Scotland, depended on how far King David's authority extended over them since much of the region was still in English hands. But their hold was tenuous, for in 1356 Roger Kirkpatrick, a member of the Closeburn family, drove the English out of Nithsdale though he failed to recapture Caerlaverock and Dalswinton.† At much the same time the Steward's eldest son, John of Kyle (future Robert III), recovered much of Annandale, although Lochmaben still remained in English hands under its new keeper Sir Richard Thirlwall.

The previous year, King Edward embarked on another campaign in his war with France. Therefore, invoking the Franco-Scottish alliance, the French king John II called on the Scots for military help, bribing them with a large sum of money to carry out a diversionary raid on northern England. The Scots responded by dispatching a contingent of soldiery to France under William Douglas, while the veteran earl of March captured Berwick town and laid siege to the castle. Later that year, following his return from France, Edward launched a retaliatory invasion of Scotland. Having lifted the siege of Berwick, relieved the garrison, and recaptured the town, he went on to spend the winter at Roxburgh.

In early 1356 he received a visit from Edward Balliol. His position in Scotland was crumbling fast. Bereft of all support in the south-west, and with his ancestral castle of Buittle in Bruce hands, he was forced to take refuge on Hestan island, his last redoubt in Scotland. The final straw came when the French king John II confiscated his lands in Picardy on the pretext that, being Edward's vassal, he was automatically an enemy of France. Yet, for all that, Balliol refused to stoop to the level of a supplicant begging for small mercies. On the contrary he drove a hard bargain with King Edward. In return for assigning him both his right to the Scottish crown and the reversion of his lands in England and Scotland, Balliol was granted a pension of £2,000 from the English crown with permission to live in England for the rest of his life.[50]

The English attributed Balliol's capitulation to his 'great age and feebleness, and his inability to continue the great labours he had to sustain'[51] – perhaps with some truth considering he was now in his mid-seventies. Still there seems to have been plenty of fight left in the old man. When it came to making a formal surrender of his kingdom, he reportedly appeared before Edward 'like a roaring lion'.[52] In a dramatic gesture expressive of his anger at Edward's abandonment of his cause, he tore the crown from

---

*   It was in consequence of this that he inherited the lordship of Dalkeith.
†   M Brown, *The Black Douglases*, 48. A man of some note, Roger (later Sir Roger) Kirkpatrick was a member of the delegation appointed to negotiate the terms of King David's release from captivity.

his head and flung it into the royal lap. Then, scraping up a handful of earth and stones he threw them down at the royal feet to symbolise his resignation of the kingdom.[53] Thereafter he spent the rest of his long life in affluent retirement at his manor in Yorkshire until his death in January 1364.

With the arrival of spring King Edward renewed his campaign. This was intended to punish the Scots for invading England, and at the same time force them into resuming negotiations for King David's release. Setting out from Roxburgh, his army advanced northwards laying waste to the countryside and burning the townships in its path until it reached Edinburgh. Because the supply ships he had been relying on failed to arrive, having been scattered in a storm, Edward was forced to abandon his plan to advance beyond the Forth. Therefore, having burnt Edinburgh his army withdrew south to Carlisle burning and laying waste to the countryside so extensively that the episode became known as the 'burnt Candlemas'.[54] But no sooner had the English crossed the border than William Douglas counterattacked, and, assisted by a number of Lothian knights, he captured Caerlaverock and Dalswinton castles,[55] which Roger Kirkpatrick failed to take the previous year.

Nevertheless the comprehensive devastation carried out by the English achieved its objective, because the Scots resumed negotiations for David's release. After some haggling, agreement was reached on all points, and on 3 October it was enshrined in the treaty of Berwick. The ransom was fixed at 100,000 merks to be paid in ten annual instalments, the first being due at midsummer 1358. Furthermore, the payments were to continue regardless of whether David should die before the ransom was fully paid. Anticipating a successful outcome, he was already on his way north. Arriving at the border, he tactfully replaced his English entourage with an impressive array of Scottish bishops, earls and knights, including Sir Roger Kirkpatrick.[56] Bower asserts that, before he was released, David was forced to give an undertaking that he would destroy the castles and forts in Nithsdale because they 'had inflicted the greatest damage on the English'. Therefore writing in the 1440s, Bower tells us that, following his return, David 'razed to the ground the castles of Dalswinton, Dumfries, Morton, Durisdeer, and nine others [which] have still not been rebuilt'.[57]

In November 1357 David convened a meeting of his Council at Scone to approve a series of measures which were designed to restore his authority. In a re-run of the situation confronting him on his return from France in 1341, much depended on the enforcement of justice, and the re-imposition of law and order which had effectively broken down under the feeble rule of the Steward. The Council remained in session for upwards of two weeks (suggesting a comprehensive agenda), in the course of which it passed a series of ordinances for the purpose. For example, they included a decree re-affirming that justices ayre should be held throughout the realm at which the king should preside in person 'to strike terror into wrongdoers'.[58]

Most important of all was the question of how to raise the money to pay his ransom. While difficult enough in any case, it was rendered doubly so by the disordered state to which the public finances had been reduced under the Steward. Nevertheless a number of measures were passed for the purpose, including the revocation of all grants of lands, rents, customs and other sources of revenue made in the course of his reign. In practice it yielded relatively little, mainly because of the numerous exemptions David had to make to keep the leading magnates, such as the earl of March, William Douglas and the Steward, on side, while others were rewards for loyalty or past service.

Another measure, namely the requisitioning of the woolcrop and re-selling it at a profit, proved a useful source of revenue. Taxation was another. It included what was effectively an income tax on rents, and a capital tax on moveable goods, crops and livestock. Neither tax was particularly remunerative; nor was the doubling of the export duty on wool, woolfells (wool with the attaching hide) and hides. Because responsibility for raising the money fell primarily on the merchant burgesses of the principal burghs, this gave them added clout – to the extent that they became a political force. This was officially recognised when they were summoned to Parliament as the third of the three estates along with the nobility and the clergy.

Notwithstanding the treaty of Berwick, negotiations over the ransom continued. Finally in 1365 King Edward fixed it at £100,000 (not merks as previously) stipulating that payment was to be made by annual instalments of £4,000 (6,000 merks), the first being due in February 1366. At the same time he granted the Scots a truce which was to last until February 1370. In May 1366 David held a Council meeting at Holyrood to decide what further measures were needed to raise the money. As a preliminary, a survey was to be made of the country's financial and economic resources to assess how much could be collected, and how often; the export duty on wool was to be quadrupled, and the ransom artificially reduced by devaluing the coinage. This was to be achieved by adulterating its silver content so that an additional ten pence could be minted from each pound of silver. Although comparatively modest, it set a precedent for further devaluations over the following centuries, to the extent that by the time of the Union the Scots pound was officially valued at one-twelfth of the English pound.

Since Parliament authorised the money raised from all sources to be used towards payment of the ransom and ordinary royal expenditure, without distinction, David took advantage of this to siphon off much of the money earmarked to pay his ransom for his own use. Not only that, but he allegedly stooped to the practice of granting – for a substantial consideration – pardons for homicide and other crimes, for which he was later rebuked by Parliament.[59] Nevertheless, through a combination of deviousness and astuteness, David ended up in a stronger financial position than any other medieval Scottish king,[60] while the ransom instalments were seldom paid – at least not in his lifetime.

DAVID II – THE LATTER YEARS

The decisions reached by the Council at Scone in November 1357 were worthless without the means to enforce them. This depended on the support of the leading magnates, generally purchasable with grants of land, exemption from taxes and other obligations, and – a novel form of bribery – the award of honours. A case in point was William Douglas. In February 1358 he was created earl of Douglas. This was no empty title because in fourteenth-century Scotland it equipped the holder with powers as a war leader and dispenser of justice. Consequently Douglas now stood in the top rank of the Scottish nobility. Nevertheless the award of an earldom was exceptional, because David generally confined himself to granting knighthoods, an example being the new Earl William's cousin and former protégé Archibald Douglas 'the Grim', illegitimate son of the 'good' Sir James.

Others included Roger Kirkpatrick. This was in recognition of past services, including in particular the recovery of Nithsdale from the English for which he had been rewarded with the lands of Glenesslin in the upper Cairn valley.[61] As a further mark of favour, David appointed him sheriff of Dumfries, and later Ayr.[62] However, in June 1358 his career was cut short with his murder at the hands of James Lindsay of Crawford.[*] The outrage took place at Caerlaverock which Kirkpatrick was occupying as the official residence of the sheriffs of Dumfries. According to Bower, Lindsay's felony was compounded by the fact that Kirkpatrick had been invited there as his guest. In an obvious flight of fancy he describes how 'after dinner when the wine had been pleasurably drained and both men said goodnight, Roger went to bed with no anticipation of evil'. Later that night his guest 'knocked and entered the bedroom with lighted candles and without further ado heartlessly cut Roger's throat'.[63] Arraigned before a specially convened assize at Dumfries, Lindsay was convicted of his murder, and on the king's orders he was executed.

At much the same time the recently knighted Sir John Herries purchased the barony of Terregles[†] from Thomas earl of Mar,[‡] the relevant charter being issued in March 1359.[64] Herries had been a member of the Scottish contingent sent to France under William Douglas in response to King John's appeal for help in his war against the English. The campaign was a disaster. In September 1356 the French army suffered an overwhelming defeat at the hands of King Edward's son, the Black Prince, at Poitiers when King John was taken prisoner. Nevertheless a number of Scots managed to escape back home. They included Douglas himself, Archibald the Grim, and Herries. Following his return to Scotland, Herries gained

---

*   Son of Sir David Lindsay of Crawford and first cousin of his close ally William earl of Douglas, he was married to the Steward's half-sister Egidia.
†   The barony extended westwards from the Nith towards modern-day Shawhead.
‡   He was the son of Earl Donald, the guardian who was killed at Dupplin. When he died without issue, the earldom passed to his sister Margaret, wife of William earl of Douglas, and from her to their son James who became earl of Douglas and Mar.

great favour with the king who raised the status of Terregles to a free barony and later a regality.[65]

More was to follow. In 1368 King David gave Herries the lands of Kirkgunzeon,[*] which had been forfeited by the monks of Holm Cultram and converted into a barony.[66] With the addition of half the barony of Urr, also given him by the king, Herries became a substantial landowner and a leading power in eastern Galloway. He was also one of the king's regular counsellors, while his standing is evident from his presence – and that of his younger son Gilbert – in the entourage who invariably accompanied King David on his visits to London. Later, David rewarded Herries with a pension of 20 merks.[67]

Meanwhile John of Kyle's recovery of much of Annandale in 1356 had rendered the English hold on the remainder of the lordship increasingly tenuous. So much so that the earl of Northampton was constrained to cede a portion of its rents and profits to King David. In terms of an agreement reached between Sir Thomas Ross (Sir Richard Thirlwall's successor as keeper of Lochmaben) on behalf of the earl, and Sir John Stewart of Dalswinton representing King David, all rents and profits, including those from judicial fines, accruing from Annandale were to be divided equally between the king and earl. The only exceptions were Lochmaben and its attaching settlements of Hightae, Smallholm and Esbie, whose profits were to belong exclusively to the earl. The agreement was formalised by an indenture which was executed in David's presence at nearby Rockhall on 1 May 1360.[68]

It was renewed at Lochmaben in June, and again in August 1364. On the latter occasion Archibald the Grim represented the king in his capacity as warden of the west marches and lieutenant of the king in Scotland. It was further renewed in December 1366.[69] On that occasion, reflecting the importance which both sides attached to it, King David was again present, while Humphrey de Bohun earl of Hereford,[†] the English-appointed lord of Annandale, was represented by the archbishop of Canterbury as chancellor, and the earl of Arundel. Its terms were a virtual repeat of the original agreement, with the further proviso that David was not to build any new fortresses in Annandale. It also confirmed the earl's exclusive right to the 'lake' (i.e. the Castle loch), park and castle of Lochmaben, and the vills of Esbie, Hightae and Smallholm. Moreover he or his agent were permitted to carry out any necessary repairs to the castle, with safe conducts issued to those responsible for collecting materials and other supplies from England.[70]

In 1363 the earl of Douglas came out in revolt against the king, in which he was joined by the Steward and his sons John of Kyle and Robert earl of Menteith (later

---

[*]   A much larger barony than Terregles, it extended from near Lochfoot to the outskirts of present-day Dalbeattie, and consisted of some 15,000 acres (6,000 ha) of land, part of which had been reclaimed by the monks of Holm Cultram.

[†]   He had succeeded to his father William's earldom of Northampton in September 1360, and to the earldom of Hereford on the death of his uncle, Humphrey de Bohun, the following year. He himself died in 1373 leaving two daughters as co-heiresses, the younger of whom married Henry of Bolingbroke, later duke of Lancaster and future Henry IV. This explains why the records of the lordship of Annandale were deposited with those of the duchy of Lancaster, where they still remain.

duke of Albany), and the seventy-nine-year-old earl of March. Ostensibly it was in protest at the money raised to pay his ransom being wasted by 'evil counsel'. In reality it was resentment of the king choosing as his advisers men of lesser rank, such as knights, burgesses and others, instead of men like themselves who in their view had a prescriptive right to act in that capacity. The earl of Douglas had particular cause for complaint – at least in his eyes. David had appointed him warden of the west marches in succession to his cousin Archibald the Grim. But, fearing that he was becoming too powerful, David had dismissed him from office and replaced him with Sir John Stewart of Dalswinton. To compound Douglas's resentment, David had rejected his claim to certain lands in Eskdale, having given them to his rival Sir James Douglas of Dalkeith.

The revolt, which amounted to little more than attacks on a number of royal castles and the capture of some royal officers, was crushed without difficulty and the leaders were forced to submit. Prudently, David refrained from punishing them, the Steward merely being compelled to renounce his bond with the two earls. They got off even more lightly, because David attempted to bring them on side with handsome concessions. In the earl of March's case he granted his heir George Dunbar[*] half the barony of Tibbers, as well as the barony of Morton which had reverted to the crown following the death of Robert Bruce's last surviving sister Christina, widow of Sir Andrew Moray, in 1357. In 1369 George Dunbar (now earl of March) assigned his share of Tibbers jointly to his sister Elizabeth, her husband Sir John Maitland of Thirlestane, and their son Robert.[†] In Douglas's case his allegiance was bought by David's undertaking to press the English to restore him to his family's lands of Fawdon in Northumberland.

In 1367 the Knight of Liddesdale's daughter Mary died giving birth to a stillborn child. She was a lady of considerable means having been adjudged the inheritor of part of his lands, including those in Eskdale. Therefore the question of who should inherit them was the subject of a dispute between her husband Thomas Erskine and her cousin Sir James Douglas of Dalkeith who claimed them as her heir-at-law. Erskine put forward an ingenious, though far-fetched and doubtless spurious claim – namely that the child had been born alive and although it died it had survived its mother. Therefore it had inherited her lands and he was entitled to them as the father.

The story goes that the issue was to be settled by a jousting match between the rival claimants in the presence of King David. But just as they were formed up ready to charge, he stopped the fight and ordered the issue to be judicially resolved.[71] He had good reason. Because Douglas of Dalkeith was a member of his intimate circle of advisers, as well as one of his most loyal supporters, David was determined that the disputed lands should go to him. Therefore, rather than chance the issue to the

---

[*] Son of Earl Patrick's first cousin, Sir Patrick Dunbar, and Isabella a sister of John Randolph earl of Moray, he succeeded to the earldom of March on the death of the eighty-four-year-old Earl Patrick in 1368.

[†] *RRS* vi, no 509. Tibbers remained in the Maitland family until 1509 when Robert's descendant, William Maitland of Lethington, sold it to Sir William Douglas of Drumlanrig (*Scots Peerage* v, 291).

uncertain outcome of a jousting match, he ensured Douglas's succession by submitting it to the due process of law where he could influence the decision. True or not, the fact remains that Mary's lands went to Douglas of Dalkeith.[72] Presumably it was for the same reason, namely to give Douglas a power base in the south-west, that in 1369 David persuaded the earl of March to hand over the barony of Morton to him.*

Besides King David and Douglas of Dalkeith, the third member of the ruling triumvirate was Archibald the Grim. As in the case of Douglas of Dalkeith, David was at pains to build up Archibald's power as a counterweight to that of the earl of Douglas. For a start he gave him in marriage Joanna Murray, an extremely well-dowered widow who brought him the lordship of Bothwell along with other lands and rights. Further honours came Archibald's way. David needed to establish a trusted supporter in eastern Galloway to fill the vacuum left by Edward Balliol, and above all someone who was powerful enough to impose his authority on the region. Therefore in 1369 he granted Archibald a charter of 'all our lands in Galloway [i.e. those belonging to the crown] between the waters of the Cree and the Nith',[73] thus establishing him as the principal power in the south-west and a formidable rival to the earl of Douglas.

Three years later, Archibald added the former crown lands in Wigtownshire to his extensive possessions. Sir Malcolm Fleming, whom King David had created earl of Wigtown, died in 1357. About the same time his grandson and successor, Earl Thomas, was given up as a hostage for David's ransom. In his absence feuding broke out among the leading Wigtownshire magnates, reducing the earldom to chaos. On his return in 1367 Thomas attempted to re-assert his authority but without success. While lack of money to pay his levies was a contributory factor, the main instigator was Archibald the Grim. Since he had his eye on the earldom and the attaching lands for himself, he was inciting the magnates to rebel and render it so ungovernable as to induce Earl Thomas to abandon it. Therefore in February 1372 Archibald persuaded Thomas to sell him both the earldom and its attaching lands for the sum of £500. This meant he was now lord of the whole of Galloway, and to emphasise the fact he embarked on the building of Threave castle, a large stone tower on an island in the river Dee, to serve as his ruling centre.

Throughout this time the Steward had remained King David's principal opponent and a constant source of trouble. By 1367 David, a much abler and far more astute man than his nephew, had succeeded in isolating him from his associates, the earl of Douglas and the new earl of March. He went further. In an attempt to drive a wedge between the Steward and his eldest son John of Kyle, he arranged a marriage between the latter and Annabella Drummond, niece of his queen, Margaret Logie.† The

---

* It was probably entirely coincidental that Douglas later married the earl of March's sister Agnes Dunbar, King David's former mistress.

† Born Margaret Drummond, she was married firstly to Sir John Logie from whom she was divorced, and in 1363 she married David, whose wife Joan had died the previous year. Six years later David tried to divorce her so that he could marry Agnes Dunbar, but Margaret contested the action and the matter was still unresolved at the time of his death.

following year, in order to bind John more closely to him and distance him still further from his father, David created him earl of Carrick.* This amounted to a tacit recognition of a Stewart succession and John's ultimate entitlement to the throne.

Evidently a forceful lady (like her niece the future Queen Annabella), David II's queen Margaret Logie persuaded him to endow her son John Logie with an access of lands as a means of establishing him as a power in the realm. They included the royal lands in Annandale, now recovered from the English, with the exception of Lochmaben.[74] Not surprisingly, Logie's advancement was widely resented. So much so that King David's loyal adherent Sir John Kennedy of Dunure was constrained to warn Logie of 'snares and plots' against him 'within the kingdom of Scotland, and chiefly within the lordship of Annandale'.[75] But Logie's tenure was brief, because his protector David died suddenly and unexpectedly on 22 February 1371 at the relatively early age of forty-six.

---

*   *RRS* vi, no 400. The title had lapsed with the death of Alexander Bruce, illegitimate son of Robert Bruce's brother Edward, at Halidon Hill. Following John of Kyle's accession to the throne in 1390 the earldom of Carrick became vested in the crown where it has remained ever since.

SEVEN

The Rise of the Black Douglases

ACCESSION OF THE STEWARTS

David II had no children by either of his wives, nor for that matter by any of his mistresses. Therefore he was succeeded by his nephew the Steward who at the mature age of fifty-five became king as Robert II. One of his first acts was to strip John Logie of the lordship of Annandale, which in consequence reverted to George Dunbar earl of March as eldest grandson of Thomas Randolph earl of Moray.

Yet King Robert never managed to impose his authority over the realm to anything like the same extent as his able and forceful uncle. This was partly because, in spite of being a grandson of the hero-king Robert Bruce, he was generally perceived as essentially a magnate, albeit one of the most powerful in the realm, rather than a member of the royal house. Altogether one gains the impression that even in his heyday he was never a very commanding personality, and became less so with age. Furthermore his poor record of government, first as guardian and later as king's lieutenant, during King David's absences told against him. At the same time he was dogged by a generally hostile administration which David had built up in opposition to him

A number of leading magnates were quick to take advantage of his perceived weakness. This became apparent at the outset when, according to Wyntoun, the earl of Douglas, Robert's former comrade in arms, challenged his right to succeed on the patently fictitious grounds that he, Douglas, represented the Balliol/Comyn faction and as such had a superior right to the throne.[1] Assisted by the earl of March, his brother John Dunbar, future earl of Moray, and others, Robert forced Douglas to withdraw his claim. However as a *douceur* he granted Douglas the lordship of Liddesdale and the lands in Eskdale which King David had awarded to Douglas of Dalkeith, claiming that, in so doing, David had acted illegally. He also appointed Douglas warden of the east marches and justiciar of southern Scotland, and in order to establish a dynastic link between their two families, he gave his daughter Isabella in marriage to Douglas's son James, the future second earl.

Unlike King David, Robert was immensely prolific having had numerous offspring by both his wives, as well as a raft of illegitimate children. By his long-dead first wife Elizabeth Mure he had ten children – four sons, including John of Kyle, now earl of Carrick, and Robert earl of Fife, and six daughters. By his second wife Euphemia, daughter of the earl of Ross and widow of John Randolph earl of Moray, he had a further two sons and two daughters. Not only that, but he had at least nine known illegitimate children, and because only males are recorded he probably had illegitimate daughters as well, in which case he must have sired upwards of twenty-three children.

But there was a problem. He did not marry his first wife – at least not in the eyes of the Church – until after their children were born. Although subsequently legitimised by papal dispensation, they were widely regarded as tainted with bastardy and therefore ineligible to succeed to the kingship. Certainly that was the view of the two unquestionably legitimate sons of his second marriage, David earl of Strathearn and Walter earl of Atholl. The latter in particular would use his half-brothers' questionable legitimacy as a pretext for claiming the throne, to the extent that in his old age he allowed himself to be inveigled into the plot to assassinate his nephew James I, with fearsome consequences for himself and his family.

Conscious of the taint of bastardy attaching to his first family, Robert attempted to put their legitimacy beyond doubt by having Parliament enact an entail to regulate the succession. This stipulated that the crown should pass from father to son, starting with his eldest son the earl of Carrick and his male issue, and so on through his younger sons in descending order. Female descendants and their offspring, on the other hand, were excluded from the succession, ironically considering Robert himself had inherited the throne through his mother. Nevertheless the fact that he had six sons all standing in line of succession rendered the point academic, particularly as they would have numerous sons of their own.

Long before his accession, while still Steward, Robert had been making provision for his sons, either by gifts of land or through marriage to well-dowered heiresses, or both. After he became king, he continued the practice of granting his sons lands and titles, to the extent that by 1377 seven of the sixteen Scottish earldoms had passed into the hands of himself and his family.[2] Although designed to bolster Robert's authority, it had the unintended effect of creating rivalries between his sons as they contended with each other for power. Worse still, they became overmighty subjects and a challenge to the royal authority.

That would come later. Meanwhile, confronted by a hostile political establishment, Robert needed to build up a group of supporters through bribery in the form of land grants to buttress his authority – in effect bargain his way to power. That said, there is no record of his using crown lands in Dumfriesshire for the purpose. True, he issued a charter in 1374 granting the lands of Durisdeer to his relative Sir Robert Stewart of Innermeath;[3] but because it proceeded on a resignation by Alexander Meyners it was most likely in implement of a sale. Although a Perthshire family, the Meyners (later Menzies) maintained their links with Nithsdale as owners of the barony of Enoch[4] for some centuries to come.

Meanwhile the fourteen-year truce which David II agreed with Edward III towards the end of his reign remained in force. This enabled Robert to concentrate on establishing his royal authority undistracted by war. In fact, such was his anxiety to avoid the risk of an English invasion to enforce payment of the arrears of King David's ransom that he ensured prompt payment of the instalments as they became due. It was a struggle, and by the time of King Edward's death in 1377 much of it had been paid. But fears of an invasion were overdone because Edward was in no fit state to lead one. Now in his mid-sixties and victim of a degenerative condition compounded by a succession of strokes, this king, who in his heyday had been one of the most renowned military commanders of the age, and the arbiter of chivalry, was reduced to what was described as a 'mindless dotard'.' Since his eldest son the Black Prince died after a long illness in 1376 and the latter's son Richard, now his heir, was under age, the old king's ruling powers were exercised by his eldest surviving son, John of Gaunt duke of Lancaster. Another martial character in much the same mould as his father and eldest brother, he would lead a number of invasions of Scotland in the course of the next few years.

Throughout this time the English remained in occupation of part of southern Scotland where they continued to hold a number of castles, including Lochmaben. Therefore, notwithstanding the truce, the Scots continued their attempts to drive them out. This involved the occasional clash such as occurred in 1378 when, on the evidence of Wyntoun, Sir John Johnstone of that Ilk, the warden of the west marches, and Gordon of Stichill defeated a superior English force 'on the Waters of the Solway' and gained a large haul of booty.[5]

By this time the Scots had recovered virtually the whole of Annandale except for the south-eastern corner (effectively the triangle between Lochmaben, Annan and Gretna) which was still in English hands. Therefore it was here that the Scots concentrated their attacks. This is evident from the accounts of William Henryson, the royal chamberlain of Lochmaben.[†] For example those for 1374 record that no rents were received from the vills of Kirkpatrick, Gretna and others at Martinmas that year because 'the tenants were totally ruined both by the English and the Scots'.[6] Those for the following year tell the same story. This time it was the vill of Annan's turn, evident from a comment that 'no tenants would hold it' (i.e. take a lease of it) because of 'the devastation of the Scots'. According to an attaching note, no rents were received from the vills of Hightae and Smallholm 'as the tenants were completely ruined by the earl of March'.[7]

Meanwhile King Robert was building up the power and influence of Archibald the Grim as a rival to that of the earl of Douglas, an example being his ratification of Archibald's purchase of the earldom of Wigtown and its attaching lands. But instead of the friendly accomplice who had incited them to rebel against Earl Thomas, the local magnates found themselves saddled with a hard, stern and even cruel master who was determined to clamp down on the slightest sign of unrest.

---

* See Ian Mortimer, *The Perfect King*, pp 382–91, which gives a harrowing description of how at his last formal reception this human vegetable had to be trussed up in specially strengthened robes which were nailed to his throne to keep him upright as he gazed down uncomprehendingly at the assembled throng.
† Royal because the castle was now in King Edward's hands as guardian of the two under-age daughters of Humphrey de Bohun earl of Hereford.

Consequently Archibald established undisputed mastery of the earldom, and with his lordship of Galloway and wardenship of the west marches he was now a dominant power in the marches.

As a man of high status, and 'ane nobilman of singulare manheid and virtew, havand [holding] priestis and religious men in gret reverence',[8] Archibald put in hand a project which was first mooted by Edward Bruce while lord of Galloway, but which his campaign in Ireland and other distractions prevented him from realising. This was to convert what was probably a disused almshouse built on land belonging to Dercongal (later Holywood) abbey into a hospital for the poor and infirm. The foundation, which would include a chapel, was to be under the charge of a secular priest with a staff of eighteen bedesmen who were responsible for praying for the souls of others – in this case Archibald himself and those of 'Robert and David, Kings of Scots, [as well as] Edward Bruce, James lord of Douglas [the 'good' Sir James], and other ancestors and successors, and of all the faithful departed'.[9] The project was approved by King Robert and the bishop of Glasgow, the king formally confirming Archibald's foundation charter in 1372,[10] although papal consent was not forthcoming until 1378.

While prepared to support Archibald's project, King Robert was clearly concerned that he had gone too far in building up his power and influence, and like the earl of Douglas he was in danger of becoming an overmighty subject. Therefore he attempted to set up his nephew Sir James Lindsay of Crawford* as a rival power in the southwest. This was to be achieved by the time-honoured method of land grants. They included the barony of Kirkmichael which formerly belonged to Lindsay's great-uncle William Lindsay.[11] But Archibald's position was unassailable because he had the power to browbeat the local magnates into supporting him. They included the influential Sir Thomas Kirkpatrick who needed little encouragement given the vendetta between his family and the Lindsay kindred stemming from his near relative Sir Roger's murder at the hands of Lindsay's father.

At much the same time, in pursuit of his policy of building up the power of his sons as a means of extending his own authority, King Robert made over the Stewardship and its attaching lands to his eldest son the earl of Carrick, later appointing him to the prestigious office of keeper of Edinburgh castle. On the strength of this Carrick set about establishing a power base in southern Scotland by enlisting the support of the principal families in the region. They included the heads of the three main branches of the house of Douglas – Earl William, Archibald the Grim, and Sir James of Dalkeith, as well as the powerful Lindsay kindred. Since his daughters were of marriageable age, Carrick used them as pawns to strengthen his ties with the Douglases. In about 1380 he arranged for his eldest daughter Margaret to marry

---

* Son of Sir James Lindsay, the murderer of Sir Roger Kirkpatrick, and King Robert's half-sister Egidia, Sir James was a close relative of the earl of Douglas and had connections with Dumfriesshire as a brother-in-law of Sir John Maxwell of Caerlaverock. (Later he would earn notoriety for the murder of Sir John Lyon of Glamis, King Robert's son-in-law and chamberlain.)

Archibald's son and heir Archibald, future fourth earl of Douglas. At much the same time he married off his second daughter Elizabeth to James Douglas, eldest son of Sir James of Dalkeith. Later a younger daughter Mary was married to the earl of Douglas's illegitimate son, George future earl of Angus.

As a further sop to Archibald the Grim, Carrick endowed his illegitimate son Sir William Douglas (described as 'a dark-skinned giant like his father and grandfather'[12]) with the lordship of Nithsdale. Later, 'on account of his skill in war', Carrick gave Sir William his half-sister Egidia (daughter of Robert II by his second wife, and reportedly 'a werry beautiful ladye'*) in marriage, while another half-sister Elizabeth became the wife of Sir David Lindsay.[†] So successful was his strategy that by 1382 he and his allies constituted what was effectively a shadow administration, ready to take over the reins of power on the old king's death which was expected – or more likely hoped for – sooner rather than later.

Meanwhile the Scots were carrying out a series of attacks on the English-held castles in southern Scotland, evident from a report submitted by the earl of Northumberland[‡] to the English Council in April 1379. This drew particular attention to the case of Sir Thomas Ughtred, the keeper of Lochmaben, who felt so threatened by the Scots that he refused to remain at his post any longer. Therefore as a temporary measure he had been replaced by a Cumbrian magnate, Armand de Monceaux. The report went on to say that the earls of Douglas and March, and Archibald the Grim, were 'harassing the English borderers by imprisonment, ransoms and otherwise'.[13] By October Sir Thomas Rokeby had been appointed keeper of Lochmaben, and the fact that Adam de Corry was a member of the garrison suggests a continuing division of loyalties within the family, and perhaps the same applied in the case of other Dumfriesshire families as well.[14]

In January 1384 the earl of March and Archibald the Grim renewed their attacks on Lochmaben. Because Sir Alexander Fetherstonehalghe, who had recently succeeded Sir Thomas Rokeby as keeper, was running out of supplies and had only a small garrison he undertook to surrender the castle unless it was relieved within eight days. Rather than face the prospect of a prolonged siege, Archibald agreed. Consequently he and his men were forced to endure a spell of miserably cold, wet and windy weather until the ninth day when, in the absence of an English relieving force, they gained possession of the castle, the last remaining English-held fortress in the south-west. Later that year, the earl of Douglas drove the English out of Teviotdale.[15] Now in his sixties this was his last campaign because he died later that year when both the title and his extensive landholdings passed to his only legitimate son Earl James.

---

*   All the king's daughters were renowned for their good looks, being described in the papal dispensation concerning their parents' marriage as 'fair to behold' (Nicholson, *Scotland: The Later Middle Ages*, 186)

†   Created earl of Crawford in 1398; the title is currently held by his remote descendant the 29th earl.

‡   So created in 1377, he was a grandson of the Henry Percy to whom Edward Balliol granted the lordship of Annandale and Lochmaben castle.

THE DOUGLAS SUCCESSION

The truce with England expired at Candlemas (2 February) 1384. The following month John of Gaunt invaded the east marches at the head of a large army and made an unopposed advance on Edinburgh. However, mindful of the hospitality he received when he took refuge there from the Peasants' Revolt three years before, he refrained from pillaging the city, although for good measure he extracted a large ransom from the citizens. King Robert's inability to defend against the invasion contributed to the political crisis which came to a head later that year. He was now nearly seventy, and in spite of Froissart's description of him as 'bowed down and blear-eyed with age' he was in fact in perfect health and looked like going on for ever. But Carrick, now approaching fifty, was impatient to take over the reins of power. Having established himself as a force in southern Scotland and gained the support of the leading magnates, he was now in a strong enough position to edge the old king aside.

In November 1384 Carrick convened a meeting of the General Council at which he organised a *putsch* (coup). At his instigation, the king was severely criticised for his inability to uphold the law and exercise justice, and in particular for his failure to curb the excesses being perpetrated in the north by his fourth son Alexander earl of Buchan (known as 'the Wolf of Badenoch'). Therefore responsibility for the enforcement of royal justice was taken out of his hands and assigned to Carrick who was appointed guardian – 'swept to power', as it was put, 'on a law and order ticket', although in the event he failed to deliver. Judging from a reference to 'the seizure of the king',[16] it seems that the king's consent was obtained by force. Thereafter he was consigned to political oblivion.

Encouraged by promises of French help, Carrick's accession to power marked a resumption of war with England. In July 1385 a combined Franco-Scottish force attacked Roxburgh castle, still in English hands, before going on to invade Cumberland. At that point news reached them that an English army under Richard II and John of Gaunt was heading north. But instead of trying to intercept it, the commanders of the Franco-Scottish force adhered to their original plan to invade Cumberland. A disastrous decision, for apart from achieving nothing it left the east and middle marches unguarded and exposed to the English invaders who swarmed across the border virtually unopposed, devastated the middle marches and sacked the Border abbeys. Advancing on Edinburgh they put the city to flames, although Holyrood was spared on the orders of John of Gaunt. This reverse, combined with growing friction between the French and Scots, forced Carrick to sue for peace. Accordingly a truce was agreed which was to last until July 1386, although subsequently extended to June 1388.

As soon as it expired hostilities were resumed. Seizing the initiative, and taking advantage of the confused political situation in England where Richard II was under challenge from a militant baronage, the Scots launched an invasion on two fronts. One army under Archibald the Grim and the king's younger son Robert earl of Fife overran the English west marches, and defeating a force of Cumbrian levies they laid siege to Carlisle. The other, under the earl of Douglas, assisted by the earl of March and his brother John earl of Moray, invaded the English east marches and plundered its way southwards as far as Newcastle.

Meanwhile the earl of Northumberland's son, Sir Henry Percy (known as 'Harry Hotspur'), mustered a force of local recruits. When the Scots were about to attack Newcastle he drove them off, and pursuing them northwards he caught up with them at Otterburn. On 5 August he forced them to give battle – unwisely, because it resulted in a Scottish victory when Percy and his brother were taken prisoner along with a number of Northumbrian knights. But it was a pyrrhic victory because the earl of Douglas was killed. The story has it that, though mortally wounded, he turned the tide of battle by ordering his retainers to hush up news of his impending death and keep his banner flying to encourage the Scots to greater efforts.

Since Douglas was one of Carrick's principal allies and a key supporter, his death left Carrick politically weakened. To compound his misfortune, it was about this time that he received a severe kick from a horse belonging to Douglas of Dalkeith – so severe that it left him permanently lame and impaired his ability to govern, which suggests he must have been in constant pain. Douglas's death had important political repercussions. Since he had no legitimate issue* and left no will, nor any instructions regarding the succession to his lands, there was considerable doubt as to who should inherit them, and who, if anyone, was entitled to succeed to the earldom.

On 18 August a meeting of the General Council was held at Linlithgow to determine the issue. While no decision was reached, it was recognised that the person with the strongest claim to the Douglas lands was Malcolm Drummond as husband of the dead earl's sister, Isabella countess of Mar.† His claim was supported by Carrick. Apart from being Carrick's brother-in-law,‡ Drummond was one of his key allies. Therefore, if his claim was upheld, it would greatly strengthen Carrick's position in southern Scotland.

This was all the more important because Drummond's claim to the principal Douglas lands was being challenged by Archibald the Grim, Carrick's main rival for power in southern Scotland. Moreover Archibald had a stronger claim as heir under the entail executed by Hugh 'the dull' back in 1342. In this he was supported by his

---

* He had two illegitimate sons – William, who had been given the barony of Drumlanrig, and Archibald, who acquired the barony of Cavers in Roxburghshire. William became a power in his own right, and his descendants became successively the earls, marquesses and dukes of Queensberry, while Archibald's descendants, the Douglases of Cavers, remained a prominent Border family.

† Unlike the Douglas earldom, which was limited to male heirs, that of Mar was open to female succession. Therefore Countess Isabella inherited the title on the death of her brother Earl James. He in turn had inherited it from their mother Margaret countess of Mar, wife of William first earl of Douglas and sister of the indigent Thomas earl of Mar.

‡ Carrick was married to Drummond's sister Annabella – a match which, it will be remembered, had been arranged by David II at the behest of his second wife Margaret Logie (née Drummond) who was Annabella's aunt.

long-standing ally Sir James Douglas of Dalkeith. He too had territorial ambitions. As nephew and heir of the Knight of Liddesdale, he set his sights on recovering the lordship of Liddesdale and the baronies of Staplegorton and Westerkirk in Eskdale, which the king had granted to William earl of Douglas. Therefore Drummond and Carrick found themselves ranged against Archibald the Grim and Douglas of Dalkeith, an overwhelmingly powerful combination.

At this point another claimant entered the field, namely the young George Douglas, illegitimate son of William first earl of Douglas by his mistress Margaret countess of Angus. She was determined to secure the Douglas lands in east Lothian, based on Tantallon castle, for her son. Meanwhile Archibald the Grim and Sir James Douglas of Dalkeith were consolidating their position in the marches by winning over the leading Border families, such as the Glendinnings, who were the principal Douglas tenants in Eskdale, the Armstrongs, Rutherfords and the Scotts of Buccleuch. This was achieved by a combination of encouragement and threats. On the one hand they held themselves out as better able to defend them than Carrick and his allies in the likely event of an English invasion, while those who refused risked devastation of their lands.

Confronted by these two powerful warlords, Drummond's position began to crumble. And, following Carrick's removal from the lieutenancy and his replacement by his brother Robert earl of Fife, the disintegration was complete.* Although never a close ally of Archibald, Fife's ascendancy was crucial to his success. This was confirmed by a Parliament held at Holyrood in April 1389 which ruled that, whereas Earl James's lands in East Lothian should go to his half-brother George Douglas earl of Angus,† Archibald was entitled to the rest, including those passing under the Douglas entail. It also confirmed Douglas of Dalkeith in possession of the lordship of Liddesdale as well as the baronies of Staplegorton and Westerkirk.

Archibald went further. He claimed the earldom itself. It was entirely spurious, but might is a powerful argument. Since Fife could not afford to antagonise him in the face of a threatened English invasion, he was forced to concede his demand. Therefore he had Archibald's claim to the earldom validated by Parliament, and in consequence he became the third earl of Douglas. But refusing to abandon his claim to the Douglas estates, Drummond appealed to the English for help to establish it by force. Responding, King Richard dispatched an army under Ralph lord Neville and the earl of Nottingham to invade the east marches. Although the army appeared a formidable host, it was riven by disputes between its leaders. Its weakness soon became apparent when it encountered a hastily mustered force under Fife and Earl Archibald, who drove it back to the river Tyne and forced the English leaders to agree a truce.

---

* Drummond was subsequently murdered in 1403 by a band of Highland marauders allegedly under the leadership of Alexander Stewart who proceeded to marry his widow Isabella.

† Progenitor of the Red Douglases, he had recently succeeded to the earldom on the resignation of his mother Countess Margaret, daughter of Thomas Stewart earl of Angus from whom she had inherited the earldom.

Archibald was the clear winner. Having started out as a landless bastard with neither prospects nor advantages save an illustrious name, a strong right arm, and an immense physique, he had come an astonishingly long way. Now in his late sixties he had reached the pinnacle of his power and influence as head of the Douglas kindred and the supreme power in southern Scotland.

Sometime before this he embarked on a project to convert the nunnery at Lincluden into a collegiate church for the accommodation of secular priests – men who had taken holy orders but not the cowl. When it was founded in 1167 provision was made for the accommodation of ten nuns. Therefore, as a preliminary, they had to be evicted and the house closed. This required papal consent, and the preamble to the petition was a masterly piece of hyperbole. 'The prioress and nuns', it went, 'have taken to leading dissolute and scandalous lives, allowing the beautiful monastic buildings to fall into disrepair and ruin through neglect, while they dress their daughters, born of incest, in sumptuous clothes with gold ornaments and pearls'.[17] Far from being the literal truth, this was merely the standard form of pleading in such cases, and as there were only about five inmates including the prioress, it is hard to imagine them getting up to such high jinks within the confines of a small institution in a relatively remote part of Scotland. Nevertheless, papal sanction was granted, and in 1389 the priory was converted into a collegiate church.

Initially it accommodated twelve canons and a provost – hence its designation as a provostry. The first provost was Elias whose successor Alexander Carnys (Cairns) combined the office with that of administrator of the Douglas lands in Galloway. Probably at his instigation the provostry took over the nearby Poor's Hospital (Earl Archibald's previous foundation) when the number of bedesmen was increased from eighteen to twenty-four. Later, the provostry was enlarged into a community of eight prebendaries (in addition to the twenty-four bedesmen), while a chapel was subsequently added by Archibald's daughter-in-law, Duchess Margaret.[*] Meanwhile the appointment of provost remained in the gift of Archibald the Grim and his successors the earls of Douglas who seem to have used it for pensioning off their senior clerks.

In April 1390 the seventy-four-year-old Robert II died at his castle of Dundonald, in Ayrshire – 'in his awin cuntrie' as the chronicler put it, emphasising the commonly held perception of him as primarily a western magnate. This meant that Fife's guardianship automatically ceased, and his consequent loss of influence was compounded by the accession of his brother, the fifty-three-year-old John earl of Carrick who had never forgiven him for supplanting him in the lieutenancy. Because the name John was thought to have unfortunate associations with the failed kingship of John Balliol, the new king took the title of Robert III. Notwithstanding that two years previously he had been declared unfit to rule, and in spite of his physical disability, he was determined to exercise full kingly powers.

---

*   Daughter of the earl of Carrick, she was married to Earl Archibald's son, the future fourth earl, who was created duke of Touraine by the French king Charles VII.

THE RISE AND FALL OF ROTHESAY

Robert II's death and the earl of Fife's fall from power must have seriously alarmed Earl Archibald and Douglas of Dalkeith, because there was every likelihood that the new king Robert might persuade the General Council to revoke its decision regarding the Douglas inheritance and award it to Malcolm Drummond instead. Robert had already shown his hand at the beginning of his reign when he pointedly confirmed Earl Archibald's rival George earl of March in possession of the lordship of Annandale.[18] As senior grandson of Randolph earl of Moray, to whom Robert Bruce had granted the lordship, he was entitled to it anyway, but it seems that the king was going out of his way to emphasise the fact.

But it was not all bad news. In May 1390, faced with the threat of an English invasion, and fearing that the king lacked the will to oppose them, the General Council deprived him of his ruling powers. Since his elder son David earl of Carrick was not yet of an age to assume the guardianship,[*] it was restored to Fife, and because he was their ally, this must have come as a considerable relief to Earl Archibald and Douglas of Dalkeith. Fife's main qualification for office was that he could be relied on to defend against an English invasion. But it never materialised, and when three years later a truce was declared there was no further need for him at the helm. In any event his nephew David earl of Carrick had a prior claim to the office; and, judging him to be old enough, the General Council appointed him guardian in his uncle's place.

Although still only fourteen, Carrick was a mature young man. Determined to become a political force in his own right, he proceeded to establish a power base for himself in southern Scotland. Since Earl Archibald was the dominant power in the region, and therefore the main obstacle to his plans, Carrick allied himself with people like the Lindsays, William Douglas of Drumlanrig and other magnates hostile to the earl, with the avowed aim of having him stripped of his title and the Douglas patrimony.

In 1394 Carrick acquired the lordship of Nithsdale. It had been granted to Earl Archibald's illegitimate son Sir William Douglas; but, following his death on a crusade in Poland, Carrick persuaded the General Council to override the claims of Sir William's son and grant the lordship to him. The threat to Earl Archibald soon became apparent when Carrick pointedly styled himself lord of Nithsdale on a visit to Dumfries in December that year.[19] And to emphasise the fact, he was accompanied by Sir James Lindsay of Crawford and other members of his kindred, all of them hostile to Earl Archibald.

While Carrick probably commanded only limited support among the Nithsdale landowners, he could at least count on that of Sir Robert Danielston. The owner of Glencairn,[20] Robert Danielston was also a prominent member of Carrick's household and keeper of Dumbarton castle, while his family had been retainers – and hence

---

[*]   At the time the king had two sons – David aged eleven and Robert, who died in adolescence. His third son, the future James I, was not born until 1394 when the king was fifty-seven.

supporters – of Robert III before his accession. But Sir Robert's support proved short-lived because he died in 1397 leaving two young daughters as co-heiresses. Thereupon his brother Walter Danielston, who was opposed to the Stewarts, arrogated the keepership of Dumbarton castle, and continued to hold it in defiance of King Robert's orders to give it up. This left the king with no alternative but to raise a force to lay siege to the castle. But humiliatingly his men were unable to take it. Later the earl of Fife persuaded Walter to surrender the castle in return for preferment to the vacant see of St Andrews, which he accepted. However, he was not to enjoy the trappings of episcopal office for long because he died in 1402.[21] Later Margaret, the elder of Sir Robert's two daughters, married Sir William Cunningham of Kilmaurs. Since she inherited a half share of the barony of Glencairn, their grandson took that as his title when he was granted an earldom.

From the mid-1390s onwards Earl Archibald found himself pitted against another rival, namely George Douglas earl of Angus. A man of vaulting ambitions who commanded much influential support, his status was greatly enhanced as a result of his marriage in 1397 to the king's daughter Mary. Having inherited his mother's lands in Angus and East Lothian, he laid claim to Liddesdale. This harked back to 1367 when the Knight's daughter Mary died in childbirth and King David engineered its award to Douglas of Dalkeith. Angus contended that Liddesdale properly belonged to his father William earl of Douglas (which was true), that the right to it had passed to his half-brother Earl James (also correct), and that he was entitled to it as his heir. Not true because illegitimate children had no inheritance rights at law.

However, ignoring such legal niceties, and determined to pursue his claim by force, Earl George attacked Liddesdale. Earl Archibald could not stand idly by. Since Douglas of Dalkeith was his close ally, he regarded an attack on Douglas's lands as tantamount to an attack on his own. More worryingly, Earl George's raid encouraged a number of Border barons to switch their allegiance to him. However, in the autumn of 1398 Earl Archibald's son, the younger Archibald,[*] made a devastating attack on Roxburgh, burning the town and rendering the castle uninhabitable. This was enough to bring the defecting Border barons like Sir Walter Scott of Buccleuch back on side.[22]

The same year Carrick and his uncle Fife, advanced respectively to the dukedoms of Rothesay and Albany, sank their differences in a bid to remove power from the king's shaky grasp (a fitting retribution for supplanting his own father fourteen years earlier). For this they needed Earl Archibald's support. Therefore he agreed to meet them at Albany's castle of Falkland when, in return for Rothesay's abandoning his opposition to him, Archibald conceded his appointment as lieutenant of the realm. Mending his fences with Rothesay suited Archibald very well because it eliminated all further risk of a challenge to his earldom and the Douglas patrimony. Therefore, to cement their new-found accord, and as a gesture of goodwill, Archibald persuaded the General Council to extend Rothesay's lieutenancy for a further three years. But it

---

* Described as 'a giant warrior in the image of his father'.

was conditional on the appointment of twenty-one magnates, including Albany and Earl Archibald, who would be responsible for supervising Rothesay's exercise of his ruling powers.

Meanwhile the Anglo-Scottish truce of 1393 remained in force. In November 1398, when commissioners for both sides foregathered at the traditional Anglo-Scottish meeting place of Lochmabenstone,* it was agreed to extend it for a further five years. It was also stipulated that the conservators, who were responsible for ensuring its observance, should be drawn from both sides. Further, that they should meet regularly either at Kirkandrews on the English side of the border, or at Lochmabenstone, to agree on the amount of compensation to be awarded for breaches of the truce by either side, and both parties undertook to punish those responsible. The Scottish conservators included five Annandale landowners – Sir John Johnstone, Sir John Carlyle, Sir William Stewart of Castlemilk, Herbert Corry and John Carruthers.[23]

Meanwhile the earl of Angus was continuing his attacks on Liddesdale and Douglas of Dalkeith's lands of Staplegorton and Westerkirk. Finally he was prevailed on to submit his claim to adjudication by the General Council. Regardless of the fact that as a bastard he had no rights to them in law, the Council found in his favour and confirmed his entitlement to them.

In 1399 Earl Archibald decided to bind Rothesay, and by extension the Stewart dynasty, to his own family by arranging a marriage between him and his daughter Mary. Rothesay sounds to have been a fickle young man having dallied initially with Euphemia Lindsay, half-sister of Sir David Lindsay of Glenesk (recently created earl of Crawford) and cousin of Sir James Lindsay the head of the family. However, Sir James's sudden death in 1396, and the consequent decline of the Lindsay power and influence, tarnished her appeal, and therefore Rothesay (or Carrick as he then was) abandoned her. Consequently he was open to other bidders.

First off the mark was George Dunbar earl of March. The foremost power in the south-east, he offered Carrick his daughter Elizabeth, gilding her attractions with a large bribe. Since it would deliver him a powerful network of allies to counter the influence of his uncle Fife, Carrick was distinctly interested. But because he and Elizabeth were within the forbidden degrees of relationship, the earl of March had to petition the Pope for the necessary dispensation. But in his hurry to grasp the prize, March rushed the marriage through before the dispensation was granted. This meant it was invalid and Rothesay was prevailed on to repudiate her. So once again he was open to offers.

Grasping the opportunity, Earl Archibald put forward his daughter Mary, coupled with the promise of a still larger bribe. Since the idea appealed to him for much the same reason as it did to Earl Archibald – namely that it would create a valuable

---

*   Situated on a stretch of level ground adjacent to the coast near Gretna, this seven-foot high boulder is believed to have served as a boundary marker and meeting place since Roman times.

dynastic link between the royal family and the powerful Black Douglas affinity, Rothesay was amenable. Accordingly the marriage took place, with the consent of his father the king, in 1400. Earl Archibald was now an old man, probably in his late seventies, and giving his daughter away must have been one of his last recorded acts, because he died on Christmas Eve that year.

Paying sycophantic tribute to the prevailing Douglas power and influence at the time he wrote his chronicle, Wyntoun claimed that 'his soul sped to Paradise',[24] while Bower asserted that 'he was called the grim or terrible [and] surpassed almost all other Scots of his time in worldly wisdom, resolution and daring'.[25] A giant of a man like all his race, it was said of him that 'he wielded an immense sword [which] scarcely any other could have lifted, and with it 'he gave such strokes that all on whom they fell were struck to the ground'.[26] Similarly the legend that at Threave castle the 'knob' (a corbel protruding over the main gate) was never without a 'tassle' (a corpse) testified to the severity with which he exercised his lordship powers.

Meanwhile the truce, which had been extended by the commissioners at Lochmabenstone in November 1398, ended prematurely. The person responsible was the earl of March. Furious at Rothesay's jilting of his 'befouled daughter' (as he described her in a letter to King Henry IV), and Rothesay's refusal to repay the bribe, March defected to Henry and encouraged him to invade Scotland. This was treason. Therefore March's lands, including his Annandale lordship, were forfeited, although strangely he was allowed to keep his title.

The invasion took place in August 1400 when King Henry crossed the border with a large army. But rather than give battle, Rothesay and Earl Archibald's son, the younger Archibald, withdrew to the comparative safety of Edinburgh castle. Consequently Henry and his army encountered minimal resistance. In fact it seems to have been a pretty tame affair altogether, for in his anxiety not to alienate March's tenants Henry ordered his troops to refrain from harrying their lands. Moreover he extended his protection to the settlements they passed as they headed for Leith. Reaching Edinburgh, King Henry declared Holyrood abbey sacrosanct in recognition of the monks' hospitality to his father John of Gaunt when he took refuge there from the Peasant's Revolt.

Meanwhile Albany was coming to the relief of Edinburgh at the head of a large army. But reaching Lothian he remained there, perhaps unwilling to risk a confrontation with the English. Bower, on the other hand, attributed his hesitancy to 'certain animosities which had previously arisen between the duke of Rothesay and himself'.[27] What they were is not known. Nevertheless the fact that Albany blamed Rothesay's jilting of March's daughter for the invasion further poisoned the already deteriorating relations between them. In the event, lack of supplies forced Henry to withdraw and by the end of the month he and his army were back in England.

In June 1401 the younger Archibald, now fourth earl of Douglas, arrogated the lordship of Annandale which had been in abeyance following the earl of March's forfeiture. Accompanied by a retinue of nobles and their levies, he arrived at Lincluden where he was joined by a group of local landowners, including March's nephew Sir Robert Maitland, the owner of Tibbers, and their retainers. Joining forces they crossed the Nith, and advancing into Annandale they took possession of the lordship including Lochmaben.[28]

Meanwhile a dispute broke out between the new Earl Archibald and Rothesay over the head of Rothesay's arrogating – unilaterally and without the authority of Parliament – the title of earl of March. Fearing this was a prelude to seizing the valuable lands attaching to the earldom in the south-east, and seeing it as a challenge to his recently acquired lordship of Dunbar, Archibald raised a formal objection. By this time Rothesay's behaviour was becoming increasingly erratic. Determined to rid himself of the constraints imposed on him by the General Council, he deliberately ignored the twenty-one magnates appointed to supervise his exercise of the lieutenancy, causing them to resign in protest. Thereafter he began behaving like the king he expected to be in the not too distant future. This finally brought him into conflict with Albany.

In January 1402 Rothesay's three-year term as lieutenant expired. Taking advantage of this, the 'powerless and decrepit' king wrote to Albany, perhaps already appointed lieutenant in Rothesay's place, ordering him to arrest Rothesay and hold him in custody until 'he had mended his ways'. In fact it was Sir William Lindsay (brother of Euphemia whom he had jilted) who had him arrested and handed over to Earl Archibald and Albany, who detained him at the latter's manor at Falkland.[29]

This raised the question of what to do with him, well knowing that if released he would scruple at nothing to exact revenge. There was only one answer. In March 1402 Rothesay died in prison – allegedly of dysentery although few believed it. Reflecting the popular view, echoed by Bower,[30] Sir Walter Scott claims in his *Tales of a Grandfather* that he was starved to death. Ever a romantic, he was unable to resist embellishing his account with the grisly detail that in an extremity of hunger Rothesay was reduced to devouring his own flesh. Nevertheless the General Council gave out that 'he had departed this life by divine providence and not otherwise'. Endorsing their verdict, the king formally absolved Albany and Earl Archibald of responsibility for Rothesay's death, and ordered that 'no-one should murmur against them'.[31]

THE ALBANY GOVERNORSHIP

Following Rothesay's death, Albany was appointed lieutenant of the realm and as such was responsible for organising the offensive against the English which was planned for the following summer. It began with a series of cross-border raids. In June one of them ended in disaster when the Scots were routed by the earl of March at the head of an English force on Nisbet Moor near Duns. Determined to hit back, Earl Archibald raised an army from among the men of the west and middle marches. In September it crossed the border and harried Northumberland as far as Newcastle. As they were heading back laden with booty, they were overtaken by an English force under Henry Percy 'Hotspur' and the earl of March near Wooler.

Seeing them approach, Earl Archibald deployed his troops along the top of the nearby feature of Homildon Hill in readiness for battle. But the English were not going to be drawn into fighting uphill. Instead, their archers fired a withering hail of arrows at the Scots, reportedly cutting them down 'like fallow deer'. Unable to withstand it, the Scots charged down the hill to engage with the English at close quarters – unwisely, because they suffered an overwhelming defeat with many killed or captured. The prisoners included Earl Archibald along with a number of fellow earls and some eighty lords. Blinded in one eye by an arrow, and losing a testicle to another, Archibald remained in captivity in England for the next five years, although allowed home from time to time on parole.

Following up Percy's success, Henry IV arrogated his right to the lands in southern Scotland which Edward Balliol surrendered to his grandfather Edward III some seventy years earlier. Therefore he unilaterally deprived Archibald of his earldom and granted it, along with most of the attaching lands, to the earl of Northumberland, while the lordships of Annandale and Galloway were awarded to Ralph Neville, now earl of Westmoreland.[32] Since they amounted to mere parchment grants, Northumberland – and his son Harry Hotspur – felt they were being short-changed. Having supported Henry IV's usurpation of the throne, and been responsible for defending the northern counties against the Scots, they expected something better. Therefore they refused to hand Archibald over to King Henry so that they could ransom him themselves and keep the money in compensation.

Indeed, such was their resentment that Harry Hotspur joined the Welsh leader Owen Glendower in his revolt against Henry. At the same time he came to an agreement with Archibald. Bribing him with his eventual freedom, and a possible waiver of his ransom, he allowed him to return to Scotland on parole so that he could raise an army in support of the revolt. On 21 July 1403 battle was joined with the king's forces at Shrewsbury. For the rebels it was a disaster. Harry Hotspur was killed, and the 'giant Douglas' (as Archibald was described), who had wreaked 'much slaughter with his great mace', was again taken prisoner, this time as a captive of King Henry – hence his soubriquet 'the tyneman' or loser.

His absence, along with that of other influential noblemen in the region, left a power vacuum in southern Scotland. Taking advantage of this, and Albany's preoccupation with affairs in the north, the old king came 'shuffling his way back into the political arena', as it was put[33] – a pale shadow of the young John of Kyle who had corralled the English into the south-eastern corner of Annandale nearly fifty years earlier, and the power-hungry earl of Carrick who had edged his father aside and usurped his ruling powers in 1384. In April 1404 he presided over a meeting of the General Council at Linlithgow which approved a continuation of Albany's lieutenancy for a further two years, attributing it to 'the king's great age and weakness.'* It also appointed commissioners to negotiate a truce with Henry IV, although the talks came to nothing.

---

* At sixty-seven the king was a mere three years older than Albany who was still in his prime.

In the autumn of 1405, after a brief Indian summer, the king retired once more to his native west – probably on account of illness, and this time for keeps. Since Albany was still preoccupied with affairs in the north, and most of the southern magnates were either in captivity or paroled by the English against the surrender of hostages, power passed to a triumvirate of lesser nobles – Henry Sinclair earl of Orkney, Sir David Fleming of Biggar, and Bishop Wardlaw of St Andrews.

The following year a dispute arose between Orkney and Fleming acting for the king, on the one hand, and Margaret countess of Angus on the other. At issue was which of them – king or countess – should be tutor-at-law to their grandson William earl of Angus.* This was important, for on it would depend control of his extensive lands. Acting in the king's name, Orkney and Fleming decided to resolve the matter by force. Therefore mustering an army, they attempted to capture the Angus ruling centre of Tantallon castle. Accompanying them was the king's eleven-year-old son and heir, James earl of Carrick. However, on approaching the castle they found themselves confronted by a superior force under Countess Margaret's ally, James Douglas of Balvenie.† Unwilling to risk a confrontation, and fearing that the young prince might be captured, Orkney and Fleming dispatched him in a rowing boat, along with a few companions, including Orkney himself, to the temporary safety of the Bass Rock. The rest of the army fled. But overtaken by Douglas of Balvenie's force on Long Hermiston moor they were routed, many of them being killed including Sir David Fleming.

Meanwhile James and his companions were compelled to remain on the Bass Rock among the gannets for a month until they were picked up by a Danzig-bound trading vessel on its return voyage from Leith. On 14 March it was intercepted by an English merchantman off Flamborough Head. James was captured, and on King Henry's orders he was consigned to the Tower. The following month the old king died at his ancestral home of Rothesay castle on Bute having allegedly composed an epitaph for his tombstone: 'Here lies the worst of Kings and the most wretched of men in the whole realm.'[34] As the sixteenth-century historian John Mair observed of him and his father, 'many Scots are accustomed to compare [them] to the horses in the district of Mar which in youth are good but in their old age bad'.

Albany was now supreme, and in June 1406 he had himself appointed governor. The following year he strengthened his position in southern Scotland by gaining the support of the now exonerated earl of March. The price was restoration to his former lands including the lordship of Annandale. However, Earl Archibald's return to Scotland on parole later that year‡ risked upsetting the arrangement. Furious at being deprived of his Annandale lordship, he embarked on a campaign to undermine March's position in

---

* His father Earl George had been captured at Homildon Hill and died of the plague while a prisoner in England. The young earl's mother, on the other hand, was the king's daughter.

† Younger brother of the fourth earl of Douglas, he subsequently became the seventh earl.

‡ Although his parole was due to expire at Easter 1409, he ignored it and remained in Scotland – presumably sacrificing the hostages left behind as security for his return.

the south-east. Therefore he proceeded to distribute lands in his lordship of Dunbar as a means of building up a group of loyal supporters and dependants in opposition to him. They were mostly local lairds although there were some exceptions. For example at least three of them were Dumfriesshire landowners – William Johnstone, Sir Robert Maxwell of Caerlaverock, who was given the lands of West Pencaitland,[35] and Gilbert Grierson whom Archibald appointed bailie of the lordship.[36]

Meanwhile, perceiving Earl Archibald as a potential threat, Albany decided to come to an accommodation with him. Therefore in June 1409 they entered into a power sharing agreement, in terms of which Albany would govern the region beyond the Firth of Forth and Archibald southern Scotland. As an English chronicler put it, 'during the whorlle bourlle [hurly-burly] in Scotland the duke of Albanye governyd Scotland beyond the Scottish sea. And in the same wyesse dydde th'erlle [of] Douglas both governe and reule over this side [of] the Scottishe see'.[37] Furthermore, under pressure from Albany, Archibald promised to abandon his campaign against the earl of March and undertook to hand over the lordship of Dunbar to him. In return, March consented to Earl Archibald's restoration to the lordship of Annandale and with it Lochmaben castle.[38]

The following year the agreement between Albany and Earl Archibald was sealed with the marriage between Albany's second son, John earl of Buchan, and Archibald's daughter Elizabeth. Dynastic marriages such as this were a tried and tested way of cementing political alliances, love being purely incidental. Another example was the marriage which Archibald arranged between his niece Egidia, daughter of his illegitimate half-brother Sir William Douglas of Nithsdale, and Henry Sinclair earl of Orkney (King James's former companion on the Bass Rock). This was intended to gain his support, which would prove still more important when he and Egidia inherited Nithsdale.*

Now restored to Annandale, Archibald proceeded to exercise his lordship rights. For example, when he held a court at Lochmaben in 1411 it was attended by an impressive array of local landowners, apparent from the witnesses to the charters he issued there. They included among others Sir Thomas Kirkpatrick and Herbert Maxwell, who had recently succeeded his father Sir Robert as lord of Caerlaverock.† As a mark of confidence in him, Archibald appointed Sir Thomas Kirkpatrick sheriff of Dumfries while confirming him in possession of the barony of Closeburn.[39] Similarly Maxwell was given the prestigious office of steward of Annandale. However, it seems that his appointment was not universally popular among the Dumfriesshire lairds, perhaps because the Maxwells were regarded as primarily Nithsdale landowners and therefore outsiders. At the same time Archibald appointed his

---

*   Following the duke of Rothesay's death, Nithsdale was restored to Sir William Douglas's son, also William, as the rightful owner, and when he died unmarried in 1419 the lordship passed to Egidia and Earl Henry.

†   Others were John Carlyle, Humphrey Jardine, Thomas Murray, Robert Herries, Gilbert Grierson and Simon Carrithers (*RMS* I, 920)

long-standing supporter Michael Ramsay chamberlain and chancellor of Annandale, and in 1421 he was given a liferent of the keepership of Lochmaben.[40]

Initially the Maxwells probably felt scant affinity with the Douglases. Indeed they may well have regarded them as *parvenus*. This would stand to reason, for when members of the Maxwell family held the prestigious offices of sheriff of Teviotdale and royal chamberlain, the Douglases were landowners of small consequence in the bleak uplands of south Lanarkshire. But, although they may have been resentful of the Douglases' growing power and influence, the Maxwells were forced to accept reality. In 1400, when faced with a likely resumption of hostilities with England, Herbert Maxwell's father, Sir Robert, acknowledged Archibald the Grim's lordship in return for his protection. From Archibald's point of view Sir Robert was a useful ally given the importance of Caerlaverock as a principal fortress in the south-west. Later Sir Robert and his son Herbert were among Archibald the fourth earl's principal advisers and members of his council. Therefore they would have been in regular attendance on him during his visits to Annandale and Nithsdale.[41] Moreover Herbert Maxwell and his son Herbert (later first lord Maxwell) would remain committed supporters of the earls of Douglas until their fall from power.

EIGHT

The Black Douglas Ascendancy

ARCHIBALD EARL OF DOUGLAS

Like his father, Earl Archibald was a generous benefactor of the Church. Besides taking a keen interest in its welfare, his role in ending the Great Schism so far as it affected Scotland raised his reputation to new heights. The Schism began in 1378 following the death of Pope Gregory XI when the Roman faction elected their own pope Urban VI, while the opposing faction at Avignon elected Clement VII, later referred to as the antipope. The ensuing rivalry between the two popes was so damaging to the Church that in 1408 their respective colleges of cardinals convened a meeting of the General Council of the Church at Pisa to resolve the issue. After a lengthy debate they elected a new pope, Alexander V, and unilaterally deposed both the Roman pope Gregory XII and the Avignonese antipope Benedict XIII. Since neither would accept their 'deposition' there were now three popes, prompting the observation that 'the infamous duality has spawned an accursed trinity'.

When the 'Pisan' Pope Alexander V died in 1410, he was succeeded by Cardinal Baldassare Cossa, who took the title of John XXIII* – an extraordinary aberration considering he was a former pirate and widely suspected of poisoning his predecessor. A pirate was essentially what he remained, as well as being a notorious lecher, giving point to the observation that 'morally and spiritually he reduced the papacy to a level of depravity unknown since the days of its tenth century pornocracy'.[1] This bizarre situation with three popes publicly vilifying each other could not be allowed to continue. Therefore the influential Sigismund of Luxemburg, future Holy Roman Emperor, took matters in hand. In November 1414 he convened a meeting of the General Council of the Church at Constance, and the following May it deposed the 'Pisan' pope John XXIII,† and similarly the eighty-seven-year-old antipope Benedict XIII, while the still older Roman pope Gregory XII was persuaded to abdicate. In their place, and after some haggling, the Council elected Cardinal Oddone Colonna as sole pope, who took the title Martin V.

The Scots refused to recognise him, and following Albany's lead they continued to regard the antipope Benedict as the rightful pope. Not so Earl Archibald, who

---

* Because his election as pope was regarded as invalid, Cardinal Roncalli took the same title on his election as pope in 1958.
† In fact he had already fled the country and put himself under the protection of the duke of Austria, being convicted in his absence of 'piracy, rape, sodomy and incest', an impressive array of crimes!

undertook to persuade the Scots to change their minds and fall into line with the rest of Christendom by recognising Martin's papacy. This earned him a fulsome letter of praise from Pope Martin. 'Magnificent prince', it went, 'we place great trust in your gracious promises [to give help] in the cause of God.' This inspired Archibald to become the spearhead of the growing opposition to Albany's stance, and in 1419 he persuaded the prestigious St Andrews University, hitherto a supporter of Benedict, to join him in recognising Pope Martin. Finally, appreciating the strength of support for Pope Martin, Albany abandoned his stance and sent procurators to Martin to render him obedience on behalf of the Scots.

In recognition of Earl Archibald's part in this, Pope Martin issued letters describing him as 'high before God' and praising him for 'the consummation of the union of the Church and the utter uprooting of ill-favoured schismatics', achieved without 'sparing labours, dangers or costs'. Archibald must have appreciated the accolade all the more since it effectively placed him on the European stage, where he aspired to be. Concluding his encomium, Pope Martin described Archibald as his 'devoted and eldest son in the realm of Scotland'.

A leading magnate who consistently refused to acknowledge Martin's papacy was the earl of March – a fact which appears to have earned some unwelcome judgements in the papal court. Therefore when the papal representative arrived at Dunbar castle armed with letters from the pope authorising him to enforce the judgements, he was arrested. The letters were forcibly extracted from him and destroyed, and on the countess's orders he was flogged. To compound matters, the earl and countess's younger son Columba Dunbar, archdeacon of Lothian, declared that 'his holiness the pope has little holiness about him'. Writing to the pope as 'your devoted servant', Archibald gleefully reported these transgressions to him.[2] They were sufficiently serious to warrant the most extreme penalties, but papal thunder was averted by the octogenarian earl's death shortly afterwards.

The closing years of the Great Schism were marked by a growing threat of war involving England, Scotland, France and Burgundy – troubled waters in which King James, still a prisoner in England, attempted to fish in the hopes of regaining his freedom. While pretending to endorse James's efforts to secure his release, Albany did little to help – understandably, because James's return would mean the end of his governorship and probably worse. Aware of Albany's reluctance to co-operate, and acting on his own initiative, James wrote to eighteen influential Scots soliciting their support. Using Sir William Douglas of Drumlanrig as an intermediary, he attempted to establish a rival king's party to advance his cause – with evident success because the General Council was persuaded to send envoys to Henry IV to negotiate his release. But in March 1413, just as they were on the point of reaching agreement, Henry IV died. Because it suited his son Henry V to keep James in custody, he broke off the talks and returned him to the Tower.

But Henry was preoccupied with more important matters than deciding what to do with the king of his impoverished northern neighbour. This was because he was about to invade France in a bid to recover the duchy of Normandy. The circumstances were favourable – even propitious, because a civil war had broken out there. This harked back to 1392 when the French king Charles VI suddenly went mad. Having killed four of his companions, he was about to set upon his brother the duke of Orleans when he was overpowered. Thereafter his bouts of insanity became increasingly prolonged and frequent. This resulted in a power struggle between his uncle, Philip duke of Burgundy, and his brother, Louis duke of Orleans, for the regency. In 1404 Duke Philip was murdered by an Orleanist, and three years later his son Duke John retaliated by having Duke Louis of Orleans assassinated. This precipitated a civil war between the Burgundians on the one side, and Duke Louis' son Charles, supported by his father-in-law the count of Armagnac, on the other.

Since it was essential to make peace with the Scots to avoid the risk of attack from the rear, Henry sent envoys to Scotland to negotiate a truce and agree a ransom for Albany's eldest son Murdoch who had been captured at Homildon Hill. Having (as he thought) protected his rear, Henry sailed for France with an army of some 10,000 men. Landing at the mouth of the Seine, they captured the important coastal town of Harfleur before setting out for Calais. But no sooner had Henry and his army left for France than the talks broke down, whereupon Earl Archibald invaded the English west marches and burnt Penrith. Retaliating, a group of northern lords invaded Annandale when they looted and burnt Dumfries.

On 24 October, in the course of its advance on Calais, King Henry's now attenuated force was intercepted by a greatly superior French army. The following day battle was joined at Agincourt when the English scored a resounding victory with some 10,000 Frenchmen killed, while Charles duke of Orleans was among the many prisoners taken. Following his success, King Henry continued his advance on Calais, and arriving there at the end of the month he took ship back to England. Once again, he attempted to secure Scottish neutrality by authorising negotiations for a truce and offering to ransom Albany's son Murdoch. But because this would mean releasing King James as well, and knowing full well the danger this would pose to himself and his family, Albany was unwilling to agree. Therefore James remained a prisoner, and so did Murdoch, although the latter was released soon afterwards.

Despite his failure to persuade the Scots to agree a truce, King Henry continued his preparations for another invasion of France. In August 1416, in order to create an anti-French alliance on its eastern border, he concluded a treaty with Sigismund count of Luxemburg and the shifty and unreliable Duke John of Burgundy. At the end of July 1417 Henry set sail again for France with a large army, accompanied this time by the youthful King James to whom he appears to have taken a liking. Landing once again near the mouth of the Seine, Henry and his army headed for Paris capturing town after town – Caen, Falaise, Rouen and others, while the garrisons of the principal castles almost fell over themselves in their haste to surrender. Thus by the end of February 1418 Normandy (which had been seized by the French king Philip Augustus as long ago as 1202) was once again a dependency of the English crown.

By this time the civil war between the Orleanists and the Burgundians had split the French king Charles VI's immediate family. On the one side was his queen, the formidable Isabelle of Bavaria who allied herself with the Burgundians, while on the other was the dauphin Charles who was supported by Duke Charles of Orleans and the latter's father-in-law the count of Armagnac.

Meanwhile, alarmed by the extent of the English successes, the Duke John of Burgundy was making overtures to the dauphin Charles. However, when in September 1419 they met on the bridge over the Yonne (near its confluence with the Seine) at Montereau to seal their alliance in person, the duke was brutally struck down and killed by an Armagnac supporter. Despite the fact that the dauphin was not an accomplice, this threw the Burgundians back into the arms of Henry V, and both they and Queen Isabelle appealed to him for help against the Orleanists and Armagnacs. Henry could demand almost any terms he wanted, and in May 1420 their agreement was confirmed by the treaty of Troyes. In terms of this, King Henry was recognised as heir to the kingdom of France, to the exclusion of the dauphin, and appointed regent during King Charles's lifetime. Finally it was sealed with the marriage between King Henry and Charles's daughter Katherine, and in February 1421 Henry returned to England with his new queen.

Meanwhile the dauphin appealed to the Scots for help in recovering his rights of succession to the throne. Responding, the General Council raised a force and sent it to his assistance. This was put under the joint command of Albany's son, John earl of Buchan, and the younger Archibald Douglas, earl of Wigtown.[*] The 6,000-strong force consisted of levies contributed by members of the Douglas kindred, including Sir William Douglas of Drumlanrig. Joining forces with the dauphin's supporters, the combined army embarked on a campaign which culminated in a victory over a joint English and Burgundian force in an engagement at Baugé in March 1421.

Meanwhile, back home, Earl Archibald was hedging his bets. On the one hand, using his son Archibald and son-in-law the earl of Buchan as intermediaries, he was in contact with the dauphin. Yet in May 1421 he attended the court of Henry V. His main object was to secure James's release, doubtless hoping that the resulting credit would redound to the benefit of himself and his family. As a *quid pro quo*, Earl Archibald agreed to become Henry's man and at the same time undertook to provide him with 200 men-at-arms and a like number of archers on request. But it seems that the offer was not taken up, for when King Henry returned to France in June 1421 he was accompanied by an exclusively English army. However, on 31 August 1422, after spending a year trying unsuccessfully to bring the dauphin to battle, King Henry died, followed three months later by the mad King Charles. Consequently Henry's infant son Henry VI was proclaimed king of France. On the other hand, the

---

[*]   Subsequently fifth earl of Douglas, his father Earl Archibald had revived the earldom of Wigtown in his favour in order to give him the same status as Buchan.

Orleanists – and indeed the French people as a whole – supported the dauphin, recognising him as King Charles VII. But it was an empty title, and would remain so until he and his allies had driven the English out of France – a formidable challenge which would take him upwards of thirty years to achieve.

Meanwhile, desperate to secure Scottish help, King Charles offered Earl Archibald the royal duchy of Touraine and other inducements if he would raise an army and come to his assistance. The bait was taken. Archibald raised a force of some 6,500 men, and in February 1424 he sailed for France, having appointed his son Archibald, now returned to Scotland, lieutenant and governor of Annandale. Landing at La Rochelle, he was invested with the duchy of Touraine* and spent the next few months on a progress throughout northern France parading himself as the European prince he aspired to be. Finally on 16 August he encountered the English army at Verneuil. The following day battle was joined, and in the hardest-fought engagement of the war, described by the English as a second Agincourt, the Franco-Scottish army was annihilated. Of the original 6,500-strong Scottish army only forty escaped the field, while Earl Archibald was killed along with his younger son, Sir James Douglas, and his son-in-law the earl of Buchan.

Meanwhile King James had returned to Scotland, his release being deliberately delayed by Murdoch, now duke of Albany. Ransomed in 1415, he had succeeded his octogenarian father Duke Robert in 1420 and been appointed governor. Knowing the threat which James's return would pose to himself and his family, he did his best to prevent it, but had been overborne by Earl Archibald and a majority of the General Council. Therefore, notwithstanding that a Scottish force was fighting against the English in France at the time, a delegation was sent to England to negotiate his release. His ransom was fixed at 40,000 pounds (60,000 merks) payable by annual instalments of 4,000 pounds over the next ten years.

But it was no more than a temporary accord, because the English commissioners were under strict orders not to agree a final peace so long as a Scottish force was fighting against them in France. However, King James, now on his way north, proposed a compromise. While admitting that it was beyond his power to recall those Scots such as Earl Archibald who had gone to France, he promised that no more troops would be sent there. His assurance was accepted and a seven-year truce was agreed.[3] By April 1424 James was back in Scotland accompanied by his newly wedded wife Joan Beaufort,† a free man after eighteen years' captivity.

---

*   The dukedom was not heritable, being personal to Earl Archibald, and therefore it lapsed on his death. Nevertheless his wife Margaret (daughter of Robert III) continued to style herself duchess of Touraine throughout her widowhood as she was entitled to do.

†   Her father John Beaufort earl of Somerset was a son of John of Gaunt by his mistress (subsequently his third wife) Katherine Swynford, and therefore a half-brother of Henry IV.

A ROYAL TYRANT

King James was crowned at Scone on 21 May 1424. Now almost thirty, active, vigorous and energetic, he was determined to establish a forceful and assertive personal rule of a kind unknown since the reign of David II. His aim was to ensure, as he put it, that 'there shall be no place in my realm where the key shall not keep the castle and the bracken-bush the cow'. But, such were the lengths he went to in his efforts to achieve it that many of the nobility came to regard him as a tyrant and an oppressor of the people. This did him less than justice, because the people regarded him as a suppressor of evil-doers, as well as being responsible for restoring law and order, securing a longed-for peace with England, and establishing a measure of stability throughout the realm.

Before he could embark on his reforms, James had to crush those magnates who were determined to thwart his efforts to reduce their power. The first opportunity came when he was presented with a list of hostages to be given up to the English as security for his ransom. It had been drawn up by Duke Murdoch in consultation with other members of the nobility, including Earl Archibald. Fearing that James had them in his sights, they made sure that the list consisted mainly of his adherents since their absence would make it easier for Duke Murdoch and his confederates to protect themselves, as well as block his reforms. James probably took one look at it and tore it up. He produced a new list which included a number of potentially hostile barons and knights whom, as he was well aware, would stop at nothing to obstruct him.

Duke Murdoch had good cause to be apprehensive. Within a matter of months James turned on him, and indeed the whole Albany Stewart faction. And the brutality with which he secured their downfall – and that of other leading magnates – earned him a reputation for vindictiveness. He had no alternative. The Albany Stewarts had dominated Scottish politics for over thirty years, had a large network of allies and supporters, and were still extremely powerful, notwithstanding the loss of the governorship. Besides, Duke Murdoch posed an added threat as heir-presumptive to the throne, while James harboured a personal grudge against him for being instrumental in prolonging his captivity.

But first of all James needed to build up his strength against an inevitable showdown. Therefore he set about winning over a number of northern magnates whom the Albany Stewarts had alienated for various reasons (and whom he would subsequently turn on). They included his uncle, Walter earl of Atholl, the last surviving legitimate son of Robert II, described as the 'old serpent of Scottish politics'. At the same time the three principal magnates in the south – George Dunbar who had recently succeeded his father as earl of March, William earl of Angus, and Archibald earl of Wigtown, representing his father Earl Archibald who was in France – declared their support for James, no doubt hoping it would gain them credit, by no means assured despite Earl William and Archibald being his nephews.

At the Parliament held at Perth in May 1424 James opened his campaign against the Albany Stewarts when he ordered the arrest of Duke Murdoch's eldest son Walter Stewart. Convicted of treason, he was consigned to imprisonment on the Bass Rock. The following March, James had Duke Murdoch himself arrested along with his wife, her aged father the earl of Lennox, and their second son Alexander Stewart. Initially confined to the castle at St Andrews, Murdoch was later transferred to the custody of Herbert Maxwell at Caerlaverock.[4]

The Parliament held at Stirling the following May appointed a grand jury to try them. Leaving nothing to chance, James made sure that the jury was packed with his supporters and those seeking favours from him. Therefore they included people like his nephew Archibald, now fifth earl of Douglas, Sir James Douglas of Balvenie, and the earls of Angus and March, as well as the recently knighted Sir Herbert Herries of Terregles.[5] The result was a foregone conclusion. Convicted of 'robbery [i.e. extortion]', Walter Stewart was beheaded at Stirling castle. Next day his grandfather the earl of Lennox, Duke Murdoch himself and his son Alexander, all convicted of treason and other crimes, followed him to the block. Since their estates were forfeited they virtually doubled the crown lands, adding significantly to the royal revenues.

Only one member of the Albany Stewarts avoided the pogrom. This was Duke Murdoch's third son, James 'the fat', who was probably out of the country at the time. However, on his return, he revenged himself for his family's slaughter by burning the town of Dumbarton, and killing the king's uncle Sir John Stewart of Dundonald,[*] and many others, before taking refuge in Ireland. As heir-presumptive to the throne, James 'the fat' continued to pose a threat to King James, although later diminished when the queen gave birth to twin sons in October 1430. Nevertheless James the fat's actions played into the king's hands because they lent substance to the charges of treason laid against his family. King James's treatment of the Albany Stewarts left a legacy of hatred which surfaced twelve years later when Lennox's grandson, Sir Robert Graham, was among those responsible for his assassination.

James's elimination of the Albany Stewarts was the prelude to further attacks on his opponents, and those he perceived as potential enemies. Here his success was due to a skilful combination of ruthlessness and opportunism. His next target was his nephew Archibald fifth earl of Douglas. Notwithstanding that Archibald's father, the fourth earl, had been among those responsible for securing James's release, and that Archibald himself had supported his attack on the Albany Stewarts, James was determined to curb his power.

But rather than risk an armed confrontation with an uncertain outcome, James was more circumspect. First, he sought to reduce Earl Archibald's power by causing a break-up of the network of bonds and alliances which his father the fourth earl had built up with other magnates and lesser barons. This had been achieved mainly on the strength of the prestigious public offices he held, since they gave him the means

---

[*] An illegitimate son of Robert II.

to protect their interests. Because these offices lapsed on his death, and James deliberately refrained from granting them to Earl Archibald, it meant that Archibald was unable to extend the same degree of protection to these magnates and lesser barons. Consequently his father's network of bonds and alliances began to fall apart.

At the same time James deprived Archibald of the help of his powerful and influential uncle Sir James Douglas of Balvenie. This was readily achieved by purchasing that notoriously rapacious nobleman's support with additional lands. Similarly, James denied Archibald the lordship of Galloway by granting it to Archibald's mother (James's sister), Margaret duchess of Touraine.[6] Finally he set about building up the power and influence of William earl of Angus as a rival to Earl Archibald in the marches. A man of consummate ambition like his father Earl George, Angus was determined to recover the lands which formerly belonged to his grandfather the first earl of Douglas. To begin with, James confirmed him in possession of Liddesdale and his lands in Eskdale, while supporting him in his feud with the earl of March. Later, following the latter's forfeiture, James granted Angus the lion's share of the earl's lands in the south-east. This enabled him to build up a network of allies and supporters, including his near relative Archibald Douglas of Cavers, sheriff of Roxburgh and bastard son of James second earl of Douglas, Walter Scott of Buccleuch and others, to rival that of Earl Archibald.

Having suppressed – or at least silenced – the opposition, James proceeded with his reforms. His first priority was to enforce law and order throughout the realm. A start was made at the Perth Parliament of May 1424 when at his instance it enacted a number of measures for the suppression of lawlessness. For example, those rebelling against 'the kyngis persone' would stand to forfeit their 'lif, landis and gudis', and if anyone responsible for administering justice showed undue leniency he would be required to answer for it. The main purpose of these and other measures was to ensure that 'firm peace be maintained throughout the realm and among the lieges of our sovereign lord the king'. In other words, there were to be no more private feuds and vendettas which had been such a drag on his predecessors' efforts to deliver firm government.

Since the English were preoccupied with their war in France, James was able to proceed with his reforms without fear of invasion. True, a 'cold war' still existed between the two countries because an attenuated Scottish contingent was fighting for Charles VII against the English in France. Indeed, there was a danger of it escalating into all-out war when King Charles, invoking the Franco-Scottish alliance, pressed James to send reinforcements. But anxious to avoid provoking the English, he stalled. Instead he palmed Charles off by suggesting a betrothal between his three-year-old daughter Margaret and Charles's five-year-old son the dauphin Louis.

There were also outbreaks of violence on the marches when cattle raiding forays erupted into skirmishes or pitched battles. But both sides were determined to put a stop to it. Therefore in June 1429 Parliament appointed commissioners to meet an English delegation at 'Hawdenstank' in order to 'redress march offences and treat for peace' as it was put. In the light of this, Parliament drew up a list of conditions which was stated to be 'for the observance of order on the marches'. Supplementing the existing march laws, they stipulated that regular meetings were to be held between commissioners for both sides at certain designated places to hear complaints.[7] This was followed by another meeting in January 1430, and in December a local truce was declared.[8]

Both sides appointed conservators to ensure its observance. The principal Scottish representative was Sir James Douglas of Balvenie, now the king's staunch supporter and a leading member of his Council. Those from the south-west included Herbert Maxwell of Caerlaverock, Earl Archibald's steward of Annandale and his leading adherent in Dumfriesshire; Michael Ramsay, the keeper of Lochmaben and a member of the royal household; and Sir Thomas Kirkpatrick. Supporting them were a number of lesser lords such as Simon Carruthers of Mouswald and Matthew Glendinning the bailie of Eskdale.[9]

Meanwhile James's ransom had still to be paid. The Parliament of May 1424 passed a series of measures for the purpose of raising the money. These included imposing export duties on horses, sheep and animal skins – and also herrings, of which there was still an abundance in Scottish waters. It also stipulated that pensions and annuities granted out of the customs and other crown revenues were to be rigorously investigated for the purpose of rescinding those deemed controversial or unwarranted. Similarly, the validity of grants of crown lands made during the previous three reigns were to be examined with a view to possible revocation.

Yet, by taking advantage of the English preoccupation with their French war, and their consequent inability to extract payment by force, James managed to avoid paying any instalments of his ransom. True, it meant that the hostages given up in security for it would find their stay in England prolonged indefinitely. But because they were mainly James's potential opponents (which accounted for their choice in the first place) this would have suited him very well. Therefore, notwithstanding that successive Parliaments voted him the money to meet these instalments, he diverted it to his own uses, embellishing his court with an ostentatious display of pomp. Although intended to convey the impression of a powerful and prestigious monarchy, it gave point to Pope Pius II's denunciation of him as a 'greedy, passionate and vindictive prince'.

In 1433, despite the fact that he had supported him in his campaign against the Albany Stewarts, James turned on the earl of March. Using his father the tenth earl's treason as a pretext, he made an apparently unprovoked attack on March's lands, seizing Dunbar castle, and depriving him of the wardenship of the east marches. The following year Parliament declared both the earldom and its attaching lands forfeit.[*]

---

[*]   The earldom was never restored. When Earl George's descendant Andrew Dunbar died in the mid-sixteenth century, survived by four sisters as co-heiresses, the senior branch of the Dunbar kindred died out in the male line.

While there was no evidence of treason on March's part, Bower implies that, like his father, he was a man of fickle loyalties. Therefore James may have regarded him as unreliable, particularly in view of the feud that existed between him and James's close ally the earl of Angus. In any event he may have suspected that March was about to defect to the English. True or not, March's subsequent actions put the matter beyond doubt.

March appealed to the earl of Northumberland for help in recovering his lands which, because the Anglo-Scottish truce had recently expired, he was able to do. Therefore summoning his levies, Northumberland and March invaded Berwickshire and advanced up the coastal route towards Edinburgh. But at Cockburnspath they encountered a force under the earl of Angus who drove them back across the border. In August 1436 James followed up Angus's success by laying siege to Roxburgh castle, one of the last two Scottish strongholds in English hands (the other was Berwick). Anticipating an easy success, he conducted the siege in person, and for two weeks his troops continued to bombard the castle with their cannonry. But when news reached them of the approach of an English relieving force, they broke off the siege and in their hurry to escape they left most of their siege equipment behind. Not James's finest hour.

This encouraged a group of covertly hostile magnates to instigate a revolt. The issue came to a head at a Parliament in late 1436. When James, who was present, demanded that it vote him an additional tax it refused. The decision was announced by Sir Robert Graham, doubtless with some glee since James was responsible for ordering the execution of his grandfather the earl of Lennox. In fact Graham went further; he planned to have James arrested while attending the Parliament. But James got wind of it and arranged for armed men to be posted outside the building. At a signal they rushed inside and arrested those who had voted against James's request. They included Graham, who was spared the death penalty and sentenced to exile. However he managed to escape to 'the cuntrie of the Wild Scottis [the Highlands]' where he and other like-minded noblemen plotted to murder the king.

Although not directly implicated, the conspiracy had the blessing of the powerful Walter Stewart earl of Atholl, King James's last surviving uncle. Although he was formerly an ally of James, relations between them had soured, and fears that the seizure of the earl of March's lands might be the prelude to an attack on his own may have encouraged him to support the conspirators. To compound his guilt, his grandson Sir Robert Stewart was one of the ringleaders, notwithstanding his recent appointment as chamberlain of the royal household.

The attack on the king took place on 21 February 1437 when he and his courtiers were staying at the house of the Blackfriars in Perth. That evening, while playing cards, they were interrupted by the sound of armed men outside. They tried to bar the door to prevent the men from breaking into the chamber. But, finding the bolt had been removed,* the courtiers attempted to hold off the intruders while the king

---

* Deliberately on the orders of Sir Robert Stewart using (or rather abusing) his authority as chamberlain.

grabbed a poker, and prising open some floorboards he tried to escape through the sewer underneath. Unfortunately he had recently ordered the outlet to be bricked up to prevent tennis balls from rolling into it. Consequently he found himself trapped, while his movements were restricted by the fact that he had become massively over-weight, or as it was put 'oppressed with much fat'. Nevertheless he managed to kill the first two assailants who leapt into the sewer after him until Sir Robert Graham, who was immediately behind, stabbed him to death.

The conspirators would have killed the queen as well, but she managed to escape. They too escaped but were subsequently rounded up and taken prisoner. Meanwhile Atholl had carefully distanced himself from the outrage by remaining at his castle of Methven. He was probably counting on – and may even have arranged for – his allies among the nobility to summon a Parliament to have him adjudged king as the undis-puted legitimate male heir of Robert II. But the queen trumped him by hurrying off to Edinburgh castle where she took possession of her son the six-year-old James II. Acting in his name, she pre-empted Atholl and his associates by summoning a Parliament at which the assassins (identified by Sir Robert Graham under torture) were brought to trial. Convicted of regicide, they were sentenced to death with vary-ing degrees of cruelty. Although peripheral to the conspiracy Atholl was sufficiently implicated to merit conviction. Consequently this seventy-six-year-old senior member of the house of Stewart was consigned to the block.

THE KINGSHIP UNDER THREAT

The Parliament of March 1437 at which James I's assassins were brought to trial formally declared his son king as James II. It further ordained that his ruling powers were to be exercised by the queen mother, Joan Beaufort, William earl of Angus and William Crichton. Lord of the barony of Crichton in Lothian, William Crichton had risen to prominence in the service of James I, first as chamberlain and later as master of his household. Also appointed to the prestigious offices of sheriff of Edinburgh and keeper of the castle, he was now a man of high standing.* In the event, the tenure of power held by the queen mother, Angus and Crichton lasted a mere two months, because in May the Council removed them from office and replaced them with Archibald fifth earl of Douglas, who was appointed lieutenant-general of the realm.

Rapacious like all the Black Douglases, Earl Archibald used his newly acquired powers to add to his already substantial landholdings. Taking advantage of the earl of Angus's death in October, and the succession of his under-age son James, he seized the forest of Jedworth.[10] He also set his sights on acquiring the lordship of Nithsdale. Although of limited value in itself, it was an important base from which to mount a campaign to wrest control of Galloway from his mother Duchess Margaret. As a first

---

* He was described by Sir Walter Scott as 'a consummate statesman according to the manner of his age [and] as destitute of faith, mercy and conscience as of fear and folly' (*Provincial Antiquities*, 167–8).

step he launched an attack on Nithsdale, evident from a complaint by Egidia, dowager countess of Orkney and lady of Nithsdale,* to the General Council that he was plundering it – an action which, as Brown tantalisingly observes, 'may be connected to later accounts of his reign of terror in Annandale'.[11] However, Earl Archibald's territorial aspirations were cut short by his death in June 1439, reputedly a victim of the plague, when he was succeeded by his under-age son William as sixth earl.

Earl Archibald's death heralded a rivalry between William Crichton (now styling himself lord Crichton) and Sir Alexander Livingston, keeper of Stirling castle, for political power, notwithstanding that there were occasions when events forced them to co-operate. That political power should devolve on two such relatively minor families was a product of the prevailing unique situation where there was only one adult earl (Crawford) in Scotland, the others being either under age or in captivity. Crichton's power derived from his custody of the king who was kept in virtual confinement at Edinburgh castle. However, the queen mother, previously Crichton's associate but now a supporter of Livingston, removed the young king from his control. Smuggling him out of Edinburgh castle she took him by boat, allegedly hidden in a chest, from Leith up the Firth of Forth to Stirling where she handed him over to Livingston.[12] However, when in July 1439 she married Sir James Stewart the 'Black Knight of Lorne', Livingston, seeing them as a potential threat, ungratefully consigned them to prison – but only briefly, because in September the Council ordered their release.

Since custody of the king held the key to political power, the unfortunate youth continued to be used as a shuttlecock between the Livingston and Crichton factions. Soon afterwards the pendulum swung back to Crichton when his henchmen ambushed the king while out riding in Stirling park, and bringing him back to Edinburgh castle they delivered him into Crichton's custody. Meanwhile Earl Archibald's son, William the sixth earl, was asserting his claim to the power and influence exercised by his father, as well as the offices of state, including that of lieutenant-general of the realm, which had lapsed on his father's death. Perceiving him as a threat, Crichton and Livingston sank their differences in the interests of ridding themselves of this arrogant and dangerously unpredictable young man.

At Crichton's instigation, abetted by Livingston, and with the connivance of their great-uncle Sir James Douglas of Balvenie, now earl of Avondale, who had much to gain from their deaths, the earl and his brother David were allegedly invited to a dinner at Edinburgh castle. Later historians add further embellishments to the 'Black Dinner' as it was called. At the end of the banquet a black bull's head is said to have been placed on the table which, as Pitscottie observed, was 'ane signe and taikin (token) of condemnatour to death'.[13] So it proved. The brothers were seized, subjected to a mock trial in the presence of the king, and promptly dragged out on to the castle

---

* Born Egidia Douglas she was the daughter of Archibald the Grim's bastard son Sir William Douglas of Nithsdale.

hill where their heads were hacked off. Consequently the Douglas earldom passed to their great-uncle the earl of Avondale.

Second son of Archibald the Grim, and described as 'ane man of gryit stature and verrey fat' (hence his soubriquet James the Gross), the new earl had been a political (and physical) heavyweight for almost half a century. Already notorious for his rapacity, having amassed a substantial landholding in the north-east, his acquisition of the earldom merely whetted his appetite for more. Not content with inheriting the lands passing under the Douglas entail, and those acquired by his father Earl Archibald, he was determined to recover the lands which had devolved on other members of the family. For example the lordship of Bothwell had been awarded to the widow of Archibald the fifth earl in satisfaction of her legal rights, although he soon recovered it from her. On the other hand, the lordship of Galloway, which included the earldom of Wigtown, belonged to fourth earl's widow Duchess Margaret.

Her heiress was her granddaughter Margaret, sister of the murdered earl and known as the 'Fair Maid of Galloway'. Therefore, in order to gain possession of the lordship, Earl James arranged for her to marry his eldest son William. But because they were within the forbidden degrees of relationship papal dispensation was necessary. A petition was presented to the papal court, but by the time the dispensation was granted in 1444 Earl James had died, although the marriage between William, now eighth earl, and the Maid Margaret went ahead as planned. Founding on her reversionary right to it, Earl William began styling himself lord of Galloway, notwithstanding that it still belonged to his grandmother, Duchess Margaret. But not for long, because he forced her to resign it. Thereafter she retired to the collegiate church of Lincluden where she died at an advanced age in 1450.

Earl William's takeover of Galloway must have been a source of considerable apprehension to William Crichton, because Earl William was now in a position to obstruct his efforts to build up a power base for himself and his family in the south-west. Despite being a Lothian-based family, the Crichtons were already well entrenched in Dumfriesshire. In the early fourteenth century William's ancestral uncle, William Crichton, forebear of the earls of Dumfries, acquired half the barony of Sanquhar through marriage to Isabel, the elder of the de Ros co-heiresses, subsequently purchasing the other half from her nephew Donald Edgar.[14] Sometime before 1361 William Crichton's grandfather and namesake acquired the de Boys lands in Dryfesdale through marriage to the heiress of Sir Humphrey de Boys who fell at the battle of Dornock in 1333.[15] There is also a reference to his uncle acquiring lands in the barony of Carruthers,[16] and finally in 1440 he himself purchased part of the barony of Kirkmichael from the earl of Crawford.[17]

Later, his near relative Sir George Crichton, future earl of Caithness, acquired the barony of Morton in Nithsdale. This formerly belonged to Sir James Douglas of Dalkeith, but following his death in about 1441 it was assigned to his widow Janet Borthwick in satisfaction of her legal rights. Therefore Sir George acquired it by the simple expedient of marrying her (she being his second wife and he her third husband). He went further. In her right he attempted to take advantage of her stepson James Douglas of Dalkeith's insanity to gain control of the lordship of Dalkeith. But he was thwarted by James Douglas's brother, Henry Douglas of Borgue, who arrogated it for himself.

Meanwhile Earl William allied himself with the Livingstons in a bid to secure the downfall of the Crichtons. As a first step, summonses were issued to William and George Crichton, and other members of the family, ordering them to appear before the Council on charges of corruption. They refused. Therefore the Council stripped William Crichton of the chancellorship, he and his family being denounced as rebels and sentenced to outlawry. Crichton took refuge in Edinburgh castle whereupon Earl William and Livingston laid siege to it. But having failed to take it after nine weeks' bombardment, they came to an agreement. In terms of this Crichton undertook to surrender the castle in return for an unconditional pardon and the abandonment of all charges laid against himself and his family.

By July 1444 the Douglas/Livingston faction, now the supreme power in the realm, persuaded the Council to declare the fourteen-year-old James of age to rule. Since he was under their control it meant that, by claiming to act in his name, Earl William and his Livingston allies could cloak their actions against their opponents with a veneer of legality. It also meant they could lawfully denounce them as rebels, notwithstanding that they included some of the most important magnates in the realm – people like the queen mother, the young earl of Angus, William Crichton and Bishop James Kennedy.[*]

As the senior member of the Douglas/Livingston alliance, Earl William was primarily responsible for the defence of the realm. Therefore, when in October 1448 an English force under the earl of Northumberland's younger son, Thomas Percy, invaded the west marches he ordered his brother the earl of Ormond to raise a force to repel them. Although mainly recruited from Ayrshire, it included levies from Annandale under lord Maxwell,[†] Sir Adam Johnstone of that Ilk, Sir William Stewart of Dalswinton, and others. When they encountered Percy's force at Lochmabenstone, near the mouth of the Sark, a hard-fought engagement took place when a large number of Englishmen were taken prisoner, the rest being driven back across the border. Such was the haul of booty taken, and the ransoms exacted from the prisoners, that as Pitscottie put it 'thair was sic an abundance of riches, silluer and gold, [that] never was the lyke sene in na man's tyme befoir'.[18]

In December 1448, anticipating a retaliatory invasion, Earl William held a meeting of local landowners at Lincluden to discuss how best to defend the region. In the end, it was decided that beacons should be established on ten hills in Annandale, and

---

[*] Son of Sir James Kennedy of Dunure and Mary, daughter of Robert III and formerly wife of George Douglas first earl of Angus.

[†] Formerly Herbert Maxwell of Caerlaverock, he had recently been created a lord of Parliament.

a further eight in Nithsdale,* ready to be lit in the event of an attack. This was to be a signal for all able-bodied men to muster at their local assembly points in readiness to repel the invaders. These precautions were soon put to the test (and evidently failed), for in the early summer of 1449 the English invaded the south-west and burnt Dumfries. Thereafter they continued to harry the region until a truce was declared, when they withdrew across the border.

In July 1449 King James married Mary, daughter of Arnold duke of Gueldres. Although Gueldres itself was a small principality in the Low Countries, it was nevertheless a prestigious match because Mary's mother, Duchess Catherine, was a niece of Philip duke of Burgundy, one of the most powerful rulers in western Europe. Also one of the richest, he undertook responsibility for Mary's dowry. This was to be paid in instalments and subject to certain conditions, one being that Mary should be endowed with lands of a specific value. Since James was not yet able to do so, the dowry was withheld until he could.

Following his marriage and his arrogation of full ruling powers, James turned on the Livingstons. While his main object was to recover their appropriated crown lands, both as a source of revenue and as a means of endowing his queen, he also had a personal animus against them. This stemmed from his treatment at their hands during the time he was in their power, as well as resentment of their imprisoning his mother Queen Joan in 1439. Meanwhile, to put them offguard, he allowed them to remain at court and appointed Sir Alexander an envoy to negotiate with English commissioners for the truce which was intended to put an end to their harrying of the south-west. In September 1449 he pounced. The leading members of the family were arrested. Convicted of a number of crimes, including the unlawful imprisonment of the queen mother, they were stripped of their offices and deprived of the keepership of the royal castles. And whereas most were imprisoned or exiled, two of them including Sir Alexander were executed.

Earl William made no attempt to come to their rescue. He had been prepared to co-operate with them so long as they were of use to him, but because this was no longer the case he actively supported the royal attacks on them. Besides, he had much to gain from their downfall having been awarded a large share of their forfeited lands. Nevertheless King James must have perceived him as a threat to his own position. But he was forced to bide his time until he was in a strong enough position to risk a confrontation. Therefore his award of the Livingston lands was doubtless intended to

---

* Those in Annandale were Trailtrow hill (the site of Repentance tower), Penteth hill (near Mouswald), Bailie hill (in the parish of Dalton), Burrain Skelton (in the parish of Appegarth), Cowdens (above Castlemilk), Quhytewoollen (near Lockerbie), Brown hill (also in the parish of Applegarth), Blaze (in the parish of Wamphray), Kinnel-knock (in the parish of Johnstone), and Gallowhill (near Moffat). Those in Nithsdale were Wardlaw (above Caerlaverock), Rachochtoun (almost certainly Trohoughton, south of Dumfries), Beacon hill (between Torthorwald and Hightae), Malow hill (unidentifiable), Corsancon (on the Ayrshire border), Cruffel (presumably Criffel), Dowlarg (in the parish of Troqueer), and Watchfell (possibly the Watchman, above Duncow). See McDowall, *Dumfries*, 153–4fn (quoting from the Beacon Act *APS* i, 716).

keep Earl William on side. In January 1450, as a further sweetener, he issued a charter endorsing Duchess Margaret's resignation of the Galloway lordship and its grant to Earl William.[19] Finally he acknowledged the right of the earl's brother James to succeed to his lands and lordships in the event of his dying childless.

In October 1450, confident of the strength of his position, Earl William embarked on a pilgrimage to Rome to celebrate the Jubilee Year proclaimed by Pope Nicholas V. Evidently a gala occasion it brought an estimated 100,000 pilgrims flocking there, lured by the promise of a plenary indulgence for their sins. Earl William's large and splendidly equipped retinue included his brother James and other magnates, as well as a number of landowners such as Charles Murray of Cockpool. When he arrived at Rome in January 1451 it created such an impression that he was said to have been 'commended by the supreme pontiff above all pilgrims'.

He had been too complacent. While he was flaunting himself in Rome, King James was busy undermining his position at home by allying himself with Earl William's Crichton enemies. A later chronicler asserts that, at their instigation, the king 'besieged all the castles of the earl [of Douglas] and slew many free tenants, and received the rest to his peace on oath'.[20] Perhaps an exaggeration, but clearly James and his Crichton allies were taking advantage of Earl William's absence to curb his power. The death of Duchess Margaret in 1450 gave James an excuse for seizing the lordship of Galloway, alleging that it had reverted to the crown. Since it included the earldom of Wigtown, he transferred its attaching lands to the queen in part payment of her endowment. But because the seizure was in flagrant breach of his charter of January 1450 confirming Earl William in possession of it, this was tantamount to throwing down the gauntlet.

Nevertheless it gave Sir William Crichton, now restored to the chancellorship, the opportunity to strengthen his position in the south-west. This was achieved partly by entering into bonds with like-minded landowners, and also through the king's influence. Therefore when the latter held a justice ayre at Lochmaben in January 1451 he ensured that, in a public demonstration of Sir William's power in the region, he was among those in attendance.[21] At much the same time, the king granted the superiority of the lands and barony of Tibbers to Sir George Crichton (although the fee remained in the hands of Sir Robert Maitland).[22]

When news of the king's actions reached Earl William, he cut short his junketing in Rome and hurried home. But instead of heading back to Scotland his immediate destination was England. Arriving there in late February 1451, he sent his brother James and others ahead to Scotland to find out what was happening so that he could decide what to do. However, when he returned to Scotland in early April, doubtless intending to take up arms against the king, he must have been disconcerted at finding himself received with every show of friendliness. Not only that, but as signal honour he was appointed a commissioner to go to England to discuss recent violations of the truce.[23]

At the Parliament held the following June, Earl William made a show of loyalty and obedience to the king by surrendering all his lands and titles. They were immediately returned to him, and in October he was restored to the earldom of Wigtown, the queen being compensated with lands elsewhere.[24] But it was a hollow truce and Earl William, who was clearly under no illusions, proceeded to build up support and form alliances to strengthen his position against an inevitable show-down. Ominously, he entered into a bond with the earls of Crawford and Ross – not the sort of people with whom he would normally associate, particularly as Ross's wife was a granddaughter of Sir Alexander Livingston for whose execution he was partly responsible. Moreover, the fact that both Crawford and Ross were among his leading opponents aroused James's deepest suspicions.

Pitscottie gives some lurid examples of Earl William's violent and arbitrary treat-ment of those of his tenants whom he suspected of co-operating in the royal takeover of Galloway. Although perhaps erring on the fanciful, they go far to explain why many landowners in the south-west, notably Sir William Douglas of Drumlanrig, defected to the king. A case in point was a certain Sir John Herries who was described as 'a faithful subject to the Kingis majestie at all tymes', which was doubtless why Earl William is alleged to have incited 'sum theiffes of Douglasdaill' to harry his lands. Taking matters into his own hands, Herries had them arrested and summarily executed. Retaliating, Earl William reportedly had Herries 'castin in yrrones and hangit schamefullie as [if] he had bene ane thief, nochtwithstanding [that] the king commandit in the contrair'.[25] Although Sir John Herrries has not been identified, the essence of the story is probably true enough.

Another example concerned Earl William's alleged imprisonment of Maclellan, the tutor of Bombie. This was because loyalty to the king prevented him from turning out in support of the earl – or as Pitscottie put it, 'he wald on na wayis ryd with the erle of Douglas'. When the king sent Maclellan's uncle, Sir Patrick Gray, to Threave with a letter demanding his release, Earl William gave him a courteous welcome, entertained him to dinner and 'maid him guid cheir' having in the meantime ordered Maclellan's execution. Therefore, when dinner was over and the earl escorted his guest out into the courtyard, he is alleged to have remarked: 'Schir Patrick ye ar come a litill too leit; yondar is your sistir sone lyand, bot he wantis [lacks] the heid. Tak his bodie and do with it quhat ye will.'[26] Since these stories give credence to the earl's hostility to the king, it was probably in a genuine attempt to resolve their differences that the latter summoned Earl William to meet him at Stirling castle. But things did not go according to plan.

THE FALL OF THE BLACK DOUGLASES

Earl William responded to the summons. But mistrusting the king, he took the precaution of demanding a 'special assourans' or safe conduct. This was duly forth-coming, and to give it added weight it was issued under the privy seal and subscribed by the king in person. When the earl arrived at Stirling on 21 February 1452, the king greeted him with every show of friendliness, and next day – at his invitation – the earl 'dynit and soupit' with him and his courtiers. However, when dinner was over and the king and earl got down to business, the atmosphere rapidly soured as their exchanges became increasingly acrimonious.

What happened next is described by the Auchinleck chronicler in such graphic detail as to suggest that he was a witness. When the king demanded that the earl break his bond with the earls of Crawford and Ross, the latter refused saying that 'he mycht not nor would nocht'. At this the king lost his temper. 'Fals traitour', he exclaimed, 'sen yow will nocht I sall'. So saying he drew his knife and stabbed the earl in the neck, Then, grasping the opportunity to revenge himself for his nephew's execution, Sir Patrick Gray split his head open with 'ane poll ax', whereupon the other courtiers fell on the dying earl, wielding their knives to such effect that by the time they had finished their gory work his corpse was lacerated with twenty-six wounds.[27]

This was slaughter under trust, and the fact that it was about the most flagrant violation imaginable of the medieval code of honour would have outraged the king's contemporaries far more than the murder itself. For James it could have been cata-strophic, except that many of those who had professed loyalty to Earl William were quick to recant now that he was dead. Some of the more courageous had opposed him from the start. They included Sir Alexander Boyd of Drumcoll (Duncow) and Sir Simon Glendinning, who were among the assassins.[28] Meanwhile James moved fast to catch the earl's supporters by surprise before they had time to rally. The ensuing campaign took him to Dumfriesshire. In early March he was at Lochmaben. From there he went on to Dumfries accompanied by a group of southern magnates, includ-ing lord Maxwell* and Sir Walter Scott of Buccleuch, and by 8 March he had reached Sir George Crichton's stronghold of Morton castle.

While at Dumfries the king took the opportunity to advance the power of the Crichtons. It was doubtless at his instigation that an assize of local men decided that the nearby barony of Preston in Kirkcudbrightshire properly belonged to Sir George Crichton in right of his wife the former Janet Borthwick. Like the barony of Morton, it had been awarded to her in part satisfaction of her legal rights in the estate of her former husband Sir James Douglas of Dalkeith. The king went further. In June 1452 he caused Parliament to approve the grant to Sir George of the earldom of Caithness and its attaching lands,[29] while the chancellor William Crichton's son James was adjudged earl of Moray in right of his wife Jonet Dunbar, the elder daughter and co-heiress of the previous earl, John Dunbar.† Finally in November the king appointed Sir Robert Crichton of Sanquhar sheriff of Dumfries, an office which later became hereditary in his family.[30]

Meanwhile Earl William's brother, James the ninth earl, embarked on a campaign of vilification of the king. Raising a force of some 600 men, he advanced on Stirling

---

* Otherwise Herbert Maxwell of Caerlaverock, he is first referred to as lord Maxwell in a charter of July 1445.
† *Scots Peerage* ii, 327. Following his death in 1454, Earl William's brother Archibald Douglas began styling himself earl of Moray in right of his wife Elizabeth, who was Jonet's younger sister and co-heiress.

where he had his brother's safe conduct tied to a horse's tail and paraded through the streets as evidence of the king's treachery. At the same time he caused his heralds to 'blow out twenty-four hornis attains [at once or simultaneously] upon the king [for] the foul slauchter of his brother' and otherwise 'spoke rycht slanderfully of [him]'. Instead of wasting time trading insults, King James spent the next few months attempting to subvert Douglas adherents with grants of land and other rights. A case in point was Sir Charles Murray of Cockpool who had accompanied Earl William on his pilgrimage to Rome. James won him over by confirming him in possession of his lands of Ruthwell, and granting him those of Coklakkis (Cocklicks) and Pyhillis (Phyllis) 'to the south of the forest of Dalton'.[31] Later, Murray was appointed warden of the west marches.

At King James's instigation a Parliament which was held in June absolved him of guilt for Earl William's murder on the unlikely grounds that the earl had renounced the royal protection the day before his murder. In spite of the Parliament's denouncing the Douglases and their supporters as rebels, James was reluctant to risk a confrontation with them. However, at that point Earl James and his brothers handed him a valuable propaganda advantage by entering into the allegiance of Henry VI – an act of treason which caused a number of their adherents to defect to the king. This put him in a much stronger position, as well as giving him a respectable excuse for taking up arms against the earl and his supporters.

In July the king summoned an army to muster on Pentland moor near Edinburgh. From there it advanced south through the Border country. Continuing up the Teviot, it crossed into Eskdale, and from there into Annandale eventually reaching Dumfries. In the course of their campaign they harried the Douglas lands in the region – unwisely because it alienated the very people the king was trying to win over. Since Earl James was busy mustering support in the north, the king was under pressure to reach an accommodation with him to avoid the risk of civil war.

In late August a meeting between them took place at Douglas castle. Because it was one of Earl James's principal strongholds, this must have involved the king in a considerable loss of face. Nevertheless an 'appoyntement' was concluded between them, in terms of which the king promised the earl that he would be left in peaceable possession of his lands. In return, Earl James undertook to renounce all bonds 'contrare' the king, to forgive him for 'arte and parte' in the slaughter of his brother, and not to seek 'entry in the lands of the earldom of Wigtown' without the queen's consent (these having been restored to her). This was merely papering over the cracks, because the king was determined to crush the Douglases once and for all. But fearing that a royal triumph might herald a return to the kind of tyranny exercised by James I, Parliament refused to support him.

This forced King James to make further concessions. In January 1453 he and Earl James entered into a very one-sided agreement, in terms of which the king undertook to restore Douglas to the earldom of Wigtown, and to assist him in obtaining papal dispensation for his marriage to his brother's widow Margaret of Galloway.

This must have been extremely galling for the king, the more so because it meant restoring the Douglas power in the south-west which he hoped – and probably thought – had been broken. Therefore it is bound to have reinforced his determination to crush the Black Douglases. In the event, papal dispensation was forthcoming, and the luckless Margaret was forced into what she later described as an 'ungodlie and wickit marriage'.[*]

Meanwhile the king's apparent capitulation to Earl James cost him much valuable support because many feared that, if the earl were to triumph, the lands and rights which the king had granted them in reward for their support would be revoked – or, as the chronicler put it, they 'wald nocht stand'. Nevertheless the Crichtons remained loyal (they had no alternative), as did many influential Border magnates – notably George Douglas earl of Angus,[†] Sir Walter Scott of Buccleuch, and Douglas of Cavers. The king needed all the help he could get because Earl James was busy mustering support against a showdown which both knew was inevitable. Since the current truce denied him English help, Earl James had to win over people like Sir William Douglas of Drumlanrig who had turned against Earl William. In fact he was even prepared to make peace with Sir Simon Glendinning, one of Earl William's assassins, for the sake of mustering support in Eskdale. In his anxiety to gain as much help as possible he is believed to have visited Galloway no less than three times in a drive to win over the local landowners.

In Dumfriesshire loyalties were mixed. Whereas the Johnstone and Herries families were supporters of Earl James,[‡] the king's adherents included the Maxwells, who were allies of the Crichtons (John master of Maxwell having recently married the earl of Caithness's daughter Jonet). Cussedness induced some landowners to support the opposite side from those with whom they were at feud, a case in point being John Carruthers of Mouswald who as keeper of Lochmaben was a man of considerable influence. Notwithstanding that his family had benefited considerably at the hands of Earl James's predecessors, he allied himself with the king, mainly because he was at feud with the Douglas-supporting Johnstones.

But the situation was about to change. William lord Crichton's death in 1454, followed almost immediately by those of his son James earl of Moray and George earl of Caithness, resulted in a break-up of the network of bonds and alliances which they had established with other local landowners in the south-west. The consequent weakening of the king's position there forced him to bring the Johnstones on side, flagrantly bending the law, and letting down his supporters, in his efforts to do so. For example,

---

[*] Pitscottie, *Historie and Cronicles of Scotland* i, 125. King James seems to have had some sympathy for her, because after her divorce from Earl James he arranged for her to marry his half-brother John earl of Atholl and endowed her with the forfeited Douglas lands of Balvenie. By him she had two sons and two daughters – Jean who married the third earl of Huntly, and Katherine who married the sixth lord Forbes. Both left numerous descendants, as did her elder son the earl of Atholl.
[†] He had succeeded his childless brother James the third earl in 1446.
[‡] Which suggests that the Sir John Herries whom Earl William allegedly put to death must have been an exception.

when two sons of Adam Johnstone of that Ilk captured Lochmaben 'throu treason of the portar',[32] the keeper, John Carruthers, a supporter of the king, appealed to him for redress. To show willing, the king sent his justiciar lord Abernethy to Annandale to adjudicate the matter. But doubtless at his prompting, and in defiance of all canons of justice, Abernethy ruled that the Johnstones were entitled to remain in possession, when they appointed a relative, Herbert Johnstone, as keeper in place of Carruthers.[33]

The final showdown arose as a result of a dispute over the lordship of Dalkeith. Since James Douglas, the second lord, had been declared insane, control of the lordship was in the hands of his acquisitive brother Henry Douglas of Borgue as curator. On the strength of this, Henry Douglas attempted to appropriate the lordship for himself to the exclusion of James Douglas's son and heir, another James.* Because King James was the younger James's guardian, he could not allow him to be defrauded of his inheritance and was prepared to defend his rights by force. As brother-in-law of Henry of Borgue (who was married to his sister) Earl James was drawn into the dispute.

Both king and earl set about raising an army, and in March 1455 the army invaded the Border country, systematically looting and burning the lands, settlements and keeps of all known Douglas supporters in the region. Then, heading north it laid siege to Earl James's stronghold of Abercorn on the shores of the Forth. Although the garrison held out, Earl James was torn between coming to their rescue or abandoning them to their fate. While he dithered, unable to make up his mind, lord Hamilton,[†] his closest adherent and foremost supporter, lost patience and defected to the king. This left the earl gravely weakened, and when Abercorn was taken he hurried south in a vain attempt to secure English help. This played into James's hands, and in early 1455, at his instigation, Parliament issued summonses to the Douglases and their supporters to appear before it on charges of treason.

The summonses were ignored. Instead, Earl James's brothers, the earls of Moray and Ormond, and John Douglas of Balvenie, in defiance of the king and Parliament, proceeded to raise an army. They invaded the Border country and ravaged the lands belonging to the king's supporters before moving on to Eskdale. Here they encountered levies raised from Annandale by lord Maxwell and John Johnstone (now in the king's allegiance), and from Teviotdale by Sir Walter Scott of Branxholm, at Arkinholm.[‡] In the ensuing engagement the Douglases were routed – Moray was killed, Ormond captured and executed, while John of Balvenie alone escaped. When Parliament met in early June, the Douglases were convicted of a whole series of crimes – conspiracy, rebellion, treasonable dealings with the English, and violent

---

*   He was created earl of Morton on his marriage in 1458 to King James's deaf and dumb sister Joanna.
†   Formerly Sir James Hamilton of Cadzow, he later married King James's daughter Mary, the divorced wife of Thomas Boyd earl of Arran. Their son James Hamilton was created earl of Arran and controlled the regency during the minority of James V.
‡   The battle took place above the confluence of the Esk and the Ewes Water, just north of Langholm, on 1 May 1455.

plundering. Consequently decree of forfeiture was passed on their lands and titles. Nevertheless James continued to style himself earl of Douglas, being so recognised by the English, until his death some forty years later.

King James's triumph was incomplete, because Threave castle, the Douglas ruling centre in Galloway, still held out. Situated on an island in the river Dee, its capture presented a daunting challenge, because its walls were so massive that only the 'great bombard', a new and improved type of cannon recently imported from the Low Countries, was capable of breaching them. Since the only one in Scotland was at Linlithgow and had to be hauled across country to Threave, the preparations for the siege took time. In fact longer than expected, for while the 'great bombard' was being manoeuvred across Crawford moor one of the wheels broke. Because attempts to extricate it merely caused it to sink deeper into the morass, troops had to be summoned from Edinburgh to help pull it out.

In a final attempt to secure English help, Earl James agreed to hand over the fortress to the English king Henry VI in return for the promise of £100 for the 'succour, victualling, relief and rescue' of the castle by mid-July. But it was too late. Sceptical of Earl James's ability to raise the siege, and overawed by the sight of the 'great bombard' positioned menacingly on the bank of the river facing the castle, the keeper Sir John Fraser surrendered the castle in return for a large bribe and safe conducts for himself and the garrison. So ended the power of the Black Douglases which in its heyday reached an eminence which has never been equalled in Scotland before or since. Thereafter Earl James remained a pensioner of the English crown, making an occasional foray into Scotland in a forlorn attempt to recover his former lands.

They were extensive. Whereas some were used to reward the king's supporters, the remainder fell into the crown and constituted a huge addition to the royal demesne. In Galloway, for example, the forfeited lands are identifiable from the Exchequer Rolls which detail the rents received for each individual property. On the other hand there were none in Annandale because all the Douglas lands there had reverted to the crown following the death of the sixth earl.[34] In Eskdale there is a reference to lands accruing to the crown 'through the forfeiture of its lord James, former earl of Douglas'.[35] They were subsequently granted, along with others in neighbouring Ewesdale, to the king's supporter George Douglas earl of Angus to add to those he already owned there.[36]

Following the Douglas forfeiture, King James conferred the lordship of Annandale, along with other titles including the lordship of the Isle of Man, on his one-year-old second son Alexander, later duke of Albany. Investing him with the lordship of Man amounted to a mere parchment grant, for it had long been annexed to the English crown. Indeed fifty years previously Henry IV had granted it to Sir John Stanley whose grandson Sir Thomas was the present lord. Nevertheless the king intended that it should crystallise in the hands of the young Alexander in the event of his recovering the island by force.

The appointment of an English bishop to its see was the pretext. Claiming that it was part of the diocese of Sodor, which was a Scottish bishopric, and that the appointment was unlawful, James dispatched an expedition from Kirkcudbright to seize control of the island, ostensibly to enforce the bishop of Sodor's jurisdiction over it. The attack was beaten off, and the following year Stanley's son, Thomas, retaliated. Joining forces with the ex-earl James they attacked Kirkcudbright from the sea, and having reduced that recently created royal burgh to ashes they went on to plunder the west marches. Although repelled by a hastily mustered local force, the attack was a salutary reminder of the Douglases' continuing nuisance value and the ever-present threat of an English invasion. Therefore in November 1457, in order to deny the ex-earl James further help from that source, the existing truce with England was extended for a further four years and ratified by the king on 31 December.[37]

Yet, notwithstanding the truce, King James was determined to capture Berwick and Roxburgh, the last two castles remaining in English hands. In July 1460, taking advantage of the English preoccupation with the Wars of the Roses, he laid siege to Roxburgh. As a preliminary he ordered all available cannonry to be assembled on the opposite bank of the Tweed in preparation for bombarding the castle. He had always been fascinated by gunnery, and this was to prove his nemesis. His obsession with monitoring the performance of the cannons caused him to stand too close to them, and when one accidentally exploded he suffered fatal injuries. So died this able, energetic, ruthlessly determined – and at times duplicitous – king within two months of his thirtieth birthday.

NINE

The Later Middle Ages

A KING IN ADVERSITY

James II was succeeded by his eight-year-old son James III. Taking advantage of her rival Bishop Kennedy's absence on a mission to the Continent, Mary of Gueldres, the determined and capable queen mother, had herself appointed guardian, effectively regent. To ensure the bishop's exclusion from power, along with her other political opponents such as George Douglas earl of Angus, she filled the principal offices of state with her supporters. They included James Lindsay, provost of Lincluden, who became keeper of the privy seal and later treasurer. Therefore when Bishop Kennedy returned the following year he was enraged to find himself deliberately sidelined.

A source of controversy between them was which side to support in the Wars of the Roses – the Lancastrians or the Yorkists. Following the Yorkist victory at Northampton in July 1460 Henry VI was taken prisoner when, threatened with death, the feeble-minded king acknowledged the duke of York, the head of the Yorkist faction, as his heir. Outraged at the exclusion of their son Edward prince of Wales, Henry's wife the redoubtable Margaret of Anjou was determined to fight for his rights. Therefore she sought the assistance of the Scots, and, having agreed to support her, Queen Mary invited her to Dumfries to discuss terms. From there the two queens went on to Lincluden where they are said to have stayed for ten or twelve days, James Lindsay the provost doubtless acting as host. Events justified Queen Mary's decision to support Margaret – at least in the short term, for on 30 December 1460 the Lancastrians won a significant victory at Wakefield when the duke of York was killed. News of this sent Margaret hurrying south with 'a great army of Scots, Welsh, Northmen [i.e. Highlanders] and other strangers' to exploit their success.[1]

In February 1461 the situation was reversed when the duke of York's son, Edward earl of March, defeated the Lancastrians at Mortimers Cross. But in a rapid change of fortune the Yorkists themselves were defeated later that month at the battle of St Albans. The story goes that in the aftermath of the battle two Yorkist knights who had been charged with guarding King Henry, and whom he had implored to stay with him as he watched the battle from under a nearby tree, were taken prisoner. Brought before Margaret, she asked the seven-year-old prince of Wales what she should do with them. 'Fair son', she is supposed to have said, 'what deaths shall these two knights you see before you die?' 'Cut off their heads', came the young prince's brutal reply. And so it was done. Meanwhile the Scots, who had systematically ravaged the countryside far and wide as they headed south, were already making their way home with as much loot as they could take with them.

In March 1461 the situation changed again following the Yorkist victory at Towton, when Henry VI was deposed and the earl of March was proclaimed king as Edward IV. Refusing to accept defeat, Queen Margaret returned to Scotland, accompanied this time by Henry, the prince of Wales and a number of supporters, to seek further assistance. Again Queen Mary was prepared to help. But it came at a price – namely the surrender of Berwick castle and a promise to cede Carlisle. Although Berwick, the last remaining stronghold in English hands, was delivered up, it was not possible to cede Carlisle castle because it had been recovered by the Yorkists.

Queen Margaret remained in Scotland for the best part of a year until April 1462. Having raised a loan from Queen Mary, she left for France to try to enlist the help of King Louis XI. But no sooner had she departed than Queen Mary entered into talks with Edward IV's envoy, the earl of Warwick.* Her change of heart has been attributed to resentment of the Lancastrian duke of Somerset's boasting of a clandestine affair with her, but more likely she was hedging her bets in case Queen Margaret returned empty-handed. Unnecessarily as it turned out, because Margaret managed to raise a large French contingent, and with their help she recovered the principal Northumbrian castles. But only temporarily, for with their new and improved artillery the Yorkists quickly re-took them having blasted whole sections of the castle walls to smithereens. Therefore once again Margaret, Henry and their supporters were forced to seek refuge in Scotland.

In January 1463, Henry and the two queens, accompanied by the youthful James III, invaded England at the head of a Franco-Scottish force. Having retaken Alnwick, they laid siege to Norham castle. But warned of the approach of a much larger Yorkist army under Warwick, the ex-Earl James and his brother John Douglas, they withdrew. Pursuing them across the border, the Yorkist army laid waste to the marches, including Annandale where they sacked Lochmaben town and laid siege to the castle. However, it was relieved by a Scottish force which drove the invaders back across the border, in the course of which John Douglas (formerly of Balvenie) was captured and executed. Meanwhile Queen Margaret left Scotland having committed Henry to the care of Bishop Kennedy at St Andrews. This time she headed for Burgundy in a vain attempt to seek the help of Queen Mary's elderly uncle Duke Philip.

Queen Mary died in November 1463, and because the earl of Angus predeceased her in March, political power passed to Bishop Kennedy. Fearing that the Yorkists, now in the ascendant, might invade Scotland, he appointed commissioners to meet a delegation at Lochmabenstone to negotiate a truce.² This suited the Yorkists because it would deny Scotland as a base from which King Henry and his supporters could stage a possible comeback. Therefore on 1 June 1464 their negotiations culminated in a fifteen-year truce.

---

* Grandson of Ralph Neville earl of Westmorland, the English-appointed lord of Annandale, and known as 'the kingmaker', Richard Neville earl of Warwick was effectively the head of the Yorkist faction.

When Bishop Kennedy died in May 1465 custody of the young king James was granted to his elder brother Gilbert lord Kennedy. However, in July the following year Kennedy's rival, Robert lord Boyd, captured the king while out hunting near Linlithgow. According to one source Boyd felled Kennedy with a single blow and seizing hold of the king he carried him off to Edinburgh castle where his brother Sir Alexander Boyd of Drumcoll (Duncow) was keeper. To secure his position, Boyd attempted to gain the support of Archibald Douglas, who had recently succeeded as fifth earl of Angus, by arranging a marriage between Douglas and Boyd's daughter Elizabeth. Still more ambitiously, Boyd arranged for his son Thomas, newly created earl of Arran, to marry King James's sister Mary. Forced to consent to such a *mésalliance*, as he perceived it, the young king allegedly wept tears of shame at their wedding.[3]

Most important of all, Boyd retained custody of the king. Nevertheless he had to wait until Parliament met in October to obtain the necessary authority, and until then he kept the king a virtual prisoner for fear of a Kennedy-inspired attempt to rescue him. Therefore, accompanied by his brother Sir Alexander and the royal court, Boyd took the king on an extended progress – probably a justice ayre – throughout the realm, in the course of which they stayed at Lochmaben.[4] From there they returned to Edinburgh in time for the October Parliament which duly ratified Boyd's custodianship of the king.

In July 1469 James married Margaret, daughter of Christian I king of Denmark and Norway who, in terms of the marriage treaty, ceded Orkney and Shetland to the Scottish crown. Now turned seventeen, James was declared of age to rule. This meant that the Boyds' custody of him – and hence their tenure of power – automatically ceased. Grasping the opportunity to revenge himself for his treatment at their hands, James caused charges of treason to be raised against them. Accordingly they were summoned to stand trial at the next Parliament. Aware of the magnates' hostility towards him and his family, and the virtual certainty of conviction, Boyd and his son Thomas earl of Arran fled to the Continent along with the latter's wife (King James's sister) leaving his brother Sir Alexander to face the music.

Sir Alexander vigorously denied the charges and demanded to be tried by an assize. A jury consisting of fifteen nobles, including the earl of Morton (formerly James Douglas of Dalkeith), was duly empanelled. Sir Alexander was convicted of treason and sentenced to execution on the castle hill at Edinburgh, while Boyd and Arran were condemned to death and forfeiture in their absence. Two years later, they moved from their refuge on the Continent to England, where they were given sanctuary by Edward IV. From there Arran sent his wife Mary to Scotland to plead with her brother the king to rescind the sentence passed on him and his father. In vain. Not only did the king refuse but he detained her in Scotland, and having compelled her to divorce Arran he married her off to his supporter James lord Hamilton. Arran died shortly afterwards, while his father lord Boyd remained a pensioner of the English crown for the rest of his life.[*]

---

[*] Later Arran's estates, which included much of Arran itself, were granted to James Hamilton and Mary's son James, who was created earl of Arran and was a regent during James V's minority.

In October 1474 James concluded a treaty with Edward IV which was sealed with the betrothal of his eighteen-month-old son James (future James IV) and Edward's five-year-old daughter Cicely. Although the treaty was generally popular – particularly with the people of southern Scotland who had suffered so much from the English invasions – it was not welcomed by the southern magnates, such as the king's brother Alexander duke of Albany as lord of Annandale, and Archibald Douglas earl of Angus as lord of Liddesdale. This was because they were benefiting handsomely from cross-border raiding, which was one of the many reasons why they turned against James. He seems to have gone out of his way to court unpopularity. For example his revocation of grants of land made during his minority made him many enemies, while there was widespread resentment of his choice of favourites, notably William Scheves. Starting out as a royal servant responsible, among other things, for sewing the king's shirts, Scheves had risen through the ranks of the royal household. Finally, overlooking his stigma of illegitimacy, the king engineered Scheves's appointment to the recently constituted archbishopric of St Andrews.

Another beneficiary was Sir John Carlyle. A loyal supporter of James II, he had been appointed keeper of Threave and Lochmaben castles, as well as justiciar of Annandale. Recently he had been sent to France to solicit promises of help against a possible renewal of war with England. In 1474 he was created a lord of Parliament when he took the title lord Carlyle of Torthorwald, and three years later King James gave him Sir Alexander Boyd's forfeited barony of Drumcoll (Duncow). This was stated to be in reward for 'his frequent expenses and great labours to the danger of his person at sundry times in the King's affairs outside the realm with the King of France and elsewhere'.[5]

Meanwhile an escalation of cross-border raiding by the southern magnates, local barons and (to quote Pitscottie) 'the theiffis of Annerdaill'[6] in breach of the truce rendered the prospect of war increasingly likely. Since the duke of Albany was warden of the marches, and therefore responsible for maintaining law and order in the region, he was held to blame. This gave the king, already jealous of Albany's popularity, an excuse to have him arrested on charges of treason, when he was warded in Edinburgh castle pending trial. However, he made a dramatic escape and fled to France. Although his lands were forfeit he remained a constant threat to the king for some years to come.[7]

Meanwhile, determined to maintain peace with England, come what may, James attempted to bribe Edward IV's co-operation by offering his sister Margaret in marriage to Edward's brother-in-law Earl Rivers. But the plan came to nothing when it transpired that Margaret was already pregnant by William lord Crichton.[*] As a notorious lecher himself Edward was no doubt privately amused, but publicly his

---

[*]   Son of James Crichton, and grandson of William lord Crichton, the former chancellor, his affair with the king's sister Margaret, who was described as 'a.lady of great beauty but with a reputation that was more than loose' (*Scots Peerage* iii, 64), was allegedly in retaliation for the king's seducing his wife. The outcome of their affair was a daughter Margaret, who married the earl of Rothes.

reaction was one of outraged honour. In 1480 the peace with England was further imperilled when the earl of Angus raided Northumberland and burnt the town of Bamburgh. Retaliating, the duke of Gloucester (future Richard III) prepared to invade Scotland. In vain, James sent envoys to Edward IV offering to redress breaches of the treaty on a reciprocal basis. But Edward refused to meet them and instead dispatched a fleet to the Firth of Forth.

James responded by summoning Parliament. It enacted a series of measures for the strengthening of the country's defences. For example there were to be regular 'wappinschaws' while James undertook to put the main Border castles in a proper state of repair and 'stuff them with victuals and artillery', as it was put.[8] Each was to be garrisoned by a hundred men – fifty pikemen and a like number of archers – to be recruited by the keeper, and everything was to be in place by 1 May 1482. The castles included Lochmaben, which was put under the captaincy of Thomas Kirkpatrick of Closeburn.[9] At the same time, Robert Charteris of Amisfeld was put in charge of the smaller peles of Castlemilk, Annan, and Bell's Tower, being allocated a hundred troops to be distributed between them.[10]

Meanwhile Edward IV authorised the duke of Gloucester and the ex-earl James to promise lands and rewards to any Scotsmen willing to support the intended invasion.[11] King James countered with an offer of a thousand merks and lands worth a hundred merks a year to anyone who delivered ex-Earl James to him dead or alive. At the same time he gave the ex-earl's supporters twenty-four days in which to obtain remission and forgiveness for past misdeeds. But not people like Alexander Jardine, younger of Applegarth, who had been the ex-earl's principal adherents and were regarded as beyond the pale.[12] To discourage any disaffected Scots from joining the English, James offered them a general amnesty for all past misdeeds. Additionally he bribed the support of his half-uncles, the earls of Atholl and Buchan, and Andrew Stewart bishop-elect of Moray,* with promises of land and high political office.

King Edward enlisted the support of the duke of Albany, now residing at the English court. In terms of the indenture concluded between them, Albany, optimistically styling himself 'Alexander king of Scots', promised that once in possession of the realm he would perform homage to Edward, acknowledge him as overlord, and break the French alliance. Further, he undertook to hand over the castles of Berwick, Roxburgh and Lochmaben to him, and surrender the lordships of Annandale, Eskdale, Ewesdale and Liddesdale.[13] In July an English army under the joint command of Albany and Gloucester, the largest to have invaded Scotland for over eighty years, crossed the border and advanced up Lauderdale towards Edinburgh.

Raising an army, James advanced south to meet it. But, on reaching Lauder, the Scottish leaders, knowing that they were heading for certain disaster, refused to go any further. Long dissatisfied with James's inept rule, and resentful of his appointment of low-born favourites to high office, they decided to mutiny. They met in secret

---

* Sons of James I's widow Queen Joan Beaufort by her second husband Sir James Stewart of Lorne.

in a local church to discuss plans and appoint a leader – not easy given the general reluctance to assume the role. Apparently the situation was compared to a group of mice trying to decide who should hang a bell round the cat that preyed on them. And because the earl of Angus is supposed to have volunteered for the role, it earned him the soubriquet Archibald 'Bell-the-Cat'. As a first step the Scottish leaders seized the royal favourites and hanged them from Lauder bridge before arresting the king.

Taken back to Edinburgh, the king was warded in the castle and placed in the custody of his uncle, the earl of Atholl. Meanwhile the Scottish host was disbanded, allowing the English army free passage to Edinburgh. In desperation the townsfolk offered them a bribe of 80,000 merks to spare the city, which was enough to persuade them to withdraw to Berwick. Albany might reasonably have expected the English success to win him the throne. Not so. Aware of his promises to King Edward, neither the Scottish people, nor crucially Parliament, would stand for it. Therefore he was forced to lower his sights to securing the restoration of his lands and titles. But even that was uncertain given his continuing intrigues with King Edward. Indeed, consorting with the enemy like this made him so unpopular that he was compelled to return to England. Some months later King James was freed by his uncles on condition that he handed over effective control of the government to them.

Edward IV died in April 1483, and following the deposition (and subsequent disappearance) of his twelve-year-old son Edward V later that year, the duke of Gloucester became king as Richard III. But faced with mounting baronial opposition, and widely suspected of being responsible for the murder of Edward V and his brother the duke of York, he could not afford the distraction of a Scottish war. Therefore he abandoned Albany. Undaunted, Albany joined forces with the ex-Earl James, and together they invaded Annandale with the aim of capturing Lochmaben. No sooner had they crossed the border than the warning beacons were lit and the landowners mobilised their levies. Led by the master of Maxwell, they included John Johnstone of that Ilk, Cuthbert Murray of Cockpool, and Sir Robert Crichton of Sanquhar, as well as Thomas Carruthers of Holmains and Sir Robert Charteris of Amisfield.[14] On 22 July, when the invaders descended on Lochmaben town in the middle of a fair, they were attacked by Maxwell's levies and driven back across the border.

The ex-Earl James was taken prisoner. Now an elderly man, he had fought bravely until unhorsed and taken prisoner by Alexander Kirkpatrick.[*] He must have fully expected to be put to death, but with unexpected leniency King James ordered him to be confined to the abbey of Lindores in Fife, and there he remained until his death in 1491, latterly granted a pension by James IV. Meanwhile Albany escaped to England, and from there to France where he was killed two years later in a jousting match with the duke of Orleans (the future King Louis XII). The Scottish casualties included Sir William Douglas of Drumlanrig and the master of

---

[*]   Brother of Sir Thomas Kirkpatrick of Closeburn.

Maxwell, the latter being stabbed in the back by one of his men who bore a grudge against him.[*]

The victors were well rewarded with forfeited lands. Most of the barony of Kirkmichael, which had reverted to the crown following the dispossession of William lord Crichton (the despoiler of the king's sister and now living in exile), was given to Alexander Kirkpatrick as a reward for capturing the ex-earl James,[15] the remainder being given to Herbert Johnstone the keeper of Lochmaben.[16] Notwithstanding William lord Crichton's forfeiture, other members of the family benefited. Sir Robert Crichton of Sanquhar's sheriffship of Dumfries was made hereditary, while his brother Edward was confirmed in possession of the lands of Kirkpatrick.[17] Similarly Andrew Herries, son and heir of Herbert lord Herries, was confirmed in those of Terregles, Kirkgunzeon and half the barony of Urr, as well as being given lands in Dumfriesshire.[†] Other beneficiaries included Thomas Carruthers, who 'for good service in the defence of the realm against Sir James Douglas and other rebels' was given the forfeited lands of Corrie.[18]

In September 1484 a three-year truce was concluded with the English when it was agreed that regular meetings should be held near the border, generally at Lochmabenstone, for the settling of disputes arising in the west marches.[19] The arrangement remained in force notwithstanding Richard III's death at the battle of Bosworth and the succession of Henry VII in 1485. In May 1486 Thomas lord Dacre, warden of the English west marches, was authorised to punish breaches of the truce and grant safe conducts to the Scottish envoys commissioned to negotiate its renewal.[20] In December John fourth lord Maxwell, warden of the west marches, was granted a safe conduct to meet lord Dacre on the English side of the border,[21] presumably to arrange compensation for breaches of the truce and hand over the guilty parties.

Although restored to a semblance of power, James's ill-conceived policies continued to alienate a large section of the baronage. In the south he came up against the powerful Home family and their allies the Hepburns, both former Boyd supporters. The quarrel soon spread, and other members of the nobility including the earl of Angus were persuaded to join them. James attempted to bribe the support of the lesser baronage with the grant of honours. Those in the south-west included Sir Robert Crichton who was appointed a lord of Parliament with the title of lord Crichton of Sanquhar, while Alexander Cunninghame lord Kilmaurs was created earl of Glencairn, and lord Carlyle's son and heir William was given a knighthood.

Meanwhile King James became morbidly suspicious of those around him, his courtiers and others, convinced that they were plotting against him. They included his immediate family – notably his fourteen-year-old son James duke of Rothesay,

---

[*] *Scots Peerage* vi, 477. John master of Maxwell has generally been referred to as the third lord Maxwell notwithstanding that he predeceased his father Robert the second lord.

[†] *RMS* II, 1654. They were Moffatdale and Evandale, Tundergarth, Lockerbie and Hoddom.

who was suspected of being in league with his uncle Albany. Eventually, fearing that his father intended to have him put to death to make way for his brother the duke of Ross, the younger James sought refuge in Stirling castle whose keeper James Schaw of Sauchie was a Home relative. According to Pitscottie, the Homes bribed Schaw to hand over the prince to them, which he did. Consequently the younger James found himself propelled into the nominal leadership of a rebellion against his father.

Since the nobility were also under suspicion, King James looked to the lesser baronage for support. Those from the south-west included men like Sir Thomas Kirkpatrick of Closeburn, Sir Robert Charteris of Amisfield and Cuthbert Murray of Cockpool. Since Murray was at feud with lord Maxwell, the latter defected to the rebels, along with most of his kindred.[22] So too – ungratefully considering that James had recently ennobled him – did Robert lord Crichton.

By March 1488 the rebellion had spread to the extent that King James's supporters persuaded him, much against his will, to leave Edinburgh for his own safety. Therefore, having looted the royal treasury for money to pay his troops, he took ship for Fife. There he raised an army, and heading south he encountered the rebel host at Sauchieburn near Stirling. Consisting mainly of men from southern Scotland, specifically Annandale, Liddesdale and Galloway, it was led by the Homes and Hepburns under the nominal command of the duke of Rothesay. By contrast some Dumfriesshire lairds supported the king. They included the earl of Glencairn, who was killed in the battle, Cuthbert Murray of Cockpool, his brother Sir Adam Murray of Drumcrieff (the main instigator of the family's feud with the Maxwells), Sir Robert Charteris of Amisfield,* and the earl of Morton.

Battle was joined on 11 June 1488 close to the field of Bannockburn. It appears to have been a relatively one-sided affair because the men of Annandale wielded their long spears to such effect that they put the king's army to flight. James himself may have been killed in the battle, although Buchanan asserts that when his companions saw it going against him they persuaded him to flee. While heading for the safety of a ship anchored in the Forth his horse is supposed to have stumbled and thrown him to the ground. As he lay there helpless, his pursuers caught up with him and allegedly hacked him to death with their swords.

COUNTRY LIFE

From the early fifteenth century onwards the climate became progressively colder. The growing season was correspondingly shorter, while the cooler and wetter summers were responsible for more frequent harvest failures and the spectre of hunger and starvation. Contemporary chroniclers testify to this. According to Bower the winter of 1431–2 was particularly hard with 'ice and gales' causing 'widespread

---

* King James's armour-bearer who fought for him at Lochmaben and Sauchieburn, he represented the Dumfriesshire barons in Parliament.

losses of sheep and cattle' while 1435 was a year of 'great food shortage'.[23] The year 1484 seems to have been bad too, because meteors reportedly 'filled the skies as dread harbingers of calamity'. On 25 September 'three moons' are said to have 'appeared in the firmament' accompanied by 'much fyre, thunder and raine'.

Because farming was the mainstay of its economy, Scotland was particularly badly affected. Therefore it is hardly surprising that foreign travellers from the fourteenth century onwards described it as a very poor country. The effects of the deteriorating climate were compounded by plague epidemics – perhaps not as serious as those of 1349 and 1362, but bad enough to cause a significant number of deaths.[24] The people of Dumfriesshire were particularly at risk, for the fact that these epidemics generally spread from England meant that they, like the inhabitants of the east marches, were most exposed to them. But not invariably, because some epidemics are thought to have originated from infected crews of foreign ships landing at the east-coast ports.

To add to their woes, the people of Dumfriesshire were regularly victims of the depredations resulting from the feuds between the leading families in the region, as well as the English invasions. The inhabitants of eastern Annandale, Eskdale and lower Liddesdale were at particular risk, for their proximity to the main western route into Scotland meant that they were particularly exposed to the damage and destruction associated with these invasions. To make matters worse, they were the main target of cross-border raids – or 'reiving' – which was endemic throughout the region, and would remain a serious blight on it until suppressed by James VI following the union of the crowns. Small wonder that, as Froissart observed, when the English invaded Scotland they took their provisions with them because there was so little available there.

Since the region was under constant threat of attack (Anglo-Scottish truces counted for little on the marches) and growing crops routinely destroyed, much of it remained uncultivated as farmers turned increasingly to livestock rearing.[25] This was partly because the Scots at that time were primarily meat eaters – unlike their eighteenth-century descendants whose staple diet was oatmeal. This is evident from the observations of an English traveller that '[the Scots] eat flesh and fish to repletion and bread only as a dainty', while Hector Boece who visited the south-west in 1527 described it as containing a 'store of bestial'.[26] Sheep farming, on the other hand, was not practised to the same extent as in the heady days of the thirteenth century. True, the market for wool staged a temporary recovery, and as late as 1471 the duty collected on its export – mainly to England – accounted for three-quarters of the total customs for that year,[27] but the market subsequently declined to a point where sheep farming was barely profitable.[28]

There were a number of reasons for this. One was the practice of smearing sheep with a mixture of tar and butter (it would continue until well into the twentieth century), which although intended to protect them against blowfly strike and maggot infestation made the fleeces difficult to clean and therefore less readily marketable. Another was the increase in the export duty on wool. This was intended to divert

Scottish-produced wool to the home market in order to encourage the domestic manufacture of woollen goods. Fine in theory, but it had unintended consequences. Because wool manufacturing was a cottage industry carried out on a piecework basis, mainly by the womenfolk to supplement their husbands' wages, they could not afford to pay more than a minimum price for wool. And because this rendered sheep farming uneconomic many turned to cattle rearing instead. Sheep farming continued to be practised, albeit on a reduced scale. But it was a precarious form of husbandry, because sheep – like cattle – were in constant danger of being driven off by marauding bands of robbers who constantly preyed on farmers.

Houses and settlements were just as liable to be destroyed in the course of these raids. But the fact that they could readily be rebuilt – within a matter of days assuming the (very basic) materials were available – helped mitigate the plight of a people already inured to hardship. This was because their hovels amounted to little more than rudimentary shelters which gave a modicum of protection against wind and rain. The walls consisted of stakes driven into the ground and strengthened with interleaved brushwood. Infilled with earth and stones, they were plastered with mud or clay, or even cow dung, which when dried and hardened rendered them tolerably weatherproof; branches laid across the top at wallhead height, and covered with turf divots, sufficed for a roof. Heather and rushes, on the other hand, were seldom used because they were too inflammable in the event of an attack.[29]

A later more sophisticated type of roof was the A-frame timbered cruck which was bonded by a collar at the top and a rafter above head height. Examples have come to light at Torthorwald and at Prior's Linn, Canonbie.[30] The hovel provided accommodation for the peasant farmer and his family at one end, while the other was occupied by his livestock, who provided a source of warmth in winter. Bastel-houses and pele-houses, on the other hand, were the preserve of minor lairds and freeholders. A bastel-house was a single-storey building with a vaulted basement where livestock, particularly cattle, could be accommodated in an emergency. There are no examples in Dumfriesshire, the nearest being at Elvanfoot a few miles beyond the county boundary in Lanarkshire. A pele, on the other hand, was a basic stone-built, two-storey tower house.

The period from about the mid-1400s onwards witnessed the final development of the multi-tenanted ferme-toun with its infield and outfield system of farming.[31] Whereas the latter was common to all the tenants, the infield consisted of the cultivable land where cropping was generally limited to bere (a form of barley) and oats, although farmers were statutorily required to grow a limited amount of pease and beans.[32] Another leguminous crop was lucerne. This was introduced into Scotland by the Cistercians, and that it was grown by the monks of Melrose on their lands in Eskdale is apparent from the discovery of traces preserved in a ditch at Over Rig near Eskdalemuir.[33] Because western Dumfriesshire is generally more fertile than the east, besides being less exposed to English invasions and cross-border raiding, it could be cropped more extensively. But this was limited by the general acidity of the soil – a characteristic of most of Scotland at the time, while much of the lower-lying regions of Annandale and Eskdale were too waterlogged to allow for cultivation.

Cattle numbers, on the other hand, were limited by the constraints of winter. Whereas in summertime it was possible to graze any amount of stock, in winter numbers were limited by the amount of fodder available. This was frequently supplemented by broom, and an Act of 1454 enjoined all landowners to require their tenants to grow it as a crop.[34] But it was a poor substitute for straw, and in any case there was never enough to feed the entire cattle stock. Therefore with the approach of winter the surplus had to be slaughtered, although farmers would invariably try to keep more than they could adequately feed. Inevitably many died of starvation, and with the arrival of spring the survivors were in such poor shape that some had to be physically carried out to the new grass – hence the term 'lifting day'.

The evidence suggests that, notwithstanding the high infant mortality, general malnutrition among the poorer classes, and the incidence of disease,[35] the period from the mid-fifteenth century onwards witnessed a rapid population growth. Possible confirmation of this comes from Pont's late-sixteenth-century map of Nithsdale, which shows some three hundred settlements, many of them identifiable from existing place-names.[36] Almost all were situated near the Nith and its tributaries, and doubtless the same applied elsewhere in Dumfriesshire. This put increasing pressure on the land, and therefore much of the wasteland which was previously used for summering cattle was brought into pasture, while swathes of native woodland were cut back.

On the other hand, certain officially designated forests were sacrosanct ('forest' in this sense meaning hill country as well as woodland). There were a number in Dumfriesshire. For example there is a reference to the king collecting herbage and foggage (rents for summer grass and winter grazing) from Cocklicks, Woodcockair and Phyllis Park, in the *forest* of Dalton,* for the year 1452, while there was another in the vicinity of Lochmaben. In Nithsdale there were at least three officially designated forests: Dalswinton, 'Herys' and Irongray. The last of these may be identifiable with the forest of Dalquhairn to the west of Cairn Water, which was traditionally the hunting preserve of the bishops of Glasgow.[†]

The pressure for increased production to feed the growing population was responsible for the passing of a number of statutes for the purpose of improving farming practices. For example an Act of 1452 prescribed the date by which corn had to be threshed, while

---

* It was about this time that Dalton, which had previously been incorporated in the forest of Annandale, was established as a separate forest, as was happening throughout Scotland where the large hunting preserves of the twelfth century were being divided into smaller ones (J M Gilbert, 'Medieval woodland management in southern Scotland' *TDGNHAS*, lxxxvi 2012).

† Hunting at that time was not the same as the modern concept of the sport. It was then the practice for the deer to be rounded up by a large number of people conscripted for the purpose. Under the direction of the huntsman, and assisted by packs of hounds, the deer would be driven into a pre-constructed trap, usually a declivity in the ground. There they would be held while the sportsmen shot at them with their bows and arrows until the requisite number had been killed when the survivors were released.

requiring farmers to grow a specified amount of pease and beans.[37] Harvest failure and the resulting food shortage were responsible for the Acts of 1449 and 1482 which forbade the practice of regrating, namely the hoarding of grain in order to sell it into a dearer market, while another of 1468 banned the export of sheep and cattle.[38]

The fact that sheep were generally ranched out on the common land meant that, as well as being prey to robber bands, they were vulnerable to predation. Worst of all was the wolf which remained a constant – and dangerous – threat to domestic live-stock until they died out in Scotland during the eighteenth century. In fact, so extensive was the damage they caused to livestock that in 1457 Parliament passed an Act requiring landowners to have their tenants take part in four wolf hunts during the spring and early summer each year in order to 'chase and seek quelpes of the woolf, and gar slaie them'.[39] However the landowners appear to have been somewhat lax in complying, because another Act of 1458 assigned responsibility for organising the hunts to the local sheriff or bailie. It went on to stipulate that three hunts were to take place between 25 April and 1 August each year, and that anyone responsible for killing a wolf would be rewarded with one shilling, or six pence for a fox – that perennial threat to the lamb population.[40]

The period from the 1400s onwards witnessed a burst of settlement formation as more land was taken into cultivation.[41] Since most were spawned from existing ferme-touns, it became the practice to distinguish them from the parent holding by adding prefixes such as 'upper' and 'lower', 'east' and 'west', 'north' and 'south', and 'meikle' and 'little' or 'laigh', or simply adding the name of the owner or principal tenant. There are a number of examples in Dumfriesshire – Dormont and Upper Dormont near Dalton; North Carthat and South Carthat, and East Raffles and West Raffles, part of the former Refholes estate near Carrutherstown. Similarly East Bretton and West Bretton, close to the former Annan power station, East Scales and West Scales near Gretna, and Broomrigg and Over Broomrigg adjacent to the Nith. Significantly most of these are situated in the more fertile parts of Dumfriesshire where there was scope for expansion.

The system of land tenure varied considerably. Whereas landowners would let most of their lands to farm tenants, they generally kept some in hand to enable them to maintain an establishment appropriate to their status. Since it was no longer the practice for cottars and others to pay their rent in the form of labour service, land-owners had to rely on paid labour to do the farm work, most of them being cottars or landless men available for hire. Whereas lands were traditionally let to the joint tenants of ferme-touns, it was becoming increasingly the practice to lease them to single tenants who were generally known as husbandmen. According to the register of the barony of Morton, the Douglases of Dalkeith had been doing this since as early as the 1370s. That the family appears to have been ahead of their time in the field of land management is evident from the estate rental for 1376–8 which shows that they were already leasing out larger holdings, with husbandmen being granted tenancies of up to 50 acres, and cottars anything from 5 to 10 acres.[42]

During the fifteenth century it became the practice to grant longer leases. Whereas the Morton estate rental shows one- to five-year leases as the norm, with the emphasis on the former, John Mair writing in the 1520s observed that it was the custom to grant leases for four or five years.[43] Military service was still a requirement, and those tenants whose annual income exceeded £10 were statutorily obliged to keep themselves armed and horsed in readiness to turn out for their lord when required. As John Mair went on to observe, 'They keep a horse and weapons of war, and are ready to take part in [their lord's] quarrel, be it just or unjust, with any [other] powerful lord, [and] if need be to fight to the death.'[44]

Yet the fact that they could be evicted at the whim of their landlord meant that tenants had no security of tenure. And because there was no guarantee of renewal at the end of their leases – or the 'ish' to use the technical term – it frequently resulted in severe hardship. Indeed an Act of 1469 refers to the uproar that invariably accompanied the evictions at the Whitsunday and Martinmas term days.[45] Aware of this, and as an encouragement to farmers to take on leases, Parliament passed a number of measures for the purpose of improving their conditions of tenure. For example an Act of 1400 protected them from liability for their landlord's debts for which they had hitherto been responsible as a last resort. In 1429 James I issued a decree ordering his barons to refrain from summarily evicting their tenant husbandmen,[46] while an Act of 1449 gave them the right to continue in occupation of their holdings notwithstanding a change of ownership of the land.[47] But these measures were dictated by self-interest rather than concern for the tenants. This was because two of the three estates of Parliament, namely the clergy and secular magnates, were themselves landowners. Therefore it was in their interests to persuade farmers to take on tenancies, in order to maintain their rental income. And doubtless it was hoped that, because it was in their interests to do so, longer leases would encourage the tenants to carry out improvements to their holdings.

The ultimate step was to grant lands in feu-ferme, a form of tenure which became increasingly common from the fifteenth century onwards. This was a lease (effectively a grant) of land in perpetuity, subject to the payment of a capital sum known as a *grassum* and a fixed annual rent or feuduty. The Church had already set a precedent by disposing of land on much the same terms since as early as the 1100s. But at that time it was the exception, and would continue so for the next three centuries until James II started feuing off crown lands as a means of raising money.[48] Other landowners followed suit, encouraged by the Act of 1449 which gave tenants the right to have their leases converted into a feu, while a later one of 1458 ordained that the king would ratify and approve all such grants.

Thereafter the practice became widespread, and many an old-established landed family today acquired their lands by feu charter. This applied in particular to the cadet branches of the principal families in the region, i.e. those descended from a younger son. Whereas in the past it had been the practice to provide for younger sons by granting them a lease (or tack) of part of the family lands, it was becoming increasingly common to grant them a feu. This accounted for the establishment of a number of cadet branches of the Maxwell, Johnstone, Irving, Carruthers, Kirkpatrick and other families, as landowners in the region.

Both parties – the landlord and the tenant – stood to gain from converting a lease into a feu. For the landlord the *grassum*, effectively the purchase price, constituted a welcome addition to his normally slender resources, while there was the added bonus of an annual feuduty payable in perpetuity. At the same time a tenant could now carry out improvements to his holding in the knowledge that he or his successors would reap the benefit. However, the rampant inflation, which was a feature of the following centuries, penalised the landowner in that it reduced the value of his feuduty in real terms, while benefiting the tenant (now the feuar) who also profited from the inflation-driven escalation in land values.

For the landowners the depreciation of their feuduties in real terms rendered it difficult, if not impossible, for many of them to run their estates on the same lines as before. Still less maintain the standard of living, and generous hospitality, to which they had been accustomed. But rather than retrench, they attempted to meet the shortfall by rent increases, and thanks to the higher prices obtainable for their produce most tenants could probably afford it – up to a point. But many landowners tried to squeeze them too hard, and this contributed to a souring of landlord–tenant relations which would persist throughout the following centuries.[49] Others were compelled to dispose of land, and in the event of a distress sale the price would be discounted accordingly. Consequently there were enterprising people who were ready to pick up land at bargain prices and sell it at a profit. In fact there are a number of landowning families today whose fortunes were founded on successful land speculation in the late Middle Ages.

THE BURGHS

The principal Scottish burghs such as Dumfries had been growing in importance ever since the reign of David II when burgesses were called to Parliament and became the third of the three estates. Hand in hand with this went an increasing affluence, mainly on the back of Scotland's expanding trade with the Continent which was a feature of the fifteenth century. Since it accrued almost entirely to the merchant class, to the exclusion of the craftsmen and others, this delivered them effective control of the burghs. The fact that Dumfries was accessible to the sea, the Nith being navigable as far as Glencaple, or Kingholm Quay for smaller craft, meant it was well placed to benefit from the lucrative maritime trade, and similarly Annan given its proximity to the Solway Firth.

The inland townships in Dumfriesshire, on the other hand, were burghs of barony which were established to serve as local markets, mainly within the founder's estates. There were only four at this time, although others were added later. Apart from the de Brus creation of Lochmaben, the others were Staplegorton, founded by Sir James

Douglas in 1320, and Torthorwald and Sanquhar, one established by Sir John Carlyle in 1473 and known as 'Cairleill', the other founded by Sir Robert Crichton (future lord Crichton) in 1484.* Later, two more were added – namely 'Ruvale' (Ruthwell) and 'Herys' (Terregles), respectively the creations of Sir John Murray of Cockpool and Andrew second lord Herries in 1508 and 1510.

The practice continued into the following century. In 1613 James VI granted a charter to Sir John Charteris of Amisfield erecting the township of Amisfield into a burgh of barony, with the right to hold a Tuesday market and a fair at Michaelmas. In 1621 Robert earl of Nithsdale was granted a royal charter creating Langholm a burgh of barony. Charles I was responsible for raising some to the status of burghs of regality, the main difference being that they enjoyed more extensive jurisdictional rights than burghs of barony. For example, in 1637 he granted a charter to William earl of Queensberry creating Dalgarnock a burgh of regality, and another to John Johnstone of Corehead in 1648 raising Moffat to a similar status.[50]

In the principal burghs the merchants had long enjoyed the exclusive right to deal in merchandise, while the craftsmen (invariably regarded as second-class citizens) engaged in trades which were mainly geared to local demand. Nevertheless the number of craftsmen, and the range of services available, was increasing rapidly – to the extent that by the end of the fifteenth century they had begun to organise themselves into separate guilds, such as smiths, tailors, tanners, cordwainers, shoemakers, hatters, glovers, and others. In Dumfries there were at least eleven different craft guilds, although they were eventually amalgamated into a single corporation.[51]

That came later. Meanwhile each guild was responsible among other things for regulating their members' conditions of work, and for establishing the rules of admission for new entrants. They were required to serve a lengthy apprenticeship in order to acquire the skills necessary to produce goods to their guild's exacting standard.[52] The person responsible for the conduct of the guild members, and for supervising their activities, was the deacon or dean, an elected official whose existence was first recognised in an Act of 1424. This authorised them to approve the quality of the goods produced by their guilds so that, as it was put, 'the Kyngis lieges be nocht defrauded [as] thai have been in tyme bygone through untreu [unqualified] men of craftis'.[53]

The merchants' superior status was confirmed by a number of Acts of Parliament dating from the second half of the fifteenth century onwards. These gave them a virtual monopoly of power and authority within their burghs, which meant that the provost, bailies, magistrates and members of the burgh council were invariably drawn from their ranks. This had not always been the case, for in the past all freemen were entitled to have a say in the election of these officials. But 'the great trouble and contention [of] the multitude, and [the] clamour of common, simple persons', as it was described, which invariably occurred at these elections rendered this

---

*   It was created a royal burgh by James VI in 1598.

impracticable. Therefore in 1469 Parliament passed an Act which limited the suffrage by ruling that henceforth burgh councils would be elected by the outgoing council, and that both councils sitting together should choose the provost and bailies. As a concession, the craft guilds were allowed to appoint a delegate to vote at the election of these officials. But because they were invariably outnumbered, and hence outvoted, it amounted to little more than a token gesture.[54]

The merchants' position within the burghs was further strengthened by an Act of 1504 which stipulated that the provost, bailies and others 'having jurisdiction within the burgh' were to be re-elected each year, and that only merchants engaged in overseas trade were eligible for office.[55] The drawback to giving legislative preference to the merchant class was that it allowed them to become self-perpetuating oligarchies with consequent scope for graft and corruption, as became apparent. Nevertheless their powers were circumscribed by the influence of the local magnate. This was a consequence of the prevailing lawlessness which encouraged burghs to put themselves under the protection of a powerful local magnate. In the case of Dumfries the people naturally looked to the lords Maxwell as their protector, and in the sixteenth century the Maxwells built a town house for themselves – 'Maxwell's Castle'* – which enabled them to supervise, and if necessary control, the affairs of the burgh and ensure the appointment of amenable officials.

Occasionally a craftsman might aspire to become a merchant, probably as a reward for some particular service to the burgh. This was exceptional, and even then it was a condition of his acceptance as a merchant burgess that he renounced the trade with which he had 'soiled his hands'[56] and abandoned the practices associated with it. For example, when in the following century an Edinburgh skinner was admitted to its merchant guild he was obliged to give an undertaking that neither his wife nor his servants would cook anything outside his house, nor carry 'meat dishes or courses through the town', nor appear in the street wearing aprons.[57] Nevertheless the statutory relegation of craftsmen to second-class citizens was widely resented and would eventually lead to civil disturbances.

Through course of time the wealthier merchants aspired to the status of landownership. An early example was John Maxwell, who in 1536 purchased the lands of Auldgirth, Blackcraig and Fyrach from John Fergusson of Auldgirth, a member of the Craigdarroch family.[58] Another was the McBrairs, an old established family of Dumfries merchant burgesses who regularly feature in the burgh records as far back as the fifteenth century. In terms of a retour of 1573 Archibald McBrair, then provost of Dumfries, was served heir to his great-grandfather William McBrair in the lands of Almagill near Dalton.[59] This suggests that the latter must have acquired sufficient wealth to purchase the estate by the beginning of that century or earlier. Other burgesses married into local landed families which would have given them added status within the community. Some might aspire to an heiress and thus acquire the

---

*   This occupied a site which broadly corresponded with the present Greyfriars Church.

family lands in her right, although there is no evidence of this in Dumfriesshire. Conversely, it became increasingly common for the younger sons of landed families to settle in the towns, become burgesses, and marry the well-dowered daughters of wealthy merchants. However, the evidence suggests that, whereas in the sixteenth century such unions were exceptional, they subsequently became commonplace.

The provost, bailies and magistrates were in overall charge of the administration of the burgh. This meant they had virtually unlimited powers to regulate the lives of the indwellers, control the affairs of the community, and pass statutes for the purpose. They included the power to punish wrongdoers – by flogging, branding, ducking, consignment to the stocks, and the like, necessary in view of the frequency of neighbourly brawls and the propensity to violence among the citizens. In extreme cases the magistrates were entitled to exercise the death penalty, usually by hanging.

As time went on, Parliament intruded to an increasing extent into the conduct of burghal affairs. This was reflected in the passing of a number of Acts which defined the functions of the burgh councils and determined their powers. They included the power to regulate prices and supervise the quality of goods offered for sale in the market. This is evident from the Burgh Court books of Dumfries for the sixteenth century which contain a number of entries stipulating the maximum price which purveyors were allowed to charge for beer and wines. Similarly there was a firm rule (doubtless often abused) that the burgh council had a right of pre-emption over all goods brought to the market.[60] That it applied in the case of imported goods is evident from the case of a Dumfries merchant who had shipped a cargo of wine from France. Because it came to light that he had sold it privately before offering it to the burgh authorities the entire cargo was confiscated,[61] although it is unlikely to have gone to waste!

By the same token there was an absolute prohibition against buyers waylaying vendors on their way to market and forcing them to sell their goods to them at a knockdown price so that they could sell them on at a profit. This was regarded as a serious crime and if detected could entail harsh punishment. Similarly merchants were forbidden to withhold their goods, mainly corn and other foodstuffs, in time of scarcity in order to sell them into a dearer market. Known as forestalling or regrating, this too was regarded as a serious crime, and during the fifteenth and sixteenth centuries no fewer than five Acts of Parliament were passed condemning the practice.

The burgh council was also responsible for administering the common good. In the case of Dumfries this included supervising its fishing rights in the Nith, whereas those of Annan and Lochmaben were responsible for their respective stretches of the Annan. The common good included the bridges and the right to levy tolls on users, which was conditional on the burgh keeping them up to standard. The main – indeed the only – bridge at Dumfries was the stone-built one attributed to Duchess Margaret, widow of the fourth earl of Douglas. This would have replaced the wooden bridge which is said to have been erected by Dervorguilla Balliol in the late thirteenth century.*

---

* The stone bridge, a narrow footbridge, wrongly referred to as Dervorguilla's bridge, still exists today.

The administration of the common good extended to supervising the mills and other pertinents, as well as the burgh land. Most if not all the burgh land was leased to individual burgesses for pasturing their livestock, the rents being applied to the common good. Later, financial stringency forced Dumfries – and doubtless other burghs – to start feuing out the burgh lands. In practice the feuars were most likely members of the council, or their friends, who probably secured their feus on concessionary terms.

All burgesses were required to carry out watch and ward duties to guard against a possible attack, and to help maintain law and order. This meant they had to be ready to intervene in the (not uncommon) event of an affray breaking out in the streets. Perhaps more importantly, they had to keep a constant watch for outbreaks of fire which would have been a constant hazard since the houses were mainly timber-built and roofed with readily combustible thatch, heather or rushes.

Most important of all, the civic authorities were responsible for the defence of the burgh. Given the proximity of Dumfries, Annan and Lochmaben to the border, this was vital – particularly during the sixteenth century when Dumfriesshire was the target of repeated English invasions. The English were not the only threat, because Dumfries was equally likely to be attacked by people like the Murrays and the Johnstones with whom the Maxwells were at feud. Therefore all burgesses were required to have a helmet, a suit of armour, sword, pike and other weaponry available in readiness to answer a call to arms. This inevitably led to cases of theft where someone finding himself short of an essential piece of equipment would try to make good the defect at his neighbour's expense.

Public health was another of the council's responsibilities, but given the foul conditions that prevailed in contemporary burghs they were fighting a losing battle. For one thing accommodation was extremely cramped. Since no house exceeded two storeys at most, and each was occupied by several families, this would have contributed immeasurably to the prevailing squalor. Indeed it is hard to imagine the extent of the all-pervading filth. Since it was the practice to tip the contents of chamber pots, human excrement and other household waste into the streets, the resulting mounds of garbage forced passers-by to keep to the centre. Because everyone did so, and the gap between the piles of refuse was generally quite narrow, there would have been frequent squabbles, sometimes erupting into violence, when people coming from opposite directions refused to give way.

In the main street, which served as the market place, conditions were incomparably worse, simply because there was more space for dumping refuse. To add to the stench, the forestairs of the furriers and skinners would be hung with what the records aptly term their 'stynkand goods'. Similarly the fleshers and fish dealers, ignoring the statutes forbidding the practice, threw their trimmings into the street to be scavenged by prowling dogs and swine. To add to the general filth, cattle which grazed the common land by day were driven inside the town wall at night, when they were left to roam at will until released the following morning.[62]

Nevertheless the market place was the hub of community life, for it was here – traditionally at the market cross – that public proclamations were made. It was here, too, that animals were slaughtered and butchered, their entrails frequently left where they dropped. Round the perimeter were the craftsmen's booths. Whereas some were permanent erections, most were temporary ones set up by itinerant vendors at the time of the annual fair. In Dumfries the market place occupied the ground between the present-day High Street and Queensberry Street, and extended roughly from the site of Greyfriars Church to beyond the Mid Steeple. Nearby was the tollbooth. Built in about 1481, this was where the burgh council conducted its business and where the public weighbeam – or tron – was accommodated, while the dungeon underneath served as the prison.

Adjacent to the market cross were the stocks, and it was here that gallows were erected for hanging convicted felons. Those guilty of lesser offences might find themselves forced to sit there exposed to public view wearing a paper hat specifying the nature of their misdemeanour. These could include the kind of ruses frequently indulged in by traders, such as selling fish in bundles where good, big, fresh fish were displayed on the outside to conceal inferior ones inside. Similarly there was a prohibition against selling victuals in sacks which looked sound enough on the surface but were rotten underneath (gilding the top of sand barrels has a long and dishonourable history). The market cross was where (in extreme cases) public executions were carried out and the dismembered limbs of traitors and other criminals were displayed.

The kirk yard (yard meaning a large open space) attaching to St Michael's Church, which was the main church in Dumfries, would have been the venue for dances, as well as serving as a sports ground. Although a popular game, football was generally frowned on by the authorities because it was seen as a distraction from military training. As well as being a haunt of beggars (begging was rife and frequently accompanied by violence), the kirk yard generally served as a public convenience and a dumping ground for refuse, as well as a trysting place for lovers.

The most important event in the life of the burgh was the annual fair, the right to hold it being generally authorised by royal grant. These were the occasions of the greatest commercial activity, mainly because of the influx of visitors and itinerant pedlars who descended on the town to take part in (and profit from) the festivities. It was also one of the few times in the year when the townspeople would make merry with a vengeance. Because civic pride demanded that the burgh should present itself to best advantage, efforts were made to have the streets cleared of the rotting piles of garbage. Labourers, frequently supplemented by others from outside the burgh, were hired to do the work, for which they were paid according to the number of roods cleared.*

Inevitably the all-pervading, rat-infested filth was a breeding ground for disease, and there was the omnipresent threat of the dreaded plague. Although in the

---

* A rood was 5½ yards or roughly 5 metres

following century the Dumfries burgh council, in common with other burghs, introduced measures to ensure that refuse was regularly cleared away from the streets and vennels, they appear to have had limited effect. Or so it would seem from the observation of a contemporary writer that the inhabitants were 'subiect tyl al sortis of sickness' because of 'the corrupit infection and evyl ayr'. Commenting on their limited life expectancy, he went on to say that most of them 'endis their dais in there grene youthe'.[63] Sadly all too true.

A RENAISSANCE PRINCE

James IV's accession heralded a new regime which was dominated by the Hepburns and the Homes.[*] Patrick Hepburn lord Hailes, the head of the family, had himself appointed to the prestigious offices of master of the royal household, sheriff of Edinburgh and keeper of the castle, as well as being created earl of Bothwell. His uncle John, prior of St Andrews, became keeper of the privy seal, while other relatives appointed to high office included William and Alexander Hepburn, who became clerk register and sheriff of Fife respectively. Similarly Alexander master of Home, later second lord Home, was appointed chamberlain and keeper of Stirling castle.

Archibald 'Bell-the-Cat' earl of Angus was rewarded with a number of prestigious offices, including the wardenship of all three marches. Therefore he was responsible, along with John fourth lord Maxwell as steward of Annandale, for seeking out 'trespassours' – namely thieves, reivers and those guilty of 'utheris innormities' – in Dumfriesshire, with power to punish them on the spot. The more serious offenders were sent for trial before the king and probable execution.[64] Earl Archibald's tenure of office was brief. Since the Hepburns regarded him as a rival power in the Borders, they caused the packed Parliament of October 1488 to strip him of his appointments, including the wardenship of the marches. Whereas Bothwell appropriated the middle and west marches, along with the keepership of Lochmaben, the wardenship of the east marches went to Alexander Home.

Taking his removal from office in bad part, Angus entered into secret – and treasonable – negotiations with the English. In 1491 they concluded an agreement whereby the English undertook that, in the event of war, they would spare Angus's lands, including Liddesdale. In return, he promised to retain control of Hermitage castle, or deliver it up to them on request. Yet Angus seems to have been playing a double game, for at the same time he remained on friendly terms with the king, frequently playing cards and dice with him.[†] And, perhaps tiring of her, he allowed

---

[*]   Home or Hume, the spelling varied because it was only later that the name became fixed as Home.

[†]   Both he and the king engaged, with two companions, in a marathon card-playing session which lasted for three days from 26 to 28 November 1490 (Macdougall, *James IV*, 87).

the king to take over his mistress Janet Kennedy.* But when Angus's dealings with the English came to light, he was stripped of the lordship of Liddesdale, which was given to the earl of Bothwell,† while he took refuge in his castle of Tantallon. The king laid siege to it, but in October he and the earl were reconciled and the siege was lifted. In 1493 Angus was appointed chancellor, and as such was responsible for negotiating a truce with the English.[65] Notwithstanding that he was later replaced by the earl of Huntly, he remained a prominent political force throughout James's reign.

The Parliament of October 1488 was responsible for setting up judicial tribunals to put James III's former supporters on trial for treason. They included a number of Dumfriesshire landowners, including lord Carlyle and his sons-in-law Adam Murray of Drumcrieff and Herbert Herries of Terregles. Carlyle seems to have got off comparatively lightly. Although decree of forfeiture was passed against him, this was limited to his recently acquired barony of Drumcoll because he appears to have retained the rest of his Dumfriesshire lands.‡ Others included Cuthbert Murray of Cockpool, and also Sir Robert Charteris of Amisfield, who had been much in favour with James III, having been mainly responsible for defeating the ninth earl of Douglas at Lochmaben in 1484.[66]

Charteris was a man of considerable local prominence having represented the Dumfriesshire barons at the Parliament of 1481 and again in 1487. But he seems to have been prone to falling out with his neighbours (not uncommon among contemporary Dumfriesshire landowners), one of them being Robert lord Crichton. There was already bad blood between them, but it came to a head over Crichton's theft of twenty-five oxen and cows belonging to Charteris which were valued at £50. Charged with this, Crichton claimed that it was to settle a debt owing him by Charteris, which the latter indignantly denied. The matter was remitted for adjudication by the local sheriff. Since he happened to be Crichton himself, the outcome was predictable. Furious at such a blatant miscarriage of justice, Charteris appealed to the lords of Council. Accepting his assertion that he owed Crichton nothing, they overturned the judgement and ordered Crichton to indemnify Charteris for the value of the livestock.[67] Crichton was forced to comply, but it merely added fuel to their mutual animosity which persisted for long afterwards.

Forfeitures were personal to the individuals concerned. Whereas they themselves were dispossessed, their heirs were entitled 'to buy brieves of service in their lands from the new king'.[68] In other words, heirs were given the option to buy back their

---

* The heroine of Pamela Hill's novel *Flaming Janet*, and unchivalrously dubbed 'Janet bair ars', she was a daughter of John second lord Kennedy. She had three children by James, including James Stewart earl of Moray (not to be confused with the Regent Moray who was an illegitimate son of James V).

† On the other hand he retained his lands in Eskdale and Ewesdale.

‡ *Scots Peerage* ii, 384. According to a royal charter of 1487 they consisted of 'the lands of Kinmount with mill, Locharwood with mill, Dornok with mill and advowson [right of patronage] of the church, Middlebie with the same, Kirkconnell with the same, Luce with the same, Annan with fishing, Kirkpatrick with mill, as well as Brumell, Marjorybank, Oulcotis, Ecclefechan, Ryhill [Ruthwell], Cummertrees, Torduff, Bengall, Dalibank, Brydekirk and Lochmaben'.

fathers' forfeited lands. A case in point was the earl of Glencairn, who was killed fighting for James III at Sauchieburn. Although his lands, including the barony of Glencairn, were forfeited, they were restored to his son for a consideration. Some of James III's supporters who came to terms with the new regime were spared forfeiture, one example being John fourth lord Maxwell. Having come into James IV's peace, he was appointed steward of Annandale and later given the wardenship of the west marches, an office that would become a virtual perquisite of his family.[69] Many of the forfeited estates were used to reward James's supporters – notably Patrick Hepburn, the newly created earl of Bothwell, who was given an access of lands in southern Scotland, including William lord Crichton's forfeited lands in Dryfesdale, as well as the barony of Kirkmichael.*

The Parliament of January 1489 enacted a number of measures for the purpose of imposing law and order, and enforcing justice, which had effectively broken down under the incompetent rule of James III. They stipulated that justices ayre were to be regularly held throughout the realm and supervised wherever possible by the king. A man of dynamic energy in contrast to his indolent father, James readily agreed – the more so because it gave him an opportunity to combine work with pleasure. His first justice ayre in February 1489 took him to the south-west where the rule of law had pretty well ceased to exist ever since the fall of the Douglases. On the 25th he was at Dumfries, from where he went on to preside over courts at Kirkcudbright and Wigtown, and finally Ayr. The records suggest that the scales of justice were heavily loaded against his father's supporters. Those brought to trial at Dumfries included John Carruthers, who was charged with being party to the burning of Thomas MacLellan of Bombie's manor of Lochfergus, near Kirkcudbright. In the event the case was dismissed, probably because MacLellan had been a supporter of James III. Contrast this with the sentence passed on Adam Murray of Drumcrieff, who was tried at the same assize. He was charged with attacking and burning Sir William Stirling's lands of Keir. But because Murray had been an adherent of James III, whereas Stirling was a supporter of James IV, he was fined the huge sum of £1,000.

The same Parliament provided for the erection of the see of Glasgow into an archbishopric. This was to put it on a par with St Andrews, an implied snub to Archbishop Scheves who had been a placeman and close associate of James III. The first incumbent was James IV's supporter Robert Blacader, who had held the bishopric of Glasgow since his translation from Aberdeen in 1483. But because Glasgow's elevation required papal consent the inevitable delay meant that it did not actually become an archbishopric until January 1492. At the same time Whithorn was declared a suffragan see, thus severing its already tenuous links with York.

---

* *RMS* II, 1784, 2452. Specifically they comprised the following: le Faranis, Blakhil, Mylnehil, Coilanehous, Aikhorneholm, Greneside, Bektoun, Lammynby, Bettishill, the mill of Dryfesdale, le Torwood, Belhill, le Quawis, the tenement of Carruthers, le Respond and Powlin, le Hessilschaw, Gilgone, le Tounlandis, Over Kirkmichael, Nether Kirkmichael, Raehills, Molyn, Monygap and Cronyantoun.

The following year marked the expiry of the truce with England. Although renewed from time to time, it failed to put an end to cross-border raiding which would continue to plague the region for a further century. Meanwhile relations between James IV and Henry VII remained distant, not helped by James's support for Perkin Warbeck's rebellion. A Flemish imposter, he affected to be Richard duke of York (the younger of the two princes murdered in the Tower) and therefore the rightful king. Nevertheless, to avoid the risk of James entering into a hostile alliance with the French king Louis XII, Henry proposed a marriage between him and his elder daughter Margaret. Since it would greatly enhance his standing among his fellow European rulers, James readily agreed, and the marriage took place in August 1503.

This put the seal on a treaty of perpetual peace between the two realms – a peace that was to prove anything but perpetual. Its provisions included certain refinements to the laws of the marches. Although originally framed by English and Scottish commissioners in 1249, they had been altered by mutual agreement from time to time. Therefore these provisions were merely the latest of a series of amendments. One of them provided that, if an Englishman committed a crime in Scotland such as a robbery, or a Scotsman did the same in England, the victim could lodge a complaint with his warden. He would then take the matter up with his opposite number who was bound to produce the responsible party at the next truce day to answer for his alleged crime. That at least was the theory, but adherence to the letter of the law depended on the state of relations between the two countries, and more particularly between the wardens themselves.

The laws provided that truce days should be held once a month, those on the west march generally taking place on an open field at places near the Solway, such as Lochmabenstone or Gretnakirk, or at Rockcliffe on the English side of the border. But a warden could generally find an excuse for postponing a truce day if he found it inconvenient, or if he was not prepared to meet his opposite number. When they did confront each other, both at the head of an armed following, it must have been a tense moment for it sometimes happened that a truce day ended in violence and bloodshed. On the other hand, if all went well the wardens would agree an armistice. This would generally last until sunrise the following day, although it might be extended depending on the amount of business to be transacted. But at least it was long enough to allow everyone to return home in safety.

In August 1503 James was back in Dumfries conducting another justice ayre. As usual he was accompanied by harpists, pipers and a band of musicians – and more mundanely an executioner. Since the administration of justice would have kept him less than fully occupied, this jolly, gregarious king and his court had ample time to enjoy themselves. This is evident from the royal accounts, which show payments to musicians, as well as for feasting and general revelry, while an entry of 13 August records a payment of thirteen shillings to 'pyparis from Dumfries' to supplement the minstrels in his entourage. James remained at Dumfries for only a few days before going on to Lochmaben, accompanied by an armed escort as well as a retinue of bards, singers and bagpipers. There was also a priest, referred to as 'the cruikit vicar of Dumfries', who was paid fourteen shillings for singing to him at Lochmaben.[70]

The treaty of perpetual peace seems to have allowed for a good deal of cross-border fraternising. For example James is recorded as playing cards with Thomas lord Dacre, the warden of the English west marches (and a future commander at Flodden), at Lochmaben when he lost the sum of 46s 8d.[71] Similarly, Sir John Musgrave sent 'twa wiffis' with a present of some ale for which they were duly rewarded, while the prior of Carlisle sent him a butt of Malvoisie.[72] Since James spent much of his time indulging his passion for hunting (he was reputedly a crack shot with a bow and arrow), Musgrave also sent him his huntsmen to assist in the chase. Leaving Lochmaben, James went on to Eskdale determined to stamp out the 'greit misruelle' which was reported to exist there. The main perpetrators were hunted down and brought to Canonbie,* where they were hanged.[73] Following this, James returned to Dumfries, where we are told he stayed for twenty-three days overseeing the work of his justiciar, Andrew lord Gray, and frequently dispensing justice himself.

Hanging the ringleaders at Canonbie was intended as a deterrent to others who might be tempted to follow their example. Another victim was Gilbert Thomesone who was hanged for the theft of forty-five sheep belonging to a Dumfries merchant; similarly Adam Baty who was convicted of associating with the king's rebels in Eskdale. In some cases remissions were granted, usually for a substantial consideration. For example Robert Grierson who was convicted of being party to the slaughter of John McBrair, a local chaplain, had his sentence remitted. Another was James Monse (Mounsey). He had been ordered to submit himself to 'the king's will' for destroying the woods at 'Lochmabane, Bakrig, Heichrig, Rammerskalls and Rowekelpark [Rockhall park]'. Under normal circumstances this would have been a hanging offence, but Monse was spared the gallows, probably because Gavin Murray, brother of Cuthbert Murray of Cockpool, agreed to stand surety for his future good behaviour.

Having men of substance act as guarantors generally ensured leniency. For example when William Jardine,† Robert Dunwoody, son of the laird of Dunwoody, and a party of Johnstones were convicted of the theft of four horses valued at £40, two candlesticks, one goblet, and other goods worth £20 from Bartholomew Glendinning, Sir Thomas Kirkpatrick agreed to stand surety for Robert Dunwoody. Similarly Adam Johnstone stood surety for his relatives, although there is no record of anyone guaranteeing William Jardine's future conduct. Since remissions frequently came at a high price, they were a lucrative source of revenue to the crown. But it was at the cost of one law for the rich and another for the poor.

William Jardine's criminal association with Robert Dunwoody was significant in view of the feud that had recently broken out between the two families. This was the

---

*   James would have been expected to lodge at the priory; but because the quarters assigned to him were considered insufficiently sumptuous he brought with him, at considerable inconvenience and expense, his own royal pavilions instead.
†   A grandson of Sir John Jardine of Applegarth.

result of a raid by a band of armed men on Dunwoody tower in the course of which Thomas Dunwoody, the head of the family, was killed. Because John Jardine, the tenant of Sibbaldbieside, was thought to be responsible he was arrested and charged along with Robert Brig, a servitor of Alexander Jardine (possibly William's brother). But when brought to trial they produced (no doubt expensive) remissions from the king and were acquitted.[74] So says McDowall, although according to another source the perpetrator was Thomas Bell of 'Curre' who is recorded as having 'escaped trial'; in other words he fled the country.[75] Reid confirms Bell's flight but claims that it followed the slaughter of Simon Carruthers of Mouswald when Bell's partner in crime was Stephen Johnstone.[76] While the accounts may differ, both agree that Bell fled abroad, so all the justiciar could do was publicly denounce him as a rebel. Nevertheless it seems that suspicion of a Jardine involvement lingered, and this was enough to cause a feud between the two families.

Another feud, this time between the Maxwells and the Crichtons, came to a head in 1508 when John lord Maxwell was about to attack Robert lord Crichton, the sheriff of Dumfries while in the act of holding court.* But forewarned, Crichton abandoned it and took refuge, along with his supporters, in a nearby redoubt. When Maxwell, accompanied by William Douglas of Drumlanrig, John Ferguson of Craigdarroch, and others stormed it, a 'grate feight' took place, when Crichton and his men were driven out of the town.[77] Breaking up what was effectively the king's court and inter-fering with the judicial process was an extremely serious offence which could well have cost Maxwell his head. As it was, he was sentenced to a term of imprisonment and fined the huge sum of £3,745, later reduced to £1,000.[78] Since there is no record of proceedings being taken against Douglas or Ferguson, it seems that the fine was intended to cover their malfeasances as well. At the same time the Maxwells were engaged in another feud with the Murrays, which reportedly stemmed from Cuthbert Murray of Cockpool's murder of John master of Maxwell.† But the bitterest and bloodiest of all was the century-long feud which broke out between the Maxwells and the Johnstones in the following reign.

In the autumn of 1504 James was back in the south-west – in considerable force because his purpose was to suppress another outbreak of unrest in lower Eskdale and the Debateable Land,‡ this time in co-operation with lord Dacre. His immediate destination was Dumfries where he held another justice ayre and consigned a batch of convicted felons to the gallows. Moving on from there, he joined forces with lord Dacre at Canonbie before embarking on the campaign. The revolt appears to have

---

* This was despite Maxwell's wife Janet being a near relative of Crichton.

† *Scots Peerage* i, 220. Yet there is no reference to the feud, nor is John master of Maxwell identifiable from the article on the Maxwell earls of Nithsdale in vol vi of the work.

‡ Lying between the rivers Esk and Sark, and extending northwards from the Solway to almost as far as Canonbie, there was no certainty as to which realm it belonged. Since neither would recognise the ownership of the other, it was regarded as a no-man's land. Consequently it became a haven for thieves and other fugitives from justice, thus assuming a nuisance value out of all proportion to its size. This remained the situation until 1552 when it was divided between the two realms by mutual agreement.

been suppressed without difficulty, and the ringleaders were quickly brought to justice. The king and Dacre then returned to Canonbie where they spent the next few days hawking and playing cards while the captives were summarily hanged.

James's perambulations throughout the realm were not devoted exclusively to work and pleasure. A man of noted piety, he regularly undertook pilgrimages to the better known shrines, his favourite being St Ninian's at Whithorn, which he visited on a number of occasions. One occurred in 1507 after the queen had given birth to their firstborn son. It had been a difficult birth, and because she was gravely ill and the child was thought unlikely to survive, James probably undertook the pilgrimage in a quest for divine help. Because self-mortification may have been thought to improve his chances of success, he made the journey on foot. This took him by way of Leadhills and across the Lowther hills to Durisdeer where he spent the night as a guest of the vicar, and where he was regaled with 'tales' by 'ane puir man'. Fording the Nith, the royal party went on to Penpont where he rewarded a woman who sang to him with 28s, while a 'fithelar' who entertained him on his fiddle received 29s. But the cobbler who soled his shoes was given a mere 1s 4d – a poor reward by comparison considering how essential it was to completing the pilgrimage.[79] If soliciting divine help was the object of the exercise it was only partially successful, for although the queen recovered the child died the following February.

Throughout this time the treaty of perpetual peace remained in force. However, following Henry VII's death in April 1509 and the accession of the egocentric and power-hungry Henry VIII, it began to unravel. Although renewed in June 1509, it came under increasing strain, mainly as the result of a number of hostile acts committed by the English on the high seas. The breaking point came in 1511 when Henry decided to invade France. This put James in a quandary. Should he observe the treaty of perpetual peace, which meant siding with Henry, or adhere to the traditional Franco-Scottish alliance? Since he already had close links with France and its king Louis XII, he was naturally inclined towards the latter, the more so because he well knew that if Henry defeated the French he would almost certainly turn on him. Therefore, responding to the pleas of their queen, Anne of Brittany, he entered into an offensive and defensive alliance with the French.

In June 1513 King Henry invaded France having charged lord Dacre, James's former card-playing companion, with the defence of the north – necessary because James was already mustering an army in preparation for a diversionary invasion of England. On 22 August the army – the largest ever to have done so – crossed the Tweed. By early September it had established itself in a strong defensive position on Flodden Edge on the foothills of the Cheviots overlooking the valley of the Till. Meanwhile the seventy-year-old earl of Surrey, a veteran of the Wars of the Roses, had mustered an army and was on his way north to join lord Dacre and his levies in resisting the invasion. Fording the Till further upstream, the combined army took up a position on Branston Hill to the north-west of Flodden Edge to cut off James's retreat.

Battle was joined on 9 September with a preliminary exchange of artillery fire. Whereas the Scots, unable to find the correct range, generally missed their mark, the English fire was deadly accurate. Eventually, unable to withstand their cannonade, the Scots were forced to abandon their position and charge pell mell across the intervening ground in wind and rain to close with the English. A hard-fought battle ensued with James well to the fore as commander of the centre division. However, the long pikes of the Scottish footsoldiers proved too unwieldy compared with the shorter English halberds which combined a spear with an axe-head and gave them the upper hand.

The battle became a massacre, and the remnants of the Scottish army were driven from the field leaving it strewn with the corpses of twelve earls, fourteen lords, one or more members of almost every leading family in the land, and thousands of 'mere uncounted folk'. The principal victims among the south-western nobility included John lord Maxwell and his four brothers, Andrew lord Herries and his brother Mungo, Sir William Douglas of Drumlanrig, Edward Irving of Bonshaw,[80] and (probably) Robert lord Crichton. Worst of all, they included the king himself, whose body was found within a spear's length of Surrey's command post, his head transfixed by an arrow and his skull cleaved by a halberd. So perished in his forty-first year one of the most attractive and enlightened of all the Scottish kings.

Since lack of provisions prevented Surrey from following up his success, he withdrew south and disbanded his army. Not so lord Dacre whose battle-hardened levies proceeded to devastate the Border country, including parts of Dumfriesshire. In the course of it families were burnt out of their houses and forced to take refuge in the damp woods and upland shielings until they could safely return to their blackened settlements.[81] Early the following year, Dacre's brother Edward conducted another punitive campaign in the south-west. Within a matter of weeks he was able to report to Henry VIII and his Council that he had devastated Eskdale and lower Annandale, reducing them to a barren wasteland, and had destroyed Annan, as well as some thirty-three townships. Finally he promised to 'continue his service with diligence to the utmost annoyance of the Scots'.[82] However, the conclusion of an Anglo-Scottish truce in March pending negotiations for a permanent peace marked a longed-for – if temporary – cessation of hostilities.

A ROYAL AUTOCRAT

James IV was succeeded by his seventeen-month-old son James V for whom his mother Queen Margaret Tudor acted as guardian and effective regent. But when she married the earl of Angus[*] the following year, the Council edged her aside and invited John duke of Albany, the heir presumptive to the throne who was living in France, to

---

[*] Archibald Douglas sixth earl of Angus. He had recently succeeded his grandfather Archibald 'Bell-the-Cat', his father George, master of Angus, having been killed at Flodden.

come to Scotland and assume the governorship.[*] Following his arrival in May 1515, the queen mother was compelled to give up custody of the young king, and she and Angus were banished from the realm.[†] They took refuge in England but were allowed to return on sufferance the following year.

In 1517 Albany returned to France having appointed a commission of regency to govern the realm in his absence. It consisted of the two archbishops – James Beaton of St Andrews and Gavin Dunbar of Glasgow – as well as the earl of Angus (now back in Scotland), James Hamilton earl of Arran, and others. As next in line to the throne after Albany, Arran effectively controlled the regency, but on his return to Scotland the following year Albany resumed the governorship. Meanwhile the threat of an English invasion polarised Scottish politics. On the one hand was the pro-English party headed by Angus, his Douglas relatives and, notwithstanding her and Angus's recent estrangement, the queen mother. Opposing them was the pro-French party, effectively a resistance movement, led by Albany, Arran and others. They were supported by a large contingent of French troops based in Scotland – a dubious advantage since they had made themselves extremely unpopular.

So long as Albany remained governor the French party was in the ascendant, but when he returned to France for good in 1524 the situation was reversed. Following his departure, Arran (a habitual trimmer like all his family) defected to the English party who in consequence gained custody of the thirteen-year-old king. A packed Parliament declared him of age to rule, and because he was under their control the queen mother, in co-operation with Angus and Arran, exercised full ruling powers in his name. However, Angus and his supporters staged a coup, and edging Arran and the queen mother aside (thus driving them into the arms of the French party) they gained possession of the king and hence political power.

This raised the question of how Angus and his supporters were to share custody of the king among themselves. Eventually a compromise was reached whereby it was agreed that he should be rotated among them, each retaining custody of him for four months at a time, with Angus taking first turn. However, when his turn came to an end he refused point blank to give up the king. Consequently he retained political power and proceeded to fill the principal offices of state, and the leading positions in the royal household, with his relatives and supporters. A case in point was his brother-in-law James Douglas of Drumlanrig, who was appointed a member of the royal household as master of the wine cellar, while Angus appointed himself chancellor. Meanwhile the king was kept in virtual captivity in Angus's stronghold of Falkland.

Attempts were made to rescue him. One took place in 1526 when Angus was taking the king on a progress through the Border country and Sir Walter Scott of

---

[*]   Son of James III's brother Alexander duke of Albany who had retired to France following his unsuccessful bid for the throne.

[†]   The same year she gave birth to a daughter Margaret who subsequently married Matthew Stewart earl of Lennox. Their elder son, Henry Stewart lord Darnley, became the second husband of Mary Queen of Scots and father of James VI.

Buccleuch (known as 'wicked Wat') invited them to stay at his castle at Branxholm. No sooner had Angus accepted than Scott mustered a large force of Scotts, Elliots and Armstrongs with the aim of ambushing the royal party at the bridge over the Tweed at Melrose while on their way to Branxholm. But things did not go according to plan. A skirmish, known as the battle of Darnick, took place when Angus, assisted by a force of Homes and Kerrs, put Scott and his men to flight. This resulted in a feud between the Scotts and the Elliots on one side, and the Kerrs on the other, which would continue for virtually the rest of the century.

Their feud was symptomatic of the lawlessness which prevailed throughout the south and south-west under Angus's rule. Another example was that which broke out between the Maxwells and the Johnstones. So long as James Johnstone of that Ilk was alive, relations between the two families seem to have been reasonably amicable, probably because Johnstone's wife Mary was a sister of Robert fifth lord Maxwell.[83] But following James Johnstone's death in 1524, and his son John's accession to the headship of the clan,* relations between John and his uncle lord Maxwell rapidly worsened.

This drove Maxwell into an alliance with Johnstone's enemies the Armstrongs who were based in Liddesdale. In fact this suited him very well, because the Armstrongs were the worst troublemakers in the region. Therefore, having them on side greatly facilitated the task of imposing law and order in the region, for which he was responsible as warden of the west marches. In 1525 Maxwell concluded an agreement with John Armstrong (known to his contemporaries as 'Black Jock' and the romanticists as 'Johnnie'), the acting head of the clan, at Dumfries. In terms of this, Armstrong granted Maxwell a bond of manrent whereby he undertook to become his man and serve him in war and peace. In return, Maxwell extended his protection to Armstrong and at the same time granted him a lease of lands in the vicinity of Canonbie where he built the stronghold of Holehouse or Hollows.[84]

At Maxwell's instigation Armstrong carried out a series of raids on John Johnstone's lands. In 1527 Johnstone retaliated by murdering 'Meikle Sim' Armstrong. The following year the earl of Angus, to whom Johnstone was bound in manrent, responded with a punitive raid on the Armstrongs' base in Liddesdale. This brought Maxwell into the conflict when he came to the Armstrongs' rescue and forced Angus to withdraw. Thereafter he encouraged them to continue their attacks on Johnstone's lands. With Angus's connivance, Johnstone retaliated by plundering the barony of Duncow which Maxwell had recently acquired from the crown. So began the century-long feud between the Maxwells and the Johnstones which would be the longest and bloodiest in the whole history of the Borders.

In 1528 James managed to escape from Falkland to the sanctuary of Stirling castle, where he was joined by Angus's opponents. Acting in his name, they charged Angus

---

* It should be noted that although the word 'clan' has come to be associated exclusively with the Highlands, it applied as much to other parts of Scotland, including the Borders where the alternatives 'kindred' and 'family' are frequently used.

and his supporters with treason, summoning them to appear before the next Parliament to stand trial. But the problem was that Angus and his men were in control of Edinburgh which meant they were able to prevent the holding of the Parliament. However, as sheriff of Edinburgh, Maxwell succeeded in driving Angus and his men out of the city, for which he was rewarded with the Angus-supporting John Lindsay's forfeited lands in Wauchopedale.[85] At much the same time he added to his already substantial landholdings with the purchase of Locharwood, near Ruthwell, from Michael fourth lord Carlyle.[86]

When the Parliament was held, Angus and his supporters refused to appear. Therefore, in their absence they were convicted of holding the king against his will and conniving at the felonies committed by John Johnstone. They included harrying and burning 'with a company of thieves and evil-doers at divers times the corn, lands, lordships and houses in the sheriffdoms of Annandale and Niddisdale which pertain to [King] James, and other divers buildings, lands and houses within the said sheriff-doms'[87] (obviously a reference to the raid on Duncow). Consequently Parliament decreed the forfeiture of their lands and goods, and condemned them to death.

Passing sentence was easy enough, but enforcing it proved well-nigh impossible because Angus and his supporters withdrew to the safety of Tantallon. Perched on a clifftop above the Firth of Forth, it was virtually impregnable. And because Angus and his men resisted all attempts to take it, James was forced to parley. After lengthy negotiations Angus agreed to withdraw to England. But it proved a far from satisfactory arrangement because he remained a constant source of trouble to James throughout the rest of his reign and beyond.

In late 1528, flushed with his triumph over the Douglases, King James embarked on a campaign to impose his authority on the Border country, which despite the efforts of the wardens was in a state of virtual anarchy. Because the Armstrongs were the principal troublemakers, James was determined to crush them before turning on other notoriously unruly Border families. Since most of them had put themselves under the protection of a leading local magnate, in many cases the head of their kindred, James took pre-emptive action. He summoned the principal magnates, including lord Maxwell, Douglas of Drumlanrig, John Johnstone, Sir Walter Scott of Buccleuch, lord Home and others, to Edinburgh ostensibly to discuss the situation in the Borders. But no sooner had they arrived there than he had them imprisoned in the castle to prevent them from coming to the rescue of those in their allegiance.

Meanwhile James caused summonses to be issued to all able-bodied men between the ages of sixteen and sixty, mainly from the sheriffdoms of Roxburgh, Dumfries and Wigtown, to take part in his campaign. Notwithstanding the many backsliders who produced all sorts of excuses for non-compliance – sickness, licence from the king's lieutenant, rivers in flood which prevented their passage, and others – James succeeded in raising an army of some 8,000 men. Advancing by way of Teviotdale and Eskdale, it reached Staplegorton from where James dispatched a letter to John Armstrong inviting him and his closest adherents to meet him at Carlenrig at the head of Teviotdale.

It is not known whether what followed was a deliberate act of treachery on James's part, and that he intended to have Armstrong put to death, or whether he genuinely meant to parley with him. His letter is believed to have been couched in the friendliest terms, perhaps implying a safe-conduct. This may have been designed to put Armstrong offguard; otherwise he would have taken the precaution of turning up with a large following instead of the twelve unarmed men he did. It has been suggested that they were too gaudily dressed, and this so enraged the king that in the heat of the moment he ordered their execution.[88] What is known is that, as soon as the unsuspecting Armstrong and his companions arrived at Carlenrig they were promptly seized and hanged from the nearest trees, their bodies being dumped in a communal pit.[*] Therefore it is difficult to avoid the conclusion that James, who was noted for his deviousness, intended treachery all along.

The expedition was only partially successful. Although Liddesdale was brought under control, many Armstrongs established themselves in the Debateable Land or settled in Cumberland from where they continued their reiving activities. Nevertheless, in the short term James achieved his objective. Having cowed the other clans and kindreds into submission, he freed the imprisoned magnates against their promise to 'keep good rule on the marches'.[89] Additionally Maxwell was required to give an undertaking that as warden of the west marches he would keep the peace and maintain the royal authority in Ewesdale, Eskdale, Wauchopedale and Annandale, while John Johnstone was taken bound to do the same with regard to 'Moffat, Lochmaben and other areas under his control'.[90]

Meanwhile the three-year truce with England, agreed in January 1526, remained in force. Yet, on the west marches, both the English and Scottish wardens suspected their opposite number of being less than assiduous about rounding up fugitives for handover at truce days. William lord Dacre, the warden of the English west marches, certainly thought so. Therefore, taking the law into his own hands, he carried out a raid on the Debateable Land to apprehend some English fugitives who had taken refuge there. Lord Maxwell responded by conducting a sortie across the border, in the course of which he burnt the Graham stronghold of Netherby.[91] In a tit-for-tat retaliation Dacre plundered the lands in the vicinity of Canonbie and burnt the Armstrongs' newly built keep of Hollows. When Maxwell remonstrated with him at the next truce day, Dacre brushed him off claiming – with some justification – that it was 'but a parcel of the debateable grounde' where it had been agreed that no building would be allowed.[92]

Sometimes the preparations for a truce day could take a curious turn. For example the story has it that, in anticipation of a truce day held in about 1540, Sir Thomas Wharton, the deputy warden of the English west marches, had undertaken to hand over to lord Maxwell a certain Andrew Bell, who was being held prisoner at Carlisle

---

[*] An inscribed stone marks the spot where the hangings took place. This quotes one source as claiming that 'the englische were glad' adding that 'so might the Americans have received news of the death of Al Capone'.

castle, in exchange for a number of Englishmen in Scottish hands. But because Bell managed to escape back to Scotland, Wharton had to swallow his pride and admit that he was unable to keep his side of the bargain. The result was farcical. When the Scottish authorities apprehended Bell they handed him over to the English so that, come the truce day, Wharton could deliver him to lord Maxwell in exchange for the English prisoners![93]

Robert fifth lord Maxwell was the most powerful magnate in the south-west. Born in about 1492, he had succeeded his father John the fourth lord, who was killed at Flodden. He himself had been on a mission to France, but having been stormbound on the way back he missed the battle. Reflecting his local standing, he was appointed keeper of Threave and Lochmaben castles and steward of Kirkcudbright, as well as being appointed to the wardenship of the west marches in place of his father. This plethora of appointments was matched by further additions to his already substantial lands. In about 1530, following his suppression of the Armstrongs, King James granted him a share of John Armstrong's forfeited lands, including Dawblane, Balgray and part of the barony of Stapleton,[94] along with other lands in Eskdale forfeited by Armstrong's supporters.* Honours were bestowed on him as well. Besides the provostship of Edinburgh, he was appointed captain of the king's guard, master of the royal household, chief carver to the king, and an extraordinary lord of King James's recently established Court of Session.[95]

Finally in 1536 Maxwell was appointed a member of the regency council charged with governing the realm in the absence of the king while he went off on a bride-hunting expedition to France – an enterprise which culminated in his marriage to Madeleine, daughter of King Francis I.[†] A prestigious body, the regency council included the two archbishops – Beaton of St Andrews and Dunbar of Glasgow – and the earls of Eglinton, Huntly and Montrose. They were equipped with extensive powers, including that of raising – and commanding – an army in the event of an English invasion, a distinct possibility given Henry VIII's opposition to James's marriage, although in the event it never materialised. Nevertheless, on his return in March 1537, James rewarded Maxwell with the lands of Logan and others in Annandale.[96] Additionally he issued a charter confirming him in his lands in eastern Annandale, Wauchopedale and Eskdale which was stated to be 'in consideration of the good service performed during our absence in France'.[97]

A girl of weak constitution, Madeleine died in July 1537 within a month of her seventeenth birthday and a mere six months after her arrival in Scotland. Nevertheless James, permanently short of money, contrived to retain her dowry of 100,000 crowns

---

*   *RMS* III, 1199. They included Johnstone of Gretna, Kirkpatrick of Knock, Irving of Stakeheugh, and Glendonwyn (or Glendinning) of Parton, as well as members of the Graham, Little and Baty families – all notorious Border reivers.
†   In fact his original intention was to marry Marie de Bourbon having negotiated a large dowry with her father. However, she turned out to be a hunchback and altogether so unattractive that he abandoned the idea and switched his attentions to Madeleine whose charms were enhanced by an equally large dowry.

(equivalent to more than 100,000 pounds Scots). Within a year he had married again, this time to the twenty-two-year-old Marie of Guise, widow of the duke of Longueville and mother of two sons. A tall, graceful lady, and member of one of the most powerful families in France, her importance in the marriage market was such that Henry VIII, whose third wife Jane Seymour had recently died, made overtures to her as a possible bride. However, mindful of the fate of Anne Boleyn, she reportedly claimed that she had too slender a neck for safety and accepted his nephew's hand instead. As Great Admiral of Scotland, Maxwell was put in charge of the deputation appointed to go to France and escort her to Scotland. The wedding took place by proxy in May 1538 and in person at St Andrews Cathedral on 12 June, immediately after Marie's arrival in Scotland. Within a year she had produced an heir, James, while the spare – Arthur or Robert – followed in April 1541. However, they both died young, and the only surviving child was their daughter Mary, future Queen of Scots.

Meanwhile relations between James and his uncle Henry VIII remained edgy, and certainly not helped by Henry's giving sanctuary to James's enemies the earls of Angus and Bothwell. Yet a quiescent peace existed between the two realms. This was partly because Henry feared that war with James would drive him into renewing the 'auld alliance' with France and encourage the Catholic nobility in the north to come out in rebellion, as happened in 1536. However in 1542 relations between uncle and nephew finally broke down. This is popularly attributed to Henry's fury at being stood up by James who, having agreed to meet him at York, failed to turn up. The real reason was James's refusal to give Henry an assurance that, in the event of his invading France, he (James) would refrain from invading the northern counties of England, as he was bound to do in terms of the long-standing Franco-Scottish alliance.

Meanwhile incidents on the marches contributed to a further souring of relations between the two kings.[98] One concerned James's refusal to arrest and hand over those English Catholics who had taken refuge in Liddesdale and elsewhere in the Borders on the grounds that they were victims of religious persecution. Henry, on the other hand, regarded them as rebels; and for good measure he complained that lord Maxwell had twice failed to turn up for a truce day. Claiming that it was to protect against possible Scottish incursions across the border, Henry sent a force under Sir Robert Bowes to garrison the strongholds of the English east and middle marches.

James responded by mustering an army. Bowes did the same, and crossing the Tweed at Berwick (when the bridge broke and five of his men were drowned) he invaded Scotland. But he was defeated at Haddon Rig when a number of prisoners were taken, including Bowes himself. The rest managed to escape, one being the earl of Angus, who was Bowes's principal lieutenant. Furious at the reverse, Henry ordered the duke of Norfolk to raise an army and invade Scotland. But it amounted to little more than a spoiling campaign, in the course of which his troops burnt Kelso and Roxburgh as well as a number of townships. Finally they ran out of provisions, and Norfolk was compelled to withdraw to Berwick.

Meanwhile Sir Thomas Wharton, the deputy warden of the English west marches, was warned by spies, including a servant of lord Maxwell, that the Scots were planning a retaliatory invasion. True enough, because James was indeed raising an army to invade the English west marches. But in an attempt to draw Wharton and his men away, James let it be known that he intended to attack the English east and middle marches. To give it credence, he publicly ordered Maxwell to recruit an army from the south-west and join him at Selkirk. But the venue was secretly changed to Langholm, from where the combined army would invade the English west marches as James intended. Meanwhile, basing himself at Lochmaben, he made a disastrous decision. Instead of giving Maxwell command of the army – an obvious choice given his pre-eminence in the region, he entrusted it to his favourite, Oliver Sinclair, who had neither the prestige nor the qualifications for it.

Undeceived by James's ruse, Wharton remained at Carlisle. When news reached him that the Scots were at Langholm ready to march, he set out to meet them. Knowing they would have to cross the Esk by a ford near present-day Longtown, he set a trap. Placing his cavalry along its tributary the Lyne, he sent a party of light horsemen under Sir William Musgrave to ambush the Scots at the ford. While they floundered across the Esk, which was swollen by recent rains, Musgrave and his men sprang from their hiding place and tore into their ragged flanks. As the Scots gained the east bank Musgrave's men continued their attacks, darting in and out of their flanks 'pricking' them with their spears before withdrawing and re-forming for another attack – classic hit and run tactics. Finally Wharton's cavalry fell on the Scots, now hemmed in between the two rivers, and forced them back across the Esk onto the treacherous Solway moss. There they were annihilated, some 1,200 being taken prisoner and 'uncounted numbers' killed or drowned.

The prisoners included lord Maxwell. A covert Protestant, and resentful at being denied command of the army, he allegedly took advantage of the confusion to defect to the English and allowed himself to be captured. If true, it was the height of treachery considering the trust James had placed in him. Of all the nobles taken prisoner, Maxwell was by far the greatest prize – apparent from a list of their assets which was drawn up for the purpose of assessing their ransoms. This showed him as having annual revenues of 4,000 merks and goods worth 3,000.[99] He was replaced as warden by John Johnstone, who had been interned in Dumbarton castle and therefore missed the battle.[100] Notwithstanding the defeat, King James was determined to continue the campaign; but in the event he was prevented by illness. Thought to have been dysentery, it proved fatal, and this able, ruthless and somewhat sinister monarch died on 14 December 1542 at the relatively early age of thirty, six days after the birth of his daughter Mary.

TEN

Towards the Reformation

THE CHURCH IN DECLINE

Constant shortage of money inhibited King James V's ability to deliver effective government – at least to begin with. This was not due to extravagance on his part. Far from it, because contemporary writers lay stress on his miserliness and 'keenness for money'. As Sir Thomas Wharton observed to Henry VIII's principal adviser Thomas Cromwell, 'the kynge inclynethe daylye more and more to covitousenesse'.[1] Not for nothing was he a grandson of the close-fisted Henry VII.˙ The fact is that it was forced on him by the parlous state to which the royal finances had been reduced through the profligacy of Albany's governorship, compounded by Angus's alienation of crown revenues to bribe the support of leading magnates.

This meant that James was compelled to resort to every possible means to raise money, and no source of revenue was overlooked however small. Taxation was an obvious answer. But the difficulty was that it needed the consent of Parliament, and when Parliament did approve a tax it was generally burdened with so many conditions as to render it almost valueless. Yet in spite of that, no less than thirteen taxes were imposed during the period of James's personal rule. Since Parliament would generally grant them for a specific purpose, James usually managed to ensure that the proceeds exceeded the sum required so that the surplus could be diverted to his treasury. Another source of revenue was charging for the issuing of charters to landowners whose titles were defective, incomplete or under challenge, as seems frequently to have been the case.[2] Yet another was to encourage crown tenants to convert their leases into feus so that he could benefit from the up-front capital payments or *grassums*. Even gold mining at Crawfordmuir – and possibly at Leadhills where the metal was known to exist, and at Wanlockhead in Nithsdale – constituted a modest source of revenue.

During the early years of his personal rule James's financial situation was such that he was reduced to taking some of the royal lands in hand and farming them himself. That he should stoop to such a practice so appalled his uncle Henry VIII that he instructed Sir Ralph Sadler, the English ambassador to Scotland, to take James to task

---

˙ One gets the impression that he took after the Tudors rather than his jolly, gregarious and pleasure-loving father, James IV.

for it. Lecturing him on the subject, he told James that it was beneath his kingly dignity to meddle in such a 'lowly and unkingly' pursuit as to 'gather into his hands numbers of sheep and other such mean and vile things however profitable it might be'.[3] Instead, he advised him take a leaf out of his uncle's book by dissolving the religious houses and appropriating their lands. No doubt a tempting thought, but in the circumstances not an option; and in any case, as a devout Catholic, James would never have contemplated it.

On the other hand he was ready to seize every opportunity to acquire lands through forfeiture. Notable examples were those belonging to the earl of Angus, which included Liddesdale and his lands in Eskdale, and those forfeited by the earl of Bothwell for his treasonable dealings with the earl of Northumberland as warden of the English east marches. In 1540, at James's instigation, Parliament passed an Act of Revocation[4] which authorised him to exact large sums of money by way of composition[5] – in other words the enforced settlement of debts owing to the crown. Besides ratifying the forfeiture of the Angus earldom and its attaching lands, the Act validated the confiscation of those belonging to John lord Glamis,[*] and those of Sir James Hamilton of Finnart, the controversial bastard son of the first earl of Arran who was executed for plotting to assassinate the king.

While James would not have been in a position – or indeed would have wished – to follow his uncle's example by dissolving the religious houses, the Church's vast wealth was potentially an extremely valuable source of revenue if only he could tap into it. Imposing a tax was the answer, but the difficulty was that it would require papal consent which for obvious reasons would be hard to obtain. On the other hand, the blatant corruption of the Church and the scandalous lifestyle of many of its senior dignitaries, itself the product of its flagrantly ostentatious wealth, would render such a tax politically acceptable. But that was not enough and James had to bide his time.

Other sources of revenue included the sale of dispensations for irregularities. For example a priest could purchase the right to hold a number of livings, albeit at the cost of the pastoral care and spiritual welfare of the parishioners, while priests and laymen could have their bastard offspring legitimised – at a price. Records show that during the thirty years before the Reformation 350 bastard sons and 50 daughters of men in holy orders were legitimised, and because this only applied where an inheritance was at stake the actual number was probably much higher. While most clergymen doubtless exercised their spiritual and pastoral duties with care and diligence, the fact remains that pamphlets imported from abroad inveighing against 'the corruption of morals and the profane lewdness of life [of] incontinent, intemperate and negligent churchmen' struck a popular chord.

---

*   The seventh lord Glamis, he was sentenced to death for treason but his execution was deferred until he had attained his majority. Fortunately for him, James V died during the interim when he was released from prison and restored to his lands.

Much of the Church's wealth was derived from the teind income, or tithes, of the parish churches with which abbeys, priories and other religious foundations had been endowed over the centuries. This had grown to such an extent that by the time of the Reformation it is estimated that the revenues of nearly 90% of the parish churches of Scotland were being diverted to the Church and its institutions. To put its wealth into perspective, its annual revenue is estimated to have been approximately ten times that of the crown.[6] True, these institutions were responsible for ministering to the spiritual needs of the parishioners of their dependent churches, but most of the underpaid clerks appointed to these livings lacked the necessary qualifications. In many cases they were so ill-educated that they could do little more than intone the Liturgy, while the fact that it was in Latin, which was incomprehensible to all but the educated few, was a further source of resentment. Consequently there was a widespread demand for the Liturgy and the Bible to be rendered in the vernacular.

Nevertheless the combination of these factors – the immorality of senior Church dignitaries, the inability of many vicars and curates to minister to the spiritual and pastoral needs of their parishioners, the rendering of the Liturgy in Latin, and other sources of dissatisfaction, probably counted for little when compared with the ostentatious wealth of the Church and its senior dignitaries. For a people living close to subsistence level it must have been particularly galling to witness the Church dignitaries' outrageously self-indulgent lifestyle when much of it was paid for by the hard-won teinds they were obliged to render the Church.

Already in the previous century dissatisfaction with the Church had led to the emergence of an Ayrshire-based reforming movement known as the Lollards of Kyle. But the catalyst occurred in 1517 when Martin Luther, a German priest and professor of theology, nailed his ninety-five theses attacking the sale of indulgences[*] to the church door at Wittenburg. The intrusion of his preaching into Scotland caught on to such an extent that in 1525 Parliament passed an Act condemning the 'dampnable opunzeounis of the heretick Luther and his discipillis' and banning the importing and possession of his tracts under threat of severe penalties. In 1528 a particularly brutal example was made of Patrick Hamilton. Nephew of the earl of Arran, and of royal descent, he was convicted of heresy and condemned to be burnt at the stake. This took place at St Andrews when it was said that the smoke 'infected [i.e. converted] all whom it blew upon'.

Determined to suppress the reformist movement in Scotland, James fully endorsed these punitive measures. At the same time he was determined to press ahead with his plans to impose a tax on the Church. But to disguise his real intention, which was mainly to fill the royal treasury, he had to put forward a convincing case for it – at least one that he could sell to Parliament, and more importantly the Pope. Here

---

*   An indulgence was a highly priced forgiveness of sins which the purchaser was induced to believe would enable him to avoid consignation to Purgatory in the afterlife.

Archbishop Dunbar, his former tutor, came up with an ingenious proposal. Public resentment of the Church was making it increasingly difficult for its functionaries to collect its revenues. And because the Church courts appeared unable to enforce payment, he suggested that the solution was to found a College of Justice equipped with powers to punish non-payers. And because it would be for its benefit, it was both logical and right that the Church should bear the cost. Accepting the argument, Parliament approved the imposition of a tax on the Church to finance it, and at James's instigation this was fixed at £10,000 a year. Because this was far in excess of the cost of founding the College he was able to divert the surplus to his own use.

So far so good, but the tax still needed papal consent. The time was propitious. Because England was threatening to go schismatic, Pope Clement VII, fearing that Scotland might follow suit, and therefore all the more anxious to keep James on side, readily assented. Not surprisingly, the imposition of the tax drew howls of protest from the clergy – most of all from Archbishop Beaton. However, James effectively silenced him by threatening to have him put him on trial for treasonable dealings with England.[7] In the end, James compounded for a lump sum of £72,000 payable over four years, known as the Great Tax. Meanwhile, doubtless at James's prompting, Parliament stipulated that the Church would remain liable for the payment of £10,000 a year until the Great Tax was fully paid. Since the money could only be raised by selling off Church lands, there was a considerable delay before this could be achieved, and meantime James continued to receive his £10,000 a year.

In fact Church lands were already being alienated, if only to a limited extent. For example, by the latter half of the fifteenth century the monks of Melrose were finding it difficult to maintain their daughter house at Friars Carse. Therefore the abbot and chapter decided to dispose of its lands, and in 1465 they feued off those of Dalgonar and Ellisland to John Kirkpatrick, a member of the Closeburn family. But the sale was conditional on Kirkpatrick and his successors entertaining the abbot and monks, and their retainers – and pasturing their horses – while on their way to and from the abbey's grange lands in Carrick.[8] Since these churchmen were accustomed to doing themselves well it must have proved a heavy imposition.

In many cases the disposal of Church lands was instigated by local landowners for the benefit of themselves and their relatives. This was achieved by taking advantage of a practice which was becoming increasingly common among ecclesiastical institutions – namely, that of acquiring the protection of a powerful local lord by appointing him, or a member of his family, as its head. Because they were laymen, and therefore not qualified to exercise the spiritual functions of abbots and priors, they held office *in commendam* and were therefore known as commendators. So, whereas the abbot or prior continued to supervise all matters religious and spiritual, the commendator controlled the institution's secular interests which in turn gave him a say in the disposal of its lands.

The imposition of the Great Tax merely accelerated the process, the main impetus coming from the institutions themselves who were under pressure to meet their share of the tax. But there were other considerations as well. Perceiving the inevitability of a reformation of the Church in Scotland, and the likely confiscation of their lands, as was happening in England, these institutions were anxious to feu them off while the going was good so that they could at least benefit from the proceeds of sale. In the event their fears proved groundless, for it was not until the passing of the Annexation Act of 1587 that all the remaining Church lands and superiorities were vested in the crown. But by then most of them had passed into private hands.

By far the largest ecclesiastical landowner in Dumfriesshire was Holywood. This was effectively controlled by the Maxwells who in consequence were well placed to acquire much of its lands. In the late fifteenth century John Maxwell became abbot – probably through the influence of his brother John fourth lord Maxwell (they had the same name in spite of being brothers). Abbot John first appears on record in 1495 when he constituted his brother the fourth lord and the latter's two infant sons, Robert (future fifth lord Maxwell) and Herbert, bailies of the abbey lands.[9] This would have given them a say in their disposal, and presumably accounted for Herbert's acquiring the lands of Clowden (Cluden).[10] Also for Robert fifth lord Maxwell's obtaining a charter of the lands of Keir, Barjarg and others which stated that it was in consideration of 'the counsel and help given, or to be given, to the abbey by him, his heirs and successors'.[11]

Other relatives acquired a share of the abbey lands. For example Sir John Maxwell, a nephew of the fourth lord Maxwell, obtained those of Cowhill[12] while another nephew acquired the lands of Glenesslin.[13] In 1544 Commendator William feued the lands of 'Porterrack' (Portrack) to Robert Maxwell, a descendant of Homer (or Aymer) Maxwell, younger brother of the third lord Maxwell.[14] In terms of the Annexation Act of 1587 the remaining abbey lands became vested in the crown. Some thirty years later, James VI had them constituted a barony which he gave, along with that of Lochmaben, to John Murray,* a gentleman of the bedchamber and his current favourite. Part of the abbey lands lying to the west of the Nith was incorporated in the newly established parish of Keir of which a portion was acquired by the Edgar family. Possible descendants of the lords of Nithsdale, they were long-established tenants of the abbey in the neighbouring parish of Glencairn.[15]

As the dominant power in the south-west, Robert fifth lord Maxwell contrived to have himself appointed bailie of the abbey lands of Holywood, Sweetheart, Tongland and Dundrennan, as well as preceptor of Trailtrow and provost of Lincluden.[16] On his death in 1546 the provostry of Lincluden reverted to the crown. The following year James Douglas of Drumlanrig, the other major power in Nithsdale, prevailed on the earl of Arran as governor to appoint his illegitimate son Robert Douglas as provost. When the provostry was closed in 1565 Robert Douglas sold off the collegiate lands

---

* A younger son of Sir Charles Murray of Cockpool, he was later knighted. In 1624 he was created earl of Annandale and in 1637 he inherited Cockpool on the death of his brother Sir Richard Murray.

at Drumsleet,* along with those at Kirkpatrick Durham in Kirkcudbrightshire, to his nephew James Douglas of Pinzearie.[17]

In 1603 this James Douglas gave the lands to his son William on the occasion of his marriage to Agnes daughter of John eighth lord Maxwell. Seven years later, William was sentenced to death for being in treasonable communication with his brother-in-law John ninth lord Maxwell, who had fled the country following his murder of Sir James Johnstone.[18] Consequently his lands were forfeited to the crown. In 1611 James VI granted them jointly to John Murray of Lochmaben and Robert Gordon of Lochinvar, both gentlemen of the bedchamber. Because the arrangement proved unworkable, it was agreed that Gordon should take the lands at Crossmichael, and Murray those at Drumsleet, which he later sold to Robert Maxwell first earl of Nithsdale.

At the opposite end of the county the lands belonging to Melrose in upper Eskdale were acquired by the earls of Morton. In 1568 Sir William Douglas of Lochleven, the future sixth earl, procured the appointment of his young son James as commendator. This was so that he could exercise the office himself as his son's tutor-at-law and thus influence (in effect direct) the disposal of the abbey lands. Not surprisingly he secured the major portion for himself! On his (the sixth earl's) death in 1606 they passed to his grandson William the seventh earl, who had the lands in upper Eskdale converted into a temporal lordship, known as the barony of Dunfedling; he later sold it to Walter lord Scott of Buccleuch.[19]

In 1619 Walter lord Scott, now earl of Buccleuch, acquired the former priory lands of Canonbie.[20] Following their reversion to the crown under the Annexation Act they were converted into a secular lordship and granted to Alexander first earl of Home.[21] In 1611 Earl Alexander resigned it to the crown in exchange for other lands closer to home. The following year the former priory lands were purchased by Sir John Ker of Jedburgh, who subsequently acquired the neighbouring lands of Tarras. In 1619 Ker sold his lands in eastern Dumfriesshire, including Canonbie, Tarras and others, to Earl Walter.[22] Unfortunately Earl Walter had over extended himself so that not only was he unable to come up with the purchase price but he found himself beset by creditors. Evidently he was about to flee the country to avoid them. But at that point his kinsman Walter Scott ('Auld Wat') of Harden persuaded some prominent Border lairds, including Sir Gideon Murray of Elibank, to mount a rescue operation. They persuaded the creditors to refrain from taking further action in return for granting them a personal bond undertaking to repay them. However, this was conditional on Earl Walter handing over the management of his estates to Scott of Harden, Murray and others as his trustees.

Within a few years Scott of Harden and his fellow trustees had restored the Buccleuch estates to solvency and were able to hand them back to Earl Walter free from all encumbrances. Then what did Earl Walter do but contract with Robert

---

* On the opposite side of the Nith from Dumfries and now part of Maxwelltown.

Maxwell, earl of Nithsdale, to purchase the barony of Langholm. Not surprisingly he was unable to pay for it. So once again Scott of Harden and others had to come to the rescue. Scott himself died in 1629 when he was succeeded by his son Sir William of Harden. Earl Walter died in 1633 with the purchase price of the Langholm estate still unpaid, having appointed Sir William and others as curators to his infant children, including his only surviving son, the seven-year-old Earl Francis.* Therefore, as curators, they were responsible for the administration of the Buccleuch estates which they managed so successfully that they were able to settle the purchase price of the barony of Langholm for the sum of 105,050 merks.[23] Not only that, but in the following decade they purchased the lordship of Dalkeith for Earl Francis from William seventh earl of Morton who contributed the proceeds to the royalist cause during the Bishops' War.

The only religious house of note in Annandale was the preceptory of Trailtrow, which belonged to the Knights of St John of Jerusalem. Otherwise known as the Knights Hospitaller, their Order was dedicated to founding hospitals, originally for pilgrims to the Holy Land but latterly for the poor, the needy and the sick. While those in Dumfriesshire had long since disappeared, their former existence is preserved in place-names like Spittal, Spittalfield and Spittalridding, the hospital at Trailtrow being the only survivor. In 1574 the preceptor feued its lands at Hoddom to Sir John Maxwell fourth lord Herries.[24] Following this, Maxwell built Hoddom castle† and the more modest Repentance Tower on top of Trailtrow hill, which would have served as a watchtower.

Their sister Order, the Knights Templar, owned small parcels of land in Dumfriesshire. Originally founded for the protection of pilgrims to the Holy Land, they amassed considerable wealth and began buying up land throughout Europe, including Scotland. In 1307 the Pope ordered all Christian monarchs to arrest them and seize their lands. But defying the papal injunction, the excommunicate Robert Bruce, who had nothing to lose by doing so, gave them sanctuary. Identifiable from place-names appearing in the records pre-fixed by 'the temple lands',‡ an obvious example being Templand near Lochmaben, their lands in Dumfriesshire would also have passed into private hands.

One of the smallest ecclesiastical institutions in Dumfriesshire was the Convent of the Greyfriars in Dumfries. By 1560 the chapter had been reduced to a mere five people including the warden, Charles Home, who was described as 'the last survivor of the Franciscans of Scotland of whom any record survives'. He would have been responsible for the gift of the friary lands, properties and other assets to the burgh of Dumfries in April 1569.[25] Finally there were the Brothers of the Order of the

---

* The foregoing information is based on a Memorandum entitled 'Ane Account of What Kindness the family of Harden did for the family of Buccleugh', a transcript of which is in the possession of Scott of Harden's descendant Lord Polwarth to whom I am indebted for a copy.

† Subsequently much enlarged it now belongs to Hoddom and Kinmount Estates.

‡ McDowall gives numerous examples in his *History of Dumfries*, p. 249.

Star of Bethlehem, who owned land at Langbetholm (formerly Langbethlem) in the parish of Kirkpatrick Juxta.[26]

In her article 'The Feuars of the Kirklands'[27] Dr Sanderson concludes that, generally speaking, the break-up of the monastic lands resulted in a wide distribution of land among the tenant class and incomers from the burghs. While perhaps true of elsewhere in Scotland, the evidence suggests that this was not the case in Dumfriesshire where the Maxwells, the Murrays, the Douglases, and (indirectly) the earls of Buccleuch, were the principal beneficiaries.

THE MINORITY OF MARY QUEEN OF SCOTS

James V had stipulated that in the event of a royal minority the earl of Arran[*] should be put in charge of the government, not on grounds of merit but simply because he was next in line to the throne, the duke of Albany having died in 1536. This was formalised by the Parliament of January 1543 which appointed him governor. Other members of the Council included Cardinal David Beaton,[†] who was given the chancellorship over the head of his rival Archbishop Dunbar, James earl of Moray (illegitimate half-brother of James V), and the earls of Huntly and Argyll. Like his father, Arran was an indecisive character with no firm convictions, and as a natural trimmer he consistently nailed his colours to the fence, or at least where he perceived his best interests to lie. At this time he was inclined towards Protestantism and an alliance with England, in contrast to the arch-Catholic Beaton who was adamantly opposed to it.

Within a fortnight of James's death, Henry VIII tilted the scales firmly in favour of the English faction by offering to release the prisoners captured at Solway Moss. This was conditional on their subscribing to a bond acknowledging him as lord superior of Scotland, and promising to do their utmost to persuade the government to cede Scotland and its strongholds to him. Furthermore they were to press for the marriage of their infant queen Mary to his five-year-old son Edward prince of Wales, and to use their best endeavours to have her delivered into Henry's custody so that she would be brought up in England. Finally, if the government refused his terms and Henry decided to invade Scotland, they were to give him all possible assistance. As a pledge of their co-operation, they were required to surrender their eldest sons and other close relatives as hostages. The following month about a thousand of these 'assured Scots' were allowed to return to Scotland, and foremost among them was Robert fifth lord Maxwell.[28]

Soon afterwards the pro-English faction received a further stimulus with the return of other English-supporting Scots, including the earl of Angus who was appointed a member of the governing Council. At his instigation, Cardinal Beaton

---

[*]   James Hamilton, who had succeeded his father as second earl of Arran in 1529.
[†]   Nephew of James Beaton, he had succeeded him as archbishop of St Andrews in 1539.

was arrested and imprisoned in his own castle at St Andrews. However, escaping from prison a few months later, thanks to the connivance of well-bribed guards, Beaton made common cause with Arran's illegitimate half-brother, the forceful and staunchly Catholic John Hamilton. At that time abbot of Paisley, and later Beaton's successor as archbishop of St Andrews, he has been described as 'the nagging Catholic conscience of his natural brother Arran'.[29] Consequently he, along with Beaton, the queen mother Mary of Guise and the earl of Lennox, newly returned from France, became the leaders of the pro-French party.

In March 1543, at lord Maxwell's behest, and overriding the strenuous protests of the clerical representatives, Parliament passed an Act which decriminalised possession of the Bible in the vernacular, referring specifically to William Tyndale's translation of the New Testament into English. Later, John Knox hailed this as 'no small victory [against] the tyranny and abuse of the Roman Antichrist', observing that it was soon to be seen 'lying upon almost every gentleman's table'. In July the Scottish government, supported by the assured Scots, concluded the treaty of Greenwich with the English. This provided for the marriage of the infant Mary to Prince Edward, while stipulating that the two countries were to remain at peace until a year after the death of the survivor.

Arran made a half-hearted attempt to insist that Scotland retain its independence, come what may, and to obtain an assurance from Henry that the proposed marriage would not result in its absorption by England. Unwilling to give such an undertaking, Henry persuaded Arran to withdraw his request with hollow promises of a marriage between his son and heir, the master of Hamilton, and the princess Elizabeth (later Queen Elizabeth). Having overcome Arran's objections, King Henry attempted to browbeat the Scots into submission by threatening to send 5,000 men to enforce ratification of the treaty in the event of Parliament's refusal to do so – not unlikely given its unpopularity with the Scots. Like Arran they too had misgivings about their future independence, although as events turned out the treaty was never ratified.

Arran also had grave misgivings about handing over custody of the young queen to the English. So much so that, persuaded by his half-brother Abbot John Hamilton, he switched his support to the pro-French party. This resulted in the appointment of a new governing Council which included Mary of Guise, Cardinal Beaton as chancellor and Abbot John Hamilton as treasurer. Meanwhile the earl of Angus emerged as leader of the pro-English faction, being joined by the earl of Lennox, who abandoned his support for the French, perhaps influenced by his prospective marriage to Angus's daughter Margaret.* Since Parliament, under pressure from the dominant pro-French party, refused to ratify the treaty of Greenwich, Henry retaliated by attempting to impose the treaty and the royal marriage on the Scots by force. Therefore he ordered the earl of Hertford to invade Scotland and so devastate the Border country as to terrorise the Scots into compliance.

---

* They would become the parents-in-law of Mary queen of Scots.

The campaign began in May 1544. But instead of overrunning the Border country, the earl of Hertford led a seaborne expedition of some 10,000 men which landed at Leith. Capturing the town, he advanced on Edinburgh where he was joined by lord Eure, the warden of the English east marches, with a force of 4,000 footsoldiers. The burghers put up a stout resistance, because the English had to mount two assaults before they could breach the town wall when they occupied the south side of the city. Having looted and vandalised Holyrood abbey they put the rest of the city to flames, while the burghers continued to fire on them with their handguns from the burning buildings. In the end some 600 were killed at the cost of a mere seven Englishmen. Leaving the smouldering ruins of Edinburgh behind them, Hertford and his army withdrew southwards by way of Dunbar, burning settlements and devastating the countryside as they headed for Berwick. This was the first campaign in what was later referred to with grim humour as the 'rough wooing'.

Hertford's success was widely attributed to the incompetence of Arran and Beaton's administration. Moreover it caused many people to question the wisdom of the government's anti-English policy. Reflecting their lack of faith in Arran, there was a move to have him replaced by Mary of Guise, who seems to have inspired more confidence. Therefore at a convention held in June, Arran was suspended from office and Mary of Guise was appointed head of the governing Council. Taking his dismissal in bad part, Arran continued to dispute her appointment notwithstanding that they were both in the French camp.

Their principal opponent was the earl of Lennox, now a creature of Henry VIII, who in August 1544 appointed him lieutenant of the northern counties and southern Scotland. In November the conflict between Arran and Mary of Guise came to a head when they summoned rival parliaments. However an appeal for unity in the face of a threatened English invasion persuaded them to sink their differences and accept Cardinal Beaton as head of the governing Council. For the next eighteen months he persuaded them to co-operate in resisting the English. Other members of the Council included Angus, who had turned against the English – ostensibly in protest at their desecration of the Douglas tombs in Melrose abbey during the 'rough wooing', but more likely bribed with promises of a French pension.

In February 1545 Angus defeated an English invading force under lord Eure at Ancrum Moor when Eure himself was killed. Although a minor success, it was enough to encourage Parliament to persist in its refusal to ratify the treaty of Greenwich. Henry's reaction was predictable. He would hammer the Scots still harder in his efforts to grind them into submission. Therefore he planned another invasion, this time on a much larger scale with an army of some 36,000 men, mostly foreign mercenaries. It was to be on two fronts – one attacking the west march and the other the east. Whereas the former would be supported by a naval force off the Ayrshire coast, the latter was to be assisted by another fleet going up the east coast. Meanwhile the French sent a large contingent of troops to help stiffen the Scots' resistance, and in June Parliament proclaimed a Franco-Scottish alliance.

The invasion began in September – deliberately timed to destroy the harvested crops – when Hertford crossed the border with an army of 12,000 men, many fewer than originally intended. Nevertheless they proceeded to devastate the Border country, sacking Dryburgh, Melrose and Jedburgh abbeys, and according to the records they burnt 192 townships, settlements, towers, bastel houses and churches.[30] At the same time they drove off 20,000 head of cattle, while hundreds of people were taken prisoner or slaughtered out of hand.

Force was merely one arm of Henry's strategy. Another was to bribe the support of the leading Scottish nobles in the hopes of sapping the Scots' will to resist. But he was on a hiding to nothing because the French could always outbid him, and anyway Henry's record of broken promises was hardly calculated to inspire confidence. One victim of his bad faith was James Douglas of Drumlanrig, hitherto a staunch supporter of the English. He had been promised a large sum of money in return for furnishing them with information about the governing Council's campaign plans to which he had access, and which had proved extremely helpful. But his reward was so niggardly that when his brother-in-law Angus defected to the Scots he followed suit.[31]

A third arm of Henry's strategy was to undermine the pro-French regime by infiltrating agents into Scotland to disseminate reformism. In fact it merely accelerated a process that was already underway, for reformism had taken root in most of the burghs – particularly those on the east coast, while many landowners were covert Protestants and others would follow suit. One agent – by far the best known – was George Wishart. A Scotsman and member of a landowning family from Kincardineshire,* his heretical teachings had brought him to the notice of the authorities, and he was forced to flee to England to avoid almost certain martyrdom at the stake. In 1543 he returned to Scotland, ostensibly as one of the English commissioners charged with negotiating the treaty of Greenwich. Taking advantage of this, he became an itinerant preacher proclaiming the gospel in the vernacular and engaging in other heretical teaching, in which he was joined by John Knox.

He may have thought that as an English commissioner he enjoyed diplomatic immunity. He probably did, for instead of having him arrested and put on trial Cardinal Beaton hired a priest to assassinate him. But the plan miscarried because, big strong man that he was, Wishart managed to overpower the priest and disarm him. Foiled in his attempt to dispose of Wishart by treachery, and ignoring his diplomatic immunity (probably redundant anyway after Henry's 'rough wooing'), Beaton had him arrested and brought to trial before a 'kangaroo' court. Since he presided in person, Wishart's conviction of heresy was a foregone conclusion, and he was sentenced to burning at the stake. It took place a few days later at St Andrews, Beaton allegedly watching the spectacle from a window of his castle.

Six weeks later, in May 1546, Beaton himself was assassinated by a group of Fifeshire lairds who hung his corpse over the castle battlements in a public

---

* An earlier member of the family was Robert Bruce's staunch supporter Bishop Robert Wishart.

demonstration of their hatred of the French alliance. While King Henry almost certainly connived at the murder, the main instigator was the earl of Cassilis who had already approached Sir Thomas Wharton with an offer to carry out a contract on him.[32] Joined by other Protestants, the lairds proceeded to occupy the castle, which they held in the face of all attempts to retake it, relying on English promises to send a relieving force. The following Easter they were joined by Knox, who was appointed chaplain to the garrison. But there was still no sign of the promised English relieving force. However, before it could reach them it was pre-empted by the arrival of French reinforcements to assist the besiegers. Therefore when the castle fell at the end of July the garrison leaders were dispatched to prison in France, while the others – including Knox – were consigned to a harsh and rigorous existence as galley slaves, which they would remain for the next two years. Meanwhile Beaton was succeeded as archbishop by John Hamilton, while James Hamilton, another of Arran's illegitimate half-brothers, was nominated to Glasgow to succeed Archbishop Dunbar who had died the previous April.

Henry VIII died in January 1547, and Hertford – now duke of Somerset – was appointed protector of the realm for the nine-year-old Edward VI. Later that year, determined to enforce the royal marriage, he invaded Scotland at the head of an army of some 16,000 men equipped with artillery and heavy cavalry, and supported by a fleet. When they encountered the poorly equipped Scottish army at Pinkie, near Edinburgh, on 10 September, they scored an easy victory with many thousands of Scots killed or taken prisoner. To consolidate his success, Somerset established an English occupation zone based on Haddington. But at that point, fearing that his position was being undermined at home, he returned south.

Meanwhile, to avoid the risk of their young queen being captured, the governing Council, under pressure from its new king Henry II, decided to send her to France for safety. Indeed Henry made this a condition of sending further reinforcements to Scotland. Landing at Leith in June 1548, the French joined the Scots in laying siege to the English headquarters at Haddington where a Franco-Scottish accord was concluded on 7 July. This provided for the young queen's marriage to the dauphin Francis,* while guaranteeing Scotland's continuing independence as a separate nation state. Justifiably wary of French promises, Arran tried to obstruct the agreement. However, the promise of a valuable French duchy was enough to persuade him to withdraw his objections. Therefore once agreement was reached the young queen sailed for France, and in February 1549 Arran was rewarded with the French dukedom of Châtelherault.

The betrothal of their queen and the dauphin was no more popular with the Scots than the French alliance. For, notwithstanding French promises to the contrary, it was widely feared that it would lead to a French takeover of Scotland and its reduction to little more than a French province. Therefore, when Mary of Guise sailed for France

---

* Since they were aged four and three respectively, the marriage did not take place until April 1558.

in 1550 to secure further help against a threatened English invasion, she took with her a number of nobles who were opposed to the French alliance, doubtless hoping they would be seduced into changing their minds. In fact it was French gold that clinched matters, because the nobles appear to have had few scruples about abandoning their opposition in return for substantial bribes, the sixth lord Maxwell for example receiving the princely sum of 2,000 francs.[33]

In December 1553 Queen Mary attained her twelfth year. Advised by his lawyers, always ready to oblige with the required 'expert' opinion under pressure, Henry II maintained that, because this was synonymous with the 'perfect age' of twelve, she was entitled to assume full ruling powers. Since she was living in France, and likely to remain there for the foreseeable future, it was essential that she appoint a regent to govern Scotland. The choice was hers. Therefore, persuaded by her powerful Guise uncles, she chose her mother Mary of Guise, who was now a major political force in her own right. Her appointment was confirmed by Parliament in April 1554, Arran having resigned the governorship under threat of being charged with embezzling crown property during his term of office.

THE CAMPAIGNS IN THE SOUTH-WEST

The 'rough wooing' extended to a campaign in the south-west. In September 1543, some six months before Hertford's invasion took place, Henry VIII convened a conference of the northern lords which was attended by Sir Thomas (now lord) Wharton. This was to decide what should be done 'to Scotlande this winter by the Westmarchers of England'. After some discussion it was agreed that Wharton should 'burne, destroy, and maik waste [all] the towers, steids, buildings and corne' in Annandale as a preliminary to devastating Eskdale, Ewesdale, Wauchopedale and the Debateable Land. Further, that he should concentrate his efforts on ravaging the more fertile parishes,* while the people were to be warned that anyone refusing to swear allegiance to the English king would be slaughtered out of hand.[34]

Before embarking on his campaign Wharton sent spies into the region to report on the strength of the three principal castles – Caerlaverock, Lochmaben and the recently built fortress at Langholm,† which were under the keepership of lord Maxwell. At the same time he incited the notoriously unruly families on the marches – the Armstrongs, Beatties, Littles and others, as well as all 'broken' men,‡ to ravage the countryside and slay at will. This was intended to soften up the region against his

---

*   Namely 'Dronoke, Reidkyrke, Gretnoo, Kyrkpatrik, Eglefleghan, Penersarkes, [and] Carudders' in Annandale, and 'Stablegorton and Watsyrkett [Westerkirk]' in Eskdale.

†   Built in about 1526 by Christie Armstrong following the grant of land at Langholm to his brother 'Johnnie' Armstrong by Robert fifth lord Maxwell.

‡   A 'broken' man was someone who had been involved in a raid, or who had committed a murder, and was unable to find someone to stand surety for his future good behaviour, in which case he was proclaimed an outlaw and if caught he was liable to be hanged.

invasion which was to take place the following spring. The spies' reports must have confirmed that the three castles were strongly held, for instead of laying siege to them Wharton adhered to his original instructions to devastate parts of Dumfriesshire.

His troops appear to have encountered minimal resistance, except when they attacked Annan and were driven off by a party of Johnstones. Therefore, abandoning it to the Scots for the time being, Wharton and his men pressed on to Dumfries where they sacked the town, burning and demolishing most of the houses. Finally they withdrew laden with booty, and for good measure they drove away the townsfolk's livestock.[35] Heading eastwards, they ravaged the Johnstone lands on the Water of Milk, in the course of which they burnt 'threescore houses and much good corn', took a number of prisoners, and again drove away a large head of livestock.[36] But all it did was to encourage John Johnstone and his uncle lord Maxwell to sink their differences and make common cause against them.[37]

Meanwhile Wharton demanded that Maxwell surrender the three castles. Maxwell refused, whereupon King Henry ordered his arrest. Taken first to Carlisle, he was dispatched to the Tower of London where he was confined under the most rigorous conditions.[*] In his absence the Armstrongs took the castle at Langholm and delivered it up to Sir Thomas Dacre, the warden of the English west marches. Caerlaverock was held by Maxwell's eldest son Robert master of Maxwell, and Lochmaben by his second son John.[†] But instead of trying to take possession of them by force, Wharton stooped to subterfuge. He attempted to bribe Johnstone to capture the master of Maxwell and thus gain possession of Caerlaverock, so reporting to the earl of Shrewsbury. But, honouring his pact with Maxwell's father, Johnstone refused, having no doubt pocketed the bribe.

Therefore Wharton tried a different approach. Later that summer, with King Henry's approval, he offered to release lord Maxwell in return for his sons' surrendering Caerlaverock and Lochmaben, and giving themselves up as hostages for his future co-operation. But soon afterwards a party of Grahams ambushed and captured the master of Maxwell while he was conducting a raid into Wauchopedale and handed him over to their allies the Johnstones. In breach of his pact with Maxwell's father, Johnstone delivered him up to the English who held him prisoner for the next four years.[38] Meanwhile Caerlaverock, now in the keepership of a Maxwell kinsman, continued to hold out. So did Lochmaben, John Maxwell having refused to surrender it and become a hostage for his father.

This left Wharton with no alternative but to take the castles by force. Therefore on Hertford's instructions he attacked Caerlaverock. In a report to the English Privy Council based on Wharton's evidence, Hertford gave a brief resumé of the situation.

---

*   According to a report by the earl of Hertford in July the following year (1545) he was reduced to so great 'a perplexitie and hevynes that he coulde neyther eate, drynke, nor slepe' (McDowall, *History of Dumfries*, 198).

†   Future master of Maxwell, later Sir John Maxwell of Terregles and finally lord Herries, he would become a principal power in the region.

'Uppon the West Marches of Scotland', he wrote, 'the country [is] a wylde and waste ground [and] there is no exployte to be donne upon that frontier nearer than Dunfreys whiche is twentie miles [away]'. Therefore all Wharton could do was 'caste downe a certen church and steple, called the Steple of Annande, which is a thinge of litle importaunce'. Concluding, Hertford told the Privy Council that in Wharton's opinion 'the West Marches of Scotlande being so barreyn a country, and already wasted by the conteynuance of the warres, there is no exployte to be done there other than aforesaide', namely to take possession of Caerlaverock.[39]

In the event Wharton took both Caerlaverock and Lochmaben without a fight, as lord Maxwell, still a prisoner in the Tower, had authorised the keepers to give them up. Caerlaverock was surrendered in return for the promise of lord Maxwell's release (which the English were slow to honour), whereas his son John Maxwell handed over Lochmaben unconditionally. This was because he had defected to the English out of resentment at what he regarded as bad faith on Arran's part. As governor, Arran had the gift of marriage of the three Herries co-heiresses who had been made wards of court following the death of their father, William third lord Herries, the previous year. After promising John Maxwell the hand of the eldest daughter Agnes in marriage Arran reneged, having decided to earmark this valuable prize for his own younger son John (future marquess of Hamilton) instead.

Meanwhile the keepership of Caerlaverock was entrusted to the Cumbrian baron Sir Thomas Carleton. No sooner had he arrived to take up the appointment than the castle was besieged by a large force recruited from Annandale, Nithsdale and Galloway under the joint command of John Johnstone, James Douglas of Drumlanrig and Gordon of Lochinvar. Wharton was unable to raise the siege, explaining the difficulties involved in a letter to Henry VIII. '[Caerlaverock] standithe from your Highness citie of Carlisle twenty-eight myllis', he wrote, 'and there are many strait [difficult] passaiges, amongst which one is called Lokermoss'. As he went on to say, the only route across it was by a man-made earthen causeway which admitted no more than four men abreast. But the drawback was that the local people could easily breach it, in which case his army would have to make an eight-mile detour to reach the castle. Moreover, 'if the weyther chance so contagious [stormy] as at this present' the rivers between Carlisle and Caerlaverock would be impassable. Nor was it possible to make a seaborne attack because boats could not come within a mile of the castle 'except at a hie spring and a full sea'. And besides, the owners of the boats would not want to venture out into 'the troubled waters of the Solway at that time of year'.[40]

In another letter to the king dated 30 November 1545 Wharton reported that a spy had told him that Johnstone, Douglas and Gordon, the besiegers of Caerlaverock, had received a letter from the earl of Arran thanking them for their services. Nevertheless, he went on, he intended to make another attempt to raise the siege, this time with a force of 200 horsemen. Evidently he was successful – but only temporarily, for by the following May Caerlaverock was back in Scottish hands.

Meanwhile the unfortunate lord Maxwell found himself delivered from the frying pan into the fire. No sooner had he returned to Scotland following his release than he was arrested. Taken to Dumfries, he was charged with treason for having authorised the surrender of Caerlaverock and Lochmaben. But when he claimed that he had been threatened with being put to death if he refused he was acquitted. In January 1546 he was granted a formal remission, and in May Caerlaverock was restored to him following its recovery from the English.[41] In June he was reappointed warden of the west marches.[42] But he did not live long to enjoy it because he died on 9 July, still in his early fifties, probably as a result of the privations he had suffered during his incarceration in the Tower.[43] Because the master of Maxwell, now the sixth lord, was still a prisoner of the English, his brother John deputised for him as head of the Maxwells.

In November 1546 a Scottish force recovered Langholm and Lochmaben castles. Therefore, with the capture of Caerlaverock the previous May, all three were back in Scottish hands. Consequently the English position in the south-west began to crumble. Taking advantage of this, the Maxwells and Johnstones, once again sinking their differences, made a combined raid into Cumberland devastating the countryside far and wide. Early the following year Wharton retaliated by ordering Carleton, now deputy warden, to invade the south-west in order to shore up the English position and, as it was put, remind the natives of the benefits of English rule.[44]

Arriving at Dumfries after encountering minimal resistance, Carleton reported to Wharton that he had issued a proclamation summoning 'all manner of men' to assemble there to swear an oath of loyalty to the new king Edward VI. He remained there for ten days receiving oaths from those Galloway and Nithsdale lairds who answered his call.[45] A notable exception was the burgh of Kirkcudbright. Because he needed the burgh for landing supplies shipped from England, as well as a base from which to intercept communications between Scotland and France, Carleton was determined to take it. Accordingly he and his men laid siege to it. But assisted by a relieving force under Thomas McLellan the tutor of Bombie, the burghers forced them to withdraw. In retaliation the English besiegers rounded up a large head of cattle, and beating off an attack by a force of 'Galloway folk from beyond the Water of Dee' they drove them as far as Lochmaben.

In April 1547 John Johnstone was ambushed and captured by the English, who held him prisoner for the next three years.[*] At the instigation of the Armstrongs, who were still at feud with the Johnstones, Carleton went on to capture the principal Johnstone stronghold of Lochwood. Being surrounded by almost impenetrable marshes it would normally have presented a formidable obstacle, but on this occasion the garrison was absent having left two men and a girl, along with a few serving wenches, to guard it.

---

[*] *Scots Peerage* i, 244. According to this source Johnstone claimed that while he was a prisoner the English tried to poison him with 'evill and unhailsome mete and drinkis', obviously without success.

Reporting its capture to Wharton, Carleton described how he and his men negotiated their way across the marshes. Reaching the tower shortly before dawn, they hid themselves in the lee of the outer wall while the advance party scaled it. Stealing into the outhouse where the serving wenches slept, they bound and gagged them to prevent them from raising the alarm. Then they lay in wait outside the main door ready to force their way in as soon as it was opened. Come the dawn, one of the garrison climbed to the top of the tower and seeing no-one astir in the serving wenches' quarters he told the girl to go and wake them. As she opened the main door the advance party forced their way in. In vain the girl leapt back and tried to bolt it, but overpowering her Carleton's men gained access and took possession of the tower. As a bonus they found it well stocked with salted beef, malt, butter and cheese.[46]

Entrusting keepership of Lochwood to an Armstrong, Carleton went on to Moffat where he issued a proclamation similar to the one issued at Dumfries. Thereafter he remained in the south-west stamping out pockets of resistance. As he reported to Wharton, he and his men 'rode daily and nightly upon the king's enemies, looting and burning, and taking prisoners'. Finally he was able to announce that the county was 'in good quietness', and that 'the landowners [of] Annandale, Nithsdale and a great part of Galloway [as far as] the Water of Dee were come in and entered pledges'.[47]

When the Protector Somerset invaded Scotland in September 1547 he ordered Wharton to launch another invasion of the south-west. Accordingly Wharton mustered an army of some 5,000 footsoldiers and 800 light cavalry, supplemented by a large contingent of assured Scots under the earl of Lennox. Crossing the Esk and advancing north-west they took Castlemilk, and, reaching Annan, Wharton called on the townspeople to surrender. They refused. Instead they barricaded themselves in the church, whereupon Wharton bombarded it with his cannonry. As the building was about to collapse he repeated his demand. This time the townsfolk capitulated, and having undertaken to abandon all further resistance their lives were spared. The building was then blown up and the town looted and burnt.

Fearing that they too were about to be attacked, many Dumfriesshire landowners who had not already done so were quick to submit to Wharton. As well as swearing an oath of allegiance to the new king Edward VI, they were ordered to pledge a specified number of men (depending on the extent of their lands) to serve the English, and give up hostages against their continuing co-operation.[*] Their oaths proved hollow. No sooner had Lennox and Wharton withdrawn to Carlisle than the same landowners, joined by others, embarked on a campaign of subversion. But at the same time, mindful of the safety of their hostages, they made every profession of loyalty to King Edward. Unconvinced and suspecting treachery, Lennox marched on Dumfries having ordered those who had sworn oaths of loyalty to meet him there in order to

---

[*]   In his *History of Dumfriesshire and Galloway* Sir Herbert Maxwell lists forty-six landowners, including a number of Maxwells, Johnstones, Irvings, as well as the heads of the Murray, Carruthers, Jardine and Charteris families who between them pledged some 6,000 men to serve the English.

affirm their oaths. But arriving there he was enraged to find that only a few had turned up. The only nobleman was the earl of Glencairn. But instead of affirming his oath, he had come to deliver what was effectively a defiance by Douglas of Drumlanrig.

Lennox immediately dispatched a 600-strong force under Wharton's son Henry to carry out a raid on Drumlanrig. But instead of attacking the stronghold itself they ravaged Douglas's lands, destroyed the homesteads in the vicinity, and made off with his tenants' goods and livestock to the value of 2,000 merks.[48] As they were about to withdraw having completed the devastation of his lands, Douglas attempted an ambush. But he and his men were driven off, Douglas himself only narrowly escaping with his life. The ferocity of the younger Wharton's raid was clearly intended as an example to others, because it encouraged the more recalcitrant lairds to come to Dumfries and pledge their loyalty to King Edward. Lennox sent them on to Carlisle, escorted by an armed guard under John Maxwell, where they swore fealty to Wharton as the king's representative and delivered up hostages against their future good behaviour.[49]

Meanwhile John Maxwell, now master of Maxwell, was steering a devious course by professing loyalty to both sides – effectively hedging his bets in a desperate attempt to protect the Maxwell lands. On the one hand he had pledged himself to serve the English, was receiving a pension from them, and had been obliged to surrender hostages against his continuing loyalty. Yet at the same time he was secretly in league with the Scots. But he was in danger of being rumbled, because Wharton was bombarding him with requests to hand over Caerlaverock and Lochmaben castles. He tried to prevaricate, but was eventually forced to concede that it might be possible if his brother, who was still a prisoner of the English, agreed.[50]

This was not good enough and Wharton remained suspicious – the more so because about that time a number of Dumfriesshire lairds, apparently indifferent to the fate of their hostages, renounced their oaths of allegiance and began attacking the English occupying troops. Therefore when the earl of Lennox invaded Dumfriesshire to crush the revolt, Maxwell and his levies were ordered to take part in the expedition. Learning that Lennox's father-in-law, the Scots-supporting earl of Angus, had descended on northern Dumfriesshire, and that he and his men were encamped at Durisdeer, Lennox and his army pursued him there. But failing to catch him they put the village to flames and withdrew south.

Now abandoning all pretence of allegiance to the English, Maxwell openly threw in his lot with the Scots. Bribery in the person of Agnes Herries was the bait. Although Arran had earmarked her for his own son John, he clearly regarded winning over Maxwell and his kindred as more important. Therefore he decided to let Maxwell have her after all, having commissioned James Douglas of Drumlanrig (coincidentally Maxwell's uncle) to make John Maxwell an offer – namely that if Maxwell changed sides then he, Arran, would consent to Maxwell marrying Agnes. Accordingly Douglas sent emissaries to Maxwell to persuade him to meet Douglas in secret at Drumlanrig. He duly did so; the offer was made and the bait was taken.

Above. Interior of a Neolithic dwelling at Skara Brae, Orkney. (Photograph: author)

Left. The Ruthwell Cross, an example of Northumbrian sculpture. (Photograph: author)

Instruments of medieval warfare

A 'berefray' or siege tower.

A trebuchet wound down ready to fire.

Firing the severed heads of captives into a stronghold helped demoralise the garrison.

Sappers undermining the foundations of the castle walls.

Images of Robert Bruce

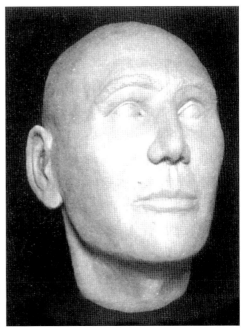

Pilkington Jackson's fancifully flattering representation of Robert Bruce. This was modelled on his skull, which was found along with his corpse in Dunfermline abbey.

Brian Hill's bland and somewhat characterless representation of Robert Bruce.

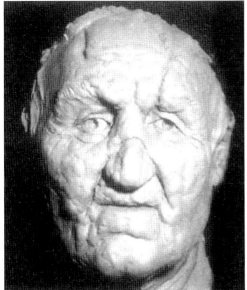

Robert Neave's more candid portrayal of Bruce. This was deliberately disfigured to show the ravages of leprosy to which the English chroniclers claimed, almost certainly wrongly, that he fell victim.

This effigy in Rosslyn Chapel is reputedly a copy of Bruce's death mask.

Caerlaverock castle. (By kind permission of the Ewart Library, Dumfries)

Imaginary siege of Caerlaverock castle.

Comlongan castle. Formerly a stronghold of the Murrays of Cockpool, it dates from about the mid-fifteenth century, the battlements being a subsequent addition. (Photograph: author)

The original part of Hoddom castle. It was built by John Maxwell 4th lord Herries in the mid-1560s following his acquisition of the Herries barony. (Photograph: author)

Drumlanrig castle, the creation of William 1st duke of Queensberry. Work was started in 1675 and continued for the next twenty-two years. The cost nearly bankrupted him and he never lived to see the castle in its finished state because he died in 1695, two years before the work was completed. (Photograph: author)

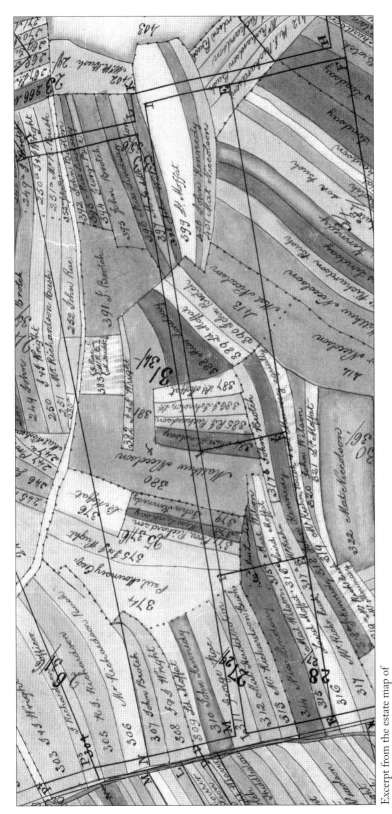

Excerpt from the estate map of Hightae illustrating the amalgamation of small runrig holdings into larger enclosed farms. (Dumfries and Galloway Libraries, Information and Archives (Archive Ref: MP 207))

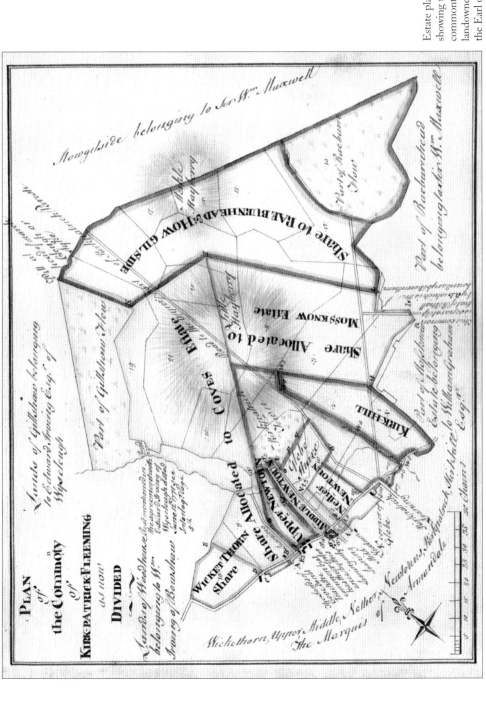

Estate plan of Kirkpatrick Fleming showing the division of the commonty between the adjacent landowners. (By kind permission of the Earl of Annandale and Hartfell)

Thomas Telford (© Highland Council (Wick Town Hall). Licensor: scran.ac.uk)

The Rev Dr Henry Duncan (© The Scotsman Publications Ltd. Licensor: scran.ac.uk)

Robert Burns by Alexander Reid (© Scottish National Portrait Gallery. Licensor: scran.ac.uk)

Scottish essayist and historian Thomas Carlyle (1795–1881). (Photograph by Time Life Pictures/Mansell/The LIFE Picture Collection/Getty Images)

Terregles House. The original part was built in 1789 for William Constable-Maxwell (great-grandson of the forfeited earl of Nithsdale) and added to by his grandson, also William Constable-Maxwell, who had the Herries barony revived following a House of Lords decision in 1858. (By kind permission of the Ewart Library, Dumfries)

The gardens of Terregles House, which were an outstanding example of the growing fashion for embellishing the surrounds of the larger mansions. Latterly they were allowed to run to seed, and isolated bits of stonework are all that remain. (By kind permission of the Ewart Library, Dumfries)

Examples of Georgian mansions

(By kind permission of the Ewart Library, Dumfries)

Dalswinton (as it was), which was built for Patrick Millar shortly after he acquired the estate in 1785.

Knockhill, Ecclefechan, which was built for Andrew Johnstone on his return from banishment to the West Indies for supporting the Jacobite rebellion.

Rammerscales, which was built at the direction of Dr James Mounsey in 1768.

Jardine Hall, Lockerbie. The original part was built in 1814 and later much enlarged. It was demolished in 1964.

Sanquhar and Kirkconnel Collieries – at the pithead. (By kind permission of the Ewart Library, Dumfries)

Sheep shearing (By kind permission of the Ewart Library, Dumfries)

Examples of nineteenth-century mansions

(By kind permission of the Ewart Library, Dumfries)

Crawfordton House, Moniaive, was built between 1863 and 1866 for Col. George (later Sir George) Walker MP and designed by Peddie & Kinnear.

Capenoch, Penpont. The original house, which dates from the late eighteenth century, was greatly enlarged by T S Gladstone during the 1850s according to a design by David Byrne.

Friars Carse. The original house, which dates from the early 1770s, was converted into a design by James Barbour whose firm, James Barbour & Bowie, was responsible for the further additions made in 1909.

Castlemilk. Designed by David Bryce for Robert (later Sir Robert) Jardine MP, the builder work was started in 1864 and completed in 1870.

Therefore, regardless of the fate of the fifteen hostages he had been obliged to surrender against his continuing loyalty,* Maxwell joined Douglas in an attack on Lennox's army at Dalswinton as it was heading south. But they were put to flight. Douglas himself, the abbot of Sweetheart, Christie Irving of Bonshaw and an unnamed brother of Charteris of Amisfield were among the prisoners taken, although Maxwell himself escaped.[51] Douglas also escaped soon afterwards having bribed his gaolers, clearly unaware of who he was, to release him. Following his success Lennox headed for Dumfries. There, on Somerset's orders, he executed some of the hostages given up by the defecting lairds (the rest were hanged at Carlisle), while his troops looted the town. Soon afterwards Arran, true to his word, consented to Maxwell's marriage to Agnes Herries. This took place in early 1548, she being fourteen while he was about thirty-six.[†]

The same year, in an act of barbarism typical of the time, the lairds of Mouswald, Kirkmichael, Kirkconnel and Logan, and other landowners, were killed by a raiding party of Grahams, stigmatised as 'sum theves of the marche'. The laird of Mouswald was Simon Carruthers. Since his daughters Janet and Marion were under age, Arran granted their wardship and marriage to James Douglas of Drumlanrig. Some years later, when they came of age, Douglas tried to force them to sell their shares of Mouswald to him on the grounds that, because it 'lay in very trublous country', it needed his protection. Whereas the more pliable Janet agreed, Marion refused. Instead she tried to safeguard her share by assigning it to her maternal uncle Charles Murray of Cockpool. Douglas tried to persuade Marion to revoke the assignation but she remained obdurate.

Shortly afterwards she died in mysterious circumstances when it was given out that she had hurled herself to her death from the battlements of Comlongan castle. This was because a suicide's lands and goods automatically escheated to the crown. Furthermore Douglas contrived to have her assignation to Charles Murray revoked on the grounds that it had been nullified by her subsequent suicide. Consequently Marion's half share fell into the crown, and at Douglas's insistence it was granted to his eldest son William Douglas of Hawick. Douglas's claim that Marion committed

---

* Fourteen of them were summarily hanged, Maxwell of Terrauchtie alone being spared on account of his youth. Remorse for his betrayal of the hostages is one of the reasons traditionally advanced for the name Repentance Tower given to the keep which Maxwell built on top of Trailtrow Hill adjacent to Hoddom. Alternatively, and perhaps more realistically, he is thought to have built it in repentance for using stones from the ruins of the still consecrated chapel at Hoddom for building the castle (see *NSA* IV (Cummertrees), 250).

† Following his marriage, John Maxwell acquired Agnes's one-third share of the Herries inheritance. A huge access of lands, it comprised the baronies of Terregles, Kirkgunzeon and half of Ur, as well as the lands of Hoddom, Ecclefechan, Warmanbie, Scales, Tundergarth and Hutton, and part of Lockerbie, Morton, Evandale and Moffatdale (*RMS* IV, 405). In 1552 John Hamilton, Agnes's unsuccessful suitor, acquired the shares of her two sisters – Catherine who married Alexander Stewart younger of Garlies, and Janet, subsequently the wife of Sir James Cockburn of Skirling. Ten years later, Hamilton sold them to Maxwell who in 1566 was granted a crown charter amalgamating all the Herries lands into the single barony of Terregles (*RMS* IV, 1728).

suicide was a fiction designed to secure her share of Mouswald, because he almost certainly had her murdered. True or not, the fact remains that Mouswald was absorbed into the barony of Drumlanrig.

Meanwhile Lennox and his army remained in occupation of Dumfriesshire where they continued their campaign of devastation, concentrating in particular on the Maxwell lands. By the following summer the situation had become so desperate that John Maxwell was compelled to appeal to Arran for help, claiming that in spite of being reduced to beggary the people had been prepared to endure it rather than give themselves up, but this could not continue indefinitely. Therefore, he went on, unless help was forthcoming they would be forced to surrender and swear allegiance to the king of England.

Appreciating the gravity of the situation, Arran led a force to the south-west in person. They captured Langholm, the garrison having surrendered after only seven shots were fired. This was intended as a prelude to recovering the other two castles which had been re-taken by the English following John Maxwell's defection to the Scots. But at that point Arran had to abandon the campaign to help the newly arrived French expeditionary force in laying siege to Haddington. Consequently Lennox remained in occupation of Dumfriesshire. But the severity of the following winter, and the consequent lack of food, compelled him to withdraw with most of his army to Carlisle, leaving only a token force to guard the region. So the situation remained until June 1551 when, through French mediation, a peace treaty was concluded between the English and Scots.

This opened the way for a partition of the Debateable Land for which lord Dacre, the warden of the English west marches, had long been pressing. The Scots were amenable. Therefore in 1552 delegations were appointed to agree a boundary line, the French king having at their joint request appointed M de Lansac as mediator. It was agreed that the march should run more or less due west from the Esk, just below its confluence with the Liddel Water, to the Sark which it was to follow down to the Solway, the line between the Esk and the Sark to be marked by an earthwork known as the Scots' Dyke which is still identifiable. Because the Debateable Land was regularly used as a haven for fugitives from justice from both countries, its division removed a long-standing bone of contention between the English and Scottish wardens, although it was not until the following century that the region was brought fully under control.

THE REFORMATION

Mary of Guise's regency augured badly because her close ties with France and her reliance on the French troops to shore up her regime made her extremely unpopular. So much so that in early 1555, within months of her assuming power, Parliament was prevailed on to pass an Act making it a punishable offence to speak evil of the queen regent and the French. Yet, in spite of being a devout Catholic, she was prepared to be tolerant towards the Protestant reformists – at least to begin with, offering sanctuary to refugees from the persecution under the English queen Mary Tudor. Furthermore, in the autumn of 1555 she allowed John Knox,* who had fled from England to the safety of Geneva, to return to Scotland. But the following year he overstepped the mark by issuing a letter demanding that she embrace reformism. This so infuriated her that, fearing retribution, Knox returned to Geneva. Yet Mary's tolerance of the reformists opened the way for a growing number of people to convert to Protestantism with impunity.

A notable example was Alexander Stewart, younger of Garlies.† He had spent time in England as a hostage for his father Sir Alexander, who was among those released by King Henry as an assured Scot. While there, the younger Alexander came under the influence of Lutheran preachers who persuaded him to convert to Protestantism. Therefore, on his return to Scotland, he was determined to spread the gospel of reformism. Since his family owned nearby Dalswinton he attempted to proselytise the burghers of Dumfries. To assist him, he enlisted the services of William Harlow, a Protestant lay preacher from Edinburgh. However, in October 1558 Harlow went too far by denouncing mass as rank idolatry. This earned him a sentence of outlawry as well as putting a temporary check on Alexander Stewart's missionary activities.[52]

Meanwhile, aware of the poor regard in which the Church was held, and the growing pressure for reform, an influential section of the clergy addressed themselves to the more pressing grievances. According to a declaration by the Provincial Council of 1549, they perceived one of the main causes of heresy as 'the corruption of morals and profane lewdness of life' among churchmen of all ranks. Therefore, in an attempt to redress the situation, the Council issued a number of edicts which were directed against 'the incontinence of the clergy, their intemperance and negligence'. One in particular forbade senior churchmen from providing for their illegitimate children out of church revenues. Other edicts were designed to ensure that priests were capable of reading and expounding the scriptures, while bishops and parsons were enjoined to preach in person at least four times a year. Hardly an onerous obligation!

In 1556 a report detailing the abuses which were responsible for the spread of reformism was submitted to Pope Paul IV, coupled with a strong recommendation for remedial action. Unfortunately he was the wrong man in the wrong place at the wrong time. As well as being the oldest pope of the sixteenth century (he was eighty),

---

* Now in his early forties and a native of East Lothian, he had been ordained a priest but became a disciple of George Wishart instead. After the latter's martyrdom he was persuaded to become a preacher himself when he denounced the Pope as Antichrist and the Roman Church as the 'synagogue of Satan'. Consigned to the galleys after the fall of St Andrews, he was released in February 1549 and settling in London he was appointed a royal chaplain and preached before Edward VI and Archbishop Cranmer. Surprising though it may seem, the latter offered him the appointment of bishop of Rochester which he declined. However, fear of persecution under the Catholic Mary Tudor caused him to take refuge in Geneva where he came under the influence of John Calvin, and it was his brand of Protestantism that Knox introduced into Scotland.

† He was married to Katherine, one of the Herries co-heiresses.

he was by far the most terrifying, and reportedly took a special delight in the Inquisition. As it was said, 'in his intolerance, his bigotry, his refusal to compromise, or even to listen to opinions other than his own, he was a throwback to the Middle Ages'.[53] Predictably the report fell on deaf ears.

In any case it was too late; the damage was done, and events were moving towards a crisis. In March 1557 a group of reformist lords who were planning to instigate a Protestant rising wrote to Knox urging him to return to Scotland and assuring him that the faithful would come out in his support. However, on second thoughts they decided it was too premature. Therefore when Knox reached Dieppe he was enraged to find letters from them advising him to remain there until the time was more propitious. In December the reformist lords and other like-minded members of the nobility formed themselves into a band. Calling themselves the Congregation of Christ, they drew up a covenant demanding the establishment of the reformed Church in Scotland. Later, styling themselves the Lords of the Congregation, many openly associated themselves with Protestant preachers, some even retaining them as members of their household. At the same time they enjoyed widespread support. But so long as Mary of Guise remained at the helm, and French troops effectively controlled the country, there was little they could do except wait upon events.

The following year the Lords of the Congregation presented a series of 'articles' to Mary of Guise. Referring to the ungodly and dissolute lives of the clergy, and the failure of the Provincial Councils to correct them, they called for curates and vicars to be better educated. They further demanded that the sacrament be administered in English,* and similarly the Book of Common Prayer and the Liturgies. Mary of Guise passed the articles to Archbishop Hamilton who summoned another Provincial Council to discuss them. Convened in early 1559, it went some way towards meeting the Lords' demands – namely, that there should be improved supervision of parishes and the private lives of their priests who were to be properly qualified to preach. But that was as far as they were prepared to go, because they refused to allow the sacrament to be administered in the vernacular, and similarly the Book of Common Prayer and the Liturgies. But it was too little too late; the time for tinkering was long past, for the winds of change were approaching gale force.

Meanwhile it was arranged that the marriage of Queen Mary and the dauphin Francis should take place in April 1558. The previous December, at the request of the French king Henry II, Parliament appointed eight commissioners to go to France to negotiate a marriage treaty. Notwithstanding French promises that Scotland would remain a separate nation state, the Scottish people viewed the prospect with alarm. They would have been even more alarmed had they known that, on the eve of her marriage, Mary was induced to sign a secret document. In terms of this she bequeathed the Scottish crown to whoever was king of France at the time of her death, were she to die childless. Apart from being extremely ill-advised, it was potentially life-threatening because it

---

* Presumably meaning Scots, which although broadly similar to English was in fact a different language.

would have given the French every incentive to have her, or any child of hers, murdered. But as a susceptible fifteen-year-old she could hardly be expected to be aware of the implications. The marriage took place on 24 April in Notre Dame Cathedral and was attended by the eight Scottish commissioners. Only four of them returned, the others having mysteriously died in France. It may have been coincidence; but it could be that they got wind of the secret document and had to be silenced.

In November the English queen Mary Tudor died and was succeeded by her Protestant half-sister Elizabeth. This gave an enormous stimulus to the reformers in Scotland, for it meant they could now look to England for help and support. Queen Elizabeth was all the more sympathetic towards them because the young Queen Mary, doubtless at the prompting of her father-in-law Henry II of France, had publicly subscribed to the Catholic view that Elizabeth was a bastard,* that she was not entitled to the English throne, and therefore it was rightfully hers as next in line.[†] To compound the offence, Mary and her husband Francis began styling themselves king and queen of England, Scotland and Ireland, and to emphasise the fact Mary quartered her royal arms with those of England.

Meanwhile Queen Elizabeth's accession, combined with pressure from King Henry of France, persuaded Mary of Guise to adopt a harsher line towards the reformers. Hitherto her policy of tolerance and compromise was intended to undermine, or at least embarrass, the Catholic Mary Tudor's regime in England. But now that the change of regime had rendered this pointless, there was nothing to prevent her from cracking down on them. As Knox put it, she began 'to spew forth and disclose the latent venom of her double heart'. Not for nothing was he described as having 'an unbridled licentiousness in speaking, mixed with a virulent frenzy of words'![54]

Following Queen Elizabeth's accession, Knox decided that he could safely return to England. But he blew his chances with the publication of his treatise 'The First Blast of the Trumpet Against the Monstrous Regiment of Women'. Far from conjuring up a stirring image of serried ranks of marching women, it referred more prosaically to the unnatural (monstrous) rule (regiment) of women. It further declared that it was contrary to the law of God and nature 'to promote a woman to beare rule, supe-rioritie, or dominion [over] any Realme, Nation or Citie'. Although it was written during the reign of Mary Tudor, and was primarily directed against her, Elizabeth saw it as an attack on herself. To compound the offence, Knox declared his refusal to recognise Elizabeth's sovereignty unless she acknowledged that she was queen by special dispensation of God, and not by any law of man.[‡] This was going too far and Elizabeth banned him from entering England.

---

*   This was because in their eyes Henry VIII's marriage to Katherine of Aragon (Mary Tudor's mother) was never annulled, and therefore it followed that his marriage to Elizabeth's mother Anne Boleyn was bigamous and that Elizabeth was illegitimate.

†   Through her grandmother Queen Margaret Tudor who was Henry VIII's elder sister.

‡   Later he wrote to the queen grudgingly conceding that if she humbled her heart she could yet prove exceptional, comparing her to the blessed Deborah in Israel – a piece of presumption to which the queen not unnaturally took grave offence!

Consequently he sailed for Scotland, informing the queen's secretary William Cecil that 'England in refusing me refuseth a friend'. Had he been granted asylum in England, the Reformation in Scotland might have followed a very different course. Arriving at Leith on 2 May 1559 he found himself plunged into the middle of a crisis. Mary of Guise's hardline attitude towards the reformers, and the consequent extinction of all hope of reaching an accommodation with them, had led to mounting tension. The crisis came when she summoned a number of Protestant preachers to Stirling to stand trial for sedition. But, publicly defying her authority, they took refuge in Perth.

Arriving there on 11 May, Knox made straight for the burgh kirk of St John the Baptist where he preached a sermon 'vehement against idolatrie' before a packed congregation. After he left the church a priest began to say mass, and when a boy tried to interrupt him the priest gave him a well-deserved clout on the ear. Retaliating, the boy threw a stone at him but missing him it shattered an image instead. At this a riot broke out and the congregation proceeded to smash the church ornaments and furnishings. Then, pouring outside they were joined by the assembled rabble – the 'rascall multitude' as Knox called them, and together they proceeded to ransack the houses of the Black and Grey friars as well as that of the Carthusian monks.

Determined to prevent further outrages, Mary of Guise sent a force of mainly French troops to Perth. But they were opposed by many of the nobility and their followers, some of whom sympathised with the reformers, while others were resentful of Mary's reliance on the French. Hearing that the earl of Glencairn had arrived with reinforcements from the west in support of the insurgents, she was forced to temporise and sent the earl of Argyll and lord James Stewart (an illegitimate son of James V) to parley with them. Consequently a truce was declared, and Mary of Guise promised a general amnesty and liberty of worship, while undertaking not to garrison Perth with French troops. But when she was deemed to have broken it by using Scottish troops in French pay, Argyll and lord James defected to the insurgents.

Meanwhile the 'rascall multitude' went on the rampage. Having pillaged the friaries at Perth, they went on to sack the religious house at nearby Scone. Then, crossing the Tay they extended their iconoclasm to the ports of northern Fife, eventually reaching the Protestant centre of St Andrews. Here on 11 June Knox, who had joined them, preached one of his electrifying sermons. Galvanised by this, the insurgents continued their trail of destruction, vandalising the churches at Stirling and Linlithgow as they headed for Edinburgh. Here the Council, fearing for the safety of the church of St Giles, hired sixty men to protect it.

By the end of June there was a stand-off. While the army of the Congregation, as the insurgents and their fellow reformers called themselves, controlled Edinburgh, Mary of Guise and her mainly French troops were in possession of Leith. This gave them the advantage because it meant they could take delivery of supplies and reinforcements coming by sea from France. On 7 July Knox was installed as the first Protestant minister of St Giles cathedral, and in October the army of the Congregation set up its own provincial government which unilaterally stripped Mary of Guise of the regency. She and her French troops retaliated by driving the army of the Congregation out of Edinburgh. Consequently they withdrew to Stirling where Knox delivered a series of rousing sermons to raise their morale.

They appealed to Queen Elizabeth for help. Hitherto she had confined herself to having small sums of money smuggled to them, but because much of it was intercepted only a small proportion actually reached them. Now the situation had changed. In July 1559 King Henry of France was killed in a jousting match and Mary's husband Francis became king. Since Mary had publicly laid claim to the English throne, Elizabeth feared – with good reason – that she and Francis were about to invade England to enforce it. Therefore, for her own protection, and because she had nothing to lose by it, she gave the reformers her unqualified support.

In January 1560 she sent a fleet to blockade the Forth in order to prevent French reinforcements from reaching Mary of Guise's troops at Leith. But it was driven off with heavy losses. Undaunted, Elizabeth went further. The following month she sent the duke of Norfolk to Scotland to negotiate a treaty with the reformers. This culminated in the treaty of Berwick which was concluded in February 1560. It provided that, in the event of the French attempting to annex Scotland, Elizabeth would take it under her protection and send English troops to help stiffen the Scots' resistance. In return, the reformers promised that if the French were to invade England they would reciprocate. Finally it was stipulated that the treaty should last for the duration of the marriage of Francis and Mary, and for one year thereafter. Because Elizabeth could not countenance a rebellion against a fellow sovereign (which effectively was what the reformers were doing), she demanded that they declare obedience to their queen and her husband the king of France.

In late March, Elizabeth sent a force to lay siege to Leith. The French garrison put up a stout resistance, but when they were reduced to near starvation the English besiegers offered them terms. However, informed that the English were also running out of supplies, Mary of Guise broke off negotiations and ordered the garrison to hold out. Meantime the ground was cut from under her feet by political upheavals in France,* as a result of which she could no longer count on French reinforcements. Instead, the new French regime was prepared to come to terms with the English. Accordingly they sent envoys, first to England and then Scotland, to negotiate peace terms. On 11 June while discussions were under way Mary of Guise died of dropsy, thus removing the last remaining obstacle to peace.

On 6 July a tripartite treaty was concluded between the French commissioners, representatives of Queen Elizabeth, and the Scottish reformers.† Known as the treaty of Edinburgh, it provided for French recognition of Elizabeth's right to the English throne and stipulated that all foreign troops, French and English, should be withdrawn

---

* This was the toppling of the existing regime which was dominated by her brothers François duc de Guise, Claude duc d'Aumale, Charles cardinal of Lorraine, and René marquis d'Elboeuf.
† Technically the treaty was between the English and French, because the French commissioners contended that their king and queen could not conclude a treaty with their own rebellious subjects.

from Scotland. Further, Mary and Francis were to abandon their claim to the English crown, while Mary was to cease quartering her arms with those of England. Additionally certain 'concessions' were granted to the Scots to settle purely Scottish questions. They included a stipulation that no Frenchman was to hold office under the crown; there was to be a general act of oblivion (i.e. an amnesty for all illegalities committed by the reformers), and that a Parliament was to be summoned the following month. Finally the French guaranteed that Francis and Mary would ratify the summoning of Parliament to render it a properly constituted body,[55] which in the event they never did. Yet the treaty was silent on all matters to do with religion.

Anxious to consolidate their success, and unwilling to wait for ratification of the treaty by Francis and Mary (well knowing they would drag their feet), the reformers unilaterally convened a Parliament. In order to convert political success into religious victory, Knox and his colleagues arranged for it to be packed with their supporters. Therefore when it met in August 1560 it was attended (with questionable legality) by over a hundred lesser barons and lairds, all committed Protestants. With their support, the Parliament proceeded to abolish the authority and jurisdiction of the pope, and all bishops and priests acting in his name. It also approved a Confession of Faith (a full statement of Protestant doctrine), and condemned all doctrine and practice to the contrary. Finally it commissioned the drawing up of a Book of Discipline to serve as a blueprint for the reformed Church in Scotland. This was submitted to a convention of nobles in January 1561.

A comprehensive document, it prescribed the new form of worship and set out the procedure for appointing office-holders such as ministers and superintendents, while making provision for their remuneration. Emphasising the importance of establishing a system of universal education, it stipulated that a schoolmaster was to be appointed for every parish, that colleges of further education be established in each of the principal towns, while Edinburgh, Jedburgh and Dumfries were to be upgraded to diocesan centres. The programme was to be funded by applying the possessions of the old Church, including its rents and other revenues, 'for the servants of the reformed Church, and for the relief of poverty'. Further, the Book of Discipline called for the abolition of the traditional Church festivals and the destruction of all abbeys, priories and other institutions. That at least was the intention. But, because the reformers lacked the means to build new churches, they were compelled to use existing ones having stripped them of all ornamentation to render them compatible with their austere form of worship.

Unlike the Confession of Faith, which Parliament seems to have passed more or less on the nod, the Book of Discipline encountered a rougher passage. When it was submitted to the convention of nobles,* many were reluctant to sanction the transfer

---

* They included John Maxwell. He continued to be styled the master of Maxwell as tutor to his nephews, Robert seventh lord Maxwell (who died aged four in 1554) and John eighth lord Maxwell, the sons of his brother Robert the sixth lord, who died in 1552.

of existing church lands and properties, in which many of them had an interest, to the reformed Church. Eventually a compromise was reached whereby bishops, abbots, priors and others were allowed to retain two-thirds of their existing revenues for life,[56] while the remainder – known as the 'third of benefice' – was to be shared between the reformed Church and the state. That at least was the theory. But because the third of benefice proved difficult to collect, the reformed Church remained seriously underfunded and would remain so for some time to come.

The convention of nobles authorised the reformed Church to appoint superintendents,[*] ministers, deacons and other officials. Nevertheless, much of the old Church remained intact with its bishops, abbots, priors and priests continuing to hold office as before. Consequently there was – at least to begin with – an uneasy co-existence between the two Churches, though it was not to last. Meanwhile the reformed Church suffered from an inherent defect in that the Reformation Parliament, to which it owed its existence, was technically illegal because it was never ratified by Francis and Mary as king and queen. Moreover the treaty of Edinburgh was invalid because Queen Mary consistently refused to sanction it. In fact it was not until after her abdication that the earl of Moray gave retrospective assent to it as regent for her infant son James VI. But disregarding such technicalities, the reformers embarked on the challenging task of establishing their Church throughout the realm. Nevertheless political and financial constraints meant that the Reformation, and the establishment of Protestantism, in Scotland was a relatively bloodless affair compared with elsewhere in Europe. The real bloodletting would occur between the rival factions within the reformed (now Protestant) Church during the following century.

THE RULE OF MARY QUEEN OF SCOTS

In November 1560 Francis II, Mary's ill-favoured and surly husband, developed a virulent ear infection. After weeks of agony the sixteen-year-old king died on 5 December leaving Mary a widow just three days before her eighteenth birthday. Francis was succeeded by his ten-year-old brother Charles IX, and because he was under age his ruling powers were exercised by his mother, the formidable and sinister Catherine de' Medici, as regent.[†] Jealous of Mary's status and influence, she engineered her exclusion from the inner circle of the royal court, effectively forcing her to return to Scotland.

---

[*]   Roughly the equivalent of bishops, they were to be put in charge of each of the ten dioceses into which the country was divided under the new church polity, while they were given overall responsibility for supervising their constituent parishes. The main difference was that, unlike bishops who in the final resort were answerable to Rome, they were accountable to the general assembly as the supreme governing body of the Protestant Church.

[†]   Niece of Pope Clement VII, she was coincidentally one of the high-born European ladies put forward as a possible bride for James V.

Refused a safe conduct to travel through England, Queen Mary sailed for Leith where she arrived on 19 August 1561. Tall, elegant and graceful, she was to all intents a Frenchwoman with an imperfect command of Scots, having forgotten much of it during her thirteen years' absence in France. She was extremely attractive to men, and even Knox conceded that she had 'some enchantment whereby men are bewitched'. But at the same time she was a notoriously bad judge of character, with no practical experience in the art of government. Through time these failings became increasingly apparent and would eventually lead to her downfall.

The Scotland she returned to with its rude and barbarous people must have come as a severe shock to her after the refinement and luxury of the French court. To add to the gloom, she found Edinburgh wrapped in a sea fog which persisted for some days after her arrival. Her realm was remote from the rest of Europe, the climate raw and chilly, while the nobility living in their primitive castles and peel towers were generally a narrow-minded, uncouth and violent lot. Furthermore, as a devout Catholic she was extremely hurt and offended at being harangued by Knox, by his denunciation of her Church as anti-Christ, and herself as a Jezebel intent on pursuing idolatry and persecuting God's prophets and people. Nevertheless he did concede her authority as queen, although tactlessly comparing himself to St Paul suffering under the Emperor Nero!

For the first few years of her reign Mary's principal adviser was her Protestant half-brother lord James Stewart, who had been jointly responsible for governing the realm since Mary of Guise's death. Notwithstanding that he was one of the main architects of the Reformation, lord James took Mary's side against Knox and insisted on her right to hear mass in her private chapel. In return she rewarded him with her confidence. Thereafter up to the time of her marriage she allowed herself to be guided by this wise and sagacious counsellor who has been described as the best king Scotland never had. At his urging she sank her Catholic principles for the sake of reaching an accommodation with the reformers, and in 1562 as a mark of confidence she created him earl of Moray.[*]

The same year Knox visited the south-west for the purpose of 'planting kirks in the sheriffdoms of Dumfries, Galloway and Nithisdaill, and the rest of the West daills', to quote from the minutes of the fifth general assembly of the reformed Church. In the course of his visit he was due to preside at the election of a super-intendent to oversee the newly established Protestant congregations in the region. One of the candidates was Alexander Gordon, a brother of the arch-Catholic earl of Huntly[†] – surprisingly, because he combined the mutually exclusive functions of a lord of the Congregation with that of a bishop in the old Church having been appointed to the see of Galloway.

---

[*]   The title continues to be held by the descendants of his daughter and son-in-law, the latter being known as 'the bonnie earl of Moray'.
[†]   Their mother Margaret Lady Gordon was an illegitimate daughter of James IV.

Evidently Mary had her doubts about him, and meeting Knox by arrangement while she was out hawking near Kinross she raised the subject of Gordon's candidature. The ensuing dialogue is recorded in Knox's *Historie*:

'I understand', said the queen, 'that ye are appointed to go to Dumfries for the election of a superintendent for those parts.'

'Yes', replied Knox, 'they have great need of one, and so have some of the gentlemen there.'

'But', countered the queen, 'I fear that the bishop of Athens˙ would be superintendent.'

'He is one', replied Knox guardedly, 'who is put in [for] election.'

'If you knew him as I do', rejoined the queen, who obviously regarded him as an apostate, 'you would never promote him to that office, nor to any others within your Kirk.'

Prevaricating, Knox replied, 'Yet madam I am assured God will not suffer his Church to be so far deceived as that an unworthy man shall be elected.'

'Well' said the queen dismissing the matter, 'do as ye will, but that man is a dangerous man.'

In a rare tribute to her, Knox conceded that 'therein was the queen not deceived, for he had corrupted [i.e. bribed] most of the gentlemen not only to nominate him but to elect him'.[57]

Knox must have heeded the queen's warning, which was probably why he delayed the election of a superintendent. Since he was unable to be present at the meeting held for the purpose, he handed over the chairmanship to the master of Maxwell, now Sir John Maxwell, coupled one would imagine with a strict injunction that under no circumstances was Bishop Gordon to be elected. In the event the successful candidate was Mr Robert Pont, an eminently suitable choice, for in addition to being a man of considerable learning and a leading reformer he was five times elected moderator of the general assembly.[58]

Knox formed a high opinion of Sir John Maxwell, evident from his *Historie* in which he refers to a discussion he had with 'the master of Maxwell [on] divers matters', describing him as 'a man of great judgement and experience'. In fact, they seem to have developed something approaching a friendship, or at least a mutual respect. Not everyone agreed with Knox's opinion. For example, in August 1567 Sir Nicholas Throckmorton, the English ambassador to Scotland, reported that 'the Lord Herries [as he had become] is the cunning horseleech and the wisest of the whole [Maxwell] faction; but, as the Queen of Scots sayeth of him "there is nobody can be sure of him"'. As he went on, 'we have good occasion to be well aware of him [but] here among his own countrymen he is noted to be the most cautelous [wily] man of his nation'.[59]

---

* Actually archbishop of Athens, an honorary title given him by Pope Julius III in 1551 in consolation for the fact that, although elected by the chapter to the vacant archbishopric of Glasgow, the prize was snatched from him through the intervention of Arran who secured it for his half-brother James Hamilton.

Later, Maxwell and Knox fell out over the issue of two Protestant ministers who, in the queen's absence, forced their way into the Chapel Royal at Holyrood and tried to prevent the celebration of mass. Knox wrote to them approving their actions, but the Council judged his letter treasonable. Taking up the cudgels on the queen's behalf, Maxwell demanded that Knox apologise to her, to which Knox replied that there was no need to because the ministers were acting strictly in accordance with the Word of God. 'Well', said Maxwell, 'do as you wish, but I think you will regret it if you do not apologise to the queen.' 'I see no reason why I should', replied Knox, adding that 'I have never been opposed to her except in matters of religion, and I am sure you will agree that I cannot apologise for that.' When Maxwell went on to warn him that the actions of the ministers would be universally condemned, Knox replied to the effect that God would be on their side, which was what mattered. As he observed, 'Never again did he and Maxwell meet in such friendship as before.'[60]

In spite of Knox's efforts to establish reformism in the western dales, it was slow to take hold, particularly in the parishes to the east of the Annan. For example none of those in Eskdale had a Protestant minister until the following century. Even in 1574, more than ten years after the Reformation, fourteen parishes in eastern Annandale were still vacant or only filled intermittently. In fact the churches of Corrie, Redkirk and Trailtrow were the only ones to have a reformist minister. That this was a matter of concern to the authorities is evident from the minutes of the general assembly of 1602 which refer to the state of the churches 'quilk hes bein desolate continuallie sen [since] the Reformation of the religioun within this countrie'.[61] From the reformers' point of view the situation to the west of the Annan was more encouraging, for by 1568 most of the churches had a resident minister or at least a lay reader. The same was the case in Nithsdale where the vicars of eight of Holywood's dependant churches were converted to Protestantism along with their parishioners.[62]

In 1563 Mary went on a progress throughout the south-west to meet and be seen by her subjects and to indulge her passion for hunting. Details of her itinerary are available from the record of expenses kept by her French equerry in the course of the tour. Arriving at Ayr in early August, she headed south to Whithorn where she stayed at the priory. Returning by way of the Wigtownshire Machars, she reached Clary where she was a guest of Alexander Stewart younger of Garlies, notwithstanding that he was a leading reformer. Crossing the Cree, she headed for Dumfries, visiting Kirkcudbright and the nearby priory of St Mary of Traill on the way. From Dumfries she made for nearby Terregles where she was entertained by Sir John Maxwell. Then on to Drumlanrig where her host was James (now Sir James) Douglas,* and finally back to Edinburgh.[63]

Meanwhile there was pressure on her to marry and produce an heir. Her choice of husband was a matter of overwhelming concern to Queen Elizabeth who feared that if Mary were to marry into one of the leading Catholic dynasties in Europe it could

---

* According to the *Scots Peerage* vol vii, 123, he was knighted 'some little time before 22 May 1549'.

jeopardise her own position. Having toyed with the idea of putting forward her favourite, Robert Dudley earl of Leicester, Elizabeth decided on lord Darnley. Now twenty, he was on the face of it eminently suitable – tall,* personable, with some accomplishments, and in her view just the sort of man who would appeal to Mary. More to the point, although a Catholic himself he was not related to any of the main Catholic families in Europe. Therefore if Mary were to marry him it would not pose a threat to Elizabeth. At the same time she perceived him for the political lightweight he proved to be. Therefore, with the enthusiastic approval of his parents the earl and countess of Lennox, she sent him north to press his suit.

Elizabeth's Protestant advisers, on the other hand, disapproved. Although they persuaded her to change her mind it was too late; Darnley was already in Scotland. No sooner had he arrived there and presented himself to Mary than she took an immediate fancy to him, describing him as 'the lustiest and best proportioned long man that she had ever seen'. It was not long before the queen, throwing discretion to the winds, fell violently, recklessly and hopelessly in love with him. Regardless of the disapproval of her Protestant subjects, and in the face of the strongest objections on the part of her counsellors, none more so than the earl of Moray, who had consistently advised against it, she was determined to marry Darnley come what may. The ceremony took place on 29 July 1565 in the Chapel Royal at Holyrood. Not only did it cost her the support of her Protestant subjects, but it caused an irreparable breach with Moray who became one of her leading opponents.

Up till now Mary's reign had been generally successful thanks to the guidance of her principal advisers, Moray and Maitland of Lethington. But after this, things began to fall apart. Beneath his courtly veneer Darnley soon revealed himself as a spoilt, petulant and self-indulgent youth whose newly acquired status went to his head, while his arrogance caused widespread offence. Egged on by his parents the Lennoxes, he demanded the crown matrimonial and when the Council denied it he became sulky – the more so because the queen's love for him failed to survive the onset of pregnancy,† and she became increasingly cold towards him. Instead she began increasingly to confide in her Italian secretary David Rizzio. Jealous of the influence Rizzio was gaining over her, Darnley was readily inveigled into a plot to murder him. The outrage took place on 9 March 1566 when the conspirators, including Darnley, burst into the queen's private apartments, and dragging the unfortunate Rizzio into an adjoining room they stabbed him to death.‡

Although Mary made a show of reconciliation with Darnley, in reality she had come to loathe him, the more so as she developed a growing partiality for her loyal supporter the ruffianly James Hepburn earl of Bothwell, with whom she soon embarked on an adulterous relationship. In February 1567 Darnley contracted

---

* He is supposed to have been six foot four inches (1.93m) – four inches taller than Mary who herself was six foot (1.82m).
† She was carrying the future James VI, who was born on 19 June 1566.
‡ The spot is still marked by a regular application of red paint.

syphilis as a result of frequenting the Edinburgh brothels. He was moved to Kirk o' Field at the eastern edge of the city which was thought to be a healthier place to convalesce than Holyrood. In the small hours of 10 February the nearby residents were woken by a loud explosion when Kirk o' Field was blown up. But Darnley's body, which was found in the garden, bore evidence of strangulation thus betraying what the explosion was designed to conceal, namely that he had been murdered.

Because he had so many enemies who were happy to see him removed from the scene, there was no certainty as to who was responsible. Nevertheless the finger of suspicion pointed firmly at Bothwell, and when in an act of unbelievable folly Mary proceeded to marry him she was widely perceived as guilty by association. At the instigation of the earl of Lennox, Bothwell was tried for Darnley's murder. It was a charade. Witnesses were intimidated into giving false testimony, and as no evidence was led by the prosecution the jury acquitted him. They had no alternative. But it failed to convince, and because the prosecution's failure to lead evidence was widely known (Bothwell's enemies saw to that) he was popularly regarded as the perpetrator.

Meanwhile the overwhelming majority of the nobility, Catholic and Protestant alike, were horrified by Mary's disastrously ill-judged marriage. Before it even took place, many of them put their names to a bond pledging themselves to 'set the queen at liberty [from Bothwell]'. No sooner was the marriage solemnised than they were determined to have it dissolved. Some went further and called for Mary's deposition. Styling themselves the Confederate lords, and determined to secure her abdication, they raised an army. Mary and Bothwell withdrew to his castle at Dunbar where they too raised a force. When the two sides met at Carberry outside Edinburgh, Mary and Bothwell's men were quickly put to flight. Bothwell escaped to Shetland from where he took ship for Norway,* while Mary gave herself up to the Confederate lords.

Brought to Edinburgh in disgrace, and jeered at by the people, she was consigned as a virtual prisoner to the Douglas stronghold of Lochleven. On 24 July 1567 she was forced to abdicate in favour of her infant son James, and the following month the earl of Moray was proclaimed regent. Having achieved their objective, namely the queen's abdication, there was nothing to hold the Confederate lords together. Consequently they split into opposing factions. Whereas the extremists banded together under Moray calling themselves the King's party, the moderates, who were sympathetically inclined towards the queen, rallied to John Hamilton,† a younger son of the earl of Arran, and became known as the Marian party.

---

*   There he fell into the hands of the relatives of a Norwegian lady whom he had seduced under promise of marriage and then abandoned. They had him consigned to a Danish prison where he was kept in such appalling squalor that by the time he died in 1578 he had become insane.

†   Arran's eldest son James had been declared *non compos mentis*. Although he succeeded to the earldom on his father's death in January 1575, his brother John was responsible for administering the family estates. Later created marquess of Hamilton he died in 1604, while Earl James lingered on until 1609 when the earldom passed to his nephew, the second marquess.

In May 1568 Mary escaped from Lochleven and headed for Hamilton-controlled Clydesdale where she was joined by a number of loyal magnates including lord Herries, his nephew John eighth lord Maxwell, and Alexander Gordon bishop of Galloway. With the Hamiltons' assistance she raised a force of some 6,000 men, and learning that Moray was at Glasgow with an inferior force she advanced to meet it. When the two armies met at Langside, on the northern edge of Fenwick Moor, Moray outmanoeuvred Mary's troops and put them to flight. Seeing that all was lost, Mary fled south, her route allegedly taking her by way of Sanquhar where she spent the night before going on to Terregles. Here the Protestant Herries gave her sanctuary. While there, she made the fateful decision to flee to England, persuading herself that Queen Elizabeth would help her regain her throne. Accompanied by lord Maxwell and a small band of supporters, she went on to Dundrennan abbey where Herries's son, Edward Maxwell, was commendator. Here she spent her last night on Scottish soil before sailing for England.

Her arrival put Elizabeth in a quandary. Helping Mary regain her throne was out of the question, if for no other reason than it would alienate her Protestant subjects. Nor could Elizabeth risk allowing Mary to go to the Continent. For, if she did, there was every risk of the kings of France or Spain, or both, using Mary as a pretext for invading England. On the other hand, if she were to remain in England she would become the focus of every Catholic dissident in the kingdom. Moreover, the fact that she had never formally renounced her claim to the English throne added to the danger. Therefore Elizabeth's only course was to keep Mary in honourable confinement as her 'guest'.

With characteristic imprudence Mary allowed herself to be inveigled into a succession of failed Catholic plots against Elizabeth. Therefore, no longer treated as a 'guest', she was transferred to a succession of prisons where she was kept under increasingly rigorous conditions. But it was her implication in the Babington plot that sealed her fate. Convicted of treason she was sentenced to death, and with the utmost reluctance Elizabeth signed the warrant for her execution which was carried out at Fotheringhay castle on 8 February 1587. This tragic end to a life, once so full of promise, has so captivated future generations that Mary Queen of Scots has become one of the best-known characters in Scottish history.

ELEVEN

The Advent of Presbytery

THE MINORITY OF JAMES VI

On 29 July 1567, five days after his mother's enforced abdication, the thirteen-month-old James was crowned king at Stirling. In a ceremony which was designed to combine the old and the reformed Churches, the crown was placed on the infant king's head by Robert Stewart bishop of Orkney, while Knox preached the sermon. But the unity it was supposed to symbolise was soon fractured by the emergence of the Protestant King's party and the Catholic Marian party, of which a leading member was Mary's loyal adherent lord Herries, now a lapsed Protestant.

Within weeks of Mary's flight to England, the regent Moray launched a punitive raid on the south-west with the aim of stamping out all remaining support for her in the region. Having destroyed the strongholds of the Marian-supporting Gordons in the Dee valley, he moved on to Dumfriesshire where he ejected Thomas Campbell, another of the queen's supporters, from the abbacy of Holywood. From there he went on to Herries's stronghold of Terregles intending to demolish it. But when it was pointed out to him that Herries was already planning to pull it down, and that he and his men would merely be assisting the work, he left it alone.[1] Instead, he went on to Annan where the castle garrison surrendered and Edward Irving of Bonshaw was installed as keeper.[2]

Irving's allies the Johnstones also submitted to Moray, and because the young John Johnstone of that Ilk[*] surrendered his strongholds of Lochwood and Lochhouse they were spared. The Carruthers family were more intransigent. Notwithstanding that the elderly John Carruthers was one of the Border lairds summoned to Edinburgh in 1567 to advise Moray on how to establish 'universall justice and quietness' on the west marches,[3] he was a Marian supporter. Therefore his stronghold of Holmains was burnt.[4] Finally Moray abandoned his campaign and returned to Edinburgh. But he was back the following year when his army was quartered on Castlemilk. While there he held a court at Annan at which John Johnstone produced for trial those of his kindred who had not submitted, having been threatened with a substantial fine should he fail to do so.[5]

Meanwhile Herries went to England accompanied by the bishop of Ross to plead Mary's cause with Queen Elizabeth. Dissembling, she told them that she intended to

---

[*] Son of James Johnstone, younger of Johnstone (who predeceased his father) and Margaret Hamilton, daughter of John Hamilton of Samuelston, an illegitimate son of the first earl of Arran, he had recently succeeded his grandfather and namesake, John Johnstone of that Ilk.

summon the rebels (as she termed them) to account for their actions in deposing Mary. Furthermore, unless their answers were sufficiently convincing she promised to restore Mary to the throne, albeit under stringent conditions. This was pure spin because Elizabeth had already assured Moray that under no circumstances would she allow Mary to return to Scotland. Nevertheless, persisting in the charade, Elizabeth arranged for a tribunal to be set up to enquire into the circumstances of Mary's deposition. Held at York, it was attended by Herries and the bishop of Ross on Mary's behalf, by Moray in person, and the duke of Norfolk and others representing Queen Elizabeth. But Moray precluded further discussion by producing the so-called 'casket letters' – copies of highly incriminating letters which Mary allegedly left behind in Scotland and which 'proved' beyond doubt her complicity in Darnley's murder. Because the originals have disappeared there is some doubt as to whether the copies were genuine or, as seems more likely, forgeries designed to incriminate Mary. Elizabeth chose to accept them as authentic since they gave her a respectable excuse for detaining Mary in England.

Following the conclusion of the enquiry, Herries went to France. There he joined the earl of Arran whom Mary, arrogating the right to do so notwithstanding her abdication, had appointed governor. On their return to Scotland, Arran and Herries declared themselves regents for the absent Mary, claiming that because her abdication was invalid, having been obtained under duress, she was still queen. Moray gave them short shrift and had them arrested. Whereas Herries was imprisoned, the more pliant Arran submitted and promised to remain in Moray's allegiance. But, when he broke his promise the following year, he was imprisoned in Edinburgh castle where he would remain until February 1573.

In late 1569 a rebellion broke out in the north of England. Headed by the Catholic earls of Northumberland and Westmorland, the rebels' objective was to depose Elizabeth and place Mary on the throne as a preliminary to restoring Catholicism in England. Initially the rebellion looked serious enough to cause Elizabeth to send a 28,000-strong army north under the earl of Sussex to suppress it. He appears to have achieved this without difficulty, and by December the rebels were on the run. Many took refuge in Scotland, including the earl of Northumberland. However in August 1570 he was betrayed by Hector Armstrong of Harelaw with whom he had sought sanctuary. Arrested, he was handed over to the English who committed him to prison, and two years later he was executed. Westmorland, on the other hand, escaped to Flanders having forfeited both his earldom and his estates.

Meanwhile in April 1570, using a cross-border raid by a party of Johnstones, Scotts and Kers as a pretext, Sussex extended his campaign into southern Scotland. His aim was to hunt down the rebels who had taken refuge there, and destroy the keeps and castles of those who had given them sanctuary or otherwise assisted them. While he concentrated on the Border region and the south-east, a separate force under lord Scrope, the English warden of the west marches, invaded Annandale. Specifically his instructions were to lay waste to the lands of lords Maxwell and Herries, Sir Charles Murray of Cockpool, and others. He was also instructed to burn the townships of

Ecclefechan, Hoddom, Trailtrow, Ruthwell, Cockpool, Blackshaw, Bankend, Lochar and Locharwood – a task which he delegated to his subordinate Simon Musgrave.

On reaching Cockpool, Musgrave and his men were surprised by a force of Dumfries burghers under lord Maxwell who drove them back to Ruthwell. But it proved a temporary reverse, for when Musgrave counterattacked he forced Maxwell and his associates, including John Johnstone and lord Carlyle, to take refuge at Blackshaw. It proved no safe haven. Catching up with them, Musgrave laid siege to it, and while Maxwell and some of his confederates escaped to the fastnesses of the Lochar moss others were taken prisoner. As for the rest, Musgrave and his men chased them back to Dumfries, whereupon the burghers barricaded the gates. Foiled in their attempt to storm the town, Musgrave's troops harried the surrounding countryside. Meanwhile, recovering from their debacle, Maxwell, Johnstone and Carlyle mustered a considerable force, and when their troops encountered Musgrave's men as they were about to burn the settlements of Bankend, Lochar and Locharwood, they gave battle. But just as Maxwell and his associates were gaining the upper hand, Musgrave was rescued by the timely arrival of a force dispatched by Scrope from Cummertrees.[6]

Scrope too had been pursuing a campaign of destruction. Whereas some strongholds such as Kirkpatrick were burnt, others like the Irving stronghold of Bonshaw were blown up, while the castles at Annan and Hoddom were demolished. Joined by Musgrave and his men following their rescue, and with the aid of further reinforcements, the combined army made another attack on Dumfries. This time they were successful. In retaliation for the burghers giving sanctuary to the supporters of Maxwell and his associates, Scrope's men spent the next few days indulging in an orgy of destruction in the course of which they demolished Maxwell's castle.

Leaving behind them 'a blackness of ashes' as it was described,[7] Scrope's men extended their campaign of devastation up Nithsdale. Their immediate objectives were the Maxwell strongholds of Tinwald and Cowhill which they demolished, the rubble from Cowhill being used to build a new stronghold. Continuing up the Nith, they captured the Kirkpatrick keep of Closeburn and blew it up. Because the septuagenarian Sir James Douglas of Drumlanrig was a leading member of the King's party, Scrope ordered that his tenants and their lands be spared. But his clemency seems to have been misplaced. For in his account of the campaign submitted to the English Privy Council, Scrope reported that Douglas's tenants 'were as cruel against us as any others', suggesting that unlike their lord they were Marian supporters.

On 23 January 1571 the regent Moray was shot and killed by a Hamilton supporter, with the connivance of Archbishop Hamilton, in the streets of Linlithgow. This led to an outbreak of civil war between the king's men, supported by an English force sent by Queen Elizabeth, and the Marian party. Meanwhile, unable to agree on a successor to Moray, the leaders of the king's party sought her advice. On her recommendation they appointed the young king's grandfather the earl of Lennox. Given his record as an oppressor of the Scots, particularly those in the south-west, and a leading instrument of Henry VIII's 'rough wooing', his could hardly have been a more controversial – or indeed unlikely – choice.

Not surprisingly there was widespread opposition to his appointment, particularly from the Hamilton faction, which merely intensified the civil war. Fearing that it was getting out of hand, Elizabeth sent envoys to Scotland to mediate. A six-month truce was agreed, but no sooner had it expired than war was resumed. In April 1571 the king's men captured Dumbarton castle and took Archbishop Hamilton prisoner. Assuming that Queen Elizabeth would demand clemency, they took pre-emptive action. A court was set up at Stirling where he was subjected to a summary trial whose outcome was a foregone conclusion. Convicted of implication in the murders of Darnley and Moray he was, on Lennox's orders, hanged at the mercat cross.

Meanwhile Edinburgh was held by the Marians under the provost Sir William Kirkcaldy of Grange. By this time support for the absent queen was beginning to crumble as some of her leading adherents defected to the King's party. In late August the King's party held a Parliament at Stirling where Sir William Kirkcaldy and a band of Marians made a surprise attack on them in a bid to capture their leaders. In the ensuing fracas the earl of Lennox was killed by a Hamilton in revenge for ordering the archbishop's hanging, his death being witnessed by his grandson the six-year-old king, while another victim was the reformist Alexander Stewart younger of Garlies.

Lennox was succeeded by the elderly John Erskine earl of Mar.[*] Although reputedly a man of integrity, which was more than could be said for most of his peers, he sounds to have been rather a lacklustre character. Since he was not committed to either party, it was doubtless hoped that he would persuade them to sink their differences and work together under his leadership. As it was, he survived for little over a year, dying – under suspicious circumstances[†] – in October 1572. Following this, a convention of the estates was held in Edinburgh at which James Douglas earl of Morton, a forceful personality and acknowledged leader of the King's party, contrived to have himself appointed regent.

Nephew of Archibald Douglas sixth earl of Angus, and therefore a relative of the king, James Douglas was married to Elizabeth, the youngest of the three daughters of James Douglas third earl of Morton.[‡] Yet in spite of his wife Elizabeth being the youngest daughter, he succeeded to the earldom. This was the result of an arrangement which harked back to 1540 when James the third earl was prevailed on by James V (apparently under threat of death) to execute a deed entailing the earldom on him (James Douglas) with remainder to his elder brother David seventh earl of Angus and his male issue.[§]

---

[*]   Coincidentally maternal uncle of the regent Moray.

[†]   See Stephen, *History of the Scottish Church* ii, 117, where he observes that 'Mar's death was not free from suspicion'.

[‡]   The other daughters were Margaret, wife of James Hamilton, second earl of Arran, and Beatrice who was married to the now-deceased Robert sixth lord Maxwell and was the mother of the eighth lord.

[§]   See G Donaldson, *Scotland: James V–James VII*, 53. It is suggested that James Douglas (the future regent) paid King James handsomely for dictating his right of succession under the entail – yet another device that grasping king resorted to in his efforts to raise money.

Therefore when Earl James died in 1548 James Douglas succeeded as fourth earl of Morton.

Now approaching sixty he already had a long experience of government, having been appointed a privy councillor by the earl of Arran in the early 1550s. With the approach of the Reformation, and seeing which way the wind was blowing, he had become a reluctant convert to Protestantism and a less-than-enthusiastic lord of the Congregation. However, English backing for the reformers, guaranteed by the treaty of Berwick, encouraged him to give them his full-hearted support. Consequently he was a signatory to the Book of Discipline. Appointed chancellor in 1563, but dismissed by Mary three years later for complicity in Rizzio's murder, he was peripherally involved in Darnley's assassination the following year. As a Confederate lord he was present at the battle of Carberry, and later commanded the vanguard of the government troops at Langside; restored to power by Moray, he was reappointed chancellor in December 1568. An unattractive character by the sound of it, he is described as 'a man of the most boorish calibre [whose] greedy eyes in his florid face betrayed the essential cruelty of his nature, [while] his pudgy hands grasped avariciously at all the rewards and benefits which were his for the taking'.[8]

His immediate objective was to crush the Marian party. But rather than confront them head-on, he came to an accommodation with their Hamilton leaders (known as the pacification of Perth). In terms of this they were promised an amnesty for their past crimes and restoration to their forfeited estates, while they for their part undertook to abandon their support for Mary and recognise Morton as regent. Not all the Marian supporters were prepared to follow suit, one of them being Kirkcaldy of Grange who continued to hold out against Morton. Deprived of Hamilton support, the Marian party were unable to prevail against Morton, who eventually forced Kirkcaldy and his hardline supporters to take refuge in Edinburgh castle, their last redoubt. Confident in its impregnability and knowing that Morton lacked the means to take it, Kirkcaldy rejected all offers to surrender even on the most lenient terms. Morton appealed for help to Queen Elizabeth, who responded by dispatching a consignment of cannonry to Leith. Finally on 28 May 1573, after eleven days' bombardment, the Marians surrendered. Kirkcaldy was executed, while his associate Maitland of Lethington (Queen Mary's former secretary) cheated the headsman by taking his own life. Morton's position was now secure. Under his firm rule, and with his authority unchallenged, Scotland would enjoy a period of unaccustomed peace for the next few years.

THE EMERGENCE OF PRESBYTERY

The defeat of the Marian party paved the way for the emergence of the reformed Church as the authentic Church of Scotland. But this lay in the future. Nevertheless, a start was made in January 1572 when the regent Mar and members of the Council met a deputation of superintendents and ministers to agree a new form of Church polity. It culminated in the Concordat of Leith which established what was, in essence, a compromise between the old and the new Churches. Effectively a hybrid Church, it included bishops and archbishops, with the present incumbents continuing to hold office, as well as retaining two-thirds of the revenues of their benefices, for life. It also provided that the existing diocesan structure should remain in place, but that whenever a bishopric fell vacant the new incumbent, although nominated by the crown, would require the approval of a committee of ministers. Further, that superintendents were to have the same authority as bishops, but they would be subject in all spiritual matters to the general assembly.[9]

The arrangement was approved by Knox. But his days were numbered. In October 1570 he had suffered a stroke which had left him partially paralysed; barely able to walk, he had to be assisted into his pulpit. Yet once embarked on his sermon he could still preach with the same vigour and warmth of language as before. By August 1572 he had become too infirm to attend the general assembly, while his last public appearance was on 9 November when he inducted his successor to the Tollbooth Church in Edinburgh. Shortly afterwards he developed bronchopneumonia and died on 24 November – the same day that Morton was appointed regent. In spite of the popular image of him as a grim religious bigot, there seems to have been a pleasantly human side to him. This is evident from his devotion to his first wife and their sons, and his much younger second wife (coincidentally a relative of the king) and their children. He much enjoyed having a relaxing game of bowls after delivering his Sunday morning sermon,[10] and was well known for his hospitality. In that connection, the story is told how on the last occasion he was able to sit at table he ordered a hogshead of wine to be broached for his guests, urging them to drink as much as they could as he would not be there to finish it himself.[11]

During the early years of his regency, Morton, in conformity with the provisions of the Concordat of Leith, nominated new-style bishops to the episcopal sees as and when they became vacant. This, however, was subject to the approval of a committee of ministers, in effect the general assembly. Nevertheless these appointees were scathingly dubbed by the extreme Presbyterians as 'tulchan' bishops (a 'tulchan' was a look-alike calf stuffed with straw to induce a cow to give milk). This was because, in their eyes, these bishops were nothing more than dummies put there to milk the revenues of their benefices and divert the proceeds to the exchequer. At the same time Morton ensured that a portion found its way into his coffers at Dalkeith castle for the benefit of himself and his immediate family, including his illegitimate sons.*

Indeed he was notorious for his nepotism, of which his securing the lands and barony of Carlyle for his half-brother Sir George Douglas of Parkhead† was an example. This followed the death of Michael fourth lord Carlyle at the hands of a party of English raiders in June 1575. His heir was his granddaughter Elizabeth, the daughter

---

* Morton had no legitimate issue, because soon after their marriage his wife Elizabeth Douglas relapsed into insanity – evidently a hereditary taint in her family because her sister Beatrix, wife of the sixth lord Maxwell, was another victim. So too was their forebear Sir James Douglas of Dalkeith, father of the first earl of Morton.

† He was an illegitimate son of Morton's father, Sir George Douglas of Pittendreich, himself a younger brother of the sixth earl of Angus.

of his deceased eldest son William; but her right to succeed to the family lands and barony was challenged by her uncle Michael Carlyle. He claimed that he had bought them from his father, the fourth lord, who in return had issued him with a charter confirming it.[12] Then, to keep her out of the way, he had his young niece abducted and spirited away to England. However, ignoring her uncle Michael's claim, Morton requested the English Privy Council to order her return to Scotland, where he he had her placed in the wardship of his half-brother Sir George Douglas. Consequently he gained control of the lands and barony of Carlyle, including the castle of Torthorwald, along with the rents. Not only that, but to keep them in the family Sir George earmarked the young Elizabeth as a prospective spouse for his son James.[13]

When Michael Carlyle (the 'wicked uncle') died in 1585 his son and heir John Carlyle of Locharthur took up the cudgels in pursuit of his father's claim. However, in 1593, the Lords of Council ruled that the charter, allegedly conveying the lands and barony to his father, was a forgery. Therefore Elizabeth was confirmed as the rightful owner.[14] Since she was now married to Douglas of Parkhead's son James, the lands and barony of Carlyle accrued to him as her husband. When he was murdered in 1608 they passed to their eldest son James, who was styled lord Torthorwald. Unfortunately he proved a waster, and towards the end of her long life (she survived until the 1640s) Elizabeth witnessed the last remnant of the extensive possessions of her forebears sold or mortgaged to William Douglas of Drumlanrig.[15]

Meanwhile the arrangement established by the Concordat of Leith was not working properly, mainly because the officials responsible were finding it difficult to collect the Church revenues – a matter in which Morton had a personal interest! Therefore he appointed a collector-general with overall responsibility for enforcing payment, equipping him with the necessary powers. But the problem was that most of the Church's patrimony had already been disposed of, while much of the remaining revenues had been remitted or burdened with pensions. This meant that the third of benefice, to which the reformed Church was entitled, was correspondingly diminished. Therefore Morton attempted to cut costs by reducing the number of parishes through amalgamation, and by extension the number of ministers on the Church's payroll. It seems to have been successful, because the period from the 1570s onwards witnessed a steady improvement in the Church's finances.

This enabled the general assembly to increase ministerial stipends, causing some to aspire to greater sartorial elegance. Or so it would appear from a deliverance of the general assembly of 1574 which forbade ministers and their wives from decking themselves out in fine clothes, adorning themselves with jewellery and wearing silk hats. Instead it recommended that 'thair hail habit be of grave colour, as black, russet, sad gray, sad browne or sicklyke',[16] although it was not until 1609 that it became compulsory for ministers to wear a black gown when conducting worship.

In 1574 Andrew Melville, that stormy petrel who would dominate the early reformed Church, returned to Scotland. Now twenty-nine and renowned for his learning, as well as being an extremely forceful character, he was a younger son of an old-established landed family in Angus. Having spent five years in Geneva he had become a fanatical adherent of the Calvinist form of Protestantism with its quasi-democratic, non-hierarchical system of Church government in which all ministers were of equal status. Therefore he was determined to rid the Church of its bishops, abbots, priests and priors, and replace them with committees of ministers, later known as presbyteries. Each would have a chairman, officially a moderator, who would be elected annually and answerable to the general assembly.

More importantly – and controversially – Melville regarded the Church and state as two separate estates, with the former predominating over the latter; and this would set him on a collision course with the king. Nevertheless his policies led to a fundamental split within the reformed Church between those who favoured a limited form of episcopacy, as provided for by the Concordat of Leith, and the Presbyterian faction who abominated episcopacy in any shape or form. Through course of time, the gulf between the two factions would become so wide, and their mutual antagonism so bitter, that it culminated in the religious wars of the following century.

Meanwhile Melville dedicated himself to imposing his brand of Church polity on Scotland to the exclusion of any compromise with the old Church. Having turned down Morton's offer of a court chaplaincy, he was elected principal of St Andrews University – a prestigious appointment since it gave him an influential voice in the Church, as well as a permanent commission to attend the general assembly. At the same time he had himself co-opted as a member of the committee appointed to draw up the second Book of Discipline. Presented to the general assembly of 1578, at which Melville was appointed moderator, it called for the whole patrimony of the Church to be applied for the remuneration of ministers, the provision of schools, and the relief of poverty. It also demanded the abolition of the whole apparatus of the existing hybrid Church with its archbishops, bishops, priests and others, and their replacement by ministers.

Because the reformed Church had hitherto been a relatively unstructured organisation, with no representative body interposed between the general assembly and individual kirk sessions, the Book (reflecting Melville's influence) called for the establishment of presbyteries and synods. Taking its cue from his perception of the Church and state as two separate estates, it postulated the view that, because the Church derived its authority from God, it should predominate and that kings were subservient to it. Thus by extension ministers were entitled to pronounce on affairs of state from their pulpits, denouncing whomever they pleased (frequently the king), claiming that in so doing they were acting as the mouthpiece of the Holy Spirit. Indeed, so committed were Melville's spiritual successors to the concept of the Church's superiority over the state that, in the following century, they were prepared to fight to the death and commit all manner of atrocities in their efforts to establish what was in effect a theocracy.

Meanwhile Morton's position was coming under threat. Notwithstanding his venality and blatant nepotism, his harsh regime had delivered firm government with all forms of lawlessness mercilessly suppressed. Crucially he had maintained peace with England. On the other hand, he had alienated a powerful section of the nobility.

They included John eighth lord Maxwell who had fallen out with him and been dismissed from the wardenship of the west marches. He was replaced by Morton's nephew, Archibald Douglas eighth earl of Angus,* an ardent Presbyterian. Another leading opponent in the south-west was Maxwell's uncle and principal supporter, John Maxwell lord Herries.

Morton had made other enemies as well. His systematic debasement of the coinage had resulted in the impoverishment of a large – and bitterly resentful – section of the mercantile community. Finally in March 1578 the eleven-year-old king was persuaded to summon a Parliament for the purpose of ending Morton's regency. Sensing which way the wind was blowing, Morton voluntarily resigned office and was excluded from power. But not for long. Within three months, through a combination of cultivating the youthful James and building bridges with the more sympathetically inclined members of the nobility, he contrived to have himself reappointed to the Privy Council. He quickly came to dominate it, thus resuming the regency in all but name.

In September 1579 King James's cousin, the thirty-six-year-old Esme Stewart seigneur d'Aubigny, arrived in Scotland. A polished frenchified dandy, he gained an ascendancy over the impressionable young king who in the following year created him earl (and later duke) of Lennox. He quickly established himself as leader of Morton's opponents, and was responsible for summoning a Parliament in December 1580 at which Morton was charged with complicity in Darnley's murder. Morton was promptly arrested. Brought to trial, he admitted to having been consulted about it but strenuously denied further involvement. Nevertheless he was convicted, and on 2 June 1581 the sixty-five-year-old former regent was executed on the maiden[†] and his lands were forfeited.

Morton's principal accuser was James Stewart a younger son of lord Ochiltree.[‡] He had recently become one of the king's favourites, been appointed to the Privy Council, and risen to become Lennox's principal lieutenant. Finally in April 1581, notwithstanding that it already existed as a Hamilton title, King James created him earl of Arran. The same year he and Lennox were responsible for granting the earldom of Morton (as a new creation) to lord Maxwell, ostensibly because he was a grandson of the third earl but in reality as a reward for his support. (Later, in January 1586, in punishment for his Maxwell kinsmen's burning the Johnstone strongholds of Lochwood and Lochhouse, and the Irving stronghold of Bonshaw, the king stripped him of the title. Refusing to accept this, Maxwell continued to style himself earl of Morton, and so did his son the ninth lord after him.)

Morton's fall from power led to renewed friction between the Protestant reformers and the still powerful representatives of the Catholic Church. They included a number

---

* He was also a brother-in-law of Maxwell who was married to his sister Elizabeth.

† An early type of guillotine, this provided for a more efficient method of decapitation than exposing the victim to the erratic marksmanship of a headsman. The main drawback from the victim's point of view was that he was placed face upwards so that in the final split second he could see the blade hurtling down on him. Ironically Morton was responsible for introducing the maiden to Scotland.

‡ Ochiltree's daughter Margaret was John Knox's second wife.

of Dumfriesshire landowners – logically because, owing to the Maxwell influence, Dumfriesshire was one of the main centres of Catholicism in Scotland. Besides lord Maxwell, the leading Catholics included James Johnstone of that Ilk, Corrie of Newby, Edward Maxwell and Charles Murray of Cockpool, evident from the fact that between 1594 and 1601 sentences of outlawry were passed on them for attending Mass and allowing their children 'to be baptised and taught by Roman priests'.

Meanwhile the Catholics and the Protestant reformers were at loggerheads over the question of whether to enter into a defensive treaty with England against the perceived Catholic threat from France and Spain (favoured by the reformers), or follow the Catholic preference for seeking closer ties with these countries. Initially Lennox and Arran, being Catholics, supported the latter policy. But when the Spaniards sent a group of Jesuit priests on a proselytising mission to Scotland, it caused a popish scare, and Lennox and Arran were denounced as agents of the counter-Reformation. Therefore they were forced to backtrack, and in January 1581 they issued a manifesto known as the Negative Confession of Faith – negative because it denied all religion and doctrine at variance with the Protestant Confession of Faith, as well as denouncing the Church of Rome as anti-Christ. This was signed by the king, by all members of the court, and by Lennox (doubtless against his conscience); and by royal proclamation it was ordered to be signed by all classes of the community.[17]

This failed to convince the Presbyterians who were at loggerheads with the government over its refusal to endorse the decision of the general assembly of July 1580 formally condemning episcopacy. The assembly went further. Usurping the government's exclusive right to do so, it unilaterally deposed the bishops and forbade them from exercising their ministry. Retaliating, the government nominated its own candidates to episcopal vacancies. Therefore, when the archbishopric of Glasgow fell vacant following the death of Bishop Boyd, Lennox appointed Robert Montgomery, a minister at Stirling, as his successor. As Stephen observed, 'a poorer type of man . . . could hardly have been found'.[18]

Notwithstanding that his nomination was rejected by the general assembly, and in defiance of its inhibition, Montgomery turned up at Glasgow cathedral determined to assert his authority. But finding a service already in progress, he attempted to pull the officiating minister out of the pulpit by brute force until he was restrained by the church officers. Indeed, such was the controversy surrounding his appointment that, when the presbytery of Glasgow met to censure him for his misconduct, they were assailed by the Montgomery-supporting corporation and citizens. The report goes on to say that, in the ensuing fray, beards were pulled and teeth knocked out until the presbytery moderator was locked up in the tollbooth. In Edinburgh another encounter took place between presbytery and corporation. This time it was a different story, and Montgomery was expelled from the city, 'the men pursuing him with batons, and wives and boys pelting him with stones and rotten eggs'.[19]

Meanwhile there was mounting (and well-justified) suspicion that, despite his subscribing to the Negative Confession of Faith, Lennox was still a Catholic at heart.

Therefore a number of Protestant nobles, egged on by Queen Elizabeth, conspired to undermine his influence. In August 1582 they carried out a *coup*, known as the Ruthven Raid, when the king was decoyed to the earl of Gowrie's stronghold of Huntingtower, near Perth, and there held a virtual prisoner. When Arran tried to rescue the king he was captured and held prisoner along with him. Meanwhile Gowrie and his fellow conspirators took control of the government, and Lennox was banished to France where he died the following year.

In June 1583 King James managed to escape to the safety of St Andrews castle where he was joined by his supporters. Driven from power, the Gowrie conspirators were declared guilty of treason; and, banished from the realm, they took refuge in England while Arran, now released from prison, was appointed chancellor. But James's wrath was directed primarily against the Presbyterians, and in particular the general assembly. He had good reason. At its meeting, held in Edinburgh in October 1582 immediately after his seizure, it warmly applauded the actions of the Gowrie conspirators and ordered all ministers to commend it to their flock under pain of ecclesiastical censure[20] – a studied insult that would earn James's undying hatred of presbytery. Fortunately for him Melville played into his hands, for in a series of sermons he overreached himself, and when summoned to stand trial for sedition he refused to submit himself to the jurisdiction of the Council. Therefore, in March 1584, to avoid imprisonment, he fled to England followed by nearly a score of ministers.

The same year, in their absence, Arran caused Parliament to pass what the Presbyterians condemned as the 'Black Acts'. These asserted the king's supremacy over Church and state, denounced 'the new pretended presbyteries', and reaffirmed the authority of the bishops. They were followed by another statute which made it a punishable offence to preach sermons critical of the king and his advisers.

About this time there arrived from France a handsome and accomplished Scot, Patrick master of Gray,[*] who soon became a favourite at court, and of King James in particular. A devious and unscrupulous character, his immediate aim was to undermine Arran's influence by advocating an alliance with England as opposed to Arran's preference for a league with Catholic France and Spain. Therefore in October 1584 James sent him to London to enter into negotiations. While there, he secured the release of the Protestant nobles associated with the Gowrie conspiracy, who were allowed to return to Scotland. With their assistance he launched a *coup*, forcing Arran to take refuge in Stirling castle. Pursuing him there, Gray and his allies took the castle, but Arran had already escaped to the fastnesses of Ayrshire, and there he remained until he was murdered by Sir James Douglas of Parkhead in December 1595.[†]

Following this, a coalition which included Gray, John Maitland of Thirlestane (brother of Maitland of Lethington), and a number of Protestant lords, took control

---

[*] Born about 1557, he was the son and heir of the fifth lord Gray, whom he succeeded as sixth lord in 1608 and died in 1612.

[†] In revenge for his securing the downfall of Sir James Douglas's uncle the Regent Morton.

of the government. Acting on their advice, James annexed all remaining Church property to the crown. Arguing that former royal endowments made to the Church had left the crown so impoverished that the measure was necessary to avoid the imposition of additional taxes, he prevailed on Parliament to pass the Annexation Act of 1587. Consequently the crown acquired all the lands and superiorities belonging to the old Church and its institutions, the only exception being the parish manses and glebes. In the event this was of minimal benefit to the royal treasury, because James converted most of the lands into temporalities (effectively baronies) and granted them to members of the nobility as a means of bribing their support.[*]

Meanwhile the fugitive ministers, who would almost certainly have included Melville, followed the rehabilitated nobles back across the border. Foregathering at Dumfries, they attempted to hold a public meeting, but, probably at lord Maxwell's instigation, they were forcibly driven out of the town.[21] From there they moved on to Linlithgow where they learnt that they had been excluded from the new regime. Nevertheless Melville and his fellow extremists were determined to repeal the 'Black Acts'. Therefore in 1592 they persuaded the Presbyterian-dominated Parliament to pass what they termed the 'Golden Acts'. These effectively restored presbytery and abolished the ecclesiastical authority of bishops. Besides forbidding them to sit and vote in Parliament, the Acts stipulated that whenever an episcopal vacancy occurred it should be filled by a minister, while all Church festivals – or Holy days – were to be abolished.[†] But James was already planning a counterattack.

SIXTEENTH-CENTURY DUMFRIES

Dumfries had not grown significantly since the thirteenth century – at least judging from the conjectural plan of its layout in about 1270 compared with that of some three centuries later (see pages 296–7). The former shows the town centre, including the market place, as extending from the old castle (between the Academy and Castle Street) as far as English Street, then known as the Lochmabengate, with vennels leading off it. According to the speculative layout of about 1560, the town had expanded as far as the Nith on the west, roughly St Michael's Street to the south, and the (now underground) Lore burn on the east. At the northern end was a church (on the site of the present-day Greyfriars church) and its 'yard', and next to it the town house of the lords Maxwells, known as Maxwell's castle.

---

[*]   The Annexation Act was later repealed by the Perth Parliament of 1606. But it was a question of locking the stable door after the horse had bolted, for by that time the Church's patrimony had been almost completely alienated.

[†]   In that connection the story is told of how the burghers of Dumfries wished to celebrate Christmas (or 'fylthie Yuell' as the reformers described it). But forbidden to do so within the confines of the burghs, they trooped out in a body to the collegiate church of Lincluden where they could celebrate it without interference from the authorities (*Stephen, Scottish Church* i, 105–6). (This was probably a different occasion from lord Maxwell's celebration of Christmas at Lincluden referred to below.)

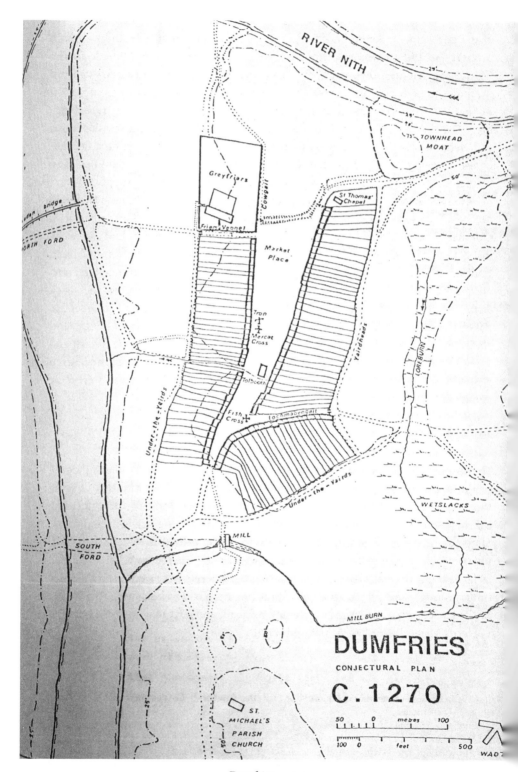

Dumfries c.1270

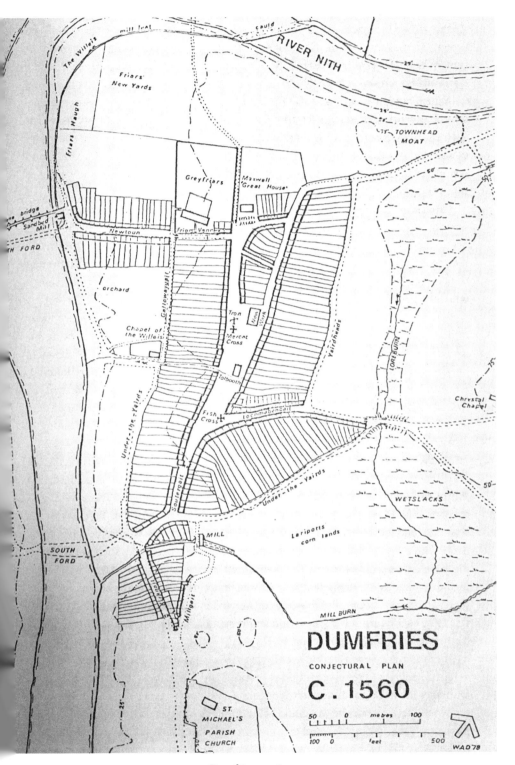

Dumfries c.1560

At that time Dumfries appears to have been a relatively affluent centre, mainly on account of its trade with the Continent, particularly France. Its merchants had representatives at Dieppe, Havre and Rouen, while its ships traded with places like Bordeaux which was a main source of wine.[22] Closer to home the merchants traded with the main Irish ports, and also the Isle of Man where they had another representative. Imports included cloth, clothing, furnishings, armour and weaponry, as well as agricultural equipment, while there is an occasional reference to the arrival of cargoes of soap and salt, and iron from Denmark (probably originating from the Åland Islands in the Baltic) and Spain. They would also have included a wide variety of foodstuffs ranging from luxuries such as raisins to more mundane corn.

Exports are not mentioned, but they probably consisted of the traditional Scottish ones of wool, woolfells, animal hides, and possibly herring although they were becoming less prolific in Scottish waters than in the past. In fact there is only one reference to them, when a certain John Edgar was accused of buying a consignment of herrings before they could be exposed for sale in the market – a serious charge which he strongly denied, although the outcome is not recorded.

References to lord Maxwell selling cargoes of salt to merchants, or more likely middlemen, in Dumfries suggests that he owned a ship himself and traded on his own account – a relatively common practice among the wealthier Scottish noblemen. On one occasion he sold a cargo of salt to Thomas Trustrie and Herbert Raining. Since there was not enough space in the warehouse to store both their shares, it led to a wrangle as to who should have priority. Evidently their argument ended in a brawl, and the matter came before the burgh court, which must have put Raining in an embarrassing position since he was a bailie.

That wine was habitually drunk by the well-to-do, and many others for that matter, is evident from the statutes issued by the burgh council from time to time stipulating the maximum price which merchants could charge for wine and ale. These were typical of the many statutes issued by the council regulating people's daily lives. Whereas some verged on the trivial, such as the stipulation that candles were to be 'sufficiently made with a small wick', others dealt with more important matters such as maintaining burgh cleanliness to which greater attention was paid than in the past. They included statutes requiring that middens were not to remain in the streets for more than twenty-four hours, and that 'fulzie' (human and animal excrement and the like) was to be cleared from the streets and vennels and carted out to the common land at least once every forty-eight hours.

These statutes were rigorously enforced. This is evident from the order issued to William Lanerick to remove a 'midden of muck and fulzie' from the back wall of John Quhinkerstane's house under penalty of eight shillings for every twenty-four hours it remained there. Clearly he was guilty of 'fly-tipping'. Another statute required that the main drain be kept unblocked at all times. In that connection John Maxwell and John McJoir were fined for not allowing 'the free passage of water (presumably sewage)' to the Nith, as they were obliged to do winter and summer. Similarly Thomas Paterson, probably a colleague, was ordered to clear 'the great drain without the west port' within twenty-four hours under threat of a fine if he failed to do so.

Such measures – and the penalties imposed for failure to observe them – were primarily intended to prevent the spread of disease, an ever-present hazard given the insanitary living conditions which prevailed in towns and burghs at the time. A common illness was 'le Quhew' probably whooping cough, although the term could have been applied to any pulmonary complaint, while another described as 'wame-ill' could refer to a number of conditions ranging from diarrhoea to dysentery to rectal or colonic cancer. Another was 'grandgore', or syphilis (significantly referred to as 'the French disease'), which was rife on the Continent, particularly (as its name implies) France. Brought to England by soldiers returning from military service it spread to Scotland, and although there is no record of it appearing in Dumfries it most likely did.

Most dreaded of all was the plague. When in 1549 it struck other parts of the country, the burgh council issued a series of measures in an attempt to prevent it from spreading to Dumfries (which fortunately it didn't). Whenever anyone fell sick, the bailies were to be notified forthwith so that a deputation could inspect the patient (no doubt at some risk to themselves) in order to determine (presumably with the aid of medical advice) whether he or she was a plague victim. If so, the patient was to be consigned to the isolation camp beyond the town wall. It was further provided that anyone exposed to infection, and therefore at risk of developing the disease, was to be confined to their house for fifteen days. Not only that, but if they had intercourse with any 'clean person' during that time they were liable to be put to death. If they survived the fifteen days without developing the disease they could be released; but only after their house had been thoroughly cleansed and fumigated 'by watter and fyre as has been usit in tyme bygone', to quote from the regulations.

There was a scare in October 1564 when the plague was rumoured to have struck Leith – not improbable since it could have spread from a visiting ship, although in the event it proved a false alarm. Nevertheless the burgh council issued a series of edicts for the protection of the people of Dumfries. They included a stipulation that guards were to be appointed to carry out a check on all travellers coming to the town, and only those who could produce a 'testimonial' from the magistrates of their home town certifying that they had not been exposed to infection could be admitted.

In 1597 plague broke out in the Borders. By the following year it had spread to Dumfries where it caused a complete dislocation of trade and a consequent food shortage. In fact, such was the resulting hardship that the burgh council was compelled to appeal to the Convention of Burghs for help. A pointless exercise as it turned out, because all it did was issue a pious injunction to seek Divine assistance, which must have been pretty cold comfort. In 1625 plague was raging in England. Therefore, to minimise the risk of it being brought to Scotland by those attending the annual fair at Dumfries, the event was cancelled by order of the Privy Council. This was followed by two further outbreaks – one in 1637 when a few cases were reported, and the other in 1644 when plague was brought to Scotland by soldiers returning from the siege of disease-ridden Newcastle. Nevertheless Dumfries escaped infection – but only just, because there was reportedly an outbreak as close at hand as Lochar moss.[23]

One of the most challenging, and indeed the most important, of the burgh council's responsibilities must have been maintaining law and order. In that connection a fascinating insight into contemporary burghal life can be obtained from the Dumfries Burgh Court Books.[*] Inevitably they are mainly concerned with brawls which ended up in court, for with people living in such close proximity to one another these would have been a regular occurrence. Some arose as a result of deliberate provocation. For example, John Tynding, a merchant and shipowner, and therefore a man of substance, was charged with stabbing Christian Maxwell's cow in the belly with his sword and killing it because it had broken into his yard. Herbert Maxwell was accused of slaughtering his neighbour's geese. On another occasion a fight actually broke out in the burgh courtroom when John Maxwell punched Stephen Palmer in the face and brained him with his keys. That the assault took place in open court was a particularly serious offence, although there is no record of the outcome.

Women were equally culpable, although their methods were rather more subtle. According to an entry of April 1579, Margaret Maxwell was ordered to appear in church the following Sunday and bring with her four of her nearest neighbours as character witnesses. This was so that they could swear before the congregation that she was innocent of sowing John Scott's yard 'at the stynkand vennel fute' with 'gouldseid' (a particularly obnoxious plant) and other weeds. She must have been unable to produce the neighbours, or perhaps they were disbelieved, because she was committed to the tollbooth to await trial, while her husband and others connected with the offence were ordered to get rid of the weeds. Since a man's yard (basically a smallholding) was where he grew cereal crops and vegetables, as well as keeping his cows, sheep, pigs and poultry – usually all he had to live on – adulterating it with weeds was regarded as a serious offence, and justifiably so.

Another miscreant was Jonet Kirkpatrick, who was convicted of pouring brewer's malt over lengths of cloth which Robert Rae and other stallholders were exhibiting for sale in the market place, and ruining them beyond redemption. But here again the records fail to divulge the punishment. That women were the victims of male attackers is evident from the case of George Fruid who was convicted of bruising and blooding Margaret Carruthers, for which he was sentenced to a spell in the stocks. More serious was that of Robert Morton who broke into his neighbour's property and demanded that the woman of the house tell him where her husband was, denouncing

---

[*] These are preserved in the local archives. Given the difficulty in deciphering contemporary handwriting, the aspiring historian owes much to the late Alfred Truckell who was responsible for transcribing the entries relating to the latter part of the sixteenth century. They are the subject of two articles which he contributed to the *Transactions of the Dumfries and Galloway Natural History and Antiquarian Society*, namely 'Dumfries Burgh Court Books in the Sixteenth Century' Part I (vol. lxxiii, 1999) and Part II (vol. lxxiv, 2000).

him as 'a naughty thief and a loon'. When she refused, he struck her several blows with a big stick leaving 'blaa straiks' (blue weals) which she was obliged to exhibit in open court. Then, having felled her with his stick, Morton went out into the yard and cut down her husband's fruit trees. Punishment was appropriately harsh; he was ordered to be put in irons or the stocks at the magistrates' pleasure.

There were cases of women becoming embroiled in an argument with members of their own sex – obviously a 'stairheid brawl'. For example Christian Montgomery had an altercation with Agnes Kent which culminated in Christian pelting her with stones and causing her severe injuries. They must have been serious because Christian was consigned to the dungeon beneath the tollbooth which served as the prison. Then it transpired that she was pregnant; but while in prison she suffered a miscarriage and was consequently released. However, it was suspected that the miscarriage had been deliberately induced by means of an abortifacient smuggled in to her by a visiting relative. Therefore she was summoned to appear before a jury of 'famous [i.e. prominent] men and women' to answer the charge that she had purposely engineered the miscarriage to secure her release. Since she failed to turn up she was ordered to be punished, but how is not divulged.

Another example of how quickly tempers could flare up is reported at some length in the Burgh Court Books. This occurred as a result of Nicol Newall's impatience at the length of time it was taking his tailor Martin Rawling to alter some clothes for him. A comparatively trivial matter one would have thought, and not such as to cause him to overreact in the way he did. According to Rawling's account, Newall descended on his booth while he, Rawling, was 'at gode's peace & the Kyngis' and tried to take the clothes away. But because Rawling had still to add the finishing touches he refused to let them go, whereupon Newall seized him by the throat, ripped the buttons off his coat, tore open his shirt, and 'would have slain him' but for the fortuitous arrival of Bailie Herbert Raining. Ordering Newall to desist, Raining commanded him to appear before the provost, bailies and council the following day, at which Newall slunk off muttering threats of vengeance.

They were no idle threats. Next day he returned to Rawling's booth accompanied by his nephews Archibald and Jamie Newall when they proceeded to belabour him with their clubs, causing him to turn tail and flee to the sanctuary of Bailie James Lindsay's house. But he never got there. Catching up with him and pinning him to the ground, Newall and his nephews continued to bludgeon him until some neighbours came to the rescue, and overwhelming them they relieved the Newalls of their clubs. Nevertheless the Newalls continued to hit and kick Rawling in spite of being ordered by Bailie Lindsay to desist, until finally they were dragged away. Brought before the magistrates, they were charged with committing 'great and manifest oppressions against Rawling' and disobeying the order of a bailie. They were released on bail of £100 each (an enormous sum), and ordered to appear before the provost, bailies and council at the tollbooth and submit to whatever punishment they thought fit.

That members of the cloth were equally vulnerable to attack is evident from the case of the Reverend Peter Watson, an early minister of the reformed Church in Dumfries. Although his appointment was endorsed by the burgh council, the fact that he was an incomer was widely resented, especially by Archie Newall (perhaps the same person as Rawling's attacker) who in the minister's absence broke into his house, denounced his wife Christian as a whore and threatened to 'cut ane lug [ear] off hir heid and cupill it to the Kirtill Taill'. For good measure he denounced her husband as 'ane myschaivit beist' and cursed them for being incomers. When the minister's sister tried to intervene Newall turned on her and, as Christian alleged, would have 'slane' her had not John Bryce come to her rescue. Newall fled the town. But the following month he was apprehended and consigned to the local prison in irons pending trial. Convicted of assault, he was sentenced to appear in the kirk on three successive Sundays (twice in his underclothes) to crave the pardon of the minister, his wife and sister. Which seems remarkably lenient in the circumstances.

While the burgh court records contain numerous cases of assault, there are very few involving sexual misdemeanours or adultery – probably because lack of privacy meant that it was virtually impossible to conduct a clandestine affair. In fact there is only one instance of the latter although it was never proved. It concerned an allegation by John Gledstanes that Thomas Gowdie had committed adultery with his wife. Since Gowdie was able to prove his innocence, Gledstanes accepted that his allegation be struck from the record – or, in the forthright language of the time, it was to 'be extinguisit & put on perpetuall oblivion'. Another case concerned Jonet Bell who claimed a sum of ten pounds Scots from Hector Rae, which he had promised her in compensation for 'defloring hir virginitie & getting ane barne with her'.

Other offences were more trivial, such as name-calling. An example was the complaint by Robert Maxwell that he had been stigmatised as an 'evill saul', while Adam Walker a flesher was accused of 'blasfemyng' the provost, bailies and judges of the town. Another involved a complaint by James Copland that Archie Newall (perhaps the same person mentioned above) had called him 'a knave and a loon in the tyme of the wappenschawing', adding for good measure that he (Newall) had refused to salute the provost when ordered to. Similarly Robert Murdoch, a tailor, admitted having told James McCaul in the presence of Bailie Herbert Raining that he was a treacherous deceiver, a thief and a loon – hardly the most opprobrious of insults one would have thought. Still it earned Murdoch a spell in the stocks notwithstanding that he claimed to have been drunk at the time. Finally there was the case of John Carruthers who was convicted of attempting to pass a counterfeit thirty shilling piece in the market, although once again details of his punishment are not recorded.

Punishment could range from incarceration in the stinking prison under the tollbooth, to a spell in the stocks where the miscreant was liable to have filth and muck flung at him by the self-righteous populace, to a fine, depending on the gravity of the offence. Banishment from the town was another, but it generally only applied in the case of vagrants. A case in point was that of Archie Maxwell, evidently a well-known troublemaker, who was described as a vagabond (itself an offence) with 'neither stob nor stake in the town', implying that he was an outsider. He was banished under threat that if he ever ventured back and caused trouble again 'his lug [would] be nailit to the tron [the public weighbeam]'.

Another instrument of punishment, which was mainly reserved for cases of cursing and swearing, or spreading false rumours, was the 'bracks'. It consisted of a headpiece which was clamped over the offender's head, and a sharp spike which was inserted into the mouth to prevent the tongue from wagging. As it was said, 'when husbands unfortunately happened to have scolding wives they subjected them to this instrument and led them through the town exposing them to the ridicule of the people'.[24] That gypsies were particularly unwelcome is evident from a mandate issued to Andrew Maxwell, a glover who had been harbouring some 'Egyptians', ordering him to expel them from his house within three hours. Failure to do so would result in him being held responsible for any goods they might happen to steal.

In the case of able-bodied miscreants punishment could include sentencing to forced labour on public works and other projects. Where there were not enough felons to carry out the work, additional help had to be drafted in. One such project was the building of a new prison which was to be paid for by selling off part of the common land at auction. A major undertaking, it required quarriers to extract 'great whinstones' from the vicinity of the Lochmabengate, as well as an army of men to haul them on sledges to the site. Since there were insufficient miscreants to execute the work, the burgh council drew up a list of able-bodied men to be pressed into service, while draught horses were commandeered to help drag the sledges. Most important of all, the burgh council was responsible for the defence of the town, which was essential given Dumfries's vulnerability to attack during the English invasions of the sixteenth century.

This period witnessed some rapid changes in the provostship. In 1581 it was held by Archibald McBrair, whose forebears had held it off and on since the previous century. But his tenure was brief. The same year he was sentenced to hanging for killing a man in the street; and to compound the offence it took place the day before the king was due to visit Dumfries. Although his sentence was commuted to imprisonment in Edinburgh castle, he was (unsurprisingly) dismissed from the provostship. Three years later Simon Johnstone, a relative of the recently knighted Sir John Johnstone of that Ilk, was elected provost. This was at the instigation of the chancellor Arran and intended as a deliberate snub to the eighth lord Maxwell whose family effectively controlled the burgh. Maxwell was quick to retaliate. Mustering his retainers, and assisted by some Armstrongs, with whom the Johnstones were at feud, he forcibly prevented Simon Johnstone from taking up his appointment. Johnstone complained to Arran, who in the king's name passed sentence of outlawry on Maxwell. Undeterred, Maxwell contrived to have his cousin John Maxwell of Newlaw*

---

* Fifth son of Maxwell's uncle, John Maxwell fourth lord Herries.

elected provost, and he in turn appointed his relatives Homer Maxwell of Speddoch and Herbert Raining as bailies.[25] But such brazen defiance of the king's authority could not be tolerated, and in 1586 Arran ordered Maxwell of Newlaw's removal from the provostship.

The following year he was murdered by a party of Irvings. This was the result of a blood feud between the two families which originated from the time of Maxwell's father, lord Herries's, wardenship of the west marches. Evidently an Irving had committed a felony in England, had escaped back to Scotland, been arrested, and Herries duly handed him over to the English warden at the following truce day. He was subsequently tried in an English court and, convicted of the felony, he was hanged. Therefore this was the Irvings' revenge. The Privy Council records contain a gruesome account of the incident. Felled to the ground with multiple stab wounds, Maxwell lay 'bullerand in his blood' (i.e. with blood gushing out of him). Thinking he was dead, his attackers 'wasched their hands in [it], feeding their cruell hairtis with the abominable spectacle [and] schortlie thairafter he depairtit this lyfe'.[26]

His successor as provost was Herbert Raining (possibly the same Herbert Raining who had been involved in the punch-up with Thomas Trustrie and had rescued Martin Rawling the tailor from the enraged Nicol Newall). Interestingly, Raining's daughter was married to Francis Irving, a member of the Bonshaw family. Because Raining himself was a relative of the Maxwells, with whom the Irvings were at feud, this was an example of how marriages sometimes transcended family feuds giving point to the tag _amor vincit omnia_. Francis Irving was himself a prominent merchant burgess of Dumfries having made a large sum of money as a wine-importer from Bordeaux.[27] Early the following century he became provost, and so too in the course of time did his son and grandson. This is an example of how control of the burgh was monopolised by relatively few families like the Irvings, Rainings and McBrairs, and later the Corsanes.

By this time it was becoming increasingly the fashion for well-to-do burgesses to aspire to landownership, since this was traditionally regarded as a step up the social ladder. An early example was William McBrair, who purchased Armagill and other lands near Dalton.[28] In 1617 Francis Irving purchased part of the former barony of Dalswinton from Sir Alexander Stewart, future first earl of Galloway.[29] The same year Stephen Laurie, a prosperous Dumfries merchant, acquired the Glencairn estate, later re-named Maxwelton. Married to an Irving, Laurie was the grandfather of Annie Laurie who is immortalised in the well-known song, while the estate remained in the hands of his descendants until 1968. Another example was John Rome who in 1625 purchased part of the former barony of Dalswinton which he re-named Dalswinton-Rome.* Two years later, John Craik, a merchant burgess and bailie of Dumfries,

---

* Following his death in 1637 it changed hands several times before ending up in the hands of John Maxwell. An advocate, he was described as 'a shady character who was familiar with the inside of the Tollbooth in Edinburgh'. Thereafter it remained in the hands of his descendants until 1785 when the last of them sold it to Patrick Millar.

bought the lands of Stewarton in the upper Cairn valley.[30] At much the same time John Corsane, who became provost in 1618, acquired the property of Meikleknox, near Buittle, in Kirkcudbrightshire. These examples illustrate how the fortunes of a number of long-established county families were originally founded on trade.

FACTION AND FEUD

The feuding between the baronial families in the Borders and the south-west, which was such a lamentable feature of the fifteenth and sixteenth centuries, was mainly attributable to the fall of the Black Douglases. Such was their power and influence that, so long as they remained at the helm, they could keep the regional baronage under control; but after their fall there was no other family of comparable power to replace them. Consequently the long-standing rivalries between the baronial families came to the surface as they began to compete, squabble and feud with one another in the resulting power vacuum.

Although the Maxwells became pre-eminent in Dumfriesshire, the fact that they lacked anything like the power of the Douglases meant that, instead of being able to control the quarrelling barons, they found themselves drawn into their feuds. For example, in the late fifteenth century they were at feud with the Murrays of Cockpool. However, a reconciliation took place in 1486 when Cuthbert Murray came to Dumfries accompanied by his kin and friends, apparently to seek the forgiveness of John fourth lord Maxwell.[31] Thereafter the two families appear to have become allies, confirmed some thirty years later when George Murray, a younger son of Cuthbert, entered into a bond of manrent with Robert fifth lord Maxwell.[32] Other Maxwell supporters included the Stewarts of Dalswinton and Garlies, their alliance being sealed with the marriage between John fourth lord Maxwell and Agnes daughter of Sir Alexander Stewart.[33]

Initially the Maxwells were at feud with the Douglases of Drumlanrig, the other major power in Nithsdale. But they must have made it up by 1509 when Robert, future fifth lord Maxwell, married Janet daughter of Sir William Douglas of Drumlanrig. Later the Maxwells became involved in a long and deadly feud with the Johnstones, and by extension with their allies the Irvings and the Grahams. Conversely, the Maxwells allied themselves with the Johnstones' enemies, the Armstrongs of Liddesdale. Since the Armstrongs had established a presence in the Debateable Land, this inevitably brought them into conflict with the Grahams who were also established there. Because the Grahams were at feud with the Carlyles and the Bells, it followed that these two families supported the Armstrongs, and hence the Maxwells. Besides, Michael fourth lord Carlyle and Robert fifth lord Maxwell were first cousins – not that blood relationship counted for much in these situations. On the other hand, the fact that Maxwell's sister Agnes was married to Robert Charteris of Amisfield, while another sister Elizabeth was the wife of Humphrey Jardine, younger of Applegarth,[34] meant that these two important families were Maxwell supporters. However, a third sister Mary was married to James Johnstone of that Ilk.[35] Yet, so long as he was alive, relations between the Maxwells and the Johnstones never plumbed the depths they subsequently did.

Meanwhile the Scotts of Buccleuch vied with the Kers (of Ferniehurst and Cessford) and the Elliots for supremacy in the middle marches. Lesser lairds who lacked the means to protect themselves and their families would almost invariably enter into a bond of manrent with their own chief, or the chief of one of the leading kindreds in the region, one example being George Murray's entering into a bond with lord Maxwell. In terms of this, Murray undertook to become Maxwell's man and remain unswervingly loyal to him in peace and war. In return, Maxwell took him under his protection and would provide for him as if he was a member of his own family, giving him food and shelter when necessary. Furthermore, if Murray was killed in his service, then Maxwell was bound to provide for his family, and if possible avenge his death.

The heads of a number of families entered into bonds of manrent with the Maxwells, reflecting their power and influence. They included Robert fifth lord Maxwell's brother-in-law James Douglas of Drumlanrig, who entered into a bond with him in 1518.[36] So too, three years later, did Maxwell's cousin Sir Alexander Stewart of Dalswinton and Garlies.[37] In 1525 John ('Black Jock') Armstrong entered into a similar bond with him,[38] and some thirty years later, in 1557, the alliance between the two families was confirmed by a bond between Armstrong's son Cristell (or Christie) and Sir John Maxwell (future lord Herries) as tutor to his under-age nephew John eighth lord Maxwell.[39] Others examples included William Jardine of Balgray and Thomas Kirkpatrick of Closeburn, who entered into bonds of manrent with the fifth lord Maxwell in 1530, and the sixth lord in 1550.[40] With the addition of John Grierson of Lag and John Crichton (brother of William lord Crichton of Sanquhar), who entered into bonds of manrent with the sixth lord in 1549 and 1550 respectively,[41] the Maxwells built up a powerful following in Dumfriesshire.

They needed to, for by this time they were engaged in their notorious feud with the Johnstones. Notwithstanding that Robert fifth lord Maxwell and his nephew John (later Sir John) Johnstone occasionally sank their differences in the interests of making common cause against the English, the vendetta between the two families would continue for another seventy years, being kept alive by their respective descendants. Later it was compounded by rivalry for the prestigious – and potentially lucrative – office of warden of the west marches. Sir John Johnstone died in 1567 and was succeeded by his grandson, another John Johnstone. When in 1579 the latter was appointed warden of the west marches, John eighth lord Maxwell, who regarded the office as belonging to his family,[42] took it as a personal affront. Therefore he refused to recognise Johnstone's authority and ordered his supporters to follow suit. Together they added up to an impressive following. Besides James Douglas of Drumlanrig,*

---

*   He had recently succeeded his grandfather (Maxwell's great-uncle), the octogenarian Sir James Douglas, his father Sir William Douglas of Hawick having died some years previously.

and the Armstrong, Charteris and Jardine families, they included the Carruthers and Kirkpatricks.

James Douglas's support for the Maxwells may have been responsible for his attack on their Irving opponents in 1583. Assisted by his uncle Robert Douglas provost of Lincluden, and a large following, James Douglas forced his way into the Irving stronghold of Bonshaw and 'maisterfully set at libertie sum notorious offendouris, rebellis and disobedient personis' who had been imprisoned there on the orders of John Johnstone, the warden.[43] Johnstone also had a powerful following. Besides the Irvings, he could count on the support of the Grahams, as well as the Scotts and the Elliots (who had presumably composed their differences). Similarly the Bells and Carlyles who had defected to them, although they soon returned to the Maxwell fold.

The rivalry between the Maxwells and the Johnstones for the wardenship of the west marches was mirrored, if to a lesser extent, by their vying with each other for control of Dumfries. When John eighth lord Maxwell was declared an outlaw for having prevented Simon Johnstone from taking office as provost of Dumfries, the chancellor Arran ordered Sir John Johnstone* to arrest him, and dispatched two companies of mercenaries to his assistance. However, they were intercepted on Crawfordmuir and killed almost to a man by Maxwell's illegitimate half-brother Robert Maxwell of Castlemilk.

The Johnstones retaliated by devastating the Maxwell lands of Cummertrees, Duncow and Cowhill. Robert Maxwell responded by burning the Johnstone strongholds of Lochwood (when all the family's writs and charters went up in smoke) and Lochhouse, as well as taking a number of prisoners. From there he went on to lay siege to the Irving stronghold of Bonshaw where Johnstone had taken refuge.[44] Bombarded by Maxwell's cannonry, the garrison was on the point of surrender when lord Scrope, the warden of the English west marches, intervened and persuaded Maxwell to withdraw. Since lord Maxwell was held responsible for his half-brother's actions, he was stripped of his earldom of Morton† – a forfeiture which Maxwell refused to recognise.

His defiance took a more practical form. The following year he and his supporters devastated the Johnstone lands round Moffat, and having burnt some three hundred houses they carried off an estimated three thousand head of cattle. Lockerbie was also partially burnt, and for good measure a number of Johnstones were hanged. The king and Arran retaliated by declaring all-out war on Maxwell. Determined to crush him and his supporters, they summoned an army; but no sooner had it mustered than plague broke out in its ranks and it never marched.

In the autumn of 1585 the situation changed to Maxwell's advantage. When the king's new favourite, Patrick master of Gray, assisted by the Protestant nobles newly

---

* He was knighted in 1594.

† This had been conferred on him by the earl of Lennox in 1581. Since the Regent Morton's earldom had passed to his nephew the earl of Angus, this was a new creation.

returned from England, laid siege to Stirling castle where Arran had taken refuge, Maxwell contributed a force from Nithsdale. He was duly rewarded. His servants and allies, including the Armstrong, Bell and Carruthers families, were granted an indemnity for any unlawful acts they had committed since April 1569,[45] while he himself was reappointed warden of the west marches in place of Sir John Johnstone whom he promptly consigned to prison.[46]

That Christmas, perhaps presuming too much on his favour with the new regime, Maxwell made a public display of his Catholicism. He summoned his followers and all local adherents of the old Church to join him at his castle in Dumfries, from where they trooped out in a body to Lincluden to celebrate the festival in the collegiate chapel.[*] On hearing this, the king summoned Maxwell to Edinburgh to answer for his actions. Maxwell must have failed to give satisfaction because he was warded in Edinburgh castle and deprived of the wardenship of the west marches, which was restored to Sir John Johnstone, newly released from prison.

Johnstone immediately avenged himself by attacking Maxwell's castle at Dumfries, as well as William lord Herries's stronghold at Annan,[†] and destroying a dozen Maxwell settlements. From there he went on to devastate the Maxwell-supporting Sir John Jardine's lands of Applegarth. In a tit-for-tat retaliation Maxwell's supporters burnt a number of Johnstone settlements and harried their lands in Dryfesdale, as well as those 'on the Water of Milk'. Doubtless the Johnstones were preparing for a return match, but at that point the situation changed. In June 1587 Sir John Johnstone died, while the marriage of his twenty-year-old son and heir James to Herries's sister, Sara Maxwell, some months later led to a temporary reconciliation between the two families.

The same year Maxwell was released from prison and sent into exile, when he took ship for Spain. While there he tried to persuade King Philip to send his armada to Scotland and use it as a base for invading the northern counties of England where he could count on strong Catholic support. A vain hope because King James, unwilling to peril his chances of succeeding to the English throne, had already declined the Spanish ambassador's request to allow the armada access to Scottish ports.[47] Returning to Scotland in April 1588 without the king's permission, Maxwell landed at Kirkcudbright where he was joined by several Catholic nobles and a large body of retainers. As soon as he heard this, the king summoned him to Edinburgh to answer charges of treason.

Ignoring the summons, and anticipating the dispatch of an army to enforce it, Maxwell began fortifying the castles of Dumfries, Caerlaverock, Langholm and Lochmaben. He judged correctly. King James mustered an army and led it in person to the south-west. When he appeared before the gates of Dumfries, the citizens

---

[*]   This was a different occasion from the time the burghers of Dumfries trooped out to Lincluden to celebrate 'filthie Yuell' there.

[†]   He had succeeded his father, the fourth lord, following his sudden death from a stroke in January 1583. This occurred in Edinburgh where he had left his lodgings to go and watch 'the boys bicker' having claimed to have felt too unwell to go to church (*Scots Peerage* iv, 411).

surrendered having held out long enough to allow Maxwell to escape. James occupied the castle and garrisoned it with his troops, while the keepers of Caerlaverock, Langholm and Lochmaben were ordered to surrender them. The first two complied, but because Lochmaben continued to hold out against him James went on to besiege it. Meanwhile Robert Maxwell of Castlemilk laid waste to the surrounding countryside with the aim of cutting off food supplies to James and his troops – evidently with some success, because the king offered a reward for his capture dead or alive. Fearing this might tempt some of his followers to betray him, Robert Maxwell abandoned his campaign[48] and allowed the king to take Lochmaben; he then appointed James Johnstone as keeper.[49]

Meanwhile, having escaped from Dumfries, Maxwell headed for Kirkcudbright where he took ship for the Continent. But, intercepted, he was forced to make a landing on the Ayrshire coast where he was captured and taken to Edinburgh for trial. Although he was convicted of treason, the king spared his life for fear of offending the still powerful Catholic faction – not to mention the kings of France and Spain with whom he was anxious to maintain friendly relations. Instead, he warded Maxwell in Edinburgh castle, where he remained until May 1590 when he was released under the general amnesty declared in celebration of the coronation of the king's newly wedded wife Anne of Denmark.

During the early 1590s the fortunes of Maxwell and Johnstone continued to fluctuate. To begin with, Johnstone was in the ascendant. But in 1592 he most ill-advisedly supported an abortive attempt by the maverick earl of Bothwell to kidnap the king at Falkland. Therefore he was imprisoned in Edinburgh castle, stripped of the wardenship of the west marches and replaced by Maxwell.* In June 1593 Johnstone contrived to escape, and in spite of being declared an outlaw and publicly he made his way back to Lochwood. Later that year he and Maxwell entered into a bond of mutual assurance which it was hoped would bring peace to the marches.[50]

The following year William Johnstone of Lockerbie and his supporters attacked the lands of Sanquhar belonging to lord Crichton, a Maxwell ally. But the attack miscarried because Johnstone was captured and hanged from the nearest tree. Retaliating, his Johnstone kinsmen made a furious descent on the lands of the Crichtons and their supporters in Nithsdale, destroying houses and habitations far and wide, and massacring the people indiscriminately. In desperation a group of widows took their murdered husbands' blood-stained shirts to Edinburgh in the hopes of persuading the Council to bring the Johnstones to justice. Because the councillors declined to meet them, the women took their campaign to the streets where they caused such an outcry that the king was forced to intervene.

He ordered Maxwell as warden to arrest Johnstone who, although not personally involved in the raid, was held responsible for the actions of his kinsmen. If Johnstone refused to surrender, Maxwell was instructed to raze his castle of Lochwood to the

---

* Hardly, one would imagine, the king's first choice but there was probably no-one else with the necessary power.

ground. Reluctant to break his recent accord with Johnstone, Maxwell demurred. However, the king was adamant. Therefore, warned of the impending attack, Johnstone raised a 500-strong force, including a contingent of Elliots and Grahams. Maxwell mustered a force double that size recruited mainly from Nithsdale. The story has it that he offered a reward of land worth ten pounds* to anyone who brought him Johnstone's hand or head. Implying that Maxwell was worth less, Johnstone allegedly countered with an offer of land of half that value for Maxwell's hand or head.

Battle was finally joined on 6 December 1593, when Maxwell and his men encountered the Johnstones drawn up on a feature above the Dryfe Water near its confluence with the Annan. Being on lower ground, and therefore at a disadvantage, Maxwell was reluctant to give battle. Perceiving this, Johnstone sent his light cavalry or 'prickers' to attack Maxwell's flanks and force him on to the offensive. It worked. Maxwell was lured into fighting uphill, exposing his troops to repeated assaults by Johnstone's men from above. The result was a rout. Maxwell's men fled, many being cut down by their pursuers, and many more drowned as they tried to cross the Annan.

Some managed to escape, including Sir James Douglas of Drumlanrig† and the lairds of Closeburn and Lag. Not so Maxwell. While galloping from the field he was overtaken by William Johnstone of Kirkhill who knocked him off his horse. Being a tall, heavy man weighed down by armour, Maxwell was unable to get up, nor could he prevent Johnstone from cutting off his hand and taking it away with him to claim his reward. The story has it that, as Maxwell lay groaning in agony under a thorn bush, he was spotted by the wife of Johnstone of Kirkton who proceeded to dash his brains out with the castle keys she happened to be carrying with her. When a party of Johnstones arrived on the scene they cut off his arm, and carrying it away as a trophy they nailed it above the entrance to Lochwood tower. Following Maxwell's death, the king appointed lord Herries as warden. But he proceeded to use – or rather abuse – his office by inflicting such 'great skaithis of fire and heartless slaughters on [the Johnstones]', as it was put, that he was replaced by Sir James Johnstone.

The feud between the Maxwells and the Johnstones rumbled on for another fifteen years. Maxwell's son, John the ninth lord, was determined to avenge his father's death; but because he was a minor he was forced to bide his time. In 1605, at the king's instigation, a show of reconciliation took place. But there was no real accord as Maxwell, now of full age, was still determined on revenge. The opportunity came three years later. Using his cousin Robert Maxwell of Orchardton as a go-between, Maxwell proposed a friendly meeting with James Johnstone, each to be accompanied by a single attendant, to settle their differences. Since Robert Maxwell was his brother-in-law,‡ as well as a trusted friend, Johnstone accepted the offer in good faith.

---

*   Meaning land yielding an annual rent of ten pounds.
†   He was knighted in 1590.
‡   Second son of Sir John Maxwell fourth lord Herries, Sir Robert and James Johnstone were doubly brothers-in-law, Johnstone being married to Sir Robert's sister Sara, while Sir Robert was the husband of Johnstone's sister Grizel.

The encounter took place near Trailtrow church on 6 April 1608 when Maxwell planned to kill Johnstone in such a way as to make it look like an accident. At his suggestion Johnstone agreed that they should leave their attendants behind and ride forward a short distance so that they could confer in private. Meanwhile Maxwell had arranged that, just as he and Johnstone went off to confer, his attendant Charles Maxwell would pick a fight with Johnstone's attendant, William Johnstone of Lockerbie. This would cause Maxwell and Johnstone to turn back and intervene to break up the fight when Johnstone would be 'accidentally' killed. But the plan miscarried. Losing his temper in the heat of the squabble, Charles Maxwell shot and killed his opposite number before Maxwell and Johnstone could reach them. Panicking, Maxwell shot Johnstone at point blank range and killed him.

Since Maxwell had guaranteed Johnstone's safety, this was slaughter under trust which was a capital offence. Therefore Maxwell fled to France. Sentence of death and forfeiture were passed on him in his absence and publicly proclaimed from the market crosses of Dumfries and Lochmaben. Two years later in 1610 the king granted most of Maxwell's forfeited lands to his current favourite Robert Ker, future earl of Roxburghe and a gentleman of the bedchamber.[51] The following year Ker sold the barony of Tinwald to Sir John Charteris of Amisfield,[52] while Lochmaben went to another favourite – namely John Murray future earl of Annandale.[53]

In 1612 Maxwell ventured back to Scotland, no doubt hoping that his crime would have been forgotten about, or even pardoned. News of his return soon got out. A hue and cry was raised against him and he was forced to spend the next few months hiding in the Border country trying to evade his pursuers. Finally he decided to escape abroad again – this time to Sweden. The earl of Caithness offered him sanctuary in the north until he could find a ship to give him passage there. Since Caithness was his relative by marriage, Maxwell took him at his word. But no sooner had he got there than, anxious to ingratiate himself with the king, Caithness handed him over to the authorities. Consequently on 21 May 1613 Maxwell was executed at the market cross in Edinburgh and his title forfeited.

John Maxwell was succeeded by his brother Robert, who was later restored as tenth lord. Evidently a more emollient character than John, he helped put an end to the feud with the Johnstones. He was doubtless encouraged by the king who was determined to stamp out what he termed 'the auld and detestable monster of deadly feud' and the lawlessness associated with it. Maxwell seems to have gained the king's favour, for in August 1620 he became earl of Nithsdale.˙ The following year he was restored to the family estates,[54] with the exception of the barony of Lochmaben,

---

* *RMS* VIII, 79. This was not a new creation but simply a change of name to avoid the confusion arising from the existence of two Morton earldoms. The first was created in 1458 when James Douglas of Dalkeith became earl of Morton, and the second in 1581 when John eighth lord Maxwell was also created earl of Morton. Although his earldom was forfeited at the instance of Arran in 1586, King James subsequently revoked Arran's decree and restored it to Robert the tenth lord, having changed the title from Morton to Nithsdale.

which had been given to John Murray future earl of Annandale.˙ Finally in 1623 the king effected a reconciliation between the Maxwells and the Johnstones, when the earl of Nithsdale and the eighteen-year-old James Johnstone (future earl of Hartfell) formally shook hands in the presence of the lords of Council. Thus ended the bitterest and bloodiest of all the Border feuds which had lasted for almost exactly a century.

---

* On his death in 1640 Lochmaben and his other lands passed to his son the second earl. When he died childless in 1659 they passed to his kinsman, David Murray fourth viscount Stormonth, and his descendants the earls of Mansfield.

TWELVE

Sectarian Strife

THE BORDER REIVERS

For many centuries people on both sides of the border had lived by reiving, namely raiding and driving away each other's livestock. Robbery and blackmail were part of everyday life, and arson, kidnapping and extortion a regular occurrence. Consequently no-one dared stir abroad unarmed; no householder could sleep in the confidence of being left unmolested, and no livestock could be left unguarded. This was not confined to depredations by English against Scots, and vice versa; it was frequently the result of inter-family feuds, and other disputes, when the participants would sometimes enlist the help of families on the opposite side of the border. Although the depredations of these raiders, freebooters and plunderers have been glamourised in the ballads of starry-eyed romanticists as stirring deeds of valour, they were nothing of the sort. The sordid reality was that they were simply predatory raids, often accompanied by extreme cruelties, and motivated by a hankering to settle old scores and above all the lure of booty.

In 1580 the young James VI consulted lord Herries as to the reason for the prevailing lawlessness. Now an old man with unrivalled experience of Border affairs, having served as warden of the west marches, he was probably better qualified than anyone to give an opinion. According to his account, it harked back to the early years of the reign of James V when some disaffected Scotsmen settled on the English side of the border. Clearly he was referring to 'Long Will' Graham* who had fallen foul of the law and incurred a heavy fine which he was unable to pay. Therefore he was banished from the realm, and he and his eight sons took refuge in the Debateable Land.[1] This was regarded as a safe haven, for the fact that neither the English nor the Scottish wardens were prepared to exercise jurisdiction over it, each regarding it as the other's responsibility, meant it was effectively outside the law.

A violent and bloodthirsty race, the Grahams were among the 'theves of the marche' who were responsible for the murder of lord Carlyle and the lairds of Mouswald, Kirkmichael, Kirkconnel and Logan, and 'many other landit men' in 1548. As time went on, the Grahams multiplied and used their wealth derived from robbery, blackmail and extortion to build 'eight or nine great stone houses [i.e. fortifications]'.

---

* 'Possibly identifiable with William Graham of Mosskesswra, 'Long Will's eldest son Richard was the ancestor of the Grahams of Esk and their cadet family the Grahams of Netherby.

Proof against all efforts by the Scottish warden to take them, these strongholds served as a base from which to harry their neighbours' lands. As to their numbers, Herries opined that at the time of James V's death in 1542 there were 'not more than twenty or thirty at most, but now [1580] they are sixteen to eighteen score' and all of them 'well horsed'.[2] Concluding, he added that the Grahams had secured their paramountcy in the region by forcing their neighbours to take their daughters in marriage without a dowry under threats to devastate their lands if they refused.[*]

Herries' assertion that the prevailing lawlessness of the Borders harked back to the early years of the reign of James V was not strictly true, because unruliness and reiv-ing had long been endemic in the region. So much so, that in the 1520s, in order to bring the full weight of the Church to bear in his efforts to suppress the practice, Archbishop Dunbar issued letters of cursing. An extraordinary farrago of ecclesias-tical thunder, they were issued in the name of the Holy Trinity, all the saints (specifically named), the pope, and the whole Church hierarchy; they cursed the reivers generally and each and every part of their anatomy in particular. They cursed them wherever they were and whatever they were doing, continuing in the same vein at inordinate length. In a final flourish he consigned their souls to 'the deip pit of hell', while their bodies were to be hanged and ripped apart by 'dogges, swine and utheris wyld beists abhominable to all the warld'. Nevertheless his curses appear to have been as so much water to the proverbial duck's back because reiving continued as relent-lessly as ever.

It was partly driven by hunger, because there was not enough land to support the population of the Border region, which was considerably higher than now. This is evident from Pont's map of Liddesdale which was drawn up in the 1580s and 1590s, and which shows many more place-names, most of them ferme touns or other settle-ments, than exist in the relatively barren region it is today.[3] The population numbers of Redesdale in Northumberland support this. During the sixteenth century it is known to have been three times what it was at the end of the eighteenth,[4] which was probably typical of the border region as a whole. Generally speaking, the population of the Scottish marches is thought to have been somewhere in the region of 45,000 to 50,000 – less than half that of the English marches which is reckoned to have been about 120,000.[5] This was mainly because of the greater fertility of the English marches compared with the Scottish ones which consisted for the most part of barren moor-land and extensive morasses.

Wherever possible the marauders were hunted down, and when brought to justice they were liable to be fined, imprisoned or hanged. Most managed to elude the less-than-effective vigilance of the authorities and continued to plunder as ruthlessly as ever, while anyone attempting to resist was killed out of hand. If, on the other hand,

---

*   R C Reid, 'The Border Grahams, their Origin and Distribution', *TDGNHAS*, xxxviii (1959–60), 105. There are such striking parallels between the story of the Grahams and that of the Doones in R D Blackmore's *Lorna Doone* that one wonders whether he had the Grahams in mind when he wrote it.

the victim proved to be a man of substance who had put himself under the protection of a local chief this would invite reprisals, with every likelihood of its escalating into a major conflict. In cases where an English reiver was apprehended by the Scottish authorities, or vice versa, he would be consigned to prison and handed over to his own warden at the next truce day for punishment. But if the prisoner escaped, as Andrew Bell did, the consequences could be embarrassing.

There were occasions when a victim's retaliatory action was more subtle. For example the story is told of how a marauding band of Robsons from Tynedale carried out a raid on their long-standing enemies, the Grahams of Netherby, when they made off with a large number of sheep. Anticipating this, the Grahams had mixed some scab-infected sheep with their flock so that when the Robsons returned home with their plundered sheep the disease spread among their own stock. Retaliating, the Robsons carried out another raid on Netherby. In the course of it they caught and hanged seven Grahams, allegedly attaching a note to one of the corpses to the effect that 'the next time gentlemen come to tak your scheip they are no' to be scabbit'.[6]

One of the most notorious reivers was William Armstrong, laird of Woodhouselees in lower Eskdale. Otherwise known as Kinmont Willie, he along with his sons and other families, including the Grahams with whom he was temporarily in league, conducted numerous predatory raids on the people of Cumberland and Westmorland. Over the years the Armstrongs and Grahams each built up a sizeable army of thieves, 'broken' men, and other desperadoes, many of whom were used as enforcers of the lucrative protection racket which they operated on both sides of the border. In 1593 lord Scrope, who had succeeded his father as warden of the English west marches,[*] was determined to put a stop to the practice. Therefore he planned to ambush and capture Kinmont Willie while he was conducting a raid on Tynedale. But Kinmont Willie had a spy in the enemy camp, namely Scrope's principal lieutenant Thomas Carleton, who happened to be his son-in-law. Therefore, tipped off in time, he avoided the trap.

Nevertheless Scrope was determined to bring him to book. The opportunity came three years later when Kinmont Willie was on his way home from a truce day which had been held near Kershopefoot. Overtaken by a party of Englishmen who had also been attending it, he was captured and handed over to Scrope who imprisoned him in Carlisle castle. Now it was the custom, indeed a golden rule, that all those attending a truce day (normally a gala occasion) were protected by an implied safe conduct which lasted until sunrise the following day, or longer by mutual agreement. This was to allow everyone to return home in safety. Since it applied to Kinmont Willie as much as everyone else, his apprehension was regarded as such a flagrant breach of the convention that it scandalised people on both sides of the border. The more so because it meant they could never entirely rely on implied safe-conducts in future.

Since the capture took place in Liddesdale where Sir Walter Scott of Buccleuch was the keeper, he took it as a personal affront and was determined on revenge. Therefore,

---

[*]   The father was the lord Scrope who invaded Annandale in 1570.

assisted by Walter Scott ('Auld Wat') of Harden, their fellow clansmen and other supporters, the combined force broke into the castle and rescued Kinmont Willie under the very nose of the English. Retaliating, Scrope raided Liddesdale with a force of some 2,000 men and took many prisoners. But fearing that the situation was getting out of hand, James VI intervened by asking Queen Elizabeth to order Scrope to refrain from carrying out further pointless raids merely to salve his wounded pride. Consequently Kinmont Willie, already in his mid-sixties, died an old man and in peace.

The Armstrongs, of whom Kinmont Willie was a prominent member, are reckoned to have been among the most turbulent and aggressive of all the Border clans, rivalled only by the Grahams. Although members of the family had settled in the Debateable Land, their principal base was Liddesdale, where the king's writ barely ran. Consequently anarchy prevailed to the extent that it had to be detached from the middle march and designated a separate entity. And it was because a powerful Border baron was needed to control the region and its people that Sir Walter Scott of Buccleuch was appointed keeper.*

During the early part of the sixteenth century the Armstrongs appear to have undergone a population explosion. As a result, some settled in lands given them by the fifth lord Maxwell in neighbouring Eskdale, and it was here in about 1525 that they built their stronghold of Holehouse or Hollows. Three years later it was burnt on the orders of lord Dacre on the pretext that it was situated in the Debateable Land where no building was allowed.[7] At much the same time the Grahams, described as 'that viperous generation', who had been driven out of Scotland in about 1515, settled in the southern portion of the Debateable Land. Broadly comprising the parish of Kirkandrews, it was here that they built their stronghold of Netherby.[8] For most of the time the two clans were at daggers drawn. Yet there were occasions when a truce was declared so that they could make common cause against the English, and there were one or two instances where it was sealed by a marriage between the two families.

The Debateable Land had long been a source of contention between the English and Scottish wardens. And because both countries claimed it, neither would allow subjects of the other realm to settle there. The result was that by the turn of the sixteenth century it had become a no-man's land. Nothing was allowed to be built there, the only concession being that cattle were permitted to graze there by day as long as they were driven away at night. Both sides were quick to punish any infringement of the rule. A case in point occurred in 1517 when John Charteris and the warden's brother Herbert Maxwell, accompanied by a force of some 400 men, drove off 700 cows and oxen belonging to an offending Englishman.[9]

In 1525 the arrangement was formalised between the earl of Angus, as warden of the west marches, and his opposite number William lord Dacre, when it was

---

*   Created lord Scott of Buccleuch in 1606, he was the father of Walter Scott, later first earl of Buccleuch, who over extended himself in the land purchase.

stipulated that 'if any house shall be built therein [i.e. on the Debateable Land] it may lawfully be destroyed without restitution'.[10] Hence lord Dacre's sanctioning of the burning of the Armstrong keep of Hollows as the prelude to a systematic devastation of the region.[11] Thereafter raids by the Scottish and English wardens were a regular occurrence throughout the next twenty-three years until 1551 when lord Maxwell, the Scottish warden, so ravaged the region that not a single building was left standing. A pointless exercise as it turned out, because the following year a partition of the Debateable Land was agreed between the two countries. Consequently the Grahams who, broadly speaking, occupied the parish of Kirkandrews, became subjects of the English king Edward VI, while the Armstrongs were mainly confined to the parish of Canonbie, which was part of Scotland. So their feuding continued as before, punctuated by the occasional marriage.

Most cross-border marriages resulted in a conflict of loyalties which could seriously obstruct the wardens' efforts to maintain law and order. An obvious example was Scrope's trusted lieutenant Thomas Carleton forewarning his father-in-law Kinmont Willie of the plan to capture him. It also meant, as frequently happened, that reivers enlisted the help of friends and relatives on the opposite side of the border to rob their compatriots. The English and Scottish wardens tried to put a stop to it by forbidding cross-border marriages. But because English and Scots regularly encountered each other at local markets, truce days, and the like, this was difficult to enforce. Conversely, the wardens did their best to encourage marriages within the same clan or kindred, or between allied families on their own side of the border.

This was peripheral to their principal duties which were mainly to do with guarding the marches, conferring regularly with their opposite number on matters concerning the maintenance of law and order in the region, appointing deputies, and ensuring that the principal strongholds were kept in a proper state of repair. Additionally they were responsible for suppressing crime, obtaining redress against offenders, the pursuit of fugitives and handing them over to the appropriate authorities, holding courts and generally administering effective rule. A formidable list, but amply compensated by the prestige attaching to the office.

One of the most important duties of a warden was to arrest reivers from the opposite side of the border, almost invariably in the course of a raid. Instead of punishing them himself, which no doubt frequently happened (his ruling centre would invariably be equipped with gallows), convention dictated that he retain the miscreant for handover to his opposite number at the next truce day to be dealt with as appropriate. The warden was also responsible for ensuring that the victims were properly compensated for loss or damage suffered. Nevertheless the maintenance of law and order was very largely dependent on the relations between the two wardens. Sometimes they worked well together, but not always. For example lord Maxwell was on such consistently bad terms with lord Scrope that co-operation between them was all but impossible.

A warden was also responsible for gathering intelligence about what was happening on the other side of the border. Here the Scots appear to have had the edge over the English, because it was said that little happened on the English side of the border that was not quickly known about in Scotland.[12] In wartime the warden was responsible for raising an army and assuming command unless or until another commander was appointed in his place. A classic example was Robert fifth lord Maxwell, who took command of the Scottish army in the run-up to Solway Moss only to be superseded by the king's favourite, Oliver Sinclair.

Notwithstanding the attaching responsibilities, the office was much coveted – partly for its status, and also for the opportunities it offered for self-enrichment through the acquisition of forfeited lands. Hence the eighth lord Maxwell's resentment of his dismissal from the wardenship by the regent Morton in 1577, compounded by the fact that he was replaced by Johnstone. Although appointments to the wardenship depended on whichever of the two families happened to be in royal favour at the time, the frequency with which it changed hands meant it was difficult, if not impossible, to establish a clearly defined policy, let alone develop a good working relationship with the English wardens.

The wardens were theoretically responsible for breaking up the lucrative protection rackets which were more or less standard practice throughout the region. Since it was not unknown for the wardens to have a hand in these themselves, their efforts were frequently less than wholehearted. Most Border families – certainly the more powerful ones – operated a protection racket of sorts. So did the more prominent reivers, and even some outlaws – or indeed anyone who was capable of looking after the interests of those paying them protection. Generally the latter were farmers and small tenants, while the person to whom they paid protection was known as the 'superior'. In return, the superior was obliged to protect them from other raiders, and where possible recover their stolen goods and livestock. But if for any reason, be it hardship or impoverishment, the tenant or farmer defaulted on his payments he could expect little mercy.

Eventually blackmail became so commonplace, and the methods so sophisticated, that it became a major industry with the blackmailers employing collectors and enforcers. The latter were generally 'broken' men or other outlaws – essentially thugs whose rough and ready methods would extend to killing or maiming non-payers and their families, or burning their settlements, or both. The most notorious blackmailers of all were the Grahams who refined the practice to a point where it could be likened to a modern insurance company. Not all that far-fetched given that, in return for the payment of a levy (essentially a premium) by a small farmer, they would extend him their protection and possibly compensate him for loss or damage suffered. Blackmail included kidnapping, a legacy of the days when it was customary to hold prisoners to ransom. The main difference was that, whereas in the past it only happened in time of war, now it was commonplace for reivers to carry off ransomworthy people, as well as their livestock and other goods.

During the last decade of the sixteenth century reiving became increasingly widespread due to indifference on the part of the authorities. This was because both countries were at peace, and in the eyes of their governments the border region amounted to little more than a small localised pocket of unrest. And because only a tiny proportion of the population were affected, it was not worth the trouble and expense of suppressing it. However, when King James VI and I succeeded to the English throne in 1603 he was determined to bring the region properly under control, although it would take him upwards of seven years to achieve.

His campaign began with the issue of a proclamation against 'all rebels and disorderly persons', commanding that no supplies be given them, 'their wives or their bairns', and that they were to be prosecuted 'with fire and sword'.[13] Next, James abolished the marches on both sides of the border which in future were to be known as the middle shires (the name never caught on and was eventually abandoned). He also rescinded the march laws, while declaring that robbery, blackmail and extortion would be punished with the utmost severity. The reivers attempted to resist. But they had lost a cardinal advantage, namely that because the two countries were united under a single crown it was no longer possible to play one off against the other.

Responsibility for the pacification of the Borders was assigned to Alexander lord Home (later first earl of Home) and his deputy Sir William Cranston, both supported by a large body of troops. They were responsible for rounding up a number of malefactors who were sent to Dumfries for summary trial. Justice was swift and merciless: thirty-two were hanged, fifteen banished, while the rest were outlawed.[14] This was merely a start. On the instructions of the Border Commission, set up for the purpose, Cranston and his men scoured the countryside arresting people on the slightest pretext, frequently reviving old charges against them, all appeals for clemency being dismissed out of hand. 'Broken' men were forbidden to absent themselves from their homes for more than forty-eight hours without a licence. Sleuth hounds were used to hunt down offenders, and 'sworne men' (informers) and 'rypers' (searchers) were planted in every parish to report suspects to the authorities.[15]

Cranston's brutality earned him universal hatred. So much so that on one occasion when he turned up in Dumfries the townsfolk tried to lynch him and he only escaped after three or four horses had been shot under him. In fact Dumfriesshire remained the last outpost of resistance and a refuge of thieves and outlaws until the very end. But resistance finally crumbled in the face of well-armed troops, and the knowledge that anyone captured would automatically be consigned to the gallows. When taxed with exercising summary justice like this, Cranston's reply was that time did not allow for long and involved arguments for the defence. Therefore he was forced to make a 'quicke dispatche' of the felons – hence the term 'Jeddart [Jedworth] justice'.*

Since they were the principal troublemakers, King James was determined to cleanse the region of Grahams altogether. Many were shipped off to the Low Countries to assist the Dutch in their war of independence, no doubt in the hopes that they

---

* So named after Jedburgh (or Jedworth) which was one of the centres, along with Dumfries and Carlisle, where hangings were mainly carried out.

would end up victims of Spanish cannonry. Some did not, and within a year most of the survivors had made their way back to Dumfriesshire where they were reportedly given sanctuary by the Carlyles, Johnstones and other prominent families. The Border Commission now tried a different approach. This time they transported them en masse to Ireland where Sir Ralph Sidley, a Roscommon landowner, had offered to accommodate them on his estate. Grasping the opportunity, and no doubt thinking Sidley must have been mad to make such an offer, the commissioners set about raising (or extorting) the wherewithal to meet the re-settlement costs. By this time the Grahams had become so reduced as a result of death, outlawry and banishment that there were only about fifty families left. The settlement was a failure from the start. Sidley's estate turned out to be an unproductive wasteland with neither wood nor water. Worst of all, the Grahams had no money, most of the cash subscribed towards the re-settlement costs having apparently found its way into Sidley's pocket. (So perhaps he was not so mad after all!) The result was that within two years there were only about half a dozen families left, the rest having dispersed. Some returned to the Border country where their descendants continue to be well represented today.

Meanwhile the work of bringing the region under control continued, and in July 1609 there was a mass hanging of captured felons at Dumfries. But another two years were to elapse before the Border Commission could report that there was 'perfect and settled peace and quietness' in the region, when Cranston resigned office. In 1620, in order to save costs, the King's guard, a company of mounted police who were responsible for patrolling the region, was disbanded. It proved a false economy because it encouraged a further outbreak of lawlessness as marauding bands of moss-troopers continued to harry the remoter parts of the region, rounding up sheep and cattle as before. Responding, the Privy Council instructed the earls of Nithsdale and Buccleuch, and John Murray of Lochmaben, the principal local magnates, to assist the Border Commission in maintaining law and order.[16] Their efforts were successful to the extent that by 1625 the Border Commission could safely be wound up.

EPISCOPACY RESTORED

The Presbyterian supremacy established by the 'Golden Act' of 1592 continued for the next five years, for it was not until 1597 that King James felt himself in a strong enough position to embark on a counterattack. Anticipating this, some ministers affected to perceive the ferocious rainstorms, which were a feature of the year 1596, as an ominous portent. Similarly the beaching of 'a monstrous great whale' in the Firth of Forth.[17] True or not, they perceived correctly. In the course of the next ten years, described by an aggrieved Melville as 'the declyneing age of the kirk in Scotland', James brought about the restoration of episcopacy and the eclipse of presbytery. A formidable achievement, it was attributable to a combination of tenacity, guile, and an ability to turn events to his advantage, combined with a judicious mix of threats and bribery, laced with a good deal of chicanery – or, as he termed it, 'kingcraft'.*

His perception of ministers, particularly the extremist Presbyterians, was the subject of a royal blast in his treatise *Basilikon Doron*, an instruction written for his son Prince Henry which was published in the early 1600s. Branding them as 'fiery and seditious spirits who delighted to rule as tribunes of the people', he accused them of placing themselves at the head of every faction which had weakened and distracted the country. Warning the prince against their fanaticism, he went on: 'Take heed, my son, [of] these pests of the Church whom no deserts can oblige, nor oaths nor promises can bind, breathing nothing but sedition and calumnies [and] railing without reason.' Denouncing their actions as the product of misguided belief, and 'without any warrant from the Word', he declared that 'ye shall never find among any Highland or border thieves greater ingratitude and more lies and vile perjuries than with these fanatic spirits'.[18]

He had good reason. A number of ministers, emboldened by their newly won political dominance, arrogated the right to fulminate against him and his advisers from the pulpit. For example, in 1594 a minister at Perth denounced him as a 'traitor, a reprobate, and a dissembling hypocrite'.[19] Two years later, in the course of an interview with King James at Falkland, Melville overreached himself. Plucking the king's sleeve, and addressing him as 'God's sillie† vassal', he proceeded to lecture him on his subordination to the Church.[20] On another occasion, in October 1598, the minister of St Andrews charged James with 'manifest treachery', claiming that 'all kings are devil's children'.[21] Not only was James firmly of the opinion that preachers had no right to fulminate against their rulers, but what really infuriated him was that they were allowed to do so with virtual impunity.

Many of the more moderate ministers who regarded their fundamentalist colleagues as too extreme took much the same view. In particular they did not associate themselves with Melville's pronouncement during his interview with the king at Falkland, namely, that all temporal rulers, in effect the state, were subject to the overriding authority of the Church. As he put it, 'there are two kings and two kingdoms in Scotland. There is Christ Jesus the King and his kingdom of the Kirk, whose subject King James the Sixth is, and of whose Kingdom not a king, nor a lord, nor a head, but a member.'[22]

James proceeded to exploit the divisions between the moderates and the extremists as a means of engineering the restoration of bishops (as opposed to mere titular, or 'tulchan', bishops). And by securing their automatic representation in Parliament he contrived to overcome Melville and his fellow extremists' dominance of the general assembly. As an opening gambit, he took advantage of the provision in the 'Golden

---

*   Although equipped with all the guile and cunning his parents so notably lacked, James inherited none of their handsomeness, charm or good looks, being described as ungainly in person, and according to at least one writer his ugliness was as offensive as his personal habits.

†   'Sillie' in this sense meaning misguided.

Act' of 1592 which stipulated that a general assembly should be held once a year. Since it was an offence to convoke ecclesiastical assemblies without the king's authority, it followed that the time and place of each meeting would be announced by the king or his commissioner at the preceding assembly. This was important because it meant that James could ensure that general assemblies were held at places like Perth and Dundee where the more moderate ministers were in control, rather than the extremist Presbyterian centres such as Edinburgh and St Andrews, or indeed anywhere in Fife, Lothian and the south-east.

He went further. Through subterfuge he arrogated the right to change the date and venue already announced. At the general assembly of 1596 the king's commissioner declared that the next meeting would be held at St Andrews the following May. But James subsequently altered this by stating, with apparent insouciance, that the venue would be changed to Perth and the date brought forward to February. Officially this was because Perth was more accessible to ministers from the north-east and the Highlands, and therefore it would be easier for them to attend. In reality they were more moderately inclined, and, since they would constitute a majority in the assembly, it could be relied on to approve the proposals he intended to put before it. Bringing forward the date was calculated not to arouse suspicion. But when the assembly accepted it without demur they were falling into a trap. For their acceptance set a precedent, in that by agreeing to the principle of the date being changed they could hardly object to it being put back on future occasions. Or, as subsequently happened, prorogued from year to year.

At the Perth general assembly it was agreed among other things, and after considerable debate, that ministers should not pronounce on affairs of state, nor attack people by name, from the pulpit. Further, that no conventions of ministers however informal should take place without the king's consent, the only exception being ordinary meetings of presbyteries and synods. Encouraged by what he perceived as a significant step forward, James summoned another assembly to meet at Dundee in May 1597.[23] At his suggestion it appointed a commission of fourteen leading ministers (excluding Melville at his special request) for the apparently unexceptional purpose of having regular discussions with him on matters to do with the well-being of the Church. These commissioners carried weight with the general assembly, and the fact that James, who was no mean theologian himself,* could generally out-argue them and persuade them to his view, meaning he could bring some influence to bear on it.

Finally it was moved that, because the clerical estate in Parliament was under-represented, it should be supplemented by ministers. This suited James. Not only did he see an increased clerical presence as a counterweight to an unreliable nobility, but he could ensure that they were his nominees and would therefore vote in accordance

---

*   He would frequently interrupt a preacher in the course of his sermon to challenge him on points with which he took issue.

with his wishes. Therefore in November 1597, at his behest, Parliament passed an Act authorising him to nominate ministers as titular bishops to the vacant sees, carrying with it the right to sit and vote in Parliament. Not what the assembly had in mind. Consequently it was denounced at the general assembly held at Dundee in March 1598, and none more so than by Melville.

But James outmanoeuvred him. Melville had assumed that the rectorship of St Andrews University (to which he had been appointed in 1590) entitled him to a permanent commission to attend the general assembly, as indeed was the case. Except that on this occasion it had been agreed that the university should be represented by three commissioners, but Melville was not one of them. Aware of this, James challenged his right to attend the assembly and Melville was forced to withdraw from it. Nevertheless the assembly overplayed its hand by calling for a representation of fifty-one ministers in Parliament, which would have been enough to out-vote the other two estates. Further, they were to be elected annually, act under the direction of the assembly, and be subject to its authority.[24] Or so the assembly may have hoped, but James's control of Parliament ensured that the proposal remained a dead letter.

The following year the extremists suffered a blow when James contrived to have Melville dismissed from the rectorship of St Andrews University. Since this deprived him of much of his authority, as well as denying him his permanent commission to attend the general assembly, it meant he could no longer influence its proceedings.

In August 1600 there occurred the Gowrie conspiracy when Alexander Ruthven[*] lured the king to his brother the earl of Gowrie's town house at Perth. This was on the pretext that he wanted the king to examine a man of suspicious character who had allegedly been found to have a pot of foreign gold hidden under his cloak. An unlikely sounding story, and therefore all the more surprising that the normally hard-headed and sceptical James should have fallen for it. But fall for it he did. When he got there he found himself confronted by a would-be assassin. Fortunately he happened to be near an open window, and, hearing his shouts for help, a band of armed men forced their way into the house, and in the ensuing fracas both Gowrie and his brother were stabbed to death.[25] Because they were leading supporters of the extremist faction within the Church, James could convincingly assert that the radical ministers had connived at the plot to assassinate him – a claim that earned him considerable support among the moderates.

Nevertheless many extremist ministers were becoming suspicious of James's motives for tampering with the place and date of the meetings of the general assembly. Therefore, when he deferred the meeting which was to be held at Aberdeen in July 1604 to the following July and then, despite petitions to the contrary, prorogued it indefinitely, a group of extremist ministers decided to make a stand. Acting on their own initiative, they announced that a meeting of the general assembly would be held at Aberdeen in July 1605. The king bided his time. The meeting was duly held, but no

---

[*]   Son of the earl of Gowrie who was responsible for kidnapping the king back in 1582.

sooner had it been constituted than the ministers were ordered in his name to disperse. They did so, but not before they convened another meeting for the following September. Since this was strictly the prerogative of the king or his commissioner, it constituted a serious breach of the law. Accordingly the ringleaders were brought to trial and convicted of illegally convoking assemblies. Fourteen of them were sentenced to imprisonment, while a further six were banished for life.

At the same time James was steadily filling the vacant sees with his nominees. Starting with those of Aberdeen, Ross and Caithness, he appointed John Spottiswoode, minister of Calder, titular archbishop of Glasgow. At the same time Bishop Gladstanes of Caithness was promoted to the senior archbishopric of St Andrews. (When he died in 1615 Spottiswoode was appointed his successor.) In 1609, in an access of Protestant zeal, Spottiswoode was responsible for desecrating the church attached to Dervorguilla's foundation at New Abbey – an act of vandalism which earned him official thanks. This was stated to be for 'going to the town of New Abbey, and there breaking up the chamber door of Mr Gilbert Broun [the abbot]'. Having found 'a grite number of bookis, copes, imageis and such uther popische trasche', he proceeded 'most worthelie and dewtiffulie' to burn them in the presence of 'a grite confluence of people in the hie street of the Burgh of Dumfries'.[26]

Meanwhile in September 1606 King James summoned the two archbishops (Gladstanes and Spottiswoode), the bishops of Galloway and Orkney, and eight extremist ministers, including Melville, to a conference at Hampton Court to discuss what he described as 'the unhappy state of the Church in Scotland'. When Melville arrived he launched into an impassioned speech in defence of the imprisoned ministers. But when he went on to compound the offence by criticising the sumptuousness of the furnishings of the chapel royal, the king was so enraged that he ordered him to appear before the royal court at Whitehall on a charge of lese-majesty. When Archbishop Bancroft declared his offence treasonable, Melville unwisely grasped the sleeves of his rochet and shaking them vigorously he denounced them as 'Romish rags'. Finally he was committed to the Tower where he was detained until 1611. Following his release, he accepted a professorship at the University of Sédan in France where he died wracked by gout in 1622. Meanwhile Melville's colleagues were also detained in London until they too were banished from the realm.

The king's, and by inference the state's, newly won authority over the Church is well illustrated by the saga of the Durisdeer corpse, namely that of William Menzies the infant son of Adam Menzies. The family were former owners of Durisdeer, while Adam himself had recently inherited the barony of Enoch. When the infant William died in December 1606, his father had him buried in the family vault in Durisdeer church. But, claiming that the church belonged to him, Sir James Douglas of Drumlanrig ordered Menzies to remove the corpse. He refused. Therefore, taking matters into his own hands, Douglas mustered a band of retainers, and armed with a warrant from the local presbytery they disinterred the forty-day-old corpse and buried it in a shallow grave outside the church.

On hearing this, Adam Menzies retrieved the remains and had them replaced in the family vault. Retaliation came the following Sunday when Douglas and a group of armed men surrounded the church while a service was in progress, and demanded that Menzies remove the remains under pain of death. When he refused, Douglas once again had his men disinter them, whereupon Menzies appealed to the Privy Council. Ruling in his favour, it ordered the presbytery to rescind its warrant and allow the remains a decent burial in the family vault. The presbytery refused, and instead tried to excommunicate Menzies for disobedience. Once again he appealed to the Privy Council. This time it forced the presbytery to give way and allow what was left of the corpse to be replaced in the vault.[27]

The removal of Melville and his fellow extremists cleared the way for James to integrate bishops into the framework of Church government, and ultimately to restore them to the power and privileges enjoyed by their predecessors before the Reformation. At his instigation, the Parliament of July 1606 passed an Act 'for the restitution of the estate of bishops', which he justified on the grounds that episcopacy was essential to the constitution of the realm.[28] Since it was to be achieved in the first instance by having them appointed permanent moderators of synods, this required ministerial approval.

Therefore in December 1606, anticipating obstruction from the general assembly, James by-passed it by summoning 136 (specially selected) ministers to a convention at Linlithgow. Pointing out that the prevailing practice of electing moderators of presbyteries and synods to serve for a year at a time risked the appointment of men who were unable to resist the (largely hypothetical) papist threat, he argued that they should choose more experienced people who were better equipped to do so and elect them as permanent moderators. Combined with a judicious admixture of threats and bribery, this was enough to persuade the majority of the ministers to agree to the appointment of constant moderators for presbyteries. But when the convention baulked at applying the same principle to synods, James simply had the minutes altered to show evidence of its consent.[29] Because the Act of July 1606 already provided for constant moderators to become titular bishops, it opened the way for the establishment of an episcopacy under his control.

This arrangement was confirmed by the Glasgow general assembly of 1610. It was effectively a packed assembly, in that James reimbursed the travelling expenses of those ministers, particularly from the more remote regions, who could be relied on to co-operate. Archbishop Spottiswoode was elected moderator, and that an archbishop, albeit titular, should be appointed to that position was a measure of how far James had succeeded in restoring episcopacy. At his instigation, the assembly approved a number of articles which effectively restored bishops to their former power and position. It was further stipulated that, at his induction, every minister would be required to swear an oath of obedience to the king. These articles were ratified by the Parliament of 1612 which effectively rescinded the 'Golden Act' of 1592.

The one remaining formality was the consecration (i.e. the laying on of hands) of the new bishops. Since there were no surviving bishops of the old Church in Scotland to perform the office, it had to be done by English bishops. But to allay any fears that, in so doing, they were submitting themselves to the authority of the Anglican Church, it was specifically provided that they would not be required to accept Anglican ordination, that no English archbishop would participate in the proceedings, and that all it would amount to was confirmation of their spiritual status. Therefore in September 1610 King James summoned Archbishop Spottiswoode and two other bishops – Lamb of Brechin and Hamilton of Galloway – to London. There they were consecrated by four English bishops so that they in their turn could consecrate their fellow bishops in Scotland. Unfortunately these bishops were, by and large, men of indifferent calibre who lacked the qualification needed to deal with a difficult, and indeed an embarrassing, situation. And the fact that they failed to do so was to a large extent responsible for the unpopularity of episcopacy in Scotland.[30]

Public opinion was divided over the restoration of episcopacy. The Protestant nobility were generally acquiescent, although some who had acquired or inherited former Church lands feared that, instigated by the new bishops, the king would demand the return of at least part of their former ecclesiastical lands and rentals for the support of the episcopate. The ministers, too, were divided. Whereas support for presbytery was most strongly entrenched among the ministers from Fife, Lothian and the south-east, and to a lesser extent Ayr and Lanark, those from elsewhere were generally supportive of episcopacy. The great majority of the people, on the other hand, were probably indifferent, being concerned above all to accept whatever was agreed on by Parliament and the general assembly for the sake of peace and order.[31] Because the general assembly was not formally suspended, it continued to meet at irregular intervals until August 1618 when James prorogued it indefinitely. Twenty years were to pass before it met again. But by then the circumstances were entirely different, and the political situation had changed beyond all recognition.

THE BISHOPS' WAR

King James died in March 1625 having reigned for almost fifty-eight years – the longest in Scottish history. He had ruled in person for some forty-five of them, and it was tribute to his political astuteness – or kingcraft – that he had succeeded in establishing his authority over the Church and nobility, had improved the lot of the lairds and burgesses, had rendered life less precarious for the poor, and above all he had left a country at peace. A remarkable achievement considering the appalling state to which Scotland had been reduced – by civil war, feuding and general lawlessness – at beginning of his reign.

Tragically his eldest son Henry, a young man of great promise, predeceased him in 1612. Therefore the crown passed to his second son Charles. A victim of rickets in childhood which had stunted his growth, he compensated for his lack of inches by an exaggerated self-importance. Although born while his father was king of Scots, he spent his formative years at the English court becoming a man of more polish than his father (which is not saying much!). But that, and the fact that he was a devoted family man, is about all that can be said for him. He had none of his father's guile, nor his political astuteness, and knew nothing about – and was not remotely interested in – Scottish affairs, or his Scottish subjects. (It was not until 1633 that he first visited the country to have himself crowned, although the delay was partly due to lack of money to pay for his coronation.) And imbued with the concept of the divine right of kings, he invariably adopted (until forced to do otherwise) a confrontational approach to all opposition. He was to be faced with much, and most of it was his own making.

Nowhere was his political incompetence and religious bigotry more apparent than in his dealings with the Scots and their Church, and in particular his Act of Revocation. This rescinded all disposals of Church lands made since 1542, subject to the payment of token compensation to the present owners. His intention was to apply the proceeds to the Church in order to enrich the clergy, and thus strengthen their power and influence. But because money was not available to pay the compensation, the Act was effectively a dead letter. Therefore all it did was sow distrust among the owners of former Church lands without doing anything for the clergy.

Worse still, financial stringency compelled Charles to impose an annual tax on his Scottish subjects. Not surprisingly this was widely resented. In fact he seems almost to have gone out of his way to court unpopularity. Even his coronation at Holyrood in 1633 caused offence, mainly because it was accompanied by an excessive display of pomp and ceremony which was widely seen as smacking of popery. Not only that, but it was perceived as an extravagance which the country could ill afford.[*] During his stay in Edinburgh he stirred up further controversy by causing Parliament to pass a number of ill-conceived measures which were designed to enhance the prestige of the clergy. One in particular, which reaffirmed an earlier Act of 1606, authorised him to prescribe clerical dress. Therefore, ignoring representations to the contrary, Charles decreed that ministers should wear surplices, and that bishops abandon their traditional black gowns for the more resplendent vestments traditionally worn by their Anglican counterparts.

The following year, he ordered the Scottish bishops to draw up a Scottish Prayer Book along the lines of the English one. The work was completed in 1637, much of it bearing Charles's fingerprints. But it was regarded as too High Church – more than the Scots were prepared to stomach, and when it was first introduced at St Giles' Cathedral in Edinburgh it caused a riot. In the course of the next few months, numerous petitions were presented to the Council calling for its withdrawal, and crowds of protesters poured into Edinburgh from Fife and the Lothians. But, instead of

---

[*] The occasion was marked by a bestowal of honours, a case in point being James Johnstone of that Ilk who was created lord Johnstone of Lochwood.

attempting to meet their objections, Charles issued a proclamation ordering them to disperse, at the same time instructing the Council to round up and punish the ring-leaders. It provoked a further protest – this time by members of the nobility and gentry, as well burgesses and ministers. In November, when their representatives met in Edinburgh to co-ordinate their opposition, they established a body known as the Tables* which rapidly assumed the functions of government. Nevertheless the king was adamant; the Book of Common Prayer and the Liturgy were there to stay and would remain the standard form of worship in Scotland.

The Tables responded by commissioning the drawing up of a manifesto known as the National Covenant. This was primarily the work of Archibald Johnston of Wariston, of whom it was said that, far from being a mere religious fanatic, he was a man 'walking on the dizzy verge of madness'.[32] The initial draft was submitted to representative committees of the nobility, gentry, burgesses and ministers for approval. Prefaced by a re-statement of James VI's Negative Confession of Faith, and the various Acts of Parliament which condemned popery and established the reformed religion, the subscribers pledged themselves to defend 'the true Protestant religion' (i.e. presbytery) against all comers. Because it was thought to be verging on treason, it was returned to the authors for re-drafting. Therefore the final version was so framed as to be directed not against the king himself but rather his policies. Accordingly the subscribers pledged themselves to 'stand to the defence of the King's majesty in the defence and preservation of the foresaid true religion'.[33]

It was subscribed in Greyfriars churchyard in Edinburgh in early 1638, first by the leading nobles and lairds, and later by ministers and burgesses. Copies were issued to every burgh and parish for subscription by burghers and parishioners alike, those refusing to do so being blacklisted. This time the king made a show of compromise by ordering the marquess of Hamilton to meet representatives of the subscribers to the Covenant, or the Covenanters as they were known. Although officially Charles authorised Hamilton to proclaim the suspension of the Prayer Book provided the Covenant was rescinded, his real intentions were apparent from his secret instruction to him to 'flatter them [the Covenanters] with what hopes you please until I be ready to suppress them'.

But the Covenanters were not to be moved. Correctly anticipating the king's inten-tion to impose the use of the Prayer Book and Liturgy by force, they took precautionary measures. They embarked on a drive to raise money for the purchase of arms and equipment from the Low Countries. This caused the king to back down. Therefore, when Hamilton returned to England having failed to persuade the Scots to rescind the Covenant he conceded the revocation of the Prayer Book and authorised the summoning of a general assembly. This was a gift to the Covenanters, for the fact that they could virtually dictate the choice of commissioners meant they could pack the assembly with their supporters.

---

* So called because their representatives sat at separate tables in Parliament House.

It met at Glasgow in November 1638 when Hamilton was appointed the king's commissioner. But the bishops, not daring to attend for fear of their lives, left the Covenanters and their supporters in control of the proceedings.[*] They overplayed their hand. When at their instigation the assembly threatened to punish the bishops for their non-attendance, Hamilton ordered the moderator to dissolve it. But threatened with reprisals if he did, the moderator refused, whereupon Hamilton left the assembly. Effectively flinging down the gauntlet, the commissioners continued to sit as an illegal body, and throwing caution to the winds they denounced as unlawful all assemblies held since 1606, thus abolishing episcopacy and re-establishing the rule of presbytery. They went on to declare the Book of Common Prayer and the Liturgy illegal and deposed the bishops. A confrontation was inevitable, and both sides – the king and his supporters (the latter being dubbed malignants) and the Covenanters – spent the following winter preparing for war.

The Tables appointed War Committees for each county, charging them to raise money from men of substance and to enlist recruits. The committee for Dumfriesshire consisted of representatives of the local nobility and landowners;[†] not that they were necessarily dedicated to the Covenanting cause, but because it was in their interests to comply. Since most of the people would have followed suit, the committee appears to have had little difficulty in fulfilling its quota. The main Catholic families, on the other hand, refused to comply. Notably the Maxwells whose chief, the earl of Nithsdale, was the leading royalist supporter in the region. Therefore the king ordered him to garrison Caerlaverock and Threave, and to ensure that they were fully provisioned against a possible siege.[‡] Meanwhile the mutual antagonism between the Covenanters and the king's supporters erupted into occasional outbreaks of violence. For example Nithsdale's nephew, lord Herries,[§] was attacked by a band of Covenanters who forced their way into the grounds of Terregles and looted the house.

Between them the War Committees raised an army of some 30,000 men. This was put under the command of Alexander Leslie, a soldier of fortune who had fought under the Swedish king Gustavus Adolphus in the Thirty Years' War. King Charles raised an army of much the same size, but it was little more than a rabble of ill-trained men, and lacking muskets they were mostly armed with pikes. Yet his plan was ambitious. While he would cross the border with the main army, Hamilton was to launch a seaborne attack on Aberdeen before linking up with the marquis of Huntly, Charles's

---

[*] The commissioners representing the Dumfries presbytery included John Irving, ex-provost of Dumfries, and Sir John Charteris of Amisfield (McDowall, *Dumfries*, 369)

[†] They included the recently ennobled William Douglas earl of Queensberry, his son James lord Drumlanrig (who was appointed a colonel in the Covenanting army), James Murray earl of Annandale, lord Johnstone, and members of his family, as well as Sir John Charteris of Amisfield, Grierson of Lag, Kirkpatrick of Closeburn, Jardine of Applegarth, and many others (see McDowall, *Dumfries*, 387).

[‡] The attack on Caerlaverock took place in August 1640 when a Covenanting force under Colonel Home bombarded it into surrender, although Nithsdale himself escaped to join the royalist army in England.

[§] Son of Nithsdale's sister Elizabeth and John sixth lord Herries, he would succeed Nithsdale's childless son Robert as third earl in 1667.

leading supporter in the north. At the same time Thomas Wentworth, his lieutenant in Ireland, was to send an Irish force to Dumbarton, while the royalist earl of Antrim would invade Kintyre.

The plan never got off the ground. Neither Wentworth nor Antrim delivered on their promises while Hamilton, unable to make headway against the earl of Montrose in the north-east, was reduced to cruising ineffectively off the Aberdeenshire coast. Then no sooner had the king's army crossed the border than it was driven back by the Covenanters under Leslie. Consequently Charles was forced to negotiate a truce – the Pacification of Berwick, in terms of which the Covenanters agreed to give up the royal castles. In return, Charles undertook to summon a Parliament and a general assembly, and both sides promised to disband their armies.

It proved a hollow truce. The Covenanters made no attempt to disband their army, while Charles refused to attend either the Parliament or the general assembly. When the latter met in August, it not only confirmed the deliverances of the Glasgow assembly condemning episcopacy as unconstitutional but it went on to declare the office of bishop contrary to the law of God – an assertion the king could not possibly accept. Nevertheless the Covenanter-controlled Parliament which met later that month endorsed the assembly's deliverances, giving them the force of law. At much the same time, the Tables was replaced by the Committee of Estates as the governing body of Scotland.

Crucially the Parliament endorsed the assembly's decision to make subscription to the Covenant compulsory under threat of severe penalties. This put it on a slippery slope towards extremism, for instead of being a bond of defence the Covenant was now an instrument of oppression. As a first step, members of the clergy who refused to subscribe were deprived of their livings. Meanwhile Charles was powerless, because acute shortage of money made it impossible for him to raise an army. Therefore in desperation he convened an English Parliament to vote him the necessary funds. But resentful at being sidelined for the past eleven years, its members refused. Therefore Charles dissolved it after it had sat for only a matter of days – hence its name the Short Parliament.

This left him with no alternative but to borrow money from a generally supportive nobility. And although supplemented by secret donations from his Catholic subjects, it was barely enough to raise a token force. The result was inevitable. When it encountered a Covenanting force under the earl of Montrose at Newburn-on-Tyne it was put to flight. By the end of August the Scots had captured Newcastle and the king was forced to sue for peace, when he undertook to ratify the legislation passed by the Scottish Parliament, thus giving legal effect to the deliverances of the general assembly. This was a humiliating retreat because it meant sanctioning the abolition of episcopacy, and hence the deposition of the existing bishops, the repeal of all Acts objectionable to presbytery, and the withdrawal of the Common Prayer Book and Liturgy.

In August 1641 Charles returned to Scotland with the aim of exploiting the divisions which were opening up between the moderates and extremists within the

Covenanting movement. But it was a pious hope. At a Parliament, which he attended in person, he was forced to concede it the right to appoint councillors, officers of state and judges. In a desperate attempt to build bridges with the Covenanting leaders he showered them with honours; Leslie was created earl of Leven, while others were knighted or appointed to influential positions in the government. But it was to no avail. In November Charles returned to London having done much for his enemies for no return, and nothing for his friends.

Meanwhile his relations with the Puritan-dominated English Long Parliament went from bad to worse. Eventually in June 1642 it presented him with a list of far-reaching demands which amounted to a virtual surrender of his sovereignty over Church and state. Since agreement was out of the question, Charles was compelled to resort to arms. On 22 August he raised his standard at Nottingham in a declaration of war on Parliament, thus precipitating that hard-fought and extremely bloody conflict, the Civil War. Charles's initial success caused the Parliamentarians to seek an alliance with the Scottish Presbyterians. Seeing this as an opportunity to impose the Covenant – and hence presbytery – on England and Ireland, they responded with alacrity, expressing the hope that their two countries might be united by a single Church professing one faith, one form of worship and the perpetual abolition of episcopacy. Notwithstanding their reservations, the Parliamentarians sent commissioners to attend the next meeting of the general assembly, now in effective control of the government, to negotiate terms.

As a result the Scots agreed to send an army to the Parliamentarians' assistance, while the English commissioners undertook to enter into a Solemn League and Covenant.* This provided for 'the preservation of the reformed faith in Scotland, the reformation of religion in England and Ireland in doctrine, worship, discipline and government according to the Word of God and the example of the best reformed Churches'. In addition, provision was made for the assimilation of their Churches, the extirpation of popery and prelacy, the preservation of the rights and privileges of the parliaments and the liberties of the kingdom, and 'the firm peace of union' of England and Scotland.[34]

Since the English Parliamentarians regarded subscription to the Solemn League and Covenant as merely a temporary expedient to help them out of a temporary difficult, they paid no more than lip service to it. Indeed their commissioners were under instruction to ensure that any agreement reached with the Scots should contain a let-out clause. Therefore, once the war began to go their way, the Solemn League and Covenant was tacitly ignored. The Scottish Presbyterians, on the other hand, regarded it as sacrosanct – to the extent that the Covenanter-controlled Committee of Estates stifled all opposition to it by issuing a copy to each parish and enforcing subscription by all parishioners under pain of forfeiture. Faced with a choice of

---

* It was from this rather than the 1638 Covenant that the Covenanters of the following decades took their name.

subscription or beggary, the people were forced to submit to what was in effect a religious tyranny.

In January 1644 an army of some 20,000 men was dispatched under the earl of Leven to assist the English Parliamentarians. At the same time, the Long Parliament sought the co-operation of the Scots in maintaining contact with their army, which was suppressing a rebellion in Ireland. This was to be achieved by establishing an overland postal service as far as Portpatrick on the west coast of Wigtownshire, and from there by sea to Ireland. Because the route beyond Carlisle passed through Scottish territory, the Parliamentarians needed the consent of the Committee of Estates. This was duly given, and it was arranged that men – usually innkeepers – of approved honesty would be responsible for supervising the various stages, one being the section between Carlisle and Annan, another from Annan to Dumfries, and so on through Galloway.

But the Scottish Presbyterians were by no means united behind the Committee of Estates' support for the English Parliamentarians. Many took the view that, because the king had subscribed to the Covenant, their object had been achieved and there was no further need to oppose him. That was certainly the view of the earl of Montrose. Hitherto one of Leslie's leading commanders, he was so appalled by the Presbyterians' fanaticism, and the tyrannical imposition of the Solemn League and Covenant on the Scottish people, that he abandoned them and offered his services to the king, with whom he had already been in touch. In August 1640, following his victory at Newburn, he had written to the king urging him to return to Scotland and adopt a more conciliatory attitude towards the Scots. When the Committee of Estates heard of this they imprisoned him for treason, and there he remained for over a year until released at the intercession of the king during his visit to Scotland. Since then Montrose had been living in retirement on his estates in Kincardineshire. But concerned to protect the royal authority against Covenanting pretensions, he was ready to take the field again – this time in support of the king who appointed him Lieutenant-Governor and Captain General of Scotland.

Equipped with a hundred horse, which was all that could be spared, Montrose recruited some 2,000 horse and footsoldiers from Cumberland for an invasion of Scotland. His plan was to advance as far as Dumfries, where he expected to find a force of 10,000 Irishmen promised by the earl of Antrim waiting for him. Crossing the border at Gretna in April 1644, he was joined by the earl of Nithsdale and lord Herries, along with other prominent landowners, including the earl of Queensberry. Some had been members of the War Committee for Dumfriesshire but had turned against the Covenanters, notwithstanding the imposition of heavy fines and excommunication by the local synod.* In Nithsdale's case the Covenanters revenged

---

* They included the earls of Queensberry and Hartfell (formerly James lord Johnstone), their kin and others, including Sir John Charteris of Amisfield.

themselves by laying siege to Caerlaverock, and when it fell after thirteen weeks' bombardment much of it was demolished.

When Montrose reached Dumfries the burghers opened the gates to him, and there he raised the royal standard. On hearing this, the grateful king created him a marquess. Meanwhile Montrose waited in vain for the arrival of the Irishmen. But when news reached him of the approach of a Covenanting army he fell back on Carlisle. While there he was ordered to send his troops to the assistance of the hard-pressed royalist army which was reeling from its defeat at Marston Moor. Now on his own, but determined to restore the royal authority, Montrose decided to open up a campaign in the Highlands. Making his way there in disguise, and accompanied by a small band of supporters, he rallied the clansmen and embarked on a year-long, hard-fought campaign. In the course of it he scored a series of brilliant successes* culminating in the capture of Edinburgh and Glasgow.

Thereafter he set his sights on recovering southern Scotland for the king. But his clansmen had had enough. Anxious to return home they were rapidly melting away, forcing him to scour southern Scotland for recruits. Not easy, and certainly not helped by the royalist defeat at Naseby in June. Therefore when Montrose encountered a Covenanting force under General David Leslie at Philiphaugh, near Selkirk, on 13 September 1644 his army was routed. In the sanguinary aftermath the victors, goaded by their chaplains into believing it was the will of God, ran amok and slaughtered the prisoners, including women and children, to the bloodthirsty yells of 'Jesus and no quarter'. The vanquished Montrose managed to escape from the field, and having made his way back to the Highlands he took ship for Norway where he sought temporary refuge. Meanwhile his defeat cost Charles all hope of recovering Scotland.

ENGLISH CONQUEST

By early 1645 the Scots were tiring of the war, and besides they were finding it increasingly difficult to raise the money needed to keep their army in the field. Their war-weariness was compounded by suspicions that, because the English Parliamentarians were gaining the upper hand in the Civil War, they were tacitly ignoring the Solemn League and Covenant. This was true enough. Their hearts were never in it, and now they had to all intents and purposes abandoned it; but at the same time they professed continued adherence to it simply to keep the Scots on side.

In May the following year Charles was beleaguered in Oxford, while the main royalist strongholds were steadily falling into the Parliamentarians' hands. However, informed by a French agent that the Scots had given a verbal undertaking regarding his personal safety, and that he would not be pressed to do anything against his conscience, Charles decided to throw himself on their mercy. Therefore, slipping out of the city disguised as a servant, he made his way to the Scottish army which was

---

* At Tibbermore (Tippermuir), Aberdeen, Fyvie, Inverlochy, Auldearn, Alford and Kilsyth.

besieging Newark. There he gave himself up to the earl of Leven. But when, contrary to what he had been led to believe, the Scots pressed him to subscribe to the Solemn League and Covenant and become a Presbyterian he refused. This put them in a quandary as to what to do with him. Finally they decided to hand him over to the Parliamentarians in return for a payment of £400,000, prompting the jibe that 'the Scots had sold their king for a groat'. Or as Charles himself allegedly remarked, 'it was cheap at the price'.

The Parliamentarians consigned him to Hampton Court Palace under house arrest. But persuaded that his life was in danger, Charles escaped to Carisbrooke Castle on the Isle of Wight, where the governor was thought to be more sympathetic. This was probably true, at least to the extent that Charles was allowed to receive visitors. Taking advantage of this, and using the earl of Lauderdale as an intermediary, Charles entered into negotiations with the more moderately inclined Scots. In December 1647 this culminated in an agreement known as the Engagement.

In terms of this, Charles undertook to subscribe to the Solemn League and Covenant although he insisted as a condition that no-one should be compelled to do so against their conscience. Whereas a substantial majority of the Committee of Estates accepted both the Engagement and Charles's condition, the commissioners for the general assembly objected on the grounds that his concessions did not go far enough. They insisted that he should give nothing less than a cast-iron guarantee that he would become a Presbyterian, and that he should use his best endeavours to impose the Solemn League and Covenant on his English and Irish subjects. Further, that he would ensure the establishment of presbytery throughout his realm to the exclusion of any other form of church government. Meanwhile they ordered every parish minister to preach against the Engagement.

Since the three estates of the Scottish Parliament were under the control of the moderates, it was generally supportive of the Engagement. But its influence was diminished as a result of military disaster. In March 1648 the Scottish Parliament decided to invade England in support of the king. Led by the incompetent duke of Hamilton,* the invasion took place in the summer of 1648. It proved a fiasco. Hamilton lost half his army in a running fight with Cromwell on the Lancashire moors, while the other half surrendered at Preston.

Taking their cue from the general assembly, the presbytery of Dumfries condemned the Engagement in the strongest terms. Whereas most people followed suit, some did not. This is evident from the presbytery minutes of 1647 and 1648 which contain numerous references to people being cited to appear before it on charges of 'Covenant-breaking', 'malignity and hostility', 'taking part in James Graham's [i.e. Montrose's] invasion' and in 'the lait sinful engagement under the Duke of Hamilton'. Prominent among Montrose's supporters was Sir John Charteris of Amisfield. Originally a member of the War Committee for Dumfriesshire, he like Montrose had switched his

---

* The king's commissioner to the general assembly of 1638, he had been advanced to a dukedom in 1643.

support to the king. But nemesis caught up with him. In 1647 he was summoned to appear before the general assembly where he admitted to having joined 'the late rebellioun, and been accessory to the shedding of the bloode of the people of God [i.e. the Covenanters]'. It decreed that he should undergo penance in the kirk of Dumfries and also in his local parish church of Tinwald.[35]

In December 1648 the general assembly ordered copies of the Solemn League and Covenant to be circulated to all presbyteries for subscription by every parishioner to affirm their commitment to it. The Dumfries presbytery went so far as to single out certain individuals who in their view were 'manifestly unworthy to sign it'. They included those who had mustered on Annan moor in readiness to join the duke of Hamilton's campaign, those who had taken part in it, or contributed troops or provisions, and even 'all women malignantly disposed'.[36] However, they were the exception, because most people in the south-west supported both the 1638 Covenant and the Solemn League and Covenant. Indeed, many men had gone into hiding to avoid being conscripted for service in Hamilton's campaign.

His defeat sparked off a rising by the extremists in the south-west. Already in June 1648 a mob of local Covenanters who were opposed to the Engagement had gathered on Mauchline moor, in Ayrshire, where they publicly proclaimed their refusal to take part in an invasion which was intended to restore the king. Although they were dispersed by government troops under Colonel Middleton, news of Hamilton's defeat encouraged them to renew their campaign. Calling themselves 'the slashing communicants of Mauchline', and joined by many local supporters, they marched on Edinburgh where the citizens opened its gates to them. Known as the 'Whiggamore Raid' it so alarmed the engagers, their morale already shaken by Hamilton's defeat, that they fled the city, abandoning control of Parliament to the hardliners.

Since they dominated the general assembly, it meant the hardliners were in full control of the government. Therefore a new administration was set up under the extremist marquess of Argyll. But lacking popular support, the hardliners attempted to shore up their position by securing an alliance with Cromwell, now the Parliamentarians' leading general – an unlikely league considering that all they had in common was a mutual hatred of monarchy. Perceiving it as a means of gaining Scottish support, Cromwell was amenable. But his co-operation came at a price. He insisted that the government eject from their charges all ministers tainted with – or suspected of being tainted with – support for the Engagement, or who refused or omitted to preach against it, and replace them with hardliners.

When Cromwell visited Edinburgh in October 1648 he demanded that the purge be extended to the civil administration. In January 1649 Parliament responded by passing the Act of the Classes. This specifically forbade the supporters of Montrose's 'horrid rebellioun', those associated with the 'unlaufull engagement' or 'censured for malignancie', and anyone guilty of immorality or neglect of family worship, from holding public office both at national and local level. The purge extended to the army, and military tribunals were set up to weed out 'all engagers, malignants and other backsliders' from its ranks. Because many of the victims were seasoned veterans with extensive military experience gained from service in the Thirty Years' War, it left the army gravely weakened, as would become disastrously apparent.

Since the majority of the influential laity and almost all the nobility were opposed to the hardliners, and therefore excluded from the government, political power passed to narrow-minded extremists who were demonstrably unfit to hold public office. The same applied in the case of the Church where the upstart replacements of the ejected ministers incurred the odium of the nobility and gentry in particular. As Sir Ewen Cameron observed, 'every parish had a tyrant who made the greatest Lord in the district stoop to his authority. The kirk was the place where he kept his court; the pulpit his throne or tribunal from where he issued his terrible decrees; and twelve or fourteen soure, ignorant enthusiasts, under the title of elders, composed his council.' Thus was established a fundamentalist clerical dictatorship supported by a hard core of unrepresentative narrow-minded extremists.

On 30 January 1649, one week after the passing of the Act of the Classes, King Charles was executed. Notwithstanding their opposition to him, this horrified the Scots of all classes who proclaimed his eighteen-year-old son king as Charles II. In March commissioners were sent to meet him in Holland, where he had taken refuge, to persuade him to accept the Scottish crown. But it was conditional on his subscribing to the Solemn League and Covenant and undertaking to impose the presbyterian form of Church government on England and Ireland. At first Charles prevaricated, pinning his hopes on Montrose, who was in the north rallying the clansmen to his cause. But the response was so disappointing that he was left with no alternative but to submit. Therefore on 17 April, salving a conscience he seldom allowed to interfere with political expediency, he conceded the Scottish demands, thus leaving Montrose in the lurch.*

When Charles arrived in Scotland in June 1649 he was compelled to undergo a penitential indoctrination by the fundamentalist clerics who were determined to purge the soul of this pleasure-loving young man and bring him into 'the true faith'. Forced to listen to their interminable sermons (six in a day on one occasion), with his attendants dismissed and replaced by dour presbyterians, he was obliged to submit to the most intimate scrutiny of his private life. Finally he was compelled to sign a humiliating denunciation of his parents. Small wonder that he conceived an abiding hatred of presbytery in general, and the extremists in particular, which would become abundantly apparent.

That lay in the future. Meanwhile Charles's presence in Scotland was perceived by the English Parliamentarians as a threat to their regime, the more so because there was still strong royalist support in England. In June 1650 the English Council of State

---

* Ten days later Montrose was defeated at Carbisdale and later captured. Taken to Edinburgh he was tried, convicted of treason, and in May 1650 he was hanged. A gifted commander, as well as a man of principle and humanity, he is justly regarded as an iconic figure in the annals of Scottish history.

ordered a pre-emptive invasion of Scotland. Therefore the following month a 16,000-strong army under Cromwell crossed the Tweed. The Scots responded by sending a numerically superior army under David Leslie to oppose him. But recognising that the army had become so debilitated as a result of the purges that it was no match against Cromwell's ironsides, Leslie fell back on Edinburgh. Cromwell pursued him as far as the outskirts of the city where he set up camp, and a stalemate ensued.

Meanwhile with a lack of realism of which only religious zealots are capable, the commissioners of the general assembly ordered a further purge of the army to rid it once and for all of anyone suspected of being an engager or a malignant. This was in the belief that if it were to consist exclusively of 'God's elect', and undefiled by anyone deviating from Holy Writ, He would deliver them victory against the English sectarians. Despite Leslie's vehement protests the purge went ahead. Accordingly some 3,000 suspected engagers and malignants, who at this of all times could least be spared, were dismissed.

But Cromwell himself was encountering difficulties as his army was being steadily reduced by a combination of disease and the effects of enduring a typically wet Scottish summer without tents. Since he was cut off from Leith, and therefore unable to take delivery of supplies by sea, he decided to withdraw to Dunbar where supplies could reach him without risk of interception. Leslie and his army gave chase and took up a position on the edge of the Lammermuirs overlooking Dunbar. Convinced that the Lord of Hosts would deliver victory to their 'purified' army, his chaplains persuaded him against his better judgement to abandon his position and attack Cromwell's army as it lay encamped outside the town.

Their faith proved woefully misplaced. The Scots were outmanoeuvred and suffered a crushing defeat. On 7 September, following on the heels of the panicking survivors, Cromwell entered Edinburgh and took possession of the city, the extremist leaders having fled to Stirling. Since the majority of Scots were not prepared to submit, the young King Charles became the main focus of resistance. At the time he and Colonel Middleton were busy rallying support in the north-east, traditionally a centre of Catholicism, where the people were generally sympathetic to his cause. The south-west, on the other hand, was a Covenanting stronghold, and it was there that the extremists raised an army. Known as the Western army, its recruits were mainly drawn from the counties of Lanark, Ayr, Renfrew, Kirkcudbright and Wigtown.* Their leaders included ultra-extremists like Gilbert Ker who took the view that only if the Covenanting cause were served by a force of godly men untainted by association with the king and his cause would it stand any chance of success.

At a meeting of the Glasgow synod on 2 October they drew up a 'remonstrance' for submission to the Committee of Estates. This attributed the defeat at Dunbar to a want of commitment to the 'true cause' on Charles's part, and his failure to expel 'all

---

* But not apparently Dumfriesshire which could be taken to suggest that support for the Covenant – or at least the fundamentalists – was less strong there.

disaffected and profane persons' from his company. In their view, this was responsible for incurring the wrath of God, and defeat was His punishment. It was followed by a second 'remonstrance' which was proclaimed at Dumfries. In terms of this, the remonstrants, as they called themselves, declared their refusal to support Charles until he 'had given satisfactory evidence of sincere repentance' and promised to 'abandon the company of malignants'. The remonstrances were presented to Parliament and the general assembly for approval which in both cases was readily forthcoming.

In the event the Western army, re-named the Holy army, proved a broken reed. In early December it was routed by an English force under Major-General Lambert at Hamilton. This created a split within the Covenanting movement. On the one hand were the fundamentalist remonstrants who held that the Act of the Classes had not been applied strictly enough and were determined that the army should be purged still more rigorously. Later known as the protesters, the remonstrants were the spiritual forebears of the radical Covenanters who would become such a thorn in the government's flesh during the reign of Charles II.*

Opposing them was the moderate majority who, more realistically, used their voting strength to pass the 'first public resolution'. This opened the way for all who were not 'excommunicated, forfeited, notoriously wicked, or enemies of the Covenant' to be readmitted to the public service and re-enlisted in the army. The only proviso was that they should make abject atonement for their perceived apostasy to their local presbytery. This concession appalled the remonstrants and left a legacy of mutual hatred between the two factions – the remonstrants (later the protesters) and the resolutioners – which far exceeded the animosity that had existed between the presbyterians and episcopalians.

Meanwhile the remonstrants' defeat at Dunbar meant that control of the Committee of Estates passed to the moderate resolutioners, and they were responsible for having Charles crowned king of Scots on 1 January 1651. But it was little more than a charade, for the fact that Cromwell was in control of southern Scotland meant that Charles's rule was limited to the region beyond the Forth and Clyde, and even that was tenuous since Cromwell was already extending his campaign to northern Scotland. However, at that point Cromwell fell ill and the offensive stalled. But following his recovery in July, the English were on the march again and by the end of the month they had reached Perth.[37]

Meanwhile David Leslie, now restored to command of the Scottish army, decided that instead of confronting Cromwell with the virtual certainty of defeat his only course was to give him the slip by invading England. Therefore on 6 August, joined by King Charles and his supporters, he crossed the border. Cromwell immediately split his force. Leaving part of it under General Monck to continue the campaign

---

* These fundamentalists are habitually referred to as the Covenanters, which is a fallacy because they merely represented the extremist wing of the Covenanting movement.

against the Scots, he headed south with the rest of his army in hot pursuit of King Charles and Leslie. Notwithstanding that the hoped-for support from the English royalists failed to materialise, King Charles and Leslie continued their advance southwards and by 25 August they reached Worcester where Charles was proclaimed king of England. Five days later Cromwell caught up with them, and on 3 September a battle took place at which the Scots were heavily defeated. Leslie was among the many prisoners taken, while Charles, having narrowly escaped capture and almost certain execution, managed to reach the safety of the Continent.

THIRTEEN

Church Versus State

THE COMMONWEALTH

General Monck's suppression of the remaining Scottish resistance was achieved by a steady process of attrition. His immediate objective was to capture Stirling and arrest the Committee of Estates who had taken refuge there. The town surrendered, but only after the Committee of Estates had escaped to Dundee where they set up an embryonic government. Meanwhile the castle garrison held out. But not for long. Monck brought up his siege artillery and bombarded them into submission, when he took possession of the Scottish records, but not the Scottish regalia, which had been removed to the temporary safety of Dunottar castle on the north-east coast.* Having installed a garrison, Monck headed for Dundee, determined to run the Committee of Estates to earth. But once again they gave him the slip, escaping this time to Kirriemuir, and from there to Alyth where they were finally captured in August 1650. Meanwhile a Scottish force of 300 footsoldiers and some horse had been installed at Dumfries castle to defend the south-west. But when word came of the approach of a detachment of English troops, they fled the town together with many of the inhabitants.[1]

By October Scotland was to all intents and purposes a conquered country, with only the Highlands remaining unoccupied. Nevertheless Monck ensured that the region was effectively isolated to prevent outbreaks of unrest from spreading south. Presciently the English Council of State, advised by Cromwell, decided that, rather than treat Scotland as a conquered country, they should incorporate it into the Commonwealth, officially as an equal partner but in reality very much the junior one. Accordingly the English Parliament appointed eight commissioners to meet Scottish representatives to negotiate (in effect dictate) the terms of its incorporation. The fact that the commissioners included three generals, a colonel and a major emphasised the essentially military character of the new regime.

In mid-January 1652, having established themselves at Dalkeith castle, the commissioners instructed all burghs and shires to send deputies there to be informed of the English proposals for the 'settlement of Scotland'. Certain smaller burghs such as Sanquhar, Annan and Lochmaben were exempted 'on account of their poverty',

---

* Removed from there the following May, shortly before the castle fell to the English, it was hidden under the floor of the church at nearby Kinneff where it remained until after the Restoration.

while others ignored the request. They included Dumfries. No reason was given, but it was most likely in protest at Scotland's absorption into the Commonwealth.[2] The majority of the burghs and shires were more compliant. Once assembled at Dalkeith castle, the deputies were presented with the Tender of Incorporation which set out in detail the English Parliament's proposals for the governance of Scotland. A lengthy document, it provided among other things for the establishment of a system of justice, as well as religious toleration for all except 'prelatists and papists'. This was anathema to the protesters and resolutioners alike, the more so because it was in clear breach of the terms of the Solemn League and Covenant to which, in their view, the English were still committed.

To forestall any prevarication on the part of the deputies, by for example claiming that they would need to refer to their burgh or shire for instructions, it was stipulated that they were there as plenipotentiaries. This meant they were fully empowered to subscribe to the Tender of Incorporation without having to obtain the consent of their principals. Moreover it was made plain that a refusal would cost them their goods and property. This was enough to enforce compliance, but the fact that some declined was a measure of the depth of Scottish hostility to the union.[3]

Generally speaking, the provisions of the Tender of Incorporation were fair and reasonable. The only contentious issue, at least in the eyes of the resolutioners and protesters, was the grant of religious toleration. This was about the only common ground between them; otherwise the two factions remained fundamentally opposed to each other, the one advocating a degree of moderation while the other continued intransigent. Their mutual antagonism came to a head at a meeting of the general assembly in July 1652. Because it had been convened by the resolutioners, a group of protesters objected to it claiming that it was unconstitutional. When they appealed to the commissioners for support on the grounds of their mutual hatred of 'Charles Stuart, crowned king', the resolutioner-dominated assembly threatened them with the full panoply of ecclesiastical retribution unless they withdrew their objection.

By this time the commissioners had had enough of these bickering clerics. Therefore, when the next meeting of the general assembly was held in an Edinburgh church in July 1653, a detachment of English soldiery was posted outside. No sooner had the moderator delivered the opening prayer than their commander Colonel Cotterel forced his way in to the church accompanied by a group of armed men. Addressing the moderator, he demanded to know on what authority the assembly had been convened. The moderator replied that it was a court of Jesus Christ 'that meddled not with civil affairs' (patently untrue), and that its authority stemmed from God. But the colonel was not there to engage in semantics. Without further ado he ordered the ministers and commissioners out of the church. They tried to protest, but when loaded muskets were turned on them they meekly obeyed. Once outside they were marched under armed guard to the Bruntsfield links beyond the city wall. There their names were taken and they were ordered never to meet again under pain of death. That was the last general assembly to be held until 1690. Nevertheless the presbyterian form of Church government with its kirk sessions, presbyteries and synods continued as before.[4]

Once the deputies had subscribed to the Tender of Incorporation they were invited to present proposals – or 'Desires' – to the English commissioners, in other words any additional provisions or qualifications they deemed appropriate. Some did. They included the deputies for Dumfriesshire and other Border counties, and it was a reflection of the prevailing unrest that they asked that the Tender should include a provision for the suppression of lawlessness in the region.[5]

In March the Tender was presented to the English Parliament along with the 'Desires' put forward by the deputies. Accepted without qualification, they were incorporated in a document ponderously entitled *The Declaration of the Parliament of England, in order to the Uniting of Scotland into one Commonwealth with England*. On the instructions of the English Parliament, the commissioners ordered it to be published throughout Scotland. Following this, the burghs and shires were directed to send representatives to Edinburgh to elect twenty-one deputies – fourteen for the shires and seven for the burghs – for the purpose of determining the shape of the new regime.

Once again Sanquhar, Lochmaben and Annan were exempted on grounds of poverty, while Dumfries refused to send a representative. The county, on the other hand, appointed a Fifeshire laird, George Blair of Garvock. In the event the whole exercise was a charade, for when the representatives met the English commissioners they found that, far from being allowed to take part in the discussions, they were merely there to provide information. The imposition of both the Tender and the Commonwealth regime on their country was a source of widespread resentment among the Scots (notwithstanding that for a conquered people they were being remarkably well treated), one disaffected minister comparing their position to that of 'the poor bird [who] is embodied in the hawk that has eaten it up'.

In the event there was a considerable delay before Scotland was fully incorporated into the Commonwealth. This was because Cromwell's quarrels with successive Parliaments meant that the union did not receive legislative sanction until 1657. Meanwhile the country continued to be governed by the commissioners on an *ad hoc* basis under the overall supervision of the army. Their rule was both fair and moderate, the diarist John Nicoll being particularly complimentary about the impartiality of those appointed to the seats of justice. 'To speak treuth', he wrote, 'the Englische wer moir indulgent and merciful to the Scottis nor [than] wes the Scottis to their awin cuntriemen and nychtbouris', going on to say that 'they also filled up the roumes of justice courtes with very honest clerkis and memberis of that judicatory'.[6]

In 1653 the outbreak of war between England and Holland forced the English to scale down their military presence in Scotland in order to provide additional troops for service in the campaign. Similarly, the need to finance the war meant they had to cut down on the occupation costs and impose additional taxes to cover the deficit. Most important of all, it meant the departure of General Monck, who was given command of the expeditionary force. He was replaced by Colonel Lilburne, a subordinate commander, but as a lower ranking officer he lacked Monck's authority.

Taking advantage of Monck's departure, Charles, who had established a court-in-exile on the Continent, sent the earl of Glencairn to Scotland to raise a rebellion in the Highlands where royalist support was strongest. A former Engager, he had taken part in Hamilton's ill-fated campaign of 1648 and was now one of Charles's trusted supporters. On the face of it the prospects boded well. The presence of the English soldiery was deeply unpopular, notwithstanding that they were under strict orders not to oppress the Scottish people. So too were the taxes imposed to meet the occupation costs. Above all there was widespread resentment of English rule.

Landing on the north-west coast in August 1653, Glencairn found himself confronted with the challenging task of persuading a group of quarrelling clan chiefs to sink their differences and make common cause against the English occupiers, rendered the more difficult because he himself was a Lowlander. Nevertheless he succeeded in raising a force of some 5,000 men, and by the end of the year his campaign, having begun with a series of violent clashes, had grown into a full-scale rising which extended well beyond the Highlands. Notwithstanding the substantial English presence in the region, another revolt broke out in the south-west. By December 1653 it had spread to the extent that Colonel Lilburne authorised the formation of a local guard to apprehend 'all Moss Troopers, Tories, and other disturbers of the public peace'.[7] Many noble and landed families attempted to safeguard themselves and their property by hedging their position. Thus, whereas the father remained at home professing loyalty to the Commonwealth, the sons joined the rising as his proxies.

The rebellion forced the Commonwealth administration into a change of policy. Since it was apparent that, despite their protestations of loyalty to the existing regime, the nobility and gentry were royalist sympathisers at heart, they were disqualified from holding public office. Nor were they allowed to carry arms. Yet such was the prevailing lawlessness in the Highlands that, appreciating the need for them to defend their lands and property, and indeed their lives, Lilburne allowed the local nobility and gentry to organise armed guards. In December 1653 – presumably for the same reason – the privilege was extended to landowners in the south-west.[8]

In early 1654 Charles replaced the earl of Glencairn with the more dynamic Colonel Middleton, relegating the earl to a subordinate command. It proved a serious mistake. A tough, hard-drinking ex-ranker who had served as a pikeman in the Covenanting army, Middleton was a competent enough soldier; but, essentially a man of the sword, he lacked the diplomatic skills needed to persuade the fractious clan chiefs to work for the common cause. Worse still he fell out with Glencairn, and their inability to co-operate was mainly responsible for the failure of the rising.

Its fate was sealed with the ending of the Dutch War in April 1654, because Middleton was denied the reinforcements he had been counting on from the Continent, while the English army of occupation was strengthened by the return of battle-hardened veterans from the war. Most important of all, it marked the return of General Monck, who put fresh heart into Lilburne's somewhat lacklustre campaign. One of his first acts was to force the noble and landed families to come on side by giving them three weeks in which to declare for the Commonwealth or face severe penalties. During the summer of 1654 he scored a number of tactical successes, steadily wearing down the royalists' resistance. Following a reverse on the shores of Loch Garry, Middleton returned to Charles's court-in-exile leaving Glencairn in charge. But after his defeat in a skirmish at Dalnaspidal in July 1654, the rising fizzled out, and by the end of September most of the leaders had submitted.

Appreciating that punitive reprisals would be counterproductive, Monck's surrender terms, incorporated in the Act of Pardon and Grace, were generally lenient. They stipulated that if those who took part in the rising surrendered their arms and entered into bonds for their future good behaviour they would be granted an amnesty. Nevertheless some of the leading participants were heavily fined, the earl of Queensberry* for example being mulcted in the sum of £4,000 while others had their estates forfeited. In many cases fines were tantamount to forfeiture because the victims were compelled to borrow money on the security of their estates to pay them, and if unable to repay they were forced into sequestration.

The Commonwealth government went further. Reflecting its determination to widen the scope of landownership, it introduced a measure which compelled lenders to accept land instead of money in satisfaction of their debts. In some cases fines were reduced, or remitted altogether, in recognition of subsequent loyal service to the Commonwealth. A case in point was James Johnstone second earl of Hartfell. Initially he was fined the sum of £4,000 which was later reduced to £2,000. However, when he abandoned (or professed to abandon) his support for the royalist cause by sitting in the Commonwealth Parliament as member for Dumfriesshire, he was granted a full remission.[9]

Following the suppression of the rebellion, the English Council of State scaled back the military aspect of the Scottish administration and introduced a measure of devolved government. Accordingly in May 1655, with Cromwell's approval, it established a Council of nine – seven Englishmen including Monck, and two Scots – who were responsible for the civil administration of Scotland, although it was not until September that the new regime took power. The first president was Roger Boyle lord Broghill. An Irishman and a younger son of the earl of Cork (as well as being a noted dramatist), he had fought for the royalists in Ireland. Later he changed his allegiance and was appointed to a leading position in the Commonwealth government of Ireland where he served with such distinction that Cromwell put him in charge of the civil administration of Scotland.

An early priority was the reform of the justice system. A start had been made in 1652 when the commissioners responsible for the government of Scotland appointed

---

* He had already been fined 180,000 merks for taking part in Montrose's campaign, of which he had paid 120,000, the balance of 60,000 merks being remitted (*Scots Peerage* vii, 135).

four Englishmen and three Scots as commissioners for justice, as well as appointing sheriffs for each county. The Supreme Court of Justice was composed mainly of Scots, and in 1654 an ordinance was passed abolishing the landowners' baronial courts. In the burghs the election of councillors and magistrates was suspended from 1652 until September 1655 when the ban was lifted. After that it was open to anyone to stand for office except those with a record of opposition to the Commonwealth, or who declined to take the oath of allegiance to it.

In order to render justice more accessible at local level, Broghill arranged for members of the Supreme Court of Justice to conduct regular 'assizes' or circuit courts throughout Scotland, and in May 1656 there is a record of one being held at Dumfries.[10] He was also responsible for the introduction of justices of the peace. Their duties were wide-ranging. Although primarily concerned with the maintenance of law and order, they were also responsible for ensuring that roads and bridges were maintained to a usable standard, for taking appropriate measures in the event of an outbreak of plague, and – reflecting the essentially puritanical character of the Commonwealth regime – for punishing 'fornication, swearing, and the breaking of the Lord's Day'.

Meanwhile the mutual antagonism between the resolutioners and the protesters continued unabated. In view of its destabilising influence on the Commonwealth regime in Scotland, Cromwell summoned their leaders to a conference in London in an attempt to persuade them to sink their differences. But such was their intransigence and refusal to compromise that he was forced to intervene. Although naturally drawn to the protester minority on account of their shared hatred of the monarchy, he found them so impossible to deal with that, notwithstanding their royalist sympathies, he came down on the side of the resolutioners, persuaded by the arguments of their silver-tongued spokesman James Sharp (or Sharp of that Ilk as he referred to him). But this was conditional on their undertaking to support the government and abandon the practice of praying for the king, which they were enjoined to do under threat of forfeiture of their livings and hence their stipends.

Cromwell died on 3 September 1658 having nominated his son Richard to succeed him as Protector. Although accepted by the army, it soon became apparent that he had no real authority. Therefore, in an attempt to strengthen his position, he summoned a Parliament from which all royalists were excluded. In Scotland the elections were rigged to the extent that all candidates had to be approved by the Council of State. Of those standing for the twenty-eight Scottish seats, seventeen were Englishmen. They included Major Jeremiah Tolhurst, a former governor of Carlisle castle, who was returned as member for the Dumfries burghs.[11]

Meanwhile Generals Lambert and Fleetwood, and other military commanders, determined to assert the supremacy of the army, claimed that it was a separate estate independent of the civil authorities. Because this was quite unacceptable to Parliament, it enlisted the support of Richard Cromwell as Protector. But it was fighting a losing battle, and four months later the army forced its dissolution.

Consequently political power passed to a military junta headed by Lambert and Fleetwood, and Richard Cromwell was forced to resign.* In May 1659, to give their actions a veneer of legitimacy, the generals recalled the Rump Parliament which Cromwell had dissolved in April 1653. Because this rescinded all legislation passed by subsequent Parliaments, including the Tender of Incorporation, it meant that technically Scotland was no longer part of the Commonwealth and the judiciary was deprived of its authority.

By October 1659 tensions between the civil and military authorities had become so acute that Lambert and Fleetwood expelled the Rump Parliament and established a Committee of Safety. But it soon became apparent that they failed to carry the army with them, because a substantial minority continued to support the Rump. Unable to control the situation, Fleetwood resigned leaving the more emollient Lambert to negotiate terms with the Rump Parliament. But because it lacked the authority to deal with a situation which was rapidly getting out of hand, many people looked to General Monck with his well-disciplined army of occupation in Scotland, purged of all unreliable elements, as the one man capable of restoring order.

For the previous few months – ever since the Commonwealth was dissolved – Monck had been governing Scotland on an *ad hoc* basis using the army to enforce law and order. During August and September 1659 it had to deal among other things with large-scale outbreaks of cattle-thieving in Annandale and Nithsdale.[12] In early December, Monck established his headquarters at Coldstream ready to march, and on 1 January 1660 he crossed the Tweed. At this stage his main concern was to defend the authority of Parliament, the question of Charles's restoration probably being the last thing on his mind. Nevertheless, on reaching London he soon found himself at odds with the Rump Parliament. Therefore, to dilute its membership, he recalled those who had been excluded by Pride's Purge[†] for their suspected royalist sympathies. This effectively restored the Long Parliament, and in March it dissolved itself to allow for the election of a Convention Parliament. It met in April, and because the majority of its members were strongly pro-monarchy a Restoration of the monarchy began to look increasingly likely. Recognising this, Monck sent emissaries to Charles at Breda in Holland to negotiate the conditions of his return. These were incorporated in the Declaration of Breda, and following its acceptance by Parliament on 1 May Charles was proclaimed king.

The impending Restoration encouraged Sharp and his colleagues to travel to Breda to meet Charles in the hopes of enlisting his support for presbytery, and in particular the resolutioners. But he was not going to be drawn into committing himself; nor obviously was he going to reveal his plans for dismantling the presbyterian system of

---

* He retired to France to avoid his creditors, but later returned to England where he lived in obscurity until his death in 1712 at the age of eighty-five.

† This took place in December 1648 when a detachment of troops under Colonel Pride forcibly prevented those members of Parliament known or suspected of being sympathetic towards Charles I from entering the building, thus ensuring a majority in favour of putting him on trial for treason.

Church government. Therefore he dissembled. While professing a 'great affection for our country and kirk', he blandly assured Sharp that he had no desire 'to wrong the settled government of our Church', promising him that 'he would reserve a full communing about it until his coming to England'. Fine words, but the reality was not what Sharp and his colleagues hoped for, least of all expected.

RESTORATION AND RETRIBUTION

Charles's return on 29 May 1660 – his thirtieth birthday – was celebrated with scenes of wild jubilation throughout the land. In Edinburgh bells were rung, cannons roared, trumpets sounded and there was dancing in the streets. As Johnston of Wariston, the principal author of the Covenant, sourly observed, 'there was a great ryot, excess [and] profanitys', adding the prayer that 'the Lord be merciful to us'.[13] A timely invocation as events would prove. At Dumfries the burgh council obsequiously voted to present a loyal address to the king, while the local kirk session, bowing to reality, ingratiatingly set aside a day of thanksgiving for his restoration.[14]

Meanwhile the commissioners appointed by Monck continued to govern Scotland until they were replaced by a restored Committee of Estates. At Charles's insistence one of their first priorities was the suppression of presbytery, in particular the protester faction. Apart from holding a deep-seated personal grudge against them for their treatment of him at the time he was forced to rely on their support, he regarded their insistence on his acceptance of presbytery and the enforcement of the Solemn League and Covenant as dangerously subversive. 'Not a religion for gentlemen' as he observed dismissively. Although not naturally vindictive, he was determined to suppress these fundamentalists who had caused his father so much trouble and looked set to become a thorn in his own flesh as well.

Therefore one of the Committee of Estates' first acts was to order the arrest of eleven protester ministers who had come to Edinburgh to present a petition to Charles. Reminding him of the promise he had given at the time of his coronation in 1651, the petition urged him to procure the observance of the Solemn League and Covenant throughout the realm – a piece of temerity that earned them a spell of imprisonment. The Committee of Estates proceeded to ban unlawful meetings and conventicles, while the presenting of seditious petitions and remonstrances was made a punishable offence. Special retribution was reserved for those protesters who had associated themselves with the Western Remonstrance of 1650. They included men like Johnston of Wariston, his fellow extremist James Guthrie, and others, who were convicted of treason and sentenced to execution. They were followed to the block by the extremists' leader, the marquess of Argyll, despite his having placed the crown on Charles's head at his coronation.

On the other hand, those who had remained loyal to the royal cause were handsomely rewarded. A notable example was James Johnstone second earl of Hartfell. Notwithstanding that he had come to terms with the Commonwealth regime and was appointed member of Parliament for Dumfriesshire, he had suffered losses in excess of £24,000, been imprisoned and narrowly escaped execution for supporting the royal cause. Therefore he was compensated with appointment to the Privy Council, and confirmation in his family's hereditary offices of steward of Annandale and keeper of Lochmaben. Further, in 1661 he was given the additional title of earl of Annandale, and in April the following year a charter was issued under the Great Seal creating him earl of Annandale and Hartfell.*

Statesmanlike, King Charles's choice of ministers to govern Scotland included men with a Covenanting past (in fact he would have been hard put to it to find anyone who had not subscribed to the Covenant, voluntarily or otherwise). A prime example was the earl of Lauderdale. A former subscriber, he had been among those responsible for negotiating the terms of the Engagement with Charles's father, and was later captured fighting for Charles himself at Worcester. Thereafter he had been incarcerated in a succession of English prisons until released in March 1660. He was appointed Secretary of State with overall responsibility for the conduct of Scottish affairs. Another subscriber to the Covenant, and later an Engager, was the earl of Glencairn, who was appointed Chancellor, doubtless in reward for co-ordinating the rising. Others with a Covenanting past included the earl of Rothes who had been captured at Worcester and was now appointed Lord President of the Council.

Finally there was John Middleton, a man with a somewhat chequered career. A veteran of the Thirty Years' War, he had served in the Covenanting army under Montrose (before the latter switched his support to the king) and rose to become David Leslie's second-in-command at Philiphaugh. Later he was captured while taking part in the duke of Hamilton's abortive campaign of 1648. Escaping from prison, he took refuge in Holland where he joined King Charles, and it was mainly on account of his military experience that Charles sent him to Scotland to take charge of the Glencairn rising. Now earl of Middleton, he was appointed king's commissioner to the new Scottish Parliament which was convened in January 1661.

On Charles's instructions, Parliament decreed a state funeral for Montrose. Accordingly his remains were disinterred and placed in a suitably magnificent coffin along with his skull, which was removed from the spike on the Edinburgh tollbooth

---

*   See Genealogical Table 6. Earl James died in 1672 and was succeeded by his eldest surviving son William, who in 1701 was created marquess of Annandale. William was twice married. By his first wife he had a son James who succeeded him as the second marquess, and a daughter Henrietta who married the first earl of Hopetoun and was the ancestress of the Hope-Johnstones. By his second wife, William had another son George who succeeded his half-brother as third marquess of Annandale. When George died without issue in 1792 the marquessate became extinct, and similarly the earldoms of Hartfell (under the 1643 creation) and Annandale (under the 1661 creation). Claims to the Annandale earldom by descendants of Countess Henrietta (the second marquess's sister) in 1844 and 1879 were rejected on the grounds that the succession was limited to *heirs male of the body* of Earl James, and that these titles became extinct on the death of George the third marquess. When in 1983 Patrick Hope-Johnstone claimed the earldom of Annandale and Hartfell under the 1662 creation, the House of Lords judges (sitting as the Committee of Privileges) ruled that, because the succession was open to Earl James's *heirs male general*, he was entitled to it as the senior male representative of Countess Henrietta.

where it had remained for the past ten years. After the funeral, his coffin lay in state in the abbey church of Holyrood for upwards of a year before it was moved to its final resting place in St Giles' Cathedral. Montrose deserved no less; but it was ironic that his funeral should be ordered by a king who had left him in the lurch and organised by Middleton who had fought against him at Philiphaugh.

In March 1661, at King Charles's behest, the Scottish Parliament passed the Act Rescissory which affirmed his right to appoint all officers of state, including privy councillors and judges, to summon Parliament and raise an army. As its name implied, it declared all Parliaments held since 1633 invalid, except that of 1651 which was held while Charles was king of Scots. Consequently all Acts giving legislative effect to the Covenant, the Solemn League and Covenant, and the Westminster Confession of Faith were rescinded. Thus the whole basis of presbytery and its system of Church government was swept away. Fears that this was a prelude to the restoration of episcopacy prompted a number of synods to lodge a formal protest to which the government turned a deaf ear.

The Act Rescissory was followed by another Act declaring the king's intention to maintain the Church's doctrine and worship as it was established in the reigns of his father and grandfather. It further provided that the government of the Church would be secured 'in such a way as shall be most agreeable to the Word of God, most suitable to monarchical government and most complying with the public peace and quiet of the kingdom', thus giving legislative effect to Charles's intention to restore episcopacy. When in April the synod of Dumfries, following the example of those of Glasgow, Ayr and Fife, was about to issue a proclamation threatening to depose all ministers who accepted episcopacy, its proceedings were forcibly terminated.[15]

In July 1661 Parliament, in effect the Committee of Estates, was prorogued. Thereafter responsibility for the government of Scotland devolved on the Privy Council which would remain the principal instrument of Charles's Scottish policy throughout the rest of his reign. In September he issued a letter to the Council effectively ordering it to establish episcopacy as the standard form of Church government in Scotland. Accordingly it appointed compliant resolutioner ministers to the episcopal sees which had remained vacant since 1638, and at the same time it legislated for the inclusion of the Lord's Prayer and the Apostles' Creed in church services. This was anathema to the protesters who denounced them as 'rotten wheelbarrows for carrying souls to Hell'. In December, four of the newly appointed bishops travelled to London for consecration by their Anglican counterparts. They included James Sharp. A leading resolutioner he had accepted the appointment of archbishop of St Andrews, thus incurring the undying hatred of the protesters who branded him a Judas and a betrayer of presbytery. Returning to Scotland the following April, he and his colleagues consecrated the other bishops, thus putting the seal on the restoration of episcopacy.

In May 1662, on the king's instructions, the Privy Council issued a proclamation prohibiting all meetings of presbyteries, synods and kirk sessions without the consent of their diocesan bishop. A far-reaching measure, it effectively subordinated presbytery to the episcopacy. Furthermore, all ministers were required to take an oath of allegiance to the king and acknowledge his supremacy under pain of deprivation of their livings. Among the many recusants was John Brown, minister of St Mungo, who was ejected from his living. Additionally he was charged with denouncing those of his colleagues who had taken the oath as 'perjured knaves and villains', and following his conviction he was ordered to be kept 'a close prisoner in the Tollbooth' in Edinburgh.[16]

Later that year the campaign against presbytery was extended to the civil service, when the Privy Council demanded that all those in public employment should swear an oath abjuring the Covenants and pledge their allegiance to the king. Failure to do so would result in their instant dismissal. The Council went further. In a measure that was deliberately aimed at the protesters, it required all ministers to have their appointments collated (i.e. confirmed) by their diocesan bishop. Those failing to do so by 1 November (the deadline was extended to 1 February 1663) would be deprived of their livings and forced to remove themselves from the bounds of their presbyteries. Since many protester and some resolutioner ministers chose deprivation rather than collation, nearly a quarter of all parishes were left without a preacher, while more than half the ministers in Dumfriesshire were 'outed'.[17] Of the twenty in lower Nithsdale and the adjacent part of Galloway only two were prepared to conform, while the rest were deprived of their livings.[18] They included John Welsh, a great-grandson of Knox and later a leading opponent of the extremists, who was ejected from the parish of Irongray.

The deprived (or 'outed') ministers were replaced by men drawn mainly from the north where support for episcopacy was strongest. Not surprisingly these intruded curates, as they were known, were extremely unpopular. Consequently they found themselves preaching to depleted congregations as their parishioners deserted them for the more wholesome religious fare meted out by the deprived ministers at conventicles held in private houses or out on the hills and moors. In his *History* Bishop Burnet was particularly scathing about the intruded curates: 'These new incumbents', he wrote, 'were very mean and despicable in all respects; they were the worst preachers I ever heard; they were ignorant to a reproach, and many of them were openly vicious. They were a disgrace to their orders, and indeed were the dregs and refuse of the northern parts.' He was hardly less scathing about some of the ejected ministers whom he described as 'generally sour little men [with] narrow souls and low notions, [having] little learning among them'.[19] There were times when public resentment of the intruded curates erupted into violence, and on one occasion Welsh's replacement at Irongray had to take to his heels when he was assailed by a volley of stones flung at him by the women of the parish. Eventually the pulpits of the outed ministers were filled, but in some cases troops had to be drafted in to protect their replacements.

In June 1663 Parliament passed an Act known as 'the bishops' dragnet' which banned the holding of conventicles. Additionally it prohibited deprived ministers from exercising their ministry under pain of being charged with sedition, while the people were ordered to attend their parish church or suffer heavy fines. The fines were indeed heavy: for example a laird could be fined up to a quarter of his annual rental, a tenant a fourth part of his moveable goods, and similarly burgesses who suffered the additional penalty of forfeiture of their right to trade. Parliament went further. In August it passed the Mile Act which forbade deprived ministers from living within twenty miles of their former churches, six miles of a major city, and three miles from a burgh, under similar penalties.

Nevertheless the hardline protester ministers continued to preach at conventicles where the faithful were prepared to risk crippling fines rather than compromise their principles by attending services conducted by intruded curates. As often as not, refusal to pay a fine resulted in troops being quartered on the delinquent's home until they paid up. Troops were also used to break up conventicles, often leading to bloody clashes with the communicants. When in 1665 war broke out between England and Holland,where many deprived ministers had taken refuge, fears that they might instigate a full-scale rising led to further repression.

In fact a rising did occur, although not at the instigation of deprived ministers. It arose as a result of a comparatively minor incident. In November 1666, learning that a troop of soldiers were about to roast a local farmer from Dalry, Kirkcudbrightshire, over a griddle for non-payment of a fine, a group of local sympathisers came to his rescue, and driving off the soldiers they wounded one of them. Knowing that reprisals would be swift and merciless, the rescuers struck first. A call went out to the faithful to assemble at Irongray kirk in readiness to march on Dumfries. This met with an overwhelming response, and many flocked to join them.

Meanwhile Sir James Turner,* the commander of the troops in the south-west, summoned a company of troops to join him at Dumfries to be issued with powder and shot in readiness for an encounter with the rebels. But the rebels got there first. When they attacked Turner's headquarters, he was caught in the act of escaping, still in his 'nightgown, nightcap, drawers and socks'. Although his life was spared, the rebels proceeded to ransack his house, impounding a quantity of money (presumably the soldiers' pay), before heading for the market cross. There, incongruously, they declared their loyalty to the king and drank his health before embarking on a recruiting drive throughout the south-west.

They succeeded in raising a 1,000-strong force supplemented by some horsemen from Galloway.[20] Armed mostly with scythes, pitchforks and staves, they assembled at Lanark before advancing on Edinburgh. They claimed it was a peaceful demonstration and that all they wanted was to petition the privy councillors to redress their grievances. Evidently the privy councillors thought otherwise, because they sent a

---

*   A rough soldier of fortune he had served in the Thirty Years' War. Returning to Scotland, he enlisted in the Covenanting army until the time of the Engagement when he switched his support to the royalists and later took part in the Glencairn rising. Imagination boggles as to how he came to earn the epithet 'Bloody bite-the-sheep'!

force under General Dalyell to intercept them.[*] The encounter took place in late November 1666 at Rullion Green, on the lower slopes of the Pentlands, when Dalyell's troops scored an easy victory and took many prisoners. Some died of their wounds but most were banished to Barbados, while about thirty were hanged in batches. Here a problem arose, because the public hangman, sympathising with the victims, refused to carry out his orders. It was solved when one of the condemned men was offered a reprieve if he would hang the others, including the recalcitrant hangman, which he did.[21] Once the grisly task was completed, the victims' heads and hands were cut off and dispatched to the principal towns in the south-west for public display as a discouragement to others from following suit.

In May 1668, in the aftermath of the rebellion, a proclamation was issued for the apprehension of about a hundred known rebels. Because some came from Dumfriesshire, the inhabitants of every burgh in the region were required to subscribe to a declaration denouncing the rising. It stated that they 'deteste and abhor the rebellioune laitly broken out in Galloway, and in other places in the west', and that they would not 'in any way whatever assist or intercommune' with those implicated in it. Further, that they were ready to risk their 'lives and fortounes against these traitours for suppressing their horrid traysone and rebellioune'. As an inducement to subscribe, it was intimated that a refusal would be regarded as tantamount to support for the rising and treated as such.[22]

The Privy Council went further. In September the earl of Annandale and Hartfell was commissioned to raise a local force to suppress dissent in Dumfriesshire. It was to consist of 88 horse and 800 footsoldiers, the earl being appointed Colonel, and William Douglas master of Drumlanrig[†] his second-in-command. Levies were to be raised from every parish, as well as from the burghs of Dumfries, Annan, Sanquhar and Lochmaben. But it proved easier said than done and was only achieved through threats to take punitive measures against recusants.[23]

In 1669, following the co-option of moderates like the earls of Tweeddale and Kincardine, and Sir Robert Moray, and encouraged by Bishop Leighton of Dundee (soon to become archbishop of Glasgow), the Privy Council adopted a more conciliatory approach. In June that year it issued an Indulgence which allowed deprived ministers to return to their former livings subject to certain not-too-onerous conditions. Accordingly forty-two ministers were restored to their livings, while a second Indulgence of 1672 resulted in the return of a further ninety. In virtually every case they were welcomed back by the parishioners of all classes, including the local gentry.

The intransigent minority who refused the Indulgences branded these backsliders as 'dumb dogs who have ceased to bark',[24] claiming that they had betrayed their

---

[*] A dedicated royalist untarnished by any links with the Covenant, Thomas Dalyell fought for King Charles at Worcester and had been a principal commander in the Glencairn rising. Escaping from Scotland following its suppression, he took service with Tsar Alexei of Russia, hence his epithet 'the Muscovy beast'. On his return he was appointed commander of the government troops in Scotland.
[†] Future third earl (and first duke) of Queensberry.

principles, had rendered their ordination null and void, and were no longer entitled to preach. Defiantly these hardliners set about ordaining their own ministers so that they could preach at conventicles. The Privy Council responded by introducing measures which rendered such illegal ordinations punishable by imprisonment or banishment.[25] Unlicensed ministers were to be fined, while preachers at field conventicles were liable to be put to death. Troops were used to break up these conventicles, and in Dumfriesshire Robert lord Maxwell (future fourth earl of Nithsdale) was commissioned to raise a force in co-operation with government-supporting landowners and the principal burghs.[26]

These landowners had been put under extreme pressure to conform. They were liable to be fined not only if any of their tenants or servants were caught attending conventicles, but also if conventicles were held on their land, even without their knowledge or consent. The Privy Council went further. In 1675 it introduced a measure which required landowners to deliver up bonds guaranteeing that no-one living on their estates would attend conventicles. But this was legislating for the impossible. Since the conventicles were becoming ever larger and more militant, there was no way that landowners could subscribe to a bond prromising compliance.

Ignoring their predicament the duke of Lauderdale,[*] the main architect of repression, responded with a policy of coercion. Since arranging for troops to be quartered on the homes of non-payers of fines had proved effective in the past, he arranged for a large number of men from the north to be billeted on recalcitrant landowners to enforce compliance. Although pejoratively referred to as the 'Highland Host', implying that they were a horde of savages, in reality they consisted of some 5,000 men drawn from the more civilised southern and eastern parts of the Highlands rather than the Gaelic heartland. Nevertheless these unwelcome intruders were forced on their reluctant hosts, eating them out of house and home throughout the months of January and February 1678. But it proved counterproductive, because all it did was to alienate many landowners and encourage them to connive in the activities of the extremists.

In spite of all the Privy Council's attempts to suppress them, conventicles continued to grow in size and strength. An example was the three-day conventicle held on Skeoch Hill in the parish of Irongray at which John Welsh was a preacher. The site is a natural amphitheatre almost entirely surrounded by higher ground, which was ideally suited for maintaining a watch against the approach of government troops. Responsibility for this was assigned to a regiment of horse under Gordon of Earlstoun who succeeded in beating off a party of dragoons under the earl of Nithsdale when it attempted to break up the conventicle. According to the inscription on the obelisk marking the site, it was attended by 3,000 people, testimony to the strength of local support for the Covenanters.[†]

---

[*] Formerly earl of Lauderdale, he had been advanced to a dukedom in May 1672.

[†] A distinction should be drawn between those who subscribed to the Covenant of 1638 and who are known as Covenanters, and the extremist protesters who were particularly active in the south-west where they are traditionally, but inaccurately, referred to as the Covenanters.

Nevertheless many were openly critical of their excesses. For example a group of sympathetically inclined Ayrshire lairds sent a deputation to the Privy Council expressing their detestation of the conventiclers whom they described as 'a few unsound turbulent and hot-headed preachers, most part whereof were never ministers of the Church of Scotland'.[27] But because it was those 'unsound, turbulent and hot-headed' preachers who were the main inspiration behind the Covenanters' resistance, and were primarily responsible for inciting these excesses, rebellion was inevitable.

THE TRIUMPH OF PRESBYTERY

The rebellion was precipitated by the murder of Archbishop Sharp, which occurred on 3 May 1679 while he was on his way from Edinburgh to St Andrews. As he was crossing Magus Moor on the final stage of the journey, his coach was held up at gunpoint by a group of local Covenanters who dragged him outside and hacked him to death with their swords in front of his terrified daughter. True, he was a man of limited principles with a permanent eye to the main chance, but that was no justification for his murder. In any case all it did was cause the Privy Council to redouble its efforts to suppress dissent, while government troops were deployed to hunt down the murderers. But it was too late, for they had already escaped to the Covenanting heartland in the west.

The murder opened up divisions within the ranks of the non-indulged ministers. Whereas most regarded the murderers' actions as indefensible, the hardline minority applauded what they perceived as a blow against prelacy. On 29 May they issued a manifesto stating their position in uncompromising terms. Known as the Rutherglen Declaration, it denounced the statutes rescinding the Covenant and the Solemn League; it condemned as illegal all Acts of the Privy Council, and in particular those ejecting ministers from their parishes. This was tantamount to a declaration of war on the government, and to put the matter beyond doubt the authors issued a call to arms.

Meanwhile John Graham of Claverhouse, the sheriff-depute of Dumfries and Annandale, was engaged in suppressing local dissent, his dragoons being quartered at Annan, Moffat and Lochmaben. But it would seem from his letters to his commander, the earl of Linlithgow, that he was fighting a losing battle. Writing to him from his headquarters at Moffat in late 1678, he reported that a number of 'great field conventicles' had been held in the vicinity to the fury of the 'regular clergy' (i.e. the local indulged ministers). Later, Claverhouse moved his headquarters to Dumfries from where he wrote to the earl again, this time complaining that conventicles were being held 'at [under] our nose' beyond the Nith and that he was unable to break them up because his authority did not extend there. Writing again in February 1679, he told the earl that he had made an example of the dissenting Carruthers family by sending a contingent of dragoons to seize their strongholds of Holmains, Dormont and Denby.[28]

In May 1679, following Archbishop Sharp's murder, the Privy Council extended Claverhouse's authority to cover the whole of the south-west, and sent him reinforcements. Later that month, while he was at Strathaven, word reached him that a large conventicle was about to be held at Darvel, some ten miles away. He immediately rushed there with a body of troops intending to disperse it and arrest the ringleaders. But they got wind of his approach. Therefore, when he encountered the Covenanting force at Drumclog on 1 June, he found it drawn up ready for battle. In the ensuing skirmish his troops were driven off; he himself only narrowly escaped on a wounded horse.

Inspired by its success, recruits flocked to the Covenanting army, swelling it to some 5,000 well-armed men all eager to fight. But as it grew in size so did dissension within its ranks. Whereas some were prepared to acknowledge the king's authority, asking only for a representative Parliament and the restoration of the general assembly, the more intransigent vowed that under no circumstances would they recognise the authority of a government which refused to accept the Covenant. As a result the army became hopelessly divided, with the more tractable refusing to serve under the hardline extremists, and vice versa. Therefore, when it encountered a 10,000-strong government force under King Charles's illegitimate son the duke of Monmouth at Bothwell Bridge on 22 June, it suffered a crushing defeat when some 400 insurgents were killed and a further 1,200 taken prisoner.

Following his triumph, Monmouth was appointed Lauderdale's deputy – in fact acting Secretary of State and effective head of the government since Lauderdale was incapacitated as the result of a stroke. Unlike his chief, Monmouth was prepared to exercise clemency and only two of the ringleaders were hanged. Because there was insufficient space to accommodate the prisoners in the local gaols, many were penned up in Greyfriars churchyard. Most were released on condition of their subscribing to an undertaking never to take up arms against the king again, although thirty-five Dumfriesshire lairds suffered forfeiture. A hard core of recusants were dispatched as slave labour to Barbados. But they never got there because their ship was wrecked in a storm off Orkney. Most were drowned while the survivors submitted and signed the undertaking in return for their liberty.[29]

Still prepared to be conciliatory, Monmouth granted a third Indulgence – these being contemptuously dubbed by the extremist Covenanters as 'blinks' between the 'killing times'.[30] Because the Indulgence allowed conventicles to be held in private houses, a number of ministers who had refused the previous Indulgences were encouraged to submit and have their licences to preach restored. Whether Monmouth's accommodating approach would have yielded results is impossible to say, because it was never given a chance. Soon afterwards he was recalled and replaced by the king's brother, James duke of York.

His appointment marked a return to a policy of repression. Anticipating resistance, the duke of York expanded the army, and additional horsemen were ordered to be raised from Dumfriesshire and the stewartry of Kirkcudbright. Quartered on

Dumfries castle, their task was to stamp out every sign of Covenanting activity with gun and bayonet. Meanwhile contributions were levied on 'the several parishes in the sheriffdom of Nithsdale, the stewartry of Annandale, and the Five Kirks of Eskdale' towards the cost of maintaining them. In January 1680, at the duke of York's behest, the Privy Council ordered Claverhouse to 'punish all disorders, disturbances of the peace and Church irregularities [i.e. non-attendance at church] in Kirkcudbright, Annandale, Wigtown and Dumfries'.[31]

On 22 June 1680 Richard Cameron, a leading extremist, and his fellow hardliner Donald Cargill played into the government's hands by issuing an inflammatory manifesto in much the same terms as the Rutherglen Declaration. Known as the Sanquhar Declaration, it formally renounced in the name of all true Protestants and Presbyterians their allegiance to 'Charles Stewart that has been reigning, or rather tyrannising, on the throne of Britain these years bygone'. When in the following month Cameron was killed in an encounter with government troops at Airds Moss, Cargill became the leader of the extremists (now referred to as the Cameronians). In September 1680, at a conventicle held in the Torwood near Stirling he formally excommunicated the king, the dukes of York and Monmouth, and the leading members of the government. The Privy Council responded by deploying troops to hunt him down, and in April 1681 he was captured along with other leading dissidents and hanged.

These successes encouraged the duke of York to persevere with his policy of repression. In May 1680 he had rescinded Monmouth's decree allowing conventicles to be held in private houses, while the licences of all but one of the ministers indulged by Monmouth were revoked. Similarly, dissenting ministers were forbidden to attend presbytery meetings, this being intended – among other things – to limit their scope for plotting a rebellion. They were also required to sign a bond undertaking not to take part in conventicles and to attend their parish church. The resulting emasculation of these hardline Presbyterians, and the perceived suppression of the Cameronians, must have given the government cause to hope that dissent was finally crushed.

Not so. In August 1681 it effectively shot itself in the foot by passing the Test Act. An ill-conceived measure, it required all holders of public office, civil as well as ecclesiastical, to swear adherence to the (half-forgotten) Protestant Confession of Faith of 1560, to acknowledge the king as the supreme authority and head of the Church, and to renounce the Covenant of 1638 and the Solemn League and Covenant. Commissions were set up in each of the western counties for 'tendering the Test to the Gentry and Commons'. Many could not in conscience subscribe to it. For example, Catholics like the earl of Nithsdale and his family had to refuse the Test since they could not possibly subscribe to a Protestant Confession of Faith. Nor could some of the episcopal clergy, while some fifty indulged ministers who refused the Test were deprived of their livings, forcing them to throw in their lot with the resurgent Cameronians. In January 1682 the Cameronians issued another manifesto, the Declaration of Lanark, which denounced all Acts of the Privy Council as illegal on the grounds that, in passing them, it was acting beyond its powers.

This gave the duke of York an excuse for reinforcing his policy of repression. Claverhouse was its chief instrument, and to equip him for the task he was confirmed as sheriff of Dumfries and given the sheriffship of Wigtown, while Sir Robert Grierson of Lag was appointed his principal lieutenant.* Specifically he was ordered to prosecute all dissenters who refused to sign a bond undertaking not to take part in conventicles and to attend their parish church. They were harried relentlessly; soldiers were quartered in their homes, their houses were pillaged, and their families reduced to near starvation. In Claverhouse's words, he 'so rifled their houses [and] ruined their goods that their wyfes and schildring were brought to sterving', while his dragoons scoured the countryside day and night in their efforts to hunt down recusants. As a result people started flocking back to the churches, and by April Claverhouse was able to claim that 'this contry nou is in parfait peace'.[32] But this was counting chickens, because the extremist Covenanters in Ayrshire and Lanarkshire remained intractable, and Claverhouse had to keep up the pressure to bring them to justice. Although a slow process, it began to show results as the Cameronian remnant, already weakened by divisions within its ranks, became increasingly powerless.

The duke of York returned south in May 1682, but there was no let-up in the policy of repression. This was mainly because the moderate members of the Privy Council had been dismissed for refusing the Test and replaced by hardliners. They included William Douglas, now earl of Queensberry, whose advancement to a marquessate in 1682 and a dukedom two years later was tribute in part to his success in bringing extremist Covenanters to justice. Commissions of justiciary were routinely set up, while the government adhered ever more rigorously to its policy of fining dissidents and quartering troops on them to enforce submission.

The following year the Privy Council introduced further punitive measures against the hardline Covenanters and their supporters. On 13 April it issued summonses to those suspected of harbouring rebels to appear before their local circuit court (these were established in all the principal burghs in the south-west including Dumfries[33]) to prove their innocence. At the same time commissions of justiciary were issued to reliable men of substance, equipping them with powers to 'cause sentence to be pronounced and justice to be done' on those suspected of aiding the rebels. Initially this applied to the counties of Dumbarton, Lanark, Dumfries, Kirkcudbright and Wigtown, although it was later extended to Ayrshire and Renfrewshire.[34]

The discovery of the Rye-house plot to assassinate the king and the duke of York, and the fact that a number of Scotsmen were implicated, prompted fears of another rebellion. This led to a further crackdown. In May 1684 a proclamation was issued

---

* McDowall, *Dumfries*, 462–3. The others were Colonel James Douglas, brother of the earl of Queensberry, Sir Robert Dalziel, Sir Robert Laurie of Maxwelton, Sir James Johnstone of Westerhall, Captain Inglis and Captain Bruce.

naming some 2,000 people whom the Privy Council singled out for punishment. The Cameronian remnant responded by issuing another manifesto, the *Apologetical Declaration*. Approved by their new leader James Renwick (a native of Moniaive who had recently returned from Holland), copies were nailed to the market cross of every town, and displayed on the walls of every parish church, in Ayrshire, Lanarkshire, Dumfriesshire and Galloway. It reiterated their denunciation of the king and speci-fied certain categories of people who were to be punished as 'enemies of God and the covenanted work of [the] Reformation'. They included 'bloody militia men, malicious troopers, soldiers and dragoons', and 'likewise viperous gentlemen and commons', as well as 'murderous bishops and curates'.[35]

Like the Rutherglen Declaration, this was tantamount to a declaration of war. The Privy Council responded by decreeing that all who supported the declaration, or refused to disown it, were to be put to death. Retribution extended to moderate Covenanters as well. In November 1684 the government effectively revoked the Indulgences by ejecting many indulged ministers from their livings for having alleg-edly broken the conditions of their reinstatement. Attributing their plight to the activities of Renwick and his extremists, these deprived ministers denounced him as 'the great cause and occasion of all the troubles of the country'.

By this time the Privy Council's policy of repression was starting to produce results, because many ministers came in from the cold and accepted its terms for reinstatement. To encourage the more intransigent to follow suit, it issued a procla-mation denouncing the *Apologetical Declaration* and reiterating its commitment to have all its supporters put to death. In order to identify them, a roll-call was to be taken of the inhabitants of every parish south of the Tay, and each person was required to swear an oath of allegiance to the king, while those who refused were publicly denounced as a rebel or executed out of hand. Numerous tales are told of these extremists being hunted down and killed by the dragoons. Although pejoratively referred to by Wodrow, that arch-apologist for the Covenanters, as 'the killing time', it has been suggested that the number of atrocities allegedly committed has been grossly exaggerated.[36] In fact it is reckoned that about a hundred extremists were executed during the 1680s, with perhaps eighty more hunted down and killed by government troops.[37]

Yet later writers, subscribing to the view sedulously promoted by the Church of Scotland – namely that it owed its existence to the 'sufferings' of these extremists – have hallowed them as martyrs and even saints. To so dignify these men who were essentially terrorists dedicated to the cause of establishing rule by presbytery – in effect a presbyterian theocracy – is to misread the facts. For it was not they but the great majority of ministers who suffered deprivation and exile in the cause of presby-tery, and thus kept it alive, who were responsible for its ultimate triumph.

King Charles died in February 1685. Since he had no legitimate issue, he was succeeded by his brother the Catholic duke of York, who became king as James II (and VII of Scotland). Ironically, in view of his hardline policy towards the

Covenanters while in charge of the government of Scotland, his accession marked a return to a more conciliatory approach, evident from the passing of the Act of Indemnity. But because the extremist Covenanters refused to comply with its requirement that they subscribe an oath of allegiance to him as sovereign, James reverted to his policy of repression. Therefore the Parliament of April 1685, besides reaffirming the Test Act, imposed severe penalties on all dissenters, while those attending field conventicles risked death or forfeiture.[38]

Meanwhile James Renwick and his dwindling band of extremists refused to have any truck with the Indulgences. In May 1685, responding to the Privy Council's denunciation of the *Apologetical Declaration*, he published a manifesto known as the Sanquhar Protestation. Branding King James a murderer who 'hath shed the blood of the Saints of God', it concluded with an appeal for comfort to a 'poor wasted, wronged, wounded, reproached, despised and bleeding remnant of the pure Presbyterian Church of Scotland' (as they saw themselves). The Privy Council responded by redoubling its efforts to apprehend Renwick. Notwithstanding the price of £100 on his head, he continued to preach at conventicles throughout the south-west until February 1688 when, in the course of a routine search, he was discovered hiding among some contraband goods. Tried and convicted of treason, he was sentenced to be executed – a fate he bore with a fortitude that earned him the accolade of 'dying like a ripe Christian'.[39]

When Parliament met in April 1686 it refused King James's request to exempt Catholics from the penalties imposed on dissenters. Therefore he prorogued it and resorted to rule by royal prerogative. In February 1687 he issued an Indulgence granting religious toleration to Roman Catholics and nonconformists such as Quakers, subject to certain conditions. It was followed by a second Indulgence which allowed all his subjects, including Presbyterians, to 'meet and serve God after their own way, be it in private houses, chapels, or places built for that use'.[40] This transformed the situation, for it meant that Presbyterian preachers were now able to conduct worship in field conventicles and in private houses, or wherever, with impunity. Consequently parish ministers found themselves once again preaching to depleted congregations as the people deserted their churches for conventicles. As a further concession, non-indulged ministers who had been committed to prison were released, while dissident ministers who had taken refuge in Holland were encouraged to return home.

In November 1688 King James withdrew his army from Scotland to help defend against the invasion by his son-in-law William of Orange, who was rapidly gaining control of the west country. Deprived of the army's support, the Privy Council was finding it increasingly difficult to maintain law and order. Taking advantage of this, the extremist Covenanters in the south-west revenged themselves on the intruded curates in a shameful episode known as 'the rabbling of the curates'. Deliberately timed to start on Christmas Day 1688, the perpetrators were mainly roving bands of Cameronians assisted by a willing peasantry.[41] Arming themselves with pitchforks, staves and clubs, they forcibly ejected these curates from their churches and manses, many suffering the indignity of having their vestments cut off and burnt. Their manses were ransacked and the contents set on fire, while they themselves were driven out into the cold to make shift for themselves as best they could. The pogrom continued until well into the new year, and in the course of it some two hundred intruded curates are believed to have been evicted.[42] Knowing what was in store for them, some abandoned their charges and fled. Among them was George Graham, the curate of Kirkpatrick Juxta and a well-known persecutor of the Covenanters, who took refuge in Edinburgh.[43]

Meanwhile, having failed to contain William of Orange in the west country, and deserted by many of his leading commanders, James was unable to prevent William's army from advancing on London. Finally, abandoning all hope, he fled to France. The English Parliament formally deposed him and declared William and his wife Mary (James's daughter) joint king and queen. Because the Committee of Estates declined to follow suit, James remained king of Scots. But not for long.

In March 1689, in the face of mounting pressure, a Convention of the Estates was summoned to determine the issue. Letters from both King James and William were read out to the members. James's hastily scribbled note offered a free pardon to all who returned to his allegiance within a month, denounced as traitors those who refused to do so, and studiously omitted any safeguards for Protestants. On the other hand, William's more moderate letter expressing the wish that the Convention should settle the religion of the country on a broad and liberal basis was enough to gain the support of a majority of the representatives. Therefore, when a number of King James's adherents, including Claverhouse (now viscount of Dundee), withdrew from the Convention, William's supporters were left in control. On 4 April it declared that King James had forfeited his right to the crown, and proceeded to draw up a Claim of Right. This laid down certain constitutional principles, while condemning prelacy as 'a great and insupportable grievance and trouble to this Natioun'.[44]

On 11 April the Scottish Convention proclaimed William and Mary as king and queen, and a high-ranking delegation headed by the earl of Argyll was sent to London to offer them the crown. This was accepted, although whether it implied acceptance of the Claim of Right was never entirely clear. The main sticking point was William's objection to the clause in the coronation oath which required him to purge the realm of heretics, since he refused to be responsible for their persecution. However, when the earl of Argyll blandly assured him that its inclusion was merely a matter of form, William withdrew his objection and accepted the crown in good faith. Exercising his kingly powers, he declared the Convention a Parliament and two days later it enjoined all ministers to proclaim his and Mary's joint rulership from their pulpits, and to pray for them, under pain of deprivation. A few diehards refused and were ejected from their livings. But that was only a start. When Parliament issued a further order enjoining congregations to report their minister to the authorities if he omitted to pray for the king and queen, the number of deprivations rose to almost two hundred.[45]

The next Parliament was dominated by the Presbyterians, notably the duke of

Hamilton, lord Melville and the Dalrymples, father and son. In July 1689 it passed an Act abolishing prelacy but without specifying what form the established Church should take. Meanwhile Claverhouse was raising a rebellion in the north where there was widespread support for King James. This, combined with fears of an invasion by Irish Papists, caused the Parliament of April 1690 to pass an Act which restored the presbyterian form of Church government as prescribed by the 'Golden' Act of 1592. It also provided for the reinstatement of those ministers who had been ejected from their livings in 1662 for refusing to accept collation by their diocesan bishop.[46]

A general assembly was convened for the first time since its members were ejected at musket-point in 1653. It met in Edinburgh on 16 October 1690. But it was hardly a representative gathering because the hundred and twenty or so attending ministers came from south of the Tay where the Covenanters were most strongly entrenched. This meant that its proceedings were dominated by the old-fashioned protester ministers, referred to as the 'antediluvians', now restored to their former livings. Three Cameronian ministers were invited to attend, which they did. But it was at the cost of being disowned by their colleagues who refused to have anything to do with their fellow Presbyterians – at least, not until they had publicly confessed their backsliding from the Covenants and repudiated their 'sinful' acknowledgement of the supremacy of a king who had not subscribed to them.[*]

Determined above all to establish the undisputed authority of presbytery, the 'antediluvian' ministers were primarily responsible for the act of the general assembly which required all ministers, elders and other churchmen to subscribe to the Westminster Confession of Faith of 1647. It also nominated two commissions of visitation – one for the presbyteries north of the Tay, and the other for those in the south. Composed of men of the same mould as the 'antediluvians', their task was to purge the Church of 'all inefficient, negligent, scandalous and erroneous ministers' who in consequence were deprived of their livings.[47] This extended to the universities where those suspected of being tainted with prelacy were dismissed from their posts.

King William repeatedly urged moderation, but he was powerless to intervene. Therefore, ignoring his pleas, and with scant regard for truth, law or justice, the commissions continued their work with uncompromising zeal until all the charges were filled by men of their persuasion. Thus there emerged from the 'Revolution Settlement' a presbyterian Church which, freed from the restrictions which King William and the more moderate magnates sought to impose on it, would continue to dominate the lives of the Scottish people for the following two centuries, and which is represented by the established Church of Scotland today.

---

[*] The Cameronians continued to survive as a small extremist splinter group, and later merging with the Seceders they called themselves the Reformed Presbyterians. They had their own meeting-houses (effectively churches), one being at Quarrelwood near Duncow, and their continuing presence in Dumfriesshire is referred to by a number of contributors to the *Old* and *New Statistical Accounts*.

AN OPPRESSIVE MINISTRY

The antediluvian and other like-minded ministers were now the dominant influence in the Church. Fearing a Jacobite counter-revolution, they purged the ministry of all those suspected of Jacobite leanings, or of heresy in any form, or indeed anyone who refused to subscribe to their dogma. Consequently these hardliners exercised a tyranny over the people which far exceeded that of their predecessors. The rigid social discipline which they imposed on their flock was enshrined in an act of the general assembly of 1707. This set out a comprehensive list of transgressions for which people were answerable to their kirk session, or in more serious cases to presbytery. If guilt was established they were forced to undergo punishment.

The transgressions included such things as fornication, adultery, blasphemy, irregular marriage (one which had not been formalised in the eyes of the Church), cursing and swearing. The last was punishable with particular severity if the person sworn at was a churchman or someone in a position of authority. For example John Wright, a resident of Dumfries, was charged with denouncing his parish elders as 'whited sepulchres', the minister as 'ane hypocrite', and the magistrates as a pack of 'rogues and knaves'. In spite of making abject apologies and professing repentance he was banished from the town.[48] These fundamentalist clerics arrogated the right to pry into every aspect of people's private lives, viewing with extreme disapproval the most innocent amusements. Card games were regarded as dangerously secular; the theatre the devil's playground, while the popular pastime of 'promisky' dancing was seen as an incentive to lust, and dancing assemblies the recruiting grounds for Satan.

The Church seems to have been obsessed above all with sexual immorality, which in spite of all efforts to suppress it appears to have been rampant. The minutes of the kirk session of Holywood, doubtless typical of others, speak to this. Many cases involving sexual peccadilloes which were brought before it appear to have been based on nothing more than gossip, rumour and innuendo. Some, on the other hand, were to do with an unmarried woman or a young widow who was pregnant or had given birth out of wedlock. Where guilt was admitted she would be put under extreme pressure to name the father. If he accepted responsibility the couple would be forced to stand before the (doubtless self-righteous) congregation, dressed in sackcloth, for ten or more Sundays in succession when they would be subjected to excoriating denunciations from the pulpit. Small wonder that some wretched girls were reduced to killing their bastard offspring to avoid having to undergo such a penance.

On the other hand, there were occasions when the man named by the accused claimed that she was promiscuous, and therefore there was no certainty that he was the father. Or he might attempt to have her procure an abortion, or simply bribe her to name another man as the guilty party. Nevertheless it appears from the minutes of the Holywood kirk session, and doubtless others as well, that there was one law for the gentry and another for lesser mortals. For example, the Maxwells of Cowhill and other heritors were accused of fathering children with their female servants, but through a combination of procrastination and employing clever lawyers they gener-ally managed to avoid punishment. Some bolder spirits simply defied their kirk session and refused to undergo penance, risking the sentence of 'greater excommu-nication'.[49] This was the ultimate deterrent since it meant that the victim was 'delivered over to Satan', banished from the Church, and denied the sacrament.

It seems that such cases were more common in country rather than in urban parishes simply because it was more difficult for town dwellers to conceal their misdemeanours, given the close proximity of their doubtless prying neighbours. There was however one case, which perhaps because of its perceived seriousness, was referred by the kirk session to the magistrates of Dumfries. This concerned 'the filth-iness committed by Robert Turner with Agnes Harbertsone and Janet Turner living all in one hous and lying together in one bed for a long space'. In the event the magis-trates decided that all three were to be 'scourged instantly thru the chief streits and banished forthwith'.[50]

The Church regarded with particular disapproval 'penny weddings', so-called because everyone contributed a penny, or food and drink, towards the festivities, for it was on these occasions that people really let their hair down and enjoyed them-selves. While some of these jamborees may have degenerated into uninhibited debauchery, the Church made no distinction between youthful high spirits and more serious dissipation, castigating both indiscriminately and punishing the participants, dancers and musicians alike. The practice was condemned by the general assembly of 1701, while an act of 1706 enjoined all presbyteries to persuade their local magis-trates to enforce with added rigour the laws against 'these promiscuous gatherings in which delicacy and decency are alike discarded'.[51]

Drunkenness seems to have been a common offence. For example the minutes of the kirk session of Mouswald cite the case of John Rae, who was accused of 'filthy and scandalous drunkenness' at a wedding, while Edward Ferguson was so drunk that 'he was not able to keep his cloaths from burning'. Another case concerned Agnes Greir and Isobel Rome who were accused of 'fighting on the Lord's Day', while Robert Craik was ordered to undergo rebuke for 'laughing and sporting in time of divine worship'.[52] This was a punishable offence under an act of the general assembly of 1707 which stipulated that people were not to 'loll, talk or fidget' during the service.[53] On the same theme, an act was passed by the assembly of 1709 enjoining churchgoers to refrain from bowing or offering 'other expressions of civil respect', and not to 'entertain one another with discourses [in other words gossip] during divine worship'.

The severest punishment of all was reserved for those convicted of witchcraft. Indeed the pogrom waged by the civil and religious authorities against anyone suspected, however remotely, of trafficking with the devil was a terrifying reflection of the prevailing mass hysteria. Although witch-hunting had become endemic throughout northern Europe in the early years of the sixteenth century, it was not until the time of the Reformation that it spread to Scotland. The earliest recorded legislation touching on the subject was an Act of Parliament of 1563. This extended the right to try cases of witchcraft, sorcery and necromancy (hitherto the preserve of the Church courts) to the civil courts, stipulating that where guilt was established the accused was to be put to death, frequently in the most horrific circumstances.* The pogrom continued throughout the reign of James VI who took a special interest in the subject and even published a treatise on it. Such was the prevailing mania that trumped-up charges, almost entirely groundless and some of them quite preposterous, were levelled against harmless, and in some cases slightly demented, or merely eccentric, people – frequently hapless old women.

Various methods were used to establish proof, the most common being the detection of a 'witch's mark' on the body of the suspect. This was done by pricking the skin with a sharp, needle-like instrument. If no pain was felt nor blood drawn, guilt was established (the victim presumably being blindfolded to avoid a feigned reaction). Consequently the appearance of a witch-pricker must have caused near-panic in a community, the more so because these people were paid by results. Confessions were frequently obtained under torture, and conviction almost invariably meant strangulation and even burning at the stake.

Witches are supposed to have frequented Dumfriesshire. For example, witch festivals or similar gatherings reputedly took place on Locharbriggs Hill and at Powfoot.[54] Tradition has it that a large rock overlooking the Crawick Water near Sanquhar, known as the 'Witches' Stairs', was the venue for a witches' convention where they would come from all over the country to plan their evil deeds and cast spells on those against whom they bore a grudge. The spells they are alleged to have cast were quite mundane, as might be expected in a farming community. For example, a farmer's best cow might cease to give milk, or a much-prized mare abort a foal, or a consignment of cream could not be churned into butter. In such cases the finger of suspicion would, as like as not, be pointed at some hapless old crone. This was enough for her to be arrested, in which case she was presumed guilty unless or until she could prove her innocence.

In that connection the story is told of how Robert Stitt, a local miller at Sanquhar, refused to give some meal to an importuning old woman, not realising that she was a member of a local coven. Therefore when Robert, attempting to open a sluice gate, fell into the mill dam and was drowned, this was attributed to her machinations. One of the most famous witches of tradition lived in the parish of Corrie. She was suspected of revenging herself on those who had crossed her by visiting accidents or misfortunes on them. Moreover she was alleged to have paid them nocturnal visits in the form of a wild cat or a weasel which not only kept her victims awake at night but reduced them to such a state of terror that they were in danger of losing their sanity.

Witch-hunting was pursued with particular rigour during the latter half of the seventeenth century. In Dumfriesshire, as elsewhere, most trials were heard before

---

* A case in point was that of the Brahan seer, a native of Ross-shire, who was crammed into a tar barrel. Nails were then driven through its sides, and set alight it was rolled down a hill.

the local presbytery. The more serious cases came before the High Court of Justiciary on the occasions when it sat in Dumfries, such as those of Elizabeth Maxwell and Euphame MacThynne which took place in May 1657. Elizabeth Maxwell was charged among other things with exercising magical powers in such a way as to cause the deaths of humans and animals, while witnesses claimed to have seen her 'riding upon a cat and leading two in her hand'. In fact she died in prison before the court could pass sentence. Euphame MacThynne was charged with going into hiding to avoid the witch-pricker, which was presumed to imply guilt. A further accusation laid against her was that, having seen some fishermen haul a quantity of fish out of Sir Robert Grierson of Lag's stretch of the Nith, she asked if they would give her one. When they refused she allegedly threatened to cause them harm. Next day when the fishermen drew their nets all they found was 'a great toad'. The same day Sir Robert fell ill and three days later he died 'like unto a mad man'. Although reportedly convicted by the jury on a majority verdict, her fate is not recorded.[55]

In April 1659 the Dumfries presbytery records refer to the passing of a resolution appointing eight local ministers to oversee the burning of a batch of witches at the stake on the Whitesands. A similar fate awaited two unfortunate women, Janet Mildritch and Elspeth Thomsone, who were convicted of witchcraft in May 1671. However, with unwonted clemency, the High Court of Justiciary ordered them to be strangled rather than burnt at the stake, although their corpses were to be consigned to the flames. In 1709 Elizabeth Rule was tried before the same court on charges of witchcraft for having issued threats against certain people who in consequence suffered misfortune. Some of their friends died; they lost some cattle, while one went mad. This was enough to secure a conviction: the court ordered her cheek to be branded and sentenced her to perpetual banishment. The story goes that the branding was carried out so hamfistedly that the iron burnt through her cheek and smoke came billowing out of her mouth.

Finally Janet McMurdoch, a prisoner in the tollbooth in Dumfries, was accused of having given herself up to the service of Satan, taken his marks on her body, and used 'devilish charms, witchcraft and sorcerie' to cause the deaths of innocent people. Worse still, she was charged with 'having carnal dealings, or copulation, with the devil, thus defiling her body which should have been a temple of the Holy Ghost'.[56] That qualified – and presumably experienced – justices should have taken such preposterous charges seriously is a measure of how far even educated people had fallen victim to the prevailing hysteria. In all, surviving records show that during a century or so of persecution some seventy-five people – mostly women – were burnt to death in Dumfries and Galloway, the last occasion being in 1722. But this pales into insignificance when compared with the 4,000 or more who perished at the stake in central and eastern Scotland during the same period.[57] Moreover these figures conceal the grim fact that many more would have been strangled.

People of those days were prey to all sorts of superstitions. For example, when someone was on the point of death it was the custom to keep the outside door ajar to allow the spirit to escape from the cottage. Once it was supposed to have departed, the deceased's eyes were closed and a copper coin placed on each eyelid. Regardless of the season, all farming activity was suspended, the period of enforced inactivity being known as the 'dead days'. Finally a bowl of salt was placed on the body, perhaps because it was regarded as a symbol of perpetuity but more prosaically it was thought to prevent it from bloating.

Meanwhile a vigil was maintained over the corpse night and day, because tales of dead people coming back to life were widely believed. During the daylight hours friends and neighbours would visit the deceased's cottage. Where permitted they would kiss the corpse, for it was thought that this would help them ward off illness and disease (although it was more likely to have had the opposite effect). When it came to placing the body in the coffin it was customary for the minister – or at least an elder or a deacon – to be present. While doubtless there to console and sympathise with the bereaved, it was also to ensure compliance with an Act of 1686 which, in the interests of promoting the linen trade, stipulated that all shrouds were to be made from home-produced linen.

In cases where the deceased's family could not afford a coffin, the parish slip-coffin was used instead. A comparatively recent innovation, it was equipped with a hinged bottom which was released by a bolt. Therefore when the coffin was lowered part way into the grave the bolt was removed and the body fell with a thwump into its final resting place. Before carts came into general use, the coffin was carried to the grave on two long poles supported by the pallbearers and covered with a mortcloth. This was generally hired out by the kirk session, the charge being applied to the poor's fund. Sometimes a mishap occurred. On one occasion a funeral party was making its way through the snow from Eskdalemuir to the kirkyard at Moffat, the coffin being carried on a horse-drawn cart behind them. But when the party reached the kirkyard where the interment was to take place, it was found that the coffin had slid off the cart somewhere on the way, and no-one had noticed. So the committal had to be postponed while the funeral party retraced their steps in the hopes of finding the coffin with the body still inside.[58]

The funeral itself was followed by the 'wake', an event of great social importance where wine (generally claret) and spirits (usually rum, whisky or brandy) flowed freely. These celebrations were apt to become so rowdy that, as early as 1645, the general assembly passed an act suppressing them. This seems to have had little or no effect; nor did the passing of a subsequent act in 1701. The custom extended to all classes, and the higher the status of the deceased the more lavish the wake. For example when Sir Robert Grierson of Lag (known as Aul' Lag) died in 1733 the bill came to £240 Scots.[59] The story goes that he had become so corpulent that, when rigor mortis set in, his corpse could not be manoeuvred down the narrow spiral stairway of his town house in Dumfries. Therefore a section of the outside wall had to be knocked away to enable it to be levered out and presumably lowered to the ground with ropes.

The previous year there occurred the first of the secessions which would continue to bedevil the Church until the Disruption of 1843 and beyond. This was primarily over the issue of patronage which had been a bone of contention within the Church ever since the passing of the Patronage Act of 1712. This restored to the patron (normally the principal landowner in the parish) the right to present a nominee to a vacant charge – a measure which was widely resented since it flew in the face of the popular view that the choice should be left to the congregation. On this occasion the issue came to a head when a group of ministers were so strongly opposed to the principle of patronage that they split off from the Church, they and their followers being known as Seceders. Later they themselves separated into the Burghers and the Antiburghers, both being represented in Dumfriesshire. That the *Old Statistical Account* refers to the existence of other splinter groups, including a surviving remnant of the Cameronians, suggests that the influence of the established Church had become less pervasive than in the past. This was mainly because a more enlightened generation was becoming increasingly sceptical of the threats of hellfire and damnation with which the old-time ministers would browbeat their forebears into abject submission to their authority.

FOURTEEN

The Union and Jacobite Opposition

PRELUDE TO THE UNION

At the beginning of the eighteenth century Scotland was essentially a peasant society whose farming practices were among the most antiquated in Europe.[1] Generally speaking, the countryside consisted of open, treeless moorland interspersed with patches of broom and whins, with here and there isolated settlements and ferme-touns, islands of cultivation in the bare, bleak landscape. Much of the low ground was too waterlogged to allow for tillage, and therefore it was abandoned as a wild-fowl sanctuary. Because Scotland was such a dirt poor country, it is hardly surprising that as contemporary travellers squelched their weary way across the endlessly boggy and windswept landscape they formed the lowest opinion of the land and its people.

One of them, Richard French, who visited Scotland in 1656, recorded his impressions in a booklet entitled *Northern Memoirs*. 'At Sanquhar', he wrote, 'the ale was so thick and ropy [full of dregs] that you might eat it with spoons'. The linen supplied at his lodgings was 'little or nothing different from the complexion of those females who never washed their faces', while he claimed to have encountered 'more sluts than cooks' and that 'in every house there were foul women, foul linen and foul pewter'. Throughout the night he was constantly 'worried by lice', and next morning he found his skin had become 'mottled and dappled like an April trout'.[2]

Another intrepid traveller – a woman this time – described her experiences when she visited Scotland in 1697. 'From there [Longtown] I went into Scotland', she wrote, adding that 'all the people about here, who are called the Borderers, seem to be very poor'. Entering an inn, she described how the household slatterns consisted of 'two or three great wenches, as tall and big as any man, hovering between their bed and the chimney corner, all idle and doing nothing tho' it was nine of the clock in the morning'. She herself on the other hand had already travelled 'seven long miles'.[3] In the summer of 1701 Sir John Perceval, another English traveller, visited Scotland and left an account of his experiences. Arriving at an inn at Langholm where he planned to spend the night, he was so disgusted by what he encountered that he could not bring himself to do so – or anywhere else for that matter. Instead he roughed it as best he could out in the open, and the following day he headed back to England.[4]

Admittedly these travellers were seeing conditions at their worst, because the 1690s was a time of famine which began in 1695 and continued for the next four years.* Drawing harrowing pictures of people falling by the wayside and left to die of hunger, infants starving to death through lack of mother's milk, and dying people crawling to the kirkyard on their hands and knees in their desperation to ensure a decent burial, the Jacobite propagandist Sir Robert Sibbald has dubbed this episode the 'ill-years' of King William's reign. By distorting the facts to equate them with the biblical seven plagues of Egypt, he was implying that it was divine retribution for the dethroning of King James VII. In fact it was merely the last, and not necessarily the worst, of the four famines which affected Scotland – and indeed Britain as a whole – during the course of the century.[†]

There were other natural disasters as well. For example, the winter of 1614 was so severe that large numbers of livestock perished, and sixty years later another particularly harsh winter was responsible for widespread sheep losses throughout the Southern Uplands.[5] People perished from the cold as well, because their primitive dwellings offered little protection against the elements. Described by travellers as filthy hovels, these dwellings consisted of a single room; the family occupied one end, where a scattering of straw covering the bare earth sufficed for a floor, and cattle were tethered at the other. In the centre was the fire. But because there was no chimney, and ventilation was minimal, the occupants would have lived in a constant cloud of smoke. A slight improvement was the two-roomed 'but and ben' where the family occupied the 'ben' while the livestock were confined to the 'but', both using the same entrance.

Yet at the same time the privileged few were building substantial houses for themselves. An outstanding example was Drumlanrig Castle, the creation of the earl (later duke) of Queensberry, which was built on the site of a partially demolished house to serve as the family's principal seat. Earlier in the century Queensberry's grandfather, the first earl, had purchased the barony of Sanquhar from William lord Crichton, and thereafter the family used the castle there (actually a peel tower) as their principal residence. But because Drumlanrig was the family home, as well being more central to his extensive landholdings,[‡] he decided to move back there and build a castle which was compatible with his status. A major undertaking, the work was started in 1675 and took twenty-two years to complete.[§] Unfortunately the duke did not survive

---

* This was not specific to Scotland because famine was widespread throughout northern Europe and elsewhere. Modern research suggests that it was associated with a significant diminution in the amount of energy radiating from the sun which was a feature of the seventeenth century (Lenman, *An Economic History*, 47). In fact the period from the mid-fifteenth to the mid-nineteenth century was marked by heavy rainfall, frequent storms, summer droughts and some of the severest winters since the last Ice Age, and the late seventeenth century in particular was a time of intense cold and hardship (McKirdy, Gordon and Crofts, *Land of Mountain and Flood: The Geology and Landforms of Scotland*, 197).

† They occurred in 1622–23, 1649–51 and 1655–56 when the harvest failed, and in an access of hunger farmers were forced to eat their seed corn so that there was nothing left to sow for the following year's grain crop.

‡ At the time of his son the 'Union' duke's death in 1711 they extended to approximately 110,000 acres, situated almost entirely in Nithsdale.

§ The story has it that, when the castle was rendered partially habitable, the duke (as he had become) intended to take up residence there. But during the first night he was taken ill, and because the servants were out of earshot and failed to respond to his shouts for help he was left writhing in pain. So the following day he returned in disgust to his peel at Sanquhar having spent only one night at Drumlanrig.

to see its completion, because he died in 1695 having virtually bankrupted himself in the process.* Other houses dating from around that time were built on a more modest scale, notably Dornock House and Gretna Hall. The latter was commissioned by Colonel James Johnstone in 1710, but it was later converted to an inn to accommodate stagecoach passengers travelling between England and Scotland.

One of the few bright spots in the prevailing depression was the cattle trade with England. Although it had existed for a long time, it took off from the early seventeenth century onwards, mainly as a result of the suppression of reiving, which allowed cattle a virtually risk-free passage to England. By the 1630s drovers were taking large numbers of cattle to the market at St Faith's in Norfolk and other English fairs – an arduous journey for man and beast alike. As to provisions, one old drover reportedly claimed that the only food he took with him was enough oatmeal to supply a pound a day for himself and another for his dog. His portion was made into a kind of brose, and for lack of any other receptacle he ate it out of his boot.[6]

In 1667 the trade from south-west Scotland received a massive boost when importing Irish cattle was banned by order of the Scottish Privy Council. This, combined with the growing demand for meat from the rapidly expanding London market, encouraged landowners in the region to extend their cattle-rearing activities. The conditions were favourable, for its relatively mild climate, long growing season and abundance of grass ensured an ample supply of fodder. Moreover the area's proximity to England meant that cattle had a shorter distance to travel than those from elsewhere, and so reached their market in better condition. Being situated at a key point on the road to Carlisle and the south, and being at the centre of a predominantly livestock-rearing district, Dumfries was the main collecting point for cattle from Galloway and Nithsdale. Its pre-eminence is evident from its weekly markets and three annual autumn fairs which date back to at least the seventeenth century.

An early pioneer of cattle rearing in the south-west was Sir David Dunbar, who enclosed a large park on his Baldoon estate in Wigtownshire. This was to enable him to carry out a controlled breeding programme for the purpose of improving the native stock. Other landowners followed suit by enclosing their estates with dykes. But because it meant evicting the sitting tenants, without making any provision for their re-settlement, it put them to severe hardship. So much so, that in the 1720s many of the victims banded together and revenged themselves by tearing down the dykes and (inexcusably) maiming cattle. Known as the levellers' revolt, it was mainly confined to Galloway where it became so widespread that the military had to be called in to suppress it. Nevertheless it was a salutary warning to other landowners, who in consequence were more circumspect about evicting their tenants to make way for improvement. Indeed, some went to considerable lengths to provide mutually profitable alternative employment for them.

---

* In fact he was so appalled at the cost that he is alleged to have written on the bundle of accounts for the builderwork 'De'il pike oot [gouge out] the een [eyes] that look herein.'

Overland trade was not limited to black cattle, because other goods were exported to England as well. They included wool, cheap woollen cloth known as 'pladding' and linen, products of local cottage industries, as well as barrelled beef and mutton, cotton yarn, shoes and clogs.[7] There was also a flourishing maritime trade with the principal Cumbrian port of Whitehaven, which was a source of coal and lime, and with the ports on the lower Clyde. Similarly Liverpool where potatoes and grain were exported in return for goods such as ironmongery, high-quality English cloth and tobacco. (It was only after the Union that Scottish merchants were given access to the English tobacco trade with the American colonies, notably Virginia.) Initially foreign trade was concentrated on Dumfries which already had well-established links with a number of French ports, including the main entrepot of Bordeaux. Writing in 1684, Symson refers to fish and tallow being exported in exchange for prunes, wine and brandy.[8]

Norway was the principal source of timber, tar and deal, which were needed for the reconstruction of towns and villages devastated by war and civil unrest. This led to the opening up of trade with northern Europe, and by the 1680s linen and skins were being exported to Rotterdam. In 1682 the Dumfries merchants opened up trade with Danzig (Gdansk), and in the course of the next few years they sent fifteen ships there. This expanded to include trade links with the Swedish ports of Gothenburg and Stockholm which were a source of timber, tar, flax and hemp, as well as iron, steel, copper and glass.[9] During the following century the merchants of Annan established their own trading links with Gothenburg, from where they imported iron, timber and deal, the last two being used specifically for its boatbuilding industry.

Additionally, the Dumfries merchants established – or more likely revived – trade links with the Low Countries. This was the source of a wide range of imports, including luxuries such as sugar and Barbados ginger, as well as more mundane products like iron pots, shovels and turpentine. Exports consisted of the kind of merchandise normally associated with a backward rural economy – namely wool and woollen products, as well as tallow, beeswax, resin and animal skins. These included the skins of brown hares, dogs, cats and rabbits, as well as polecats, otters, foxes and badgers.[10]

Towards the end of the seventeenth century the Scottish government was prevailed on to support a visionary project which its promoters guaranteed would earn the country sufficient wealth – more than sufficient it was claimed – to lift it out of its current poverty. Known as the Darien Scheme, it envisaged the establishment of a colony adjacent to the Gulf of Darien on the Atlantic side of the isthmus of Panama. It would be open to ships from every country in Europe, as well as traders from Africa, the plan being that their cargoes would be offloaded there and transported across the isthmus to the Pacific side where they would be traded for calicoes, spices and other exotic goods, as well as precious metals, brought from the Orient, in particular the East Indies. Not only would this avoid the long and perilous voyage round Cape Horn, but the colony would become an immensely profitable staging post on the principal – indeed the only – trade route between east and west.

The Darien Scheme was the brainchild of William Paterson, a brilliant Scottish businessman and a co-founder of the Bank of England. A native of Dumfriesshire, he was born in 1658 at the farm of Skipmyre in the parish of Tinwald. He had already acquired some knowledge of region, having spent time in the Bahamas where his scheme was originally formulated. Returning to Europe in the 1680s, he attempted to sell it to the English government, but without success. Having tried to interest the governments of the Holy Roman empire and the Dutch Republic in the project with equal lack of success, he joined the Merchant Taylors' Company in London where he made a fortune out of foreign trade – mainly with the West Indies.

Meanwhile his enthusiasm for the project remained undiminished. In 1694 he approached the Scottish government and persuaded them with silver-tongued eloquence that the colony would infallibly become a virtual Eldorado and make Scotland one of the richest nations on earth. The government was duly convinced and agreed to give him its full backing. Therefore, the following year, Paterson was responsible for setting up a consortium known as the 'Company of Scotland Trading to Africa and the Indies'. Its aim was to secure Scottish control of the trade between America, Africa and Asia, free from all customs, excise and other duties, for twenty-one years. The company was incorporated under an Act of the Scottish Parliament which received the royal assent in June 1695. The share capital was to be £360,000, a huge sum in relation to Scotland's poverty-stricken economy.

It was not long before the English began to interest themselves in the scheme. Indeed, so eager were the London merchants to participate that they persuaded the Scottish directors to increase the share capital to £600,000, notwithstanding that it meant losing control of the company. The omens were favourable and it looked as though there was every chance of the share capital being fully subscribed. Then everything turned sour. This was mainly because of the strenuous opposition of the East India Company, who feared that their monopoly of trade with the East would be broken and their hugely profitable business ruined. Since they controlled a number of parliamentary seats, they were in a position to persuade the English government not only to withdraw its support for the project but to threaten the directors of the company with impeachment. This was enough to induce the English investors to withdraw their money and leave the Scots in the lurch.

Undeterred, the Scots decided to go it alone and raise a sum of £400,000 – a vastly ambitious target which is believed to have represented as much as a fifth of the total wealth of Scotland. But swept away by their enthusiasm for the project, and their blind faith in its success, the Scots wilfully ignored the harsh reality that they had no experience as colonisers, and very little of trade on the scale envisaged by the scheme, nor did they have the resources to survive any reverse. People of all classes subscribed to the scheme, to the extent that the promoters succeeded in raising the entire sum. The duke of Queensberry, for example, subscribed £5,000, and Dumfries burgh council, who saw the project as giving a valuable fillip to its trade, contributed a similar amount. So, too, did the merchants and other prominent burgesses who acquired shares on their own account, while Paterson's Dumfriesshire connections would have encouraged many local people, including a number of landowners, to do so as well.

Their optimism proved woefully misplaced, because the promoters had no conception of just how inhospitable the local conditions were – the prevalence of disease, the hostile climate, the swampy terrain, and above all the insuperable difficulties involved in trying to transport goods across the mosquito-infested tropical jungle which separated the two oceans. Nor do they appear to have anticipated the hostility of the Spaniards who claimed sovereignty over the territory. Nevertheless in July 1698 a fleet of five ships carrying 1,200 aspiring settlers, blissfully unaware of the difficulties that lay ahead, set out from Leith. Among them was Paterson himself together with his wife and son, neither of whom would survive the expedition.

Unfortunately the voyage was marred by feuds which broke out among the leaders, and which continued to fester after they landed in Panama. To add to their woes, the settlers found themselves desperately short of food and a prey to disease. Meanwhile, anxious to avoid the risk of being dragged into a war with Spain, the English government forbade their colonists in North America and the West Indies from coming to their rescue. Worse still, the settlers found the Spaniards openly belligerent, having intercepted a ship dispatched from the Clyde with much-needed provisions. Eventually the exhausted survivors decided to abandon the colony and sail for home, although only one ship and a mere quarter of the original pioneers who had set out with such high hopes made it back to Scotland. Meanwhile, unaware of the difficulties involved, a second expedition had already set sail. But no sooner had it reached Darien at the end of November 1699 than disaster struck. Although the expedition succeeded in making landfall, the people found themselves under attack from the Spaniards, and unable to hold out against them they were forced to capitulate, albeit on honourable terms. So the colony was abandoned.

The failure of the project provoked outrage throughout Scotland where almost every family of consequence suffered loss. Their fury was directed primarily against the English, who were blamed for withdrawing their financial support, and whose lack of co-operation and refusal to rescue them from the Spaniards was seen as responsible for its failure. However, the failure also forced many of the Scottish establishment to recognise the unpalatable fact that Scotland could never become a major power on its own. Therefore they perceived that the best way forward was union with England, for only then could Scotland benefit from its international trade and achieve a measure of prosperity.

THE UNION

King William died in March 1702* and was succeeded by Queen Anne. Since she had no surviving issue,† there was a distinct possibility that on her death the crowns of England and Scotland would go their separate ways. This was the result of the Act of Settlement, which was passed by the English Parliament in 1701 to ensure a Protestant succession. As things stood, it meant that the English crown would pass to the dowager Electress Sophia of Hanover‡ as the queen's nearest Protestant relative. But, resentful at not being consulted about the Act, the Scottish Parliament asserted its right to legislate for a Catholic succession, in which case its crown would pass to the queen's half-brother Prince James.§

In that event it was feared that this would re-ignite the traditional hostility between the two countries, fuelled by Scottish resentment of the English indifference to their sufferings during the famines of the 1690s, and their perceived responsibility for the failure of the Darien Scheme. The crisis came when the Scots found themselves dragged on the English coat-tails into the War of the Spanish Succession against their traditional allies the French. But what really infuriated them was that it was achieved through sharp practice. By law a Scottish Parliament had to be convened within twenty days of Queen Anne's accession. But because it was certain to vote against participating in the war, the summonses were deliberately delayed so that in its absence the more amenable Scottish Privy Council would follow the English lead by declaring war on France.

When Parliament did eventually meet, the duke of Hamilton, who was adamantly opposed to being drawn into the war, declared the actions of the Privy Council illegal. But it was too late to disengage, and when he failed to carry his point he and his supporters withdrew from the Parliament. This meant that control of its proceedings passed to the queen's commissioner, the rabidly pro-union duke of Queensberry. Meanwhile, determined to exclude her Catholic half-brother from the succession to the Scottish crown, Queen Anne appointed commissioners to negotiate a union of the Parliaments, while Queensberry persuaded the Scottish Parliament to reciprocate.

The prospects could hardly have been less favourable, because neither country liked or trusted the other. As it was put, 'the English hated Scotland because Scotland had successfully defied them [while] the Scots hated England as an enemy on the

---

* As a result of being thrown from his horse when it accidentally stumbled on a molehill. Hence the Jacobite toast to 'the little gentleman in black velvet'.

† She had eighteen children of whom at least twelve were stillborn, the last survivor being the eleven-year-old William duke of Gloucester who died in 1700.

‡ Like Queen Anne's father James VII, this septuagenarian princess was a granddaughter of James VI. As it happened, she died six weeks before Queen Anne and therefore the crown passed to her son the Elector George who became king as George I.

§ Dubbed by Queen Anne as the Pretender, and otherwise known as the Chevalier, this son of James VII by his second wife was later referred to as the Old Pretender to distinguish him from his son Prince Charles Edward, better known as the Young Pretender or 'Bonnie Prince Charlie'.

watch to make them slaves'. Neither country really wanted a closer association, the Scots fearing that it would open the way to English domination, while the English had no wish to open their borders to a flood of beggarly Scots. As the English parliamentarian Sir Edward Seymour put it, 'all the advantage we shall have [from a Union with Scotland] will be no more than what a man gets by marrying a beggar – a louse for her portion',[11] which was not far from the truth since Scotland was virtually bankrupt. Not surprisingly the talks broke down.

In 1703 there was a Scottish general election. It resulted in the appointment of a new broad-based administration in which Queensberry continued to serve as queen's commissioner, although with reduced power and influence. Determined to assert its right to act independently of England, and overriding Queensberry's wishes, the new Scottish Parliament passed an Act which proclaimed its right to dissent from English foreign policy, particularly in matters to do with war and peace. In a further act of defiance it passed the Wine Act which authorised Scottish merchants to continue trading with France notwithstanding that it was at war with England. Finally it passed the Act of Security. This provided that the successor to the Scottish crown should be nominated by the Scottish Parliament, be of the royal line, and a Protestant. It further stipulated that unless the English Parliament legislated to secure 'the honour and sovereignty of this Crown and Kingdom' (i.e. unless it endorsed the Act of Security) that successor would not be the person who stood to inherit the English crown.[*]

The following year the Act of Security received the royal assent and became law. This was not at all to the liking of the English government, who placed little faith in Scottish assurances that whoever succeeded to their throne would be a Protestant. With good reason, because there was a distinct possibility that a Stuart king might be forced on the Scots by the French with Jacobite assistance. Moreover it raised the prospect of the French allying themselves with the Scots and using them as second front in their war with England. Therefore the English government insisted that the Scottish Parliament legislate for a Hanoverian succession; and it was the Scots' refusal that decided the English to force a union on them, come what may. So once again they appointed commissioners and invited the Scottish government to do the same in order to treat for 'a nearer and more complete union'.

In February 1705, by which time it was clear that the talks were getting nowhere, the English Parliament effectively blackmailed the Scots into compliance by passing the provocative Alien Act. This stipulated that, unless the Act of Security was repealed, and either the Hanoverian succession was accepted, or negotiations were under way for a treaty of union by Christmas Day 1705, all Scots (except those domiciled in England) would be treated as aliens. Furthermore an embargo would be placed on Scottish trade with England and Ireland. This was deliberately intended to beggar Scotland's economy since it would ban the export of cattle on which Scotland so

---

*   Which raised the interesting possibility that in such a case the person who stood to succeed to the Scottish crown would be the anti-union duke of Hamilton.

largely depended, and thus hit the landed classes in particular. Not only would they stand to lose out the most from the ban, but the fact that the embargo would extend to wool, woollen goods and linen would render them doubly vulnerable, because it was only by selling their home-produced linen and woollen goods that most of their tenants could afford to pay their rent. Still more potent was the threat that, if the Alien Act were to come into force, Scotsmen would be disqualified from owning or inheriting land in England. Consequently those who owned lands in England stood to lose them.

In July 1705 draft legislation for a treaty was introduced into the Scottish Parliament. Predictably it was the subject of heated debate, one of the points at issue being the choice of commissioners to agree the terms of a union with their English counterparts. This was vitally important, for on it could hinge the success or failure of the negotiations. Therefore, to ensure the appointment of like-minded commissioners, the pro-unionists stooped to chicanery. When the debate ended inconclusively and most members had left the chamber, the suitably bribed,* hitherto anti-union, duke of Hamilton did a complete *volte-face* by moving that the choice be left to the queen, and by implication her pro-union ministers. A division was immediately rushed through. Yet in spite of every effort on the part of the pro-unionists to whip up support, the motion was carried by a mere four votes.

Notwithstanding the strenuous objections of Queen Anne, who detested him, Queensberry was appointed leader of the Scottish commissioners. As she observed to her chief minister Godolphin, 'it grates my soul to take a man into my service that has not only betrayed me but tricked me several times, but one that has been obnoxious to his fellow countrymen these many years, and one that I can never be convinced can be of any use'.[12] Since Queensberry and his fellow commissioners were strongly pro-union, as were their English counterparts, the negotiations went comparatively smoothly in spite of their sitting in separate rooms and communicating with each other by written notes.[†]

Negotiations began in April 1706. Within ten days the commissioners had agreed the shape of the treaty, and three months later they had drawn up the twenty-five Articles of Union. The first three – namely that the united kingdoms were to be known as Great Britain, confirmation of the Hanoverian succession, and the stipulation that there should be a single Parliament of Great Britain – met the English government's minimum requirements. The others consisted of concessions to the Scots and consequential adjustments. For example, there was to be complete freedom of trade for all British subjects, English and Scots alike. There was to be a standardisation of weights and measures on the English model, while a conversion rate of

---

* Presumably with an up-front cash payment, while he was later given an English dukedom (Brandon), the Garter and the Thistle, as well as being appointed ambassador to Paris. Not bad for a turncoat!

† This would have been partly due to language difficulties because English and Scots were barely mutually intelligible. So much so that when Scottish members were elected to the combined Parliament at Westminster they had to learn English to make themselves understood.

twelve pounds Scots to the English pound was agreed. The law of Scotland was to be preserved, except where amended by Acts of the united Parliament, and there were to be no appeals to English courts except the House of Lords.

Finally the Scots were to be paid a sum of just under £400,000. Known as the Equivalent, it was ostensibly a *quid pro quo* for the Scots' acceptance of liability for part of the English national debt. In fact, much of it was used to reimburse share-holders for the losses they had incurred as a result of the collapse of the Company of Scotland (the Darien Scheme), while some was applied towards the development of Scottish industry such as the linen trade and the manufacture of coarse wool. As to the rest, part was used to pay arrears of government salaries and pensions, while a proportion found its way into the pockets (allegedly as gratuities) of the commission-ers responsible for negotiating the treaty.*

A sticking point was the question of representation in the united Parliament. Eventually a compromise was agreed whereby the Scots were given forty-five seats in the House of Commons – fifteen allocated to the burghs,† and thirty to the shires, while sixteen elected peers would be entitled to sit in the House of Lords. The propos-als were incorporated in a draft treaty, and given that the annual revenue from Scotland was about one-fortieth that of England, which was a measure of just how poor a country it was, the terms were not ungenerous.

Nevertheless it soon became clear that an incorporating union, such as had been agreed, was extremely unpopular with the Scots who feared that they would be consistently out-voted by an English-dominated Parliament. Given the uncertainty as to whether the Scottish Parliament would accept the Articles of Union, the pro-union ministers resorted to every possible stratagem in their efforts to generate support for it. For example, payment of arrears of salaries to office-holders was made conditional on their supporting the treaty, while there was a wholesale distribution of patronage, including the award of peerages, to bribe the support of leading politi-cians. The English played their part as well, because a sum of £20,000 sterling was secretly dispatched to the earl of Glasgow, the Scottish treasurer, to bribe the support of uncommitted members of the Scottish Parliament.[13]

On 3 October 1706 the duke of Queensberry as commissioner opened what was to be the last session of the Scottish Parliament. When the first Article of Union was read out and put to the vote it became clear that, in spite of every effort by the pro-union ministers to canvass support for the treaty, it would only be approved by a small majority – much less than expected. Therefore in November, in an attempt to placate the Church which was using its considerable influence to stir up opposition to it (the treaty was formally denounced by a commission of the general assembly), a

---

* For example Queensberry received a payment of in excess of £12,000, and this was in addition to his reward from the English – namely a lump sum of £10,000, a pension of £3,000 for life, and the English dukedom of Dover.
† Those in Dumfriesshire were Dumfries, Annan, Lochmaben and Sanquhar which together comprised one seat.

bill was passed guaranteeing the Presbyterian settlement of the Church. This was enough to buy it off.

Nevertheless, reflecting popular hostility to the Union, demonstrations were held in Edinburgh where pro-union statesmen were threatened, and anti-unionists cheered as the country's champions. Queensberry's carriage was regularly stoned as it passed up and down the High Street from his official residence at Holyrood to Parliament House and back. Riots broke out in Glasgow as well, and a force of 200 dragoons was sent there to restore order. But no sooner had they been withdrawn than rioting broke out again. The same happened in Dumfries where a riot was instigated by the Cameronians. The townspeople eagerly joined in, and nailing a manifesto declaring their opposition to the treaty to the mercat cross they ceremonially burnt a copy of the Articles.[14] In fact the disturbances reached such a pitch that the English sent a force to the border in readiness to march at Queensberry's request.[15]

The Church's acquiescence in the union, combined with skilful management on the part of the earl of Mar as Secretary, was enough to secure the passage of the remaining Articles through the Scottish Parliament. On 16 January 1707 it finally passed the Treaty of Union, but only by a majority of forty-three, and in the face of protest meetings up and down the country, while petitions for its rejection poured in from burghs and shires alike.[16] On 19 March the treaty was ratified by both houses of the English Parliament having been driven through the all-important committee stage of the Commons in a single sitting. Finally on 28 April the Scottish Parliament was dissolved by proclamation of the Privy Council. But, as Sir John Clerk, one of the commissioners, admitted, the Articles had been carried 'against the inclinations of at least three-fourths of the kingdom'.[17] It was doubtless for that reason that the government decided not to call a general election for the time being. Instead it nominated thirty commissioners to represent the Scottish shires and fifteen the burghs.

Contrary to the optimistic forecasts of the pro-unionists there was no sudden burst of prosperity following the Union, because it was only later that the benefits began to show through. While the English could hardly be blamed for the bad harvest of 1709 which resulted in much suffering and a general decline in economic activity, they were nevertheless guilty of acts of bad faith. A case in point was the proposal to extend the Malt Tax to Scotland, notwithstanding that it was in direct contravention of the terms of the Treaty of Union. In the event it provoked such an outcry that the measure was suspended. True, a bill was introduced into Parliament for the purpose of promoting the Scottish linen industry, but it was defeated by the Irish linen lobby. In fact about the only branch of commerce that continued to thrive in the immediate aftermath of the union was the cattle trade.

The Scots were hardly on the side of the angels either, because their merchants had compromised themselves at the outset by engaging in some sharp practice which although perfectly legitimate was calculated to arouse English suspicions. When the union looked like becoming a reality these merchants bought up large quantities of French wines, brandy and tobacco, taking advantage of the fact that these could be imported into Scotland virtually duty-free, whereas in England they were subject to heavy customs. Then once the Treaty of Union was passed, and the trade barriers were removed, they flooded the English market with these goods and made a substantial killing.[18] That apart, the supposed benefits from the union were so slow to materialise that dissatisfaction with it – among English and Scots alike – reached such a pitch that in 1713 the Scottish members of Parliament made a determined effort to have it dissolved. Indeed, it was a measure of its unpopularity that when a motion to that effect was introduced into the House of Lords it was defeated by a mere four votes. As Jonathan Swift, reflecting the widespread hostility to the union, wrote:

> *Strife and faction will o'erwhelm*
> *Our crazy, double-bottomed realm.*[19]

THE 1715 REBELLION

Queen Anne died in August 1714 and in terms of the Act of Settlement she was succeeded by her Hanoverian cousin George I. Nevertheless there was still widespread support for the Stuarts in Scotland, which was understandable considering that they had reigned there for well over three centuries. Already in 1708 the Jacobite supporters, encouraged by promises of French help, were poised to come out in rebellion against the Treaty of Union and the prospect of a Hanoverian succession. But it never got off the ground because the French expedition sent to help them was intercepted by the English navy and forced to return home. Consequently no landing was made and not a Jacobite stirred. In fact all it achieved was to cause Parliament to extend the English treason laws with their draconian penalties to Scotland.

The chief instigator of the 1715 rebellion was the earl of Mar. Notwithstanding his role in piloting the Treaty of Union through the Scottish Parliament, he had been dismissed from the secretaryship by George I. Smarting at what he regarded as a deliberate and very personal insult, he switched his allegiance to the Jacobites (earning the nickname 'Bobbing John') and supported the claim of Queen Anne's half-brother Prince James to the throne. Taking ship on a collier bound for Scotland, he landed at Elie on the coast of Fife from where he made his way to Braemar. There on 26 August he held what was ostensibly a hunting party. In reality it was a meeting of Jacobite chiefs from the Highlands and the Lowlands (the latter including the earl of Nithsdale[20]) for the purpose of organising a rebellion. Once again the French king Louis XIV promised to help, but he died on 1 September, and the duke of Orleans, as regent for his great-grandson Louis XV, reneged on the old king's undertaking.

Undaunted, Mar proceeded to raise a rebellion. On 6 September he hoisted his standard at Braemar and proclaimed the twenty-seven-year-old prince as King James VIII, while similar proclamations were made at Aberdeen, Dundee, Perth, Inverness and elsewhere. Two weeks later he set out for Perth at the head of an army of some

5,000 clansmen. There he remained for some weeks awaiting the arrival of Prince James from France, and for news of the promised outbreaks of rebellion in the Lowlands and northern England. But neither of them materialised, nor did the prince show up. Meanwhile recruits drawn from other parts of the Highlands flocked to his banner swelling his army to some 12,000 men.

In Dumfriesshire loyalties were mixed. On 29 May 1715, the anniversary of the Restoration, a group of Jacobite-supporting gentry, including representatives of the Maxwell and Johnstone families,* Carruthers of Rammerscales and others, fore-gathered at the town cross at Lochmaben. There in front of a large crowd, and on bended knee, they drank 'their king's [James VIII's] health, invoking perdition on the heads of those who refused to join in'.[†]

Following the outbreak of Mar's rebellion, the Hanoverian-supporting Sir James Kirkpatrick of Closeburn and Alexander Ferguson of Craigdarroch, both prominent Nithsdale landowners, proceeded to raise a defence force in co-operation with other local lairds. At the same time they pressed 'the well-affected nobility, gentry and citizens within the shires of Clydesdale, Renfrew, Ayr, Galloway and Nithsdale, and the Stewartries and bailiaries thereof' to contribute levies. This was to defend against a Jacobite uprising in the region, which was a distinct possibility given the strong Catholic presence there. Kirkpatrick and his colleagues were fully supported by the local ministers, as well as the magistrates of Dumfries, who in addition to contributing money for the purchase of arms and equipment undertook to train their recruits in the use of firearms.[21]

Meanwhile, warned of Prince James's plans to come to Scotland, and fearing that he might land at Loch Ryan in Wigtownshire, or nearer still at Kirkcudbright from where he was bound to advance on Dumfries, the burgh council took precautionary measures. Its defences were repaired, while all able-bodied men were enlisted to be ready to repel the expected attack, and a military guard was posted at each of the main gates. At the same time the Incorporated Trades raised seven companies of sixty men each, all to undergo rigorous training.[22] Following their example, many local landowners enlisted recruits from among their tenantry, and similarly ministers from their parishioners, while the authorities in Edinburgh sent Major James Aikman, a professional soldier, as their training officer.

On 10 August Sir Thomas Kirkpatrick and Sir Alexander Gordon of Earlstoun held a review of recruits from Upper Nithsdale in the grounds of Closeburn castle. At the same time they convened a meeting of all Hanoverian-supporting lairds in Nithsdale who undertook to raise volunteer companies. Finally it was agreed that in the event of a rebellion breaking out in Nithsdale there was to be a general muster at Sanquhar as a preliminary to taking on the insurgents.[23] But events overtook

---

*   Specifically Francis Maxwell of Tinwald, his brother Robert, and Robert Johnstone of Wamphray.
†   W McDowall, *Dumfries*, 519 quoting from the Rev Peter Rae's *History of the Rebellion*. This asserts that the event took place on 29 May 1714, which cannot be right because Queen Anne was still alive.

them. While the earl of Mar was waiting at Perth for the arrival of Prince James, the government ordered the duke of Argyll to raise a force and occupy Stirling to prevent his army from advancing south. Having established himself there, Argyll sent letters to 'well-affected' individuals and burghs requesting them to send him all the troops they could.

The 'well-affected individuals' included Ferguson of Craigdarroch who was ordered to come in person and bring as many well-armed men as possible. Accordingly he proceeded to Keir moss, near Penpont, with some sixty men raised from the parishes of Glencairn and Tynron. There he was joined by other local landowners, including Sir Thomas Kirkpatrick and James Grierson of Capenoch, with their levies. Joined also by Provost Corbet of Dumfries and a number of local ministers with their levies, the combined force set out for Stirling to join the duke of Argyll – all except Provost Corbet, who returned to Dumfries allegedly to supervise its defences. No sooner had Ferguson, Kirkpatrick and their levies reached Stirling than news came that a rebellion had broken out in the south-west. Therefore they were ordered back there post haste to suppress it. In fact there were two rebellions, one in Dumfriesshire and the other in north-west England. Whereas one was instigated by the earl of Nithsdale, the other – more serious – rebellion was being co-ordinated by viscount Kenmure. Assisted by lord Derwentwater and other local magnates, he was recruiting an army from Cumberland and the northern counties.

Fearing that Kenmure intended to attack Dumfries, the marquess of Annandale as lord lieutenant, supported by his deputies,* issued summonses to all able-bodied men to assemble on Locharbriggs hill in readiness to defend the town. No sooner had they mustered than Sir William Johnstone of Westerhall arrived with news that he and his levies had been attacked by a force under Kenmure near Lochmaben and had barely escaped with their lives. Further, that the rebels had made off with all their arms and equipment and were advancing on Dumfries. This was indeed the case. But as Kenmure and his rebel force were approaching the town, he received a letter from the earl of Nithsdale (hidden by the messenger in the lining of his bonnet) warning him that it was defended by a much larger force than they realised, or indeed was the case. Since he had only about a hundred and fifty horse, Kenmure decided to defer his attack and withdrew to Lochmaben.

Arriving there he went straight to the market cross where he proclaimed Prince James as king, the centre of the town having been cleared of cattle which had been penned up in a temporary enclosure. The story has it that during the night the cattle broke out, and when some strayed into a townsman's yard he shouted at his dog to drive them away. It so happened that the dog's name was 'Help'. Therefore when Kenmure's men heard him shouting 'Help, Help' they assumed they were being attacked. So, half-dressed as they were, and with no time to saddle up their horses,

---

* Kirkpatrick of Closeburn, Ferguson of Craigdarroch, Johnstone of Corehead, Grierson of Capenoch, Maxwell of Dalswinton, and Johnstone of Broadholm.

they tried to flee on foot, some cutting up their boots in their hurry to put them on – until the mistake was discovered and order was restored.[24]

The following morning Kenmure and his men set out for Ecclefechan. But no sooner had they arrived there than the sudden descent of a troop of horse on the town caused a near-panic until it transpired that they were fellow Jacobites under Sir Patrick Maxwell of Springkell. Joining forces, they went on to Langholm from where they advanced up Ewesdale and across into Teviotdale, gathering recruits as they went, until they reached Kelso, by which time their army had swollen to some 2,000 men.[25] There they met up with Mackintosh of Borlum,[26] one of the earl of Mar's principal lieutenants. He had been dispatched with a force of some 1,500 men to join the rebels in northern England as a preliminary to attacking the duke of Argyll's army at Stirling from the south.

Meanwhile, learning that Kenmure was making for the Border country, and confident that the danger had passed, the defenders of Dumfries relaxed their guard, and the men assembled on Locharbriggs hill were allowed to return home. But news that Kenmure had joined forces with Mackintosh shook the burgh council out of its complacency. Fearing that the combined army would attack the town, since it held the key to the south-west, they ordered its defences to be further strengthened. At their urging Argyll sent a number of officers, presumably military engineers, to supervise the work. Ditches were dug and filled with water diverted from neighbouring burns, earthworks were thrown up, and the town gates barricaded. Even the chapel, which had been erected by Robert Bruce's sister Christina to the memory of her husband Christopher Seton some four hundred years previously, was pulled down to provide material for the walls. At the same time, responding to the council's pleas for reinforcements, a force of some 2,000 well-armed volunteers raised from the local parishes arrived to help man the town's defences.

Meanwhile punitive measures were taken against Jacobite fifth columnists. Some were spreading false rumours for the purpose of creating alarm and despondency among the townspeople, while others resorted to sabotage. For example, a Jacobite supporter was caught in the act of laying a trail of gunpowder to a cluster of thatched houses near the town centre. In the event only one caught fire, but it was put out before it spread to the others. The records do not divulge what happened to the perpetrator, although he was presumably hanged.

The measures taken by the burgh council appear to have been timely. In late October word came that Kenmure was on his way back to Dumfries, this time with a much larger force. He had reached Langholm where he was joined by the earl of Nithsdale and his kinsmen, as well as other Jacobite-supporting lairds.[*] Meanwhile a detachment of 400 horse under the earl of Carnwath had reportedly reached Ecclefechan on its way to meet him. The situation was indeed menacing. However,

---

* William Gierson of Lag, his brother Gilbert Grierson, John Maxwell of Steilston, Edmund Maxwell of Carnsalloch, William Maxwell of Munches, his brother George Maxwell, and Charles Maxwell of Cowhill.

the danger was averted when Kenmure was persuaded by his English followers to abandon his plan to attack Dumfries. Instead he was prevailed on to head south and join forces with the rebels in northern England. A disastrous decision, as it turned out, because on 14 November his army was routed by a government force at Preston. Worse still, he and the other leaders including Nithsdale, and most of the rest of the army, were taken prisoner.[27]

Throughout this time the earl of Mar had remained at Perth waiting for the arrival of Prince James. Fearing that if he delayed any longer his army would melt away, he decided to attack Argyll's force which was still in occupation of Stirling. Although his army was three times the size of Argyll's 4,000 men, the latter consisted of seasoned troops, properly disciplined and well led, which Mar's were not. Therefore, accepting the challenge, Argyll advanced out of Stirling and taking up a position on Sheriffmuir above Dunblane he forced Mar to give battle. Since the right wing of each army prevailed, it was technically a drawn battle, but Argyll held the field, which was what mattered. Therefore Mar was compelled to fall back on Perth. Although this did not mark the end of the rebellion it was effectively doomed.

On 22 December Prince James finally landed at Peterhead. By then it was too late. In any case he proved a charmless, uninspiring character and completely lacking in the qualities needed to put fresh heart into his supporters. This became evident when he held a brief court at Scone where he cut a poor figure and made a very indifferent impression on the assembled company. Meanwhile his demoralised troops, short of food and weaponry, were forced to retreat in the face of the advancing government force. Finally on 4 February, abandoning his supporters to their fate, Prince James took ship for France never to return.

In the aftermath of Preston the captured officers were shot out of hand, while the rank and file were dispatched as slave labour to the American plantations. The ringleaders were taken to London and consigned to the Tower pending trial for treason. Following their conviction, Nithsdale and Kenmure were stripped of their titles,* had their estates forfeited and were sentenced to execution. The earl of Mar met a similar fate, except that in his case the sentence was commuted to banishment for life.† The earl of Carnwath was also sentenced to death, but unlike Mar he was eventually pardoned although he forfeited his estates,‡ while other leading participants were also pardoned.

---

* The Nithsdale earldom was never revived. However, in 1848 the earl's great-great-grandson William Constable-Maxwell petitioned the House of Lords for the restoration of the Herries barony. This was opposed by William Maxwell of Carruchan who claimed the title as the senior male heir of the sixth lord Herries. The suit was protracted, for it was not until 1858 that the House of Lords pronounced in favour of William Constable-Maxwell who in consequence became tenth lord Herries.

† Although he was stripped of his earldom it was subsequently restored to his great-grandson by an Act of Parliament of 1824.

‡ In 1723 they were bought by his lawyer William Veitch, with the exception of Elliock, which reverted to the duke of Queensberry as feudal superior. Later, in 1734, Veitch restored them to the earl shortly before the latter's death in 1737, and Glenae continued to belong to his Dalzell descendants until the 1930s (*Scot Peerage* ii, 415–6).

On 22 February, two days before his execution was due to take place, Nithsdale, assisted by his wife Countess Winifred and a female accomplice, made a dramatic escape from prison. Having remained at large for some time, he found sanctuary in the Venetian embassy where he was hidden by a servant without the ambassador's knowledge. A few days later, when the coast was clear, the servant conveyed him disguised in the ambassador's livery to Dover where he managed to take ship for France. Later that year he was joined by his wife, and thereafter they lived – often in considerable poverty – at Prince James's court in Rome.[28]

In the normal course of events Nithsdale's estates would have fallen to the crown. However, in 1712 he had the foresight to execute a deed entailing them on his successors. Therefore the question of whether or not the forfeiture superseded the deed of entail was the subject of a protracted hearing before the Judicial Committee of the House of Lords. Finally in 1723 it was decided that the entail should stand. Nevertheless it was decreed that, although the ex-earl's life interest was forfeit, it would pass to his son William as the heir of entail on his death. It is pleasing to record that, when the younger William came into his inheritance following his father's death in 1744, he was able to send money to his widowed mother from time to time to ensure her a comfortable old age until her death in 1749.[29]

TRADE, LEGAL AND ILLEGAL

Nowhere was Scottish disenchantment with the Union more apparent than among the merchant community. True, their right to trade with the English colonies was enshrined in the Treaty of Union; but because most merchants lacked the necessary capital, let alone ships which were capable of venturing across the Atlantic, few were able to take advantage of it. Those who did had to charter English vessels, but the combination of the hire charges and the inflated insurance premiums rendered it barely profitable.[30] This remained the case until some merchants, mainly from Glasgow and other western seaports such as Dumfries, began to acquire larger ships. This brought them into competition with the merchants of Whitehaven, Liverpool and Bristol who complained to Parliament – with some justification – that Scottish merchants were bribing the customs officials to waive the duty on their imports and thus undercutting them. But when their grievances were investigated, it was found that the English merchants were doing exactly the same!

Nevertheless the Scottish customs service was purged, and in 1723 new customs officers were appointed to the ports of Greenock and Port Glasgow.[31] At much the same time a customs office was established at Dumfries, the officer in charge being responsible for supervising the ports along the inner Solway, including Kirkcudbright where the customs service established a subsidiary office. This operated on a shoe-string with a staff of only nine – a collector, a surveyor, six excisemen and tidewaiters, and a clerk,[32] while the main office at Dumfries was allocated a mere fifteen men, which was barely enough for it to function properly. [33]

As Scottish merchants acquired larger ships they began trading more extensively with the English colonies in America – particularly Virginia which was the main source of tobacco. Since much of it was re-exported to the Continent where it fetched a high price, the trade was extremely profitable. The only drawback was that, because customs duty of one penny per pound was imposed on imported tobacco, it put the trade beyond the reach of smaller merchants. Nevertheless tobacco became the staple of Dumfries's foreign trade.[34] But it was not to last, for the greater accessibility of the Clyde to vessels trading with America meant that the tobacco trade became concentrated on Glasgow – to the extent that it was mainly responsible for the city's growing prosperity.

A major disadvantage of free trade with England was that it brought the Scottish wool and linen manufacturers into direct competition with their English counterparts. This was greatly to the detriment of the Scots, because their products – particularly linen cloth – were coarser and generally inferior to the English and therefore less readily marketable. Besides, they seem to have been less than pristine – at least judging from the observation of a contemporary Dutch merchant that 'your Scots houses, as well as spinners' fingers, are not so clean [as in England]'.[35]

Nevertheless by the early eighteenth century the production of linen cloth had replaced the manufacture of woollen goods as the main cottage industry. Indeed it was second only to agriculture as a source of employment, understandably since it took some five workers (mainly women) to process the flax or lint into enough yarn to keep a single weaver fully occupied. Because the proceeds of sale represented an important part of a cottager's income, and payment of his rent depended on it, landholders had a vested interest in promoting the industry. Moreover they were concerned that their tenants and workers should be kept fully occupied, for mindful of the maxim that 'idleness breeds disaffection', it was seen as a means of keeping social discontent under control and thus suppressing political unrest.[36]

Such was the importance attached to the linen industry that a supervisory body – the Board of Trustees for Fisheries and Manufactures – was established under the auspices of the Society of Improvers in the Knowledge of Agriculture to control it. The Board was responsible among other things for maintaining and improving the workers' skills, and hence the quality of the finished products. In 1727 the industry received a bonus. Under the Treaty of Union an annual sum of £2,000 was set aside for the improvement of the Scottish woollen industry, and because much had remained unspent there was a considerable accumulation of arrears. Therefore it was decided to hand it over to the Board of Trustees for the improvement of linen manufacture instead. Some of the money was used to raise the standard of home-grown flax by importing high-quality seed from Estonia and other Baltic provinces, as well as encouraging 'flaxmen' from countries like Holland to introduce new and improved methods of production.

The linen industry was the success story of the eighteenth century, and much of its expansion – particularly in the early years – was attributable to the efforts of the

Board of Trustees. Reflecting this, linen production doubled roughly every twenty or twenty-five years, resulting in a sixfold increase during the period from about 1730 to the end of the century – a trend which would continue at an accelerating rate until the post-Napoleonic War slump. But the growth was far from uniform because there were two major setbacks. One occurred in the 1750s following the temporary withdrawal of the 'bounty' (a subsidy paid to linen exporters to help them undercut foreign competition), while the other was the closure of the American market following the outbreak of the War of Independence. Nevertheless by the end of the century, thanks to the efforts of the British Linen Company,* linen manufacture had not only recovered but continued to flourish, although by that time it was being overtaken by cotton.

The extension of English import duties to Scotland, provided for in terms of the Treaty of Union, gave a massive stimulus to the smuggling trade. This involved the illegal importing of dutiable goods such as tobacco, wines and spirits (rum, brandy and geneva or gin), and also silk, cloth and lace, as well as spices and salt. It began in about 1670 when a company of adventurers from Liverpool established a base at Douglas on the Isle of Man where a wide range of commodities could be imported virtually duty-free. Therefore merchants were encouraged to take advantage of this by landing cargoes there, so that the goods could be shipped in smaller craft to the coast of Dumfries and Galloway and thus evade customs duty. As well as being conveniently close to the Isle of Man (it's only about thirty miles away at its nearest point), this was a fairly remote part of the country, yet within striking distance of Edinburgh, Glasgow and Carlisle. There was also the advantage that the local customs service was so undermanned that it was all but impossible for them to suppress the trade,[37] which meant that contraband goods could be landed at secluded inlets along the Solway coast with minimal risk of detection.

It was generally the practice to ship the goods to within easy reach of the mainland, where they were transferred to wherries, yawls and luggers, and ferried under cover of darkness to secret hiding places along the coast. Whereas the wine and brandy came from France, the more exotic commodities such as spices came from the East Indies on ships owned by the East India Company who had a monopoly of the trade. Therefore the company established bases in Europe for purposes of organising their freightage to temporary entrepots – mainly Ostend, the island of Guernsey, and the Isle of Man. There the goods would be held until conditions were right for a run ashore, those landed on the Solway coast being stowed in caves, or remote farmhouses with concealed cellars known as 'brandy holes', or simply buried in the ground. Local farmers and cottagers would then take them under cover of night to the main collecting points for delivery to the middlemen who would transport them on pack horses to the principal markets.

---

* Despite its name this was a Scottish enterprise which was founded in 1746 for the purpose of encouraging the export of Scottish linen. Although it branched out into banking as early as the 1760s, it was not until 1906 that it became the British Linen Bank which was taken over by the Bank of Scotland in 1971.

Apparently some pack horses were so well trained that they could find their way to the collecting points on their own. Therefore if an exciseman happened to encounter them when fully laden he could hardly arrest them, and all he could do was impound the goods.[38] Some participants in the trade went so far as to buy coastal farms with suitable caves where the contraband goods could be hidden until conditions were right to take them to the local collecting point. Altogether it was an extremely profitable business for everyone concerned – the producers, the importers, the merchants on the Isle of Man and other entrepots, the ferrymen, the local farmers and cottagers, and the middlemen who sold the goods to the retailers. Furthermore there was enough left over to bribe the excisemen and other officials to turn a blind eye, which appears to have been almost standard practice.

Inevitably there were clashes between smugglers and excisemen. On one occasion, in April 1711, the sight of two small boats hovering off the coast near Ruthwell alerted the suspicions of the local excisemen that a drop was about to be made. As indeed it was, because the next morning tell-tale tracks along the sand led them to the hiding place where they seized a cask of brandy. Impounding it, they locked it up in a local customs shed intending to take it to Dumfries. But before they could do so 'upwards of a hundred women broke the doors and windows of the place where it was kept' and carried off the liquor.[39]

The following month a similar affray took place further along the coast when an exciseman was tipped off by a local fisherman that a notorious smuggler, Morrow of Hidwood, had landed a cargo of contraband goods from the Isle of Man. When he raided Morrow's house he found a stack of contraband tobacco. But no sooner had he impounded it than he was attacked by 'a multitude of women' armed with clubs and pitchforks who forcibly relieved him of the tobacco and made off with it. The exciseman gave chase, but when he caught up with them these amazons turned on him, beat him up and carried him off to the smugglers' stronghold of Hidwood House, although he was later released.[40]

The same year a band of smugglers and their accomplices, having acquired a duplicate key, broke into the customs house in Dumfries and made off with five hundredweights (about 250 kg) of tobacco. In another instance a consignment of four casks of brandy was impounded at Annan and taken to the principal warehouse at Dumfries where it was put under guard. However, the smugglers overpowered the guards, and forcing their way into the warehouse they recovered the brandy. These people enjoyed much popular support, while many of the gentry, and even some clergy, connived at their activities if only to fill their cellars with cut-price wine and their pipes with cheap tobacco.[41] In September 1722 the collector at Dumfries reported that he and his men had impounded a cache of five casks of brandy but were forced to abandon them when they were attacked by a group of local men armed with stones, clubs and firearms. On another occasion a band of raiders equipped with a crowbar forced open the doors of the warehouse where the impounded goods were stored and made off with five casks of brandy.[42] Small wonder that, as the collector observed in his Report, 'the whole coast from Cummertrees to Sarkfoot is populated by nothing but a set of smugglers'. Or, as the Whitehaven customs officers concluded, 'the smuggling trade from the Isle of Man is notoriously carried on upon the coast of North Britain, especially near Annan'.[43]

Because there were insufficient excisemen to keep watch over the whole coastline, they concentrated their efforts on places where smuggling was known to take place, such as Ruthwell, Powfoot, Annan, Dornock, Torduff and Gretna. On at least four occasions James Johnston, the exciseman responsible for supervising the coast between Annan and Sarkfoot, was beaten off by smugglers. The first occurred in March 1721 when, observing some people carrying casks, which he assumed were full of brandy, he attempted to seize them. But he and his men were driven off by a mob of 'near and hundred people, men and women'. In May 1724 his attempt to seize two boats loaded with casks of wine from the Isle of Man was equally unsuccessful. As the collector observed, 'it is not in the power of my officers to hinder them [the smugglers] from doing what they please, for there will be two or three hundred men and women assisting at the unloading of a small boat, and they give no regard to [the] law'.[44]

In January 1725 a band of smugglers forcibly prevented Johnston from seizing three cargoes of brandy. Because one of his men was badly wounded in the fray, Johnston complained to the collector that 'he is very much threatened by the country people on that account' – evidence of the widespread popular support for the smugglers. His fourth misadventure occurred in February 1727 when a Manx wherry landed at Torduff Point and seven or eight armed men prevented him from boarding her. By the time he returned with a police escort most of the cargo had vanished, apart from a few casks of brandy. Although he took possession of the wherry and its remaining cargo, it became grounded on a sandbank and he was unable to get it afloat. However, he was rescued by an English vessel whose captain suggested that he transfer the cargo to his own boat in order to lighten the load. It worked, but by the time the wherry was floated the English captain was already on his way to Whitehaven with the cargo to claim the prize. To cap it all, the unfortunate Johnston's consistent lack of success earned his dismissal from the service the following year.[45]

From about 1724 onwards, tea featured prominently among the contraband goods as the habit of tea-drinking began to catch on. Initially there was a strong prejudice against it – a 'vile drug' as the peppery Mackintosh of Borlum,* that stalwart imbiber of Scotland's native drink, dubbed it. Echoing his view, the provost and magistrates of Dumfries passed a resolution in 1744 deploring its use by the lower classes as a pernicious luxury.[46] That year, along with other burghs and county authorities, they issued a manifesto denouncing the practice of smuggling, claiming that it was illegal (which was stating the obvious), that it caused thriftlessness and encouraged idleness and luxury. Moreover the fact that most of the contraband goods came from France

---

* He, it will be remembered, was one of the earl of Mar's principal lieutenants during the 1715 rebellion.

meant that the smugglers were giving aid to the king's enemies and were therefore guilty of treason.* Not that this did much to discourage such a popular, and for many such a lucrative, trade which was rendered all the more profitable as a result of the raising of the Malt tax in 1726.

The unpopularity of a tax on alcohol was evident from the popular reaction to a proposal by the provost and magistrates of Dumfries to impose a duty of two pence Scots on every pint of beer or ale brewed and sold in the burgh. Ironically the proceeds were to be used to build a new church. Inevitably it drew howls of protest from brewers, retailers and customers alike – the more deafening because there were no less than ninety-one brewers and retailers in the burgh. Although in the end about a third of them complied, the rest refused. The law was invoked. But when the sheriff officers attempted to impound the defaulters' goods, the town's beer-drinkers rallied to their defence. Having sent these minions of the law packing, they proceeded to storm the council chamber breaking the windows and hurling stones and 'softer unsavoury missiles' at those inside. Then forcing open the door, they physically assaulted the magistrates before retiring in triumph. The matter did not end there. At the request of the burgh council, criminal proceedings were instituted against the brewers. They retaliated by appealing to the Court of Session to have the duty annulled on the grounds that the council was not entitled to impose it. Eventually a compromise was reached whereby the council agreed to withdraw the duty, and both sides undertook to abandon their actions. Nevertheless the church was built.†

The smuggling trade continued throughout the rest of the century and beyond, while the raising of duties to an extortionate level to help finance the American War gave it a further stimulus.[47] That the excisemen were fighting a losing battle against the smugglers is evident from a Report by the Board of Customs in Edinburgh to the government in 1764. This stated that 'many unsuccessful attempts have lately been made by the surveyor-general at Annan to intercept the smugglers in the act of conveying goods, but frequently to little other purpose than getting him or his assistants severely beat and abused'. Worse still, 'the parties of soldiers on such occasions being on foot, are not able to overtake or keep up with the smugglers [because they] are generally well-mounted'.[48]

Perversely, the law seems to have discriminated against the excisemen. An example occurred in 1764 when Patrick Houston, the captain of the King's boat, and his crew were attacked while attempting to destroy five Manx boats. Although they overpowered the attackers, the authorities were prevented from taking proceedings against the miscreants because the law stipulated that hostile craft such as these were to be disabled, but not destroyed. Therefore, in attempting to destroy them, Patrick Houston and his crew were guilty of an offence. The same happened some months later when, in the absence of Houston who was 'confined to his house through

---

* Britain and France were on opposite sides in the War of the Austrian Succession.
† McDowall, *Dumfries*, 563–5. It was replaced by the present Greyfriars Church in 1865.

sickness', the attackers struck again. Again the crew overpowered them and seized their cargo, and again the attackers could not be prosecuted because in Houston's absence the crew had no authority to impound their cargo. Indeed there were occasions when the authorities seem almost to have gone out of their way to accommodate the smugglers. When in 1766 the Board of Customs decided to dispose of Houston's vessel, which was 'very much spoiled by being exposed to the inclemency of the weather', it was sold for a knockdown price to John Rome, a well-known smuggler.[49]

During this time agricultural improvement, and the landowners' increased rental income, created more spending power and hence a growing demand for contraband goods. The government responded by increasing the number of excisemen (one being Robert Burns), while an Act of 1784, known as the Hovering Act, provided that any vessel found at anchor on the Solway coast, or even within four miles of it, was to be searched. But judging from the criticism levelled by the Westminster government at the Scottish authorities for their laxity in enforcing the anti-smuggling laws, it would appear to have had little effect.

Part of the difficulty was that there seems to have been a lack of co-operation, or worse, between the excisemen on the one hand, and the tidewaiters on the other, the latter being responsible for boarding vessels carrying suspect goods and impounding them. An example occurred in early 1797 when some excise officers asked a couple of tidewaiters to help them seize a Manx boat which was unloading a cargo of smuggled salt at Powfoot. Although the tidewaiters responded to the extent of boarding the boat with the excisemen, that was as far as they were prepared to go, for no sooner had they done so than they started drinking with the smugglers. Nor did they come to the rescue of the excisemen when the smugglers forced them into a small boat and left them to make for the shore as best they could.[50]

This was not an isolated incident, because collusion between the authorities and the smugglers appears to have been rife. For example Robert McDowall of Sarkfoot, a well-known smuggler, owed much of his initial success to the co-operation of Robert Carmichael, the captain of the King's boat at Carsethorn. The arrangement was that McDowall would inform Carmichael where he had landed part of his cargo so that he could impound it, and as *quid pro quo* McDowall would be allowed to land the rest with impunity. Unfortunately for him, on one occasion Carmichael was not on duty, and in his absence other customs officials, unaware of the arrangement, seized a large haul of contraband goods which he had contracted to purchase but had not paid for. Unable to settle with his creditors, McDowall was forced into bankruptcy and fled to America.[51]

Yet there was a downside to the smuggling trade. For one thing it risked bringing the law into disrepute, for if the laws banning the import of contraband goods could successfully be flouted, it could lead to other laws being disregarded as well. Also cheap spirits were available to a much wider section of the population. This in turn led to an alarming increase in drunkenness, and a consequent sloth and inability – or disinclination – to work. As Sir Robert Chambers observed, 'it was nothing unusual for a whole family – men, women and children – to continue in a state of intoxication for three days and nights without intermission'.

The practice was almost universally condemned by the contributors to the *Old Statistical Account*, while ministers railed and the general assembly thundered against it. But ministerial fulmination was no deterrent to those practitioners of free trade who stood to gain so much from it, particularly when members of the clergy were known to be on the take. However it was a change in the law rather than clerical denunciation which was responsible for the decline of the trade. This was because the government's long overdue reduction in excise duty in the 1820s meant that smuggling was no longer sufficiently profitable to justify the accompanying risks.

THE 1745 REBELLION

Some thirty years had passed since the Jacobite rebellion of 1715 and times had changed. As the benefits of the Union were beginning to become apparent it had come to be more widely accepted, and only in the wild and inaccessible Highlands where the king's writ barely ran was there lingering support for the Jacobite cause. However, in 1740 it received a stimulus when Britain found itself pitted against the French in the War of the Austrian Succession. Perceiving the Jacobites as a means of attacking England in the rear, the French encouraged them to come out in rebellion with promises of military support.

This begged the question of who should lead it. Now in his late fifties Prince James, discouraged by the failure of his rebellion, decided he was too old. Therefore the mantle fell on his son Prince Charles Edward. A handsome dashing young man in his mid-twenties and possessed of infinitely more charm than his father (hence the soubriquet Bonnie Prince Charlie), he was determined to recover the crown of his ancestors to which he saw himself (or his father) as rightfully entitled. Therefore he was readily persuaded to undertake the assignment. The French promised to equip him with 3,000 troops and supply him with arms and money, on the understanding that he would persuade as many clan chiefs as possible to come out in his support.

The French expedition set sail in 1744, but blown off course by violent storms and intercepted by the Royal Navy it was forced to turn back. Consequently the prince was left in the lurch. Nevertheless, young and full of optimism, he was determined to persevere, although one wonders whether he fully appreciated just how daunting a challenge he was undertaking, and how great were the odds against success. Despite his abandonment by the French, he set sail from Nantes in June 1745. After a hazardous month-long voyage he landed on Eriskay in the Outer Hebrides with only seven companions – three Scots, two Englishmen and two Irishmen. Seeing this was all he had, the local chiefs urged him to abandon the enterprise and return to France. But the prince was undeterred. Sailing on to the west coast, he and his companions landed at Loch nan Uamh in Arisaig before continuing to Loch Moidart. Basing himself on the MacDonald stronghold of Kinlochmoidart, he spent a week issuing letters to the local clan chiefs soliciting their support before heading for neighbouring Loch Shiel.

On 19 August he raised his standard at Glenfinnan, at the head of the loch, having persuaded a hesitant Cameron of Lochiel to join him with his clansmen. This was crucial, for such was Cameron's influence that it encouraged other clan chiefs to follow suit. Indeed, had it not been for his support, the enterprise would probably never have got off the ground. More Highland chiefs joined him, along with their clansmen and other Jacobite supporters, as he headed south. The most important recruit was lord George Murray. Younger brother of the duke of Atholl and a veteran of the 1715 rebellion, he was to prove a brilliant general, and despite their frequent differences he became the prince's right-hand man. On 4 September the prince captured Perth, and on the 17th, having overcome a token resistance, he took possession of Edinburgh. Finally on 21 September he defeated a Hanoverian army under Sir John Cope at Prestonpans. This effectively gave him control of Scotland, and for the next six weeks he remained in Edinburgh holding court at Holyrood. Meanwhile the castle remained in the hands of government troops, though there was little they could do apart from firing off an ineffective salvo from time to time.

Following the victory at Prestonpans, the prince's secretary, Murray of Broughton, issued letters to the provosts of all the burghs in southern Scotland demanding a contribution towards his war effort, the amount to be determined according to their customs revenues. Dumfries burgh council ignored the request. However, a second letter, threatening reprisals if they failed to comply, caused them to think again. At a meeting held on 21 October it was decided to appoint a committee to recommend how the sum should be raised.[52] The council's attitude was typical of the majority of the people of southern Scotland where there was only limited support for the Jacobite cause, mainly because of its association with Catholicism.

While at Holyrood the prince decided – after acrimonious debate among his advisers, and against the advice of lord George Murray – to invade England. Because an English army under Marshal Wade was in control of the north-east, the prince took the western route. But first he split his army in two. One division under his command would make for Jedburgh, and from there through the Border country to Brampton to intercept Marshal Wade should he decide to advance on Carlisle. The other division was put under lord George's brother, the duke of Atholl, assisted by the duke of Perth. This was to head via Peebles to Moffat, and from there through Annandale and on to Carlisle.

Since the people of Dumfriesshire were generally hostile to the Jacobite cause,* it was feared that the duke of Atholl might attack Dumfries. Therefore on 2 November, hearing that he was at Moffat, the burgh council held a crisis meeting to decide

---

* Notable exceptions included Robert Carruthers of Rammerscales and William Maxwell of Nithsdale although, fortunately for Maxwell, he was dissuaded by William Craik of Arbigland from joining the rebels.

how best to defend the town. But the measures they took were hardly equal to the occasion, since they amounted to little more than ordering a check to be made on the available weaponry and have any deficiencies made good.[53] Nothing was done about having its defences put in order, nor was the militia called out, nor even the gates barricaded.

The expected attack never materialised – at least not for the time being, because the duke of Atholl had arranged to join forces with the prince at Carlisle. The story goes that, in the course of their advance through Annandale, a party of Highlanders who had become separated from the rest of the division encountered the funeral cortege of the minister of Wamphray as his coffin was being conveyed to its final resting place on a horse-drawn cart. Following it to the local kirkyard, they had the grace to wait until the coffin had been lowered into the grave before impounding the horses.[54]

Apparently the going was so bad that the duke of Atholl's baggage train was unable to keep up with the rest of his division. Therefore, on his instructions, thirty cartloads of stores were left behind under guard at Ecclefechan.[55] When news of this reached the burghers of Dumfries, a group of enterprising citizens hurried there, and overcoming the guards they seized the baggage and brought it back with them. It included a large haul of weaponry which looked promising until it transpired that the duke had taken all the guns and ammunition with him leaving only a collection of rusty pikes and scythe blades behind.[56] On 9 November Atholl's division reached Gretna and by the 15th it had crossed the Esk.

Meanwhile the bickering between the prince and his commanders, and among the commanders themselves, continued. In the course of it the prince fell out with the blunt-speaking and forthright lord George Murray, who detested the Irish cronies to whom the prince habitually deferred. The crisis came after the capture of Carlisle when the prince dismissed lord George. But when his Highland chiefs told him in no uncertain terms that they were not prepared to serve under anyone else, the prince was compelled to reinstate him. Everything now turned on whether the English Jacobites would rally to his standard. But as the army advanced through Cumberland and Lancashire it became clear that no support was forthcoming, and worse still the Highlanders were beginning to desert.

When the army reached Derby on 4 December the dispute between the prince and his commanders reached a climax. Encouraged by his Irish cronies, the prince was determined to press on to London. But supported by the Highland chiefs, lord George Murray argued that, with Marshal Wade's army in their rear and the presence of another in the Midlands, such a move would be fatal. The result was that a sulky and embittered prince was compelled to order a withdrawal. He would have been still more aggrieved had he known that his successes had so alarmed King George II that he was ready to abandon the country for his native Hanover.

Anticipating that the presence of Marshal Wade's army in the north-east would compel the prince to return by the western route, the men of Annandale were ordered to guard the line of the Esk and drive the Highlanders back into the river if they so much as dared cross it. But cross it they did, on 20 December near Longtown, at the cost of some camp followers being swept away by the current and drowned. Having put the men of Annandale to flight, the prince sent a detachment north under lord George while he and the rest of the army headed for Dumfries determined to punish the citizens for the theft of the duke of Atholl's baggage train. Swatting aside a token force which had volunteered to defend the bridge at Annan, the prince and his army, cold and wet from their plunge into the Esk, continued along 'excessively bad roads'[57] to Comlongan where they commandeered all the horses.

From there they advanced on Dumfries which they proceeded to occupy.[58] According to a contemporary report 'they were most rude in the town, pillaged some shops, and pulled shoes off gentlemen's feet in the street'. Finally they demanded a further thousand pairs of shoes, the surrender of all arms, ammunition and other weaponry, and payment of a fine of two thousand pounds sterling by the following evening, failing which the town would be sacked and put to flames. Fortunately some of the leading burgesses came to the rescue by offering to lend the burgh council enough money to make a substantial payment to account. In return, the council undertook to repay the sum out of the proceeds of a property-based tax to be levied on the citizens. As it happened, this proved unnecessary because after the rebellion was suppressed the duke of Queensberry and Sir James Johnstone of Westerhall, the member of Parliament for the Dumfries burghs, prevailed on the government to repay the loan out of the proceeds of sale of forfeited Jacobite estates.[59]

On 22 December the prince himself reached Dumfries where he commandeered lodgings at the foot of the High Street to serve as his headquarters.[60] In his *Tales of a Grandfather* Sir Walter Scott recounts how the Jacobite soldiery were about to burn down the house of John Corsane, a prominent burgess, but had the grace to keep his six-year-old daughter Janet out of harm's way before doing so. Too young to be aware of the danger, she asked the Highland officer who was holding her to show her the pretender. This the good-natured fellow promised to do on condition that she addressed him as prince, which she did. Consequently the house was spared.[*]

The Jacobite occupation of Dumfries was cut short when a messenger, apparently an acquaintance of the prince, arrived with news that an army under George II's son, the duke of Cumberland, had recaptured Carlisle and was advancing on Dumfries. In fact it was a false alarm, because the messenger had been taken in by a disinformer whom he had encountered in a public house in Annan. Nevertheless everyone fell for it, including the prince, because the following day he and his army abandoned the town (doubtless to the vast relief of the citizenry) and headed for Drumlanrig, taking

---

[*]   McDowall, *Dumfries*, 589–90. The story is well authenticated because Janet Corsane's daughter, Elizabeth McCulloch, married Sir Walter's brother Thomas Scott. Since Janet herself survived until 1824, Sir Walter's claim to have heard it at first hand would have been true enough.

with them two leading burgesses as hostages in security for payment of the balance of the fine.[61]

Arriving at Drumlanrig the prince ordered James Ferguson of Craigdarroch, the duke of Queensberry's commissioner, to provide accommodation for himself and his retinue in the castle, as well as quarters for his troops, and to supply them with quantities of meal, black cattle and sheep. Reporting to the duke on the state of the castle following the prince's departure, Ferguson told him how they had killed about forty sheep, 'most of them in the vestibule next the low dining room [at] the foot of the principal stair which they left in a sad pickle, as they did the whole house'. Their horses were kept 'under the gallery', while the troops had 'destroyed [presumably consumed] all the spirits and most of the wine in your Grace's cellars', and 'would have destroyed more' had he, Ferguson, not ordered the servants to hide as much as possible, while most of the pewter was melted down. Nevertheless, he went on, '[the troops] would have done much more mischief had not the duke of Perth stayed until most of them were gone', adding that the duke had relieved the troops of the sheets and blankets they attempted to carry away with them. Concluding, Ferguson told the duke that 'by the nearest computation I can make, at least two thousand were lodged in the house and the stables'.[62]

On 17 January 1746 the retreating Jacobites defeated a combined English and Hanoverian army at Falkirk. But supplies were running low, and having failed to capture Stirling castle they withdrew northwards. Meanwhile the duke of Cumberland's army was shadowing them up the east coast, and on 16 April the two armies met on Drummossie moor, near Culloden. But the Jacobites stood little chance. Whereas they were a half-starved and ill-disciplined rabble, Cumberland's army was well provisioned and well equipped with artillery. Lord George Murray strongly advised against giving battle on such unsuitable ground, recommending that they should conduct a guerrilla campaign in the mountains instead. But he was overruled by the prince and his Irish cronies, who were determined to fight. It was a disastrous decision. When battle was joined, the yelling Highlanders were soon silenced as, ripped apart by musket balls or impaled on English bayonets, they died in their thousands.

When at last the survivors turned and fled they were mercilessly hunted down by Cumberland's redcoats. Reprisals were the order of the day, and the fleeing rebels were shot out of hand. Ghastly atrocities were committed – on men, women and children alike – earning Cumberland the epithet 'the Butcher'. The lands of Jacobite supporters were systematically ravaged and their squalid settlements routinely torched as young and old, and the sick and the lame, were driven out on to the moors. Meanwhile Prince Charles fled the field. Finally on 20 September, after five months of hiding in the Highlands and Islands, with a price of £30,000 on his head, he managed to take ship for France. Returning to Rome where his father Prince James maintained an embryonic court, he remained there dissolute, morose and embittered until his death in January 1788. Although the rebellion ended in failure, the fact that having started out with a mere seven companions he had gained temporary control of Scotland, and had come close to establishing his claim to the throne, was a remarkable achievement by any standard.

Nevertheless the consequences for Scotland – and particularly the Highlands – were dire, because the rebellion was followed by a pogrom which was aimed at extinguishing the entire Highland culture. For example the Disarming Act of 1746 proscribed all forms of Highland dress, and anyone caught wearing the kilt, plaid, trews and tartan was liable to be deported to the American plantations. Similarly the Gaelic language (referred to as Yrische) was forcibly suppressed, and even speaking it was a punishable offence. All musical instruments traditionally associated with the Highland culture, such as bagpipes, the harp and the clarsach, were banned; and similarly the carrying of guns, swords, pistols and other weaponry. In July 1746, having completed the subjugation of Scotland, the duke of Cumberland returned south leaving behind the strongest military presence the country had ever seen.

Finally the already moribund clan system was suppressed, and in order to strip the Highland chiefs of their residual powers the government passed the Heritable Jurisdictions (Scotland) Act of 1747. Notwithstanding that these powers had been guaranteed under the Treaty of Union, it abolished heritable jurisdictions such as hereditary sheriffships and the right of landowners to dispense (a limited form of) justice in their baronial courts. Although mainly intended to curtail the powers of Highland chiefs to eliminate the risk of another rebellion, it affected all Scottish landowners. Despite receiving large sums of money in compensation, the same landowners protested loudly and vehemently against the loss of their hereditary rights.

Ironically the abolition of hereditary jurisdictions did not go unmourned by those who claimed that they 'aye liked gentlemen's law', meaning that they preferred to be tried by people to whom they owed instinctive deference rather than the upstart professional lawyers who replaced them. Yet it undoubtedly led to an improvement in the quality of local justice which could all too frequently be arbitrary and capricious, many of those responsible for administering it having little knowledge of the law and unaware of the finer points at issue. Others were simply bored with listening to the lawyers and their complicated pleas, dismissed by one tetchy landowner as 'blethering loons'. But the days of such arbitrary justice were over, and the new breed of lawyers who presided over the local courts could be relied on to take their duties more seriously and apply the law with greater fairness and impartiality.

FIFTEEN

Early Improvement

EARLY IMPROVERS

The eighteenth century witnessed Scotland's transformation from a poor backward country to one of incipient prosperity. This was attributable to a combination of land improvement, the introduction of more efficient farming practices, better communications and early industrial development. During the first half of the century a few enterprising landowners began improving their estates, but it was only later that others started to follow suit. Writing at the end of the century, many of the contributors to the *Old Statistical Account* claimed that the appearance of the countryside had changed beyond all recognition. That may have been true, but improvements were still patchy, and according to the contributors to the *New Statistical Account* much had yet to be done.

Since it was a precondition of improvement that the land had to be cleared of the existing small-time tenants and cottars, it came at a heavy cost in human terms. Even at the best of times their quality of life was basic in the extreme. This is evident from a letter written by John Maxwell of Munches, near Dalbeattie, to his neighbour William Herries of Spottes in February 1811. In it the 91-year-old Maxwell, harking back to his youth in the 1730s, described how the people lived 'very meanly on kail, goat's milk, graddon [coarse oatmeal] ground in querns, and grain dried in a pot, with a crock [diseased] ewe now and then about Martinmas'. Their clothing generally consisted of 'cloth made of waulked plaiding, black and white wool mixed, very coarse and rarely dyed [while] their hose [trousers] were made of white plaiding cloth sewed together, with single-soled shoes, and a black or blue bonnet'.* 'None wore hats', he went on, '[except] the lairds who thought themselves very well dressed for going to church on Sundays with a black-kelt coat of their wife's making'.

The initial spur to improvement came from the black cattle trade, and the enclosing of grass parks to facilitate their selective breeding and management; Sir David Dunbar's park at Baldoon was a notable example. Said to be two-and-a-half miles long by a mile-and-a-half wide,[1] it was here that he experimented with improving the native cattle. Initially he crossed them with bulls from Ireland, but when importing Irish cattle was banned by order of the Privy Council in 1667 he is believed to have

---

* This was worn at all times, indoors and out, and only removed during prayers and the singing of the psalm in church.

used bulls from Cumberland instead. Whatever their origin, their progeny grew to such a size that on one occasion, while a herd of them was being driven south, they were mistaken for illegally imported Irish cattle and the authorities ordered them to be 'knocked on the head'. Eventually realising their mistake they rescinded the order, but not before sixty cattle had been killed.*

Cattle had regularly been exported to England in the past despite the risk of attack by reivers, and the later imposition of customs duties. Since payment of the latter was readily avoidable, assertions that the king was being defrauded by the loss of revenue from the export of sheep and cattle were responsible for an order issued by the Privy Council in 1612 requiring that tolls be paid on all livestock crossing the border at 'the kirk of Graitney in Annandale' under pain of confiscation.[2] Meanwhile King James VI's success in bringing the Border region under control gave added stimulus to the cattle trade, to the extent that it led to complaints about a shortage of meat in Scotland. Therefore in the autumn of 1612, in an attempt to discourage the trade, the export duty on cattle was raised to £10 Scots per head and £5 for calves (a colossal sum).[3] Yet it seems to have made little difference, and because the trade continued as buoyant as ever, the authorities went further. In 1625 commissioners were appointed to restrict the export of cattle from Nithsdale, Annandale and Roxburghshire.[4]

They were fighting a losing battle, because the trade grew exponentially. By the 1630s it was already well established, Symson describing how drovers were taking large numbers of 'bestiall' to sell at St Faith's in Suffolk and other English markets.[5] By 1663 the number of cattle, for which toll (at eight pence per head) was paid at Carlisle, exceeded 18,500. But they were making such a mess of the place and causing the citizens so much annoyance that, as a discouragement to the drovers, the authorities imposed a tax of two shillings a head on all cattle crossing the border between 20 August and 20 December. This meant that drovers simply by-passed Carlisle, and the resulting loss of revenue forced the authorities to withdraw it. Instead, they imposed a levy of six pence per head on all cattle entering Cumberland, Westmoreland and Carlisle.

Meanwhile the trade continued to grow, and by 1662 some 3,000 cattle were passing through Carlisle daily during the season.[6] By the time of the Union upwards of 30,000 were being exported to England annually, most of them bound for the principal markets in Norfolk. The purchasers were generally grassland farmers in the Home Counties who would fatten up the cattle for sale at Smithfield, the principal market for the exploding population of London. The trade continued to expand, to the extent that by 1750 the number crossing the border annually had risen to 80,000, and by the end of the century it was 100,000.[7]

A further incentive to land improvement came from reports by Scottish peers and members of Parliament who in the course of their journeys to Westminster following

---

* A Symson, *A Large Description of Galloway*, 25. In fact the authorities may have been right after all, for in 1670 Sir David Dunbar was fined for importing Irish cattle in defiance of the ban (see A R B Haldane, *The Drove Roads of Scotland*, 162).

the Union witnessed the changes that were taking place in farming practices in England. Here farms were being consolidated, fields enclosed with hedges, while turnips and red clover – hitherto unknown in Scotland – were being grown. Labour-saving farm implements were coming into general use, while a more advanced system of crop rotation had been developed to improve productivity. Inspired by these innovations, some landowners introduced them to their own estates, one of the earliest in the south-west being the earl of Stair. A former soldier and diplomat, he devoted his latter years to improving his estates in Wigtownshire and West Lothian. An advocate of enclosure, as well as draining and liming, he was among the first to grow turnips and cabbages in Scotland.

Turnip-growing in particular was regarded with grave suspicion by Scottish farmers. Not only did the earl of Stair's tenants refuse to grow them, but when they saw the size his turnip-fed bullocks grew to compared with their own stunted creatures they refused to handle such monsters. Indeed, such was the opposition to turnips that it was not until the following century that farmers came to appreciate their importance for fattening livestock, particularly sheep.* The same applied to potatoes. Although first grown in the south-west in the 1720s, it was only later that people came to accept them as a vital constituent of their diet.

Since large-scale improvements were expensive, and the benefits in the form of increased rental were slow to materialise, some of the early pioneers overreached themselves. Unable to stay afloat until the rewards began to show through, they were forced into bankruptcy. Land improvement was necessarily a slow process, not least because, mindful of the excesses of the Galloway levellers, landowners in Dumfriesshire and elsewhere were more circumspect. Therefore, instead of arbitrarily evicting their tenants, they kept strictly within the law and waited until their leases were about to expire before serving them with notices to quit.† Although the process may have been slower, it appears on the whole to have been relatively trouble-free. At least there is no record of any major disturbances, while a number of landowners went to considerable lengths to provide mutually advantageous employment for their displaced tenants.

As early as 1723 a group of far-sighted landowners, encouraged by the earl of Stair and others, formed an association – the Society for Improving in the Knowledge of Agriculture – for the purpose of disseminating information about new farming practices. William Craik of Arbigland, whose long life spanned virtually the entire century, was a prominent member. A man of wide-ranging interests and immense energy, he was regularly out supervising his experiments before dawn, while coercing his tenants into adopting his innovative farming practices. For example he forbade them to grow more than two cereal crops in succession, insisting that the ground be left fallow for

---

* Even as late as 1773 turnips were regarded as such a rarity that they were served as a dessert at Edinburgh dinner parties (Haldane, *The Drove Roads of Scotland*, 215).
† It was not until the end of the previous century that it had become the practice for landowners to issue their tenants with written leases specifying their duration and the expiry date.

at least a year afterwards. Instead of allowing weeds to take over, which was the traditional practice, he encouraged his tenants to smother them by growing green crops such as cabbages and turnips, and to undersow their cereal crops with rye grass or clover to restore fertility to the soil.

He was particularly interested in developing new and improved types of farm implements. For example he was responsible for introducing the English type of plough into south-west Scotland. Unlike the traditional Scottish four-horse plough which could barely scratch half an acre a day and was 'more fit to raise laughter than raise soil', as lord Kames put it, this had a curved metal mouldboard and could be drawn by two horses. It was normally his practice to plough a field one way, and then crossways, in order to eliminate the weeds and produce a friable seedbed – so friable that to walk on it was said to be like walking on snow. At the same time the clods of earth were broken up with the aid of a granite roller, another of his inventions and a vast improvement on the traditional method of pounding them with a mallet. Another of his labour-saving devices was a rudimentary threshing machine for separating the grain from the stalk. This, too, represented an enormous improvement on the traditional method of beating the corn with flails on a threshing floor. The only drawback was that this traditional source of winter employment became less readily available. Nevertheless Craik's reputation as the father of agriculture in Dumfries and Galloway was eminently well deserved.

The earliest pioneer of enclosure in Dumfriesshire was the third duke of Queensberry. Already in the 1740s he was building drystone dykes on his Drumlanrig estate, and later he was responsible for establishing a rudimentary road system in Upper Nithsdale.[8] But it was not until the latter half of the century that land improvement in Dumfriesshire began to take off. An early pioneer was Alexander Johnstone, a London chemist who acquired the property of Carnsalloch in lower Nithsdale. In his contribution to the *Old Statistical Account*, the minister of Kirkmahoe describes how Johnstone bought the estate in about 1750 when 'improvements had not yet started' and 'became one of the first in this part of the country to exert himself in draining, enclosing and planting trees'. He continues: 'neighbouring landowners soon followed [his] example and consequently, instead of being comparatively unproductive, the parish became remarkable for its cultivation'.[9]

That the work of improvement was so long delayed was due to a combination of inertia and a prejudice against innovation on the part of many lairds. But perhaps most of all it was attributable to lack of capital. A further impediment was that in many cases their estates were entailed. This was a legal device introduced by an Act of 1685 which enabled landowners to protect their estates from creditors in the event of bankruptcy. Although designed to preserve them for future generations, the fact that they could not be sequestrated rendered them unacceptable to Banks and other lending institutions as security for loans. However, the situation was partially rectified by the Montgomery Act of 1770. This enabled landowners (technically the heir of entail), within certain limits, to borrow money on the security of their estates to improve them.

But it was not without its risks, a classic example being the failure of the Ayr-based Bank of Douglas, Heron & Co. Many looked to it for loan finance, mainly because of its accessibility, and the fact that both Douglas and Heron were local landowners. More to the point, credit was readily available. Too readily as it turned out. The Bank was founded in 1769 and, trading on their kinship, Douglas persuaded the duke of Queensberry to become chairman and endow it with the prestige of his name. Many landowners in southern Scotland subscribed for shares, thus incurring unlimited liability for its debts.

However the directors appear to have been extraordinarily unbusinesslike, being obsessed above all with building up a prestigious clientele by advancing loans to privileged customers without properly investigating the projects they were intended to finance. Small wonder, therefore, that they were described as acting like 'fools to a major degree and knaves to a lesser'. With a culpable lack of commercial sense they took over the ailing Ayr Bank, and consequently incurred liability for its debts. Therefore when it failed in June 1772 the Douglas & Heron Bank was forced into liquidation, and the shareholders became personally liable for its debts, while the liquidators foreclosed on the outstanding loans. As a result it is reckoned that a hundred and forty Scottish lairds were ruined.[*]

This inevitably retarded the process of land improvement. But not for long, because it was steadily gaining momentum – to the extent that it was becoming very much the fashion. And besides, it made – or could make – sound commercial sense. This was because the resulting increase in the landowners' rental usually justified the cost of the improvements, despite the rising cost of labour which virtually tripled between the 1770s and the 1790s.[10] Land improvement also had the advantage of providing employment for the victims of enclosure. But there were other sources of employment as well. For example, some were hired to work on the new farms, or they became landless labourers available for hire, or they might be taken on by the small industrial concerns which were being started up on the initiative – or with the encouragement – of the more enterprising landowners. Others settled in the planned villages which were being established at the time to become self-employed craftsmen. Still others would have moved to central Scotland in search of work in the growing urban and industrial centres,[†] probably as a last resort given the appalling working conditions which prevailed there. But needs must. A few emigrated to the Colonies although the number would increase dramatically during the following century.

---

[*] Besides the dukes of Queensberry and Buccleuch, the Dumfriesshire lairds who took a substantial hit, although not actually bankrupted, included Ferguson of Craigdarroch, Sir William Douglas of Kelhead, William Maxwell of Dalswinton, Gilbert Gordon of Halleaths, Dr William Graham of Mossknowe, John Carruthers of Holmains, William Hay of Crawfordton, and Sir Robert Laurie of Maxwelton (see McDowall, *Dumfries*, 627–8).

[†] So much so that in the last two decades of the eighteenth century, and the first two of the nineteenth, Scotland experienced the fastest urban growth rate in western Europe: in 1700 one in ten of the population were urban dwellers; by 1821 this had risen to one in three (Aitchison and Cassel, *The Lowland Clearances*, 3).

Land improvement could be a long, costly and laborious process. First of all the land had to be drained. This was done by digging open drains (tiled drainage had not yet been invented), which meant that it was only possible where there was sufficient gradient to allow the water to run off. The land was then divided into farm units and the fields enclosed with stone dykes, or more often hedges. They were then cleared of stones and comprehensively limed to improve their fertility, while new and superior farmhouses and farm steadings were built. Improvements did not extend to farm-workers' cottages, which generally remained as before, although it would seem from the *New Statistical Account* that on a number of larger estates they were being upgraded as well.

The new farms were generally let by public roup. While this may have been regarded as the most effective way of maximising the rent, it did not necessarily ensure a satisfactory tenant. Some were incomers who had experience of modern farming techniques elsewhere, but found to their cost that these were unsuited to local conditions, and in some cases they were forced to abandon their leases. Since it was generally the practice to grant leases for nineteen – and on some estates upwards of twenty – years, this was long enough to encourage the tenants to carry out improvements themselves in the knowledge that they would reap some of the benefits. In fact this was normally a condition of their leases, to the extent that from about the 1790s onwards improvements were generally the work of tenant farmers rather than land-owners, as in the past. Yet the tenant farmer received no compensation for these improvements, nor for the enhanced value of his holding, which accrued exclusively to the landlord.

Since most tenant farmers lacked the means to carry out improvements them-selves, the landowner would frequently supply them with the materials, or advance them the money to do so at a modest rate of interest. One example was the Rev. James Stuart-Menteth who extended credit on accommodating terms to his tenants to enable them to carry out improvements to his newly acquired Closeburn estate. Another was the fourth duke of Queensberry's chamberlain John McMurdo who was responsible for the management of the duke's Dumfriesshire estates. He advanced money on the duke's behalf to his tenants in the parish of Mouswald, and doubtless elsewhere, to finance improvements to their holdings. In their case interest was charged at 5% which, as the local minister claimed, they willingly paid. But the improvements carried out by his Mouswald tenants were partly negated when the duke sold off the woods in the parish for clear-felling, thus exposing the land to the sea winds.[11] Evidently McMurdo went to some lengths to encourage the ducal tenants to fertilise their lands, because they seem to have been given *carte blanche* to help themselves to the duke's marl deposits in Dryfesdale.[12]

The duke himself appears to have taken little interest in his estates in Dumfriesshire (and doubtless those elsewhere), because he was a notorious example of the type of absentee landowner who exploited his lands to subsidise an extravagant lifestyle in London and on the Continent. Not for nothing was he known as 'the rake of Piccadilly' or more familiarly as 'Old Q'.* In fact he was said to have visited Drumlanrig only once and that was to negotiate the sale of the woods for clear-felling, a policy which he seems to have applied to the rest of his estates in Upper Nithsdale.† Hence the minister of Kirkconnel's complaint that 'there is not a single tree of any value within the portion of this parish which originally belonged to the duke',[13] although did concede that the situation was being rectified by the present duke.‡ Old Q's reluctance to carry out improvements to his Dumfriesshire estates is evident from the minister of Sanquhar's observation that the ducal lands in his parish were 'bare and unenclosed'.[14] This is said to have been dictated by a personal dislike for the third duke of Buccleuch, who stood to inherit his title along with the entailed estates on Old Q's death. Therefore, in order to spite him, Old Q deliberately reduced their value by granting nineteen-year leases of the farms for a nominal rent, but with an inflated up-front capital payment from which he would benefit to the exclusion of his successor.

The foremost improver in Dumfriesshire was George Johnstone marquess of Annandale, who was the second largest landowner in the county (after the duke of Queensberry), where he had estates in five different parishes.§ In fact he himself was *non compos mentis*,¶ and therefore the person immediately responsible was his curator, namely his nephew and heir John second earl of Hopetoun.** One of his first acts on taking over the management of his uncle's estates was to commission a survey of each individual farm in order to assess its quality and value, and hence the scope for improvement. The same applied to the woods. These had been completely neglected, the public having been allowed to cut down the trees for firewood more or less at will,[15] so much so that it was said the Raehills estate did not contain a single tree on which 'even a cat could be hanged'. Therefore a comprehensive re-planting programme was put in hand as a matter of urgency. Although the improvements must have involved some evictions, the evidence suggests that the earl was at pains to

---

* He was described as 'a little sharp-looking man, very irritable, and swore like ten thousand troopers'.

† The proceeds of sale were allegedly applied towards the provision of a dowry for Maria Fagliani, the duke's putative illegitimate daughter, on her marriage to the earl of Yarmouth. But the duke's friend George Selwyn claimed her as *his* daughter, bestowing a large fortune on her as well, although it was generally supposed that neither of them was the father!

‡ This refers to Walter fifth duke of Buccleuch and seventh duke of Queensberry. When Old Q died in 1810 the dukedom passed, along with the entailed estates, to the third duke of Buccleuch. But, already an elderly man, he survived for just over a year, and was succeeded in 1812 by his son Duke Charles. who died prematurely in 1819, when Duke Walter inherited the family titles. Old Q was also marquess of Queensberry. But because the title was held under a different destination, it passed (following a House of Lords decision) to his nearest heir in the male line and remote kinsman, Sir Charles Douglas of Kelhead, who became the fifth marquess. Old Q's earldom of March, on the other hand, passed to the earl of Wemyss who was another relative.

§ Kirkpatrick Juxta, Johnstone, Hutton and Corrie, Dryfesdale, and Kirkpatrick Fleming.

¶ Evidently he spent the last twenty years of his life in an asylum. According to Reid he was the victim of delusions, one being that he had written a novel (presumably a horror story) which had driven all its readers mad! (Reid MSS)

** Son of the marquess's much older half-sister Henrietta and Charles Hope first earl of Hopetoun, Earl John was sixteen years older than his uncle (actually half-uncle) the marquess.

keep them to a minimum. Moreover, as we are told, once 'the fields were divided, hedges planted, and trees planted on the line of the fences, all under his direction', those tenants who were not in arrears with their rents were given a right of first refusal to take on leases of the new farms.[16]

When Earl John died in 1781 his eldest son James succeeded him as third earl of Hopetoun. He also became curator to his great-uncle the marquess on whose death in 1792 he inherited the Annandale estates.* Despite the improvements carried out under his father's management, there was still much to be done, and the fact that lime had to be carted some distance – either from Closeburn, Comlongan or Kelhead – added to the cost. Nevertheless the work of draining and enclosing the arable land continued apace although, like his father, Earl James was at pains to evict as few tenants as possible and none at all on his Wamphray estate.[†]

Once the land was enclosed, comprehensively limed, and new farm steadings built, it was estate policy to grant leases for twenty-one years. This was long enough for the tenants to benefit from the improvements which they were required to carry out under the terms of their leases. These specified the kind of farming practices to be adopted. For example there was to be a 'well-chosen rotation of crops' and 'a regular cessation of tillage' (meaning that the rotation was to include periods of fallow to rest the ground). Significantly the earl abolished thirlage, the iniquitous system whereby tenant farmers were obliged to have their grain ground at the estate mill with the miller effectively holding them to ransom.[‡]

At much the same time, the earl of Mansfield was establishing woodlands and generally improving his lands in Dryfesdale. As the local minister observed, 'the new method of farming, [and] the enclosing of land with stone fences [i.e. dykes] continues to flourish'.[17] His colleague at Hoddom was equally complimentary about the improvements which the earl was carrying out to his estate there.[§] 'About twenty-two years ago', he wrote, 'not a fence or dyke of any kind was to be seen in the whole parish. Now almost every farm is surrounded by a good fence, either of stone or hedge, mostly the latter.' He goes on: 'the improvement of the soil has been great, rapid and substantial, mainly because lime can be transported a considerable distance without difficulty and in all seasons'. This was attributed to the rapid improvement of

---

*   On his death in 1817 the Annandale estates passed to his eldest daughter, who was the ancestress of the present earl of Annandale and Hartfell. The earldom of Hopetoun, on the other hand, passed along with the attaching estates to his half-brother, the fourth earl, and his descendants the marquesses of Linlithgow.

†   This was acquired by his father Earl John from Colonel Robert Johnstone in 1747 (J T Johnstone, 'Moffat and Upper Annandale in the Middle of the Eighteenth Century' *TDGNHAS*, i (1912–13), pp 191ff.)

‡   *OSA* (Hutton and Corrie), xiii, pp 567ff. In fact thirlage was abolished by statute in 1799.

§   This had been purchased in the previous century by the earl's predecessor John Murray first earl of Annandale from the earl of Nithsdale. When his son James the second earl died without issue in 1659, the Murray estates in Dumfriesshire appear to have passed to his widow Jean Carnegy, and hence her second husband David Murray fourth viscount Stormont (a kinsman of her first husband), the earl of Mansfield's great-grandparents.

the existing roads and the formation of new ones which were currently under way. Waxing almost lyrical, he went on to observe that, 'to the traveller coming from Dumfries who has to pass through a wild, bleak and treeless tract of country, this vale [lower Annandale] with its enclosures fenced with hedges and interspersed with clumps of oak and ash appears like a paradise'.[18]

The earl of Mansfield appears to have made over his lands at Lochmaben and Ruthwell to his nephew and successor David viscount Stormont. Commenting on the latter's lands at Ruthwell, the local minister observed that 'the system of enclosing in this and many other parishes has produced an extraordinary rise in rents in the last twenty years, which so far from injuring or impoverishing the tenantry has contributed to their prosperity'.[19] On the other hand, the farms which lord Stormont was establishing at Lochmaben were described as 'generally very small'.[20]

Another improving landowner in Annandale, if on a smaller scale, was Sir William Maxwell of Springkell in the parish of Halfmorton. A prominent banker he was jointly responsible for financing the development of the New Town of Edinburgh. In common with the earls of Hopetoun and Mansfield, and William Graham of Mossknowe, he owned lands in the parish of Gretna. Therefore he would have been entitled to a share of the local minister's eulogistic praise that the annual production 'has been greatly increased by the improvements carried out on the initiative of the proprietors'. He went on: 'they financed the enclosing of the arable land, [and] several of the farms are in a very high state of cultivation, while the rest are daily improving'.[21]

The foregoing are merely some examples of the late-eighteenth-century improvers. There were many others. For example, in the parish of St Mungo, admittedly a relatively fertile parish, the minister refers specifically to four improving landowners – Colonel Alexander Dirom of Mount Annan, Robertson Lidderdale of Castlemilk, Lady Douglas of Kelhead (the heiress of the Johnstones of Lockerbie) and her son Sir Charles Douglas (future fifth marquess of Queensberry). As he put it, 'about the year 1769 the spirit of improvement was introduced into the parish, the good effects of which are apparent from the substantial farm houses, enclosures, and the general appearance of the inhabitants'. He goes on: 'the whole parish is now enclosed, and the commons are under cultivation which must in a few years greatly increase both the rents and the number of inhabitants'.[22] In sum, therefore, even if by the end of the century improvements were still patchy and incomplete, significant progress had been made and would continue at an accelerating rate until well into the following century.

FURTHER IMPROVEMENTS

The latter half of the seventeenth and early eighteenth centuries witnessed extensive land improvement in Nithsdale. Here the principal landowners led the way, and foremost among them was the third duke of Queensberry. He was enclosing the newly established farms on his Drumlanrig estate, while his contemporary William Maxwell of Nithsdale* was doing the same on his lands at Caerlaverock, Terregles and Kirkgunzeon. Here Maxwell's son-in-law, William Haggerston Constable, continued his improvements, to the extent that by 1793 the rental of Caerlaverock had doubled since 1776 and trebled since 1756.[23] And doubtless the same applied to his lands of Terregles and Kirkgunzeon.

Meanwhile Patrick Miller was busy improving his newly acquired Dalswinton estate. A banker by profession (he was Deputy Governor of the Bank of Scotland) he purchased it in 1785 from Major William Maxwell, a victim of the collapse of the Douglas & Heron Bank. Apparently Miller bought it sight unseen. Furthermore, as he later admitted in a letter to his son the younger Patrick, when he did eventually visit the place he was so disgusted with it that he vowed never to come back. However, he must have had second thoughts, because he embarked on building the original part of the present house and forming a loch out of an area of boggy ground in the immediate vicinity.

He also embarked on an ambitious programme of improvements. Too ambitious as it turned out, because they nearly bankrupted him. In fact he was reduced to such a state that, as he admitted in another letter to his son, he had given up his carriage and 'kept only one pony to enable me to attend to my farming'. Further, he had given up all visiting and entertaining; and, as he went on to say, 'I didn't drink a bottle of wine in a month'. However, he kept his nerve, observing that 'a life of useless sloth was ever despicable, if not criminal, in my estimation', and managed to ride out the storm.[24] A man of inventive turn of mind, he devised the original paddle wheel and the means of propelling it by steam. In fact it was the brainchild of John Taylor, the tutor to his children who, being conversant with steam engines, persuaded Millar that they were powerful enough to propel a boat. Millar's curiosity was aroused, so he arranged for an engine to be manufactured and fitted to a small vessel equipped with paddle wheels. When in October 1788 a successful trial was carried out on the Dalswinton loch, it could arguably be claimed that he was the pioneer of steam navigation.[25]

He also acquired a colliery in southern Ayrshire to cash in on the expanding demand for coal. This was for firing the kilns to convert raw lime into fertiliser for land improvement. Fortunately his various enterprises paid off and he became extremely rich – he bought 22,000 acres of land in America, mainly as a hedge against the country's possible defeat in the Napoleonic War. He died in 1815 at the age of eighty-three, and so extensive were the improvements he carried out to Dalswinton that when his executors sold the estate in 1822 it fetched £120,000 compared with the £25,000 he originally paid for it.[26]

Immediately to the north, the Rev. James Stuart-Menteth was improving his Closeburn estate. A native of Perthshire and rector of Garrowby in Lincolnshire, he

---

* Son of the forfeited earl of Nithsdale, he was – fortunately for him – dissuaded more or less at the last minute from coming out in support of the Jacobite rebellion of 1745. When he died in 1776 the Maxwell estates passed to his only child Winifred and her husband William Haggerston Constable of Everingham, in Yorkshire.

purchased it from Sir James Kirkpatrick's trustee in bankruptcy in 1783, when it was claimed that 'agricultural improvements may be said to have commenced in this part of the county'.[27] It was his policy when granting leases of the estate farms to require his tenants to lime part of them each year. Since the coal to fire the kiln at Closeburn had to be carted from his colliery at Mansefield, near New Cumnock, it added considerably to the cost of the lime, thus putting it beyond the reach of his tenants. Therefore he supplied it to them at his own expense and charged them interest. The result was, as the local minister put it, 'rents have more than doubled, yet the farmers lead incomparably better lives than they did when they paid half the current rents'.[28]

Meantime Stuart-Menteth developed and expanded the estate lime quarry which had been opened up by Sir James Kirkpatrick in about 1774. Initially it would have amounted to little more than excavating a large hole in the side of the hill and leaving the tenants to dig out and cart away whatever they needed. Stuart-Menteth was responsible for its expansion into a much larger enterprise. The lime was excavated with the aid of dynamite, and a kiln was built to burn the raw lime in order to convert it into fertiliser. Two large waterwheels were constructed, one for hauling, with the aid of belts and pulleys, trucks loaded with untreated lime up a 200-yard inclined wooden railway to the head of the kiln into which it was dumped. The other powered the bellows to heat the kiln, the furnace in the estate smithy, and also drove the sawmill.[29]

Water to turn the wheel was drawn from the Garroch Water, in the hills six miles away. This was conducted to the quarry by a watercourse which was excavated at Stuart-Menteth's direction, and which crossed two watersheds by means of finely adjusted levels. An artificial pond, the Heathery Dam, was excavated near the site to serve as a holding tank from which water was released by means of sluices as and when required.* At much the same time, other limeworks were being opened up on the opposite side of the Nith at Barjarg and Porterstown.

Similar developments were taking place in Eskdale where the third duke of Buccleuch was undertaking a comprehensive programme of land improvement. Other local landowners were following suit. Among them was Sir James Johnstone of Westerhall who was responsible for opening up an antimony mine, known as the Louisa mine (after his wife), in the Meggat valley. Another was the Rev. Robert Graham of Netherby. In the *Old Statistical Account* the local minister credits him with rescuing his tenants from 'the state of idleness and dissipation' to which they had become accustomed by 'encouraging them into the pursuit of industry'. The result was that during his tenure of the estate, from about 1760 until his death in 1782 the annual rental rose from £2,500 to £8,000 while the tenants were said to have 'lived more comfortably than formerly'.[30]

---

* The limeworks have been the subject of a detailed study by the late Dr Richard Clarke, a retired civil engineer, who contributed a series of articles on the subject to the *Transactions*. The watercourse is still identifiable from a line of rushes which marks the underlying clay bedding.

The duke of Buccleuch's improvements were not invariably successful. For example draining his lands at Eskdalemuir encouraged a proliferation of moles that scraped up a black mould, and unless dispersed this produced a coarse type of grass which was harmful to sheep.[31] Nor – initially at any rate – was he able to make proper use of the marl deposit on the farm of Megdale up the Meggat Water. This was because the tenant tried to prevent other farmers from gaining access to it, having a rooted (and understandable) objection to having his land poached by their horses and carts.[32] He is unlikely to have got away with it for long.

Further south, the arable lands on the duke's Langholm estate were almost completely enclosed. Because it meant amalgamating seven or eight smallholdings to form each new farm, this was achieved at the cost of a displacing numerous small-time tenants and cottars, evident from the fact that the number of families living on the estate was reduced from eighty to just fourteen. However, some of the tenants and cottars appear to have found employment as weavers, either on contract or as workers in the recently established industrial enterprises at New Langholm. Others probably became self-employed craftsmen for which there was a growing demand, while some were compelled to seek employment in the newly established industrial concerns in central Scotland.

The new farms were generally let by public roup, the new tenants being obliged to carry out improvements, and build farmhouses and steadings for which they were supplied with the necessary materials. Further down the Esk, the minister of Canonbie was fulsome about the improvements the duke of Buccleuch was carrying out to his lands there, observing that 'new roads were made, [and] farms laid out where the plough had never penetrated before'. As he went on to say, 'the land was divided into enclosures with a hedge or ditch, leases [were] given at a moderate rate [and consequently] heath, bent and moss have given place to luxuriant crops of corn'.[33]

Yet it appears from the *Statistical Accounts* that in almost every parish at least some – and frequently a majority – of the landowners were absentees. As the minister of Dornock observed, 'it is certainly unlucky for this district, as well as for many others in Scotland, that the land has fallen into the hands of people who draw their rents and spend them either in London or in foreign parts'. 'If only', he went on, 'they would live at home and invest their rents in promoting manufactures, commerce, and improvements of every kind, it would be of incalculable service both to the district itself and the kingdom in general'.[34] It would indeed, because it seems from the observations of the contributors to the *New Statistical Account* that the improvements carried out before the 1790s, when the previous *Account* was published, were less extensive than the latter would have one believe.

Nevertheless estate rentals were increasing and the landed classes were becoming generally wealthier. This is evident from the number of mansions being built at the time. No longer designed for defence like the earlier tower houses, they were much more aesthetically pleasing, combining spaciousness with comfort. Whereas windows were formerly narrow slits to give maximum protection against missiles in the event of an attack, they were now much larger, designed to harmonise with the external appearance of the house while admitting as much light as possible. It was also the fashion to embellish the immediate surrounds with a flower garden, and – less obtrusively – a vegetable garden to provide for the owner, his family and the indoor staff.

Besides Drumlanrig castle, Dornock House and Gretna Hall, an early example was Craigdarroch near Moniaive, which was built for Alexander Ferguson in 1728 according to a design by William Adam. In the following decade Adam was commissioned by Charles Erskine, the Lord Advocate, to draw up plans for Tinwald House which was completed in 1740. It was preceded by Springkell, another medium-sized Palladian mansion which was built for Sir William Maxwell in 1734. Those dating from the second half of the century included Carnsalloch, built for Alexander Johnstone in the early 1750s, and Moffat House, Mossknowe and Rammerscales, which date from the following decade. Designed by John Adam, and commissioned by the second earl of Hopetoun as curator for his uncle the marquess of Annandale, Moffat House originally served as the family's town house, and is now a hotel. Mossknowe was built for Dr William Graham in 1767* and is thought to have been designed by William Craik of Arbigland, while Rammerscales was built the following year for Dr James Mounsey, former chief director of the Medical Chancery of Russia.

Bonshaw and Knockhill date from the 1770s. The former was built immediately adjacent to the existing tower while the latter, which was completed in 1777, was commissioned by Andrew Johnstone. A former Jacobite supporter, Johnstone had fought for Prince Charles Edward in the 1745 rebellion and been sentenced to transportation to the West Indies, although subsequently reprieved. The original part of Raehills – that 'new and elegant palace' as the minister of Dryfesdale described it[35] – was commissioned by the third earl of Hopetoun as agent and curator for his great-uncle the marquess of Annandale in 1782.

A number of houses in Nithsdale date from this time, a prominent example being Dalswinton. Commissioned by Patrick Miller shortly after he acquired the estate in 1785, it is thought to have been designed by the landscape painter Alexander Nasmyth. Further down the Nith, Cowhill was built in 1788–9 for the new owner, George Johnstone, a Liverpool merchant, and remains in the hands of his descendants. At the same time nearby Terregles was built for William Haggerston Constable and his wife Winifred Maxwell,† while Glenae was built according to a design by Thomas Boyd in 1789–90.‡

---

* Before he became a victim of the collapse of the Douglas and Heron Bank.

† Now demolished, further embellishments were added to it in the 1830s by their grandson William Constable-Maxwell (later 10th lord Herries).

‡ The foregoing is merely a sample of the country houses in Dumfriesshire at the time because there were many others. For example, the minister of Dryfesdale described in his contribution to the *Old Statistical Account* the number of 'gentlemen's seats' which could be seen from the high ground in his parish – namely Kirkwood, Denbie, Whitecroft, Rammerscales, Holmains, Newmains, Fourtowns, Halleaths, Castlemains, Lochmaben, Elsieshiels, Rigghead, Todhillmoor, Kirkmichael Place, Hillside and Balgray.

Improvements extended to raising the quality of livestock, to which a number of farmers and landowners, encouraged by the prospect of the higher prices, devoted considerable time, effort and expense. An early pioneer was William Craik who, in addition to his other activities, built up a large cattle-rearing enterprise, to the extent that by 1748 he was exporting 1,700 black cattle annually to England. They made a name for themselves on account of their size, which was achieved by crossing his cows with bulls he purchased from Robert Bakewell, a well-known cattle breeder of Dishley Grange in Leicestershire.[36] While no doubt expensive, it was money well spent, for not only did Craik obtain a high price for their progeny but he would have profited from hiring out bulls with a proven record of siring good quality stock to other farmers.

While most cattle breeders were in the business of producing beef cattle for the English market, some Ayrshire farmers were developing a milk-producing cow. Being horned, these could be dangerous to handle, and because Ayrshire bulls are notoriously aggressive they were not popular with farmers. As the minister of Johnstone observed, 'a strong prejudice prevails all over the country against horned cattle'.[37] Yet, to quote from his colleague at Dunscore, 'Mr Robert Burns, a gentleman well known for his poetical productions who runs a farm in this parish [Ellisland] is of the opinion that the west-country cows give a larger quantity of milk'.[38] It was not until the following century, when the advent of railways enabled milk to be transported to a much wider market while remaining fresh, that the Ayrshire came into its own.

Attempts were made to improve the quality of the sheep by importing selected breeding stock from England and the Continent. There was clearly a need for this because the native stock seems to have deteriorated since the Middle Ages. By the eighteenth century the sheep had reverted to small animals, described as having 'a black or sometimes grey face, black legs and wool of very poor quality – not worth the cutting' as it was put. Other sheep were distinguishable by their physical peculiarities. As the minister of Moffat observed, 'it is not long since the sheep in this part of the country were of the four-horned kind [presumably Jacob sheep], and a few of them are said to remain in parts of Nithsdale'. 'But now', he went on, 'attempts have been made by certain farmers in the parish to breed for an improved quality of wool'.[39] This was not always successful, because many hill farmers failed to appreciate that a softer fleece impaired a sheep's ability to withstand the rigours of a Southern Uplands winter.

The results were not always successful on the lower ground either. Broadly speaking, there were three types of imported sheep; the long-woolled breed from Lincolnshire known as muggs, the long-bodied and broad-backed type bred by Robert Bakewell, and finally Spanish sheep. On the face of it, the muggs sound an unlikely choice. Described as 'large, scraggy animals with voracious appetites, very slow to fatten, and with poor-quality meat', their one redeeming feature was that they produced more wool, and of finer quality, than the native stock. They are known to have been introduced into the parish of Holywood,[40] and doubtless elsewhere in

Dumfriesshire. However the Rev. Dr Bryce Johnston, the contributor for the parish, omitted to say whether or not they were successful – perhaps because it was too early to judge by the time the *Old Statistical Account* was published.

Like the muggs, the Bakewll-bred sheep were prized for their wool. There is mention of them being introduced into the parishes of Sanquhar, Hutton and Corrie (encouraged by the earl of Hopetoun), and Holywood (presumably to see how they compared with the muggs). Evidently they were a failure at Sanquhar because the soil was described as 'inadequate', suggesting that there was insufficient grass of suitable quality and that the climate was too harsh.[41] The only reference to Spanish sheep in the *Old Statistical Account* concerns those imported by Patrick Miller. But this was not a success because the ram promptly died while some of the ewes were barren.[42]

By the end of the century, improvement had become all the rage, evident from the founding of the ponderously titled 'The Practical Farming Society of the Shire of Dumfries and the Stewartry of Kirkcudbright'. But there was an obverse side. Whereas the more far-sighted landowners were prepared to grant longer leases as an encouragement to their tenants to carry out improvements, others were too greedy. This was because it was a time of escalating rents, itself a product of the growing profitability of farming. This in turn was fuelled by a rapid rise in commodity prices on the back of an expanding population and an increasing demand for food. Therefore some landowners attempted to cash in on the boom by granting short-term leases in the expectation that when they expired the farms could be re-let for a higher rent. This meant that the tenants had no incentive to improve their holdings since they would be unable to reap the benefits. As it was said, 'short tacks make thriftless tenants'. Nevertheless the boom continued throughout the Napoleonic Wars until the bubble burst, and the resulting depression would last until the 1830s.

IMPROVING COMMUNICATIONS

Land improvement depended on a serviceable road system in place of the ill-defined tracks which had hitherto sufficed for overland communications. Ill-defined was exactly what they were, for as each track became churned up by human and animal traffic a parallel one was opened up instead. Eventually there was such a multiplicity of tracks that it was often hard to distinguish the actual highway. Worse still, they were invariably reduced to quagmires in wet weather and morasses in winter. Therefore one can readily understand how it was that the duke of Atholl's baggage train was unable to keep up with the rest of the division as it ploughed its way through Annandale in the course of the 1745 rebellion. Hitherto the only means of transporting goods overland was by pack horse, or people simply carried the goods on their backs like their Stone Age forebears. However, the development of a road system led to a growing use of carts, which was a subject of comment by nearly all the contributors to the *Old Statistical Account*.

During the previous century sporadic attempts were made to render the existing tracks usable, an early example being the laying out of a drove road from Annan to Gretna in 1619. Two years earlier, Parliament had passed an Act, confirmed by a later one of 1661, which empowered justices of the peace to improve the tracks leading to market towns, seaports and parish churches. The first officially designated highway in Scotland was the route between Carlisle and Portpatrick, which was established in 1642 to enable the English parliamentarians to maintain contact with their army in Ireland. But it could hardly be described as such, because all it amounted to was marking out a line of existing tracks.

Later, the Highways and Bridges Act of 1669 introduced a system of statute labour. This required all tenants, cottars and farm servants to give up to six days' work on the roads during the months of June and July each year – inconveniently because it coincided with hay and harvest time when demand for labour was at its peak. The work consisted mainly of repairing, ditching and fencing highways, which were required by law to be at least 20 feet wide.[43] A further Act of 1686 rendered the commissioners of supply and the justices of the peace jointly responsible for the repair and maintenance of the roads in their district. But it was an unsatisfactory arrangement, because it was virtually impossible to get them to agree on – let alone co-ordinate – an overall plan. Therefore the work was necessarily haphazard, while the statutory labour was grudgingly given and amounted to little more than filling in the potholes gouged out by human and animal traffic.

By 1697 the cattle trade had expanded to a point where a petition was presented to the Privy Council for authority to establish an officially designated highway for driving livestock through Galloway to Dumfries and beyond. It was represented that while the drovers followed a line between New Galloway and Dumfries there was no properly defined track. And because cattle could be troublesome to the owners and tenants of the lands they passed through (to say the least!), there were occasions when owners and tenants tried to stop the drovers by force, and the resulting clashes frequently ended in bloodshed. Alternatively, owners and tenants tried to impose 'illegal exactions of money on the cattle to the great damage of the trade', in effect holding drovers to ransom. Therefore a commission was appointed to mark out a highway between New Galloway and Dumfries.[44]

Through time the shortcomings of the statute labour system became so apparent that in 1751, under pressure from the commissioners of supply, Parliament passed an Act empowering them to levy a charge of £1 10s (£1.50) per £100 of their rent-roll on landowners, and a per capita charge of 2s 6d (12½p) on all householders and mechanics (i.e. labourers). The proceeds were to be applied towards the cost of repairing and improving the roads on a contract basis. Meanwhile the system of statute labour remained in force, for it was not until 1777 that an Act was passed authorising the commissioners of supply to commute it to a monetary payment. In Dumfriesshire, and doubtless elsewhere, the proceeds were used to improve the minor cross-country roads and build feeder roads.

The 1751 Act further provided for the creation of turnpike roads to replace or complement existing ones. Therefore it gave members of the public, generally local landowners and other interested parties, the right to petition Parliament for authority to establish a turnpike trust. This would be equipped with powers to build a new highway, or upgrade an existing one to a usable standard. The cost of the work was to be met by levying tolls on users, except for those going to church or a funeral, and later on mail-coaches which were initially exempt from tolls. Consequently tollhouses or tollbars were established at regular intervals – usually every six miles – along the route, and also at ferries and bridges. The Act further empowered the trustees to raise loans on the security of future tolls to finance the building of the turnpike. On the other hand, some roads were paid for by public subscription, one example being the road from Dumfries to Moffat which broadly followed the line of the present A701. A later Act of 1767 made it compulsory to erect milestones along the main turnpikes, partly as a guide to travellers and also to help mail-coaches keep to schedule.

One road had a curious origin. This was the forerunner of the present road from Lockerbie to Annan. In the *Old Statistical Account* the Rev. William Burnside, the minister of Greyfriars, Dumfries, explained how it came about: 'Around the beginning of the century [i.e. about 1700] an English visitor bought a large quantity of tobacco, but left without giving instructions as to where it was to be delivered.' Having made repeated attempts to trace him without success, the burgh council petitioned the Court of the Exchequer for authority to sell the tobacco and account to the purchaser for the proceeds. Still unable to track him down, the council decided to apply the proceeds, together with the original purchase price of the tobacco, towards the cost of making of a new road (it must have been a huge sum), and this was their choice.[45]

The first positive step towards road improvement in the south-west came in 1757 when it was planned to build a government-funded road from the Sark bridge to Portpatrick as an extension of the main highway from the south. According to the initial survey report, the object was 'to open a speedy and certain communication between Great Britain and Ireland, especially with regard to the passage of troops from one kingdom to the other whenever required'. Since the work was carried out by army engineers, it was known as the military road. Although the section from Dumfries to Portpatrick was stated to have been completed in 1763,[46] that this was clearly not the case is evident from a complaint some thirty years later that the final section in western Wigtownshire was 'almost impassable for carriages of any kind [because] only a small part of it has yet been formed'. There was considerable delay in completing the section between the Sark bridge and Dumfries as well, because work on it was not started until 1773[47] and only completed in 1776,[48] while tollbars were still being built in the 1790s.[49]

Further north, a track followed the course of the old Roman road from Elvanfoot up the Daer Water and over the pass to Durisdeer, and from there into Upper

Nithsdale. This had been brought up to a usable standard by the third duke of Queensberry in 1736, and when a new road was cut through the Dalveen Pass in the late 1760s he, along with other landowners in Upper Nithsdale, paid the lion's share of the cost, the balance being met by the commissioners of supply.[50] In 1786 John McMurdo, the fourth duke's chamberlain, gave an undertaking on his behalf to meet the cost of repairing and maintaining the road, for which the duke remained liable until about 1810 (the year of his death) when the road was turnpiked.[51]

In 1776 an Act of Parliament was obtained authorising the construction of three turnpike roads in Dumfriesshire. One was to connect Gretna with Moffat via Ecclefechan and Lockerbie, broadly the forerunner of the M74. Another would replace (or rather upgrade) the existing road from Dumfries to Moffat, while the third was to link Annan via Kirkpatrick Fleming with the road from Carlisle to Langholm. In each case the trustees were empowered to levy tolls every six miles. In fact the first of these, namely the proposed road from Gretna to Moffat, had already been incorporated in a planned turnpike from Carlisle to Glasgow which was authorised by a separate Act of Parliament. This road was duly built, and the first mail-coach from Glasgow to London passed along it in 1788.*

So too did an estimated 20,000 head of cattle each spring on their way to the English markets.[52] But they reduced the road to such a quagmire that by 1795 the section from the upper Clyde over the Beattock summit to the Evan Water had become impassable to mail-coaches and the service had to be suspended. This was serious because the road was the only link between central Scotland and the south; and besides it was of the utmost importance that nothing should interfere with the mail service. Although the road would have been repaired as a matter of urgency, it was decided to build an alternative route which would be denied to livestock. Accordingly in 1798 the Evan Water trustees obtained an Act of Parliament authorising them to build a new road which would connect it with the Edinburgh, Moffat and Dumfries turnpike. Because the government declined to subsidise the cost, it was funded by the Glasgow merchants since they had a vested interest in the project. Even so the road was not completed until 1808,[53] the delay being due in part to the need to build a bridge over the Evan Water. Unfortunately in October that year torrential rain caused it to flood and part of the bridge was washed away. Unaware of this, a passing coachman failed to stop his horses in time, with the result that they went careering over the edge dragging the coach and its occupants after them. The coachman and a number of passengers were killed while others were left permanently maimed.[54]

In 1815 the Carlisle–Glasgow road was designated one of national importance. Therefore Parliament granted a facility of £50,000 towards the cost of upgrading it,

---

*   To begin with, mail-coaches were exempted from paying tolls. But these four-horse coaches caused so much damage to the roads that in 1813 Parliament, bowing to pressure from the turnpike trustees, passed an Act removing the exemption (N and M Miller, 'Improvements to the Glasgow-Carlisle Road 1815' *TDGNHAS*, lxvii (1992), 67).

while Thomas Telford* was appointed to supervise the work on the section between the Sark bridge and Hamilton. In fact Telford's plan was more radical than originally proposed, because he re-aligned the road from its original course via Longtown to follow the existing one to Dumfries and Portpatrick as far as Gretna.[55] This added considerably to the cost, and, because the tolls were insufficient to cover it, the trustees were forced to cut corners where they could. Nevertheless they were statutorily obliged to maintain ten broken stone deposits per mile, and to employ one man for every five miles of road or less depending on usage. In winter their main task was to clear the road of mud and water, and in summer to fill the potholes with stones (leaving it to wheeled traffic to compact them), clear the side drains, and repair the retaining walls where necessary. By 1836 the cost overrun was such that the government had to increase the facility to £86,000.[56]

Meanwhile the turnpike from Dumfries to Moffat was completed, while the section of the old military road from Annan to Dumfries was altered to keep to the higher ground to the north, thus reducing the distance by some miles. At much the same time a separate Act of Parliament authorised the building of a turnpike from Carlisle to Langholm, and this was extended up the Ewes Water via Teviothead to Hawick.

The year 1790 saw the completion of a turnpike up Nithsdale. This replaced – or at least upgraded – the existing highway known as 'the old great road' which broadly followed the course of the present A76 from Dumfries to Sanquhar and Kirkconnel, and on to Ayr. The work involved levelling sections of the existing track to render the new highway accessible to carriages. Since upgrading the road was crucial to the improvements he was carrying out on his estates in mid- and upper Nithsdale, the third duke of Queensberry took over responsibility for completing the 22-mile stretch which passed through his lands.[57] Once completed, the road allowed for the institution of a regular mail service between Dumfries and Ayr, a post office (reputedly the oldest in the world) having been established at Sanquhar as early as 1712.

The improved road network enabled a regular mail service to be established throughout much of the country. One of the earliest was the service between Edinburgh and Glasgow, which was introduced in 1749. But the roads were so bad that it took 12 hours to complete the journey. By 1780 they had been improved to the

---

* Born in 1757 he was a shepherd's son from Glendinning on the Westerhall estate. Left fatherless at the age of three, he was reared in poverty by his mother and largely self-taught. His talents were first recognised by Sir William Chambers who was responsible for building the additions to Somerset House. In 1787, through the influence of William Johnstone Pulteney, the local member of Parliament and younger brother of Sir James Johnstone of Westerhall, he was appointed surveyor of public works in Shropshire when he established a commanding reputation as a builder of bridges, and later canals. In 1801 he was commissioned to draw up a plan for the improvement of communications in the Highlands, a project that would occupy him for the next twenty years. This included cutting the Caledonian canal, re-designing sections of the Crinan canal, and building some 920 miles of new roads and over 1,000 bridges. In 1808 he was commissioned by the king of Sweden to build a canal linking Gothenburg with Stockholm, while he continued to mastermind many other projects until his death in 1834.

extent that it was possible to run faster and more regular mail services. Edinburgh was now the hub of the postal system in Scotland, and regular deliveries were made to Carlisle, Aberdeen, Stirling and Dumfries,[58] although it was not until 1788 that the first mail-coach completed the 60-hour journey from Glasgow to London.

Bridges, particularly those across the main rivers, were integral to the road system. The earliest in Dumfriesshire was the stone bridge which was built by Duchess Margaret over the Nith at Dumfries in the 1430s to replace the wooden one attributed to Dervorguilla. All cattle coming from Galloway to England were driven across it, earning the town some £200 annually in tolls. But, as the Rev. William Burnside pointed out in the *Old Statistical Account*, the bridge was too narrow to accommodate them, and besides it was becoming ruinous. Therefore it was decided to build a new one which was to be 'more spacious and elegant'.[59] This was the Buccleuch Street bridge, which was designed by Thomas Boyd[60] (who was responsible for Glenae House); the work was put in hand in 1791 and the bridge was completed three years later.

In the previous century the Highways and Bridges Act of 1669 assigned responsibility for maintaining the bridges in their shire to the justices of the peace, although there were probably relatively few in Dumfriesshire at the time. The bridge over the Water of Milk, where the 'commoun hieway passed southwards towards London', was an early one. This was built by public subscription organised by a group of local ministers on the instructions of the Privy Council.[61] Another was a bridge over the Nith at Sanquhar. This had a long history: James VI's charter of 1598 making Sanquhar a royal burgh included a grant to the provost and others of 'the bridge of the said burgh', which suggests that it had already existed for some time, possibly since the previous century. Eventually it fell into disrepair, and because the burgh lacked the means to rebuild it the Scottish Parliament passed an Act in 1661 authorising the levying of contributions on the local heritors to help fund the cost. At the same time the burgh was authorised to levy tolls on the users.[*] In 1706 a bridge was built over the Crawick Water near its confluence with the Nith at Sanquhar, allegedly at the expense of the 'Union' duke of Queensberry.[62]

Further downstream there was probably already a bridge at Auldgirth, because one was reported to have existed there 'for a long time' before 1740 when the local justices of the peace were ordered to keep it in a proper state of repair. Evidently they failed to do so, because by 1777 it had become so ruinous that it had to be replaced with a new bridge. This was completed in 1782, one of the masons employed on it being James Carlyle, father of Thomas Carlyle. The contractor, William Stewart, went on to build bridges over the Ae and the Shinnel, which were completed in 1783 and 1786 respectively. He was also responsible for the bridges at Collin and Dunscore, as well as those crossing the Dryfe, the Dalquhat, the bridge over the Nith downriver from Drumlanrig, and finally the Buccleuch Street bridge at Dumfries.

---

[*] The right to levy tolls was finally abolished by the Highways and Bridges Act of 1887.

In about 1745 a three-arched bridge was built at Canonbie. This was primarily to enable the townspeople living to the west of the river to get to the church on the opposite side. Hitherto the only way they could do so was by wading the river or crossing it on horseback, and if it was in flood they had to use a boat. This could be risky: on one occasion the boat capsized and a number of people were drowned. But it was only after others had lost their lives that, in response to popular agitation, the bridge was built. Later, in about 1790, a second bridge was built by the third duke of Buccleuch a mile or so upstream near Hollows to provide a shortcut to his colliery at Byreburnfoot.[63] Meanwhile in 1782 the earl of Hopetoun was responsible for building St Anne's bridge over the Kinnel Water, and rebuilt in 1797 it was later widened and improved when the road from Dumfries to Moffat was turnpiked.[64]

The latter half of the eighteenth century witnessed the construction of other bridges in Eskdale, one example being the Ewes Bridge which was built over the Ewes Water just north of Langholm in 1763. This was followed in 1775 by a three-arched bridge, immediately below the confluence of the Esk and the Ewes Water, which was financed by public subscription.[65] Now part of the B708 road from Langholm to Eskdalemuir, it was here that the young Thomas Telford was employed as a journey-man mason, evident from his mark which is incised on some of the stone blocks. In 1813 the first iron bridge in the county was built across the Esk at Langholm Lodge (now part of a public walkway). Known as the Duchess's Bridge, it replaced a dilapi-dated wooden bridge and set the fashion for building other iron bridges. One example was the Boatford Bridge, known as the 'swing brig', which was built about a mile downriver in 1871 to replace an existing ford and enable workers to reach the mills in New Langholm dryshod. Its inauguration nearly ended in disaster. No sooner was it formally opened and the barriers at either end removed than such a crowd rushed on to it that it gave way in the middle. Both sections subsided into the river, but slowly enough to allow the people to scramble to the safety of the nearest bank, fortunately without any casualties.

During the latter part of the eighteenth century canal-building was all the rage in England, and this extended – albeit on a much smaller scale – to neighbouring Kirkcudbrightshire. But not Dumfriesshire. That said, there was a proposal to cut a canal to connect the Lochar moss with the sea. The purpose was to drain the moss as a preliminary to reclaiming it as farmland, as well as allowing small boats access from the sea as far as the parish of Kirkmahoe.[66] But for various reasons the plan was abandoned. There was another proposal to cut a seven-mile canal, following what is thought to have been the original course of the Annan, from Dormont to Powfoot.[67] This, it was hoped, would reduce the cost of transporting coal, lime and manure, as well as wood, iron and slate, from Cumberland to upper Annandale.[68] Although an ambitious, not to say a visionary, scheme it never amounted to anything more than a bright idea.

INDUSTRIAL DEVELOPMENT

Industrial development was the logical progression from the traditional cottage industries of carding and spinning wool, knitting, carpet weaving, and the manufacture of linen and linen cloth. This was generally done by the womenfolk, although the men would help out during the winter months when there was less work available on the farms, while the children carded the wool and turned the wheel which operated the loom. The finished products were sold at the local fair or market. As well as being a vital supplement to their hand-to-mouth existence, the cottars relied on the proceeds to pay their rent. During the 1760s weaving was revolutionised by James Hargreaves' invention of the spinning jenny which was patented in 1764, and Richard Arkwright's spinning frame, a water-powered device for spinning cotton which was patented five years later. This resulted in the industry becoming concentrated in purpose-built mills in the vicinity of a river or stream where the flow turned the waterwheel which powered the looms.

Throughout the eighteenth century there was a growing emphasis on the production of linen and linen cloth, but latterly it was overtaken by cotton. Therefore it followed that the first two mills in Scotland – at Rothesay and Penicuik – were cotton mills, the latter being founded by Sir James Clerk on the banks of the Esk in 1778. In 1785 a Mr Hurst established a cotton mill at Annan, and the following year David Dale was responsible for building the cotton mills adjacent to the Clyde at New Lanark. In 1799 they were taken over by his son-in-law Robert Owen, a philanthropist and social reformer who, unlike the great majority of millowners, went to considerable lengths to provide for the welfare of his workers and the education of their children.

In Dumfriesshire industrial development was focused primarily on the woollen industry, one of the main centres being Sanquhar – logically, because it is situated at the heart of extensive sheep country. In 1721 Provost John Crichton set up a wauk mill on the banks of the Crawick Water, and in 1735 he was the promoter and principal partner in a wool manufacturing enterprise which was established in Sanquhar itself.[69] Although the latter went out of business in 1741 Crichton kept on the mill at Crawick, while his son – also John Crichton – converted it into a blanket mill. Later, in about 1790, a carpet mill was established on the opposite side of the Crawick Water. Once up and running it contained fifty-four looms, and as such was a major source of employment in the district, while the carpets earned a reputation for durability which extended far beyond the British Isles.

Langholm was also becoming an important industrial centre, and here the emphasis was on the production of woollen goods and linen – wool because, like Sanquhar, it was the centre of extensive sheep country, and linen because flax or lint was widely grown by farmers and villagers alike. Langholm had the further advantage of being situated at the confluence of three rivers – the Esk, the Ewes Water, and the Wauchope Water – which meant there was ample water power available. And because it is only about fourteen miles upriver from the sea, the finished products could readily be exported.

Although Langholm was the centre of a long-established cottage-based woollen industry, the first mill to be established there was a cotton mill, the Meikleholm Mill. This was founded in 1789 by a group of Carlisle manufacturers, probably encouraged by the duke of Buccleuch* to set up in business in the new town which he was in the process of developing as an industrial centre. Unfortunately the mill fell victim to the financial crisis, and the accompanying dearth of credit, which followed the outbreak of war with France in 1793 and went out of business. Fortunately most, if not all, the weavers were taken on by several Carlisle manufacturers, notably Dickson, Forrester and Ferguson, as contract labour working from home. Meanwhile the abandoned Meikleholm mill was taken over by John and James Carruthers who were soon producing some 20,000 yards of cotton checks and coarse linen annually.

The first woollen manufactory in Langholm was the Whitshiels Mill which was situated about a mile upriver of the town on the Ewes Water. This was founded by Irvine & Co. in 1797 and employed some fifty workers, mainly in spinning and knitting. At much the same time, a stocking-knitting manufactory was founded by T & A Renwick in the new town. This was intended to cater for the revival in demand from the former American colonies following the end of the War of Independence. Notwithstanding that there was a factory in Dumfries turning out similar articles to supply the local market, the demand was such that, as the contributor to the *Old Statistical Account* put it, 'the manufacturer [Renwick] cannot answer his orders'.[70]

The fact that so many workers were employed on contract working from home was responsible for the survival of the traditional cottage industries in the face of progressive industrialisation. Added to which, many small-time tenants and cottars who had been evicted from their holdings to make way for land improvement became full-time weavers. This is evident from the *Old Statistical Account* where they feature prominently in the list of tradesmen returned for each parish. As the minister of Dryfesdale observed, 'every family is a small factory for the manufacture of both linen and woollen cloth'.[71]

While the duke of Buccleuch may have been responsible for encouraging the Carlisle manufacturers, and Irvine & Co, to establish the Meikleholm and Whitshiels Mills, he seems to have decided that enough was enough. That at least is the conclusion to be drawn from his agent's reply to George Maxwell of Broomholm's request in his letters of 1808 and 1809 for permission to tap into a water supply on the duke's lands to power a mill he was planning to build on his estate. To lend force to his petition, Maxwell went on to extol the benefits of manufacture.

The duke disagreed. Although consenting on his behalf, the agent explained the duke's reservations. They had 'not had the effect of advancing his rents in the least degree', while 'the mills already [established] have been prejudicial to his property,

---

* The third duke, he was known as 'the good Duke Henry'.

and his residence there [Langholm Lodge] has been rendered very disagreeable, if not disgusting'. In his view 'manufacturing in general has been pushed too far in Great Britain [and] has withdrawn capital which might have been used in cultivation'. Expressing a view shared by many of his peers, the agent quoted the duke as saying that industrialisation was 'the source of riot and disorder'.[72] It may be that his aversion stemmed from the fact that, at the time of writing, six factories producing cotton checks, thread and stockings, and two dyeing plants had been established at Langholm. While perhaps not to the duke's liking, it certainly benefited the community because it was responsible for the rise in the population to some 2,500 making it the second largest town in the county after Dumfries.

By this time most factories were steam-powered, thanks to James Watt's invention of the steam engine which, patented in 1769, heralded its replacement of water as the main source of power. This revolutionised the whole textile industry because it meant that factories no longer needed to be situated in the vicinity of a river or stream. Therefore industry became increasingly concentrated in central Scotland where there was an abundance of coal for firing the boilers to produce the steam. Here Langholm had the advantage of a readily available supply of coal from the pits at nearby Canonbie.

The earliest reference to its existence comes from Lowther's *Tour of Scotland* in 1629 in which he observed that '3 miles from Langham is my L Bucp's [Buccleuch's] colepits'.[73] These were probably the pits on the west side of the Esk which provided coal for the limekilns at Holehouse, for it was not until 1768 that the third duke took over the recently sunk mine at Byreburnfoot and brought in colliers from his mines at Sheriffhall near Dalkeith to work it. Two years later, in 1770, the coal seam to the west of the Esk was exhausted and the mine closed. Meanwhile the mine at Byreburnfoot was badly affected by drainage and ventilation problems, not helped by the fact that during a spell of exceptionally wet weather the Byre burn burst its banks and flooded it, putting it out of commission.

Later the Canonbie coalfield was leased to a Mr Lomax on condition that he provided the local people with a regular supply of coal at an affordable price.[74] Because the need to install a pumping engine and drainage equipment would be so costly as to render it uneconomic, Mr Lomax decided not to re-open it. Instead he dug an opencast pit at nearby Archerbeck where coal could be produced more cheaply. It was not a success. In fact Lomax was only saved from bankruptcy when by a happy chance a flood exposed a thick seam of coal further downstream. During the subsistence of his lease he sank some seventy pits of varying depth, employing horse gins to raise the coal to the surface, while a steam engine was installed to pump out the water. Following his death in 1837, the coalfield reverted to the duke of Buccleuch.[75]

Because Mr Lomax decided not to re-open the Byrburnfoot mine, the duke took it over himself for the purpose of 'affording the public the happy prospect of a prompt and ample supply of this necessary article of life'.[76] To render it more accessible, he was responsible for building the bridge over the Esk at Hollows and for diverting the high road from the west to the east bank of the river. At the same time he appointed a manager to run the mine. But judging from the minister of Kirkpatrick Fleming's complaint about the scarcity of coal, due to 'the miserable management which [the mine] has [for] some years been under', he was clearly not up to the mark. Nevertheless, the minister went on to concede that 'attempts are being made to introduce better management',[77] for it was about that time that the duke installed a new type of pump designed by William Keir, his factor at Canonbie.

The other main source of coal in Dumfriesshire were the mines at Sanquhar and Kirkconnel in Upper Nithsdale. For centuries it had been known to exist there, although it was not until later that the coalfield was found to extend to some six square miles.[78] The earliest reference to the existence of coal in the district comes from an entry in the municipal accounts of Dumfries for 1638 which records a payment of £1 4s for 'fetching coals out of Sanquhar'.[79] In 1768 Robert Barker, a native of Derbyshire, leased the coalfield from the duke of Queensberry,[80] and in the following decade Sanquhar burgh council granted Robert McMath the right to dig for coal on the burgh muir.[81] Evidently with some success, because in 1792 it encouraged the council to open a pit themselves. Therefore after a preliminary survey, and on the advice of Barker and McMath, they opened one at Knowehead near Sanquhar.[82]

Initially, flooding was a problem since it made it impossible to dig anything other than a shallow pit. In an attempt to solve it, a winch was erected to enable water to be hauled to the surface in buckets fixed to a chain, the winch being turned by horse gins. But this rather primitive method of disposing of water failed to solve the problem because the mine quickly filled up again. In the 1790s Thomas Barker, who had succeeded his father Robert as lessee of the duke of Queensberry, installed pumps which were powered by a waterwheel driven by the Nith. But the mine was too close to the river because the water broke through and flooded it, though fortunately without loss of life.[83] Therefore Barker installed a steam-driven pump instead, evident from the local minister's reference in the *Old Statistical Account* to a 'fire or steam engine lately erected for draining the mines'.[84]

Throughout this time the miners were effectively serfs, following an Act of the Scottish Parliament of 1606 which bound all hewers of coal (and salters) to their colliery (or saltpan) for life, and forbade them from seeking alternative employment. In terms of two subsequent Acts of 1641 and 1661 this was extended to surface workers as well. Consequently they became pertinents of the mine, and therefore transferable with it in the event of a change of owner or leaseholder. This remained the case until the system was abolished by an Act of 1775. However, in his *Upper Nithsdale Coalworks*, J C I McConnel, formerly the Assistant Managing Director of Sanquhar and Kirkconnel Collieries Ltd, states categorically that there was no evidence of this form of servitude applying to the Upper Nithsdale pits, nor of any women being employed underground.[85]

This would imply that the ban extended to children as well. In which case, it was probably atypical of the coal industry as a whole where children were employed to move coal from the face to the main shaft. Traditionally it was carried by miners in creels on their back, but from about the 1770s onwards wooden rails were installed in the mines to enable coal to be transported in wheeled boxes instead. Therefore boys and girls as young as five or six were yoked to them by means of a harness known as a 'girdle and chain' and made to pull them to the foot of the mineshaft from where the coal was winched to the surface. In the Upper Nithsdale pits, on the other hand, the wagons or boxes, known as 'hutches', were drawn by horses – necessary given that each box would generally contain as much as half a ton of coal.[86]

It was unfortunate that the two main sources of coal in Dumfriesshire were at opposite ends of the county, because the cost of carting it to the limeworks for firing the kilns rendered lime prohibitively expensive, and this may to some extent have inhibited land improvement. True, coal was readily available from Cumberland, but it was rendered virtually unaffordable by heavy import duties,* a subject on which the contributors to the *Old Statistical Account* – particularly those from the southern parishes – wax vitriolic. According to the minister of Cummertrees numerous petitions were made to the government calling for their abolition. But in spite of it, he went on, 'the measure remains unrepealed – to the great obstruction of the improvement and cultivation of the country'.†

Canonbie also boasted a deposit of iron ore. Here ironworking dated from at least 1699 when Anne duchess of Buccleuch‡ allowed a group of English entrepreneurs to build a forge there and undertook to supply them with timber to provide the charcoal to fire it. That she gave them the right to build more than one forge suggests that there were several pockets of iron ore in the vicinity. However, the enterprise seems to have been a failure because the ironworks were abandoned. In 1715 Duchess Anne tried again. This time she leased them to two other Englishmen – chancers by the sound of it, because their lease was abruptly terminated when they were outlawed (no reason given) and declared bankrupt. Undaunted, she made a third attempt. This time she contracted with a Mr Brooke, a London merchant, and his partner Mr Dod to take over the ironworks and run it. Holding themselves out as respectable businessmen, they assured the duchess that the foundry would be used for converting scrap iron into cast iron. When it transpired that they were manufacturing counterfeit Irish halfpennies, their lease was abruptly terminated, [87] though what became of the forgers is not known.

At the opposite end of the county there was an abundance of lead, and some gold, at Leadhills and Wanlockhead. A survey carried out in the reign of James IV listing

---

*   This is strange considering it was of the essence of the Treaty of Union that there should be a free movement of goods between England and Scotland.

†   In fact the measure was repealed in 1793 just as the *Old Statistical Account* was going to press. But in practice it made little difference because the Cumberland coalmasters took advantage of it to raise their prices.

‡   Heiress of the Scotts of Buccleuch, her first husband was Charles II's illegitimate son the duke of Monmouth who was executed in 1685.

the places where gold was found stated that 'sundrie workmen afirme that at Wanlock Water, and in sundrie other places, they have founde gold in bigness of cherristones', and that '[it] hath been gotten from the workings' in the 'Langham' Water and the Meggat Water.[88] This together with similar reports doubtless encouraged Sir Bevis Bulmer, the master of Queen Elizabeth's mint, to obtain a licence from the Regent Morton to prospect for gold in the vicinity of Wanlockhead.* With some success, for in the course of several summers his (mainly German) workforce are said to have mined up to £100,000 worth of the metal,[89] some of it being used to make a gold porringer for presentation to Queen Elizabeth. In fact nuggets of anything up to 30 ounces (825 grams) were reportedly found there during the early years of the nineteenth century.[90]

Forty-seven veins of lead have been found at Wanlockhead, and approximately a further twenty-three at Leadhills. It has been claimed that the lead was first discovered by Cornelius Hardskins, one of Sir Bevis Bulmer's workers, in the course of his search for gold. However, this is wrong, because there is a reference to lead in Sir David Lindsay's charter of 1239 granting land at Crawfordmuir to the monks of Newbattle.[91] Later, in 1529, James V granted a licence to Ninian Crichton, the parson of Sanquhar, to 'work in the mynes of lead within the barony of Sanquhar for three years'.[92] Finally in 1562 Johne Achisone and John Aslowane were granted the right to 'work and wyn lead in the mines of Glengonar and Wanlock', the ore being shipped to Flanders in exchange for silver.[93]

In 1675 the earl (later first duke) of Queensberry granted a lease of the mine at Wanlockhead to Sir John Stampfield and two other entrepreneurs from Newcastle. But they encountered endless difficulties – obstruction from their rivals at Leadhills, a recalcitrant workforce (understandably given their primitive working conditions) and an embezzling manager, as well as drainage problems. Therefore when their lease expired they declined to renew it. In 1691 Matthew Wilson and another Englishman took a nineteen-year lease of the mine, but they were handicapped by a lack of capital needed to develop it. When their lease expired in 1710, the 'union' duke of Queensberry re-let the mine to the London Lead Company who introduced the practice of using coal instead of peat for smelting the ore. They continued to work the Old Glencrieff and Belton-grain veins, but without much success, until they struck the Lochnell and New Glencrieff veins which proved much more productive.

The London Lead Company and its successors continued to work the mine until 1755 when it was leased to Ronald Crawford, Meason & Co. By this time the rising price of lead rendered it a profitable concern, to the extent that they are reported to have employed a workforce of some 360 men. But they were the victims of ruthless exploitation. They were paid according to the amount of lead produced, and then only infrequently. Because they lacked the means to purchase the necessities of life

---

* The price of the licence was the delivery of a tenth share of any gold recovered to Morton in person (Porteous, *God's Treasure House*, 38).

during the interim, they were allowed to do so on credit at the only shop in the village. Since this was owned by the company, it effectively held the workers to ransom by charging them exorbitant prices, not only for food and other essentials, but also for the tools and candles (the only sources of light in the mine) which they were required to provide at their own expense.

The work was dangerous too. Apart from the constant risk of rockfalls, the smelting process was particularly hazardous because the fumes given off were extremely toxic. And, lacking any form of protection, many workers died prematurely from the effects of lead poisoning. Moreover they were accommodated in the most basic hovels which were so badly thatched that it was said that 'no sooner does the rain fall but it comes down through the roof and runs out through the door'. The high rainfall which is a feature of the region compounded the problem of flooding in the mine. In 1778 Ronald Crawford, Meason & Co installed the first of three water-powered beam engines in the mine (the other two were installed in 1812 and 1817). Designed by James Watt, it was capable of pumping out between fifteen and twenty gallons of water a minute, which was a measure of how quickly it accumulated in the mine.

Meanwhile the company continued to prosper on the back of the growing demand for lead, fuelled by the American War and latterly the Napoleonic War, and also by a construction boom at home. But it was not to last, because the slump in the price of lead in the aftermath of the Napoleonic War forced a cutback in production and workers began to be laid off. In 1827 the effects of the downturn were compounded by the removal of the import duty on foreign lead, and the resulting glut pushed the price down to a point where the mine was no longer viable. However in 1830 the situated was partially redeemed when hydraulic pressure engines were installed to replace the water-powered ones. This made it possible to extend the mine, besides making it easier (and hence cheaper) to extract the ore. Consequently the mine was restored to profit and further redundancies were avoided.

A vein of lead was discovered at Broomholm near Langholm, and in 1762 the proprietor, Maxwell, established a small opencast mine there. In the event only a minimal amount of lead was extracted, and therefore it was closed soon afterwards. Nevertheless it seems to have been enough to encourage Sir James Johnstone of Westerhall to scour his Eskdale lands for the metal. In 1788 metal was indeed discovered – to the east of the Meggat Water opposite the farm of Glendinning, but it turned out to be antimony.* A company was formed – the Westerhall Mining Company – to extract it. This was 50% owned by Sir James while the other 50% was shared between a Captain Cochrane and a Mr Tait. Operations began in 1793, and in the course of the next five years the mine – the Louisa mine – produced approximately a hundred

---

* The (doubtless apocryphal) story has it that the name of the metal was derived from 'antimoine' or 'anti-monk'. This was because a German monk observed that, when fed to pigs, the mineral caused them to put on weight, and therefore he tried it out on his more cadaverous brethren to see if it would do the same for them, But the experiment proved a failure because they all died! *OSA* (Westerkirk) xi, pp 514–31.

tons of antimony.[94] When Sir James Johnstone died the following year, his share in the company passed to his brother Sir William Johnstone Pulteney.*

The company was reported to have built a fine smelting house for processing the ore and employed a workforce of forty men plus an overseer. Foreshadowing Robert Owen's concern for the welfare of his workforce at New Lanark, the company provided the workers and their families with comfortable accommodation for a modest rent in a purpose-built village called Jamestown on the Meggat Water. It boasted a school, and by 1790 the company was in the process of setting up a contributory scheme to provide for the workers in sickness and old age – in effect a Friendly Society, of which a number were established in Dumfriesshire at the time.

Jamestown was an example, albeit a small one, of the many planned villages which were founded in Dumfriesshire, and indeed throughout Scotland, during the eighteenth and early nineteenth centuries. They were either new settlements or an extension of an existing one like New Langholm and Lockerbie. Whereas most were founded by individual landowners, there were exceptions such as Gasstown on the outskirts of Dumfries which was established by the burgh council.†
Those dating from the eighteenth century were usually associated with agricultural improvement. Therefore they were designed to accommodate casual labourers, self-employed tradesmen such as masons, joiners and blacksmiths, as well as those employed in the upkeep and improvement of landed estates. Most were dispossessed small-time tenants and cottars, many of whom set themselves up as weavers. They frequently formed themselves into small co-operatives, with each member performing an allotted task, be it carding, spinning or weaving – effectively becoming small-time factories.

Planned villages also served as markets for people to sell their surplus produce. In many cases, perceiving it to their financial advantage, the founding landowners encouraged entrepreneurs to establish small industrial concerns as a source of employment. Indeed, landowners actively encouraged people with particular skills to join the community, frequently advertising for suitable applicants in a local or national newspaper. As an added incentive, these settlers were almost invariably allotted a feu of a piece of land, known as a toft, as part of their accommodation. Effectively an area of cultivable garden ground, it was generally sufficient to accommodate a house cow and some pigs, generally for home consumption. Indeed the provision of a toft, otherwise known as a yard, was integral to the layout of virtually all planned villages.

The earliest in Dumfriesshire was Lockerbie. This was founded in 1730 by Johnstone of Lockerbie who expanded the existing settlement by feuing out building plots.[95] In the late 1740s Dumfries burgh council founded a residential development

---

* He changed his name following his marriage to the fabulously wealthy Frances Pulteney.
† So called after Joseph Gass who was responsible for its founding, and for supervising its initial development.

at Glencaple to accommodate the harbourmaster, the ancillary staff needed to run its recently enlarged harbour, and a small merchant community. This was followed by another at Kingholm Quay immediately downriver from Dumfries. The 1760s witnessed the founding of further planned villages, notably Moffat and Newton Wamphray, the creations of the second earl of Hopetoun, the former on behalf of his uncle the marquess of Annandale and the latter on his own account. The combined village of Dunreggan and Moniaive was founded by Ferguson of Craigdarroch.

In 1778 the third duke of Buccleuch embarked on the creation of New Langholm on the opposite side of the Esk from Langholm itself. Following his death in 1812, his son the fourth duke carried on the work, and by the time he died in 1819 the new town was virtually complete. It consisted of 142 terraced cottages consisting of one or two storeys, each with its own yard. Meanwhile the 1780s witnessed the opening up of the limeworks at Closeburn and the establishment of the villages of Croalchapel and Park, while those at Barjarg on the opposite side of the Nith spawned the village of that name, and also Porterstown, both of which have since disappeared. Other planned villages dating from around that time include Kirkconnel, which was established for the accommodation of coalminers, Patrick Miller's creation of Dalswinton, and Marmaduke Constable-Maxwell's estate village of Terregles,* as well as Ruthwell which was founded by lord Stormont, and the fishing village of Powfoot.

Some sixteen villages were founded during the 1790s and the 1800s, including the duke of Buccleuch's creation at Canonbie. Another was Kelhead, near Kinmount, which was founded by Sir Charles Douglas (future marquess of Queensberry) to accommodate the workers in his newly opened lime quarry. A third was Brydekirk. This was founded in 1800 by Major-General Dirom, who established a woollen mill there. A fourth was Druidsville adjacent to the Nith, and presumably so-called after the stone circle known as the Twelve Apostles in the vicinity. This was founded by the Rev. Dr Bryce Johnston, the minister of Holywood and clearly an enterprising member of the cloth. But it never came to anything and was eventually superseded by the modern village of Holywood. Some villages were established at the intersection of turnpikes to cater for passing traffic, such as Springfield near Gretna which was built at the junction of the road to Dumfries and the main Carlisle–Glasgow road.[†]

The three outstanding examples of a planned village developing into a thriving town are Moffat, Lockerbie and Langholm. Some like Kirkconnel, Moniaive and Canonbie have grown into townships,[‡] while places like Eaglesfield, Kelhead, Duncow, Dalswinton, Crawick, Croalchapel and Park survive as small settlements

---

* This has since disappeared, the modern village of Terregles being situated about half a mile to the west.
† Other planned villages dating from this time include Carronbridge, Craigielands (the forerunner of Beattock), Crawick Mill (near Sanquhar), Collin, Cummertrees, Eaglesfield, Keir Mill, Penpont, Racks and Waterbeck.
‡ Others include Beattock, Brydekirk, Carronbridge, Clarencefield, Closeburn, Collin, Cummertrees, Glencaple, Kingholm Quay, Penpont, Powfoor, Racks, Ruthwell, Springfield and Wamphray.

or clachans. Others like Porterstown have disappeared and remain as mere names on the Ordnance Survey map. Of the four which were founded after 1810, namely Corrie, Carrutherstown, Fairyhall and Hollie, only Carrutherstown survives. Nevertheless, successful or not, they all played a part in shaping the history of Dumfriesshire during the eighteenth and early nineteenth centuries.

SIXTEEN

Eighteenth-Century Life

CONTEMPORARY LIFE

Land improvement, the creation of planned villages, developing industry, work on the newly created farms and their ancillary trades, not only provided employment for many of the victims of enclosure but it was also responsible for the expanding population of Dumfriesshire. This is evident from the statistics. In 1755 Dr Webster put it at about 45,000, whereas the returns of the contributors to the *Old Statistical Account* show it to have been 53,600, an increase of just over a quarter in the space of forty years. Nevertheless the rate of increase (and decrease) varied widely between parishes. Predictably, those with the largest increase (i.e. over 50%) were where there was industrial development (Dumfries, Annan and Canonbie), limeworks (Ruthwell, Closeburn and Dunscore) or extensive land improvement (Gretna, Mouswald and Cummertrees).

Exceptionally, the population of Lochmaben more than doubled. Similarly the parish of Morton where, according to the contributor, 'labourers and tradesmen find plenty of employment [in Thornhill] and the immediate vicinity'. He goes on: 'when not occupied in cultivating their small farms, those who have horses carry coals from Sanquhar for hire'.[1] Conversely, the decrease in the population of outlying parishes such as Glencairn, Hutton and Corrie, Ewes and Eskdalemuir shows that there was already a drift away from the landward areas. Commenting on this, the minister of Eskdalemuir asserts that 'the population is considerably reduced in the memory of the present inhabitants', attributing it to the conversion of 'several of the smaller farms into a large one'.[2] Perhaps so, but because the population in 1792 was a mere 36 less than Webster's figure of 675 in 1755 the decline was hardly significant.

Some of the victims of enclosure emigrated to the American colonies. As the Rev. William Sibbald, the contributor for Johnstone, observed, 'emigration was frequent until the last nine years'. 'But now', he went on, 'there is employment for both parishioners and incomers'.[3] The facts bear this out, because the population of his parish was on the increase, and the trend would continue at an accelerating rate throughout the 1790s and beyond – tribute to the extensive improvements being carried out by the earl of Hopetoun. Therefore, judging from his observations, and the increase in the population of Dumfriesshire as a whole, it would seem there was only limited emigration from the region at this time, although numbers would increase dramatically in the course of the following century.

The minister of Cummertrees was the only other contributor to the *Old Statistical Account* to touch on the subject. 'Twenty-five years ago', he wrote, 'about forty people, some of them farmers, but mostly labourers and tradesmen, emigrated to America lured there by advertisements sent by those who had acquired tracts of land there and wanted people to come and work on them'. It proved a major disappointment for, as he went on to say, 'when they arrived there, they were miserably deceived and disenchanted, and those who had money enough for their passage home returned bemoaning their credulity'.[4] Word would have got around and no doubt acted as a deterrent. Added to which, it was a hazardous undertaking since not all vessels made it safely across the Atlantic, some being shipwrecked in storms. Not only that, but in order to cut costs conditions on board were so disease-ridden and insanitary that Parliament was compelled to address the issue. In 1803 it passed what was known as the Passenger Act which required the provision of certain basic essentials, such as adequate food supplies, proper berthing arrangements, and the services of a qualified medical practitioner. Some able-bodied men, mostly from the south-eastern parishes, moved to England attracted by higher wages. Consequently local farmers and employers were forced to improve their workers' wages to discourage them from following suit.[5] This would no doubt have accounted – at least in part – for the three-fold increase in wages which occurred during the latter part of the eighteenth century.

Since there is no record of a major influx of people to the region, other than the swarm of Irish beggars who were widely perceived as a blight on the district, the population increase must have been attributable to births exceeding deaths – inevitably given that large families were the norm (contraception being unknown). On the other hand, infant mortality was distressingly high. Those who survived infancy were exposed to a host of diseases such as diphtheria, typhus, scarlet fever, measles and whooping cough. A major killer was smallpox. Although inoculation was tried out in Dumfriesshire as early as 1733 it was potentially dangerous, and it was not until the 1770s that a safer form of vaccination was introduced.[6] But the damage was done, and the practice was regarded with widespread suspicion, and even downright hostility – a view that persisted long after the benefits became apparent.

The aversion to inoculation is commented on by most of the contributors to the *Old Statistical Account*, almost all of whom touch on the health of their parishioners (which they were asked to do). Most refer to the prevalence of rheumatism, asthma, ague (less apparent than formerly) and 'nervous disorders', ascribing them to the wet weather, constant wearing of wet clothes, and the dampness of their living conditions. Exceptionally, the minister of Canonbie referred to the incidence of scrofula.* While expressing doubt as to whether it was indigenous or imported by infected spouses from elsewhere, he claimed it was 'an established fact that it may be propagated through a series of generations'. 'Therefore', he went on, 'much caution ought to be

---

* Defined as tuberculosis of the lymph nodes, especially in the neck, which caused glandular swellings and eczema.

used in forming matrimonial connections [as being] the only effective way of prevent-ing the entail of this malignant disorder upon posterity.'[7]

Yet the rigorous living conditions bred a toughness and hardihood that enabled some people to survive to extreme old age. This is apparent from the *Old Statistical Account* which contains frequent references to people in their nineties and even some centenarians. For example, the minister of Tynron referred to one old lady who died in 1787 at the age of 102,[8] while his colleague at Kirkmichael had a 103-year-old on his communion roll.[9] Not to be outdone, the contributor for Middlebie referred to a woman of the parish who died 'a few years ago' aged 109.[10]

However, the record was broken by two veritable Methuselahs. One was John Taylor. A native of Wanlockhead, he was born about 1637, evident from the fact that he was old enough to remember the total eclipse of the sun which occurred in 1641. Therefore when he died in May 1770 he must have been about 133 years old! A lead miner to trade, he was described as 'a thin, spare man, black-haired, with a ruddy face and a long visage'. His breakfast usually consisted of oatmeal porridge, with meat and broth for dinner, while his favourite drink was malt liquor.[11] Scarcely less impressive was his contemporary Thomas Wishart. A tenant farmer at Wysebie, he was born in September 1635 and died in December 1759 at the age of 124. According to the local contributor 'he retained his faculties to the end, had lost none of his teeth, could thread a needle with the naked eye, [and] not two days before his death he walked six miles over very uneven ground'. In fact the only time he ever grumbled was at funer-als when he complained that 'everyone can die but me'.[12]

At the time of his death living conditions were still primitive. But, writing some thirty years later, a number of contributors to the *Old Statistical Account* commented on how much they had improved since then. This was because the tripling of farm workers' wages meant they outpaced living costs, notwithstanding that these had more than doubled. The result was that, as one contributor put it, the annual expend-iture of a married farm labourer with five or six children was reckoned to be around £16. Although his wages came to about £13, paid partly in kind, his wife made up the difference by spinning during the winter and helping out with the hay and harvest in the summer. By the time the children reached the age of seven or eight they, too, contributed to the family budget by tending livestock during busy times of the year.

More specifically, the minister of Holywood observed that a labourer could live 'tolerably comfortably, and give his children an education proper to their station provided he and his wife are sober, industrious and frugal'.[13] The standard of accom-modation had improved – at least to the extent that the interior walls of the cottages were plastered and properly finished. According to one source, this made them 'exceedingly warm and comfortable', notwithstanding that the roof consisted of straw, heather, turf or bracken (only the houses of the gentry and some manses had slate roofs).

Similarly the eating habits of the people had improved. No longer did they subsist on a monotonous diet of oatmeal in its various forms, because the potato – hitherto regarded with grave suspicion – was now accepted as the main constituent. As Lenman put it, '[its] impact was probably more significant as a cause of sustained population growth than all the activities of the medical profession'.[14] It had the additional advantage that it could be grown on ground which was unsuitable for grain crops, and being less weather dependent it was an invaluable stand-by in the event of a bad harvest. It was also recognised as a valuable source of energy, and would continue to feature prominently in the diet of hill shepherds until well into the twentieth century.

It was found that, when fed on potatoes, pigs put on so much weight, and so rapidly, that potatoes were grown as much for them as for the people themselves. Consequently every householder kept a pig or two in his yard. As the *OSA* contributor for Mouswald observed, 'Whereas forty years ago there was not a single pig in the parish, now almost every cottager buys one, fattens it and kills it for eating, [so that] their diet consists mainly of pork and potatoes'.[15] Pig farmers sent most of their porkers to the weekly pig sale at Ecclefechan, or to Dumfries where there was a twice weekly market on Wednesdays and Fridays. The buyers would slaughter the pigs, cure the meat and sell it as bacon – either directly or through middlemen – to the principal English markets, including London.[16] In addition to its twice weekly market, Dumfries had a long-established right to hold three fairs a year – on Rood Day in October, and at the beginning of February and July. Indeed, most towns were authorised to hold at least one annual fair. These drew itinerant merchants and pedlars from all over southern Scotland; and it was there that labourers were hired, usually on a six-month contract or longer if married.

There were fun and games as well. At Lockerbie for example curling was a popular sport. This was attended by 'scores of people' who, we are told, would 'compete with one another in the most friendly way', while 'the proceedings would generally conclude with a good dinner, drink and songs'.[17] Less respectably, cockfighting was another pastime although, writing in the 1830s, the minister of Cummertrees reported that 'this barbarous and brutalising sport is now completely laid aside'.[18] Dances were extremely popular – particularly among the young, for these were the occasions when they could really let their hair down and enjoy themselves with uninhibited abandon. Not surprisingly, marriages were frequently the outcome of events such as these which helped brighten the farming year.

Sometimes the method of choosing a partner could vary, as we are told was the practice at Eskdalemuir. Here it was apparently the custom for the youth of the district to attend a fair which was held on a meadow at the confluence of the Black and White Esk, many presumably coming from far afield. There they would choose a member of the opposite sex whom they fancied, and if he or (more likely she) was willing they would live together until the next annual fair. This form of union was known as handfasting. Effectively an open marriage, it meant that when the fair came round again it was open to either party to terminate the relationship. In that case they would look for another mate, the rejected partner being given custody of any child of the union.

On the other hand, if all went well, they might decide to commit themselves to a regular marriage.[19]

The smithy at Gretna was long regarded as a venue for informal marriages, mainly by fugitive lovers from England. The local minister was scathing about the practice. On his say-so, people were led to believe that these marriages were conducted by a properly licensed clergyman, whereas in fact they were conducted by imposters without any right to do so; still less were these imposters entitled to charge the customary fee for their services. One of those responsible for 'conducting' these runaway marriages was generally believed to be a blacksmith, although in reality he was a tobacco seller whom the minister described as 'an illiterate without principles, without morals, and without manners'. Warming to the theme, he went on: 'His life is a continual scene of drunkenness [while] his irregular conduct has rendered him an object of detestation to all the sober and virtuous part of the neighbourhood.'[20]

The minister's tirade against the ruinous effects of alcohol was echoed by many of his colleagues who railed against the popular addiction to whisky, one of them blaming it on the heavy excise duty on ale, which drove people to the 'dram shops' (where the whisky was probably contraband). Another warned that 'if a proper check shall not soon be given to the great number of whisky shops, and the cheapness of whisky, the morals and health of the lower classes will be greatly injured'. On the other hand, the minister of Dryfesdale conceded that 'even in Lockerbie where dramming does sometimes prevail, especially when there is a market, there has not been a fight for a long time'. 'This', he went on, 'is proof of the civilising of the people, and particularly the influence of the fair sex; for if the men are sometimes drunk women never are, neither at markets nor on any other occasion.'[21]

Clerical fulmination had a point because over-addiction to cheap smuggled whisky and other spirits could reduce the victims to beggary. For some begging was a way of life. In that connection, a distinction was drawn between the so-called 'sturdy' beggars (mainly Irishmen) who extorted alms under threats of violence, and genuine mendicants who were sometimes issued with a badge as proof of authenticity. In some parishes local people were forbidden to beg, in which case they simply took themselves off to another parish and became vagrants. Hence the minister of Sanquhar's complaint that his parish was 'infested with shoals of foreign beggars'.[22] Dumfries was a particular target, for many of the foreign beggars were Irish drovers returning from England who, having squandered all their money, were forced to beg their way home.

On the other hand, provision was made for the genuine poor. In the previous century a Poor Law was passed which authorised kirk sessions to levy a 'poor's rate' for their maintenance, while an Act of 1663 provided that half the sum was to be levied on the parish heritors and half on tenant farmers (presumably the more prosperous ones). This was supplemented by special collections in church, and in many cases legacies bequeathed by wealthier parishioners for the relief of poverty.[23] Where people were unable to work, as a result of injury, illness or old age, their circumstances were carefully investigated by members of the kirk session, and if found genuine they were added to the poor's roll. It frequently happened that, in cases of particular hardship and distress, friends would come to the rescue by holding a 'drinking' to which all the neighbours were invited. Here they were entertained to bread and cheese, small beer, and sometimes a tot of whisky or brandy. Music and dancing were also laid on, and as each guest was obliged to contribute a shilling this could raise anything from five to seven pounds for the indigent family – a large sum by the standards of the time.[24]

By the end of the century there was a movement which the Rev. Henry Duncan, the minister of Ruthwell, was mainly instrumental in founding – namely the establishing of Friendly Societies to encourage people to save for their old age. Forerunners of the penny-a-week insurance schemes, they were designed to help those who had fallen ill, or were otherwise incapacitated and no longer able to work, and to meet their funeral expenses (a 'good' wake was obligatory since it was a mark of status). One example was the Friendly Society of Kirkpatrick Fleming and Graitney which was established in the 1780s, while another was founded at Langholm. The members, who were required to contribute a small sum each quarter, consisted mainly of labourers and mechanics (or artisans), while a number of farmers enrolled voluntarily in order to contribute to what was regarded as a deserving charity.[25] Establishing these societies was a laudable reflection on the people's willingness to help one another in times of hardship or adversity, and they were the forerunners of a movement that would proliferate throughout the following century.

EIGHTEENTH-CENTURY DUMFRIES

For Dumfries the eighteenth century was a time of growing prosperity, stemming initially from its control of the tobacco trade. Despite its takeover by the Glasgow merchants, the burgh continued to flourish on the back of its expanding trade links with the Continent. They were concentrated in particular on the principal entrepots of Bordeaux and Nantes, and Malaga in Spain, which were the main sources of wine and brandy. Indeed, entries from the burgh account books for 1709 to 1711 reveal the use of copious quantities of brandy to lubricate meetings of the burgh council.[26] This was not specific to the Dumfries, because the same applied at Sanquhar and doubtless elsewhere. As the authors of the *Annals of Sanquhar* put it, 'the burgh fathers appear to have been unable to do anything without having recourse to the bottle. Every meeting of the magistrates or council was made an excuse for a dram, and often the cost of the drink consumed amounted to much more than the business in hand.' As to the choice of liquor, 'their favourite drink is said to have consisted of two parts whisky and one of rum seasoned with sugar and spice.'[27]

Since these councils had overall responsibility for the administration of the burgh, regular (and doubtless well-oiled) meetings were essential. On one occasion the question of appointing a public hangman was the subject of discussion by the Dumfries burgh council. Hitherto it had been the practice to bring a hangman over from Wigtown whenever there were felons to be disposed of. But because it was becoming too expensive, the council decided to appoint their own hangman. The successful applicant was George Mickle-Duff, and one of the perquisites of his appointment was the right to help himself to a ladleful of meal from every sack exhibited for sale on market days.* Nevertheless his was no sinecure, for it seems from the treasurer's accounts that the gallows were in regular use. For example one entry shows a payment of 5 shillings for '3 pynts of aill' for those responsible for setting up 'ye jeabet [gibbet]'. Another records a payment of ten shillings for six pints of ale for those responsible for conveying a felon's corpse to the churchyard, and for taking down 'ye jeabet' (the gallows were erected and taken down each time there was a hanging).

Eventually Mickle-Duff decided he had had enough of his grisly task. But when he refused point blank to carry out any more hangings he was thrown into prison. The so-called 'new prison', it was built sometime in the late 1730s in response to a petition by certain leading citizens who claimed that the existing one had become so insecure that 'several malefactors, guilty of great crimes, have made their escape to the dishonour and imminent peril of the people'.[28] Furthermore it was extremely obnoxious to its immediate neighbours, evident from the complaint by a shopkeeper whose premises lay directly underneath. He alleged that one Thomas Crosby, a 'furious and madd prisoner wanting [lacking] a tubb to ease nature Does it up and down the prison whereby my shop is rendered noisome to any people who come into it, and already the goods in [it] are greatly spoiled and abused by the same'.

Since the council lacked the means to build a new prison, it persuaded 'the gentlemen of the stewartry of Annandale' to contribute to the cost. Therefore in 1735 they concluded an agreement, to which the local justices of the peace were a party, and the new prison was built.[29] Seven years later it was partially burnt by a woman who had been consigned there for pilfering a pair of stockings, and had prevailed on an obviously simple-minded jailer to give her a lighted candle.[30] Although the damage was rectified, conditions were still rigorous. A prisoner's daily fare consisted of one pound of oaten bread – unless he had the means to pay the jailers for extra food or special delicacies. Since they were paid a pittance, the jailers relied on the turn they stood to make from accommodating the privileged prisoners. So much so that James Fraser, one of the jailers, complained to the council that because he had 'only a parcel of gypsies and vagabonds' in the prison '[he] had no profit in them'. Therefore he requested that they send him 'a better class of prisoners'![31]

The dilapidated state of the former prison was typical of much of the burgh at the beginning of the eighteenth century. In their report of 1692 the representatives of

---

* Mickle-Duff's successors continued to avail themselves of the privilege to the increasing annoyance of the merchants. The issue came to a head in 1791 when one merchant forcibly prevented the hangman from dipping his outsize ladle into his sacks. Although the offending merchant was consigned to prison, fears that others might follow his example led to the abolition of the practice in 1796 when the hangman was compensated with a salary increase of £2 a year.

the Convention of Royal Burghs claimed that numerous tenements were ruinous. Further, that those on the north side of the Lochmabengate, which had been destroyed by fire the previous year, had not been rebuilt and the site was derelict. Fire was a constant hazard since most of the houses were built of clay and wood and roofed with straw or other combustible material. One which broke out in 1701 destroyed much of the Friars' Vennel. In 1723 the council decreed that, whenever houses fronting the High Street were renovated or rebuilt, the roofs were to be slated or tiled. In fact a considerable amount of builderwork was being carried out in Dumfries at the time. The most important was the construction of a new church which was begun in 1724 and completed three years later. Known as the New Church (later replaced by the present Greyfriars Church), it was built on part of the site of the former Maxwell castle and was designed to accommodate the overflow from St Michael's Church.

The council's duties were all-embracing, one of the most important being to supervise – and where possible extend – the burgh's educational facilities. This was easier to achieve in a place like Dumfries where the council could afford good quality schoolmasters, whereas some landward parishes lacked the means to pay for a schoolmaster at all. For the fact was that the provision in the First Book of Discipline requiring that every parish have a school and a schoolmaster, confirmed by an Act of the Scottish Parliament of 1696, was legislating for the impossible. Whereas kirk sessions may have been able to provide a hovel for a school, many could not afford to employ a schoolmaster, or at least pay him a proper wage, let alone provide him with suitable accommodation. This state of affairs was widely condemned by the contributors to the *Old Statistical Account* who, as members of the cloth themselves, had a vested interest in it.

While there were undoubtedly good, bad and indifferent schoolmasters, it is to be hoped that none were in the same league as Robert Carmichael, the schoolmaster at Moffat, who punished the laird of Dornock's son with such ferocity that he 'most inhumanely' (as it was euphemistically put) beat him to death. Carmichael immediately went on the run. A warrant was issued for his arrest, and the *Edinburgh Gazette* carried a notice describing him as 'of middle stature, thin and lean, of a swarthy complexion, pock-marked and wearing his own hair which is very black'. Therefore 'all good Christians' were enjoined to look out for him, any sighting to be reported to the authorities.[32] History does not relate what happened to him, although one would imagine that he was apprehended, convicted and dispatched to the gallows.

Dumfries benefited from a number of endowments made by some of its wealthier citizens for educational purposes. For example one bequest financed the founding in 1719 of a school for girls where they were taught sewing and embroidery. In 1722 the council was bequeathed the sum of 8,000 merks for the employment of a teacher of Latin, rhetoric, the classical writers, and instruction in the New Testament in Greek. It was followed by another endowment – of 7,000 merks – for the purpose of teaching aspiring merchants the art of writing, arithmetic, book-keeping and navigation. Later, in about 1740, the council founded a music school.

Meanwhile the burgh council's building programme continued apace. But by 1730 they had overreached themselves and incurred such massive debts that they were forced to sell off part of the burgh lands. While the proceeds may have helped reduce the outstanding debts, it left nothing in hand to meet the cost of maintaining the burgh property. This is apparent from a report by a committee of the Convention of Burghs which stated that the school (unspecified) was partially ruinous, that several arches of the bridge (Dervorguilla's bridge) were in a critical state, and that the Nith had become so silted up that it was barely navigable. In an attempt to meet the cost of these and other repairs, the council petitioned for an Act of Parliament authorising it to impose certain duties and customs, including a tax on ale. Although the Act was passed in June 1737 (when the council's attempt to impose the tax caused a riot), the fact that the duties extended to imports led to fears that it would inhibit trade.[33] Not so. In fact trade increased, mainly as a result of the improvements carried out to the port at Glencaple. They included enlarging the harbour and building warehouses on land donated by William Maxwell of Nithsdale, the work being completed in 1747. This was followed by an upgrading of the facilities at Kingholm Quay which involved deepening the approach channel and removing the obstructing boulders.[34]

During the second half of the eighteenth century Dumfries was the centre of a lively social life which revolved round the main events of the year. These included the races which were held on the Tinwald Downs* in October and were attended by a large crowd, including noblemen and lairds from throughout the south-west. As the English traveller Robert Heron observed, '[Dumfries] is perhaps a place of higher gaiety and elegance than any other town in Scotland of the same size.' He went on: 'Both the Dumfries and Galloway Hunt, and the Caledonian Hunt, are assembled here [and] every inn and alehouse is crowded with guests.' Touching on burgh life at the time, he described how 'in the mornings the streets are full of hairdressers, milliners' apprentices, grooms and valets, [with] carriages driving backwards and forwards'. 'In the forenoon almost every soul, old and young, hastened out to follow the hounds or view the races.' Dances were regularly held in the Assembly Rooms at which 'there was such a show of female beauty and elegance as few country towns in Scotland or England are likely to exhibit on similar occasions'.

Throughout the time of the Scottish Enlightenment, Dumfries was second only to Edinburgh in the field of artistic endeavour, while it surpassed most other towns of similar size in Scotland as an intellectual centre. Reflecting this, a new theatre was opened in September 1792 which was much patronised by 'the upper classes of the neighbourhood', as well as the officers of the regiments stationed in Dumfries from time to time.[35] Such was the milieu which Robert Burns encountered when he moved there in the autumn of 1791 with his wife and three sons to take up a post with the customs and excise service. Taking a lease of a three-bedroom flat on the north side of Bank Street, he entered enthusiastically into the social and artistic life of the town.

---

* Comprising broadly the site of present-day Heathhall and the Catherinefield Industrial Estate.

He was no stranger to Dumfries having first visited it in June 1787, when as a tribute to his poetical works he was made an honorary burgess. The following year he took a lease of the farm of Ellisland from Captain Robert Riddell. ˙ During that time he was a frequent visitor to Dumfries where he spent many a convivial evening, his favourite hostelry being the Globe Inn which he regularly frequented after moving to Dumfries. The story goes that on a cold and frosty night in January 1796, while making his way home through the snow after a heavy drinking session, he collapsed and nearly died of hypothermia. Although rescued in time, his constitution was so weakened by rough living that he never properly recovered, and after a long battle against ill-health he died on 21 July at his house in Mill Street. This was a comparatively new acquisition, he and his family having only recently moved there. A substantial improvement on his previous lodgings in Bank Street, it would have been a handsome brick and sandstone house similar to those fronting the High Street, itself evidence of Dumfries's growing prosperity.

Population numbers speak to this. In 1727 the number of residents over the age of ten was estimated at 2,030; in 1755 Dr Webster put it at 4,517, whereas in 1792 Dr William Burnside, the minister of the New Church, reported a figure of 7,000: 5,600 in the town itself and 1,400 in the landward parts. This was in spite of the exodus of a number of young men who had left the town in search of better paid employment elsewhere. Dr Burnside attributed the increase to 'the progress of industry, the advancement of agriculture, the ending of the American War (and the consequent revival of the transatlantic trade), and the rapid recovery from the failure of the Ayr Bank'.[36]

As a further reflection of Dumfries's growing prosperity, well over a thousand indwellers were engaged in business or trade, most of them members of one or other of the seven incorporated trade guilds. The largest was the shoemakers' guild, closely followed by the squaremen (joiners and carpenters), and – in order of membership numbers reflecting their relative importance – the tailors, hammermen (metal workers), weavers, fleshers, and finally the skinners and glovers. Among the unincorporated trades were seventy-eight licensed purveyors of spirits, as well as gardeners, stocking-makers, and professionals such as apothecaries, surgeons and physicians. Non-guild tradesmen included milliners, hatters, shoemakers, clogmakers, clock- and watch-makers, and the like. The existence of so many trades was evidence of considerable spending power, reflecting an increasingly affluent society. By this time most tradesmen were running their businesses from their own houses or outbuildings, the forerunners of shops which were beginning to replace the markets as the principal retail outlets.

Last but not least were the lawyers who were generally agents for – and therefore closely associated with – one or other of the branches of the three main banks which

---

*   Described as 'a big cultivated man with a booming voice who did not mince his words', his claret-drinking competition with Sir Robert Laurie of Maxwelton and Alexander Ferguson of Craigdarroch for the silver whistle was described in verse by Burns.

were established in Dumfries. Bullion, mostly coin, would have been conveyed to them from their Head Office by the daily mail-coach from Edinburgh to Carlisle and London; and transferred (doubtless under guard) to a local coach at Gretna, it would be taken to Dumfries. Besides delivering bullion, this service would have enabled the citizens of Dumfries to keep in touch with the outside world in general, and those centres in particular.

The upgrading of the landing facilities at Kingholm Quay, and the improvements to the port at Glencaple, helped expand Dumfries's maritime trade, as it was intended to do. For the most part it was confined to the ports along the Solway coast from Balcary Bay, near the mouth of the Urr, to Sarkfoot, and across the Firth to places like Whitehaven in Cumberland which was a source of coal, lime, and limestone. Hand in hand with this went an expansion of Dumfries's overseas trade. While maintaining their existing connections with the Baltic, and the French and Spanish ports, the Dumfries merchants were establishing trade links further afield with places like the West Indies, a principal source of sugar for which there was a growing demand.[37] Meanwhile the merchants of Gretna were importing timber from the Baltic ports of Memel and Riga,[38] while their counterparts at Annan were acquiring timber from Gothenburg in Sweden, as well as iron from Demark.[39]

The transatlantic trade was temporarily killed off by the outbreak of the American War in 1775, and when three years later France allied itself with the colonists it resulted in a cessation of trade with the principal centres of Bordeaux and Nantes. This lasted until January 1783 when the end of the war led to a resumption of trade with France and America. But Britain's overseas trade was to suffer a far more severe – and much longer – disruption following the outbreak of war with France in 1793 which would continue with one short break for the next eighteen years until June 1815.

THE NAPOLEONIC WAR AND AFTER

Conversely, the war proved a boon for farmers – in Dumfriesshire as much as anywhere else. This was mainly the result of the French naval blockade which denied Britain access to the grain and other commodities traditionally imported from the Continent. True, some came from America and Canada, but because there was not enough to compensate for the shortfall it raised the spectre of a food shortage, rendered the more acute by the demands of a growing population and a succession of poor harvests. The combined effect was to drive up the price of home-grown produce to the benefit of arable farmers, while the navy's requirement for salt beef was mainly responsible for the threefold increase in the price of cattle.

The combination of rising prices and greater productivity resulting from land improvement rendered farming increasingly profitable. This in turn meant that tenant farmers could afford higher rents. Therefore, when farms became available for re-let, aspiring tenants could find themselves having to offer as much as five to seven times the former rent in order to secure a lease or the renewal of an existing one.

Rising rents led to an escalation in land values which was compounded by a spiralling competition for land. Therefore an intending purchaser would generally have to offer an inflated price to secure the property of his choice; and in addition he would most likely find himself saddled with the cost of improving it.

Higher rents meant that landowners could afford to build fine new houses or embellish existing ones. In fact they were under pressure to do so, because it was almost obligatory for every landed property to have an appropriately-sized mansion house.[40] An early example was Kinmount which was commissioned by the marquess of Queensberry in 1812 and designed by Robert Smirk, although the person immediately responsible was his assistant William Burn. Soon afterwards Burn set up his own practice, and in 1817 he was commissioned by William Younger, a wealthy Edinburgh brewer, to design Craigielands near Beattock. Although best known as a designer of churches and their interiors, Burn was employed by the duke of Buccleuch to draw up plans for a number of houses on the Drumlanrig estate, including Dabton which was built in 1820 and was traditionally the factor's house. In about 1830 he was engaged by General Sharpe* to design his proposed additions to Hoddom castle, and at much the same time John James Hope-Johnstone commissioned him to plan the embellishment of Raehills. A slightly earlier creation was Jardine Hall. Incorporating much of the original house, this was built in the classical style by James Gillespie Graham for Sir Alexander Jardine of Applegirth in 1814.[†]

Wartime prosperity was not destined to last. Having peaked in 1812 and 1813, farm prices began to fall, precipitated initially by the plentiful harvest of 1813, reputedly the best in living memory. The end of the war spelt disaster for British farmers. Following the return to peacetime conditions and the reopening of trade with Europe, the market was flooded with cheap imported grain. This led to a catastrophic drop in prices which bore particularly heavily on arable farmers. Livestock farmers were also badly affected, because the drastic cutback in the navy killed the market for salt beef, which in turn led to a slump in cattle prices. Consequently farming was reduced to marginal profitability while falling prices caused large tracts of arable land to be taken out of cultivation and put down to pasture. An example was the parish of Tynron where the minister cited this as the reason for its declining population between 1811 and 1821.[41]

The crisis came in 1816 when the ruinous effects of falling prices were compounded by atrocious weather which resulted in widespread sheep and cattle losses, and to cap it all there was a harvest failure. Many labourers were thrown out of work and soup kitchens were established in a number of parishes, as well as in towns like Dumfries,

---

* A prominent Dumfriesshire landowner, General Matthew Sharpe was in a reality a Kirkpatrick of Closeburn. His father Charles Kirkpatrick changed his name to Sharpe on inheriting Hoddom from that family, his forebear John Sharpe having purchased it from the earl of Southesk towards the end of the seventeenth century. When General Sharpe died without issue in 1846, Hoddom passed to his brother William, and following his death it was sold to Edward Brook.

† It was greatly altered and added to by David Jardine in the 1890s and demolished in 1964.

Lockerbie and Ecclefechan.[42] Many parishes provided additional relief. For example the heritors of Kirkconnel raised a subscription for the purchase of provisions for the unemployed, which was supplemented by meal and potatoes contributed by the farmers. To ensure a fair distribution, those responsible for collecting and storing them were instructed to hand out a specified amount to the most deserving for free, while others were charged a token price.[43]

The dumping of cheap imported grain on the market, and the consequent slump in prices, had such a devastating effect on the farming industry that the government was compelled to intervene. Therefore it enacted the Corn Laws which imposed a tariff on imports with the aim of creating an artificial scarcity in order to stabilise the price of grain. Not that the government was concerned so much for the plight of the farmers, but being dominated by the landowning class its main concern was that they should be able to afford their rent. Perhaps not entirely fair, but certainly that would have been the majority view.

Nevertheless there was a serious downside to the Corn Laws in that they drove up the price of bread, and as this was the staple of the urban underclasses it put them to severe hardship and possible starvation. In 1828 growing social unrest resulting from what was stigmatised as 'the dear loaf' forced the government to modify the Corn Laws. Therefore it introduced a sliding scale whereby corn would be imported duty-free if the domestic price rose above 73s (£3.65) per quarter. If, on the other hand, it fell below that level the duty was increased proportionately. But it did little to alleviate the situation.

The downturn in farm prices bore particularly heavily on those tenants who had been induced to offer inflated rents in the expectation that the rise in farm prices would continue indefinitely. No longer able to afford them, they faced bankruptcy or at the very least eviction. Nevertheless some landowners, sympathising with their plight, were prepared to be accommodating, a notable example being John James Hope-Johnstone of Annandale. Most of his farms in the parish of Johnstone had been re-let for a twenty-one-year period in 1814 just as prices were beginning to fall. Since many of the tenants were unable to pay the full rent, he granted them abatements of between 20% and 40%. Consequently very few were forced to quit their holdings,[44] and doubtless similar concessions were granted to his other tenants as well.

Meanwhile the post-war depression, combined with the rise in unemployment caused by the return of service personnel, encouraged further emigration. Certainly that was the view of the contributor to the *New Statistical Account* for the parish of Hutton and Corrie.[45] But the emigrants appear to have included some undesirables. As he went on to say, 'Much loss and mischief are occasioned by dishonest emigrants to America [of whom] a considerable portion are guilty of dishonest practice'. Further, that during his ministry 'not far short of a score have left this parish under charges of various kinds, some to avoid having to support illegitimate children, some after swindling practices and committing forgery, and others after committing frauds of all sorts with a view to emigrating with their ill-gotten gains'.[46]

The scale of emigration from Dumfriesshire is evident from the records which show 547 people embarking from Glencaple and upwards of 1,000 from Waterfoot during the six months to June 1817.[47] Here a plaque records that 'Waterfoot prospered as a port during the period 1780 to 1848. During this time emigrants from the area sailed from Waterfoot to North America. The sailing ships were not large, usually schooners and brigs of about 500 tons burthen.' In which case, it would have rendered the voyage across the Atlantic all the more hazardous. But because so many emigrants were prepared to risk it, the availability of shipping was unable to keep pace with demand; so much so that sometimes lots had to be drawn by intending emigrants to secure a place.[48]

Initially the West Indies were the main focus of emigration. But when reports came back harping on the insalubrity of the climate and other disadvantages, intending emigrants began to settle in growing numbers, and generally in small family groups, in North America and Canada. Here they were joined by other emigrants, many of them encouraged by government-inspired advertising campaigns, and in some cases grants of land. From the 1830s onwards, emigrants widened their horizons to include countries like Australia and New Zealand, some disembarking on the way to settle in South Africa. Through time emigration from the Lowlands, be it to England or the Colonies, resulted in a much more extensive clearance than in the Highlands. Yet it never attracted the same obloquy, nor has it become anything like the emotive issue which attaches to the latter. According to one authority, this was because those affected were generally better off as a result, and the process was much more gradual than the speed and brutality of the Highland Clearances.

The *New Statistical Account* speaks to continuing improvements in Dumfriesshire. For example, the contributor for the parish of Applegarth and Sibbaldbie reported that 'the farmhouses are nearly all new and in general very commodious'. If the proprietor, Sir William Jardine of Applegarth, was responsible that was to his credit. Otherwise he sounds to have been a less-than-accommodating landowner. For the contributor's observation that 'the tenant who can pay his rent without encroaching on his capital, if he has any, considers himself fortunate'[49] suggests an unwillingness on Jardine's part to grant them an abatement. That was certainly the case with some landowners in the parish of Kirkpatrick Juxta. Here the minister asserts that 'the obstacles to improvement are attributable to the fall by about one-third in the price of produce, while rents are not always abated to compensate for it'.[50] A similar situation seems to have obtained in the parish of Middlebie where the contributor observed that 'an abatement of rent would operate to the advantage of the landlord as well as the tenant'.[51]

Through time farming recovered from the post-war depression. In his *Scottish Farming* Symon attributes this to a number of factors – a downturn in rents resulting from the fall in farm profits, and the adoption of a system of crop rotation which allowed for resting the ground in place of the former practice of over-cropping with consequent diminishing yields. A third was the use of underground tile drainage which enabled much more extensive patches of boggy land to be drained than was possible with open ditches.* Perceiving the advantages of this, and anticipating a booming demand for them, the duke of Buccleuch established a brickworks at Canonbie which also manufactured drainage tiles. They commanded a ready sale, while his tenants were allowed to buy them at a discounted price as an encouragement to them to carry out their own drainage operations.[52]

The recovery from the depression stimulated a further round of country-house building. Examples include Gribton, near Holywood, which was built by Francis Maxwell, and Burnfoot Hall. Another was Kirkmichael House (now the Barony) at Parkgate. Designed by William Burn for George Lyon, a wealthy Liverpool manufacturer[†] who had purchased the estate in 1825, it earned a flattering encomium from the local minister. 'This very handsome and elegant mansion house', he wrote, 'has been erected by Mr Lyon [and] is built in the old manorial style after a plan by Mr Burn of Edinburgh'. He went on: 'It is surrounded by a very considerable extent of fine old timber; the pleasure grounds are embellished by beautiful flower-gardens and two fine artificial pieces of water. Mr Lyon has also made a very excellent walled garden and hot-house'.[53] This was in keeping with the prevailing fashion of surrounding country houses with ornamental parks and gardens, collectively known as the policies.

At much the same time Burn was responsible for drawing up plans for the Crichton Royal Institution in Dumfries. This was financed out of a legacy by Dr James Crichton, a wealthy merchant who had amassed a fortune in the course of his career with the East India Company. Returning home in 1808, he purchased the property of Friars Carse where he lived until his death in 1823. In terms of his Will, the legacy was to be spent 'for beneficent purposes' at the discretion of his wife, subject to the approval of her co-trustees. Their original intention was to use it to found an academic institution, but they appear to have encountered so many difficulties that the idea was abandoned. Therefore it was decided to establish a centre for the treatment of the insane instead. Accordingly the trustees purchased some forty acres of land on the outskirts of Dumfries, and here they built an institution which was designed to accommodate up to 125 patients. The foundation stone was laid in June 1835 and by 1839 most of the building was ready for use.[54]

Whereas tenant farmers were mainly responsible for land improvement in the nineteenth century, this is not to deny the achievements of people like the duke of Buccleuch and others. The improvements carried out to his estates included planting up woodland (many other landowners were doing the same), constructing roads and bridges, and building superior farmhouses. His achievements were the subject of fulsome praise by the minister of Canonbie. 'The great improvements carried out

---

* The drains were dug with the aid of a special type of plough invented by James Smith of Deanston in Stirlingshire.
† And member of a Scottish family of the same stock as the earls of Strathmore.

by the duke', he wrote, 'gave constant employment to artisans and labourers, [and] as the duke resided in the neighbourhood during the busiest time of the year and supervised the improvements on an almost daily basis, he had an opportunity of knowing the character of each workman'. While those who worked hard were rewarded, lazy and obstreperous workers 'not only lost their employment but were obliged to leave the parish'.[55] Although perhaps smacking of obsequiousness and a timely recall of the landowner's right of patronage, such observations were probably none the less valid for that.

Improvements extended to reclaiming marginal land to bring it into cultivation, a labour-intensive undertaking since it generally involved the removal of a mass of stones and boulders. For example when Francis Maxwell purchased the Gribton estate in 1827 this was a necessary preliminary to rendering it fit for cultivation. The work was carried out by immigrant Irish labour, and by the time it was finished they are said to have removed something like a thousand cartloads of stones.[56] The main advantage of using Irish navvies was that they were cheap and at the same time capable of prodigious feats of labour. But because they undercut local workers they were not popular, while it was claimed that wherever they established a temporary encampment they left what the minister of Kirkpatrick Juxta delicately referred to as 'improper burdens or an immoral taint behind them'.[57]

Whether attributable to landowners or tenants, the result of these improvements is the subject of glowing tributes by the contributors to the *New Statistical Account*. For example the minister of Kirkconnel claimed that 'there is now nine times the amount of land under plough' as there was forty years before.[58] In the parish of Penpont 'areas of land, indeed whole farms, can be shown to be three times more productive than they were thirty years ago',[59] while the production of the parish of Holywood 'has doubled within the last thirty years'.[60] In Middlebie the improvements in agriculture during the last twenty years are described as 'very extensive',[61] and the appearance of the parish 'has entirely changed [and] many hundreds of acres, which [thirty years ago] were lying open and waste, are now well enclosed'.[62]

The principal obstacle to land improvement in Lower Nithsdale was the Lochar moss. In 1754 the duke of Queensberry commissioned Thomas Smeaton, a leading civil engineer who was responsible for planning the Forth and Clyde Canal, to draw up a scheme for draining it. He recommended digging a canal from the mouth of the Lochar Water to the head of the moss in the parish of Kirkmahoe. But for various reasons it was judged impractical and the idea was abandoned. According to the contributors for Torthorwald and Caerlaverock the obstruction was a 'paltry mill' at Bankend, towards the southern end of the moss which 'yields very little rent to the proprietor and is hardly of any consequence to the tenants'.

The difficulty was that the weir dammed up the Lochar Water, and because it raised the water level by several feet the moss was permanently waterlogged. But for some reason the owner could not be persuaded to sell it – or, as has been suggested, he was prevented by an entail from doing so. Whatever the reason, it was claimed that 'if [the mill] were removed and a proper course cut for the water, with the necessary lateral drains, which could be done at very moderate expense', a large tract of useless ground 'might be formed into valuable meadows'. Another difficulty was that, because so many proprietors were involved, it was virtually impossible to get them to agree on a co-ordinated plan. Nevertheless, writing in October 1835, the minister of Caerlaverock expressed the hope that the situation might soon be resolved.[*]

Land improvement was accompanied by advances in farming practices, in particular the science of crop rotation and the management of livestock. While farmers developed a system best suited to their land, they invariably followed certain basic principles – namely, that cereal crops should not be grown in succession since it would exhaust the ground, with consequently diminished yields. Also, that the rotation should include root crops and several seasons of fallow when the land was put down to grass. The fact that it provided grazing, as well as yielding an annual haycrop, suited the great majority of Dumfriesshire farmers with their emphasis on livestock rearing. Additionally, farmers were much more assiduous in keeping weeds under control than in the past. As one contributor put it, 'we seldom see a field destroyed by corn marigold as was all too common in former times. Therefore no decent farmer now allows ragweed and thistles to form and scatter their seed by the wind, but they cut them down when in early flower.'[63]

Root crops consisted of turnips and potatoes. Since there is no reference to growing pease and beans in either of the *Statistical Accounts*, the old statutory requirement to do so seems to have been ignored or simply abandoned. That said, there is a reference to pease being grown in Dumfriesshire in the seventeenth century.[†] Clearly farmers had not yet realised – still less appreciated – the value of the nitrogen-fixing properties of these crops. As in the past, potatoes were grown for human consumption, as well as for fattening pigs because pig-keeping seems to have been ubiquitous. According to the contributor for Lochmaben, 'many farmers send thirty or forty carcases to market every season [while] every cottager keeps a couple of pigs'. This was essential, for, when sold fat, the proceeds helped pay the rent, while killing pigs for domestic consumption enabled them to maintain 'the common luxuries of life during the winter'.[64]

Turnip-growing was becoming increasingly popular, particularly for feeding to sheep. This was because it was found that, when grazed on turnips, wedder lambs and hoggs[‡] rapidly put on weight. As the contributor for Kirkmichael observed, 'turnips [in this parish] are cultivated to such an extent that 2,200 Cheviot and Highland

---

[*]   In fact the work of reclaiming it was put in hand shortly after the *New Statistical Account* was published. But because it was done piecemeal it took upwards of a century to complete, and even as late as the 1940s Italian prisoners-of-war were put to work on it.

[†]   W Coutts, 'Farmers in Dumfriesshire from 1600 to 1665' *TDGNHAS*, lxi (1986), p 69, which states that 'only the wealthy landlord or merchant could afford to experiment in the growing of pease, wheat and rye'.

[‡]   A ewe lamb from the time of its weaning (spaining) to its first clipping.

[i.e. Blackface] wedders, including several score of half-bred hoggs, are fattened on them annually'. Endorsing this, his colleague at Caerlaverock claimed that 'the greatest improvement is in the introduction of bone manure and the consequent extension of turnip-growing [compared with] forty years ago [when] it was a rare thing to see [them] sown'.[65] But rather than rear sheep, some farmers found it more profitable simply to buy in store sheep, run them on a field of turnips and sell them fat. Others took the easy option of renting out turnip fields to graziers on the basis that they (the farmers) would look after them.

Whereas upland farmers kept Cheviot sheep, perhaps running a few hardier Blackfaces on the high tops, low ground graziers would generally buy their cast ewes* and put them to a Leicester – or in some cases a Southdown – ram. Their lambs were fattened up for sale at the principal markets of Dumfries, Annan and Lockerbie where they would fetch between 20 and 30% more than pure-bred Cheviot lambs.[66] Most went to Dumfries from where they were taken by steamboat to Whitehaven, and from there to Liverpool which, as the contributor for Dumfries put it, was the route by which 'an immense quantity of livestock, particularly sheep, are exported to the English market'.[67]

As to cattle, the Galloway was kept to the virtual exclusion of any other breed. The one exception was the Ayrshire which was kept for its milk, most of it being processed into cheese for which there was a keen demand. Many farmers went to great lengths to improve their stock by selecting their best cows for breeding, importing quality bulls from elsewhere, and possibly hiring the services of bulls with a proven record of siring good quality stock. The outstanding characteristics of the Galloway were their hardiness, and the quality and flavour of their meat which accounted above all for their popularity. The bullocks and surplus heifers were generally sold at two to three years old, some going at an earlier age to dealers who would fatten them for slaughter. On the other hand, six-week-old calves were in particular demand by the Dumfries butchers because veal was a popular delicacy among the upper classes. But there was a downside. As one contributor pointed out, some farmers were tempted to become dealers themselves, doubtless perceiving it as a quicker way of turning over a profit than rearing cattle to maturity. Therefore they spent most of their time at the market to the neglect of their farms.[68] Nevertheless farming continued to be the mainstay of the economy of Dumfriesshire, and indeed most of Scotland, for some time to come.

RAILWAYS

The railways were a development of the wooden rail system used in coalmines. The first surface railway in Scotland was a two-mile wagonway which ran from the coalmines at Tranent to the port of Cockenzie. This was followed by others which were built to connect collieries, and in some cases industrial concerns such as the Falkirk-based

---

*   Those which had already had four or five lambings.

Carron Company, with the nearest port or canal. The first proper railway was the line established by an Act of Parliament of 1826 for transporting coal in horse-drawn trucks from the collieries belonging to the duke of Buccleuch and others in the vicinity of Dalkeith to the port of Leith. Later, when steam locomotives were introduced to the line following their successful trial on the Monkland–Kirkintilloch railway in 1831, the service became available to passengers, and this was followed by a rapid expansion of railway building.

Perceiving a rail link with England as a means of tapping into its growing industrial wealth, a group of Scottish entrepreneurs decided to investigate the possibility of building a line to connect Edinburgh and Glasgow with the main industrial centres of northern England. There the leading railway company was the Grand Junction whose directors were of the same mind, albeit for different reasons. They had already built a railway as far as Carlisle and saw an extension into Scotland as a means of developing what they perceived as a valuable market for English manufactures. Therefore Joseph Locke, a leading civil engineer, was commissioned to investigate the feasibility of establishing a route up Annandale, over the Beattock summit and down through Clydesdale to Glasgow. This would include a branch line from Carstairs to Edinburgh. Perceiving the gradient beyond Beattock up the Evan Water to the summit as too steep, Locke recommended that the line should follow a westerly route instead. This would take it via Dumfries, up Nithsdale and into Ayrshire as far as Kilmarnock to link up with the Glasgow, Paisley & Ayr railway.

However, John James Hope-Johnstone of Annandale, member of Parliament for Dumfriesshire and a man of considerable local influence, took the view that this was far too circuitous a route and was determined that the railway should follow the Annandale one. Therefore, at his instigation, Locke was persuaded to think again. This time he conceded that building a line over the Beattock summit was feasible. But because this would take it through sparsely populated country, whereas the westerly route would serve a number of thriving townships, local opinion was solidly in favour of the latter. In 1839 the government appointed a royal commission to report on the issue. After two years' deliberation it decided in favour of the Annandale route. This had one key advantage in that, taking their lead from Hope-Johnstone, most of the landowners were amenable to the railway passing through their lands.[69]

Eventually railways proliferated to the extent that the government decided that state supervision was essential. Therefore an Act was passed in 1842 which established an agency equipped with the necessary powers, while another of 1844 stipulated that every company should run at least one train a day on each of its lines. Further, that every train should have covered seating accommodation for third-class passengers, who were not to be charged more than one penny per mile.[*] Hitherto provision

---

[*] The man responsible for piloting these Acts through parliament was W E Gladstone, then President of the Board of Trade, notwithstanding his personal interest as a major shareholder in the Grand Junction railway.

for third-class passengers was minimal and they frequently found themselves travelling in open trucks, disposing themselves as best they could among the goods, and sometimes livestock.

By 1845 plans for constructing the railway up Annandale had progressed to the point where a company – the Caledonian Railway Company – was incorporated to build it, and a bill was presented to Parliament for the necessary authority. The chief promoter was Hope-Johnstone, while the others included two local landowners – Sir William Jardine[*] and Robert Johnstone-Douglas, the proprietors of Applegarth and Lockerbie estates, both of which stood to be affected by the railway. The bill was approved by Parliament and on 31 July it received the royal assent. The work was undertaken by Thomas Brassey, a leading railway contractor who hired an army of navvies to undertake the heavy work. They sound to have been an unwelcome intrusion into the district – or so it would seem from a letter written by Thomas Carlyle to a friend describing the scene at Ecclefechan his birthplace.[†] 'All the roads and lanes [are] overrun with drunken navvies', he wrote, '[and] I have not in my travels seen anything uglier than that disorganic [sic] mass of labourers, sunk three-fold deep in brutality by the three-fold wages they are getting'.[70]

Many of the navvies were Irish while others were local men. Some were ablebodied poor, and others fugitives from justice taken on with no questions asked. Housed in rough encampments near the scene of operations they did much of the work by hand, and prodigious feats were achieved with the aid of picks and shovels. Gunpowder was used to blast through rock to create cuttings, particularly on the ten-mile section between Beattock and the summit of the pass, the debris being used to form embankments further down the line. In the end a gradient of 1 in 75 was achieved, which was just acceptable although two engines were needed to haul the trucks and carriages up the slope. Basic rules of safety were consistently ignored, and the hazards normally associated with the use of gunpowder were compounded by the navvies' bravado and recklessness. Some undermined too far and were buried alive by rockfalls while others were apt to smoke their pipes in dangerous proximity to the gunpowder barrels with predictable results. Fights regularly broke out, and altogether it was a rough, harsh and even brutal existence, relieved only by their high wages.

The first section of the line between Carlisle and Beattock was opened in September 1847, passengers bound for Edinburgh or Glasgow having to complete the journey

---

[*]   Initially he was strongly opposed to the railway passing through his land, fearing that it would spoil the amenity of Jardine Hall. However when it became inevitable he abandoned his opposition and instead tried to claim as much compensation as possible. But he never came to terms with it, particularly as his son-in-law Hugh Strickland was killed in a railway accident.

[†]   Philosopher, essayist and the author of many historical works, he was born there in 1795. Following his marriage to Jane Welsh and her inheritance of the property of Craigenputtock at the head of Glenesslin near the Kirkcudbrightshire border, they lived there until 1831 when they moved to London. There he remained until his death in 1881. Meanwhile he retained strong links with his Scottish roots, remaining close to his sister Mrs Aitken whom he regularly visited at Dumfries, and also his brother Dr John Carlyle, an eminent German and Italian scholar.

by coach. Consequently it took six hours to get to Edinburgh and nearly eight to Glasgow. But no sooner was the line opened than some evilly disposed miscreants laid a tree trunk across the line on the Esk viaduct, near Gretna. Fortunately the engine driver spotted it in time; otherwise, to quote from the advertisement offering a £100 reward for identifying the culprits, 'the most frightful consequences must have ensued'.[71] Meanwhile work on the northward extension from Beattock continued apace. The section as far as the summit was completed in 1848, and the final section to Glasgow by September 1850.

Unfortunately the Board of Directors became too ambitious. Following the completion of the line to Glasgow, the company was amalgamated with the Edinburgh and Glasgow Railway, and two others, for the purpose of extending it to Stirling, Perth, and finally Aberdeen. But no sooner was the merger completed than it transpired that the Edinburgh and Glasgow Railway was being sued for large sums of money in compensation for damage caused by sparks emitted from its engines.[72] Since the Caledonian incurred joint liability, and the compensation award swallowed up all its profits, it was reduced to paying dividends out of capital, while its bankers were pressing for repayment of their loans. The situation was saved by James Baird,[*] a wealthy ironmaster and a man of considerable local influence whose large investment in the railway (paid for in cash at the last minute) was enough to restore public confidence. But it was not enough to save the Board. Some of the directors resigned, and at a meeting held in London in February 1850, at which Hope-Johnstone presided, he too resigned. Nevertheless, under the direction of the new Board, the Caledonian Railway was restored to prosperity and would become pre-eminent among the Scottish railway companies.

Notwithstanding the decision to link the English railway system with Glasgow by the Annandale rather than the Nithsdale route, a group of local businessmen decided to press ahead with the latter. Therefore they were responsible for incorporating the Glasgow, Dumfries & Carlisle Railway Company to undertake the work. The Caledonian directors seem to have had no objection since they allowed the company to use (subject to an agreed tariff) the section of their railway from Carlisle as far as Gretna, where the proposed railway would diverge to Annan, Dumfries and beyond. In 1846 the directors of the Glasgow, Dumfries & Carlisle Railway obtained an Act of Parliament authorising them to build the railway. John Miller, a leading Scottish railway engineer, was commissioned to draw up the plans, and the work was completed by September 1850.[†] At much the same time the Glasgow, Dumfries & Carlisle Railway was merged with the Glasgow, Paisley & Ayr Railway to become the Glasgow & South Western Railway.

In 1856 it obtained consent to extend the railway from Dumfries westwards via Dalbeattie to Castle Douglas, and the following year it was authorised to build a

---

[*]   Brother of Douglas Baird who purchased the Closeburn estate about the same time.
[†]   This was Miller's last contract because he retired later that year at the early age of forty-five having made a considerable fortune.

further extension via Stranraer to Portpatrick which was the main embarkation point for Ireland. A subsidiary company, the Portpatrick Railway, was incorporated to carry out the work. The line to Castle Douglas was completed in 1859 when the company embarked on the extension to Portpatrick. From Castle Douglas the line followed a course up the Dee valley, and crossing the river at Parton it struck westwards across an expanse of boggy moorland which required extensive embankment. The section between the Water of Fleet and Gatehouse station was even more challenging because it involved cutting through a large granite outcrop to achieve an acceptable gradient which added significantly to the cost. From there it descended to Newton Stewart, and crossing the Cree it continued through Wigtownshire to Stranraer. It was completed in 1861, but for various reasons – not least being a shortage of money – it took another year to build the extension to Portpatrick. Then no sooner was it completed than the embarkation point for the Irish mail was changed to Stranraer and the extension became redundant from the start.

The year 1862 marked the completion of the North British and Border Union Railway's line from Carlisle up through Liddesdale to Hawick, while the branch line which diverged at Riddings to cross the Liddel Water and snake its way up the Esk to Langholm was opened in 1864. The previous year the Caledonian Railway embarked on the construction of a branch line from Lockerbie via Lochmaben and the Locharbriggs quarry (transporting the stone, sand and gravel was a valuable source of revenue) to Dumfries.[*] In 1888 it built another branch line – the Moffat Railway – to connect Beattock with Moffat, then a noted spa town and health resort.[†] Later the 'Tinto Express', as it was called, ran a direct service to Glasgow mainly for the benefit of commuters from Moffat.

Meanwhile the Caledonian was jointly responsible for building the Solway Junction Railway. This ran from a point immediately north of Kirtlebridge across the Solway to Kirkbride in Cumberland to connect with the Silloth branch of the North British Railway. Its main purpose was to transport iron ore from west Cumberland to the foundries of central Scotland. It was opened for freight in 1869 and for passengers the following year. Its weak point was the two-mile viaduct across the Solway from Shawhill, immediately to the east of Annan, to Herdhill Scar near Bowness-on-Solway. This was because the tide can run very strongly in the Solway, particularly when the rivers are in spate, and this put severe pressure on the viaduct. For example the winter of 1881 was marked by a period of intense cold, when the ice-flows cannoned into the piers with such force as to cause several of them to collapse along with thirty-seven girders. As a result the line had to be closed for three years to enable repairs to be carried out.

In 1895, notwithstanding its disadvantages, the Caledonian took over the line and continued to run it until 1921 when the viaduct was pronounced unsafe and had to

---

* A victim of the 'Beeching axe' the line was closed in 1966.
† This was closed to passenger traffic in 1954

be closed. Nevertheless the company continued to operate a service between Kirtlebridge and Shawhill where it connected with the Glasgow & South Western railway. Meanwhile all traffic, including pedestrians, was denied access to the viaduct. Not that this discouraged those who, at risk of a heavy fine, used it to cross over to England to take advantage of its more relaxed licensing laws, which they continued to do until the viaduct was demolished in 1935.

Back in 1865 there was a plan to establish a link between Moniaive and the Glasgow & South Western railway at Thornhill. But for various reasons the company rejected it. The following year an alternative proposal was put forward – namely to construct a line from Moniaive down the Cairn valley to Dunscore to join the Glasgow & South Western railway near Auldgirth. Although perhaps acceptable to directors of the Glasgow & South Western, the promoters were unable to raise the necessary finance and the plan was abandoned. In 1870 a scheme was put forward to build a narrow gauge (and hence cheaper) railway from Moniaive to join the Glasgow & South Western line at Portrack. This seems to have been acceptable to the directors, because they agreed to build a station at Portrack where a steam-powered crane would transfer goods from the narrow gauge trucks to their own wagons. But, like the previous scheme, it was abandoned for lack of money.

In 1896 there was a plan to develop Moniaive as a health resort. To attract summer visitors it was necessary to link it with the Glasgow & South Western line, preferably at Thornhill. Therefore the promoters made another approach to the directors, gilding it with the prospect of the increased custom they would stand to gain from visitors to the proposed spa at Moniaive. As a further incentive, a highly impractical scheme was put forward to extend the railway as far as the coalfields at Dalmellington in southern Ayrshire. But the directors were not to be moved. Undaunted, the promoters came up with another scheme. This was to run the branch line down the Cairn valley to connect with the Glasgow & South Western near Auldgirth – basically a repeat of the proposal advanced in 1866. This time the directors were amenable, but only if the line was extended beyond Auldgirth to join theirs at Dumfries. This was the plan which was finally adopted. Although the necessary authority was obtained in 1897, work was not started until 1901 and the line – the Cairn Valley Light Railway – was finally opened in February 1905.[73]

It is difficult to overemphasise the impact which the development of a rail network had on the region. Above all it increased people's mobility and enabled them to travel further afield in search of higher-paid employment and better working conditions. This had a knock-on effect on wage levels generally, because there was pressure on local employers, farmers and others to bring their rates of pay into line with those available elsewhere in order to keep their staff and attract replacements. Dairying in particular stood to benefit, for the fact that milk could reach the wholesalers in Glasgow and elsewhere in central Scotland while fresh greatly expanded its market. But it was at the expense of the once prosperous cheese-making industry which went into decline. The droving trade was another casualty, because transporting cattle south by rail rendered the drovers redundant, and many were reduced to hiring themselves out as casual labourers instead. Similarly the advent of railways had a major impact on the turnpike trusts, because the diversion of traffic from road to rail so reduced their revenue that they could no longer afford to maintain the roads to the required standard. However, recognising the need for a serviceable road network, the government ordered the railway companies to pay them compensation.

By the end of the century the bicycle had come into popular use, the original pedal bicycle having been perfected by Kirkpatrick MacMillan at Keir Mill, near Thornhill, in 1839. In 1861 an improved model – the 'boneshaker' – came into production, and the fact that a larger wheel meant that a bicycle travelled proportionately further with each rotation was responsible for the development of the 'penny farthing'. This had a front wheel of over five feet in diameter, the much smaller rear one being merely a stabiliser, while the first chain-driven bicycle appeared in the 1880s. But being mainly a hobby, and only used for short distances, the bicycle never posed a challenge to the railways.

Motorised transport, on the other hand, did. Although petrol-driven motor cars (or horseless carriage as they were known) came on stream at the turn of the century, they were the preserve of the wealthy few. Most of the travelling public, on the other hand, relied on motor buses. Initially they were steam-driven, and because they lacked the power to negotiate steeper hills they were replaced by the internal combustion engine. Even so, buses offered a limited service, at least to start with, for it was only after the First World War that they came into general use. Because they served the smaller villages and most of the remoter communities, they gave people living in the landward areas access to the shops and other facilities available in the larger towns. However, it was the exponential growth of private car ownership from the 1950s onwards which was mainly responsible for drawing passenger traffic away from the railways and would account for the drastic cutback in the rail network which took place in the early 1960s.

SEVENTEEN

The Nineteenth Century

CONTEMPORARY FARMING

The development of a rail network, and the widening of the market for its products, contributed significantly to the prosperity of farming. Fuelled by a booming economy, the widespread use of tile drainage which enabled large areas boggy land to be brought into cultivation, and the advent of rudimentary mechanisation, it had staged a dramatic recovery from the post-Napoleonic War depression. Nevertheless livestock farmers had to contend with periodic outbreaks of disease, such as the foot-and-mouth epidemic of 1839. Others included the outbreaks of pleuro-pneumonia and rinderpest affecting cattle which occurred in 1860 and 1865 when all infected animals, even those at risk of infection, were compulsorily slaughtered. According to McDowall, rinderpest appeared on forty farms in Dumfriesshire of which fifteen were in the parish of Dumfries itself. In all, an estimated 710 cattle died of the disease while a further 130 infected animals had to be slaughtered.[1]

But the prosperity was illusory because the seeds of the depression which set in during the 1870s and would continue for the rest of the century were already being sown. From the mid-nineteenth century onwards, huge areas of the American mid-west were being opened up to corn production and cattle rearing. In time this would flood the European markets – including Britain – with cheap beef and grain, leading to a sharp decline in farm prices. However, the effects were masked by the American Civil War of the 1860s which put a temporary brake on the development of the mid-west, while the wars of 1866 and 1870–71 which culminated in German unification disrupted the flow of imports from the Continent.

Once the expansion of America's grain-producing regions was resumed, and the flow of imports gathered pace, the results were little short of catastrophic. For example, during the period from 1867 (admittedly a poor harvest year with consequently inflated grain prices) to 1890, the average price of wheat fell by approximately 65% from 64s 5d (£3.22) a quarter to 23s (£1.15), the lowest it had been for two hundred years.[2] The fall in the price of oats and barley on the other hand was less steep, and because these were the staple crops of Scottish farmers they were less badly affected. Besides, the demand for oats to feed the large number of workhorses on the land, and the fact that oaten bread was the staple of the urban underclasses, helped underpin the price.

In Dumfriesshire arable land was increasingly put down to pasture, with a corresponding expansion of livestock rearing, while many farmers turned to dairying. This is evident from the statistics. Whereas in 1870 just over 60% of the land was put down to temporary or permanent pasture, by 1910 the proportion had risen to almost exactly 75%.[3] Yet stockbreeders had their problems as well. This was mainly because the introduction of refrigeration meant that huge quantities of beef could be imported from America, Australasia, and later Argentina, which flooded the market and depressed prices. Moreover the government, no longer controlled by the landed interest, was unwilling to intervene since it stood to gain more votes by reducing costs to the consumer than by protecting farmers' livelihoods. Which is ever thus, except in times of national emergency when extreme measures were needed to make up for successive governments' neglect of farming.

The fall in prices is evident from the records. They show that between 1883 and 1895 the price of best quality fatstock declined by 20%, while middling quality fell by anything from 25% to 50%, and similarly beef.[4] The price of wool fell by a third, and, to compound their plight, hill farmers were badly hit by a succession of particularly cold winters which caused widespread stock losses. Yet large numbers of sheep continued to be exported from Dumfriesshire, and the south-west generally, to the principal markets of northern England – Carlisle, Penrith, Appleby, Preston, Liverpool and Newcastle.[5]

Dairying, on the other hand, remained unaffected by the downturn. Protected from foreign competition by the perishability of milk, and encouraged by the growing demand from the main urban and industrial centres of central Scotland, it continued to flourish. The breeding of the Ayrshire cow as a milk-producer was a principal feature of eighteenth-century livestock improvement. Although introduced into Nithsdale at a relatively early stage, evident from Robert Burns's reference to it, the Ayrshire was traditionally kept as a house cow to provide milk for the family rather than for profit, unlike the Galloway and other breeds of cattle. However, as a consequence of the depression and the widespread switch into dairying, it rapidly came into its own.

Because dairy farms were generally small family-run units consisting of about 100 acres or so, which was about as much as a single family could manage on its own, labour costs were minimal. This meant that dairying could be extremely profitable, so that dairy farmers from outside the region could generally afford to outbid local farmers for the lease of a suitable holding whenever one came on the market. As a commentator put it, 'Any farms becoming vacant in the counties of Wigtown, Kirkcudbright and Dumfries were generally taken by dairymen, most of whom come from Ayrshire, with a few from the counties of Lanark and Renfrew.'[6]

Since there was invariably a surplus of bull and heifer calves, only a small proportion of the latter being retained for the milking herd, it was generally the practice to put some cows to a Shorthorn bull since their progeny fattened more readily for sale or slaughter. Although a dairy farmer could generally offer a higher rent for the tenancy of a farm than his competitors, it depended on his ability to stock and equip it. Since this included the purchase of milking cows, converting the farm buildings into a byre and calf pens, and the like, it required a considerable capital outlay. Few aspiring dairy farmers had the means, so they would generally start by entering into a 'bowing' arrangement with a landlord or a well-to-do tenant farmer. In terms of this, the landlord or farmer would supply the 'bower', as he was known, with the cows, capital and fixed equipment in return for a rent based on the number of milking cows. In the 1870s the rate varied between £8 and £12 a cow, but by 1914 it had risen to between £12 and £18.[7] This gave the 'bower' the chance to acquire sufficient capital to set himself up as a dairy farmer himself.

Notwithstanding the depression, farmworkers' wages were rising, mainly as a result of competition from industry. The rates varied according to the category of the worker, of which there were basically three – or four if one includes day labourers. The first was the cottager. He was generally a married man who lived in a rented cottage, probably with a patch of cultivable ground, which went with the job. His wife would be required to give a set number of days' free labour to pay the rent, as well as providing paid labour at busy times of the year such as hay and harvest. Where there were children of suitable age they might be employed in tending livestock. This remained the situation until the 1870s when male workers' wages had risen to a level where it was no longer so necessary for the wife and children to work, and in any case school attendance was now compulsory. Known as a 'benefit' man, the cottager's annual wage at the time of the *New Statistical Account* varied from £20 to £25.

The second category consisted of the bothymen, known elsewhere as hinds, who were lodged in a crude bothy or equally rudimentary quarters. Generally young unmarried men, they were hired by the half-year at the local spring and autumn fairs. At the time of the *New Statistical Account* their wages were about £12 a year, but by the end of the century they had more than doubled to £27. The third category were those who boarded with the farmer and his family, had their meals with them, and slept in an attic or an outhouse attached to the farm steading.[8] Their wages were much the same except that a deduction was made for board and lodging. Since ploughmen were regarded as the elite of the farm workers, they were paid more – £16 16s being the norm in the parish of Morton,[9] which was probably more or less standard throughout the region.

Because women were regarded as not up to a man's work they were paid half as much. The most common type of female workers in Dumfriesshire were the farm servants. Referred to as the 'in and out' girls because they worked in the farmhouse as well as out-of-doors, they did the housework, milked the cows, helped in the fields, and generally turned their hand to whatever needed doing in and around the farm steading. They had no fixed hours, nor until as late as 1914 did they have any statutory holiday entitlement. Not surprisingly this type of work was regarded as rough, dirty and 'unwomanlike', while the long hours, lack of holidays, and limited opportunity to enjoy a social life, rendered it doubly unpopular. Therefore domestic service in the towns was regarded as preferable – and certainly more genteel – than working on a farm,[10] and this was mainly responsible for the drift of female workers to the towns.

At the bottom of the pay scale were the day labourers who were hired at the busy times of the year such as turnip-hoeing in early summer, at hay and harvest time, and to assist in potato picking and shawing turnips (both back-breaking jobs!) in the autumn. At the time the *New Statistical Account* was compiled they were paid up to 1s 2d (about 6p) a day, while general labourers were paid rather more. In almost all cases wage rates varied according to whether meals were provided, or if the worker was required to bring his own 'piece'. It depended too on the time of year, because they were generally higher in summer when people could work longer hours than in winter. Finally there were specialist tradesmen such as carpenters, masons and smiths who were employed on a daily basis at a rate broadly comparable with that of scythesmen.

Whereas wages had more than doubled by the latter part of the century, the increase in real terms was all the greater because of the fall in the cost of living which occurred during the period from the 1860s to the 1890s.[11] This meant that agricultural workers could afford a better lifestyle. Instead of being limited to a diet of milk, oatmeal and potatoes, supplemented by meat and eggs, as in the past, it was more varied. As a contemporary observer put it, 'Porridge is the chief breakfast food, [but] in many houses bread, cheese, butter and jam' are eaten instead.' He goes on: 'There are two courses for dinner, either broth and meal, or meal and pudding.' Herrings either fresh or salt are popular, and they may be seen hanging in a row outside the door of many a cottage. Eggs, too, are purchased from farmers or egglers [those who made a living from selling eggs].'[12]

Nevertheless for farmworkers it was a hard life. Their accommodation was basic in the extreme, for it was not until later that farmers and landowners were statutorily obliged to bring farm cottages up to an acceptable standard. And besides it was generally regarded as a dirty and monotonous job with long hours and few prospects. As a Dumfriesshire ploughman observed in his submission to the Royal Commission on Labour in 1893, 'To my opinion the life of the agricultural labourer is altogether colourless and sordid; in fact his life throughout is sleep, eat and work; no time for enjoyment as other labourers have; no half-holiday on Saturday, although it is earnestly asked for; no holidays as a right, only as a favour, and even then we only get three or four days a year.'[13]

The complaint that farmwork offered few prospects was fair, because generally speaking the best an agricultural worker could aspire to was to become a farm manager or grieve. The more ambitious might set their sights on acquiring the tenancy of a smallholding, but this was at the cost of saving part of their wages towards the initial outlay, and marrying an equally thrifty farm servant. Then if they were lucky, worked hard, and perhaps delayed starting a family, they might eventually

---

* Not a sweet in the modern sense, but more likely a black pudding or something of that ilk.

acquire a farm tenancy. Because they were better paid, this was more likely to have applied in the case of ploughmen, although there were instances of farm labourers becoming tenant farmers.[14]

Escalating wages encouraged farmers to cut costs through mechanisation. Consequently workers were laid off, with many having to migrate to the expanding urban and industrial centres in search of employment. This accounts – at least in part – for the decline in the population of Dumfriesshire, and the south-west generally, which occurred during the second half of the nineteenth century. Mechanisation can be said to have started in the late 1780s when Andrew Meikle devised the first successful threshing mill (presumably a more sophisticated model than William Craik's one). Although power threshing had become commonplace in most districts by the 1830s,[15] the absence of any reference to it in the *New Statistical Account* suggests that it had not yet spread to Dumfriesshire, although it soon would.

Another innovation was the horse-drawn mechanical reaper. This was a revolutionary advance on the traditional method of cutting the corn with a sickle – an infinitely slow and laborious task which remained standard practice up to the nineteenth century. By that time the sickle was beginning to be replaced by the scythe, an early pioneer being George Bell of Woodhouselees, near Canonbie. And because scythesmen had to be 'strong men capable of undergoing great fatigue' they commanded a premium wage.[16] Apart from being able to cut a field of corn more quickly, particularly when working in gangs which was the normal practice, it was possible to cut the stalk closer to the ground and thus produce more straw for fodder.[17]

Although scything corn continued to be practised on some farms until as late as the twentieth century, from about 1850 onwards the horse-drawn mechanical reaper became the norm.[18] Going round the field in an ever-decreasing circle, it cut the corn much more quickly, making it possible to 'snatch' a crop of ripe corn if rain threatened. Given the importance of weather prediction, it is hardly surprising that local folklore was (and still is) full of long-held axioms, many of which are pretty accurate. The introduction of binders and their complicated knotting mechanism enabled the corn to be bound into sheaves which were then propped up in stooks of six or eight sheaves. This gave them a measure of protection from the rain and allowed them to dry out – weather permitting, which was not always the case, particularly in a wet summer when the harvest could be lost.

Advances were continually being made in the method of preparing the ground for sowing. For example the introduction of a superior type of American plough made it possible to dig broader furrows, break up the land more effectively and bury the turf more completely, while implements like discs and spring-toothed harrows were coming into general use. Later, oil-driven engines became available for operating turnip cutters and potato sorters. At much the same time, the introduction of mechanical seeders enabled the seedcorn to be sown in drills rather than broadcast at random, and for fertilisers – mainly dung but frequently supplemented with bone meal and guano – to be spread more evenly.

Radical changes were taking place in the marketing of livestock. Purpose-built marts equipped with extensive stockpens and a weighbridge were coming into general use, one of the earliest being Dumfries mart, which was established in 1858 for the holding of a weekly sale of livestock.[19] This meant that, instead of being sold at street fairs and markets, such as those which were regularly held at places like the Whitesands in Dumfries, as in the past, livestock could be properly auctioned with all interested parties being given a chance to bid.

Significant progress was being made in the field of agricultural education. This was mainly thanks to the Highland and Agricultural Society which was founded earlier in the century for the purpose of instructing farmers in the science of animal and crop husbandry. This included selective breeding of livestock to meet consumer demand, experimenting with new methods of grassland management, developing more prolific strains of cereals, and exploring new techniques for reducing the incidence of pests and diseases. The results were disseminated through the holding of exhibitions countrywide. One of the earliest was held in Dumfries in 1830, and this was followed by others in 1837, 1845, 1860 and 1878.[20] Additionally, livestock competitions were regularly held under the auspices of its local subsidiary, the Union Agricultural Society, which incorporated the local farming clubs. They, too, helped stimulate an interest in the science of livestock improvement, although this was seldom an adequate substitute for a farmer's knowledge, experience and 'eye' for stock.

Unfortunately the Highland and Agricultural Society lacked the support of a government which consistently adopted a *laissez-faire* approach to farming. On the other hand, some universities were more supportive, an example being Edinburgh University which founded a chair of agriculture in the 1880s. At the turn of the century, an agricultural college for south-west Scotland was established at Glasgow, which was later moved to Auchencruive. In the following century an agricultural school, later upgraded to a college, was established at the Barony (formerly Kirkmichael House) at Parkgate. However, the agricultural depression of the late nineteenth century forced the government to confront the plight of farmers. Therefore in 1889 it established a Board of Agriculture for England, although it was not until 1912 that a similar board was set up for Scotland. But four years later, faced with mounting shipping losses during the First World War and the prospect of a serious food shortage, and even famine, the government was compelled to resort to much more drastic measures to encourage agricultural production.

FURTHER INDUSTRIALISATION, THE POOR AND EDUCATION

Centres of industrial development continued to flourish in Dumfriesshire throughout the nineteenth century. For example there was a thriving cotton industry at Sanquhar which employed 100 full-time weavers and 300 female embroiderers on piecework. Meanwhile the Crawick carpet mill had expanded to a point where it was employing about 130 men, women and children of both sexes. They worked a ten-hour day regardless of age or sex, the men being paid 12s (60p) a week, and the women and children proportionately less.[21] Most were accommodated in purpose-built cottages. But because these hovels lacked sanitation a large trough at the rear served as a communal *pissoir*, and in this unwholesome brew the fleeces were steeped to rid them of their greasiness. Yet the products of this unsavoury treatment were in considerable demand. A few were sold locally and some sent to London, others were exported to places like Hamburg and St Petersburg, while most went to America. In addition, the mill produced some 20,000 yards of tartan cloth annually, but it was eventually closed down, probably in the early 1860s.*

About this time, John McQueen, a blanket manufacturer, established a weaving business in Sanquhar in partnership with James Tweddel. In 1876 they took over the woollen mill at Crawick (probably the one founded by Provost Crichton), and this continued in production until 1909 when it was accidentally burnt down. Meanwhile the McKendrick brothers founded the Nithbank Mill for the manufacture of blankets. Later it was converted into a steam laundry, and later still it became the Nithsdale Creamery which produced a popular brand of cheese. Finally there was a woollen and carding mill at Euchan Foot, close to where the Euchan Water joins the Nith, immediately downstream from Sanquhar.

There were also two forges, the Riggs and the Cotts. The Riggs was founded in the 1770s and probably identifiable with the iron-plating forge referred to by the local minister in his contribution to the *Old Statistical Account*. It is described as having a 6 cwt (19 kg) hammer which struck upwards of 170 times a minute, being driven by a 14 foot diameter waterwheel.[22] The Riggs was where Robert Burns is said to have purchased his farm implements, particularly shovels, when he took on the lease of Ellisland. The Cotts was founded in 1874.

During the previous century knitting woollen stockings was an important industry at Sanquhar. Although it suffered badly as a result of the American War of Independence, and the closure of that market, it staged a recovery. However, the quality of its products appears to have varied widely. Whereas most were described as 'of coarse quality', some were so fine that it was said they could 'be drawn through a ring for the finger'. One manufacturer alone is reported to have sent 4,000 pairs south annually, and they are said to have been admired (and perhaps worn) by no less an arbiter of fashion than the Prince Regent.[23]

Nearby is the lead mine at Wanlockhead. When Ronald Crawford, Meason & Co.'s lease expired in 1842 the duke of Buccleuch took it over himself and employed a succession of managers to run it. A brave decision, and one that appears to have paid off. This was partly because the opening of the Caledonian railway in 1850 enabled the lead to be transported to the principal markets of Edinburgh, Glasgow and Liverpool much more quickly than in the past. Hitherto lead bars were taken (five at

---

* In his *History of Sanquhar*, written about 1865, Simpson states that 'the carpet works [which] have for a long time been productive of much benefit to the place are not now in operation'.

a time because of their weight) by horse and cart to Leith Docks, a journey of fifty-five miles each way which took four days to complete. From there, the lead was exported to places like Middelburg and Rotterdam.

The recovery in the price of lead from 1850 onwards rendered the mine increasingly profitable, to the extent that by 1875 it was employing 274 men. But it was not to last, because the lead-mining industry fell victim of the late-nineteenth-century depression. The mine at Leadhills was another casualty. The contrast between the treatment of its workers and those at Wanlockhead was highlighted in an article in the *Dumfries & Galloway Standard*. This stated that 'in Wanlockhead during last winter [1878–9] through the liberality of the duke of Buccleuch, although not one ton of lead had been sold for many months, the miners had their regular wages'. 'The people of Leadhills', it went on, 'are in a very different position, having got into the possession of a very grasping company who were endeavouring to draw away all they could from the works. In consequence the men are kept very poor.'[24]

In 1902 the transport of lead from the mines at Leadhills and Wanlockhead was greatly facilitated by the opening of a light railway which linked them to the main Caledonian line at Elvanfoot. Four years later, in 1906, the duke of Buccleuch leased the mine to the Wanlockhead Lead Mining Company. It had mixed fortunes. Whereas the demand for lead for munitions during the First War gave the industry a temporary fillip, the depression of the late 1920s and early 1930s, and the corresponding slump in the price of lead, forced its closure. In 1951 it was re-opened and leased to a company, the Consortium, which employed 100 men. But it was undercut by cheap foreign imports, and in 1958 the mine was again closed, this time for good.

Meanwhile coal continued to be mined at Sanquhar and Kirkconnel. In 1822 George Whigham, member of a long-established Sanquhar family, obtained a lease of the coalfield from the duke of Buccleuch. When Whigham died in 1842 the lease passed to his two unmarried daughters, Jemima and Elizabeth. The opening of the Glasgow & South Western Railway in 1850, and the consequent demand for coal to fuel its steam-driven engines, encouraged the Misses Whigham to extend their operations. They were responsible for sinking three deeper mines to tap into the better-quality coal which underlay the current workings – namely Gateside 3 and 4 (to distinguish them from the existing 1 and 2) which were opened in 1850, and Bankhead in 1857. The labour needed to work them was supplied by incomers, mainly from Ayrshire, and by the late 1870s there were approximately 140 men on the payroll.[25]

The Misses Whigham died in 1880 and 1884 respectively when the lease of the coalfield passed to their sister Mary and her husband James Kennedy, who became the manager. When he died in 1887, the Whigham sisters' 24-year-old nephew, James Irving McConnel (habitually referred to as J I McConnel),* became responsible for running the coalmines. A qualified engineer and a man ahead of his time, he was one

---

*   He died in December 1957 at the age of 95.

of the first Scottish coalmine owners to introduce electric cutters in place of the pick for hewing coal. In 1891 he was responsible for enlarging the Gateside pit, by which time he was employing about 240 men.[26] This was followed in 1896 by the sinking of Fauldhead 1 (effectively replacing the Bankhead pit). By the turn of the century the collieries were expanding so rapidly that in 1903 J I McConnel incorporated the business as the Sanquhar and Kirkconnel Collieries Ltd. It was responsible for sinking Fauldhead 3 (an extension of Fauldhead 1) and the Tower mine in 1911 and 1916 respectively.[27] It seems that under McConnell's management labour relations were good, because their workers refused to join the national strike of 1912 in spite of attempts by some 200 miners from the New Cumnock and other Ayrshire pits to bully them into it. In the end these troublemakers were driven off by a large body of police who were rushed to the scene by special train from Dumfries. Consequently the pits remained in operation throughout.[28]

Meanwhile the pits at Canonbie continued to be worked, although the coal industry here was on a much smaller scale than Upper Nithsdale. In fact it was mainly focused on the mine at Rowanburn which was operated by Canonbie Colliery. This was opened by Mr Lomax sometime before 1810, and not long afterwards another mine was sunk at Blinkbonny. Thereafter coal continued to be mined at Canonbie until 1922 when the seams were thought to be exhausted, although subsequent investigations have shown that this was not the case. During the Second World War part of the coalfield was leased to Adam Potts, who opened a drift mine on an outcrop at Archerbeck, but it was closed soon afterwards.*

According to a paper published in 1862, the mines at Canonbie supplied coal not only to the local estates but also to the Langholm gas works, the Langholm and Glentarras distilleries, Tarrasfoot tileworks and the Harelawhill limeworks. The Tarrasfoot tileworks, which was situated midway between Langholm and Canonbie, was one of nine tileworks established in the region following the discovery of local clay deposits. However, they were eventually reduced to two – namely Tarrasfoot and those at Bonshaw near Kirtlebridge. The former was established by the duke of Buccleuch in the early nineteenth century for supplying his tenants with drainage tiles on concessionary terms,[29] and it would remain in operation until the 1960s.

The Harelawhill limeworks was opened in about the 1770s and according to the local contributor to the *Old Statistical Account* its lime was of the purest quality, as well as being 'easily wrought and seems inexhaustible'.[30] It continued to be quarried throughout the following century, but latterly it was abandoned. In 1947 Buccleuch Estates persuaded Adam Potts, who had recently closed the drift mine at Archerbeck, to re-open the limeworks. But quarrying the lime proved so difficult and dangerous, as well as expensive, that the works was eventually closed for good in 1966.

---

*   I am indebted to Arthur Irving for kindly supplying me with copious information about coalmining and its associated industries at Canonbie.

This was basically the story of the lime industry in Dumfriesshire, and doubtless elsewhere. Demand had peaked during the late eighteenth and early nineteenth centuries when land improvement was all the rage, but as the impetus diminished so did the demand for lime, to the extent that by the end of the nineteenth century many quarries were closed. Although lime continued to be quarried at Park, near Closeburn, and similarly at Porterstown and Barjarg on the opposite side of the Nith, lack of demand was responsible for the closure of the limeworks at Closeburn in 1895, followed by those at Porterstown while the limeworks at Kelhead, Kirtlebridge, Caldronlea and Blackwoodridge were also closed.[31]

Meanwhile the antimony mine at Glendinning in the Meggat valley remained derelict for most of the century. Sir William Johnstone Pulteney of Westerhall (the patron of Thomas Telford), who had inherited it from his brother Sir James Johnstone in 1794, died in 1805. Since he had an only daughter, the baronetcy passed, along with the Westerhall estate, to his nephew Sir John Johnstone, who closed the mine and laid off the workforce. This remained the situation until 1888 when it was re-opened by Sir John's grandson, Sir Frederic Johnstone. Under his direction it produced nearly a hundred tons of ore. But because the cost of transporting it to the nearest smelting works rendered it uneconomic, the mine was closed in 1891, and once again the workforce was laid off. When Sir Frederic died in 1913 the baronetcy passed to his nephew Sir George Johnstone who sold the Westerhall estate to Mr F B Matthews. He was responsible for re-opening the mine to take advantage of the rocketing demand for antimony during the First World War. The old workings were drained and new shafts sunk, while a paraffin engine was installed to produce the compressed air needed to ventilate the mine. However the post-war slump in the price of antimony rendered it uneconomic, and in 1922 it was closed for good.[32]

Notwithstanding the post-Napoleonic War depression and the decline in the cotton industry, some factories remained in production. The largest was at Gretna which was run by Ferguson and Dickson of Carlisle* and employed up to 600 men, women and children. But it sounds to have been tantamount to slave labour, for according to the local contributor to the *New Statistical Account* they worked a twelve- to fourteen-hour day, the men being paid a mere 7s (35p) or 8s (40p) for a six-day week, and the women and children proportionately less. Small wonder that, as he observed, '[the men] are barely able to support their families by this mode of subsistence which weakens the body, depresses the mental powers, and engenders a spirit of improvidence and disaffection'.[33] Ferguson and Dickson operated a similar enterprise at Kirkpatrick Fleming employing about 150 weavers who seem to have been paid much the same as those at Gretna. Nevertheless, as the local minister observed, 'not being [too] crowded together [the workers] suffer no very material injury either to their health or [their] morals'.[34]

---

* The same business as Dickson, Forrester and Ferguson referred to above.

Exploiting the weavers by forcing them to work long hours for a relative pittance seems to have been standard practice. Although doubtless attributable in part to the rapacity of the employers, they themselves were victims of the blockade imposed during the Napoleonic War which cut them off from their traditional continental markets. After the war they found themselves in competition with the European manufacturers who undercut their products, forcing many firms out of business. This in turn led to widespread unemployment and social unrest, evident from the Luddite riots in England, and the militant Paisley weavers who were suppressed with difficulty, and only with the help of the militia. Although some firms managed to stay afloat, they could not afford to pay their workers more than the bare minimum.[35]

Ferguson and Dickson's factories at Kirkpatrick Fleming and Gretna were a case in point, while another survivor was the cotton factory at Annan. This was established by Mr Hurst in 1785, and by the end of the century he was employing between 100 and 130 men, women and children. In 1825 the business was taken over by W Douglas & Co. of Manchester. It proved well-timed because the market was staging a recovery from the post-war depression on the back of a growing demand for cotton and cotton products. Therefore the premises were enlarged to accommodate the additional looms needed to cope with it. At the time of the *New Statistical Account* the firm was employing between 120 and 140 weavers,[36] and in 1839 two steam engines were installed to replace the existing waterwheel.* Unlike his colleagues at Gretna and Kirkpatrick Fleming, and their damning observations about Ferguson and Dickson's exploitation of their workers, the local minister makes no such criticism of Douglas & Co, from which it may be inferred that their conditions of employment were relatively better.

By this time the Meikleholm Mill at Langholm, which had been taken over by John and James Carruthers, was employing between 80 and 100 spinners and hand-weavers. Although production peaked in the 1840s, the adverse trading conditions of the following decade forced it to suspend operations, after which the factory was converted into a corn mill. The Whitshiels Mill, on the other hand, which employed some 50 workers, continued trading until 1872 when it was accidentally burnt down.

Meanwhile the demand for knitted stockings remained buoyant, the factory established by T & A Renwick having been taken over by David Reid & Sons. By the time of the *New Statistical Account* the father David had died, while the elder son David had left the business to go into partnership with Andrew Byers, the proprietor of Byers Mill, a woollen mill which he founded in 1825. Consequently the younger son Alexander, described as 'a man of great vision and drive', continued to run the business on his own until 1848 when he went into partnership with Joseph Taylor, a draper from Brampton, and the factory was converted to a woollen mill. Thereafter, trading as Reid & Taylor, they greatly expanded the business. By 1854 the factory had

---

* The factory was subsequently burnt down in 1878 and thereafter the business turned to manufacturing wadding until it ceased trading in the early 1900s.

been enlarged, and at its peak it was employing some 400 workers, many of them working from home on contract.

The contributor for Langholm refers to the existence of a brewery, and also 'a distillery for whisky on a small scale'.[37] Thereby hangs a story. In the summer of 1849 cholera struck Langholm. Attributing this to the poor quality of the town's drinking water, the council decided to tap into the nearby Whita well instead. But because this supplied the distillery, the owner Mr Connel objected on the grounds that he had a prescriptive right to it. Not strictly true, because his predecessor had installed a pipe to divert the water to the distillery, having bribed the acquiescence of the local farmers with regular libations of whisky. Therefore the council threatened to take him to Court. Because their case was less than foolproof, they compromised by offering Mr Connel the use of another well instead. But he was not to be moved.

The issue remained unresolved until the summer of 1852 when there was a severe drought and consequent water shortage. Meanwhile water from the Whita well continued to flow to the distillery, and because this was far in excess of its requirements and the surplus was going to waste, some local youths decided to take matters into their own hands. So one night they cut a channel to divert it to the town's water supply. Mr Connel and a band of henchmen immediately rushed to the scene and in the ensuing scuffle they were driven off, although three of the youths ended up in the Dumfries jail charged with assaulting him.

Clearly matters were getting out of hand. Therefore agreement was reached whereby Mr Connel and the council would share the cost of installing a tank to capture the water from the Whita well and the neighbouring Donks well, with one third going to the distillery and the rest diverted to the town. Nevertheless the fact that the community was being deprived of what they regarded as their proper entitlement to a supply of pure and wholesome water merely to facilitate the distilling of whisky, which many regarded as a blot on the neighbourhood, was widely resented.* Indeed many continued to harbour a grudge against the distillery until it was closed in 1917.

By this time the state had taken over responsibility for the old and infirm from the Church. Hitherto parish relief was their ultimate means of support, and almost all the contributors to the *New Statistical Account* specify the number of people on the poor's roll of their parish, and in most cases the amount periodically distributed to them. The number of recipients in the country parishes seldom exceeded thirty, but in the towns it was a good deal higher – in Langholm and Canonbie for example there were upwards of sixty and seventy respectively. The figure for Annan, on the other hand, was in excess of a hundred and twenty. The sums distributed varied considerably from one parish to another, with the more affluent allocating upwards of £4 annually and the poorer little over £1.

---

* I am indebted to Ron Addison, the librarian of the Langholm Public Library, and his colleague Tom Kennedy, for kindly supplying me with this information.

In most cases the applicant was means tested to determine his or her entitlement to relief. This depended on whether a free issue of fuel or food was available, or whether the applicant was capable of undertaking part-time work, or was being supported by relatives. In at least one parish (Wamphray) some of those on the poor's roll were given rent-free housing thanks to the generosity of Dr Rogerson the principal heritor.[38] In four parishes in Eskdale – Ewes, Westerkirk, Canonbie and Langholm – and probably others as well, the rates were fixed in 1773 and had remained unaltered since then. As the cost of living was a good deal higher in the 1830s than in the 1770s this meant that the poor of these parishes were proportionately worse off. At Canonbie the situation was rather different. Here the rate of £4 annually, fixed in the 1770s, was considerably higher than elsewhere; but the parish could afford to pay it because at that time there were only twenty-four on the poor's roll. However by the 1830s the number had risen to seventy-five,[39] and as the amount of relief remained the same it must have been a considerable drain on the parish funds.

Through time there was a change of attitude among the recipients of parish relief, evident from the observations of a number of contributors. Whereas in the past it was considered demeaning to be taken on to the poor's roll, and self-respect deterred many people from applying for relief, now they had no such inhibitions and tended to look on it as a right. As the minister of Penpont aptly put it, 'the aversion to receiving parochial aid, at one time so beautifully characteristic of the Scottish people, is unhappily for the morals of the community gradually diminishing'.[40] In the same vein, his colleague at Kirkmahoe observed that 'some poor persons have been heard to say that the rich are obliged to maintain the poor'.[41] Again, some were initially reluctant to seek parish relief, but as the contributor for Tinwald put it, 'once on the roll they soon lose all feeling of delicacy and take their allowance as a right'. Furthermore, 'in some instances, instead of being thankful, they upbraid members of the session for an unfair distribution'.[42]

So where did the money come from? The answer is special collections, legacies, and levies on the heritors and principal farmers, and also the dues of proclamation of marriages, as well as fines for irregular marriages and 'immoral conduct' (whatever that might mean), the use of the parish coffin and mortcloth, and others. Finally there might be income from a trust or trusts (referred to as mortifications) established by former benefactors for the relief of poverty. Much the largest contributions came from the local landowners who were assessed according to the value of their estates. Similarly the principal tenant farmers. In some parishes, such as Annan, Canonbie and Eskdalemuir, and presumably others, tenant farmers were required to match their landlord's contribution which must have put them to considerable hardship.

By the 1840s the system of parish relief had become seriously overstretched. This was particularly apparent in the main urban and industrial centres where the population had grown exponentially. Therefore a royal commission was appointed to report on the situation and recommend improvements. Their conclusions were incorporated in the Scottish Poor Law Amendment Act of 1845. This provided for the establishment of a central board of supervisors to oversee the operation of the system, while parochial boards were empowered to raise funds locally for distribution among the poor and indigent at discretion. Because the Act shifted responsibility for the poor from the Church to the state, kirk sessions had no further say in the matter. Finally in 1894 responsibility for the poor was assigned to the newly created Local Government Board.

Education also came under state control. By the end of the previous century the drawbacks of the traditional system of control by the Church were becoming increasingly apparent. Notwithstanding the provision in the First Book of Discipline of 1560 that every parish should have a school and a schoolmaster, many lacked both. The Education Act of 1696 attempted to remedy the situation by requiring every parish without a school to make good the deficiency, while stipulating that the schoolmaster's salary was to be paid by the heritors. But even where there were schools they were generally earthen-floored hovels, testament to the parsimony or poverty of the heritors. For the same reason schoolmasters were so poorly paid that they frequently had to double up as the session clerk, or even become a grave-digger, to make ends meet. Yet in spite of this, an overture to the general assembly of 1748 petitioning for an increase in their salaries was rejected, and similarly in 1782.[43]

Finally, recognising their plight, and the need to attract suitably qualified schoolmasters to ensure a proper standard of education, the government acted. In 1803 it passed an Act enjoining kirk sessions to pay the parish schoolmaster a minimum of 300 merks annually. To fund it, they were empowered (subject to the approval of presbytery) to raise up to 600 merks (equivalent to roughly £35 sterling) a year through local taxation, this being considered sufficient to pay the schoolmaster and if necessary an assistant. Further, schoolmasters were allowed to supplement their salaries by charging tuition fees. These varied according to the complexity of the subject, and to some extent the parents' ability to pay. According to the *New Statistical Account* they ranged from 2s to 2/6 per quarter for reading and writing, to 5s (in some cases 4s and in others 7/6) for Latin and Greek, to 10/6 per half-year for French if available.* Whereas every school taught the basic subjects of reading, writing and arithmetic, others might include algebra, geometry, geography and mensuration. Exceptionally the Hutton and Corrie school taught navigation[44] – surprisingly, considering that it is a landlocked parish well removed from the sea.

Dumfries had long been a pioneer in the field of education, and as early as 1723 the burgh authorities were responsible for establishing the first writing or commercial school where the subjects included book-keeping and arithmetic.[45] Some eighty years later, in 1802, the foundation stone of the Academy was laid. It had four departments – one for Latin, Greek, French and German, another for English, a third for arithmetic and mathematics generally, while the fourth was for drawing and

---

* Equivalent of 10p, 12½p, 25p, 20p, 37½p and 52½p respectively in decimal currency.

penmanship.[46] Dumfries was ahead of its time, in that it had two girls' schools where sewing and embroidery were the principal subjects. A few landward parishes had one thanks to the generosity of a local benefactor, but they were very much the exception. Another centre of learning which made a significant contribution to local education was the Dumfries Mechanics' Institute. Founded for the benefit of working class children by the Rev. Henry Duncan, the minister of Ruthwell and a noted philanthropist, it held evening classes where the subjects on offer ranged from architectural drawing to the study of Euclid, to practical geometry and mensuration.[47]

The Disruption of 1843 led to a radical alteration in the system of Scottish education. This was the most important single event in nineteenth-century Scotland when upwards of a third of the ministers, elders and laity seceded from the Established Church and constituted themselves the Free Church of Scotland. This meant they were confronted with the formidable task of building their own churches and manses, as well as schools. The latter were important, both for providing employment for the 400 seceding teachers and to break the Established Church's control of parish schools. Therefore it was mainly thanks to the contributions from a generally supportive public that by 1851 the Free Church had succeeded in building no less than 751 schools.

Although this represented a welcome expansion of the education system, the drawback was that other denominations followed suit by setting up their own schools. But the fact that there was such a multiplicity of schools, and of such varying quality, meant that in the absence of any supervisory authority the whole education system threatened to descend into chaos. The situation was worst in the slums of the main industrial centres where 'ragged schools' were established for the frequently neglected children of the poor. Therefore it was essential that a national system of education be established under state supervision. Accordingly in 1872 Parliament passed the Education Act which assigned overall responsibility for education in Scotland to the newly created Scotch Education Department.

DUMFRIES: REFORM AND THE DISRUPTION

The outbreak of war with France in 1793 had an important impact on Dumfries because of the number of regiments stationed there in readiness to be sent abroad. Whereas the officers were readily admitted to the local society and became the mainstay of its social life, the rank and file seem to have become bored and discontented. In June 1795 this erupted into a mutiny following the arrest of a private soldier for 'impropriety in the field when under arms' (probably insubordination). Brought back to Dumfries under armed escort, he was locked up in the guardroom pending a court martial. When news of this got out, some of his friends attacked the room in an attempt to rescue him. But alerted by the noise, the adjutant and the orderly officer appeared on the scene fully armed, and forcing the mutineers out of the building at gunpoint they arrested the ringleader.

The commanding officer ordered him to be court-martialled. But, while the ring-leader was being taken to the court under armed guard, the mutineers attacked his escorts threatening to bayonet them, whereupon he escaped. Observing this, the commanding officer and the second-in-command chased him down the street to apprehend him, only to find themselves confronted by the mutineers. However, when the commanding officer drew his pistol and threatened to shoot the first man to lay hands on him they backed off. At that point other officers and men came to their rescue, and rounding up the mutineers they placed them under close arrest. Five of them were tried by court martial, four being sentenced to hanging while the fifth was given 500 lashes – probably enough to finish him off as well.[48]

In 1797 Parliament passed the Militia Act. This required every parish to draw up a list of men between the ages of eighteen and twenty-three for service in the local militia. Notwithstanding the upsurge of patriotism in response to the French declaration of war, many attempted to evade the draft by producing a whole litany of excuses – lameness, ill-health, deafness, insanity, stomach complaints, a rupture, piles, consumption, convulsions, and a hump back. Some were exempted because they were cripples, another because he was 'wanting [lacking] three fingers', while Othello Maxwell was excused service on the grounds of being a 'Blackmoor'.[49]

Later, Dumfries was earmarked along with Sanquhar, Lockerbie and Lochmaben as an internment centre for French prisoners of war, and in November 1811 a detachment of 100 prisoners, mostly officers, was dispatched there. They seem to have been well treated, being lodged in hostelries and billeted on private houses, while they were given the liberty of the burgh and allowed to wander as far as a mile beyond its limits. Writing home one of them commented that 'the town is pretty enough and the inhabitants, though curious, seem very gentle'. Questionably gentle but certainly curious, because they were at a loss to understand how the French seemed to spend so much time 'catching frogs and hedgehogs, and eating them'. On one occasion, perhaps driven by hunger, they reportedly killed and ate 'a fat cat'. After the war some remained in Dumfries, one becoming a chemist while another was employed as a French teacher at the Academy.[50]

In February 1829 a riot, described as 'far the greatest that ever occurred in recent times', broke out in Dumfries. It was sparked off by the arrival of William Hare, William Burke's accomplice in supplying ready-made corpses to Edinburgh University's medical faculty for their dissection classes. When their crimes came to light they were arrested and tried for murder. Both were convicted, and whereas Burke was hanged, Hare, who had turned king's evidence against him, was sentenced to deportation to his native Ireland. His route took him by way of Dumfries. Here he was to spend the night under guard at the King's Arms before being put aboard the mail-coach for Portpatrick next morning. However, when news of his arrival got out, a hostile crowd advanced on the hostelry threatening to lynch him, and he had to be taken down to the cellar for safety. Breaking into the building the mob came within an ace of capturing him, but he was rescued in the nick of time by some policemen who forced them out.

Next morning the Galloway mail-coach set off. Assuming that Hare was on board, a mob held it up on the Buccleuch Street bridge intending to drag him out and throw him into the Nith. But he was not there. Evidently the authorities had got wind of their plan and had whisked him away to the safety of the local prison. Again word got out, and thirsting for blood the mob descended on it pounding the main gates and hurling stones at the building. Just as they were about to set fire to it, a large body of policemen arrived, and supported by the local militia they forced the crowd to disperse. But Hare had already been spirited out of the prison – and the town – with the connivance of the authorities who were doubtless only too glad to be rid of him. *

In spite of all the improvements carried out in Dumfries during the previous century, parts of it were still in a state of utmost squalor. This combined with the polluted drinking water which was transported in filthy carts from the Nith, where most of the town's refuse was dumped, rendered them a breeding ground for disease. Outbreaks of typhus were a regular occurrence, particularly in spring and autumn; but far worse was the cholera pandemic which struck the town in 1832. The first case occurred in mid-September when the victim died within a few hours, followed by others in the course of the next two weeks. By October the daily death toll had reached alarming proportions, striking down 'high and low alike regardless of whether they lived in the stately mansions of Buccleuch Street or the vilest rookeries of the Vennel'.[51] Since the local doctors were unable to cope, the local health board had to call on the assistance of others from Edinburgh and elsewhere. But some of the relief doctors fell victim to the disease themselves.

Trade came to a virtual standstill and the weekly market, although not officially cancelled, was virtually abandoned and, as the local minister put it, 'a more than Sabbatical stillness seemed to prevail'.[52] In an attempt to purge the atmosphere, great quantities of tar and pitch were burnt in the streets and lanes; but all it did was to cover the town in a dense pall of smoke. This persisted into the following month when it was dispersed by a prolonged and violent thunderstorm.[53] Meanwhile burial pits were dug in St Michael's cemetery to accommodate the dead, the corpses being placed one on top of the other. Once filled to capacity, the pits were saturated with quicklime and overlaid with a thick covering of earth. But fear of contamination from the graveyard caused the minister to suspend services in St Michael's Church and change the venue to the courthouse instead. Even so, Sabbath congregations were reduced to a mere handful of people and, as it was said, the only occasions when the public gathered for worship was at funerals.

---

*   W McDowall, *Dumfries*, 715–18. Burke and Hare had their counterparts in Dumfriesshire. Known as the 'resurrectionists', it was their practice to exhume recently buried corpses and sell them to the medical schools for dissection. It came to light when the son of the Sanquhar doctor, himself a medical student, was horrified to encounter on the dissecting table the body of a man whose burial he had recently attended in the local kirkyard.

Because the disease was thought to be contagious as well as infectious, the victims were treated like lepers. Refused admission to the infirmary for fear of infecting the patients, they were compelled to eke out their final hours huddled together in a disused granary which served as a makeshift hospital. Meanwhile whole families fled the town for the illusory safety of the countryside, although many people already stricken with the disease died on the way. Those who made it were shunned by the countryfolk. Terrified of catching the disease themselves, no farmer, cottager or other householder would give them shelter. Consequently the refugees were forced to make shift for themselves out in the open as best they could.

Overwhelmed by the onslaught of the disease, all the authorities could do was set up soup kitchens in the streets in the hopes that it would give the starving populace sufficient strength to ward off the disease, while a tax was levied on householders to help defray the cost. The proceeds were supplemented by voluntary contributions from a number of towns in England and Scotland where there was widespread sympathy for the townsfolk of Dumfries. By the end of October the epidemic was beginning to subside, although it was not until mid-November that the daily death toll was reduced to single figures. When the disease had finally run its course, it was reckoned to have claimed upwards of 900 victims.[54]

This was followed by another outbreak in 1848 when more than 300 people died. Since the polluted water supply was seen as the main source of the disease, steps were taken to remedy the situation by having clean water pumped from Lochrutton some five miles away. Despite objections from various quarters, the scheme was sanctioned by a parliamentary committee in May 1850 when, according to McDowall, 'bells were rung and bonfires kindled to manifest the general joy of the inhabitants'. The pipe was laid in January 1851 and, as he goes on to say, 'the first instalment of the pure Lochrutton fluid emerged sparkling from the pipes in the presence of a delighted throng [when] there was an immediate improvement in the standard of public health'.[55] But the pipe proved insufficient to supply the demands of a growing population, and ten years later a larger one was laid alongside it.

This is moving ahead of events. During the first quarter of the nineteenth century the Roman Catholic population had increased dramatically, mainly as a result of Irish immigration to the south-west because of its proximity to Ireland. Roman Catholics had been under attack ever since the Reformation, with discriminatory laws passed against them from time to time. This culminated in the Revolution Settlement of 1688 when a statute was passed re-enacting these laws with added rigour. Catholic priests were banished under threat of hanging if they returned, while anyone caught hearing mass, or refusing to attend a presbyterian service, or found in possession of popish books, was liable to have his property confiscated. Furthermore Catholics were forbidden to educate their children in the Catholic faith, and prohibited from purchasing – or otherwise acquiring – heritable property (i.e. houses and land). Even retaining a Catholic servant could render the employer liable to a fine of 500 merks.[56]

Since Catholics were perceived almost by definition as Jacobite supporters, the failure of the Jacobite rebellions resulted in the passing of further proscriptive measures. These remained on the statute book until 1793 when an Act was passed repealing some of the more oppressive laws. By the turn of the century the Catholic population of Scotland was estimated to have been in the region of 30,000,[57] but a quarter of a century later it had risen to some 70,000.[58] This added to the pressure for Catholic emancipation and the repeal of the discriminatory statutes which denied them entry into the professions such as the civil service, the army, the navy and the law. Most important of all, the Catholics demanded the vote. It was an extremely controversial issue within the ruling Tory party and was only resolved in 1829 when, in a desperate attempt to stave off demands for electoral reform, the duke of Wellington as Prime Minister carried the Roman Catholic Relief Bill through both houses of Parliament.

Contrary to the duke's hopes, it failed to stem the pressure for an extension of the suffrage. The first attempt to address it came in March 1831 when the Whig government under Earl Grey, who had succeeded the duke of Wellington as Prime Minister, introduced a Reform Bill. This was intended to widen the franchise by extending the vote to tenants of land above a certain value, but not sub-tenants or anyone of comparable or lower rank. In the towns and burghs, on the other hand, the vote was to be extended to shopkeepers and the better-off artisans. Because it was designed to achieve a fairer representation in Parliament, and prise it away from the grip of the landed interest, the bill was extremely controversial. Nevertheless at a public meeting held in Dumfries on 15 March 1831 its terms were unanimously approved and endorsed by the burgh council. Three days later, a meeting of representatives of the county was held to discuss them. This time it was a different story because many landowners, seeing it as an assault on their rights, were vehemently opposed to it.

Although the Bill passed the Commons by a single vote, it had still to be sanctioned by the House of Lords where the peers were at loggerheads. In the event it was the twenty-one bishops opposed to the Bill who decided the issue by voting with the Tories to throw it out. This provoked riots up and down the country, and in Dumfries the mob went on the rampage throwing rocks and stones at the windows of suspected opponents of reform. Eventually the constabulary restored order and arrested the ringleader; but when he was committed to prison the mob stormed the building and tried to set it on fire. Finally the militia were called in. They forced the mob to disperse and leave the captive demagogue to his fate.[59] Meanwhile riots broke out in Sanquhar[60] and presumably other centres in Dumfriesshire as well.

Refusing to accept defeat, Grey asked King William IV for a dissolution of Parliament. Realising that in the circumstances a refusal might well lead to a revolution, he acceded. A general election was held in July. Contested on the single issue of reform, it resulted in the return of a Whig government with an increased majority. Nevertheless William Douglas* was returned as the Tory member for the Dumfries

---

* Younger brother of the marquess of Queensberry.

burghs,* one of the few Tories to be re-elected notwithstanding that his nomination was opposed by Dumfries and Annan. Evidently they were not alone in this, because news of his re-election was greeted with hisses and groans, while his defeated rival, General Sharpe of Hoddom, was hailed as a hero.

In September the newly returned Whig government introduced a second Reform Bill. This time it passed the Commons by a substantial majority. But, knowing that it was likely to be defeated in the Lords, Grey tried to extract a promise from the king to create enough new peers to ensure a majority in favour of Reform. When the king refused, Grey resigned and the duke of Wellington was invited to form a government. This caused mayhem up and down the country, and in spite of conceding moderate parliamentary reform Wellington was unable to hold his party together. Therefore in November he resigned. This left the king with no alternative but to recall Grey and agree to his request.

In the spring of 1832 Grey introduced a third Reform Bill. When it passed the Commons by a large majority, the king was faced with having to make good his promise – a step he deplored. Therefore in a last ditch attempt to avoid it, he instructed his private secretary to suggest to the duke of Wellington as Tory leader that when it came before the House of Lords he and his followers should abstain. Therefore when the Bill was introduced into the upper house, the Tory benches were practically empty and it was carried by an overwhelming majority. On 7 June 1832 the Representation of the People Act, otherwise known as the Reform Act, received the royal assent and became law. When a general election was held in December that year under the new rules, General Sharpe was returned as the Whig member for the Dumfries burghs having defeated William Douglas, while John James Hope-Johnstone of Annandale secured Dumfriesshire for the Tories.

While the new rules were hardly revolutionary, widening the suffrage meant that, instead of being self-perpetuating oligarchies, town councils were bound to have regard to the views of the newly enfranchised shopkeepers, artisans and householders. Similarly in the landward areas where the introduction of a secret ballot meant that tenants and feuars could vote according to their preference instead of following the dictates of their landlord. Nevertheless many working class people were aggrieved at being denied the vote, the more vociferous claiming that they had been betrayed. Consequently there was growing agitation for a further widening of the suffrage.

In 1838 it culminated in the drawing up of a People's Charter – hence the name Chartism applied to the movement. This called for an extension of the franchise to further democratise the political system. Therefore the following year a petition signed by a large number of working people was presented to Parliament. Despite the presenting of two more petitions in 1842 and 1848, it was not until 1867 that a second Reform Act was passed which went some way towards meeting the Chartists' demands. Since it was the distress of the weavers in particular which contributed to

---

* The constituency comprised the burghs of Dumfries, Annan, Lochmaben, Sanquhar and Kirkcudbright.

the rise of Chartism, and they were heavily concentrated in Gasstown, Dumfries was a prominent centre of Chartism in Scotland. The Chartists regularly held large public meetings in Queensberry Square when the populace were incited to take to the streets in support of reform. However in July 1842, when the protests appeared to be getting out of hand, the authorities banned all further public meetings.[61]

The political exclusion of the underclasses was mirrored by a similar remoteness on the part of the Church. Such was the view of its evangelical wing whose adherents were convinced that, under the influence of the prevailing moderatism, the Church was identifying itself too closely with the landed interest to the prejudice of the urban underclasses. While this was a contributory factor to the Disruption of 1843, the proximate cause was the issue of patronage, and by extension the relationship between Church and state. It harked back to 1834 when the general assembly passed the Veto Act. This provided that, where a majority of the male heads of family objected to the patron's choice of presentee to a vacant charge, presbytery was obliged to reject him.

It was almost immediately put to the test when a majority of the parishioners of Auchterarder in Perthshire objected to the patron's choice of presentee to their living. Therefore his nomination was rejected by presbytery whose decision was upheld by the general assembly. Refusing to accept it, the patron and presentee appealed to the Court of Session. In view of its importance the case was heard by a full bench of thirteen judges. By a majority of eight to five the court found in their favour, their decision being upheld on appeal to the House of Lords.[62] This precipitated what became known as the Ten Years' Conflict, in the course of which a number of similar cases were brought before the courts. The last – and most contentious – concerned the parish of Marnoch in Aberdeenshire where the objection of a majority of the parishioners to the patron's choice of presentee was sustained by presbytery and endorsed by the general assembly.

Again the patron and presentee took their case to the Court of Session who ordered the presbytery to accept the presentee's nomination. It complied, but only by a small majority. Therefore, exercising the full rigour of ecclesiastical law, the general assembly ejected those in favour of his nomination from the presbytery. It went further. It revoked the presentee's licence to preach and barred him from carrying out his parochial duties. The deposed presbytery members retaliated by successfully petitioning the Court of Session for decree annulling the assembly's sentence of deposition and ordering restoration of the presentee's licence to preach. This was granted. But when the decree was formally served on the assembly it was rejected. Deadlock ensued, and protest meetings were held up and down the country, while deputations of leading ministers and laymen tried to persuade the government to change the law. But in vain. The issue was critical, because on it depended the Church's independence of the state.[63]

Matters came to a head at the general assembly which was held in St Andrew's Church, George Street, Edinburgh, in May 1843. When it was moved that the Court of Session's decree be accepted, effectively confirming the Church's subordination to the state, some 470 dissenting ministers, representing more than a third of the entire ministry, withdrew. Led by Dr Thomas Chalmers and accompanied by a host of elders and supporters they proceeded down the hill, cheered by crowds of sympathetic onlookers, to Canonmills. Congregating in the nearby Tanfield Hall, they constituted themselves an assembly of the Free Church of Scotland (i.e. free from state control) and elected Dr Chalmers as moderator.[64] Having set themselves up as an independent Church, its members embarked on the daunting task of establishing a new church, manse and school in every parish in Scotland. Such was their zeal and determination in raising money from a generally supportive public that by 1848 they had built some 700 churches at a cost of £500,000. In addition, they had raised a further £10,000 towards the erection of manses, as well as a substantial covenanted income for the provision of ministerial stipends,[65] and by 1851 they had built 751 schools.

In 1900 the Free Chruch of Scotland joined the United Presbyterian Church of Scotland to form the United Free Church of Scotland. However, a dissenting minority of Free Church ministers remained outside the union, and claiming to represent the legitimate Free Church they continued to call themselves the Free Church of Scotland. Drawing their support mainly from the north-west and the Outer Isles, they are commonly referred to as the 'Wee Frees' – not to be confused with the 'Wee Wee Frees'. Officially the Free Presbyterian Church of Scotland, this small group had split off from the Free Church in 1893 in protest at its decision to moderate its strict compliance with the Westminster Confession of Faith,[*] their secession being symptomatic of the continuing fissiparity within the Church.

POLITICS

In July 1834 Earl Grey resigned the premiership and was succeeded by lord Melbourne. His tenure was brief. In November he was dismissed by the king who invited Sir Robert Peel, the leader of the Tory opposition, to form a government. Having failed to achieve a majority at the general election of January 1835, he resigned and Melbourne resumed the premiership. He went on to win the general election of November 1837 when General Sharpe and John James Hope-Johnstone retained their seats, the one as Whig member for the Dumfries burghs and the other as Tory representative for Dumfriesshire.

In 1839 Melbourne resigned following a defeat in Parliament, and Peel was again invited to form a government. But, faced with the demand that she exchange the Whig ladies of her household for Tories, the youthful Queen Victoria tearfully

---

[*]   Drawn up by the Westminster Assembly in 1646, it proclaimed the Church of England's stand on the issues of worship, doctrine, government and discipline in accordance with that of the Scottish Presbyterian Church who adopted it the following year. In effect it confirmed the English acceptance of the Solemn League and Covenant which was a condition of Scottish support for the Parliamentarians during the Civil War.

refused. Therefore Peel declined the commission and Melbourne once again regained the premiership which he held until his resignation following a vote of no confidence in June 1841. At the ensuing general election the Tories were returned to power, and this time Peel accepted the queen's commission (reluctantly given) to form a government. William Ewart,* who had been a member of Parliament since 1828, was elected as the Whig member for the Dumfries burghs in place of the now-retired General Sharpe, having narrowly beaten Sir Alexander Johnstone of Carnsalloch for the nomination. Meanwhile John James Hope-Johnstone was returned as the Tory member for Dumfriesshire.

Peel's administration became fatally split over the issue of the Corn Laws which by keeping the price of grain artificially high was causing widespread hardship and distress. Therefore, overriding the vested interests of his colleagues, Peel was determined to repeal them. The issue came to a head in 1845 with the failure of the Irish potato crop and the resulting famine. Peel was not prepared to wait any longer. Despite the opposition of the majority of his cabinet, he presented a Bill to Parliament for their repeal, and supported by like-minded Whigs and the Irish members it passed both houses of Parliament.

The Conservative party† was now split between the Peelites who supported repeal, and the protectionists. The result was inevitable. At the general election of August 1847 they were swept from power, and lord John Russell became Prime Minister at the head of a Liberal administration, William Ewart being returned as the Liberal member for the Dumfries burghs. Bucking the trend, lord Drumlanrig, the son and heir of the marquess of Queensberry, held Dumfriesshire for the Conservatives in place of the retiring John James Hope-Johnstone. Described as 'a man better known for his fighting abilities than his academic achievements', as well as being a keen sportsman and an inveterate gambler, Drumlanrig was a staunch Peelite (paradoxically in view of his landed background).

Peel continued to lead the Peelite wing of the Conservative party until his death in July 1850, when he was succeeded by lord Aberdeen. In February 1852 lord John Russell resigned as Prime Minister following a vote of no confidence. He was succeeded by lord Derby, the leader of the Conservative protectionists, who formed an administration from which the Peelites were excluded. Following his defeat at the general election of November that year, Derby resigned and was succeeded by the Peelite lord Aberdeen. In an attempt to strengthen his administration, he formed a coalition known as 'the Government of all the Talents' with lord John Russell as Foreign Secretary and lord Palmerston Home Secretary. Other Cabinet appointments included Gladstone, at that time a Tory Peelite, who succeeded Disraeli, then a Tory protectionist, as Chancellor of the Exchequer. Meanwhile lord Drumlanrig and

---

*   Ewart was a close friend of Sir John Gladstone, and it was on account of this that Sir John gave his fourth son, William, the future Prime Minister, the middle name of Ewart.

†   It was about this time that the Whigs began to be called Liberals and the Tories Conservatives.

William Ewart retained Dumfriesshire and the Dumfries burghs for the Conservatives and Liberals respectively.

In March 1854 the Crimean War broke out. But when the failings of the army through incompetent leadership, bad organisation, and lack of supplies became apparent, it caused a public outcry. The issue was raised in Parliament, and a motion was presented to the Commons calling for the appointment of a Select Committee to investigate it. When the motion was carried in January 1856, Aberdeen treated it as a vote of no confidence and resigned. In February, having exhausted all attempts to find an alternative, the queen was reluctantly compelled to invite Palmerston, her *bête noir*, to form an administration. Accordingly he became Prime Minister at the head of a Liberal government which included a number of Peelites whom Aberdeen encouraged to support it. As a Peelite, lord Drumlanrig was offered a position in the new government. He made his acceptance conditional on the award of an English barony, but when it was refused he resigned his seat in dudgeon and flounced out of Parliament.[*]

In April 1857, impatient with the constraints imposed on him by his Peelite colleagues, Palmerston called a general election, and having gained a working majority he formed an exclusively Liberal administration. William Ewart was re-elected as member for the Dumfries burghs having secured nomination as the Liberal candidate after narrowly defeating the radical James Hannay.[66] Meanwhile John James Hope-Johnstone, who had come out of retirement, was returned as Conservative member for Dumfriesshire.

In February 1858 Palmerston resigned following a vote of censure and was succeeded by lord Derby at the head of another weak Conservative administration. It lasted for some fifteen months until the general election of May 1859 when Palmerston was returned to power with a large majority. John James Hope-Johnstone continued to hold Dumfriesshire for the Conservatives, while William Ewart was re-elected as member for the Dumfries burghs having narrowly defeated his Conservative opponent Captain (later Colonel Sir) George Walker of Crawfordton.[67]

In July 1865 the eighty-year-old Palmerston called a general election, when his party was returned to power with a substantial majority. William Ewart was returned as member for the Dumfries burghs for a fifth time having defeated his Conservative opponent, Colonel John Clark-Kennedy of Knockgray,[†] by a large majority. John James Hope-Johnstone, who was now approaching seventy having represented Dumfriesshire off and on since 1830, stood down and was succeeded by Major George Walker (the unsuccessful candidate for the Dumfries Burghs in 1859) as Conservative member for Dumfriesshire. When Palmerston died in October, lord

---

[*]   When his father died in December that year he became the seventh marquess of Queensberry. However in August 1858 he was killed when his gun accidentally exploded although his intimates were convinced it was suicide.
[†]   Clark-Kennedy made no further attempt to enter Parliament and died two years later while serving in the Abyssinian campaign.

John Russell (now Earl Russell) became Prime Minister. The following March, Gladstone as Leader of the Commons was responsible for introducing the Representation of the People Bill for the purpose of widening the franchise. When it was defeated by the Conservatives, supported by the more reactionary Liberal members, Russell resigned. Consequently lord Derby became Prime Minister at the head of another minority government, Disraeli once again being appointed Chancellor of the Exchequer as well as Leader of the Commons.

The defeat of Gladstone's Bill fuelled public pressure for an extension of the franchise and demonstrations were held up and down the country agitating for reform. In Dumfries the local branch of the Scottish Reform League organised a rally at which a group of firebrand speakers incited the populace to take to the streets.[68] Bowing to popular agitation, Disraeli introduced a Reform Bill into the Commons. Despite fierce opposition and the need to make some concessions, the Bill was passed by the Commons, and – grudgingly – by the Lords. By enfranchising all rate-paying householders it added approximately a million new voters to an electorate of much the same number – far more than would have been allowed for under Gladstone's Bill. In some cases the proportion was much higher, the increase in the Dumfries burghs electorate for example being two-and-a-half times the previous number.[69]

In March 1868 lord Derby resigned and Disraeli became Prime Minister, Gladstone having succeeded Earl Russell as leader of the Liberal party. At the general election of December that year the newly qualified voters gave their support – not to the party responsible for enfranchising them, as might have been expected, but to the Liberals. This was enough to win them the election and Gladstone became Prime Minister. But William Ewart, who had represented the Dumfries burghs since 1841 and was now in failing health, did not seek re-election (in fact died the following month). A keen espouser of liberal causes throughout his forty-year parliamentary career, he had supported Catholic Emancipation, and later pressed for the abolition of the death penalty for such crimes as horse-, cattle-, and letter-stealing, sacrilege, and escaping from transportation.[*] He was also responsible for the Act of 1866 which encouraged the building of labourers' houses in Scotland.[70] Robert Jardine of Castlemilk, until recently the member for Ashburton, was nominated to succeed him; but his candidature was opposed by an outsider, Ernest Noel, whom he narrowly defeated. However, Noel promised his supporters that he would return to fight another day if they so wished, as he did.[71]

The swing to the Liberals was enough to topple Major (now Colonel) George Walker, who lost Dumfriesshire – by a narrow margin – to the recently knighted Sir Sydney Waterlow. But Walker had another string to his bow, because it transpired

---

[*] McDowall, *Dumfries*, 436. William Ewart was responsible for the passing of the Public Libraries Act of 1850 and its Scottish counterpart in 1853. These empowered local authorities to meet the cost of founding public libraries out of the rates. Therefore it was in recognition of this that, when in 1890 Andrew Carnegie donated a sum of £10,000 towards the cost of establishing a public library in Dumfries, he suggested that it be called the Ewart Library after him, which was adopted.

that Waterlow's family firm, of which he was a partner, had a contract for supplying stationery to the government. Therefore he claimed that as a government contractor Waterlow was disqualified from sitting and voting in Parliament. The matter was adjudicated by the Committee of Privileges who upheld Walker's claim,[*] and at the ensuing by-election in March 1869 he was returned to Parliament by a narrow majority.

At the general election of March 1874 the Liberals suffered a heavy and unexpected defeat when Disraeli became Prime Minister for a second time. Meanwhile the Dumfries burghs constituency had switched horses when the supporters of Ernest Noel contrived to have him adopted as the official Liberal candidate in place of Robert Jardine who was de-selected. Undeterred, Jardine persuaded the Dumfriesshire Liberals to adopt him as their candidate instead. However, the swing to the Conservatives proved too much and he was narrowly defeated by John James Hope-Johnstone, grandson and heir of the elder John James Hope-Johnstone (who was still alive).[72] Nevertheless, bucking the trend, Ernest Noel held Dumfries burghs for the Liberals.

In February 1880, at the request of lord Beaconsfield (as Disraeli had become) the queen dissolved Parliament. At the general election held in April the Liberals were returned to power. Having tried unsuccessfully to persuade lord Hartington to form an administration, the queen was compelled to turn to Gladstone whom she cordially disliked,[†] and who became Prime Minister for a second time. The Liberal victory was reflected in both Dumfriesshire constituencies. Robert Jardine was elected to Parliament as member for Dumfriesshire having narrowly defeated the Conservative Colonel George Walker, while Ernest Noel was returned as member for the Dumfries burghs having secured the nomination in the face of two rival contenders.[73]

Unlike his first premiership of 1868, Gladstone found himself presiding over a divided party which included a number of radical newcomers. Their leader was the firebrand Joseph Chamberlain, a successful screw manufacturer who had been elected to Parliament in 1876 after an outstandingly successful term as mayor of Birmingham. In order to keep the radicals on side, Gladstone included him in the government as President of the Board of Trade. In 1884, as a further sop to the radicals, Gladstone introduced a third Reform Bill – the Representation of the People Bill – which gave almost every adult male the vote, while a separate Act of Parliament abolished the remaining pocket burghs and divided the country into single-member constituencies.

In June 1885 his government was defeated on an amendment to the budget when the Irish members voted with the Conservative opposition. Therefore he resigned and was succeeded by the Conservative leader lord Salisbury,who formed a minority government dependent on the support of the Irish members. But they proved so

---

[*] This was by no means the end of Waterlow's political career because he went on to become Member of Parliament for Maidstone and Gravesend, and finally Lord Mayor of London from 1872 (when he was created a baronet) until 1877.

[†] She was in the habit of referring to him privately as 'merrypebble'.

unreliable that, at Salisbury's request, Parliament was dissolved later that year. At the following general election, the suffrage having been greatly increased as a result of Gladstone's Reform Bill, the Liberals gained the largest number of seats but without an overall majority. This meant that, like Salisbury, Gladstone was forced to rely on the support of the Irish members who held the balance of power. They were prepared to co-operate, but it was conditional on his undertaking to deliver Irish Home Rule. Meanwhile Sir Robert Jardine (he was created a baronet the same year) was returned as the member for Dumfriesshire having defeated his Conservative opponent the earl of Dalkeith,[*] son and heir of the duke of Buccleuch, while Ernest Noel continued to hold the Dumfries burghs for the Liberals.

In an attempt to buy off Chamberlain's opposition to Irish Home Rule, Gladstone appointed him President of the Local Government Board. Having neutralised him (as he thought), Gladstone pressed ahead with his plans to establish a parliament in Dublin with full responsibility for the conduct of Irish affairs. As he saw it, this would have the double advantage of solving the Irish question once and for all, while the cessation of Irish representation at Westminster would free him – and Parliament – of those perennially troublesome members. This was too much for Chamberlain, and the final break came at an acrimonious Cabinet meeting in March 1886 when he angrily picked up his papers and stormed out of the room. Thereafter he and his fellow radicals formed their own Liberal Unionist party.[†]

When Gladstone introduced his Home Rule Bill into the Commons, ninety-three members of his own party voted against it, along with Chamberlain and his fellow Liberal Unionists. Therefore it was thrown out. Gladstone immediately called a general election. Held in July 1886, it was fought on the single issue of Irish Home Rule. A hugely controversial issue, it caused many Liberal supporters to defect to the Conservatives who in consequence gained the largest number of seats, although they failed to win an overall majority. Accordingly Gladstone resigned and Salisbury became Prime Minister for a second time.

In Dumfriesshire Sir Robert Jardine was returned as Liberal member for the county. This was in spite of his refusal to commit himself to Irish Home Rule which was official Liberal policy, a stand that cost him the support of an influential section of the local association. They put forward Thomas McKie, one of the association's vice-presidents, for the nomination, although he lost it by a narrow margin. According to McDowall, Jardine owed his success to the intervention of lord Tweedmouth, the Liberal Chief Whip, who persuaded the majority of the association members to support him. Nevertheless the episode merely reinforced Jardine's opposition to Home Rule – to the extent that he made common cause with Chamberlain's Liberal Unionists and voted with the Conservatives.[74] Meanwhile Ernest Noel, his rival candidate for the Dumfries burghs whom he defeated in 1868 but who defeated him

---

[*] He was accidentally killed while deer stalking later that year.
[†] 'Unionist' because they supported a continuing union with Ireland.

in 1874, also declared his opposition to Irish Home Rule. Consequently he was de-selected, and Robert Threshie Reid, a barrister and a local man who had been member of Parliament for Hereford, was returned as the Liberal member in his place.

The next general election, which was held in August 1892, resulted in a narrow Liberal victory when the eighty-two-year-old Gladstone became Prime Minister for a fourth time. In Dumfriesshire Thomas McKie, now the official Liberal candidate, was defeated by his Conservative opponent William Herries Maxwell, son of the laird of Munches, while Robert Threshie Reid retained the Dumfries burghs for the Liberals.[75] In February 1893 Gladstone introduced another Irish Home Rule Bill. Although opposed by the Conservatives and the Liberal Unionists, the votes of the Irish members were enough to secure its passage through the Commons. But, following its defeat by an overwhelming majority in the Lords, the issue remained quiescent until it re-emerged with the Easter Rising of 1916.

In March 1894 Gladstone, who had fallen increasingly out of sympathy with his Cabinet colleagues,[*] resigned the premiership and was succeeded by lord Rosebery who was nearly forty years his junior. The same year, Sir Robert Reid was appointed Solicitor General for England, and being obliged to seek re-election he was again returned as member for the Dumfries Burghs. Lord Rosebery's government lasted until June 1895 when it was defeated on a snap vote in the Commons and he resigned. At the general election held the following August the Conservative/Liberal Unionist alliance scored a decisive victory and Salisbury became Prime Minister for a third time when Chamberlain was appointed Colonial Secretary. Bucking the trend, Robinson Souttar, an incomer from Oxford and the Liberal candidate for Dumfriesshire, defeated the sitting member William Herries Maxwell by a mere thirteen votes, while Sir Robert Reid (as he had become) continued to represent the Dumfries burghs.[76]

As Colonial Secretary, Chamberlain was responsible for the conduct of the South African War which broke out in October 1899. In September 1900, confident that the war as good as won, Salisbury called a general election. Known as the 'khaki' election, it resulted in the Conservatives and Chamberlain's Unionists being returned with a large majority, one of their new members being the young Winston Churchill.[†] This time William Herries Maxwell recovered Dumfriesshire for the Conservatives having defeated Robinson Souttar whose opposition to the war cost him much of his former support. In fact the Boers were far from defeated, because the war dragged on for another year and a half until May 1902. With peace secured, the ageing Salisbury resigned the premiership and was succeeded by his nephew and principal lieutenant, Arthur James Balfour.

---

[*]   In spite of being at odds with them, when it came to presiding over his last Cabinet there were tearful scenes of farewell. Gladstone was unmoved, contemptuously referring to his former colleagues as 'that blubbering cabinet'.

[†]   He delayed taking his seat until February the following year, a month after Queen Victoria's death. Had he done so earlier he could claim to have served as a member of Parliament under six different sovereigns.

His government became fatally split over the issue of Free Trade versus Imperial Preference and Tariff Reform, its leading proponent being the ever-controversial arch-imperialist Joseph Chamberlain. His time as Colonial Secretary had convinced him of the importance of removing all duty on goods traded within the British Empire, while imposing a tariff on all foreign imports, particularly from Germany and the United States. Taking the view that this would increase the cost of food, the majority of his Cabinet colleagues favoured unrestricted Free Trade. Finally in 1903, having failed to win them over, Chamberlain resigned from the government on amicable terms (Balfour having appointed his son Austen as Chancellor of the Exchequer to secure his continuing loyalty) so that he could stump the country proclaiming the virtues of Imperial Preference.* Balfour tried desperately to paper over the cracks within the party which the Liberal opposition was doing its best to exploit. But it was to no avail; the split was irrevocable and in December 1905 he resigned the premiership.

King Edward invited the Liberal leader, Sir Henry Campbell-Bannerman, to form a government in which Sir Robert Reid, the member for the Dumfries Burghs, was appointed Lord Chancellor.† This meant he had to resign his seat, but the electors were not disenfranchised for long, because in January 1906 Campbell-Bannerman dissolved Parliament and called a general election. The Liberals scored a landslide victory and John Gulland, an incomer from Edinburgh, was elected member for the Dumfries burghs. Meanwhile William Herries Maxwell had announced his intention not to seek re-election for Dumfriesshire, which was perhaps as well because the swing to the Liberals would have cost him his seat in any case. As it was, the Liberal candidate Percy Molteno, a partner in Donald Currie & Co, the Edinburgh ship-owners, defeated the Conservative J H Balfour-Browne of Goldielea, a local man, by a substantial majority. Thereafter the Liberals remained in power, initially under Campbell-Bannerman and latterly Asquith, for the next ten years until December 1916 when Asquith was forced from office and replaced by Lloyd George at the head of a Liberal–Conservative coalition government.

LANDOWNERSHIP

The 1860s was a time of rising prosperity. Britain's economy was booming, and similarly agriculture which, notwithstanding the repeal of the Corn Laws and the periodic outbreaks of disease, had flourished considerably over the past twenty years. By the early 1870s it had reached its peak and rents were higher than ever. Since the landlord–tenant system was almost universal, the owner occupier who

---

* In July 1906, immediately after his seventieth birthday celebrations in Birmingham, he suffered a stroke which left him virtually paralysed. This meant he could no longer play an active part in politics, although his interest remained undiminished, his son Austen keeping him fully informed about political events until his death in 1914.

† In recognition of his local connections he took the title lord Loreburn.

farmed his own land being very much the exception, a landowner could live comfortably off his rents and maintain a considerable style with a large staff of indoor and outdoor servants. Indeed it was regarded as something of a privilege for a young girl – or man for that matter – to go into service in the 'big hoose' and work their way up the social hierarchy that existed behind 'the green baize door'. Judged by modern standards, theirs was a very cloistered existence with long hours and hard work, and little time off to enjoy a social life. Yet, provided the employer and his family were considerate towards their domestic staff (by no means always the case), and the staff gave satisfaction, the job had its compensations in that it offered security of employment. And besides the restrictions were probably (although not invariably) accepted as the way of life.

On the larger estates, and those of the wealthier landowners, the outdoor staff would have been equally numerous – probably more so, because they ranged from gardeners and grooms to foresters, carpenters and gamekeepers. Since large-scale shoots had become increasingly fashionable, gamekeepers were the most important members of the estate staff. This was because the size of the 'bag' at each shoot (which was the subject of keen competition among landowners) depended to a large extent on the experience, effort and skill of the keepers and their assistants. This applied in particular to rearing game, notably pheasants and partridges, and killing raptors and other predators, in order to produce the best possible showing of birds at each shoot. Indeed, such was the importance attached to a good day's sport, that other estate activities were almost invariably subordinated to the shoot.

On the other hand, game – particularly hares and rabbits – caused serious damage to the tenant farmers' crops, while crops on the Solway coast suffered from the depredations of geese.* Not only that, but shooting days frequently interfered with farming activities. Worse still, the right to kill game of whatever kind belonged exclusively to the landowner, so tenant farmers had to look on helplessly as these predators destroyed their crops. If they attempted to take matters into their own hands and were caught doing so, punishment could be excessively harsh. Although it was the gamekeeper's responsibility to keep down these predators, many failed to do so, and this was a source of widespread (and well-justified) grievance. Nevertheless it was only after considerable agitation that the situation was rectified with the passing of the Ground Game Act of 1880. This gave tenant farmers the right to kill hares, rabbits and other vermin – but not game birds – on their land.

The agricultural boom was not destined to last, and the onset of the depression from the late seventies onwards was reflected in a corresponding decline in rents. Not that this deterred those who had made money in other walks of life from buying estates, partly for the enjoyment of landownership and its sporting facilities, and also

---

* As a measure of the damage they can cause, it is reckoned that four geese will eat as much grass as a sheep. Therefore, to compensate for this, some landowners allowed their tenants an abatement of rent. But they were probably the exception and certainly there is no mention of this in either the old or new *Statistical Accounts*.

for its perceived social status. In fact it was the wealthier incomers who were mainly responsible, along with the larger landowners, for maintaining the high style of country house life with its lavish hospitality, large-scale shoots, and generally leisured existence associated with the upper classes of the late Victorian and Edwardian era.

The invaluable *List of Owners of Land in Scotland*, otherwise known as the Scottish Doomsday Book, which was published in 1873, gives details of the landowners in each county, the amount of land they owned and its gross annual value. The section dealing with Dumfriesshire shows that, in almost all cases, the lands belonging to the principal improvers of the late eighteenth and early nineteenth centuries remained in the hands of their descendants. One exception was the Closeburn estate which was sold following the death of Sir Charles Stuart-Menteth in 1847. Another was Dalswinton. It was purchased from Patrick Miller's executors by James MacalpineLeny, and in 1919, following the death of his grandson James Macalpine-Downie, it was sold to David Landale.

By far the largest landowner was the fifth duke of Buccleuch whose Dumfriesshire estates extended to 253,514 acres and represented nearly 40% of the land surface of the entire county. In fact this is slightly misleading, because most of his lands in the upper Cairn valley, Upper Nithsdale, Dryfesdale and Upper Eskdale consisted of poor quality marginal or hill country. A truer comparison can be gained from their gross annual value which represented just under 16% of the total for the county. Coming a long way behind, but still a very substantial landowner, was John James Hope-Johnstone of Annandale whose landholdings amounted to 64,079 acres. Here again most of his lands in the parishes of Moffat and Kirkpatrick Juxta consisted of hill ground – very scenic but not much use for anything other than sheep farming and forestry, and now the erection of wind turbines.

The next five largest landowners, in descending order, were:

Sir Frederic Johnstone Bt of Westerhall	17,064 acres
The earl of Mansfield	14,342 acres
The heiresses of Douglas Baird of Closeburn	13,560 acres
Sir John Heron-Maxwell Bt of Springkell	13,391 acres
The marquess of Queensberry	13,243 acres

In addition, there were a further sixty-five people who owned land of more than 1,000 acres, and another 821 with less than 1,000 acres, which suggests that with the few exceptions mentioned above, landownership was quite widely diffused in Dumfriesshire.

An early example of a wealthy incomer establishing himself as a landowner in Dumfriesshire was Thomas Gladstone, a Liverpool merchant, who purchased the Capenoch estate near Penpont from James Grierson of Dalgonar in 1848. At much the same time Douglas Baird, one of five brothers who between them had built up a successful ironfounding business at Gartsherrie,* purchased the Closeburn estate. But his tenure was brief because he died prematurely in 1854 leaving the estate jointly to his two daughters Jane Isabella, later Mrs Frederick Villiers, and Charlotte Marion, who became the countess of Enniskillen.

Another was Edward Brook, a wealthy and innovative textile magnate from Huddersfield, who acquired the Hoddom estate from the representatives of William Sharpe. Some twenty years later he added to it with the purchase of the duke of Buccleuch's lands in the same parish, and by 1900 he had acquired Kinmount House and estate from the eighth marquess of Queensberry.† Meanwhile in the 1880s William Younger, member of the Edinburgh brewing family, purchased the estate of Auchencastle, near Beattock, from the Hon. Henry Butler-Johnstone of Corehead.‡ In fact William Younger already had connections with Dumfriesshire since both his father and grandfather had owned nearby Craigielands, his grandfather having been responsible for building the present house in 1817. At much the same time John Crabbie, an Edinburgh vintner, purchased Duncow from James Heron, and by the end of the century it had passed to his son Captain John Crabbe.§

The 1880s also witnessed the sale of the Lockerbie estate by Arthur Henry Johnstone-Douglas to Andrew Wright who sold it on to George Fullerton, another incomer to the region. Similarly Henry Walker, a coalmaster from Airdrie, acquired the Dalgonar estate near Dunscore from James Grierson, thus marking the final severing of that family's long-standing connection with the region.¶ In 1891 Walter Duncan, a successful tea merchant, purchased Newlands in the neighbouring parish of Kirkmahoe, and at much the same time Edward Johnson-Ferguson, a Manchester businessman and member of Parliament for Loughborough (and later a baronet), bought the Springkell estate from Sir John Heron-Maxwell.

By far the largest land purchasers in Dumfriesshire during the latter half of the nineteenth century were the Jardines. Exceptionally they were native to the region, their common ancestor Andrew Jardine being a smalltime farmer from near Lochmaben. In 1802 his eighteen-year-old younger son William, a medical graduate,

---

* One of the brothers was James Baird who was responsible for rescuing the Caledonian Railway Company from bankruptcy.

† Notoriously cantankerous, eccentric and on occasions violent, he was the originator of the 'Queensberry Rules'. His charging Oscar Wilde with having a homosexual relationship with his son lord Alfred Douglas caused Wilde to sue him for libel – most imprudently because it backfired and resulted in his being sentenced to a term of imprisonment, homosexuality being a criminal offence.

‡ A younger son of the 13th baron Dunboyne, he added the name Johnstone when his wife inherited Corehead from her uncle General Frederick Johnstone.

§ The story has it that when he was put up for membership of the New Club, Edinburgh under his original name of Crabbie he was blackballed on account of his association with trade. Therefore, to distance himself from his commercial roots, he changed his name to Crabbe, prompting some wag to observe 'if thine eye offend thee pluck it out'!

¶ It had lasted for almost half a millennium ever since his forebear Gilbert Macgregor (corrupted to Grierson), described as armour-bearer to the earl of Douglas, was granted lands there by George Dunbar earl of March in 1400.

obtained employment as a surgeon's mate with the East India Company's naval service. This entailed long sea voyages to India and China, but the fact that he was given a generous allowance of 'privilege space' enabled him to do some trading on his own account which paid off handsomely. In 1822 he established himself as a merchant in Canton, and in 1832 he co-founded with James (later Sir James) Matheson the firm of Jardine Matheson & Co, traders in a wide range of commodities and whose interests included the importing of opium from India to China.

In 1835 William Jardine took his eldest nephew Andrew Johnstone into partnership, followed in 1839 by his brother David's eldest son, Andrew Jardine. Meanwhile, alarmed by the rapidly increasing addiction to opium, and its harmful effect on the population, the Chinese authorities decided to suppress the trade. Accordingly they seized, burnt and otherwise destroyed the entire stock of opium belonging to the foreign traders in Canton, and banished them from China. They took refuge in the Portuguese colony of Macao where they continued to be harassed by the Chinese. Retaliating, Foreign Secretary Palmerston, in consultation with William Jardine and others, dispatched a fleet of gunboats from Singapore to Canton, thus precipitating the First Opium War. It lasted until 1842 when, in terms of the treaty of Nanking, the Chinese were forced to permit a resumption of the opium trade and ceded the island of Hong Kong to the British crown. Two years later, Jardine Matheson established a base there.

In 1843 David Jardine, another of William Jardine's nephews, became a partner in the business and subsequently *tai pan* (senior executive), and two years later he was joined by his next brother, Joseph. Later, in 1858, their relative William Keswick, a great-nephew of William Jardine, was taken on as a partner and in 1875 he became *tai pan*. Founder of a dynasty which has been mainly responsible for the direction of the company ever since, he remained head of Jardine Matheson until his retirement in 1906 and a director until his death in 1912. Meanwhile David and Joseph died in 1856 and 1861 respectively, and because they were both unmarried their estates – and their interest in the firm – passed to their youngest brother Robert, the future member of Parliament.

William Jardine, the co-founder, retired from active participation in the business in 1839 having set his sights on acquiring the Castlemilk estate. Since the owner refused to sell, he bought the property of Lanrick instead. But he was not ready to retire. Since it was vital that Jardine Matheson should have a voice in Parliament, and access to government circles as a means of advancing its interests, and those of the China trade generally, William Jardine had himself elected as Whig member for Ashburton. But his tenure was brief, because he died unmarried in 1843 at the relatively early age of fifty-nine. This resulted in a by-election, and in order to retain the seat for the firm, William Jardine's partner Sir James Matheson effectively bought it. He held it until the general election of 1865 when he stood down in favour of Robert Jardine. The youngest of William Jardine's nephews, Robert continued to represent Ashburton until 1868 when it disappeared under a reorganisation of the constituencies and he had himself adopted as the Liberal candidate for the Dumfries burghs instead.[77]

Four of the five sons of William Jardine's brother, David Jardine of Muirhousehead, joined the firm, and with the exception of the third son David they all acquired lands in Dumfriesshire. The eldest, Andrew, who inherited Lanrick from his uncle William, and Muirhousehead from his father, purchased the lands of Corrie and others in the parish of Hutton and Corrie, thereafter styling himself 'of Corrie'. He also acquired Halleaths, near Lochmaben, from the representatives of his cousin Andrew Johnstone, a partner in Jardine Matheson, who died in 1857. Not long afterwards Andrew Jardine sold it to Andrew Johnstone's brother John, who in about 1860 commissioned David Bryce to alter and extend the house. Andrew Jardine also purchased lands in the parish of Tundergarth, some of which he sold to his youngest brother Robert in the 1860s, and dying unmarried in 1889 he bequeathed him the remainder of his lands, including Corrie.

Having purchased the lands of Dryfeholm in the 1860s, the second son James embarked on something of a land-buying spree, mainly at the expense of the marquess of Queensberry and Sir Alexander Jardine of Applegirth (no relation). Initially he purchased the marquess's lands at Lochmaben followed by those in the parishes of Tinwald (including Tinwald House) and Torthorwald. In the 1880s he bought lands in the parish of Johnstone from Sir Alexander Jardine, who seems to have been in straitened circumstances because shortly afterwards he sold James Jardine the remainder of the Applegirth estate which had belonged to his family for well over six centuries. When James Jardine died in 1893 his lands passed to his son David, who on the strength of inheriting Applegirth styled himself 'of Applegirth'; but confusingly Sir Alexander's successors continued to do the same! On David's death in 1922 his lands passed to his daughter, Mrs Dorothy Agnes Jessie Cunningham,* who sold most of the former Applegirth estate to Chatsworth Estates in 1944, although it later became the property of the Crown Estate Commissioners.

In 1854 the fourth son Joseph purchased Castlemilk from George Armstrong (the estate his uncle William Jardine set his sights on but was unable to acquire). When Joseph died prematurely in 1861 he bequeathed Castlemilk, along with his interest in Jardine Matheson, to his youngest brother Robert. Some years later Robert had the existing house demolished and replaced by the present mansion which was designed by David Bryce in the Scottish baronial style and completed in 1870. By this time he was becoming a substantial landowner. According to the Valuation Roll of 1862–3 he had acquired lands in the parishes of Hoddom and Lochmaben, as well as others from Sir William Jardine of Applegirth, and at much the same time he purchased land in the parish of Tundergarth from his eldest brother Andrew. In the 1880s he acquired others belonging to James Alexander Rogerson of Gillesbie in the parish of Wamphray, and following his eldest brother Andrew's death in 1889 he inherited Corrie along

---

* Wife of F E Cunningham she added Jardine to her married name to become Cunningham-Jardine.

with his interest in the firm. Consequently Sir Robert Jardine (as he had become) was now the owner of extensive lands in Dumfriesshire, and having inherited his brothers' interests in Jardine Matheson he was the major shareholder in the firm. When he himself died in 1905 his landholdings passed along with his interest in the firm to his son Sir Robert William Buchanan-Jardine.*

In 1894 Sir William Harcourt, the Chancellor of the Exchequer in lord Rosebery's Liberal government, was responsible for the introduction of death duties, which in time would accelerate the decline of the landowning class. The concept of a tax arising on death was not new, because probate and legacy duty had been introduced in the previous century. But it was only with the introduction of succession duty by lord Aberdeen's government in 1853 that the tax was extended to land. The difference was that, whereas these taxes were levied on the inheritors of property, death duties were chargeable on the assets of the deceased on a sliding scale according to their total value. Although the top rate was initially a mere 8%, the advent of death duties was greeted with alarm by many landowners who feared that it would lead to the break-up of their estates – justifiably as it proved when the top rate was progressively raised to a swingeing 80%. Nevertheless some relief was available for agricultural land, while those who made a lifetime gift of their estates to their successor could avoid death duties provided they survived for five (later increased to seven) years from the date of transfer.

This lay in the future. Although the latter part of the nineteenth century witnessed the break-up of a handful of landed estates, they were the exception and probably attributable to the prevailing depression as much as anything else. One example was the former Corrie estate of Newbie which was acquired by Edward McKenzie, who sold it off piecemeal during the 1880s. Another was the Johnstone-Douglas estate of Lockerbie, while a third was the former Carruthers estate of Dornock. This passed to the Carlyle family, who were responsible for its break-up. Otherwise the structure of landownership remained more or less intact, and would continue to do so until the First World War when death duties were levied on the estates of landowners killed in action (exemption only came later and was not retrospective). This inevitably had an impact on landownership, which was compounded by high taxation, the depression, and a progressive increase in death duty rates. These combined with the effects of the Second War, discriminatory post-war legislation, and a further escalation of death duties, were responsible for accelerating the diffusion of landownership and the rise of the owner occupier.

---

* The addition of the name Buchanan was in recognition of his maternal grandfather's chieftainship of the clan.

EIGHTEEN

Modern Times

AGRICULTURE

The government's adherence to a policy of cheap food and free trade persisted throughout the latter part of the nineteenth century and well into the twentieth. Indeed nothing, not even the outbreak of war in August 1914, could shake it out of its conviction that Britain's command of the high seas would ensure a continuing flow of imports from across the Atlantic. However, mounting shipping losses in May and June 1915, and the threat of a food shortage, shook it out of its complacency, and measures were introduced to increase home production. But they were patently inadequate. County councils were instructed to appoint agricultural committees for the purpose of submitting proposals for increasing productivity. Coercion was ruled out because the government assumed that scarcity would drive up prices and encourage farmers to produce more. But continued shipping losses combined with a bad harvest in 1916 exposed the inadequacy of these measures.

Meanwhile in May 1915 wartime emergency compelled Prime Minister Asquith to bring some leading Conservatives into the government to form a National Ministry. But it was not enough to stave off the crisis. This occurred in December 1916 when he fell from power and was replaced by the dynamic Lloyd George at the head of a Liberal/Conservative Coalition. Appreciating the danger to the country's food supplies, and indeed its very survival, he forced through Parliament the kind of radical measures that were needed to encourage home production. In Scotland district Agricultural Executive Committees were appointed to advise the Board of Agriculture on all matters to do with food production in their areas. Specifically they were required to carry out a survey of each individual farm to assess the amount of land that could be cultivated, with powers of enforcement where necessary. That was the stick. The carrot was the introduction of guaranteed minimum prices for wheat and oats. They were set at a level which would encourage farmers to take pasture back into cultivation, and as a further incentive these measures were guaranteed to remain in force until 1922.

Although helpful so far as they went, they did not solve the crisis as home production continued to lag behind the nation's requirements. Because this remained the case until well after the War, farmers were under continuing pressure to bring more land into cultivation and increase the stocking levels of grassland. As an added incentive, the government issued a solemn promise that never again would agriculture be neglected as in the past. Because the guaranteed price of cereals, combined with the grants and subsidies which were now available, rendered farming increasingly profitable, this was reflected in rising rents and hence land values. This encouraged some landowners who were feeling the effects of high taxation and other fiscal burdens to profit from the boom by selling off farms. In many cases they were sold to sitting tenants who, having benefited from the upturn in farming, could generally afford to buy them. Even if they couldn't, banks and other lending institutions were prepared to assist, and this in turn gave added impetus to the trend towards owner occupancy.

Some estates were sold off in their entirety. A case in point was the Terregles estate which was sold by Herbert Constable-Maxwell-Stuart in 1920. It consisted of three separate blocks of land which would have been more or less identical with those acquired by his remote forebear Sir John Herries in the late 1300s. One was Terregles itself, while the other two comprised lands in the parishes of Kirkgunzeon and Lochrutton in Kirkcudbrightshire. Many of the farms were bought by sitting tenants, and in some cases they remain in the hands of their descendants to this day. Most of the lower-lying land at Terregles, on the other hand, was sold to the Board of Agriculture for subdivision into smallholdings for the benefit of ex-servicemen.

Another was the Closeburn estate. This belonged to Sir James Buchanan,[*] a Glasgow whisky distiller, who had recently purchased it from the trustees of Douglas Baird as a speculation. It was stripped of its timber while the farms were sold off, some going to sitting tenants. Although Buchanan is said to have disposed of them at reasonable prices,[1] the whole exercise doubtless yielded him a substantial profit. A third was the Dumcrieff estate near Moffat. It belonged to lord Rollo whose forebear Dr Rogerson, the court physician to the Empress Catherine the Great, had acquired it on his return to Scotland in the early 1800s. Here again most of the farms were sold to the sitting tenants. Finally there was the Carnsalloch estate near Duncow which was sold by Capt. Archibald Campbell Johnstone, a descendant of Alexander Johnstone the noted eighteenth-century improver. It consisted of six farms of which two went to sitting tenants, two to incomers, while Auchencrieff and Heathhall were acquired by the motor manufacturers Arrol Johnston.

The duke of Buccleuch was also disposing of lands. They included two outlying hill farms – Glencorse and Gubhill – in the parish of Closeburn which were sold to the Forestry Commission and formed the nucleus of the Forest of Ae. The Commission was established as a government-funded body under the Forestry Act of 1919 for the purpose of regenerating woodland to replace the timber felled during the War. Through time the Forest of Ae expanded eastwards to include much of the parish of

---

[*] The story goes that shortly afterwards, at the time of the honours scandal, Buchanan was approached with the offer of a peerage in return for a substantial contribution to the Liberal party. But, a canny gentleman, he asked for a guarantee that if he paid the sum indicated, a peerage would follow. Since this was not forthcoming, he is reputed to have signed the cheque 'Woolavington', which was the title he intended to take!

Kirkmichael and, following the death of Sir William Younger in 1937, the Commission acquired the Auchencastle estate in the parish of Kirkpatrick Juxta. Together with these and other purchases, it eventually built up a huge access of land which extended from the Ae valley to the Lowther hills. In the 1940s it acquired nearly as much again with the purchase of most of upper Eskdale from Buccleuch Estates.

Besides the two farms in the parish of Closeburn, the duke of Buccleuch disposed of a further five in the parish of Dornock. Four of them went to sitting tenants, while the fifth was acquired by the Board of Agriculture for division into small-holdings to accommodate ex-servicemen. In 1915 much of the land in that parish and neighbouring Gretna, which belonged to the earl of Mansfield, Sir George Johnstone of Westerhall, and William Graham of Mossknowe, was the subject of a compulsory purchase order.

This was to establish a huge factory complex for the manufacture of cordite, an essential component of high explosive artillery shells. These were primarily for use on the Western Front where the shortage and generally poor quality of the shells supplied to the army had become a national scandal. So much so that Lloyd George was appointed Minister of Munitions, an appointment specially created to deal with the crisis. The site was chosen for a number of reasons. It was generally poor quality land, partly peat-bog, remote, underpopulated and uniformly flat. Yet it was served by good rail links – to the coalfields of Sanquhar and Kirkconnel in one direction, and sources of raw material from England in the other, with good facilities for transporting the finished product, namely the cordite, to the ammunition factories in the south. Coal was also available from the pits at nearby Canonbie, and in greater abundance from the Cumberland coalfield, which was readily accessible by way of the Solway Junction Railway. It also had the advantage of being effectively out of range of German bombers. Or if any did penetrate that far they would most likely be intercepted and shot down before they could reach their target.

A top secret establishment, as well as being the largest in the world, the factory complex extended from Dornock to Longtown across the border, being nine miles long by an average of a mile and a half wide. Although officially referred to as HM Factory, Gretna, for security reasons it was codenamed Moorside, while the undried cordite was referred to as 'devil's porridge'. It consisted of three separate factories – one at Dornock, another at Gretna, and a third at Mossband which was adjacent to the lower reaches of the Esk in Cumberland. Deliberately set well apart to avoid the risk of an explosion occurring in one igniting the others, they were connected with each other by a network of 125 miles of light railway.

At the Dornock factory the imported cotton waste was treated with chemicals which were refined or distilled on site, the resulting mix being reduced to a cordite paste. This was transferred to the Mossband factory where it was mixed with further chemicals to produce a look-alike porridge (hence the name 'devil's porridge') which was extruded into spaghetti-like cords. These were cut to the required length and dried out in purpose-built ovens for dispatch to the shell factories. The factory at

Gretna, on the other hand, comprised the administrative offices as well as a hospital, an essential facility given the dangerous working conditions and the highly toxic nature of the product.

Over 30,000 workers were drawn from throughout the Empire to build the complex; and whereas some were accommodated in hostels in Carlisle, most were housed in hutted encampments thrown up near the site. Many were Irish who were renowned for their prodigious feats of labour, if less so for their ferocious consumption of alcohol and drink-fuelled violence. This accounted – at least in part – for the government's decision to impose state control over all public houses around Carlisle and south-eastern Dumfriesshire, and drastically reduce the opening hours. It also took over the Annan brewery, as well as other local breweries and distilleries. This was part of its campaign to curb excessive drinking which in its view was having a damaging effect on war production, and some of the regulations remained in force until the 1960s.

By the summer of 1916 the factory complex was up and running, and as the now-redundant workforce was transferred elsewhere they were replaced by some 20,000 operatives. Mostly women, supplemented by chemists, scientists and other specialists, they were referred to as the 'forgotten army' on account of the secrecy surrounding the establishment. Because the hutted encampments which sufficed for the navvies were considered too primitive, the women were accommodated in specially built townships at Eastriggs and Gretna which were equipped with shops, a cinema, a function hall, and other facilities, including two churches. In August 1916 the first consignment of cordite was ready for dispatch, and thereafter production quickly reached a maximum of 1,000 tons a week.

Although the women were well paid and comfortably lodged in purpose-built hostels in the new townships, theirs was unremittingly hard work, and dangerous given the extreme volatility of cordite. Temperatures had to be constantly monitored, for the least generation of heat could cause an explosion as sometimes happened. Since there was minimal protection from the effects of the chemicals, the fumes could render the women so drunk that they sometimes had to be taken to the sick-bay to sleep it off. Not only that, but mixing the chemicals with the cotton waste could cause their skin to turn yellow, earning them the nickname 'the yellow canaries'. This was no joking matter, because the condition was generally irreversible and in some cases the women's hair began falling out. Worse still, some would later die from the effects of inhaling the poisonous fumes.

After the War the workforce was laid off and the factory complex abandoned, with Eastriggs and Gretna reduced to ghost towns. The plant and machinery was sold off, and in 1924 the 600 or so lots of housing went under the hammer for knockdown prices. On the other hand, much of the land was retained by the government, and later an ammunition storage depot was established on the site of the former Mossband factory. Notwithstanding the compulsory purchase order, the earl of Mansfield, Sir George Johnstone, and William Graham were still left with a considerable amount of land in the parishes of Dornock and Gretna which they eventually sold, some of the farms going to sitting tenants. But, whether sold to sitting tenants or incomers, it contributed to the trend towards owner occupancy which would continue with added momentum throughout the rest of the century and beyond.*

Unfortunately those who bought their farms at the height of the boom proved over-optimistic because it quickly collapsed. Escalating land values were the product of farming prosperity which in turn was based on the dubious strength of government guarantees. Implementing them was easy enough during wartime, or in the immediate aftermath when a general scarcity was driving up farm prices; but to do so at a time of falling prices proved too expensive. This was the situation in 1921 when production had recovered to the point where it exceeded demand. Consequently prices fell, and wool for example sank to almost a quarter of its former level, which in turn led to a sharp fall in the price of sheep. Nevertheless, protected (or so they thought) by the Agriculture Act of 1920 which, repeating the provisions of the Corn Production Act of 1917 guaranteed cereal prices, arable farmers remained complaisant. But their illusions were rudely shattered, for in order to win the consumer's vote the government reverted to a policy of cheap food and free trade, and the resulting torrent of cheap imported grain forced prices down to a level where it could no longer afford to implement its guarantee. Therefore the legislation was repealed.

This meant that the whole structure of agricultural support collapsed. Not only that, but the price of farm produce fell to roughly half its 1920 level and, victims once again of a policy of cheap food and free trade, farmers were left to sink or swim on their own. For those who had taken out loans to purchase their farms it was a disaster. Falling land values reduced them to a position of negative equity, and unable to service their loans many were forced into bankruptcy. Consequently large tracts of arable land were taken out of cultivation and put down to permanent pasture† as farmers turned to livestock rearing and particularly dairying.

Eventually prices stabilised. But it was not to last, because it was followed by a still more severe slump in 1929 which caused both arable and pasture land to be taken out of production altogether. Finally in 1931, recognising the farmers' plight, and the need to increase productivity, the National Government (coalition) abandoned its policy of free trade and reintroduced guaranteed prices, first for wheat and later for oats and barley. Meanwhile cattle prices continued to fall, to the extent that by the following year the government was forced to limit beef imports, those from South America being reduced by 10%. Although enough to avert disaster, it did little to restore livestock farming to prosperity. In 1934 the government attempted to remedy the situation by introducing a system of grants to subsidise production costs, initially as a temporary measure although it later became permanent.

---

* And will become more or less universal as a result of the passing of the Land Reform (Scotland) Act of 2016.
† Evident from records which show a reduced area of tillage in all but seven of the forty-four parishes in Dumfriesshire.

This gave added momentum to the switch into dairying, evident from the *Third Statistical Account* where just about every contributor emphasises its importance. Indeed, in most cases more than half the holdings in the parishes were officially classified as dairy farms. As the contributor for Kirkmahoe, writing in 1953 and doubtless speaking for many others, put it: 'Over the past twenty years there has been a great swing away from mixed farming into dairying'.[2] Increased milk production required better marketing, and hence the formation of milk-selling co-operative societies. In order to maintain a balance between supply and demand, they imposed milk quotas on their members who would receive a guaranteed price for milk up to the limit of their quota, any excess being paid at a lower rate. For a time the arrangement worked well enough, but as more farmers turned to dairying the glut of milk forced the co-operatives to undercut each other in their efforts to sell into a buyers' market. Therefore it was decided to place the co-operatives under the control of a central agency which would have overall responsibility for milk marketing. Whereas most would be sold to the main retailers at an agreed price, the rest would go for manufacture. This led to the establishment of the Scottish Milk Agency in 1927. Again the system worked well for a time, but because membership was not obligatory it broke down when other producers started competing with it for the disposal of their milk.

It was now clear that for milk marketing to work properly the Milk Agency would have to be replaced by a statutory body where membership would be compulsory for all milk producers. Further, this body should be given full power to regulate the disposal of milk, to determine by agreement with the wholesalers the amount to be sold to them, and how much should be allocated to the manufacture of butter, cheese and other dairy products. It was also to have a say in controlling imports to ensure price stability. Accepting this, the government passed the Agricultural Marketing Act of 1933 which set up a Scottish Milk Marketing Board with full power to regulate the purchase and sale of milk. Following this, the Board established creameries throughout the country which were responsible, among other things, for the daily collection of milk from each dairy farm in their district. The farmer would receive a monthly cheque for the proceeds of sale, and because it ensured a regular cash flow, as well as a quick and certain profit, it encouraged still more farmers to switch to dairying.

In 1937 the government passed an Agriculture Act which extended price guarantees to oats and barley. It also established a Land Fertility Scheme, which in order to increase its stock-carrying capacity subsidised 50% of the cost of lime and 25% of basic slag applied to pasture land. In 1939, faced with the prospect of war and the need to increase home production, the government passed the Agricultural Development Act. This introduced a system of grants towards the cost of ploughing up old grassland to make good the depression-induced de-cultivation. As in the First World War, the Act required surveys to be made of every holding of five acres or more in order to assess its cropping potential. Specifically, the cultivation officers' remit was to report on the quality of the land, the calibre of the farmer, the type of soil, the acreage under crops and grass, as well as the extent of rat and rabbit infestation (rabbits were an invaluable source of food during the War). Agricultural Executive Committees were appointed for each county to advise and assist the government (or the Department of Agriculture for Scotland) on all aspects of production, with statutory powers to direct land use where necessary.

In early 1940 food rationing was introduced, while the imposition of price controls ensured that it was universally affordable. Where production costs exceeded the stipulated price, subsidies were available. These were set at a level which not only covered the shortfall but allowed farmers sufficient margin to encourage them to maximise production. Additionally they were designed to cushion farmers against any increase in costs, including the statutory wage rises which were periodically awarded to agricultural workers.

But quantity was not an end in itself, because wartime exigencies demanded that production should be concentrated on what was best suited to maintaining the strength of a population on limited rations. Therefore priority was given to cereal production rather than livestock rearing. But because milk was essential to the nation's health (expectant mothers and children were given a free issue of one pint a day), an exception was made in the case of dairying. At the same time, a variable sheep subsidy was introduced to encourage hill sheep farmers to maintain, and where possible increase, current stock levels. This was to be determined according to the ascertained profit (or otherwise) of hill sheep farming each year. It was followed by a hill cattle subsidy, while large areas of marginal land were put down to turnips and potatoes.

Meanwhile the larger houses were requisitioned for a variety of purposes. For example Halleaths was used as an army camp, the troops being billeted in nissen huts in the grounds while the house served as the officers' mess. Later it became a prisoner of war camp. Jardine Hall was one of a number of houses used for convalescing officers, in this case under the direction of the owner Mrs Dorothy Cunningham-Jardine as matron, while Hoddom was used as a hospital. Other houses such as Rammerscales and Raehills accommodated schoolchildren, mainly evacuees from Glasgow and Clydebank, while Comlongan castle was used to accommodate orphans from Dr Barnardo's who were sent there to avoid the air-raids on southern England.

Because so many farm workers were called up for war service (it was only later that farming was classified as a reserved occupation), the government encouraged young women, known as land girls, to join the Women's Land Army with the slogan 'dig for victory'. Alternatively they could join the Timber Corps where they were known as 'lumberjills'. Most came from the cities with little knowledge of the country-side (they would soon learn!), and many were billeted on Dinwoodie Lodge, near Johnstonebridge. Initially voluntary, service with these and similar organisations was rendered compulsory in 1941, and by 1943 some 80,000 young women were working either on farms or in forestry across Britain.

Later, prisoners of war who were considered trustworthy were put to work on the farms. They were graded 'white' in contrast to the hardline Nazis. Classified as 'black', the latter were confined to high security prisons or camps in the more remote places like Shetland. Because Dumfriesshire had five camps – more than any other county in Scotland, there was a readily available supply of prisoner labour. The concentration was deliberate, for the fact that it was a primarily agricultural region meant that it needed a large labour force, while its relative remoteness was a deterrent to aspiring escapists.

The largest prison camp was at the Barony near Parkgate. In 1939 it was taken over by the Ministry of Defence who employed a Jewish pioneer corps to build a hutted encampment, initially for use as a training camp. Later it became a prisoner of war camp, when a double barbed-wire fence was built round the perimeter with guard towers erected at every hundred yards. Initially it served as a transit camp for Italian prisoners of war who were employed in draining the Lochar moss. However in 1944 some 8,000 German prisoners of war, mostly non-commissioned officers captured during the campaign in north-west Europe, were interned there. Because it was classified as a working camp, the prisoners were hired out to work on local farms or in the forestry. The proceeds of hire were applied towards the cost of running the camp, while the prisoners were paid in the form of vouchers which were negotiable at the prison canteen.

As prisoners of war they continued to be employed in farm work and other activities for some years after the War. This provoked complaints from some quarters about the unethical use of 'serf labour'; but in view of the continuing food shortage it was essential for maintaining home production. In any case, the fact that so much of Europe was in ruins and swarming with displaced persons, while hunger was rife, meant that returning combatants found it difficult to re-settle. Therefore it was thought preferable – and in their interests – to organise a controlled release as and when circumstances allowed. On the other hand, those who wished were allowed to remain in Britain. Many did, frequently marrying local girls and becoming integrated into the local community.

INDUSTRY

Dr Singer's observation in the *New Statistical Account* that 'manufactures have never been very extensive in this county'[3] was as true now as it was in the 1830s. In 1958 about 22% of the workforce in Dumfriesshire was employed in manufacturing compared with roughly 40% in Scotland as a whole. Five-sixths were employed in or near Dumfries and Annan, while many worked in the mills at Langholm and in the Sanquhar and Kirkconnel coalmines. Here the escalating demand for coal during the First War was responsible for the sinking of the Tower mine, while the prosperity of the industry is evident from the increase in Sanquhar and Kirkconnel Collieries' workforce to nearly 2,000, with coal production peaking at 3,000 tons a day.[4]

That the good times were not to last is evident from the Sanquhar and Kirkconnel Collieries' Annual Report of 1927. This stated that 'the demand from the home market has not been up to expectation while the foreign markets are either in the hands of other coal-producing countries, or competition has been so keen that uneconomic prices have had to be accepted'.[5] Therefore it was no coincidence that about that time Sanquhar and Kirkconnel Collieries sold its mining interests to William Baird & Co. Later incorporated as Bairds & Dalmellington Ltd, it continued to operate the mines, notwithstanding the adverse trading conditions and the accelerating switch from coal to oil as the principal source of power, particularly in ships. However, following the nationalisation of coal in 1947, the mines were taken over by the newly created National Coal Board.

Despite the soaring costs of production and many other difficulties facing the coal industry, the Board was responsible for excavating three surface drift mines (effectively tunnels cut into the hillside) in Upper Nithsdale, namely Rig in 1948, Roger 1 and 2 in 1950, and 3 and 4 in 1956. Nevertheless the decline in the industry forced the Scottish Division of the National Coal Board to undertake a massive cutback. The first casualty among the Upper Nithsdale pits was Gateside which, victim in particular of the switch from coal-powered to diesel-driven trains, was closed in 1964. It was followed by Rig in 1966, while 1968 saw the closure of Fauldhead 1 and 3, and Roger 3 and 4, although Roger 1 and 2 remained in production until 1980. Yet, in spite of this, the Coal Board opened another pit – the Lady Ann – in 1969 although it was closed in about 1977.

Closely associated with coalmining was a brick-making industry. Although bricks had long been produced locally, the discovery of pockets of clay in 1840, combined with a growing demand for building bricks and tile drains, persuaded the duke of Buccleuch to establish a brick and tile works, known as the Buccleuch Brickworks, in 1852. Later it was acquired by Sanquhar and Kirkconnel Collieries who started up another brickworks at the Fauldhead pit in about 1912, but both have since been abandoned.

Quarrying, on the other hand, has survived in good shape. Although considerably reduced since the nineteenth century when stone was the principal building material, and the demand for gravel for bedding railway tracks was at its height, there are still a number of quarries in operation in Dumfriesshire. One of the largest was the firestone quarry at Gatelawbridge near Thornhill which had a rail link with the Glasgow & South Western Railway. The stone was used in the construction of major public buildings in Edinburgh and Glasgow, as well as in America, Canada and elsewhere. Latterly it was overtaken by the Locharbriggs quarry, and those at Morrinton and Tundergarth.

The quarries at Locharbriggs and Jericho Bridge are primarily a source of aggregates, including sand, gravel and gritstone, as well as cut stone. The main contractors are Tarmac and Hoddam Contracting, the latter operating another quarry at Annan. The cut stone, which is used in the construction of prestigious public buildings, is produced by Stancliffe Stone. Tarmac also operate the Morrinton quarry. Traditionally a source of sandstone greywackes, a type of rock that underlies much of southern

Scotland, it was used in the construction of the Cairn Valley Light Railway, and is now mainly used for roadmaking. Another major company with interests in Dumfriesshire is Breedon Aggregates. It operates sand and gravel quarries at Jericho Bridge, Barburgh Mill at Auldgirth, and Beatttockhill near Moffat.

Dunhouse Quarry Co. Ltd operate the sandstone quarries at Corncockle and Corsehill, the one near Templand and the other north of Annan. Stone from Corncockle (where fossilised footprints from an early ancestor of the dinosaur were found) was used in the construction of prestigious buildings in Edinburgh (one being the Caledonian Hotel), Glasgow, London and New York, while the quarry was linked by rail with the Glasgow & South Western Railway. Dunhouse took it over in 1982. But recently it has had to scale down its operations to avoid putting birds off their lay during the nesting season, and production is on hold. The Corsehill quarry, which is adjacent to the former Solway Junction railway, was noted for its fine-grained pinkish sandstone which was much in demand for the construction of major public buildings at home and abroad, one example being the Scottish National Portrait Gallery in Edinburgh. It was closed in about 1946, but re-opened in 1983 following its acquisition by Dunhouse to cater for a renewed demand for the stone.

The quarry at Tundergarth was opened by Grange in 2000 for the extraction of greywacke aggregates, including crushed rock, sand and gravel. In 2011 the company established a ready-mixed concrete plant at Kirkburn on the outskirts of Lockerbie, and is now one of the leading suppliers in north-west England and southern Scotland. In about 2012 it took a lease of the redundant lime quarry at Kelhead where it established a recycling plant and a facility for washing the sand prior to mixing it with concrete. Another quarry was opened at Dalton, but because it was dedicated to supplying building material for the atomic power station at Chapelcross* it has since been closed.

From the 1890s onwards a motor manufacturing industry was established at Heathhall on the outskirts of Dumfries. Among the first was McKinnel's foundry which manufactured farm implements, traction engines and bridges. Between 1905 and 1908, trading under the name of the North British Motor Manufacturing Company, it expanded into motor car production. Unfortunately the cars had defective gearboxes and the company went into voluntary liquidation. More successful was the coach-building firm of J B Penman who produced their first motor car body on an Albion chassis in 1902. In 1947, trading as A C Penman, and by then a specialist

---

* Consisting of four reactors, it was built by the UK Energy Authority to generate electricity for the South of Scotland Electricity Board. Initially it was intended to manufacture plutonium for making nuclear warheads, although it soon turned to producing electricity. Construction work began in 1955 although it didn't become operational until 1959. Latterly it was the scene of a number of accidents, including one fatality. Therefore the United Kingdom Energy Authority decided to close the plant, putting some 650 employees out of work, although it was not decommissioned until 2004.

engineering firm, it took over part of the Rosefield Mills in Dumfries˙ where it manufactured spare parts for Albion lorries and tankers, as well as locomotive turntables,
wagon tippers and cranes.

In 1913 Arrol-Johnston, a car-manufacturing firm based in Paisley, acquired the
farms of Heathhall and Auchencrieff where it established a factory for producing,
among other things, electric cars. It had the distinction of being the first factory in
Europe to replicate the layout of Henry Ford's plant at Highland Park, Michigan,
where he produced his model-T Ford and as such it has been designated a Grade A
listed building. In 1921 Arrol-Johnston established a subsidiary plant at Tongland,
near Kirkcudbright, for the manufacture of the cheaper 'Galloway' model. However
it was closed after only two years when production was moved to the company's plant
at Heathhall. In 1927 the company was merged with Aster of Wembley to become
Arrol-Aster. But the combination of a trade recession and increasing competition for
a sluggish market forced it to scale back its operations, although it continued to trade
until 1931 when the plant was closed.

During the Second War the derelict building was taken over by the Royal Air
Force and converted into a maintenance unit to service the nearby aerodrome. When
the latter was abandoned after the War, the building was acquired by the Edinburgh-
based North British Rubber Company who converted it into a factory for the
production of golf balls, hotwater bottles and flooring material. At that time it had
approximately a 1,000-strong workforce and was the biggest single employer of
labour in Dumfries and Galloway. In 1966 the company was taken over by Uniroyal
(formerly United States Rubber Company) when it branched out into the manufacture of rubber footwear such as wellington boots. In 1987 the business was acquired
by the Gates Rubber Company, an American firm based at Denver, Colorado, which
continues to manufacture similar products. Meanwhile in the early 1960s the redundant airfield[†] was taken over by the Dumfries County Council and developed into the
Heathhall Industrial Estate.

On the eve of the Second World War, Imperial Chemical Industries Ltd established a factory at Drungans on the western outskirts of Dumfries for the manufacture
of gunpowder, which it continued to do throughout the War. After the War it turned
to the production of Ardil, a synthetic fibre made from ground nut waste. Later it
branched out into manufacturing other products such as polyester film, which
it continued to do following its acquisition by Du Pont Chemicals. Latterly the factory
was closed and the building abandoned, although it has since been acquired by the
Health Board for a Scottish Government-funded hospital.

At much the same time as ICI was establishing the factory at Drungans, the
Ministry of Supply was responsible for building another one near the coast between

---

[*] A former woollen mill adjacent to the west bank of the Nith, it was owned by Charteries Spence & Co
who went out of business in 1938, and being a large complex it readily lent itself to subdivision.
[†] This was the former Tinwald Downs where the Dumfries races were traditionally held.

Annan and Powfoot. This was run by its explosives division for the manufacture of high explosives, including TNT, as well as ammunition for small arms, and medium and heavy calibre guns. At its peak it had some 4,000, mainly female, employees on its payroll; but following the post-War slump in demand it was closed down. However it was re-opened in June 1946 when production was resumed for the purpose of supplying much the same products to British and NATO forces, albeit on a smaller scale, with a workforce of between 550 and 600.[6] In 1984 it became part of Royal Ordnance plc when the workforce was further reduced to 190, and the factory was finally closed in the late 1990s.

Further along the coast the Birkenhead-based firm of Cochran & Co established a shipyard at Newbie, on the lower reaches of the Annan, in 1898. During the next three years they built some twenty iron-hulled ships, but in 1901 the shipyard was closed and thereafter the firm concentrated on manufacturing boilers, mainly for ships. During the Second World War it manufactured component parts for the Mulberry harbours which were used in the D-Day landings. By 1961 the factory was employing a workforce of over 700, and it remains a thriving business. In 1967 another engineering firm, J Boyd (Annan) Ltd, established a factory at Annan for the manufacture of cranes, wagon tippers and turntables, first for British Rail and later for the British Transport Docks Board. However it was closed in March 1984 when the company's operations were moved to Carlisle and the premises were taken over by Ker the sawmillers.

Engineering was a comparatively recent innovation at Annan, for apart from textile manufacture its traditional industries included farming, fishing, shipping, bacon-curing (during the nineteenth century), and boat-building. According to the *New Statistical Account* Annan's principal imports included timber, lathwood (or deal) and tar from America and the Baltic, much of the timber being used for ship-building.[7] A logical progression from Annan's traditional boat-building industry, the first reference to shipbuilding occurred in 1817 when John Nicholson was recorded as carrying on business as a shipbuilder at the Welldale yard. Initially his firm John Nicholson & Co. concentrated on building brigs and schooners, and whereas the earlier ones were built of locally produced timber this was later replaced by more durable Canadian timber. In the 1850s the firm switched to building tea clippers, but when they were superseded by steam-powered vessels the business went into decline. In 1867 the firm abandoned shipbuilding to become timber merchants, and later builders' merchants. The premises were eventually taken over by Jewson, while Nicholsons converted their business into the preparation and marketing of seafood.

In 1860 Robert Robinson acquired the Newbie Water Mill which was converted for the milling of oatmeal, and later rolled oats and animal feedstuffs. Later still, trading as R. Robinson & Co, he acquired the Welldale Mill, formerly part of the Nicholson shipyard, for the manufacture of feeding stuffs and pearl barley, subsequently becoming the largest miller of oatmeal in Scotland. When the Newbie Mill was burnt down in 1906, the firm moved its premises to a converted windmill in

North Street where it manufactured 'Provost Oats' a world-famous breakfast cereal. The mill continued in operation until 1946 when it was taken over by Scottish Agricultural Industries, and the site has since become a housing estate.

In 1916 Annan's reputation as a textile manufacturing centre encouraged Wolsey, a Leicester-based hosiery firm, to establish a glove-making factory. This expanded into the manufacture of socks and other articles of clothing. By the 1950s it was employing some 400 people – almost all women, of whom about half worked in the factory while the rest worked from home on contract. Because Dumfries was traditionally the principal hosiery manufacturing centre in the south-west, Wolsey established a factory there as well, and by the late 1950s it was employing about 300 people.[8] When Wolsey closed their Annan factory in 1963, the Dumfries factory took on about a quarter of its workforce until it too went out of business in the late 1990s.

One beneficiary of the closure of Wolsey's Annan factory was Barrie Knitwear, for when it established a factory at Annan in 1964 it took on many of Wolsey's redundant workers. In 1980 it moved its premises to the site of the former railway goods station, by which time it was employing about 100 women. But, like many others, it was unable to compete with cheap foreign imports and was forced to close, when its premises were acquired by the Annandale Observer Group for use as a printing works.

In 1955 Scottish Weyroc established a factory on the site of a former timber yard on the outskirts of Annan for the manufacture of chipboard, or man-made timber. The raw material consisted mainly of forestry thinnings obtained from roughly a 60-mile radius. A large area, it would have included the whole of Dumfriesshire and much of the heavily afforested neighbouring counties. Since it provided a valuable outlet for thinnings which were otherwise unmarketable, the business expanded rapidly to the point where it employed 110 workers and was producing 200 tons of chipboard a week.[9] However the business was eventually closed, and the premises were acquired by Dumfriesshire Caskets for the manufacture of coffins.

Writing in the early 1950s, the contributor to the *Third Statistical Account* for Langholm states that the town comprised five tweed mills, a dyeworks, a skinyard and an engineering workshop,[10] a significant decline from its former fifteen mills. For example, the Meikleholm Mill which had been converted into a corn mill was demolished in 1891, while the Whitshiels Mill was burnt down in 1872 and never rebuilt. Another fire victim was Reid & Taylor's factory, although unlike the Whitshiels Mill it remained in business, while the Byers' Mill was burnt down in 1950. Of the six other mills which were founded on the back of the renewed prosperity of the industry in the 1860s, two were burnt (one under suspicious circumstances prompting allegations of fraud and arson), three were demolished, while the Waverley Mills were taken over by Edinburgh Woollen Mill and have since gone out of production. A sad comedown from the days when Langholm was one of the leading industrial centres in southern Scotland, the more so because the lack of employment opportunities has reduced it to little more than a dormitory town for Carlisle.

On the other hand, carpet-making held its own, thanks mainly to a buoyant domestic market. This more than compensated for the industry's exclusion from the American and Canadian markets following their imposition of a tariff on imported carpets to protect their domestic industry. Notwithstanding that the earlier mills, which supplanted the traditional cottage-based industries, have long since been overtaken by advanced industrialisation, some still survived. One was at Cample mill, near Closeburn, which was converted into a small industrial workshop for manufacturing blankets and cloth.* Similarly Barburgh Mill near Auldgirth. Here an industrial workshop was established for the production of blankets and other woollen goods, although it ceased production in about 1950.[11] Apart from other enterprises based mainly in the principal towns in the region, the undertakings mentioned above broadly represent the extent of Dumfriesshire's industrialisation today.

TRANSPORT

During the First World War railways were vital to the direction of the home front. None more so than the Caledonian which was responsible for transporting iron and steel, and other materials, to the Clydeside shipyards, and for provisioning the Grand Fleet at Scapa Flow. In view of its importance the government ruled that, like troop trains, theirs were to have priority over all other rail traffic. This was the proximate cause of the Gretna rail disaster. A three-train collision, the worst in British railway history – worse in terms of fatalities than the Tay Bridge disaster of 1879 – it occurred at Quintinshill some two miles north of Gretna in the early morning of Saturday 22 May 1915.

Quintinshill was a wayside stop on the Caledonian line consisting merely of a signal box and a couple of loops, or sidings, one beside the northbound line and the other the southbound. According to the timetable, two express trains from Euston were due to leave Carlisle in fairly quick succession, the first which was bound for Edinburgh and Aberdeen being scheduled to leave at 5.50 am, while the other was the 6.05 to Glasgow. Like all express trains they had priority over local ones. Immediately after the departure of the Glasgow express, a local train was due to leave Carlisle for Beattock to connect with the 'Tinto Express' which ran from Moffat to Glasgow. The arrangement was that if the Glasgow express was running late, and the Beattock train left Carlisle before it, then it would be shunted on to a siding at Quintinshill to allow the express to pass.

On this occasion the first of the two expresses – the 5.50 for Edinburgh – left on time and passed Quintinshill without incident. The 6.05 for Glasgow, on the other hand, was running late. Therefore the Beattock train left before it. Normally it would have been shunted onto a siding at Quintinshill to let the Glasgow express pass, but

---

* It was later converted into a mill for grinding oats, barley and wheat which was mixed with (mostly imported) maize to produce animal feeds.

it so happened that both sidings were already occupied, the one on the northbound line by a goods train, and the other by an empty coal train. It had been delivering coal to Grangemouth for shipment to the Grand Fleet at Scapa Flow and was on its way back to Pontypool. However it had been diverted on to the siding to make way for a troop train which was due to pass through Quintinshill on the southbound line at any minute. Having left Larbert at 4.00 am, the troop train was transporting the Leith battalion of the Royal Scots to Liverpool for embarkation to the Dardanelles, and in accordance with the government directive it had priority over all other rail traffic.

Since both sidings were occupied, the Beattock train was temporarily shunted on to the southbound line to let the Glasgow express pass. After that it would be shunted back on to the northbound line to continue its journey leaving the southbound line clear for the troop train. This should have been a straightforward enough operation, except that contrary to expectation the troop train was due to arrive at Quintinshill before the Glasgow express. Since the Beattock train, being parked on the southbound line, was blocking the way, the troop train had to be stopped until the Glasgow train had passed to allow the Beattock train to be shunted back on to the northbound line.

Therefore the signalman raised the signal on the southbound line to the stop position. But culpably he omitted to put a collar on the lever operating the signal which would have prevented it from being lowered. At that point his shift came to an end, but he failed to put the relief signalman fully in the picture. Although the latter had just travelled on the Beattock train from his home in Gretna, the fact that it was parked out of sight of the signalbox meant that, equally culpably, he forgot all about it. Therefore when the troop train approached at an estimated seventy miles an hour, he lowered the signal by means of the uncollared lever to let it pass. And it was only as it roared past the signalbox that he remembered the Beattock train. But it was too late. Although the driver of the troop train had seen the Beattock train ahead of him, he was unable to stop in time and the train went crashing into it, he and the fireman being killed instantly.

The Beattock train was pushed back about a hundred yards, the engine was derailed while the rear carriages and the guard's van were uncoupled and rolled back another fifty yards or so to safety. The troop train fared worse. The engine was thrown on to its side across the northbound track, while the carriages, many of them crushed by the impact, were spread higgledy-piggledy across both tracks, many of the soldiers being trapped inside. At that point the Glasgow express came hurtling along the line at full speed. As soon as he saw it, the guard on the Beattock train whose van had been pushed back along the southbound track made a desperate attempt to flag it down. The driver tried to stop. But it was too late, and like a giant battering ram the express went ploughing into the wreckage of the troop train.

The confusion was indescribable as the engines and carriages were pushed on top of each other. Live coals ejected from the engines set the wooden carriages alight, and when the gas canisters supplying the interior lamps started exploding it became a raging inferno, burning alive the soldiers trapped inside their carriages. Those who managed to extricate themselves made desperate efforts to free their comrades, but it was to no avail and they perished excruciatingly in the flames, some shot by their officers to spare them the agonies of incineration.

Local doctors and nurses quickly arrived on the scene. But another hour and a half elapsed before an emergency train arrived from Carlisle bringing ambulance staff and equipment, and more doctors. Meanwhile it took the Carlisle fire brigade upwards of three hours to reach the scene. This was because nobody thought to warn them until a sailor, who had been on the Glasgow express and survived unscathed, hitched a lift to Carlisle and reported the accident to the duty officer at the Central Police Station. He immediately telephoned the fire brigade who rushed to the scene. But such was the intensity of the blaze that, when they finally succeeded in putting it out, it took nearly twenty-four hours for the wreckage to cool sufficiently for the breakdown gangs to start removing the debris.

Altogether there were 226 fatalities – 214 officers and men of the Royal Scots, three railwaymen including the driver and fireman of the troop train, and nine civilian passengers. In addition 246 passengers were seriously injured. Of the Royal Scots only 7 officers, including the commanding officer, and 55 other ranks escaped unhurt or with minor injuries. To compound the tragedy, more than half the survivors were killed at Gallipoli, and by July the combined result of the railway disaster and a series of costly attacks on the peninsula had reduced the 1,028-strong battalion which set out from Larbert on that early summer morning to a mere 174.

A Board of Trade Enquiry was held, and the procurator-fiscal depute at Dumfries ordered the arrest of the two signalmen pending trial. This took place before the High Court of Justiciary in Edinburgh when they were convicted of manslaughter, one being sentenced to eighteen months' imprisonment and the other three years' hard labour. Yet for certain unexplained reasons, which have been the source of much speculation amounting to suspicions of a cover-up, their sentences were remitted the following year and both were re-employed by the Caledonian.

After the War, as the railway companies began to lose out to the bus services, and later private car ownership, they became increasingly reliant on the carriage of goods. It also meant they had to cut costs. This was achieved to some extent by rationalisation and re-grouping. Therefore in terms of the Railway Act of 1921 the Glasgow & South Western, the Caledonian and Highland Railways were amalgamated to form the London Midland & Scottish (LMS), while the east coast lines were merged into the London & North Eastern Railway (LNER). Loss-making services were either reduced or cut back altogether. An early victim was the Solway Junction Railway. In 1921 the viaduct across the Solway was declared unsafe and had to be closed, although it was not dismantled until 1935.* Nevertheless the railway continued to provide a

---

* It continued to be used as a pedestrian crossing by local people to take advantage of the more relaxed English drinking laws, notwithstanding the risk of a heavy fine.

service between Kirtlebridge on the former Caledonian line and Shawhill on the former Glasgow & South Western Railway until 1931 when it was closed to passenger traffic, although it remained open for goods trains until 1939. At much the same time the light railway connecting Leadhills and Wanlockhead with the Caledonian line at Elvanfoot was closed, and similarly the Cairn Valley Light Railway in the 1940s.

Meanwhile the proliferation of bus services posed a growing threat to the railways, the more so because buses were able to deliver passengers more or less from door to door, as well as providing a service to the remoter communities. So although the population was becoming increasingly mobile, it was the bus companies which benefited to the virtual exclusion of the railways. As the contributor to the *Third Statistical Account* for the parish of Westerkirk, writing in 1950, put it: 'less than forty years ago there was no motor car in the parish; now all travelling is done by bus, or by hired or private cars'. At that time, he went on, 'many parishioners had never been in a train and some young people had never even seen one though the nearest railway station was at Langholm, six miles away'.[12]

A drawback to public transport was the poor state of the roads. Whereas the A75 from Gretna westwards was pulverised by heavy army traffic heading for Cairnryan, which was the embarkation point for Northern Ireland, during the Second World War, the A74 remained potholed until the late 1950s. However, in the following decade it was upgraded, with sections realigned to bypass townships on the way, although it was not until later that it was officially designated a motorway. The A75 has also been greatly improved, with sections being straightened out to facilitate the flow of an ever-increasing volume of traffic (mainly Irish lorries) passing along it.

In 1948 the railways were nationalised when they were vested in the British Transport Commission. But this failed to arrest their decline in the face of increasing competition from public transport, private car ownership and road haulage. By 1960 the railways were running at an unsustainable loss. Therefore Dr Beeching was seconded from ICI to become chairman of British Rail (the successor of the British Transport Commission) with a mandate to rationalise the system and cut the losses. His Report, which was published in March 1963, called for the closure of approximately a third of the entire rail network and a like proportion of stations. Almost all his recommendations were adopted, although the Carlisle to Glasgow line was spared the 'Beeching axe' as it was known. So too was the Carlisle–Dumfries–Glasgow line, but not its western extension to Stranraer which was closed in 1965. The line from Dumfries via Lochmaben to Lockerbie was another casualty. Similarly the line to Langholm which was closed to passenger traffic in 1964, although it remained open for goods trains until 1967.

Car ownership began to take off during the 1950s, and has increased exponentially ever since. Similarly road haulage which has almost entirely overtaken the carriage of goods by rail, although this is at the cost of increased traffic congestion, particularly in the south where long delays are almost invariably the norm. On the other hand, mass car ownership has led to a rapid growth of tourism, one of the mainstays of the

Scottish economy. Neighbouring Galloway with its numerous sandy beaches has benefited in particular; but because Dumfriesshire lacks these facilities it has never attracted tourists to the same extent. That said, there are exceptions such as Dumfries itself, while Moffat has long been a popular health resort, and Gretna was a popular marriage venue for eloping couples.

This had been the case since as long ago as 1754 when an Act was passed rendering marriage without publication of banns or other licence illegal in England. Since it did not apply to Scotland, and because Gretna is the nearest Scottish town to England, it was the most convenient place for eloping couples to tie the knot. This remained the situation for nearly two centuries until the passing of the Marriage (Scotland) Act of 1939 which required marriages to be conducted by a minister of religion or a registrar. Even then Scots Law did not require the parents' consent so long as the contracting parties were over the age of sixteen. Consequently eloping couples continued to flock to Gretna to be married, the only requirement being compliance with the residential qualifications. Because ministers generally refused to officiate if they thought the couples were too young to know their own mind, and were reluctant to be a party to flouting their parents' wishes, most runaway couples patronised the registrar instead.

In 1979 the removal of exchange controls, which limited the amount of money that could be taken abroad, meant that people could holiday further afield to places like the Mediterranean resorts and elsewhere, while the advent of cut-price package holidays put them within reach of a much wider section of the population. But flying was not without its risks, and one of the worst examples in recent times was the Lockerbie Air disaster. It occurred on the evening of 21 December 1988 when a Boeing 747 Pan Am flight 103 was on a scheduled transatlantic flight from Frankfurt to London Heathrow, and from there to Detroit via New York JFK. Most of the 243 passengers were American service personnel stationed in Germany who were going home for Christmas, while others had joined the flight at Heathrow. In addition there was a cabin crew of 16 making a total of 270.

Take-off from Heathrow was delayed until 6.25 pm, twenty minutes behind schedule. This was crucial, for had it been on time the explosion would have occurred over the Atlantic and all evidence pointing to the perpetrators would have been lost. As it was, the bomb exploded as the aircraft was approaching Lockerbie at a height of 31,000 feet. At 6.58 pm the air traffic controller at Prestwick saw it appear on his screen as a small green cross, and four minutes later he gave it route clearance. To his surprise the message went unacknowledged, and a few moments later he saw the green cross disintegrate into four or five blips. Almost immediately afterwards, while flying over Carlisle, the pilot of a British Airways scheduled flight from Heathrow to Glasgow reported a huge fire on the ground ahead of him.

The explosion was such as to blow the forward section of the aircraft clean off. The rest of the aircraft hurtled forward under its own momentum, ejecting passengers, their luggage, and much else besides, as it continued for almost a hundred miles along its flight path. At the same time it rapidly lost height until it was over Lockerbie when it went into a nose dive. Hitting the ground at 500 mph, it tore out a large crater in Sherwood Crescent, at the southern end of the town, destroying some of the houses and killing eleven local residents. The 200,000 lb of jet fuel ignited into a fireball which gutted all but one of the remaining houses, scorched traffic passing along the A74 and reduced what was left of the fuselage to a heap of twisted metal.

Some 500 police officers and military personnel were rushed to the scene and carried out a desperate search for survivors. But there were none. Those who survived the initial explosion were killed on impact with the ground. The forward section of the Boeing, which plunged to earth in a field adjacent to Tundergarth church,* was found to contain the bodies of the captain, two members of the crew and several first-class passengers still strapped to their seats. One of the crew members was still just alive, but he died before medical help could reach him.

An accident centre was set up at Lockerbie Academy, and by the following morning more than 1,000 police officers and 600 military personnel had arrived, together with a team of FBI agents sent from the States, to help with the investigation. Once it was clear that there were no survivors, a meticulous search was carried out by the police and military personnel, assisted by volunteers, for every piece of debris in the hopes that something might turn up which could point, however remotely, to the identity of the perpetrators. A huge operation, it involved combing some 800 square miles of south-eastern Dumfriesshire and adjacent parts of northern England. Since it included large areas of forestry, private helicopters equipped with thermographic cameras were called in to assist, and initially hampered by snow and bad weather the search continued for many months.

Every piece of debris recovered was put into a plastic bag, labelled, and taken to the accident centre which had been set up at Lockerbie Academy. There it was X-rayed, checked for evidence of explosives and laid out in the gymnasium. Altogether more than 10,000 pieces were identified and tagged. The fragments of the airliner were taken to a hangar earmarked for the purpose at Longtown where they were examined by inspectors from the Air Accident Investigation Board preparatory to being taken to the Board's headquarters at Farnborough. There a skeleton model of the airliner was built so that, once identified, each piece could be fitted to the appropriate place – an extremely complex operation but vital to the enquiry. Eventually the investigators succeeded in reconstructing almost 85% of the fuselage.

The dead were taken to a mortuary set up in the basement of Lockerbie Town Hall, and after positive identification they were flown back to the States for release to their relatives. But many of the relatives had already flown to Lockerbie in the hopes of identifying their loved ones notwithstanding that the US government had advised

---

* There is a small building within the precincts of the churchyard which serves as a memorial to the victims and where there is a Book of Remembrance containing a photograph and brief biographical details of each of them.

against it, fearing that it would hamper the investigation. Because some of the dead were disfigured beyond recognition, it took time to identify them. But failing to appreciate this, many of the relatives were becoming angry and frustrated. This put the investigators in a difficult position. While anxious to soothe relatives as much as possible, they could only give out a limited amount of information for fear that if they divulged too much it would alert the perpetrators that they were under suspicion. The same was the case with the swarm of news-hungry reporters who had descended on Lockerbie, since they could not be relied on to maintain discretion.

Meanwhile the victims' relatives and friends were interviewed in the hopes of eliciting information which might point to a lead. Because single female passengers were considered the most likely to have been used as an unwitting carrier, as had happened in the past, it was essential to find out who their friends were, and who they had been seeing recently, so that they too could be questioned if necessary. Although a laborious, time-consuming – and frequently invidious – task, it was essential to the investigation. By December 1989 some 14,200 statements had been taken from witnesses, relatives, those who had booked on to the flight but had not boarded it (one of them being a member of the Spanish royal house), and indeed anyone remotely connected with the disaster.

At the same time the search for evidence continued. While sabotage was suspected from the outset, conclusive evidence of a bomb emerged with the discovery of a hole about twenty inches square with traces of explosive which had been blown out of the side of the forward cargo hold. Further evidence pointed to the bomb originating from Malta, while the company which supplied the clothing thought to have been wrapped round it was identified from the remnants of a name tag. When Scottish detectives visited the company they were directed to its principal retail outlet on the island. Here the manager not only remembered selling the clothes but was able to describe the purchaser. On the strength of this the purchaser was identified as Abdelbaset al-Megrahi, the head of security of Libyan Arab Airlines and director for Strategic Studies in Tripoli, and allegedly an officer in the Libyan intelligence service.

In the light of further evidence pointing to the Libyan connection and Megrahi's involvement, the case against him was judged sufficiently strong to warrant his arrest. Similarly that of his associate Khalifah Fhimah, the Libyan Arab Airline's manager at Luqa airport in Malta, and also a suspected Libyan intelligence agent. In November 1991 they were indicted for murder. But first of all, the Libyan leader Colonel Gaddafi had to be persuaded to release them for trial, not easy given the fraught relations which had existed between Britain and Libya since the siege of the Libyan embassy in 1984. Nevertheless in 1999 Gaddafi agreed to release them on condition that they were tried on neutral territory. Therefore it was arranged that the trial should be held at Camp Zeist, a former US air base in the Netherlands, which was declared Scottish territory for the occasion. It was to be conducted by three senior Scottish judges and a fourth non-voting judge, but there would be no jury.

The trial began in May 2000, and the following January the judges issued their verdict. Megrahi was convicted of 270 counts of murder and sentenced to life imprisonment, while his co-accused Khalifah Fhimah was acquitted having produced a cast-iron alibi. Megrahi's conviction was regarded by many as unsafe, and certain perceived weaknesses in the prosecution's case constituted grounds for his unsuccessful appeal, which was heard within weeks of his conviction. In June 2007 the Scottish Criminal Cases Review Commission ruled that further evidence which had come to light warranted another appeal. However in August 2009, while it was still pending, Megrahi was diagnosed with prostate cancer and given three months to live. Therefore the Scottish Justice Secretary authorised his release on compassionate grounds and allowed him to return to Libya. Receiving a hero's welcome, he survived for another two years and nine months until his death in May 2012, protesting his innocence to the last.

Although Megrahi abandoned his appeal (not a condition of his release), there are those who are convinced that he was the victim of a miscarriage of justice, and that had the appeal gone ahead the guilty verdict would have been overturned. In August 2010 they presented a petition to Prime Minister Gordon Brown urging him to order a public enquiry in a final attempt to establish the truth. This was refused on the grounds that it was a matter for the Scottish Executive. But, claiming that it lacked the competence to deal with the international aspects of the case, the latter declined to pursue the matter. Therefore no action was taken.

Nevertheless the doubters refused to give up. In June 2014 they appealed to the Scottish Criminal Cases Review Commission to reaffirm its earlier decision to allow the appeal. However, in November 2015 it ruled – albeit 'with some regret' – that for the reasons stated it was unable to do so. Yet that may not be the end of the matter, because the previous month the Lord Advocate and the US Attorney General issued a joint request to the Libyan authorities for permission to question two suspects in Tripoli. So the saga continues. But with the passage of time, and apparent lack of co-operation from some quarters, it is unlikely that the truth will ever be known.

POLITICS

The fall of Prime Minister Asquith's Liberal government in December 1916 and its replacement by a Coalition under Lloyd George split the Liberal party. Whereas the Liberal Unionist majority supported Lloyd George and the Coalition, the Liberal rump remained loyal to Asquith. Nevertheless, having won the general election of December 1918, called in the aftermath of victory, the Coalition continued to hold office until the Conservatives withdrew from it in October 1922.

Meanwhile in 1918 the two Dumfriesshire constituencies, the burghs and the county, were amalgamated into a single seat. This raised the question of which of the two sitting Liberal MPs – Percy Molteno for the county or John Gulland for the burghs – should be the candidate for the new Dumfriesshire constituency. In the event the choice fell on Gulland. This was keenly resented by Molteno's supporters, and their refusal to support Gulland would have accounted for his defeat by the Conservative Unionist candidate, Major William Murray, at the December 1918 general election. At the next election held in November 1922, following the Conservatives' withdrawal from the Coalition, the Liberals were swept from power, being relegated to third place behind the emerging Labour Party. Nevertheless, defying the trend, the Liberal candidate, William Chapple, was returned as member of Parliament for Dumfriesshire having narrowly defeated his Unionist opponent Henry Keswick.[*]

Following his defeat, Lloyd George resigned the premiership and was succeeded by the Conservative leader, Andrew Bonar Law. His tenure was brief. The following year he was diagnosed with incurable cancer of the throat and resigned without nominating a successor. The most likely candidate was lord Curzon. But he had made too many enemies, and besides it was considered no longer appropriate to have a Prime Minister in the Lords. Therefore the choice fell on Stanley Baldwin, a wealthy Worcestershire ironmaster.[†] The following general election of December 1923 resulted in a 'hung' Parliament with no party gaining an overall majority. When Parliament met, the government was defeated and Ramsay Macdonald, as leader of the next largest (Labour) party, became Prime Minister at the head of a minority government. Meanwhile Dumfriesshire was held by William Chapple with a majority of some 2,000 over his Conservative Unionist opponent Brigadier-General Charteris.

The Labour government lasted a mere ten months. In September 1924 it was defeated on a vote of censure, and at the ensuing general election Baldwin was returned to power, mainly on the strength of a virtual wipe-out of the Liberal party. General Charteris was returned as the member for Dumfriesshire having defeated William Chapple by a substantial majority. This was mainly due to the intervention for the first time of a Labour candidate, Mrs Agnes Dolan, who polled some 6,300 votes almost entirely at the expense of the Liberals. Thereafter the Conservatives remained in power under Baldwin for the next four and a half years. However in May 1929, as the government was approaching the end of its statutory term, Baldwin called a general election. Contrary to expectation, Labour won the largest number of seats. Baldwin resigned, and once again Ramsay Macdonald became Prime Minister at the head of a minority government. Despite his party's eclipse, Dr Joseph Hunter was returned as the Liberal member for Dumfriesshire having defeated General Charteris, while the Labour candidate W H Marwick came in third place.

The Wall Street crash of October 1929 sparked off a worldwide depression, and in Britain unemployment rose to two and a half million. Fears that it could reach three

---

[*]   A director of Jardine Matheson & Co he was a great-grandnephew of William Jardine the co-founder.
[†]   Branded by Curzon in a fit of pique as 'a man of the utmost insignificance', this did less than justice to an extremely astute political operator. His reputation has since been tarnished by his refusal to accept – let alone take any steps to counter – the growing power of Nazi Germany. But his hand was effectively forced because the prevailing anti-war sentiment rendered it politically impossible for him to do otherwise.

million forced the Labour government to resort to drastic measures. Therefore in August 1931, in an attempt to contain the situation, it proposed a wage cut and a reduction in unemployment benefit. This was more than a party which was committed to supporting the workers could stand and nearly half the Cabinet resigned. Therefore, when in September an emergency budget incorporating these proposals was presented to the Commons, most Labour members either voted against it or abstained. The result was that, in spite of being supported by almost all the Conservative and Liberal members, it was passed by a mere fifty votes.

This caused a split within the Labour party, and the ensuing crisis was only resolved when Baldwin and his colleagues agreed to serve in a National government under Macdonald, most of his Labour colleagues having refused to join it. At the general election of October 1931 it was returned to power with a huge majority, and Macdonald retained the premiership despite having cut himself off (with considerable acrimony on both sides) from the Labour party he had done so much to create. Therefore, although he was nominally head of the government, real power was exercised by the Conservatives under Baldwin.

By 1935 Macdonald's powers were visibly failing. In June he was persuaded to resign the premiership in favour of Baldwin who gave him the face-saving appointment of Lord President of the Council. In September a by-election was held in Dumfriesshire following the death of Dr Hunter, when Sir Henry Fildes was returned as the Liberal National member after defeating his Labour opponent John Downie. In October Parliament was dissolved, and at the general election held the following month the Conservatives were returned to power, except this time they found themselves up against a far stronger Labour opposition. Meanwhile Sir Henry Fildes was returned as the member for Dumfriesshire with a substantially increased majority.

In May 1937, having successfully steered the country through the abdication crisis, the seventy-year-old Baldwin resigned. He was succeeded by the marginally younger Neville Chamberlain with whom he had been yoked in uneasy harness ever since he attained the premiership in 1923. In many ways they were exact opposites. Whereas the one was calm to the point of laziness, unflappable and emollient, as well as being a shrewd political operator, the other was abrasive, impatient to get things done, and had an unfortunate knack of rubbing people up the wrong way. Like his father Joseph, Neville Chamberlain had devoted his earlier career to local politics in Birmingham in the course of which he served as mayor.* Therefore it was not until November 1918 that at the age of nearly fifty he first entered Parliament. Within four years he had become Minister of Health and later Chancellor of the Exchequer. Although a man of considerable ability, he has gone down in history as the personification of appeasement of Hitler, notwithstanding that he was supported by most of the establishment at the time.

---

* Prompting Churchill's caustic jibe that he was in the habit of examining world problems through the wrong end of a municipal drainpipe.

Yet in spite of all Chamberlain's efforts to come to an accommodation with Hitler, war broke out on 3 September 1939. On 10 May 1940 he resigned the premiership following a highly critical debate in the Commons on the conduct of the War – the very day the Germans invaded the Low Countries. The arch-appeaser Lord Halifax was his favoured successor. But the situation was so desperate that it called for nothing less than a National government in which all parties – Conservative, Liberal and Labour – were represented. In the event the sixty-five-year-old Churchill emerged as leader – to the horror, it may be added, of many of his own party. In spite of his unrivalled experience of government, having held high office off and on for over thirty years, they regarded him as a maverick, unsound, and altogether unreliable. Not without reason given his controversial track record: he had defected from the Conservatives to the Liberals and back to the Conservatives again, and been appointed to high office under both.

The situation confronting him could hardly have been more daunting. Not only was the country in imminent danger of invasion, but he lacked the support of appeasers like Chamberlain and Halifax, notwithstanding that political considerations dictated their inclusion in his Cabinet. Although his determination to fight on proved abundantly justified, it looked a forlorn hope at the time. So much so that many influential people advocated a negotiated peace with Hitler, who had hinted through intermediaries at a willingness to come to terms. But well aware of how short-lived such an accommodation would be, Churchill would have none of it, and in a series of rousing speeches he galvanised the people into a spirit of resistance. It was a monumental gamble, for no-one knew better than he just how hollow his promises of ultimate victory really were. Still, it was tribute to his leadership that the British managed to hold off the Germans and their Italian allies until Hitler's invasion of Russia in June 1941, and the American entry into the War the following December, rendered the prospect of ultimate victory a reality. Even then it would take four long years to achieve, and at appalling cost.

When it was finally achieved, it was widely assumed that Churchill's success would ensure his return to power at the head of a Conservative government. Wrongly as it turned out. His personal popularity was not enough to prevail against the widespread view that it was time for a change, and at the general election of July 1945 Labour was swept to power on the crest of a landslide victory. A new government was formed under Clement Attlee, and Churchill became leader of the opposition.* Bucking the trend, Niall Macpherson, the Liberal National candidate for Dumfriesshire, gained a majority of upwards of 4,000 over his Labour opponent. Standing as a National Liberal, he held the seat at the general elections of 1951, 1955 and 1959, and despite his political affiliations he gained ministerial office under Harold Macmillan. In 1955 he was appointed Joint Under-Secretary of State for Scotland, Parliamentary

---

*   He eventually regained the premiership in October 1951 and held it until his retirement in April 1955 at the age of eighty.

Secretary to the Board of Trade in 1960, Minister of Pensions and National Insurance in 1962, and finally Minister of State at the Board of Trade in 1963. He resigned his seat in November that year on his elevation to the House of Lords as lord Drumalbyn of Whitesands.

At the ensuing by-election David Anderson, the Solicitor-General for Scotland, won the seat for the Conservatives, one of his opponents being the Scottish National Party's John Gair, the first time the party fielded a candidate in Dumfriesshire. Initially he polled a mere 4,000 votes although he increased it marginally at the next three elections in 1964, 1966 and 1970 when he was replaced by L A B Whitley. Having gained some 9,000 votes at the general election of February 1974, Whitley increased it to an impressive 12,500 at the October election which put him on a par with the Labour candidate (confusingly called Wheatley). After he stood down in 1979 the number of SNP votes fell away under his successors. David Anderson held the seat for only a year. Standing down at the general election of 1964, he was succeeded by Hector Monro* who would represent Dumfriesshire for thirty-three years until his retirement at the general election of 1997. During that time he fought eight general elections,† regularly polling around 20,000 votes, and was eventually appointed Minister of Sport by Margaret Thatcher, fittingly for a former Scotland rugby selector.

Labour's landslide victory in May 1997, and the virtual wipe-out of the Conservative party in Scotland, was enough to win them Dumfriesshire when their candidate Russell Brown, a local man and former branch chairman of the TGWU, was elected to represent the constituency. This was the first time it was held by Labour, and he repeated his success in 2001. On each occasion the runner-up was the Conservative candidate – Struan Stevenson in 1997 and John Charteris‡ in 2001, and regularly gaining a majority of around 10,000 Russell Brown continued to represent the constituency until the reorganisation of 2005.

As a result, Dumfriesshire was merged with Galloway and Upper Nithsdale (represented by the Conservative Peter Duncan) to become the united constituency of Dumfries and Galloway, and the Conservatives adopted Duncan as their candidate. However, at the general election held later that year he was defeated by Russell Brown. Despite Labour's defeat at the 2010 general election, Brown held the seat with an increased majority, again defeating Duncan. The rest of Dumfriesshire was included in the Dumfriesshire, Clydesdale and Tweeddale constituency, its first member being Dumfries-born David Mundell, formerly MSP for South Scotland.

The relatively modest performance by the SNP candidates for Dumfriesshire (apart from Whitley's score of 12,542 in October 1974) was atypical of a party which was gaining ground in Scotland. A strand of nationalism had existed ever since the

---

* Later Sir Hector, and ultimately lord, Monro.
† In 1964, 1967, 1970, February 1974, October 1974, 1979, 1983 and 1992.
‡ Grandson of Brigadier-General Charteris who held the seat from 1924 to 1929.

Union, fuelled by the widely held view that Scotland was betrayed by 'a parcel of aristocratic rogues' (as it was put) into surrendering its sovereignty to become very much the junior partner in an extremely unpopular federation. This is undeniable, although there is still debate in some quarters as to whether or not it was to Scotland's benefit. There were other contributory factors, including in particular an anti-land-lord bias, stemming – at least in part – from the Highland clearances, combined with a perception of landowners as an anglicised upper class, and a growing resentment of private landownership in principle. Although there is no denying the clearances, nor the accompanying hardship and brutality, they were by no means universal, being limited to a minority of admittedly large estates. Nevertheless, applying the particular to the general, social historians have hyped them up to the highly emotive issue it has become.

The Scottish National Party was founded in 1934 following a merger between the National Party* and the pro-Home Rule Scottish Party. But, rather than adopt the National Party's policy of 'self-government for Scotland with independent national status within the British group of nations', the newly founded SNP campaigned for 'a parliament which shall be the final authority on all Scottish affairs'. In early 1945 it gained its first parliamentary seat (Motherwell) at a by-election, but lost it at the general election in July. Throughout the 1950s the party remained in the doldrums, but in the following decade it became more proactive, quadrupling the number of local branches and raising its membership from some 2,000 to almost 120,000. The upsurge culminated in its capture of the traditionally safe Labour seat of Hamilton at a by-election in 1967.

The discovery of oil off the coast of Aberdeen in October 1970 transformed the party's fortunes. Representations were made to the newly elected Conservative government that the oil revenues should be assigned to a special fund for the benefit of the Scottish people. When these were brushed aside, the SNP responded by press-ing for devolution. Therefore a royal commission was appointed under the chairmanship of lord Kilbrandon to put forward proposals for implementing it. Reporting in October 1973, it recommended the establishment of a Scottish Convention consisting of 100 members elected by proportional representation which would be equipped with wide-ranging powers. Additionally there should be a Scottish Cabinet headed by a Scottish Prime Minister, while the office of Secretary of State for

---

*   One of its founder members was a Dumfriesshire man Hugh MacDiarmid (in reality Christopher Murray Grieve) who was a native of Langholm. A stormy petrel, he was a man of extreme political views which were often contradictory and, as it was said, almost entirely devoid of common sense. In 1934 he was thrown out of the National Party because of his Communism, and in 1938 he was thrown out of the Communist Party for his 'nationalist deviation'. Four years later he joined the Scottish National Party calling for 'a native species of fascism' for Scotland and then resigned from it. In 1956 he rejoined the Communist Party at the very time the Soviets were crushing the Hungarian uprising. As it was said, 'His love of bitter controversy, his extravagant invective against the English, and his woolly thinking' were enough to persuade 'many of the more sober-minded Scots [to] condemn the whole case for Scottish Home Rule out of hand'.

Scotland would be abolished. As a *quid pro quo*, there would be a reduced Scottish representation at Westminster.

Meanwhile, following the SNP's by-election victory at Govan in February 1974, pressure for devolution mounted. In late 1977 the Labour government decided to call a referendum, and a bill was introduced into Parliament providing for the establishment of a Scottish assembly with wide powers. But in order for it to pass the Commons the sponsors were obliged to concede that the referendum required the approval of minimum of 40% of the Scottish electorate. When it was held in March 1979 only 32.9% voted for it, and because it was well below the stipulated 40% the bill was dropped.

Refusing to accept defeat, the SNP tried to persuade the Prime Minister, James Callaghan, to railroad the bill through Parliament regardless of the wishes of the electorate. When he refused, its members tabled a motion of censure which the government lost by a single vote. A general election was called and the Conservatives were returned to power under Margaret Thatcher. For the SNP it was a disaster. Their parliamentary representation fell from eleven to two, while their standing in the polls crashed from the mid-30s to a mere 12%. This led to a split between the fundamentalists who argued for a more extreme agenda in order to win over Socialist voters, and the traditionalists who feared it would scare others away.

The issue came to a head at the annual conference in June 1982 when the traditionalists expelled the fundamentalists from the party. They included Alex Salmond although he was allowed to rejoin it the following year. His election as leader in May 1990 gave added impetus to the drive for independence. Nevertheless it was firmly opposed by the Conservative government, although Prime Minister John Major did eventually concede to the extent of allowing the Stone of Destiny, which Edward I had removed to Westminster almost seven hundred years before, to be returned to Scotland. A rather futile gesture which predictably cut no ice with the Nationalists.

Labour's general election victory in May 1997 heralded a more accommodating approach to Nationalist aspirations. Accordingly legislation was introduced which provided for the establishment of a Scottish Executive (later re-named the Scottish Government), in reality a cabinet, headed by a First Minister. Further, there was to be a Scottish Parliament consisting of 129 members, known as MSPs, with a Presiding Officer (effectively a Speaker) to control the proceedings. It was formally opened by the Queen in 1999. Since devolved Scottish government required the creation of new constituencies, Nithsdale was amalgamated with Galloway to form Galloway and West Dumfries. When the first elections to the Scottish Parliament were held in May 1999, the seat was won by the SNP candidate Alasdair Morgan. In 2003 he lost it to the Conservative Alex (now Sir Alex) Fergusson who retained it at the elections of 2007 and 2011. The rest of Dumfriesshire comprised a separate constituency, and at the May 1999 election it was won by the Labour candidate Elaine Murray.

At the first election to the Scottish Parliament Labour held the largest number of seats, and similarly in 2003 when it held fifty seats compared with the SNP's twenty-seven. However in the election of 2007 the latter emerged as the largest party with forty-seven seats as against Labour's forty-six. Consequently Alex Salmond became First Minister at the head of a minority government. At the following election in May 2011 the SNP gained an overall majority with sixty-nine seats. This gave added strength to their campaign for Scottish independence. In 2014 Prime Minister David Cameron introduced legislation giving the Scottish Parliament further devolved powers and providing for a referendum to be held on 19 September. The result was that, in an exceptionally high turnout of 84.59% of the electorate, 55.3% voted 'no' compared with a 'yes' vote of 44.7%. Alex Salmond thereupon resigned as First Minister and was succeeded by Nicola Sturgeon.

For the 'Better Together' campaigners it was something of a pyrrhic victory. In the latter stages of the campaign an opinion poll showing the independence supporters in the lead caused panic in the opposite camp and brought the leaders of the three main political parties hurrying north to Scotland to lend weight to their cause. Heading them was David Cameron who, without parliamentary approval, lavished promises of further devolved powers in a desperate attempt to bring the electors back on side. Therefore, notwithstanding that the vote went against the supporters of independence, he was obliged to make good his promises.

Far from regarding the referendum result as a setback, the SNP continued its campaign for further devolution as a stepping-stone to independence with unremitting vigour. Judging from the opinion polls and their increased party membership, it was extremely successful, notwithstanding the calamitous post-referendum fall in the price of oil on which the economic case for Scotland's independence so largely depends. Yet in spite of this, the success of their campaign was evident from the result of the general election of May 2015 when the SNP gained all but three of the fifty-nine Scottish seats at Westminster, including Dumfries and Galloway where their candidate Richard Arkless defeated Russell Brown. On the other hand, Dumfries, Clydesdale and Tweeddale was retained by David Mundell, and as the only Conservative MP north of the border he was appointed Secretary of State for Scotland.

The SNP success was not repeated to quite the same extent in the Scottish election of May 2016 when they lost six seats, reducing their number to sixty-three – just two short of an overall majority. The Conservatives, on the other hand, gained sixteen seats to end up with thirty-one, thus replacing Labour as the main opposition party at Holyrood. For Labour it was a disaster, and a leading casualty was Elaine Murray who lost Dumfriesshire to the Conservative Oliver Mundell, while Finlay Carson held Galloway and West Dumfries in place of the retiring Alex Fergusson.

Nevertheless the SNP continues to be well entrenched in government, and the cause of Scottish independence remains very much a live issue. The results of the June 2016 referendum, when the question of whether the United Kingdom should remain part of the European Union or not was put to the vote, have given it added momentum. For whereas the country as a whole voted to leave by a majority of 51.9% as opposed to 48.1% on a turnout of 72.2%, Scotland voted to remain by a majority of 62% over 38% on a turnout of 67.2%.

Despite the fact that over a million voted to leave, the SNP are claiming that the Scots are being forced out of the European Union against their will. Accordingly representations have been made to the European leaders entreating that Scotland be allowed to remain in the Union as a separate entity. Despite eliciting professions of sympathy, their appeals have been rejected on the grounds that Scotland is not a separate nation state. But even if they were accepted, the fact that it would require the unanimous consent of all member states, some having already declared their opposition to it, has ruled it out. Instead the SNP are now pressing to secure a place for Scotland in the European single market by joining the European Free Trade Association regardless of whether or not the rest of the UK decides to leave it. But according to constitutional experts, some of them SNP members, the legal, political and technical issues involved would render it almost impossible to achieve.

Meanwhile it is being argued that the outcome of the referendum of whether to stay in or out of Europe constitutes a change of circumstance sufficient to warrant the holding of a second referendum on Scottish independence. Therefore the threat is being used for all its worth to put pressure on the Westminster government to conclude a so-called 'soft' Brexit agreement with the European Union. But it is somewhat vitiated by current opinion polls which show a consistent lack of support for a second referendum, and indeed Scottish independence.

This was reflected in the result of the 'snap' general election of June 2017 when the SNP lost twenty-one of the fifty-six Scottish seats, which although they had enough to give them a majority was nevertheless a significant setback. One of those which changed hands was Dumfries and Galloway where the sitting member Richard Arkless was defeated by the Conservative Alister Jack. Meanwhile David Mundell retained Dumfriesshire, Clydesdale and Tweeddale which he has represented since 2005. Yet in spite of this, the cause of Scottish independence remains firmly on the agenda notwithstanding the continuing – and damaging – uncertainty, until the issue is decided one way or the other. But to separate two countries which have functioned as a single state for upwards of three hundred years raises a host of problems which have yet to be addressed, let alone resolved.

THE LAND

The end of the War brought little relief. There was a continuing food shortage and many of the wartime restrictions remained in place. The plight of Europe was infinitely worse. Since much of the continent had been devastated, and there had been a wholesale requisitioning of livestock from the occupied territories, hunger was rife. Only limited help was available from America which had been the main source of food and raw materials during the War, because most was needed for home consumption. In any case the War had left Britain's finances so depleted that, even if she could import what she needed, she lacked the means to pay for it. Therefore food rationing continued while farmers remained under pressure to maximise productivity.

But life was not easy for them – it never is. This was particularly the case with hill sheep farmers who were badly hit by the winter of 1946–47 which was the worst in living memory. Many sheep perished, and because the arctic weather continued into March, lambing was a disaster. Nevertheless the Hill Farming Act of 1946 gave the farmers some relief by allowing them to reclaim half the cost of improving their holdings, subject to an agreed plan, over a five-year period, the concession being later widened to include upland stock-rearing farms. The Agriculture Act of 1947 ensured the continuation of guaranteed prices and markets for fatstock, cereals, milk and eggs, as well as other farm produce, the price to be determined annually in advance according to prevailing market conditions. Similarly, the premium placed on milk encouraged a further switch into dairying where labour-saving milking machines had become more or less universal. These measures were extended to Scotland by the Agricultural Holdings (Scotland) Act of 1948.

Reflecting the Labour government's bias against landowners, branded by one of its leading members as 'lower than vermin', the 1947 Act gave tenant farmers lifetime security of their holdings regardless of the terms of their leases which were now transmissible to their heirs. Yet at the same time landowners were statutorily obliged to keep their lands properly fenced and drained to enable their tenants to achieve maximum productivity (at least in theory). They were also required to ensure that farm buildings and farmworkers' cottages were brought up to standard, while similar measures applied to local authority and other rented housing The resulting improvements are evident from the contributors to the *Third Statistical Account* which was published in the following decade. Nevertheless there were exceptions. A case in point was the parish of Caerlaverock where it was observed that 'most people have an electricity supply, but there is still no general water supply and some still have to carry it a considerable distance [while] sanitation, though improving, leaves much to be desired'.[13]

The government's attempts to benefit tenant farmers had predictable, if unintended, consequences. For it meant that whenever a tenanted farm became vacant, the landlord would generally put it on the market rather than re-let it. Alternatively he might take it in hand and farm it himself. This had certain fiscal advantages, in that with good professional advice he could generally offset the non-agricultural costs of running his estate, as well as a proportion of his living expenses, against the farm profits for tax purposes. Either way, the rental market virtually dried up and many an aspiring young farmer was denied an opportunity to get on the farming ladder. Other landowners simply cut their losses and, where possible, sold their farms to the sitting tenants. Since it was a buyer's market, farms generally went for a knockdown price which in the light of the subsequent escalation in land values was greatly to the tenant farmers' advantage, while it gave further impetus to the trend towards owner occupancy.

By the 1960s there was a growing feeling that farmers were getting too generous a deal and that only the most glaringly inefficient ones were being dispossessed on grounds of bad husbandry (for which provision was made under both the 1947 and 1948 Acts). Further, that increased productivity was being achieved at too high a price. This was mainly due to the removal of price controls on cereals and food-stuffs, since it meant that farmers could sell their produce in the open market. If the price was below that set by the 1947 Act, as amended from time to time, they would be reimbursed the shortfall, officially termed a deficiency payment. Not surprisingly it was widely felt that farmers were being 'feather-bedded', as it was put – a view which the sight of carparks at the principal markets filled with expensive-looking vehicles, and the well-advertised fancy prices paid for pedigree sheep and cattle, did nothing to dispel.

By this time owner occupancy was becoming the norm, and there were only a few large estates left in Dumfriesshire. In spite of sundry disposals over the years, including in particular its lands in upper Eskdale, Buccleuch Estates was still by far the largest landowner. Coming a long way behind, but still substantial, were the Annandale, Castlemilk, and the Hoddom and Kinmount, estates. In the 1920s part of the Annandale estates in the parish of Hutton and Corrie, amounting to some ten farms, had been sold off, and in 1965 this was followed by roughly a further 23,000 acres in the parishes of Kirkpatrick Juxta and Moffat which had to be sold to meet death duties. Although on the face of it substantial, this consisted almost entirely of hill ground comprising the poorer part of the estates. Another victim of death duties was the Mansfield estates, when those in Dumfriesshire were sold along with Comlongan castle following the death of the seventh earl in 1971.

Farming continued to be profitable until the 1970s when Britain's entry into the Common Market meant that control of its agriculture passed increasingly into the hands of the European ministers and their Brussels-based bureaucrats. The Common Market was established under the Treaty of Rome of 1957 when the Common Agricultural Policy (CAP) was set up to co-ordinate (or in EU jargon 'harmonise') the agricultural industries of each member state into a common entity which would be controlled by a Commission. All internal tariffs were removed to allow the free flow of agricultural produce throughout the Common Market area, while production costs were subsidised to ensure that food was available to the consumer at an acceptable price.

All very well in theory, but it raised a number of difficulties. For example, if the sale price of a particular commodity was driven down through over supply then the cost of subsidising the difference between that and the cost of production was correspondingly increased. Therefore, to avoid this, the Commission would bulk buy that particular commodity, and by creating an artificial scarcity stabilise the price. That at least was the theory, but in practice it resulted in the notorious butter mountains, wine lakes, and the like, which the Commission had to dispose of by selling them outside the Common Market and destroying the rest. Considering that so much of the world's population was living at or below subsistence level, this policy, although perhaps making sense from a strictly narrow view, was in reality quite perverse. It also proved unworkable. Therefore the only answer was to limit production. In the case of milk, for example, this was achieved by imposing a quota on all producers. Consequently many farmers went out of dairying, and because their quotas were marketable they were able to sell them to other dairy farmers enabling them increase their milking herds. The MacSharry reforms of 1992 introduced the policy of set-aside which was designed to reduce production by paying farmers to take arable land out of production for a specified period – again a policy that only made sense from a strictly narrow view.

Finally subsidies were scrapped in favour of direct payments to farmers to compensate them for the excess of production costs over the price to the consumer. Notwithstanding that the result of these measures was to reduce EU expenditure on agriculture to some 50% of its overall budget, it did not go far enough to appease its critics. Ignoring the importance of maintaining a viable farming industry, they took the view that because it did not create jobs, nor offer aspiring young farmers the opportunity of a career in agriculture, the amount of money spent on it was unjustified. The Commission responded by attempting to wrap the industry in the flag of concern for the countryside and the environment generally, effectively going a wishy-washy 'green'.

Faced with the prospect of ten new member states, most of them with large rural populations and many small farmers, joining the Union in 2004, the Commission's agricultural policy was radically altered. Known as Agenda 2000 its objectives included, for example, the improvement of food safety and quality, improvement of the environment (a typically vague concept), and the creation of alternative sources of employment in rural areas. More specifically, the proposals included a 20% reduction in the payment to cereal producers and 30% for beef, both to be phased in gradually. Similarly with dairying where the support price for milk was to be reduced in stages by 10%, although the existing level was pledged to continue until 2006.

In June 2003 agreement was reached on a further package of CAP reforms. These were designed to support farmers but without encouraging them to increase production. In EU jargon the subsidy was to be 'de-coupled' from production. This apparent paradox was to be achieved by introducing a Single Farm Payment Scheme. These reforms came into effect in 2005. But as a nod to the Greens, payment was made conditional on farmers maintaining acceptable environmental, food safety and animal welfare standards – an essentially unquantifiable yardstick. Nevertheless each member state would be allowed to vary the Scheme to suit its particular requirements so long as they conformed to the basic principles established by the EU Commissioners which were mainly to do with the environment.

The result of these measures was to reduce EU expenditure on agriculture to some 40% of its overall budget. But it was still not enough to appease its critics who pressed for more – to the extent that they eventually succeeded in having the agricultural budget capped. Therefore it was laid down that, for each of the years from 2007 to 2013, any increase would be limited to 1% per annum – a fall in real terms after inflation. If the limit was breached, direct payments to farmers would be reduced in proportion. In May 2008, in response to a growing world population, and a possible food shortage, the European Commission introduced a further set of reforms. They included the removal of all tariffs on cereals, the abandonment of arable set-aside, and the scrapping of milk quotas by 2015.

The post-2013 reforms to the CAP stated as a preamble that 'farmers should be rewarded for the services they deliver to the wider public, such as landscapes, farmland biodiversity and climate stability' – high-sounding principles although virtually meaningless in practice. More specifically, they replaced the Single Farm Payment Scheme with the Single Area Payment Scheme so that payments to farmers would depend on both the size and quality of their holding. Member states were enjoined to move towards this method of payment by the start of 2019. Other reforms included the provision of a further Green subsidy which was to come into effect from 2015. This was intended to reward farmers for maintaining permanent grassland, 'ecological focus areas' and (unspecified) 'crop diversification'.

Meanwhile the EU Rural Development Policy continued to be implemented through national and/or regional rural development programmes as before. Perhaps intended more for public relations, and effectively for show, its stated objectives sound less than specific. For example they include such things as 'enhancing farm viability', 'promoting food chain organisations [and] risk management in agriculture', encouraging 'resource efficiency and supporting the shift towards a low carbon and [a] climate resilient economy in agriculture'. On the same theme, and scarcely less nebulous, it was committed to 'promoting social inclusion, poverty reduction and economic development in rural areas'.

Because the effect of the Scheme is to render livestock rearing in the less-favoured areas only marginally profitable, all it will achieve is to encourage farmers to reduce the scale of their operations and cut back production. Given the need to feed a growing world population, this is a classic example of how decisions reached by officials with limited practical experience, or indeed knowledge, can have unintended (and frequently undesirable) consequences. Since the world population is growing exponentially, the time will come when home consumption in third-world countries will take priority over exports. This means that imported foodstuffs will be less readily available, in which case the UK – along with other importing countries – will be forced to rely increasingly on home production. As the need becomes ever more acute, many of the self-indulgent nostrums which restrict farmers' ability to manage their land to best advantage will have to go by the board in the interests of maximising production. But it may be too late, because the continuing drift of people from the landward areas to towns and cities is bound to lead to a shortage of rural-based manpower and a loss of stock management skills.

Looking to the immediate future, the decision to withdraw from the European Union is likely to have a far-reaching effect on the farming industry, if only because it will involve repatriating control from Brussels, and possibly a complete overhaul of the whole structure of support. And if Scotland were to become independent, further comprehensive changes are likely to follow, while the level of support will depend on the state of its finances, which does not augur well for the industry. So, all in all, farmers are facing an uncertain future. Nevertheless, if the worldwide food shortage were to become critical, the powers-that-be will be compelled to face reality and take whatever steps may be necessary to confront the situation. This can only be to the benefit of hard-pressed and over-regulated farmers, ever at the mercy of changing bureaucratically inspired policies and victims of that essentially cyclical industry.

Meanwhile the SNP-controlled Scottish government, dedicated to the principle that 'Scotland's land must be an asset that benefits the many, not the few', has pledged itself to 'return the land to the people'. Although a populist soundbite, the assertion that the land belongs to the few (even if not necessarily to their benefit, despite the popular perception to the contrary) has some basis in fact, since it is claimed (although admittedly without detailed evidence) that half the privately owned land in Scotland is held by a mere 432 people. But 'returning the land to the people', although unexceptionable in theory, will prove difficult, if not impossible, to achieve in practice. Resentment of the concentration of land in the hands of the few has a long history which harks back to Lloyd George's denunciation at the time of the constitutional crisis of 1910–11: 'By what right do ten thousand people own the soil of this land when the rest of us are merely trespassers'.

The Land Reform (Scotland) Act, which was passed by the Scottish Parliament in March 2016, and is to be implemented in stages, attempts to address the issue. But reflecting the inherent difficulties, its provisions are less far-reaching than the recommendations of the Land Reform Review Group in its Report of December 2014, or indeed than the campaigners for a more radical approach would wish. As one of them, welcoming the Group's recommendations, declared: 'Now a revitalised Scottish government can reverse decades of rural stagnation and unfairness, tackle soil degradation and over-grazing, [and] with democratic stewardship and new non-traditional landowners a thousand flowers could blossom'.

Part 1 of the Act obliges the Scottish Government to publish a Statement of Land Rights and Responsibilities based on the principles of human rights, equal opportunities, diversity of land ownership, 'inequalities due to socio-economic disadvantage', and other buzz-words characteristic of civil-servant-speak. Since this requires to be regularly updated, not only is it an ongoing commitment but it also gives the Scottish Government a wide discretion to amend it as they consider appropriate from time to time. In the interests of transparency the Act further obliges Scottish ministers to compile a register of landholders, and those having a controlling – or any other – interest in land. This is to be maintained and regularly updated by the Keeper of the Registers of Scotland and will be available for public inspection.

Landowners are also obliged to consult with their community about decisions affecting their land. Here one can envisage a proposal to establish such things as a factory or a quarry, or even a piggery, or indeed anything that might be regarded as detrimental to the neighbourhood. Like much else in what is essentially an enabling Act, ministers will be given a wide discretion to issue whatever guidelines they see fit. In cases where a landowner for any reason refuses to take the initiative, and where it is considered to be in the public interest to do so, local communities will be entitled to apply to the Scottish ministers (effectively the appropriate government agency) to acquire part or whole of his land to 'further sustainable development' by compulsory purchase, the price to be determined by a government-appointed valuer. This raises a number of questions. How is 'sustainable development' to be defined, where will the money to fund such projects come from, and how will the future running costs be financed, or at least subsidised? This is important because they could be substantial, particularly as experience has shown that such projects almost invariably exceed budgeted costs.

Other provisions include rights of access over land by officially designated core paths. While the overwhelming majority of users exercise such rights responsibly, there are unfortunately a minority who, perhaps unaware that farmers depend on proper stock management for their livelihood, leave gates open or allow their dogs to chase livestock with devastating consequences, particularly during lambing time. Worse still, there are those who, for reasons best known to themselves, and in some cases out of sheer devilment, commit deliberate acts of vandalism.

Part 2 of the Act provides for the establishment of a Scottish Land Commission which is a fully staffed corporate body under the direction of a Chief Executive. Broadly, its function is to advise Scottish Government ministers on all aspects to do with land management. There are five Commissioners (including a Gaelic speaker) and a Tenant Farming Commissioner, while the Commission as a whole will be entitled to acquire and dispose of land, enter into contracts, and generally exercise the wide-ranging powers conferred on it under the Act. To ensure that they are properly qualified for the task, the Act requires that, between them, the Commissioners must be conversant with – and have experience of – a variety of disciplines ranging from law and finance to less specific ones such as human rights and equal opportunities. The Tenant Farming Commissioner, who must have some knowledge and experience of farming, is responsible for the working of the landlord/tenant system, any question of law being determined by the Land Court. In the first instance he is required to draw up a Code of Practice, with full power to vary it from time to time at discretion. This will include such matters as rent reviews, tenants' improvements, compensation claims and the like.

Adopting many of the recommendations put forward by the Agricultural Holdings Review Group, commissioned for the purpose, the Act introduces extensive amendments to the law governing agricultural tenancies. The Group's remit was to recommend whatever changes to the existing system it considered necessary 'to ensure a vibrant future for the [farming] sector', as it was put. The recommended changes include giving tenant farmers the right to assign or bequeath their lease to a wide range of relatives, their spouses and civil partners, while those without a successor will be entitled to sell their tenancies. This means that only in exceptional circumstances will it be possible for landowners to regain vacant possession – unless he were to buy out the tenant's leasehold interest, as provided for under the Act. Since letting a farm would be tantamount to losing possession of it for all time, landowners will understandably be reluctant to do so. Consequently young aspiring farmers will be denied the opportunity to follow the career of their choice. Although the Scottish Government may try to rectify this by forcing the landowners' hand, this will not be easy if for no other reason than that it could risk infringing their human rights. Like much else in the Act, this represents unfinished business. Therefore Land Reform is likely to remain on the agenda for the foreseeable future. Nevertheless, regardless of who owns it and how it is managed, the land will always be there to be enjoyed, relished, appreciated, and hopefully cared for, by countless generations to come.

Notes

ABBREVIATIONS USED IN NOTES

app	Appendix
APS	*Acts of Parliament of Scotland*, 1814–75
CCR	*Calendar of Charter Rolls*
CDS	*Calendar of Documents relating to Scotland*, ed J Bain (Edinburgh, 1881–8)
CPR	*Calendar of Patent Rolls 1399–1441*, 8 vols (London, 1903–7)
Chron Auchinleck	*Auchinleck Chronicle, ane schort Memoriale of the Scottis croniklis for Addicioun*, ed T Thomson (Edinburgh, 1891–77)
Chron Fordun	*John of Fordoun's Chronicle of the Scottish Nation*, Historians of Scotland series, ed W F Skene (Edinburgh, 1871)
Chron Knighton	Henry of Knighton, *Chronicle of Leicester*, part 1
Chron Lanercost	*Chronicle of Lanercost 1272–1346*, trans Sir H Maxwell (Glasgow, 1913)
Chron Melrose	Anderson, A O and M O (eds), *The Chronicle of Melrose*, fasimile edition, 1936
Chron Rishanger	Rishanger, Willelmi, *Chronica et Annales*, ed H T Riley, Rolls series, 1865
Chron Wyntoun	Wyntoun, Andrew of, *The Orygynale Cronykil of Scotland* (ed D Laing), 1872–9
Chron Wyntoun (Amours)	*Orygynale Cronikil of Androw of Wyntoun*, ed F J Amours (Edinburgh, 1907)
Fasti	*Fasti Ecclesiae Scoticanae* (revised and enlarged edition) vol 2 – Synods of Merse and Teviotdale, Dumfries and Galloway (Edinburgh, 1917)
Foedera	*Foedora, Conventiones, Litterae et Cuiuscunque Generiis Acta Publica*, 20 vols, ed T Rymer, Record Commission edn (London (1816–69)
Grey, *Scalacronica*	*Scalacronica by Sir Thomas Grey of Heaton*, trans. Sir H Maxwell (Oxford, 1907)
Reg Hon de Morton	*Registrum Honoris de Morton* (Bannatyne Club, 1853)
NSA	*The New Statistical Account of Scotland*, 1845
OSA	*The Statistical Account of Scotland*, 1791–9

Palgrave, *Docs*	*Documents and Records illustrating the History of Scotland*, ed F Palgrave (Record Commission, 1827–)
PRS	Particular Register of Sasines, Scottish Record Office, HM General Register House, Edinburgh
Rot Scot	*Rotuli Scotiae in Turri Londinensi et in Domo Capitulari Westmonasteriensi Asservati, 1814–19*
RRS	*Regesta Regum Scottorum*, ed. G W S Barrow
RMS	*Registrum Magni Sigilli Regum Scotorum*, ed. J. M. Thompson et al., 1882–1914
SHSMisc	*Miscellany of the Scottish History Society*
Stevenson, *Docs*	*Documents Illustrative of the History of Scotland 1286–1306*, 2 vols, ed J Stevenson (Edinburgh, 1870)
Stones, *Docs*	Stones, E L G (ed), *Anglo-Scottish Relations 1174–1328: Some Selected Documents* (London) 1965
TDGNHAS	*Transactions of the Dumfriesshire and Galloway Natural History and Antiquarian Society*

Notes

CHAPTER ONE

1. J G Callender, 'Dumfriesshire in the Stone, Bronze and Early Iron Ages' *TDGNHAS*, xi (1923–24), 97 et seq.
2. C R Wickham-Jones, *Scotland's First Settlers*, 48
3. Callender, 'Dumfriesshire', 97 et seq.
4. H Mulholland, 'The Microlithic Industries of the Tweed Valley' *TDGNHAS*, xlvii (1970), 81 et seq.
5. Callender, 'Dumfriesshire', 97 et seq.
6. A Moffat, *The British: A Genetic Journey*, 84–5
7. D Maynard, 'Neolithic pit at Carzield, Kirkton' *TDGNHAS*, lxviii (1993), 25 et seq.
8. Wickham-Jones, *Scotland's First Settlers*, 106
9. G Noble, *Neolithic Scotland*, 203
10. J Williams, 'Neolithic axes in Dumfries and Galloway' *TDGNHAS*, xlvii (1970), 111 et seq: F E S Roe, 'The Battle-Axes, Mace-heads and Axe-Hammers from South-West Scotland' *TDGNHAS*, xliv (1967), 57 et seq.
11. A E Truckell, 'A Neolithic Axe Roughout' *TDGNHAS*, xlii (1965), 149 et seq: Roe, 'Battle-Axes etc'.
12. This was the subject of a Channel 4 TV documentary on 10 March 2013. Current

thinking has it that Stonehenge was a healing centre as well as being a religious focal point.

13. Truckell, 'A Neolithic Axe Roughout', 36–7

14. Callender, 'Dumfriesshire', 97 et seq.

15. Moffat, *The British*, 90

16. W F Cormack, 'Prehistoric site at Beckton' *TDGNHAS*, xli (1962–3), 111 et seq: 'Prehistoric site at Kirkburn, Lockerbie' *TDGNHAS*, xl (1961–2), 53 et seq.

17. M Kirby, 'Neolithic, Bronze Age, Anglian and later discoveries at Lockerbie' *TDGNHAS*, lxxxv (2011), 54–7

18. Callender, 'Dumfriesshire', 97 et seq.

19. I Armit, *Celtic Scotland*, 27–8

20. Callender, 'Dumfriesshire', 97 et seq; J C Wallace, 'A burial mound near Gatelawbridge' *TDGNHAS*, xxxii (1953–54), 138 et seq; W Dickie, 'Carigdarroch (Sanquhar) tumuli and others' *TDGNHAS*, i (1912–13), 354 et seq.

21. W F Cormack, 'Prehistoric site at Kirkburn, Lockerbie' *TDGNHAS*, xl (1961–62), 53 et seq; T G Cowie, L J Masters and M Harman, 'An urn burial from Burnfoot Plantation, Dowglen Hill, Westerkirk' *TDGNHAS*, lvi (1981), 31 et seq: R D Oram, *Scottish Prehistory*, 59: Kirby, 'Neolithic discoveries at Lockerbie', 57–9

22. Noble, *Neolithic Scotland*, 90

23. Oram, *Scottish Prehistory*, 49

24. *Ibid*, 49–50

25. Callender, 'Dumfriesshire', 97 et seq.

26. J M Coles, 'Bronze Age metalwork in Dumfries and Galloway' *TDGNHAS*, xlii (1965), 61 et seq.

27. *Ibid*

28. A Robertson, 'Birrens 1962–63' *TDGNHAS*, xli (1962–63), 135 et seq.

29. Callender, 'Dumfriesshire', 97 et seq.

30. *Ibid*

31. P J Ashmore, *Neolithic and Bronze Age Scotland*, 113: A Fenton, 'Plough and spade in Dumfries and Galloway' *TDGNHAS*, xlv (1968), 147 et seq.

32. Noble, *Neolithic Scotland*, 90

33. *Ibid*, 110

34. E Clarson and B Upton, *Death of an Ocean*, 201

35. N Crane, *The Making of the British Landscape*, 158

36. Oram, *Scottish Prehistory*, 62

37. *Ibid*, 56

38. Coles, *Bronze Age Metalwork*; R A Gregory, 'Prehistoric landscapes in Dumfries and Galloway Part 2: Bronze landscapes' *TDGNHAS*, lxxvi (2002), 45 et seq.

39. Moffat, *The British*, 124

40. *Ibid*, 63

41. Ashmore, *Neolithic and Bronze Age Scotland*, 118

42. I Armit, *Celtic Scotland*, 48–9; Ashmore, *Neolithic and Bronze Age Scotland*, 116

43. Callender, 'Dumfriesshire', 97 et seq.

44. Armit, *Celtic Scotland*, 82: TV programme on the Iron Age and the advent of the Celts (Neil Oliver) on 15 April 2011.

45. S P Halliday, 'Settlement, territory and landscape' *TDGNHAS*, lxxvi (2002), 91 et seq; A Wilson, 'Roman and native in Dumfriesshire' *TDGNHAS*, lxxvii (2003), 103 et seq.

46. Oram, *Scottish Prehistory*, 93

47. Gregory, 'Excavation at Hayknowes Farm, Annan' *TDGNHAS*, lxxv (2001), 29 et seq.

48. Armit, *Celtic Scotland*, 73: McCulloch, *Galloway*, 27

49. A Fenton, 'Plough and spade in Dumfries and Galloway' *TDGNHAS*, xlv (1968), 147 et seq.

50. R J Strachan, 'Excavations at Albie Hill, Applegarthtown' *TDGNHAS*, lxxiii (1999), 9 et seq.

51. Armit, *Celtic Scotland*, 75

52. J Murray, 'Archaeological landscapes' *TDGNHAS*, lxiii (1988), 22 et seq.

53. Callender, 'Dumfriesshire', 97 et seq.

54. TV documentaries to do with the Iron Age, 7 and 15 April 2011

55. Callender, 'Dumfriesshire', 97 et seq.

56. Oram, *Scottish Prehistory*, 77

57. A Wilson, 'Roman penetration in East Dumfriesshire and beyond' *TDGNHAS*, lxxii (1999), 17 et seq.

58. E Birley, 'The Brigantian problem and the first Roman contact with Scotland' *TDGNHAS*, xxix (1950–1), 46 et seq.

59. This is the interpretation placed by D Williams on the reference in a Roman text to a Brigantian attack on the '*Genounian* district whose people are subject to Rome' in his article 'The frontier policies of Antoninus Pius in Scotland and Germany' *TDGNHAS*, lvi (1981), 73 et seq.

60. The postulated road system in Dumfriesshire and the surrounding regions is the subject of an exhaustive study by A Wilson whose conclusions are published in his article 'Roman penetration in East Dumfriesshire and beyond' *TDGNHAS*, lxxiii (1999), 17 et seq.

61. R C Reid, 'Notes on Roman roads' *TDGNHAS*, xxxii (1953–4), 73–4

62. Wilson, 'Roman and native in Dumfriesshire' *TDGNHAS*, lxxvii (2003), 103 et seq.

63. P Salway, *Roman Britain*, 211

64. S Foster, *Picts, Gaels and Scots*, 77

65. A W Wade Evans, 'The year of Cunedda's departure for Wales' *TDGNHAS*, xxx (1951–52), 193 et seq.

66. D Brooke, *Wild Men and Holy Places*, 20–2: discussion with P Hill, supervisor of the Whithorn Dig.

67. See A Macquarrie, *The Saints of Scotland*, 117–144 on which this account of Kentigern's career is based.

68. W J Watson, 'The Celts in Dumfriesshire and Galloway' *TDGNHAS*, xi (1923–24), 119 et seq.

69. Macquarrie, A, 'The career of St Kentigern of Glasgow: vitae, lectiones, and glimpses of fact' *Innes Review*, xxxvii (1986), cap XXXII.

70. P Hill, *Whithorn and St Ninian*, 37

71. L Laing, 'The Angles and the Mote of Mark' *TDGNHAS*, 1 (1973), 39–40

72. Conversation with Professor Oram

73. See Brooke, *Wild Men and Holy Places*, 35 et seq.

74. R G Collingwood, 'The Ruthwell Cross' *TDGNHAS*, vii (1919–20), 97 et seq.

75. Kirby, 'Neolithic discoveries at Lockerbie', 60

76. R C Reid, 'Applegarth before the thirteenth century' *TDGNHAS*, viii (1920–1), 161

77. A A M Duncan, *Scotland: the Making of the Kingdom*, 79

78. Sir F Stenton, *Anglo-Saxon England*, 320

79. G Fellows-Jensen, *Scandinavian place-names in Dumfries and Galloway*, 80

80. R A Dodgshon, *Land and Society in Early Scotland*, 54

81. *Ibid*, 92

82. *Symeon of Durham*, 1, 208–9

83. Stenton, *Anglo-Saxon England*, 332, 340

84. *Ibid*, 359

CHAPTER TWO

1. The suggestion that the people of Galloway prevented the Strathclyde Britons from advancing beyond the Urr comes from Daphne Brooke's *Wild Men and Holy Places*, 71 where she bases her hypothesis on R D Oram's PhD thesis, 'The Lordship of Galloway 1000–1250' (St Andrews University, 1991)

2. R C Reid, 'The feudalisation of Lower Nithsdale' *TDGNHAS*, xxxiv (1955–6), 102

3. J G Scott, 'The partition of a kingdom – Strathclyde 1092–1153' *TDGNHAS*, lxxii (1997), 11 et seq.

4. G W S Barrow, *Kingship and Unity*, 11

5. G W S Barrow, *Anglo-Norman Era*, 32–4

6. Barrow, *Kingship and Unity*, 11

7. W T McIntire, 'Historical relations between Dumfriesshire and Cumberland' *TDGNHAS*, xxi (1936–8), p 74

8. *Ibid*, 18, 19, 21

9. See Barrow, *Kingship and Unity*, 8

10. Hereford, Shrewsbury and Chester which were committed respectively to William fitzOsbern, Roger Montgomery and the Conqueror's nephew Hugh d'Avranches who was created earl of Chester.

11. Scott, 'The partition of a kingdom', 19

12. Duncan, *Scotland*, 134

13. Scott, 'The partition of a kingdom', 28

14. *Ibid*, 28 and 207

15. According to R L G Ritchie, *The Normans in Scotland*, 69, the granting of the charter of Annandale to Robert de Brus in c.1124 was merely giving formal recognition to a situation that already existed.

16. Reid, 'Applegarth', 161

17. Ritchie, *The Normans in Scotland*, 44–7 and 299–304n

18. Reid, 'Applegarth', 161–2

19. G Neilson and G Donaldson, 'Guisborough and the Annandale Churches' *TDGNHAS*, xxxii (1954–5), 142 et seq.

20. *RMS* I, app i, 94

21. Examples are cited in W McDowall, *Dumfries*, 249

22. T McMichael, 'The feudal family of de Soulis' *TDGNHAS*, xxvi (1947–8), 163

23. R C Reid, 'Staplegorton' *TDGNHAS*, xxxi (1952–53), 167 et seq.

24. Barrow, *Anglo-Norman Era*, 30, 48–9

25. Duncan, *Scotland*, 442–3

26. Ritchie, *The Normans in Scotland*, 147

27. W E Kapelle, *The Norman Conquest of the North*, 197

28. A C Lawrie (ed), *Early Scottish Charters*, no. LIV, 48–9 where the charter is reproduced in its original Latin.

29. See R C Reid, 'The caput of Annandale and the curse of Malachy' *TDGNHAS*, xxxii (1953–54), 155 et seq.

30. A M T Maxwell-Irving, *The Border Towers of Scotland*, 5

31. Barrow, *Anglo-Norman Era*, 50

32. *CDS* i, 29

33. Reid, 'Staplegorton', 168

34. R M Blakely, *The Brus Family In Engand and Scotland 1100–1295*, 122, 223 app 142 (actually Robert de Hodelme, not William de Carlyle as she claims).

35. *Ibid*, 222, app 132

36. *CDS* i, 607

37. Blakely, *The Brus Family*, 221, app 128

38. Ritchie, *The Normans in Scotland* 217

39. Blakely, *The Brus Family*, 114

40. W Fraser, *The Annandale Family Book of the Johnstones* I, i–iii

41. Maxwell-Irving, *Border Towers*, 191

42. *CDS* i, 700, 704, 705

43. J B Irving, *The Irvings: An Old Border Clan*, 20

44. Maxwell-Irving, 'The origin of the Irvings' *TDGNHAS*, lxxviii (2009), 81 et seq.

45. Irving, *The Irvings*

46. See A S Carruthers and R C Reid, *Records of the Carruthers Family*, 38

47. *CDS* i, 197

48. *Ibid*, 606

49. *Ibid*, 1685

50. Barrow, *Anglo-Norman Era*, 50
51. Blakely, *The Brus Family*, 123
52. Roger de Howden, 'Chronica (732–1201)', W Stubbs (ed), *Rolls Series* no. 51 (1868–71)
53. A A M Duncan, 'The Bruces of Annandale' *TDGNHAS*, lxix (1994), 91–2
54. Blakely, *The Brus Family*, 30
55. *Ibid*, 32
56. *CDS* i, 105
57. *Liber S Mary de Calchou* II, 305
58. *CDS* i, 297
59. *Ibid*, 278
60. *Ibid*, 1683, 1685
61. *Exchequer Rolls* i, p 35
62. Fraser, *The Book of Caerlaverock* I, 586
63. *CDS* i, 1683
64. *Ibid*, 1685
65. R C Reid MSS
66. *CDS* i, 606, 607, 635, 700, 704, 1682
67. G W S Barrow, *The Anglo-Norman Era in Scottish History*, 94
68. R C Reid, 'The de Boys of Dryfesdale' *TDGNHAS*, xxiii (1940–44), 82
69. R C Reid, 'The monastery at Applegarth' *TDGNHAS*, xxxv (1956–7), 14 et seq.
70. *CDS* i, 606, 700, 704, 707
71. *Ibid*, 1682, 1683
72. Barrow, *Anglo-Norman Era*, 154
73. *RRS* i, no 491
74. *CDS* ii, 1985
75. *Ibid*, 225
76. See Maxwell-Irving, *Border Towers*, 143
77. *CDS* i, 1705
78. *Ibid*, 606, 607, 635, 704, 1763
79. *Ibid*, 1705
80. *Ibid*, 223, no 139
81. Blakely, *The Brus Family*, 141 n 45
82. *CDS* i, 635
83. *Scots Peerage* ii, 372
84. Blakely, *The Brus Family*, 144
85. *CDS* i, 606, 635, 700, 704, 707, 1763
86. Maxwell-Irving, *Border Towers*, 238
87. *CDS* i, 1685
88. R C Reid, 'The early Kirkpatricks' *TDGNHAS*, xxx (1951–2), 61 et seq.
89. Fraser, *The Annandale Book* I, ii: Barrow, *The Anglo-Norman Era*, 124
90. Reid, 'The early Kirkpatricks', 61 et seq.

91. *CDS* i, 606, 607, 705
92. *Ibid*, 706, 1680
93. Reid, 'The early Kirkpatricks', 61 et seq.
94. *Ibid*, 606
95. *Ibid*, 607, 700, 704, 707

CHAPTER THREE

1. Reid, 'The feudalisation of Lower Nithsdale' *TDGNHAS*, xxxv (9156–7), 14
2. W A Dodds, *The Medieval Town Plan of Dumfries*, 110
3. *Scots Peerage*, vi, 286
4. *RRS* i, no 230
5. *Ibid*, 267
6. Dodds, *Medieval Town Plan of Dumfries*, 113
7. *Scots Peerage* vi, 286
8. *RMS* I, app i, 94. The deed describes Richard as a son of Dunegal (and Bethoc), which is clearly an error.
9. *Scots Peerage* vi, 287
10. *RRS* ii, no 376, p 363
11. *Scots Peerage* vi, 287: McDowall, *Dumfries*, 17
12. McDowall, *Dumfries*, 17
13. *RRS* ii, no 492
14. *Chron Melrose* lib I, nos 199–201
15. D Hall, 'The rediscovery of Scotland's monastic landscapes: monastic granges in Dumfriesshire and Galloway', *TDGNHAS*, lxxxiii (2009), 55 et seq.
16. J G Scott, 'An early sheriff of Dumfries?' *TDGNHAS*, lvii (1982), 90
17. *CDS* ii, 1606
18. Blakely, *The Brus Family*, 39
19. Duncan, *Scotland*, 174
20. Blakely, *The Brus Family*, 39
21. See R C Reid, 'The early history of Eskdalemuir' *TDGNHAS*, xiv (1926–28), 324–5
22. See J M Gilbert, *Hunting and Hunting Reserves in Medieval Scotland*, 250
23. *Chron Melrose* lib I, p xvi
24. *RRS* ii, no 450
25. *CDS* i, 197
26. *Ibid*, 700, 704
27. *Ibid*, 705
28. *Ibid*, 605
29. *Ibid*, 705
30. *Ibid*, 706
31. *RMS* I, app ii, 1597
32. *Ibid*, 1682

33. *Reg Hon de Morton* I, 3
34. *CDS* i, 1683
35. *Ibid* i, 1680, 706
36. Maxwell-Irving, *Border Towers*, 77
37. See Fraser, *Book of Caerlaverock* i, 1 et seq
38. Duncan, *Scotland*, 309
39. Sir F Powicke, *The Thirteenth Century*, 572–3
40. A O Anderson, *Early Sources of Scottish History* ii, 224
41. *Chron Lanercost*, 367
42. Bower, *Scotichronicon* 5, 325
43. *APS* i, 382
44. *Ibid*, 397
45. *Ibid*, 67
46. *CDS* i, 1683
47. *Ibid*, 605
48. Dodgshon, *Land and Society*, 178–9
49. Blakely, *The Brus Family*, 225 app 153
50. Duncan, *Scotland*, 350
51. J A Symon, *Scottish Farming*, 23–4
52. *CDS* i, 2176: McDowall, *Dumfries*, 36–8
53. *APS* i, 373
54. A R B Haldane, *The Drove Roads of Scotland*, 8
55. *Ibid*, 7
56. Duncan, *Scotland*, 428
57. *Ibid*, 421
58. Bower, *Scotichronicon* vii, 157
59. I F Grant, *Social and Economic Development*, 82–3
60. *Chron Lanercost*, 14–15
61. C Innes, *Scottish Legal Antiquities*, 159
62. *APS* i, 60
63. *Chron Lanercost*, 111–12
64. R D Oram, *Alexander II*, 106
65. *CDS* i, 706, 1680, 1683, 1685; Blakely, *The Brus Family*, 229 no 176
66. Blakely, *The Brus Family*, 228 no 172
67. *RMS* I, app i, 60
68. Maxwell-Irving, *Border Towers*, 209
69. Blakely, *The Brus Family*, 227 app 163
70. Bower, *Scotichronicon* 5, 383–5
71. Duncan, *Scotland*, 400
72. *CDS* ii, 236, 237
73. M Prestwich, *Edward I*, 196

CHAPTER FOUR

1. Stones, *Docs*, no 19, 103–5
2. R Nicholson, *Scotland*, 28
3. M Prestwich, *Edward I*, 76, 318–22
4. Stones, *Docs*, 80–1
5. Palgrave, *Docs*, 118
6. *CDS* ii, 699, 852; Stevenson, *Docs* i 313, ii 348; *CCR* iii, p 295
7. *CCR* iii, p 349
8. *Scots Peerage* ii, 432
9. *CPR* (1292–1301), p 151
10. Bower, *Scotichronicon* 6, p 59
11. *Chron Lanercost*, 135
12. *Ibid*, 140–1
13. Nicholson, *Scotland*, 50
14. *Chron Fordun*, ch. xciv, 319
15. See A Cameron Smith, 'Wallace's capture of Sanquhar and the rising in the south-west', *TDGNHAS*, vol xi, 35
16. Details of Edward's itinerary from 28 March to 22 August are given in Stevenson, *Docs* ii, 25–31 and *CFR* i, 377
17. Stevenson, *Docs* ii, 431: *CDS* ii, 887
18. *Ibid*
19. *CDS* ii, 894: *CPR* (1292–1301), 253
20. *Chron Guisborough*, 295
21. See A C Smith, 'Wallace's capture of Sanquhar and the rising in the South-West', *TDGNHAS*, xi (1923–4), 21 et seq, and W Simpson, 'Sanquhar Castle, *TDGNHAS*, xiv, 335
22. Smith, 'The Estate of Dalswinton', *Ibid* ix (1921–2), 213 et seq.
23. Stevenson, *Docs* ii, 437
24. McDowall, *Dumfries*, 60
25. Stevenson, *Docs* ii, 452
26. *Ibid*, 454: *CDS* ii, 918
27. *CDS* ii, 919
28. Stevenson, *Docs* ii, 475: *CDS* ii, 1055
29. Grey, *Scalacronica*, 20
30. *CDS* ii, 920
31. *Ibid*, 961: *CPR* (1292–1301), p 315
32. Bower, *Scotichronicon* 6, p 85
33. *Chron Guisborough*, 307–8, though the chronicler omits to say which
34. Bower, *Scotichronicon* 6, 93
35. F Watson, *Under the Hammer*, 68
36. *Ibid*

37. *CDS* ii, 1009
38. *Ibid*, 1031, 1033: Stevenson, *Docs* ii, 544
39. Stevenson, *Docs* ii, 555: *CPR* (1292–1301), p 392
40. *Ibid*, 543: *CDS* ii, 1028
41. *Ibid*
42. *CDS* ii, 1949
43. G W S Barrow, *Bruce*, 104: Fisher, *Wallace*, 171–2
44. F Watson, *Under the Hammer*, 74–5
45. *Ibid*, 80–1
46. *Ibid*
47. *CDS* ii, 1088
48. *Ibid* 1067
49. *Ibid*, 1057
50. *Ibid*, 1115
51. Watson, 82
52. Barrow, *Bruce*, 107
53. *CDS* ii, 1101
54. Watson, *Under the Hammer*, 87
55. *CDS* ii, 1011, 1027, 1115
56. Stevenson, *Docs* ii, 590
57. H N Nicolas (ed), *The Siege of Caerlaverock*
58. *Ibid*, 65
59. *CDS* ii, 1162
60. *Chron Lanercost*, 170
61. *CPR* (1292–1301), 529
62. *Chron Rishanger*, 447
63. *Foedera* i, II, 925: *CPR* (1292–1301), 541
64. *CDS* ii, 1170, 1171
65. Stevenson, *Docs* ii, 611
66. *Ibid*, 612
67. *Ibid*
68. *APS* i, 484
69. *CDS* ii, 1334
70. Watson, *Under the Hammer*, 168
71. *CDS* ii, 1356
72. *Ibid*, 1351
73. *Ibid*, 1374: *CPR* (1301–07), 146
74. Watson, *Under the Hammer*, 176
75. *CDS* ii, 1417, 1418
76. Palgrave, *Writs*, 128–31, 133, 134
77. *CDS* ii, 1635
78. *Ibid*, 1646

79. *Ibid*, 1420
80. Watson, *Under the Hammer*, 210
81. *CDS* ii, 1504, Stevenson, *Docs* ii, 647
82. *Ibid*, 1687
83. Stevenson, *Docs* ii, 641: *CDS* ii, 1510
84. *Ibid*, 642
85. *CDS* ii, 1469
86. *Foedera* i, II, 965–6
87. *APS* i, 119–22
88. GWS Barrow, 'Robert Bruce and the Community of the Realm', 198–9

CHAPTER FIVE

1. Palgrave, *Docs*, no 125
2. Bower, *Scotichronicon* 6, p 303
3. *Ibid*, 305
4. *Ibid*, 311
5. Grey, *Scalacronica*, 29
6. See Bingham, *Robert the Bruce*, 120–1, 349 n 48
7. *Ibid*, 122
8. Palgrave, *Docs*, no 150, p 348
9. Stones, *Docs*, 131
10. *CDS* ii, 1754, 1757, 1766
11. *Foedera* i, II, 989
12. Barbour, *Bruce* (MacDairmid and Stevenson) II, 32
13. *CDS* ii, 1807
14. *Ibid*, 1803
15. *Ibid* v, 439
16. *CDS* ii, 1909
17. *Chron Lanercost*, 179–80
18. *CDS* ii, 1893, v, 492: *CPR* (1301–07), p 490
19. *Ibid* i, 1923
20. *Chron Lanercost*, 180
21. *CDS* ii, 1912: *CCR* v, p 490
22. *Ibid*, 1923
23. *Ibid*: Prestwich, *Edward I*, 557
24. *Foedera* II, i, 4
25. *Ibid*
26. *CDS* iii, 80
27. Barbour, *Bruce* (MacDairmid and Stevenson) II, 220–1
28. *Chron Lanercost*, 188
29. *Ibid*, 185, 188

30. Bower, *Scotichronicon* 6, p 343
31. *Ibid*, 345
32. Barbour, *Bruce* (Douglas), 230–2
33. *Rot Scot* i, 77b–78a
34. *CDS* iii, 274, 278, 281
35. *Ibid*, 304
36. Barron, *War of Independence*, 409
37. McDowall, *Dumfries*, 106–7
38. Barbour, *Bruce* (Douglas), 237–40
39. *Ibid*, 244–8
40. *Chron Lanercost*, 204
41. *Vita Edwardi Secundi*, 50
42. Bower, *Scotichronicon* 6, p 363
43. Barbour, *Bruce* (MacDairmid and Stevenson) III, 63
44. *APS* i, 464
45. *RMS* I, app ii, 323
46. *Ibid*, 306
47. *Ibid*, 32: *RRS* V, 66
48. *RRS* V, 20
49. *RMS* I, 34, app ii, 148
50. *Ibid*, app ii, 294, 505: *RRS* V, no. 503
51. *Ibid*, app ii, 303
52. *Ibid*, 33, 91, app ii, 143, 147, 205
53. *Ibid*, app ii, 293, 504
54. *RRS* v, nos 160, 201, 437
55. *RMS* I, app ii, 14, 75
56. *RRS* v, no. 143
57. *Ibid*, no. 166: *RMS* I, app ii, 224, 523
58. *RMS* I, 29, app ii, 143
59. *Ibid*, app i, 58, ii, 305, 354: *RRS* v, 189
60. *Ibid*, app i, 60, ii, 313
61. *Ibid*, app ii, 314
62. *RRS* v, no 404: *RMS* I, app ii, 510
63. *CDS* ii, 1009
64. *Ibid*, 1435, 1481
65. *RRS* iv, p 390
66. *Ibid* iii, 366
67. *RMS* I, 92, 93, app ii, 206
68. *Ibid*, app ii, 301, 534
69. *Ibid*, 300, 533
70. C McNamee, *Wars of the Bruces*, 154
71. *CDS* iii, 543

72. See Hailes, *Annals of Scotland*, 91 et seq

73. E J Cowan, *For Freedom Alone*, 76

74. *Ibid*, 5

75. *CPR* (1317–21), p 562

76. See *Old Statistical Account* vii, 239: *New Statistical Account* iv (Lochmaben), 387

77. *Chron Guisborough*, 240

78. *RMS* I, app i, 38: *RRS* v, 166

CHAPTER SIX

1. *Chron Wyntoun* (Armour) v, 403

2. Bower, *Scotichronicon* vii, 77

3. R C Reid, 'Edward de Balliol', *TDGNHAS*, xxxv, p 40, n 14

4. M Brown, *The Black Douglases*, 34

5. RC Reid, 'The de Boys of Dryfesdale' *TDGNHAS*, xxiii (1940–44), 82 et seq.

6. Brown, 40

7. *CDS* iii, 1109

8. *Ibid*, 1127

9. McDowall, *Dumfries*, 115

10. Reid, 'Edward de Balliol', 60

11. *CDS* iii, 1101

12. Reid, 'Edward de Balliol,' 61

13. *Chron Lanercost*, 290–1

14. *RMS* I, app ii, 813

15. *Ibid*, 805

16. *Ibid*, 803

17. *Ibid* I, 78

18. *Ibid*, 81

19. M A Penman, *David II*, 94

20. *RRS* vi, 282

21. *Reg Hon de Morton* ii, 89, 90, 93

22. I Mortimer, *Edward III*, 217

23. See A A M Duncan, 'A Siege of Lochmaben Castle in 1343' *TDGNHAS*, xxxi, 74–7

24. T Taylor, 'Liddel Strength' *TDGNHAS*, xvi (1929–30), 112 et seq

25. Penman, *David II*, 136–7

26. *RRS* vi, nos 89, 129

27. Bower, *Scotichronicon* vii, 271

28. *CDS* iii, 317–19

29. *Ibid* ii, 1493

30. *Ibid*, 1499

31. *RRS* vi, no 143

32. *Rot Scot* i, 704
33. *Chron Fordun* ii, 359
34. *Chron Knighton* ii, 62. Since he was an English chronicler this is doubtless a gross exaggeration.
35. *Chron Fordun* iv, 359
36. K Jillings, *Scotland's Black Death*, 34
37. Penman, *David II*, 151
38. Bower, *Scotichronicon* 7, p 273
39. *Chron Fordun*, 369
40. J Ritchie, 'The plague in Dumfries', *TDGNHAS*, xxi (1936–8), 91
41. *Ibid*
42. *APS* ii, 46
43. J Thorold Rogers, *A History of Agriculture and Prices in England* vol I
44. Dodgshon, *Land and Society*, 133–4
45. McDowall, *Dumfries*, 124
46. S G E Lythe, 'Economic Life', 84
47. *Rot Scot* i, 752–3
48. Penman, *David II*, 177
49. *RRS* vi, no 153: *RMS* i, app i, 123
50. *CDS* iii, 1593
51. *Ibid*, 1591: *Rot Scot* i, 800
52. *Chron Wyntoun* ii, 485: *Scalacronica*, 304
53. *Chron Fordun* i, p 373
54. Bower, *Scotichronicon* vii, 291
55. Penman, *David II*, 185
56. *Ibid*, 192
57. Bower, *Scotichronicon* vii, 305
58. *APS* i, 492
59. *Ibid*, 397
60. R Nicholson, *Scotland: the Later Middle Ages*, 177
61. *RMS* I, app ii, 1154
62. *Ibid*, 1272
63. Bower, *Scotichronicon* vii, 309
64. *RMS* I, app i, 192
65. *RRS* vi, no 373
66. *Ibid*, 210: *RMS* I, 282, app ii, 1574
67. Penman, *David II*, 403
68. *CDS* iv, 47
69. *RRS* vi, no 363
70. *CDS* iv, 127: *RRS* vi, no 368
71. Penman, *David II*, 376
72. M Brown, *Black Douglases*, 59

73. *RMS* I, 329: *RRS* vi, no 451: *CDS* iv, 100

74. *RSS* vi, no 354

75. Penman, *David II*, 354 (quotation)

CHAPTER SEVEN

1. *Chron Wyntoun* (Amours), vol vi, 264–5

2. R Nicholson, *Scotland*, 187

3. *RMS* I, 457

4. *Ibid*, 585

5. *Chron Wyntoun*, bk IX, chap II, 277: *Scots Peerage* v, 234

6. *CDS* iv, 223

7. *Ibid*, 231

8. D E Easson, 'The Nunneries of Scotland' *TDGNHAS*, xxiii (1940–44), p 191

9. *Ibid*, 192 (quoting from 'Vatican Transcripts').

10. *RMS* I, 488

11. *Ibid*, 590

12. Brown, *The Black Douglases*, 131

13. *CDS* iv, 260

14. *Ibid*, 280

15. See S Boardman, *The Early Stewart Kings*, 118

16. *Ibid*, 125

17. D E Easson, 'The Nunneries of Scotland' *TDGNHAS*, xxiii (1940–44), 190 et seq.

18. *RMS* I, 800

19. Boardman, *Early Stewart Kings*, 198

20. *RMS* I, 362

21. Boardman, *Early Stewart Kings*, 141, 183, 212

22. Brown, *The Black Douglases*, 91

23. *CDS* iv, 512

24. *Chron Wyntoun* xxi, 77

25. Bower, *Scotichronicon* viii, 35

26. Froissart, *Chroniques* ii, 215

27. Bower, viii, 35

28. See Brown, *The Black Douglases*, 103

29. R Nicholson, *Scotland: The Later Middle Ages*, 221

30. Bower, viii, 39

31. Nicholson, 222

32. *Rot Scot* ii, 163–4: *Foedera* viii, 289

33. Boardman, *Early Stewart Kings*, 273

34. Bower, *Scotichronicon* viii, 65

35. Fraser, *Book of Caerlaverock* ii, no. 22: *Scots Peerage* vi, 474

36. *Reg Hon de Morton* ii, no. 216

37. M Connolly, '*The Dethe of the Kynge of Scotis*: A new edition' in *SHR*, 71 (1992), 49–50
38. *RMS* I, 920
39. *RMS* I, 919
40. *Ibid*, app i, 165
41. *Ibid*, app i, 161

CHAPTER EIGHT

1. J J Norwich, *The Popes: A History*, 226
2. Bower, *Scotichronicon* viii, 199
3. *Ibid*, 949
4. Bower, *Scotichronicon* viii, 243
5. *Ibid*
6. *RMS* II, 47
7. *CDS* iv, 1029, 1030
8. *Ibid*, 1032, 1038
9. Brown, *The Black Douglases*, 244; *James I*, 131
10. Brown, *The Black Douglases*, 249
11. *Ibid*
12. *Scots Peerage* v, 426–7
13. Pitscottie, *Historie and Cronicles of Scotland i*, 41–46
14. *Scots Peerage* iii, 219–20 which is less than didactic on this point.
15. Reid, 'The De Boys of Dryfesdale', 82 et seq.
16. *Scots Peerage* iii, 220
17. *RMS* II, 226
18. *Scots Peerage* i, 76
19. *RMS* II, 309
20. C McGladdery, *James II*, 55 (quoting Law, J, *De Cronicis Scotorum brevia*, 1521, Ein. Univ. Lib. DC7, 63, f.128v
21. *Ibid*, 56
22. *RMS* II, 418
23. McGladdery, *James II*, 58
24. *APS* ii, app 31–2, 71–2: *RMS* II, 523
25. *Ibid* chap xx, 88
26. *Ibid*, 90–2
27. *Chron Auchinleck*, f. 1142
28. Nicholson, *The Later Middle Ages*, 411
29. *Scots Peerage* ii, 327
30. *Ibid*, 220: *RMS* II, 790
31. *RMS* II, 564
32. *Chron Auchinleck*, f. 112v – 113r
33. *ER* vi, p 63

34. *Ibid* v, 668–71
35. *Ibid* vi, p, 171
36. *RMS* v, 54: McGladdery, *James II*, 95
37. *CDS* iv, 1288, 1293

CHAPTER NINE

1. *Chron Auchinleck*, 21, 58
2. McDowall, *Dumfries*, 169
3. R Nicholson, *The Later Middle Ages*, 413
4. N Macdougall, *James III*, 77
5. *Scots Peerage* ii, 385
6. Pitscottie, *Historie* I, 171
7. Nicholson, *Later Middle Ages*, 485
8. *Ibid*, 493
9. *RMS* II, 1007
10. *Acts of the Lords of Council*, 60, 95
11. *CDS* iv, 1470
12. Nicholson, *Later Middle Ages*, 476
13. *CDS* iv, 1476
14. McDowall, *Dumfries*, 166
15. *Ibid*, 1603
16. *RMS* II, 1588
17. *Ibid*, 1597, 1594
18. R C Reid MSS
19. *CDS* iv, 1506
20. *Ibid*, 1519, 1520
21. *Ibid*, 1531
22. Macdougall, *James III*, 418
23. Bower, *Scotichronicon* viii, 267, 299
24. See Grant, *Social and Economic Development*, 551–2
25. McDowall, *Dumfries*, 128–9
26. P Hume Brown, *Early Travellers in Scotland*, 27: Grant, *Social and Economic Development*, 555–6: Haldane, *The Drove Roads of Scotland*, 16,
27. A Murray, *Customs Accounts*, 142
28. *Ibid*, 143
29. See A Moffat, *The Reivers*, 66
30. P Dixon, *Puir Labourers and Busy Husbandmen*, 24–5
31. Dodgshon, *Land and Society*, 191
32. Grant, *Social and Economic Development*, 193
33. P Dixon, *Puir Labourers*, 39
34. *APS* ii, 51

35. Dodgshon, *Land and Society*, 134
36. J C Stone, 'The settlements of Nithsdale in the sixteenth century by Timothy Pont' *TDGNHAS*, i (1973), 82 et seq.
37. Grant, *Social and Economic Development*, 193
38. *APS* ii, 36, 144
39. S G E Lythe & J Butt, *An Economic History of Scotland*, 81
40. Gilbert, *Hunting and Hunting Reserves*, 232
41. Dodgshon, *Land and Society*, 176
42. J A Symon, *Scottish Farming*, 66
43. Mair, *History of Greater Britain*, 31
44. R Nicholson, *Scotland: The later Middle Ages*, 261–2
45. Grant, *Social and Economic Development*, 255
46. *APS* ii, 17
47. Grant, *Social and Economic Development*,256
48. Dodgshon, *Land and Society*,101
49. *Ibid*, 134–7
50. G S Pryde, 'The burghs of Dumfriesshire and Galloway' *TDGNHAS*, xxix (1950–51), 81 et seq.
51. McDowall, *Dumfries*, 137
52. Grant, *Social and Economic Development*, 422
53. McDowall, 137
54. W Croft Dickinson, *Scotland from the Earliest Times to 1603*, 234
55. *Ibid*
56. *APS* ii, 178
57. Croft Dickinson, *Scotland from the Earliest Times,* 236
58. *RMS* III, 1652
59. McDowall, *Dumfries*, 222
60. W Dickie, 'Scottish burghal life in the sixteenth and seventeenth centuries', *TDGNHAS*, (second series) vol. xvii, 97
61. Grant, *Social and Economic Development*, 399–400
62. See Croft Dickinson, 245–6
63. Grant, *Social and Economic Development*,557
64. McDougall, *James IV*, 60
65. *Scots Peerage* i, 180–1
66. R C Reid, *Charteris of Amisfield*, 15
67. *Ibid*, 16–17
68. McDougall, *James IV*, 60
69. McDowall, *Dumfries*, 171
70. *Ibid*, 172
71. *Ibid*, 173
72. *Ibid*, 172
73. *Ibid*, 173

74. *Ibid*, 172–5

75. Maxwell, *Dumfries and Galloway*, 155

76. *Ibid*; Carruthers and Reid, *Records of the Carruthers Family*, 62

77. *Ibid*, 176–7

78. *Scots Peerage* vi, 478: Nicholson, *The Later Middle Ages*, 570

79. Wilson and McMillan, *Annals of Sanquhar*, 309

80. McDowall, *Dumfries*, 179

81. See Moffat, *The Reivers*, 145

82. McDowall, *Dumfries*, 179: G M Fraser, *The Steel Bonnets*, 218.

83. *Scots Peerage* i, 240 which asserts that John Johnstone was described as 'sister son' to lord Maxwell.

84. See Fraser, *Steel Bonnets*, 227

85. *RMS* III, 882

86. *Ibid*, 900

87. J Cameron, *James V*, 11: *APS* ii, 325

88. See Moffat, *The Reivers*, 161

89. Fraser, *The Annandale Book* i, 34

90. Cameron, *James V*, 85

91. *Ibid*, 14

92. *Ibid*, 70: Maxwell-Irving, *Border Towers*, 160

93. See G Watson, *The Border Reivers*, 48–9

94. Cameron, *James V*, 79

95. *Scots Peerage* vi, 479–80

96. *RMS* III, 1053, 1054

97. *Ibid*, 1692

98. Cameron, *James V*, 291

99. *Ibid*, 320

100. *Scots Peerage* i, 243

CHAPTER TEN

1. Cameron, *James V*, 255

2. *Ibid*, 258

3. *Ibid*, 262

4. *APS* II, 357–8

5. G Donaldson, *Scotland: James V–James VII*, 53

6. *Ibid*, 133, 135

7. *Ibid*, 47

8. McDowall, *Dumfries*, 240

9. Fraser, *Book of Caerlaverock* ii, 450 (repeated in *ibid* i, 165)

10. *Scots Peerage* vi, 478

11. Maxwell-Irving, *Border Towers*, 71

12. J Macdonald, 'Notes on the Titles of Cowhill Tower', *TDGNHAS*, iii, 225–53: Fraser, *Book of Caerlaverock* i, 594

13. *Scots Peerage* vi, 479

14. *RMS* VIII, 1392

15. Sir P J Hamilton Grierson, 'Some documents relating to Holywood', *TDGNHAS*, vii (1918–19), 168 et seq

16. Fraser, *Book of Caerlaverock* , 174–5

17. *RMS* IV, 1506, 1507 now Baitford, near Penpont.

18. *Ibid* VII, 599

19. Sir W Fraser, *The Scotts of Buccleuch* i, 251

20. *Ibid*, 252

21. *RMS* VII, 290

22. *Ibid* VIII, 145

23. Fraser, *The Scotts of Buccleuch* i, 252–3

24. *RMS* IV, 2311

25. G W Shirley, 'The End of the Greyfrairs' Convent of Dumfries and the last of the Friars' *TDGNHAS*, i (1912–13), p 313

26. *Fasti*, 203, 211, 215

27. *Scottish Historical Society* vol 52 (1973), 118 et seq.

28. M Lynch, *Scotland: A New History*, 188

29. *Ibid*, 203

30. Fraser, *Steel Bonnets*, 260

31. *Scots Peerage* vii, 120–3

32. *Ibid* ii, 468

33. Donaldson, *James V–James VII*, 80

34. McDowall, *Dumfries*, 205

35. *Ibid*, 105–6

36. Fraser, *The Annandale Book* ii, 38–9

37. *Ibid*, 39

38. R C Reid, 'Kirkandrews and the Debateable Land' *TDGNHAS*, xvi (1929–30), p 126

39. McDowall, *Dumfries* 199

40. *Ibid*, 201

41. Fraser, *Book of Caerlaverock* i, 202

42. *Scots Peerage* vi, 480

43. Fraser, *Book of Caerlaverock* i, 203, ii, 472–3

44. Fraser, *Steel Bonnets*, 263

45. McDowall, *Dumfries*, 208

46. Fraser, *The Annandale Book* ii, 44

47. *Ibid*, 45

48. Pitcairn, *Criminal Trials* i, 348

49. See McDowall, *Dumfries*, 215–6

50. Fraser, *Steel Bonnets*, 268

51. McDowall, *Dumfries*, 217
52. *Ibid*, 236–7
53. J J Norwich, *The Popes*, 305
54. W Stephen, *History of the Scottish Church* ii, 18
55. Donaldson, *James V–James VII*, 100
56. See Stephen, *Scottish Church* ii, 5
57. J Knox, *Historie* (eds Thomasson and Pullen) lib I, 343
58. *Ibid*, 353
59. A E MacRobert, 'Lord Herries and Mary queen of Scots' *TDGNHAS*, lxxxviii (2014), 79
60. McDowall, *Dumfries*, 259. This is the substance of an extremely convoluted passage which McDowall appears to have lifted straight out of Knox's *Historie*.
61. I B Cowan, 'The Reformation in Dumfriesshire' *TDGNHAS*, lvi (1981), 12 et seq.
62. *Ibid*
63. Her itinerary is described in detail in Sir Herbert Maxwell's 'The Tour of Mary Queen of Scots in the South-West', *TDGNHAS*, x (1922–23), 84 et seq.

CHAPTER ELEVEN

1. Fraser, *Book of Caerlaverock* i, 30
2. *Ibid*, 243
3. Carruthers and Reid, *Records of the Carruthers Family*, 89
4. Maxwell-Irving, *Border Towers*, 275
5. *Scots Peerage* v, 249
6. See McDowall, *Dumfries*, 270
7. *Ibid*, 271
8. Antonia Fraser, *Mary Queen of Scots*, 148–9
9. Stephen, *Scottish Church* ii, 88–9
10. *Ibid*, 221 (quoting Hessey's *Bampton Lectures*, 269, 270)
11. *Ibid*, 95
12. D M Rose, 'The abduction of a Carlyle heiress' *TDGNHAS*, xvi (1929–30), 42
13. *Ibid*, 45, 47
14. *Ibid*, 48
15. *Scots Peerage* ii, 394
16. Donaldson, *James V–James VII*, 151
17. Stephen, *Scottish Church* ii, 120
18. *Ibid*, 125
19. *Ibid*, 127 (quoting *Calderwood* iii, 577–634: *Book of the Universal Kirk*, 256–8)
20. *Ibid*, 129
21. *Ibid*, 140
22. A E Truckell, 'Early shipping records in the Dumfries burgh records' *TDGNHAS*, xxxiii (1954–5), 132 et seq.

23. Ritchie, 'The plague in Dumfries', 90 et seq.
24. *NSA* (Langholm), 421
25. McDowall, *Dumfries*, 223
26. See D C Herries, 'John Maxwell of Newlaw, sometime Provost of Dumfries', *TDGNHAS*, x (1922–3), 97–102
27. McDowall, *Dumfries*, 228
28. *Ibid*, 222
29. *GRS* xvii, 93
30. P W L Adams, *A History of the Douglas Family of Morton*, 280
31. Fraser, *Book of Caerlaverock* i, 159
32. *Ibid* ii, 486
33. *Ibid* i, 159
34. *Scots Peerage* vi, 479
35. *Ibid* i, 240 (presumed but not certain)
36. Fraser, *Book of Caerlaverock* ii, 457
37. *Ibid*, 459
38. *Ibid*, 462
39. *Ibid*, 479
40. *Ibid*, 466, 478
41. *Ibid*, 475, 477
42. *Ibid* i, 246–7
43. Fraser, *The Annandale Book* i, xc
44. Fraser, *Book of Caerlaverock* ii , 262
45. McDowall, *Dumfries*, 277
46. *Scots Peerage* i, 251
47. Stephen, *Scottish Church* ii, 147
48. *Caerlaverock* i, 278
49. *Scots Peerage* i, 252
50. *Caerlaverock* i, 285
51. *RMS* VII, 217
52. *Ibid*, 481
53. *Ibid*, 650
54. *Ibid* VIII, 228

CHAPTER TWELVE

1. R C Reid, 'The Border Grahams' *TDGNHAS*, xxxviii (1959–60), 86
2. *Ibid*, 105
3. Moffat, *The Reivers*, 41
4. G Watson, *The Border Reivers*, 21
5. Fraser, *Steel Bonnets*, 42–3
6. Watson, *The Border Reivers*, 29

7. Maxwell-Irving, _Border Towers_, 160

8. _Ibid_, 11

9. R C Reid, 'Kirkandrews and the Debateable Land' _TDGNHAS_, xvi (1929–30), 123

10. _Ibid_

11. _Ibid_, 125

12. Fraser, _Steel Bonnets_ <author to confirm>, 129

13. Moffat, _The Reivers_ 263

14. Fraser, _Book of Caerlaverock_ i, 364

15. _Ibid_, 365

16. R C Reid, 'Maxwell of Castlemilk' _TDGNHAS_, xix (1933–35), 187 et seq.

17. D G Mullan, _Episcopacy in Scotland_, 79

18. See Stephen, _Scottish Church_ ii, 177

19. _Ibid_, 164

20. Donaldson, _James V–James VII_, 194

21. Stephen, _Scottish Church_ ii, 165

22. _Ibid_, 163

23. _Ibid_, 173

24. _Ibid_, 175: Donaldson, _James V–James VII_, 202

25. _Ibid_, 179

26. F J Stewart, 'Sweetheart Abbey and its owners over the centuries' _TDGNHAS_, lxiv (1989), 61

27. R C Reid, 'The baronies of Enoch and Durisdeer', _TDGNHAS_, viii (1920–21), 164 et seq.

28. Donaldson, _James V–James VII_, 205

29. _Ibid_

30. Stephen, _Scottish Church_ ii, 206–7

31. _Ibid_, 213–14, 210

32. Donaldson, _James V–James VII_, 313

33. J Dodds, _The Scottish Covenanters_, 29

34. See Donaldson, _James V–James VII_, 332

35. McDowall, _Dumfries_, 403–4

36. _Ibid_, 405

37. Much of the foregoing information is based on Trevor Royle's _Civil War_, 592 et seq.

CHAPTER THIRTEEN

1. F D Dow, _Cromwellian Scotland_, 16

2. _Ibid_, 41

3. _Ibid_, 16

4. Stephen, _Scottish Church_ ii, 323–4

5. Dow, _Cromwellian Scotland_, 44

6. C J Nicholl, 'A Diary of Public Transactions' (_Bannatyne Club_, 1836), 95

7. Dow, _Cromwellian Scotland_, 100

8. *Ibid*, 127

9. Dow, 150, 2: *Scots Peerage* i, 259

10. *Ibid*, 178

11. *Ibid*, 238

12. *Ibid*, 244–5

13. F D Dow, *Cromwellian Scotland*, 265

14. McDowall, *Dumfries*, 421

15. I B Cowan, *The Scottish Covenanters*, 44

16. *Fasti*, 224

17. Donaldson, *James V–James VII*, 365

18. McDowall, *Dumfries*, 428

19. Wilson and McMillan, *Annals of Sanquhar*, 316

20. Cowan, *Scottish Covenanters*, 67

21. *Ibid*, 70

22. McDowall, *Dumfries*, 443

23. *Ibid*, 444–5

24. Stephen, *Scottish Church* ii, 362

25. Donaldson, *James V–James VII*, 389

26. McDowall, *Dumfries*, 445

27. Wodrow, *Sufferings* iii, 37–8

28. McDowall, *Dumfries*, 453–5

29. Stephen, *Scottish Church* ii, 388

30. *Ibid*

31. McDowall, *Dumfries*, 462

32. Cowan, *Scottish Covenanters*, 111–12

33. *Ibid*, 116–17

34. *Ibid*, 118

35. Stephen, *Scottish Church* ii, 396

36. Donaldson, *James V–James VII*, 372

37. M Lynch, *Scotland: A New History*, 295

38. *APS* viii, 461

39. J K Hewison, *Covenanters* ii, 510

40. Donaldson, *James V–James VII*, 382

41. Cowan, *Scottish Covenanters*, 135

42. Stephen, *Scottish Church* ii, 407

43. *Fasti*, 225

44. W Ferguson, *Scotland 1689 to the Present*, 5

45. Cowan, *Scottish Covenanters*, 137

46. *Ibid*, 133–4

47. Stephen, *Scottish Church* ii, 426

48. M Stewart, 'Crime and punishment in the seventeenth and eighteenth century records of Dumfries, Part II' *TDGNHAS*, lxxiii (1999), 195 et seq.

49. H Kirkpatrick, 'Holywood Kirk Session Minutes 1698 to 1812' *TDGNHAS*, lv (1980), 97 et seq.

50. Stewart, 'Crime and punishment'

51. Stephen, *Scottish Church* ii, 460–1

52. A E Truckell, 'Mouswald Kirk Session Minutes 1640–1659' *TDGNHAS*, lxxvii (2003), 168 et seq.

53. Ferguson, *Scotland*, 109

54. J Maxwell Wood, *Witchcraft in South-West Scotland*

55. P G Maxwell-Stuart, *An Abundance of Witches: The Great Scottish Witch-Hunt*

56. Truckell, 'Unpublished witchcraft trials (part II)' *TDGNHAS*, lii (1976–77), 95 et seq.

57. Truckell, 'Unpublished witchcraft trials' *TDGNHAS*, li (1975), 48 et seq.

58. Maxwell Wood, *Witchcraft*, 223

59. *Ibid*, 227

CHAPTER FOURTEEN

1. P Aitchison and A Cassel, *The Lowland Clearances*, 3

2. Wilson and McMillan, *Annals of Sanquhar*, 111–2

3. See R Fiennes, *Mad Dogs and Englishmen*, 265

4. Ferguson, *Scotland*, 87–8.

5. J A Symon, *Scottish Farming*, 103

6. W A J Prevost, 'The Drove Road into Annandale' *TDGNHAS*, xxxi (1952–53), 121 et seq.

7. T C Smout, 'The foreign trade of Dumfries and Kirkcudbright' *TDGNHAS*, xxxvii (1958–9), 36 et seq.

8. A E Truckell, 'Old harbours in the Solway Firth' *TDGNHAS*, lii (1976–77), 109 et seq.

9. C Hill, 'The mechanics of overseas trade: Dumfries and Galloway 1600–1850' *TDGNHAS*, lxxx (2006), 81 et seq.

10. Truckell, 'Some seventeenth century customs and excise records for Dumfries and Kirkcudbright' *TDGNHAS*, lxxv (2001), 173 et seq.

11. P H Scott, *1707: The Union of Scotland and England*, 21

12. G David (ed), 'Letters from Queen Anne to Godolphin', *SHR* xix, 191–2

13. Ferguson, *Scotland*, 49

14. McDowall, *Dumfries*, 508–12

15. Ferguson, *Scotland*, 51

16. M Lynch, *Scotland: A New History*, 313

17. 'Sir John Clerk's observations on the present circumstances in Scotland, 1730', *SHSMisc* x (1965), 192

18. B Lenman, *An Economic History of Modern Scotland*, 61: G S Pryde, *Scotland 1603 to the Present*, 55

19. Ferguson, *Scotland*, 61–2 (quoting from *The Poems of Jonathan Swift* ed H Williams I, 96)

20. McDowall, *Dumfries*, 518

21. *Ibid*, 520–1

22. *Ibid*, 521

23. *Ibid*, 521–2

24. *Ibid*, 530

25. Ferguson, *Scotland*, 67–8

26. McDowall, *Dumfries*, 524–31

27. *Ibid*, 532–8

28. *Scots Peerage* vi, 489

29. *Ibid*

30. See Ferguson, *Scotland*, 183

31. *Ibid*, 182–3

32. T C Smout, 'The foreign trade of Dumfries and Kirkcudbright' *TDGNHAS*, xxxvii (1959), 36 et seq

33. McDowall, *Dumfries*, 515

34. C Hill, 'The mechanics of overseas trade: Dumfries and Galloway 1600–1850' *TDGNHAS*, lxxx (2006), 81 et seq

35. A J Durie, *The Linen Trade*, 15

36. *Ibid*, 13

37. W A J Prevost, 'The Solway smugglers and the customs post at Dumfries' *TDGNHAS*, li (1975)

38. McDowall, *Dumfries*, 555

39. *Ibid*, 515

40. *Ibid*, 515–16

41. *Ibid*, 516–17

42. *Ibid*, 553–4

43. F Wilkins, 'Smuggling in Annandale' *TDGNHAS*, lxxxviii (2014), 99

44. *Ibid*, 88

45. *Ibid*

46. McDowall, *Dumfries*, 556–7

47. M Stewart, 'Crime and punishment in the seventeenth and eighteenth century records of Dumfries, Part II', *TDGNHAS*, lxxiii (1999), 195 et seq

48. Wilkins, 'Smuggling', 87

49. *Ibid*, 90

50. *Ibid*

51. *Ibid*, 103

52. McDowall, *Dumfries*, 582

53. *Ibid*, 580

54. *NSA* IV (Kirkpatrick Juxta), 133

55. W A J Prevost, 'The march of the Jacobites through Annandale' *TDGNHAS*, xlvii (1970), p 186

56. McDowall, *Dumfries*, 584

57. As reported by John Daniel, an Englishman serving with the Jacobite army (see A E MacRobert, *The 1745 Rebellion*, 81).
58. McDowall, *Dumfries*, 586
59. *Ibid*, 594–5
60. *Ibid*, 587–8
61. *Ibid*, 592–5
62. MacRobert, *Rebellion*, 84–5

CHAPTER FIFTEEN

1. A Symson, *A Large Description of Galloway*, 41
2. Haldane, *The Drove Roads of Scotland*, 16
3. *Ibid*, 16
4. *Ibid*, 17
5. Symson, *Galloway*, 41
6. W A J Prevost, 'The Drove Road into Annandale' *TDGNHAS*, xxxi (1952–3), p 122
7. M Lynch, *Scotland: A New History*, 380
8. Prevost, 'Dry stone dykes of Upper Annandale' *TDGNHAS*, xxxiv (1955–56), 84 et seq.
9. *OSA* (Kirkmahoe) ii, 31
10. *OSA* (Kirkconnel) x, 439
11. *OSA* (Mouswald) vii, 292n
12. *OSA* (Dryfesdale) ix, 428
13. *NSA* iv (Kirkconnel), 322
14. *OSA* (Sanquhar) vi, 459
15. J T Johnstone, 'Moffat and Upper Annandale' *TDGNHAS*, i (1912–13), p 96
16. *Ibid*, 210
17. *OSA* (Dryfesdale) ix, 429
18. *OSA* (Hoddom) iii, 356
19. *OSA* (Ruthwell) x, 227–8
20. *OSA* (Lochmaben) vii, 242
21. *OSA* (Gretna) ix, 524
22. *OSA* (St Mungo) xi, 388
23. *OSA* (Caerlaverock) vi, 23
24. R C Reid, 'Some letters of Patrick Miller' *TDGNHAS*, ix (1921–22), 125 et seq.
25. McDowall, *Dumfries*, 631
26. Reid *op cit*: A C Smith, 'The estate of Dalswinton', *TDGNHAS*, ix (1921–22), 213 et seq.
27. *NSA* iv (Closeburn), 82
28. *OSA* (Closeburn) xiii, 242
29. I Donnachie, 'The lime industry in south-west Scotland' *TDGNHAS*, xlviii (1971), 146 et seq.
30. *OSA* (Canonbie) xiv, 417

31. *OSA* (Eskdalemuir) xii, 615–6.
32. *OSA* (Westerkirk) xi, 524.
33. *OSA* (Canonbie) xiv, 418
34. *OSA* (Dornock) ii, 23
35. *OSA* (Dryfesdale) ix, 430
36. J Webster, *Agriculture in Galloway*, 24
37. *OSA* (Johnstone) iv, 219
38. *OSA* (Dunscore) iii, 142
39. *OSA* (Moffat) ii, 285 et seq.
40. *OSA* (Holywod) i, 31
41. *OSA* (Sanquhar) vi, 468–9
42. Reid, 'Some letters of Patrick Miller' *TDGNHAS*, ix (1921–22), 125 et seq.
43. W A J Prevost, 'The Commissioners of Supply for Dumfriesshire' *TDGNHAS*, xxxvi (1957–58), 27 et seq.
44. McDowall, *Dumfries*, 780
45. *OSA* (Dumfries) v, 128
46. A D Anderson, 'The road system in Kirkcudbright' *TDGNHAS*, lxiv (1967)'
47. A D Anderson, 'Some notes on the Old Military Road in Dumfries and Galloway' *TDGNHAS*, lxxii (1997), 79 et seq.
48. *NSA* iv (Mouswald), 447 which states that 'the great post-road from Carlisle to Dumfries and Portpatrick was finished in 1776'.
49. *OSA* (Torthorwald) ii, 6
50. A D Anderson, '"The Old Edinburgh Road" in Dumfriesshire and Galloway' *TDGNHAS*, lxxxiv (2010), p 103.
51. *Ibid*, 104; M Allen, 'Old maps and roads in Nithsdale – with particular reference to Durisdeer' *TDGNHAS*, lxxxvi (2012), 129 et seq.
52. *OSA* (Dryfesdale) ix, 428
53. W A J Prevost, 'Moffat and Beattock Inns, two mail-coach stages' *TDGNHAS*, li (1975), 76 et seq.
54. *Ibid*
55. N and M Miller, 'The Carlisle to Glasgow Road' *TDGNHAS*, lxv (1990), p 100
56. *Ibid*, 100 et seq.
57. *OSA* (Sanquhar) vi, 458n
58. Ferguson, *Scotland*, 193
59. *OSA* (Dumfries) v, 124
60. G W Shirley, 'The Building of Auldgirth Bridge' *TDGNHAS*, xxiii (1940–44), 71 et seq.
61. D C Herries, 'An Annandale minister of the seventeenth century' *TDGNHAS*, vi (1918–19), 30 et seq. This is on the B7076 which runs alongside the M74.
62. *OSA* (Kirkconnel) x, 457
63. *OSA* (Canonbie) xiv, 415
64. Prevost, 'Moffat and Beattock Inns', 76 et seq.
65. *OSA* (Langholm) xiii, 600

66. *NSA* iv (Kirkmahoe), 66
67. *Ibid* (Dalton), 372
68. *OSA* (Dalton) xiv, 102–3
69. T Wilson and W McMillan, *The Annals of Sanquhar*, 182–3
70. *OSA* (Langholm) xiii, 607
71. *OSA* (Dryfesdale) ix, 428
72. SRO, GD 224/522/3
73. RCAHMS, *Eastern Dumfriesshire: An Archaeological Landscape*, 270
74. *OSA* xiv (Canonbie), 415fn
75. RCAHMS, *Eastern Dumfriesshire*, 270
76. *OSA* xiv (Canonbie), 416
77. *OSA* xiii (Kirkpatrick Fleming), 268–9
78. *Dumfries & Galloway Standard*, 1 Sept 1897
79. Watson and McMillan, *Annals of Sanquhar*, 217
80. *Ibid*
81. *Ibid*, 219
82. *Ibid*, 220
83. J C I McConnel, *The Upper Nithsdale Coalworks*, 19
84. *OSA* vi (Sanquhar), 454
85. McConnel, *Upper Nithsdale Coalworks*, 47
86. *Ibid*, 29
87. A R MacDonald, 'The first English ironworks in Scotland?' *TDGNHAS*, lxxiii (1999), 209 et seq.
88. J M Porteous, *God's Treasure House in Scotland*, 38
89. *NSA* (Sanquhar), 299–300
90. R Brown, 'The mines and minerals at Leadhills' *TDGNHAS*, vi (1918–19), 124 et seq.
91. Porteous, *God's Treasure House*, 65
92. *Ibid*
93. *Ibid*
94. A McCracken, 'The Glendinning antimony mine' *TDGNHAS*, xlii (1965), 140 et seq.
95. D G Lockhart (ed), *Scottish Planned Villages*, which is the source of much of the information that follows.

CHAPTER SIXTEEN

1. *OSA* (Morton) x, 155
2. *OSA* (Eskdalemuir) xii,, 611
3. *OSA* (Johnstone) iv, 225
4. *OSA* (Cummertrees) vii, 305
5. *OSA* (Gretna) ix, 525n
6. S G E Lythe and J Butt, *An Economic History of Scotland*, 93
7. *OSA* (Canonbie) xiv, 412

8. *OSA* (Tynron) xiv, 275

9. *OSA* (Kirkmichael) i, 57

10. *OSA* (Middlebie) vi, 60

11. R Wood, *Upper Nithsdale Folklore*, 80

12. *OSA* (Kirkpatrick Fleming) xiii, 259–60

13. *OSA* (Holywood) i, 28

14. Lenman, *An Economic History*, 113

15. *OSA* (Mouswald) vii, 301

16. *OSA* (Hoddom) iii, 355

17. *OSA* (Dryfesdale) ix, 432

18. *NSA* iv (Cummertrees), 251

19. *OSA* (Eskdalemuir) xii, 615

20. *OSA* (Gretna) ix, 531–2n

21. *OSA* (Dryfesdale) ix, 432

22. *OSA* (Sanquhar) vi, 452

23. A McCracken, 'Some poor's house correspondence' *TDGNHAS*, lii (1976–77), 158 et seq.

24. *OSA* (Kirkmichael) i, 59

25. *OSA* (Gretna) ix, 528n

26. G W Shirley, 'Burghal life in Dumfries two centuries ago' *TDGNHAS*, viii (1920–21), 117 et seq.

27. Wilson and McMillan, *Annals of Sanquhar*, 228

28. McDowall, *Dumfries*, 499

29. M M Stewart, 'Crime and punishment in the seventeenth and eighteenth centuries: records of Dumfries' *TDGNHAS*, lxxii (1997), 69 et seq.

30. McDowall, *Dumfries*, 687

31. Stewart, 'Crime and punishment'

32. I Macleod, 'Notices in Scottish newspapers relating to Dumfries and Galloway 1699–1722' *TDGNHAS*, lxxxi (2007), 85–7

33. McDowall, *Dumfries*, 570–1

34. *Ibid*, 597–8

35. *Ibid*, 641–2

36. *OSA* (Dumfries) v, 137

37. A E Truckell, 'Old harbours in the Solway Firth' *TDGNHAS*, lii (1976–77), 109 et seq.

38. *OSA* (Gretna) ix, 524

39. *OSA* (Annan) xix, 449

40. R H Campbell, *Owners and Occupiers*, 143

41. *NSA* iv (Tynron), 476

42. E J Cowan, 'Agricultural improvement and the formation of early agricultural societies in Dumfries and Galloway' *TDGNHAS*, liii (1977–8), 157 et seq.

43. *NSA* iv (Kirkconnel), 321fn

44. *Ibid* (Johnstone), 162

45. *Ibid* (Hutton and Corrie), 539
46. *Ibid*, 552
47. R A Shannon, *Calendar of Annandale Migration*, 2
48. Aitchison and Cassel, *The Lowland Clearances*, 118
49. *NSA* iv (Applegarth and Sibbaldbie), 185
50. *Ibid* (Kirkpatrick Juxta), 127
51. *Ibid* (Middlebie), 368
52. *Ibid* (Canonbie), 498
53. *Ibid* (Kirkmichael), 71
54. See McDowall, *Dumfries*, 182–4
55. *NSA* iv (Canonbie), 492
56. *Ibid* (Holywood), 562
57. *Ibid* General Observations, 573
58. *Ibid* (Kirkconnel), 322
59. *Ibid* (Penpont), 512
60. *Ibid* (Holywood), 561
61. *Ibid* (Middlebie), 368
62. *Ibid* (Cummertrees), 252
63. *Ibid* General Observations, 578
64. *Ibid* (Lochmaben), 390
65. *Ibid* (Caerlaverock), 356
66. *Ibid* (Hutton and Corrie), 541
67. *Ibid* (Dumfries), 20
68. *Ibid* (Hutton and Corrie), 543
69. C J A Robertson, *The Origins of the Scottish Railway System*, 182
70. O S Nock, *The Caledonian Railway*, 17
71. *Ibid*, 31
72. *Ibid*, 37
73. See I Kirkpatrick, *The Cairn Valley Light Railway: Moniaive to Dumfries*.

CHAPTER SEVENTEEN

1. McDowall, *Dumfries*, 782
2. Lenman, *An Economic History*, 196
3. Campbell, *Owners and Occupiers*, 72
4. T M Devine, 'Scottish farm labour' in T M Devine (ed), *Farm Servants and Labour in Lowland Scotland*, 243
5. McDowall, *Dumfries*, 782
6. Campbell, 'Agricultural labour in the south-west' in Devine, *Farm Servants*, 69
7. *Ibid*, 62; Campbell, *Owners and Occupiers*, 90
8. I Levitt and T C Smout, 'Farm workers' incomes in 1843' in Devine, *Farm Servants*, 156.

9. *NSA* iv (Morton), 79

10. Devine, 'Women workers' in Devine, *Farm Servants*, 109, 119

11. Devine, 'Scottish farm labour', 244, 245

12. *Ibid*, 247

13. *Ibid*, 252

14. Levitt and Smout, 'Farm workers' incomes', 156

15. S G E Lythe and J Butt, *An Economic History of Scotland* 1100–1939, 123

16. *Ibid*, 131

17. *Ibid*

18. W Howatson, 'Grain harvesting and harvesters' in Devine, *Farm Servants*, 132

19. McDowall, *Dumfries*, 781

20. *Ibid*, 785

21. *NSA* iv (Sanquhar), 309

22. *OSA* x (Kirkconnel), 450

23. The foregoing information is based on R Simpson's *History of Sanquhar*.

24. *Dumfries & Galloway Standard*, 19 Oct 1879.

25. *Ibid*, 28 Aug 1880

26. *Ibid*, 30 June 1894

27. *Third Statistical Account* (Kirkconnel), 226

28. McConnel, *Upper Nithsdale Coalworks*, 47

29. *NSA* iv (Dumfriesshire), 498

30. *OSA* x (Canonbie), 416–7

31. I Donnachie, 'The lime industry in south-west Scotland' *TDGNHAS*, xlviii (1971), 146 et seq.

32. See I McCracken, 'The Glendinning antimony mine' *TDGNHAS*, xlii (1965), 140 et seq.

33. *NSA* iv (Gretna), 269

34. *Ibid* (Kirkpatrick Fleming), 285

35. See Lenman, *An Economic History*, 120–2

36. *NSA* iv (Annan), 528

37. *Ibid* (Langholm), 424

38. *Ibid* (Wamphray), 148

39. *Ibid* (Canonbie), 497

40. *Ibid* (Penpont), 515

41. *Ibid* (Kirkmahoe), 65

42. *Ibid* (Tinwald), 80

43. Ferguson, *Scotland*, 200

44. *NSA* iv (Hutton and Corrie), 545

45. Ferguson, *Scotland*, 203

46. McDowall, *Dumfries*, 678–9

47. W B de B Nicol, 'The Dumfries and Maxwelltown Mechanics' Institute 1825–1900' *TDGNHAS*, xxviii (1949–50), 64 et seq.

48. G W Shirley, 'Strathspey fencibles at Dumfries in 1795' *TDGNHAS*, iii (1914–15), 96 et seq.

49. A McCracken, 'Notes on the militia raised against Napoleon' *TDGNHAS*, xlv (1968), 228 et seq, and 'Lieutenancy Minutes for the subdivision of Eskdale' *TDGNHAS*, xlix (1972), 84 et seq.

50. J M Forbes, 'French prisoners on parole at Dumfries, Sanquhar, Lockerbie and Lochmaben' *TDGNHAS*, i (1912–13), 247 et seq.

51. *Ibid*, 736

52. *NSA* iv (Dumfries). 8

53. *Ibid*

54. McDowall, *Dumfries*, 743

55. *Ibid*, 818–9

56. Stephen, *Scottish Church* ii, 539–40

57. *Ibid*, 559

58. *Ibid*, 589

59. McDowall, *Dumfries*, 727–8

60. Wilson and MacMillan, *Annals of Sanquhar*, 264–7

61. C Troup, 'Chartism in Dumfriesshire 1830–50' *TDGNHAS*, lvi (1981), 100 et seq.

62. Stephen, *Scottish Church* ii, 596–7

63. *Ibid*, 616 et seq.

64. Stephen, *Scottish Church* ii, 623

65. *Ibid*, 625

66. McDowall, *Dumfries*, 822

67. *Ibid*, 824

68. *Ibid*, 833

69. *Ibid*

70. B Craig, 'Nineteenth century electioneering' *TDGNHAS*, xxvi (1947–48), p 60

71. McDowall, *Dumfries*, 836

72. *Ibid*, 840n

73. *Ibid*

74. *Ibid*, 840–1n

75. *Ibid*, 841n

76. *Ibid*

77. Much of the information about the Jardines and associated families has been gleaned from Maggie Keswick's *The Thistle and the Jade* updated by Clara Weatherall.

CHAPTER EIGHTEEN

1. *Third Statistical Account* (Closeburn), 220

2. *Ibid* (Kirkmahoe), 144

3. *NSA* iv (General observations), 569

4. McConnel, *Upper Nithsdale Coalworks*, 36

5. *Dumfries & Galloway Standard*, 31 Dec 1927

6. *Ibid* (Annan), 265

7. *NSA* iv (Annan), 529

8. *Ibid* (Dumfries burgh), 115, 117

9. Burgh, Parish of Annan (*County of Dumfries*), 265–6

10. *Ibid* (Langholm), 400

11. *Ibid* (Closeburn), 221

12. *Ibid* (Westerkirk), 414–15

13. *Third Statistical Account* (Caerlaverock), 157

Bibliography

PUBLISHED PRIMARY SOURCES

Record Sources

Anglo-Scottish Relations 1174–1328: Some Selected Documents, ed E L G Stones (Edinburgh and London, 1965)

Calendar of Documents Relating to Scotland vols i–iv, ed J Bain and others (Edinburgh 1881–8); vol. v; ed G G Simpson and J D Galbraith (Edinburgh, 1986) (*CDS*)

Calendar of Patent Rolls 1399–1441, 8 vols (London, 1903–7) (*CPR*)

Documents and Records illustrating the History of Scotland, ed F Palgrave (Record Commission, 1827–)

Documents Illustrative of the History of Scotland 1286–1306, 2 vols, ed J Stevenson (Edinburgh, 1870).

Exchequer Rolls of Scotland, ed J Stuart and others, 23 vols (Edinburgh, 1878–1908) (*ER*)

Foedora, Conventiones, Litterae et Cuiuscunque Generiis Acta Publica, 20 vols, ed T Rymer, Record Commission edn (London (1816–69)

Liber Sancte Marie de Melros (Bannatyne Club, 1837)

Liber S Mary de Calchou 1113–1567 (Bannatyne Club, 1846)

Regesta Regum Scotorum: Acts of Malcolm IV 1153–65, ed G W S Barrow (Edinburgh, 1960) (*RRS* i)

Regesta Regum Scotorum: Acts of William I 1165–1214, ed G W S Barrow (Edinburgh, 1971) (*RRS* ii)

Regesta Regum Scotorum handlists: Acts of Alexander II 1214–1249, ed J M Scoular (Edinburgh, 1959) (*RRS* iii)

Regesta Regum Scotorum handlists: Acts of Alexander III, the Guardians and John 1249–1296, ed G G Simpson (Edinburgh, 1960) (*RRS* iv)

Regesta Regum Scotorum: Acts of Robert I 1306–29, ed A A M Duncan (Edinburgh, 1988) (*RRS* v)

Regesta Regum Scotorum: Acts of David II 1329–71, ed B Webster (Edinburgh, 1982) (*RRS* vi)

Registrum Magni Sigilli Regum Scotorum, J M Thomson and others (eds), 11 vols (Edinburgh, 1877–1914) (*RMS*)

Registrum Honoris de Morton (Bannatyne Club, 1853) (*Reg Hon de Morton*)

Registrum Secreti Sigilli Regum Scotorum, ed M Livingstone and others (Edinburgh, 1908–) (*RSS*)

Rotuli Scotiae in Turri Londinensi et in Domo Capitulari Westmonasterii Asservati i–ii (eds) D Macpherson and others (London, 1814–19) (*Rot Scot*)

Scottish Historical Documents, ed G Donaldson (Edinburgh, 1970)

Narrative and Literary Sources

Anderson, A O (ed), *Early Sources of Scottish History 500 to 1286*, 2 vols (London, 1908, republished Stamford, 1990)

Anderson, A O (ed), *Scottish Annals from English Chroniclers AD 500–1286* (London, 1908, republished Stamford, 1990)

Androw of Wyntoun's 'Orygynale Cronykil of Scotland', ed D Laing (Edinburgh, 1879)

Auchinleck Chronicle, ane schort Memoriale of the Scottis croniklis for Addicioun, ed T Thomson (Edinburgh, 1891–77)

Barbour, 'The Bruce', ed W M Menzie (London, 1908)

Bower, Walter, *Scotichronicon*, ed D E R Watt, 9 vols (Aberdeen, 1996)

Chronica Magistri Rogeri de Houedon, ed W Stubbs (London, 1868–71)

Chronicle de Lanercost (Maitland Club, 1839)

Chronicle of Lanercost 1272–1346, trans Sir H Maxwell (Glasgow, 1913)

Chronicle of Melrose, ed A O Anderson in Early Sources of Scottish History (London, 1936: republished Stamford, 1990)

Chronicle of Walter of Guisborough, ed H Rothwell (Camden Society, 1957)

Criminal Trials in Scotland from 1488 to 1624, ed R Pitcairn (Edinburgh, 1833)

Daniel, Walter, *The Life of Ailred of Rievaulx*, ed F M Powicke (London, 1950)

Fasti Ecclesiae Scoticanae (revised and enlarged edition) vol 2 – Synods of Merse and Teviotdale, Dumfries and Galloway (Edinburgh, 1917)

Historie and Cronicles of Scotland by Robert Lindsay of Pitscottie, ed Æ J G Mackay (Edinburgh, 1899)

John of Fordoun's Chronicle of the Scottish Nation, Historians of Scotland series, ed W F Skene (Edinburgh, 1871)

Knox, John, *Historie of the Reformatioun of Religioun in the Realme of Scotland*, ed Thomasson and Pullen (London, 1644)

Lawrie, A C (ed), *Annals of the Reigns of Malcolm and William, Kings of Scotland* (Glasgow, 1905)

Lawrie, A C (ed), *Early Scottish Charters prior to 1153* (Glasgow, 1905)

Macquarrie, A, 'The career of St Kentigern of Glasgow: vitae, lectiones, and glimpses of fact' *Innes Review*, xxxvi (1986)

Mair, John, *History of Greater Britain* (Scottish History Society, 1892)

Orygynale Cronikil of Androw of Wyntoun, ed F J Amours (Edinburgh, 1907)

Rishanger, Willelmi, *Chronica et Annales*, ed H T Riley, Rolls series, 1865

Scalacronica by Sir Thomas Grey of Heton, Knight, ed J Stevenson (Maitland Club, 1836)

Scalacronica by Sir Thomas Grey of Heaton, trans. Sir H Maxwell (Oxford, 1907)

Stones, E L G (ed), *Anglo-Scottish Relations 1174–1328: Some Selected Documents* (London) 1965

REFERENCE WORKS

The Scots Peerage, Sir J Balfour-Paul (ed), 8 vols (Edinburgh, 1904–11)

The Complete Peerage, H A Doubleday and Lord Howard de Walden (eds), 13 vols (London, 1940)

Burke's Peerage, 105th edn (London, 1970)

Burke's Landed Gentry, 15th edn (London, 1937)

Burke's Landed Gentry, 18th edn, 3 vols (London, 1969)

Secondary Sources

Books

Adams, P W L, *A History of the Douglas Family of Morton* (Sidney Press, 1921)

Aitchison, P and Cassel, A, *The Lowland Clearances: Scotland's Silent Revolution 1760–1830* (Edinburgh, 2012)

Armit, I, *Celtic Scotland* (London, 1997)

Ashmore, P J, *Neolithic and Bronze Age Scotland* (London, 1996)

Barrow, G W S, *The Anglo-Norman Era in Scottish History* (Oxford, 1980)

Barrow, G W S, *Robert Bruce and the Community of the Realm of Scotland* (Edinburgh, 1988)

Blakely, R M, *The Brus Family in England and Scotland 1100–1295* (Woodbridge, 2005)

Boardman, S, *The Early Stewart Kings* (Edinburgh, 1996)

Brooke, D, *Wild Men and Holy Places* (Edinburgh, 1994)

Brown, M, *The Black Douglases* (East Linton, 1998)

Brown, M, *James I* (Edinburgh, 1994)

Burne, A H, *The Hundred Years War: A Military History* (London, 1956)

Cameron, J, *James V: the personal rule 1528–1542* (East Linton, 1998)

Campbell, R H, *Owners and Occupiers* (Aberdeen, 1991)

Carruthers, A S and Reid, R C, *Records of the Carruthers Family* (London, 1934)

Clarkson, E and Upton, B, *Death of an Ocean* (Edinburgh, 2013)

Cowan, E J, *For Freedom Alone* (Edinburgh, 2014)

Cowan, I B, *The Scottish Covenanters 1660–88* (London, 1976)

Cowan, I B, *The Scottish Reformation: Church and Society in Sixteenth Century Scotland* (London, 1982)

Cowan, I B and Easson, D E, *Medieval Religious Houses: Scotland* (New York 1976)

Croft Dickinson, W, *Scotland from the Earliest Times to 1603* (Oxford, 1977)

Devine, T M (ed), *Farm Servants and Labour in Lowland Scotland 1770–1914* (Edinburgh, 1984)

Dixon, P, *Puir Labourers and Busy Husbandmen* (Edinburgh, 2002)

Dodds, I, *The Scottish Covenanters: The Fifty Years' Struggle of the Scottish Covenanters 1638 to 1688* (London, 1868)

Dodgshon, R A, *Land and Society in Early Scotland* (Oxford, 1981)

Donaldson, G, *Scotland: James V–James VII*, Edinburgh History of Scotland series (Edinburgh, 1965)

Donaldson, G, *Scottish Church History* (Edinburgh, 1985)

Dow, F D, *Cromwellian Scotland* (Edinburgh, 1979)

Duncan, A A M, *Scotland: The Making of the Kingdom*, The Edinburgh History of Scotland, vol 1 (Edinburgh, 1975)

Durie, A J, *The Scottish Linen Industry in the Eighteenth Century* (Edinburgh, 1979)

Ferguson, W, *Scotland 1689 to the Present* (Edinburgh, 1968)

Foster, S, *Picts, Gaels and Scots* (London, 2004)

Fraser, A, *Mary Queen of Scots* (London, 1969)

Fraser, G M, *The Steel Bonnets: The Story of Anglo-Scottish Border Reivers* (London, 1971)

Fraser, Sir W, *The Annandale Family Book of the Johnstones, Earls and Marquises of Annandale* (Edinburgh, 1894)

Fraser, Sir W, *The Book of Caerlaverock* (Edinburgh, 1873)

Fraser, Sir W, *The Scotts of Buccleuch* (Edinburgh, 1878)

Fraser, Sir W, *The Douglas Book* (Edinburgh, 1885)

Gifford, J, *Dumfries and Galloway*, The Buildings of Scotland series (Harmondsworth, 1996)

Gilbert, J M, *Hunting and Hunting Preserves in Medieval Scotland* (Edinburgh, 1976)

Grant, I F, *Social and Economic Development of Scotland before 1603* (London, 1930)

Haldane, A R B, *The Drove Roads of Scotland* (Trowbridge, 1973)

Hamilton, J A B, *Britain's Greatest Rail Disaster* (London, 199)

Hewison, J K, *The Covenanters* (London, 1908)

Highet, C, *Scottish Locomotive History 1831–1923* (London, 1970)

Hill, P, *Whithorn and St Ninian* (Stroud, 1997)

Hume, J R, *Dumfries and Galloway: An Illustrated Architectural Guide* (Edinburgh, 2000)

Hume Brown, P, *Early Travellers in Scotland* (Edinburgh, 1891)

Innes, C, *Lectures on Scottish Legal Antiquities* (Edinburgh, 1872)

Irving, J B, *The Irvings, Irwins, Irvines or Erinveines, or any other spelling of the name: An Old Border Clan* (Aberdeen, 1907)

Jillings, K, *Scotland's Black Death* (Stroud, 2007)

Kappelle, W E, *The Norman Conquest of the North: The Region and its Transformation* (Chapel Hill, NC, 1979)

Keswick, M, *The Thistle and the Jade* (London, 2008)

Kirkpatrick, I, *The Cairn Valley Light Railway: Moniaive to Dumfries* (Newport, 2000)

Larner, Christina, *Enemies of God: The Witch-hunt in Scotland* (Oxford, 1983)

Lenman, B, *An Economic History of Modern Scotland, 1660–1976* (Hamden, CT, 1977)

Lockart, D G (ed), *Scottish Planned Villages* (Edinburgh, 2012)

Lynch, M, *Scotland: A New History* (London, 1992)

Lythe, S G E & Butt, J, *An Economic History of Scotland 1100–1939* (Glasgow, 1975)

McConnel, J C I, *The Upper Nithsdale Coalworks* (Gillingham, 1962)

McCulloch, A J, *Galloway: A Land Apart* (Edinburgh, 2000)

Macdougall, N, *James III: A Political Study* (Edinburgh, 1982)

Macdougall, N, *James IV* (East Linton, 1997)

McDowall, W, *History of Dumfries* (republished Wakefield, 1972)

McGladdery, C, *James II* (Edinburgh, 2015)

McKirdy, A, Gordon, J and Crofts, R, *Land of Mountain and Flood: The Geology and Landforms of Scotland* (Edinburgh, 2007)

McNamee, C, *Wars of the Bruces: Scotland, England and Ireland 1306–1328* (East Linton, 1997)

Macquarrie, A, *The Saints of Scotland: Essays in Scottish Church History AD 450–1093* (Edinburgh, 1997)

MacRobert, A E, *The 1745 Rebellion and the Southern Scottish Lowlands* (Ely, 2006)

Maxwell, Sir H, *A History of Dumfries and Galloway* (London, 1896)

Maxwell-Irving, A M T, *The Border Towers of Scotland* (Stirling, 2008)

Maxwell-Stuart, P G, *An Abundance of Witches: The Great Scottish Witch-Hunt* (Stroud, 2005)

Maxwell Wood, J, *Witchcraft and Superstitious Record in South-West Scotland* (Dumfries, 1911)

Moffat, A, *The Reivers* (Edinburgh, 2007)

Moffat, A, *The British: A Genetic Journey* (Edinburgh, 2013)

Moffat, A, *Bannockburn: The Battle for a Nation* (Edinburgh, 2016)

Moffat, R M, *A Short History of the Family of Moffat of that Ilk* (Jersey, 1905)

Moffat, F, *The Moffats* (Chichester, 1987)

Mortimer, I, *The Perfect King: The Life of Edward III* (London, 2006)

Mullan, D G, *Episcopacy in Scotland: The History of an Idea 1560–1638* (Edinburgh, 1986)

Murray, A, *Customs Accounts of Dumfries and Kirkcudbright, 1560–1660* (Dumfries, 1965)

Nicolas, H N (ed), *The Siege of Caerlaverock* (Toronto, 1828), available online

Nicholson, R, *Scotland: The Later Middle Ages* (Edinburgh History of Scotland series), (Edinburgh, 1974)

Noble, G, *Neolithic Scotland* (Edinburgh, 2006)

Nock, O S, *The Caledonian Railway* (London, 1963)

Norwich, J J, *The Popes: A History* (London, 2011)

Oram, R D, *Scottish Prehistory* (Edinburgh, 1997)

Oram, R D (ed.), *The Stewarts: Kings and Queens of Scotland 1371–1625* (Stroud, 2002)

Penman, M, *David II 1329–1371* (Edinburgh, 2005)

Porteous, J M, *God's Treasure House in Scotland* (London, 1876)

Powicke, Sir M, *The Thirteenth Century 1216–1307* (Oxford, 1962)

Prestwich, M C, *Edward I* (London, 1988)

Pryde, G S, *Scotland 1603 to the Present* (Edinburgh, 1960)

RCAHMS, *Eastern Dumfriesshire: An Archaeological Landscape* (Edinburgh, 1997)

Reid, R C, *Charteris of Amisfield* (Dumfries, 1938)

Ridley, J, *Henry VIII* (London, 1984)

Ritchie, R L G, *The Normans in Scotland* (Edinburgh, 1954)

Robertson, C J A, *The Origins of the Scottish Railway System 1722–1844* (Glasgow, 1983)

Salway, P, *Roman Britain* (Oxford, 1981)

Scott, P H, *1707: The Union of Scotland and England* (Edinburgh, 1979)

Scott, W, *Bannockburn Revealed* (Rothesay, 2000)

Simpson, R, *History of Sanquhar* (Glasgow, 1865)

Stenton, Sir F, *Anglo-Saxon England* (Oxford, 1971)

Stephen, W, *History of the Scottish Church*, 2 vols (Edinburgh, 1896)

Steuart, J, *The Bell Family in Dumfriesshire* (Dumfries, 1932)

Symon, J A, *Scottish Farming Past and Present* (Edinburgh, 1959)

Symson, A, *A Large Description of Galloway* (Edinburgh, 1823)

Watson, F, *Under the Hammer: Edward I and Scotland* (East Linton, 1998)

Watson, G, *The Border Reivers* (Morpeth, 1994)

Wickham-Jones, C R, *Scotland's First Settlers* (London, 1994)

Wilson, T and McMillan W, *Annals of Sanquhar* (Dumfries, 1931)

Wilson, W B, *The Royal Burgh of Lochmaben: its History, its Castles, and its Churches* (Dumfries, 1987)

Wilson W B, *The Royal Four Towns of Lochmaben*, 2nd edn (Dumfries, 2001)

Wodrow, R, *The History of the Sufferings of the Church of Scotland*, 4 vols (Glasgow, 1832)

Young, A. *Robert the Bruce's Rivals: The Comyns, 1212–1314* (East Linton, 1996)

Statistical Accounts

The Statistical Account of Scotland, ed Sir J Sinclair, 21 vols (Edinburgh, 1791–9)

The New Statistical Account, 15 vols (Edinburgh, 1845)

The Third Statistical Account of Scotland, ed M C Arnott and others (Glasgow 1951–62)

Articles

Allen, M, 'Old maps and roads in Nithsdale – with particular reference to Durisdeer', *TDGNHAS*, lxxxvi (2012)

Anderson, A D, 'Some Notes on the Old Military Road in Dumfries and Galloway' *TDGNHAS*, lxxii (1997)

Anderson, A D, 'The 'Old Edinburgh Road' in Dumfriesshire and Galloway', *TDGNHAS*, lxxxiv (2010)

Ballantyne, J D, 'Natural Determinants of Routes on Lower Nithsdale' *TDGNHAS*, xi (1923–24)

Barrow, GWS, 'The Pattern of Lordship and Feudal Settlement in Cumbria', *Journal of Medieval History* i, (1975)

Birley, E, 'The Brigantium Problem and the First Roman contact with Scotland' *TDGNHAS*, xxix (1950–51)

Brown, R, 'The Mines and Minerals of Leadhills *TDGNHAS*, vi (1918–19)

Brown, R, 'More about the Mines and Minerals of Wanlockhead and Leadhills' *TDGNHAS*, xiii (1925–26)

Callender, J G, 'Dumfriesshire in the Stone, Bronze and Early Iron Ages' *TDGNHAS*, xi (1923–24)

Campbell, R H, 'The Population of South-West Scotland from the mid-Eighteenth Century to 1911' *TDGNHAS*, lx (1985)

Coles, J M, 'Bronze Age Metalwork in Dumfries and Galloway'*TDGNHAS*, xlii (1965)

Collingwood, W G, 'The Ruthwell Cross in its relation to other monuments of the Early Christian Age' *TDGNHAS* v (1916–18)

Connolly, M, 'The Dethe of the Kynge of Scottis: a new edition in *SHR* 71 (1992)

Cormack, W F, 'Prehistoric site at Beckton, Lockerbie' *TDGNHAS*, xli (1962–63)

Coutts, W, 'Farmers in Dumfries from 1600 to 1665' *TDGNHAS*, lxi (1986)

Cowan, E J, 'Agricultural Improvement and the formation of early Agricultural Societies in Dumfries and Galloway' *TDGNHAS*, liii (1977–78)

Cowan, I B, 'The Reformation in Dumfriesshire' *TDGNHAS*, lvi (1981)

Craig, B, 'Nineteenth Century Electioneering' *TDGNHAS*, xxvi (1947–48)

Devine, TM and Lythe, SGE, 'The Economy of Scotland under James VI', *SHR* 1 (1971)

Donaldson, J, 'Mid-Nineteenth Century poverty in Dumfries' *TDGNHAS*, liii (1977–78)

Donnachie, I, 'The Lime Industry in South-West Scotland' *TDNGHAS*, xlviii (1971)

Duncan, A A M, 'The Siege of Lochmaben Castle (1343)' *TDGNHAS*, xxxi (1952–3)

Duncan, A A M, 'The Bruces of Annandale' *TDGNHAS*, lxix (1994)

Easson, Rev. D E, 'The Nunneries of Scotland' *TDGNHAS*, xxiii (1940–44)

Fellows-Jensen, G, 'Scandinavians in Dumfriesshire and Galloway: The Place-name Evidence', in *Galloway: Land and Lordship*, ed R D Oram and G P Stell (Edinburgh, 1991), pp 77–95

Fenton, A, 'Plough and Spade in Dumfries and Galloway' *TDGNHAS*, xlv (1968)

Findlater, A M, 'Hoddom: A Medieval Estate in Annandale' *TDGNHAS*, lxxxii (2008)

Forbes, J M, 'French prisoners on parole at Dumfries etc.' *TDGNHAS* i (1912–13).

Gilbert, J M, 'Medieval Woodland Management in Southern Scotland', *TDGNHAS* lxxxvi (2012)

Gregory, R A, 'Excavation at Hayknowes Farm, Annan' *TDGNHAS*, lxxv (2001)

Hamilton Grierson, Sir P J, 'Some documents relating to Holywood' *TDGNHAS*, vi (1918–19)

Herries, D C, 'An Annandale Minister of the Seventeenth Century' *TDGNHAS*, vi (1918–19)

Herries, D C, 'John Maxwell of Newlaw sometime Provost of Dumfries' *TDGNHAS*, x (1922–23)

Herries, D C, 'Dumfries Burghs: Sir Robert Herries MP for – 1780–1784' *TDGNHAS*, xvii (1930–1)

Hill, C, 'The Mechanics of Overseas Trade: Dumfries and Galloway 1600–1850' *TDGNHAS*, lxxx (2006)

Johnstone, J T, 'Moffat and Upper Annandale in the Middle of the Eighteenth Century *TDGNHAS* i (1912–13)

Kirkpatrick, H, 'Holywood (Dumfriesshire) Kirk Session Minutes 1698 to 1812' *TDGNHAS*, lv (1980)

Laing, L R, 'The Angles in Scotland and the Mote of Mark' *TDGNHAS*, l (1973)

Laing, L R, 'Timber Halls in Dark Age Britain – some problems' *TDGNHAS*, xlvi (1969)

McCracken, A, 'The Glendinning Antimony Mine' *TDGNHAS*, xlii (1965)

McCracken, A, 'Notes on the Militia Raised against Napoleon' *TDGNHAS*, xlv (1968)

McCracken, A, 'Some Poor's House Correspondence' *TDGNHAS*, lii (1976–77)

MacDonald, A R, 'The First English Ironworks in Scotland? The 'forge' at Canonbie' *TDGNHAS*, lxxiii (1999)

MacDonald, J C R, 'Notes on the Titles of Cowhill Tower in the Parish of Holywood' *TDGNHAS* ii (1913–14)

McIntire, W T, 'Historical Relations between Dumfriesshire and Cumberland' *TDGNHAS*, xxi (1936–38)

Macleod, I, 'Notices in Scottish Newspapers relating to Dumfries and Galloway 1699–1722' *TDGNHAS*, lxxxi (2007)

McMichael, T, 'The Feudal Family of de Soulis' *TDGNHAS*, xxvi (1947–48).

Macquarrie, A, 'Notes on some Charters of the Bruces of Anandale 1215–1295' *TDGNHAS*, lviii (1983)

Macquarrie, A, 'The career of St Kentigern of Glasgow: vitae, lectiones, and glimpses of fact' *Innes Review*, xxxvii (1986)

MacRobert, A E, 'Lord Herries and Mary Queen of Scots' *TDGNHAS*, lxxxviii (2014)

Maxwell, Sir H, 'Tour of Mary Queen of Scots in the South-West of Scotland, August 1563' *TDGNHAS*, x (1922–23)

Maxwell-Irving, A M T, 'The Origin of the Irvings' *TDGNHAS*, lxxxiii (2009)

Maynard, D, 'Neolithic Pit at Carzield, Kirkton' *TGDNHAS*, lxviii (1993)

Miller, N and M, 'The Carlisle to Glasgow Road' *TDGNHAS*, lxv (1990)

Miller, N and M, 'Improvements to the Glasgow-Carlisle Road 1815' *TDGNHAS*, lvii (1992)

Murray, J, 'Archaeological Landscapes, Recent RCHAMS Survey in South-West Scotland' *TDGNHAS*, lxiii (1988)

Neilson, G and Donaldson, G, 'Guisborough and the Annandaole Churches' *TDGNHAS*, xxxii (1953–54)

Nicol, W B de B, 'The Dumfries and Maxwelltown Mechanics' Institute 1825–1900' *TDGNHAS*, xxviii (1949–50)

Phillips, L J, 'Planned Villages in Dumfriesshire and Galloway: Location, Form and Function' *TDGNHAS*, lxxx (2006)

Prevost, W A J, 'The Drove Road into Annandale' *TDGNHAS*, xxxi (1952–53)

Prevost, W A J, 'Dry stone dykes of Upper Annandale' *TDGNHAS*, xxxiv (1955–56)

Prevost, W A J, 'The Commissioners of Supply for Dumfriesshire' *TDGNHAS*, xxxvi (1957–58).

Prevost, W A J, 'The Solway Smugglers and the Customs Post at Dumfries' *TDGNHAS*, li (1975)

Prevost, W A J, 'Moffat and Beattock Inns, two mail-coach stages' *TDGNHAS*, li (1975)' *TDGNHAS* (1975)

Prevost, W A J, 'The March of the Jacobites through Annandale in November 1745' *TDGNHAS*, xlvii (1970)

Pryde, G S, 'The Burghs of Dumfriesshire and Galloway: their origin and status' *TDGNHAS*, xxix (1950–51).

Reid, R C, 'The Baronies of Enoch and Durisdeer' *TDGNHAS*, viii (1920–21)

Reid, R C, 'Some Letters of Patrick Miller (after the Napoleonic Wars)' *TDGNHAS*, ix (1921–22)

Reid, R C, 'Applegarth before the Thirteenth Century' *TDGNHAS*, xiv (1926–28)

Reid, R C, 'The Early History of Eskdalemuir' *TDGNHAS*, xiv (1926–28)

Reid, R C, 'Maxwell of Castlemilk' *TDGNHAS*, xix (1933–35)

Reid, R C, 'The De Boys of Dryfesdale' *TDGNHAS*, xxiii (1940–44)

Reid, R C, 'The Early Kirkpatricks' *TDGNHAS*, xxx (1951–52)

Reid, R C, 'Staplegorton' *TDGNHAS*, xxxi (1952–53)

Reid, R C, 'Notes on Roman Roads' *TDGNHAS*, xxxii (1953–54)

Reid, R C, 'The Caput of Annandale, or the Curse of St Malachy' *TDGNHAS*, xxxii (1953–54)

Reid, R C, 'The Monastery at Applegarth' *TDGNHAS*, xxxv (1956–57)

Reid, R C, 'The Baronies of Enoch and Durisdeer' *TDGNHAS*, viii (1920–21)

Reid, R C, 'Kirkandrews and the Debateable Land' *TDGNHAS*, xvi (1929–30).

Reid, R C, 'Some letters by Thomas Bell, drover, 1746' *TDGNHAS* xxii (1938–40)

Reid, R C, 'Edward I's pele at Lochmaben' *TDGNHAS*, xxxi (1952–53).

Reid, R C, 'The Feudalisation of Lower Nithsdale' *TDGNHAS*, xxxiv (1955–56)

Reid, R C, 'The Border Grahams, their Origin and Distribution' *TDGNHAS*, xxxviii (1959–60)

Ritchie, J, 'The Plague in Dumfries' *TDGNHAS*, xxi (1936–38)

Robertson, A, 'Birrens 1962–63' *TDGNHAS*, xli (1962–63)

Rose, D M, 'The Abduction of a Carlyle Heiress' *TDGNHAS*, xvi (1929–30).

Rose, G D, 'Draining the Wanlockhead lead mines' *TDGNHAS*, lix (1984)

Rose, G D and Harvey, W S, 'Lead Smelting sites at Wanlockhead 1682–1934' *TDGNHAS*, liv (1979)

Sanderson, *The Feuars of the Kirklands* SHS, vol 52 (1973)

Scott, J G, 'An early Sheriff of Dumfries?' *TDGNHAS*, lvii (1982)

Scott, J G, 'The Partition of a Kingdom – Strathclyde 1092 – 1153' *TDGNHAS*, lxxii (1997)

Shirley, G W, 'Strathspey Fencibles at Dumfries in 1795' *TDGNHAS*, iii (1914–15)

Shirley, G W, 'Burghal Life in Dumfries Two Centuries Ago' *TDGNHAS*, viii (1920–21)

Shirley, G W, 'The Building of Auldgirth Bridge' *TDGNHAS*, xxiii (1940–44)

Shirley, G W, 'The End of the Greyfriars' Convent of Dumfries and the last of the Friars *TDGNHAS*, i (1912–13).

Simpson, W D, 'Sanquhar Castle' *TDGNHAS*, xxi (1936–38)

Smith, A C, 'The Estate of Dalswinton' *TDGNHAS*, ix (1921–22)

Smith, A C, 'Wallace's Capture of Sanquhar and the rising in the South-West' *TDGNHAS*, xi (1923–24)

Smout, T C, 'The Foreign Trade of Dumfries and Kirkcudbright' *TDGNHAS*, xxxvii (1959–59)

Smout, T C, 'The Lead Mines at Wanlockhead' *TDGNHAS*, xxxix (1960–61)

Stewart, M, 'Crime and Punishment in the Seventeenth and Eighteenth Centuries: Records of Dumfries' *TDGNHAS*, lxxii (1997)

Stewart, M, 'Crime and Punishment in the Seventeenth and Eighteenth Century Records of Dumfries Part II' *TDGNHAS*, lxxiii (1999)

Still, G, 'Two cruck-framed buildings in Dumfriesshire' *TDGNHAS*, xlix (1972)

Stone, J C, 'The Settlements of Nithsdale in the Sixteenth Century by Timothy Pont' *TDGNHAS*, l (1973)

Strachan, R J, 'Excavations at Albie Hill, Applegarthtown' *TDGNHAS*, lxxiii (1999)

Taylor, L T, 'Liddel Strength' *TDGNHAS*, xvi (1929–30)

Troup, C, 'Chartism in Dumfriesshire 1830–50' *TDGNHAS*, lvi (1981)

Truckell, A E, 'Early Shipping Records in Dumfries Burgh Records' *TDGNHAS*, xxxiii (1954–55)

Truckell, A E, 'A Neolithic Axe Roughout' *TDGNHAS*, xlii (1965)

Truckell, A E, 'Unpublished Witchcraft trials' *TDGNHAS*, li (1975)

Truckell, A E, 'Unpublished Witchcraft Trials (pt II)' *TDGNHAS*, lii (1976–77)

Truckell, A E, 'Old Harbours in the Solway Firth' *TDGNHAS*, lii (1976–77)

Truckell, A E, 'Extracts from Dumfries Burgh Court Records' *TDGNHAS*, lxxii (1997)

Truckell, A E, 'Dumfries Burgh Court Book in the Sixteenth Century Part I' *TDGNHAS*, lxxiii (1999)

Truckell, A E, Dumfries Burgh Court Books in the Sixteenth Century Part II' *TDGNHAS*, lxxiv (2000)

Truckell, A E (ed), 'Some Seventeenth Century Custom and Excise Records for Dumfries and Kirkcudbright' *TDGNHAS*, lxxv (2001)

Truckell, A E, 'Mouswald Kirk Session Minutes 1640–1659' *TDGNHAS*, lxxvii (2003)

Wade Evans, Rev. A W, 'The Year of Cunedda's Departure for Wales' *TDGNHAS*, xxx (1951–52)

Wallace, J C, 'A Burial Mound near Gatelawbridge' *TDGNHAS*, xxxii (1953–54)

Watson, W J, 'The Celts (British and Gael) in Dumfriesshire and Galloway' *TDGNHAS*, xi (1923–24)

Wilkins, F, 'Smuggling in Annandale' *TDGNHAS*, lxxxviii (2014)

Williams, J, 'Neolithic axes in Dumfries and Galloway' *TDGNHAS*, xlvii (1970)

Williams, J, 'The Antimony, Bismuth, Molybdenum and Tungsten minerals of South-West Scotland' *TDGNHAS*, l (1973)

Wilson, A, 'Roman penetration in East Dumfriesshire and beyond' *TDGNHAS*, lxxiii (1999)

Wilson, A, 'Roman and native in Dumfriesshire' *TDGNHAS*, lxxvii (2003)

Index